SKILLS For SUCCESS

with Microsoft® Access 2010

COMPREHENSIVE

TOWNSEND | HAYES

Prentice Hall

Boston   Columbus   Indianapolis   New York   San Francisco   Upper Saddle River
Amsterdam   Cape Town   Dubai   London   Madrid   Milan   Munich   Paris   Montréal   Toronto
Delhi   Mexico City   São Paulo   Sydney   Hong Kong   Seoul   Singapore   Taipei   Tokyo

Library of Congress Cataloging-in-Publication Data
Townsend, Kris.
  Skills for success with Access 2010 comprehensive / by Kris Townsend.
      p. cm.
  ISBN 978-0-13-508835-7 (alk. paper)
  1. Database management.   2. Microsoft Access.   I. Title.
QA76.9.D3T6862 2010
005.75'65—dc22   2010019637

Editor in Chief: *Michael Payne*
AVP/Executive Acquisitions Editor: *Stephanie Wall*
Product Development Manager: *Eileen Bien Calabro*
Editorial Project Manager: *Virginia Guariglia*
Development Editor: *Nancy Lamm*
Editorial Assistant: *Nicole Sam*
AVP/Director of Online Programs, Media: *Richard Keaveny*
AVP/Director of Product Development, Media: *Lisa Strite*
Editor—Digital Learning & Assessment: *Paul Gentile*
Product Development Manager, Media: *Cathi Profitko*
Media Project Manager, Editorial: *Alana Coles*
Media Project Manager, Production: *John Cassar*
Director of Marketing: *Kate Valentine*
Senior Marketing Manager: *Tori Olsen Alves*
Marketing Coordinator: *Susan Osterlitz*

Marketing Assistant: *Darshika Vyas*
Senior Managing Editor: *Cynthia Zonneveld*
Associate Managing Editor: *Camille Trentacoste*
Production Project Manager: *Camille Trentacoste*
Senior Operations Supervisor: *Natacha Moore*
Senior Art Director: *Jonathan Boylan*
Art Director: *Anthony Gemmellaro*
Text and Cover Designer: *Anthony Gemmellaro*
Manager, Rights and Permissions: *Hessa Albader*
Supplements Development Editor: *Vonda Keator*
Full-Service Project Management: *MPS Content Services, a Macmillan Company*
Composition: *MPS Content Services, a Macmillan Company*
Printer/Binder: *Quad/Graphics-Taunton*
Cover Printer: *Lehigh/Phoenix*
Typeface: *Minion 10.5/12.5*

Prentice Hall
is an imprint of

www.pearsonhighered.com

10 9 8 7 6 5 4 3 2
ISBN-10:   0-13-508835-6
ISBN-13: 978-0-13-508835-7

Contents in Brief

Table of Contents

Common Features

Access

More Skills

More Skills

About the Authors

Kris Townsend is an Information Systems instructor at Spokane Falls Community College in Spokane, Washington. Kris earned a bachelor's degree in both Education and Business, and a master's degree in Education. He has also worked as a public school teacher and as a systems analyst. Kris enjoys working with wood, snowboarding, and camping. He commutes to work by bike and enjoys long road rides in the Palouse country south of Spokane.

This book is dedicated to the students at Spokane Falls Community College. Their adventures, joys, and frustrations guide my way.
—KRIS TOWNSEND

Darren R. Hayes is CIS Program Chair and Lecturer at Pace University. He is also a consultant for the Department of Education in New York City, where he provides high school teachers with training in computer forensics. He is passionate about computer forensics, works closely with law enforcement, and believes that the field of study is a great way to get students interested in computing. He's not a native of New York but shares the same birthplace as Oscar Wilde, Bram Stoker, James Joyce, and Bono. On his breaks from university life, he likes to travel home to Ireland or to his wife's native Trinidad. In the summertime, you might see him and his children trekking along the magnificent bike paths of Harwich, Massachusetts.

I would like to dedicate this book to my best friend and wife Nalini, my four children, and my loving parents Ted and Annette.
—DARREN HAYES

Contributors

We'd like to thank the following people for their work on Skills for Success:

Instructor Resource Authors

Sharon Behrens	*Northeast Wisconsin Technical College*	Stacey Gee Hollins	*St. Louis Community College—Meramec*
Art Carter	*Radford University*	Yvonne Leonard	*Coastal Carolina Community College*
Barbara Hearn	*Community College of Philadelphia*	Steve St. John	*Tulsa Community College*

Technical Editors

Lori Damanti		Linda Pogue	*Northwest Arkansas Community College*
Elizabeth Lockley		Steve Rubin	*California State University—Monterey Bay*
Janet Pickard	*Chattanooga State Tech Community College*	Jan Snyder	

Reviewers

Laura Aagard	*Sierra College*	Susana Contreras de Finch	*College of Southern Nevada*
Darrell Abbey	*Cascadia Community College*	Gail W. Cope	*Sinclair Community College*
John Alcorcha	*MTI College*	Lennie Coper	*Miami Dade College*
Barry Andrews	*Miami Dade College*	Chris Corbin	*Miami Dade College*
Natalie Andrews	*Miami Dade College*	Janis Cox	*Tri-County Technical College*
Wilma Andrews	*Virginia Commonwealth University School of Business*	Tomi Crawford	*Miami Dade College*
		Martin Cronlund	*Anne Arundel Community College*
Bridget Archer	*Oakton Community College*	Jennifer Day	*Sinclair Community College*
Tahir Aziz	*J. Sargeant Reynolds*	Ralph DeArazoza	*Miami Dade College*
Greg Balinger	*Miami Dade College*	Carol Decker	*Montgomery College*
Terry Bass	*University of Massachusetts, Lowell*	Loorna DeDuluc	*Miami Dade College*
Lisa Beach	*Santa Rosa Junior College*	Caroline Delcourt	*Black Hawk College*
Rocky Belcher	*Sinclair Community College*	Michael Discello	*Pittsburgh Technical Institute*
Nannette Biby	*Miami Dade College*	Kevin Duggan	*Midlands Technical Community College*
David Billings	*Guilford Technical Community College*	Barbara Edington	*St. Francis College*
Brenda K. Britt	*Fayetteville Technical Community College*	Donna Ehrhart	*Genesee Community College*
Alisa Brown	*Pulaski Technical College*	Hilda Wirth Federico	*Jacksonville University*
Eric Cameron	*Passaic Community College*	Tushnelda Fernandez	*Miami Dade College*
Gene Carbonaro	*Long Beach City College*	Arlene Flerchinger	*Chattanooga State Tech Community College*
Trey Cherry	*Edgecombe Community College*	Hedy Fossenkemper	*Paradise Valley Community College*
Kim Childs	*Bethany University*	Kent Foster	*Withrop University*
Pualine Chohonis	*Miami Dade College*	Penny Foster-Shiver	*Anne Arundel Community College*
Tara Cipriano	*Gateway Technical College*	Arlene Franklin	*Bucks County Community College*
Paulette Comet	*Community College of Baltimore County—Catonsville*	George Gabb	*Miami Dade College*
		Barbara Garrell	*Delaware County Community College*

Deb Geoghan	*Bucks County Community College*
Jessica Gilmore	*Highline Community College*
Victor Giol	*Miami Dade College*
Melinda Glander	*Northmetro Technical College*
Linda Glassburn	*Cuyahoga Community College, West*
Deb Gross	*Ohio State University*
Rachelle Hall	*Glendale Community College*
Marie Hartlein	*Montgomery County Community College*
Diane Hartman	*Utah Valley State College*
Betsy Headrick	*Chattanooga State*
Patrick Healy	*Northern Virginia Community College—Woodbridge*
Lindsay Henning	*Yavapai College*
Kermelle Hensley	*Columbus Technical College*
Diana Hill	*Chesapeake College*
Rachel Hinton	*Broome Community College*
Mary Carole Hollingsworth	*GA Perimeter*
Stacey Gee Hollins	*St. Louis Community College—Meramec*
Bill Holmes	*Chandler-Gilbert Community College*
Steve Holtz	*University of Minnesota Duluth*
Margaret M. Hvatum	*St. Louis Community College*
Joan Ivey	*Lanier Technical College*
Dr. Dianna D. Johnson	*North Metro Technical College*
Kay Johnston	*Columbia Basin College*
Warren T. Jones, Sr.	*University of Alabama at Birmingham*
Sally Kaskocsak	*Sinclair Community College*
Renuka Kumar	*Community College of Baltimore County*
Kathy McKee	*North Metro Technical College*
Hazel Kates	*Miami Dade College*
Gerald Kearns	*Forsyth Technical Community College*
Charles Kellermann	*Northern Virginia Community College—Woodbridge*
John Kidd	*Tarrant County Community College*
Chris Kinnard	*Miami Dade College*
Kelli Kleindorfer	*American Institute of Business*
Kurt Kominek	*NE State Tech Community College*
Dianne Kotokoff	*Lanier Technical College*
Cynthia Krebs	*Utah Valley University*
Jean Lacoste	*Virginia Tech*
Gene Laughrey	*Northern Oklahoma College*
David LeBron	*Miami Dade College*
Kaiyang Liang	*Miami Dade College*
Linda Lindaman	*Black Hawk College*
Felix Lopez	*Miami Dade College*
Nicki Maines	*Mesa Community College*
Cindy Manning	*Big Sandy Community and Technical College*
Patri Mays	*Paradise Valley Community College*
Norma McKenzie	*El Paso Community College*
Lee McKinley	*GA Perimeter*
Sandy McCormack	*Monroe Community College*
Eric Meyer	*Miami Dade College*
Kathryn Miller	*Big Sandy Community and Technical College, Pike Ville Campus*
Gloria A. Morgan	*Monroe Community College*
Kathy Morris	*University of Alabama, Tuscaloosa*
Linda Moulton	*Montgomery County Community College*
Ryan Murphy	*Sinclair Community College*
Stephanie Murre Wolf	*Moraine Park Technical College*
Jackie Myers	*Sinclair Community College*
Dell Najera	*El Paso Community College, Valle Verde Campus*
Scott Nason	*Rowan Cabarrus Community College*
Paula Neal	*Sinclair Community College*
Bethanne Newman	*Paradise Valley Community College*
Eloise Newsome	*Northern Virginia Community College—Woodbridge*
Karen Nunan	*Northeast State Technical Community College*
Ellen Orr	*Seminole Community College*
Carol Ottaway	*Chemeketa Community College*
Denise Passero	*Fulton-Montgomery Community College*
Americus Pavese	*Community College of Baltimore County*
James Gordon Patterson	*Paradise Valley Community College*
Cindra Phillips	*Clark State CC*
Janet Pickard	*Chattanooga State Tech Community College*
Floyd Pittman	*Miami Dade College*
Melissa Prinzing	*Sierra College*
Pat Rahmlow	*Montgomery County Community College*
Mary Rasley	*Lehigh Carbon Community College*
Scott Rosen	*Santa Rosa Junior College*
Ann Rowlette	*Liberty University*
Kamaljeet Sanghera	*George Mason University*
June Scott	*County College of Morris*
Janet Sebesy	*Cuyahoga Community College*
Jennifer Sedelmeyer	*Broome Community College*
Kelly SellAnne	*Arundel Community College*
Teresa Sept	*College of Southern Idaho*

A Microsoft® Office textbook that recognizes how students learn today-

Skills for Success

with Microsoft® Access 2010 Comprehensive

- **10 x 8.5 Format** – Easy for students to read and type at the same time by simply propping the book up on the desk in front of their monitor

- **Clearly Outlined Skills** – Each skill is presented in a single two-page spread so that students can easily follow along

- **Numbered Steps and Bulleted Text** – Students don't read long paragraphs or text, but they will read information presented concisely

- **Easy-to-Find Student Data Files** – Visual key shows students how to locate and interact with their data files

Start Here – Students know exactly where to start and what their starting file will look like

Outcome – Shows students up front what their completed project will look like

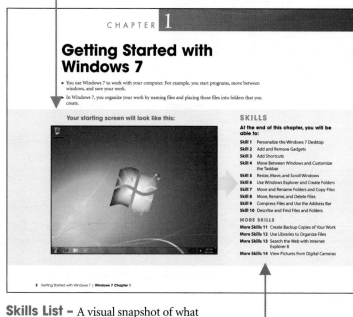

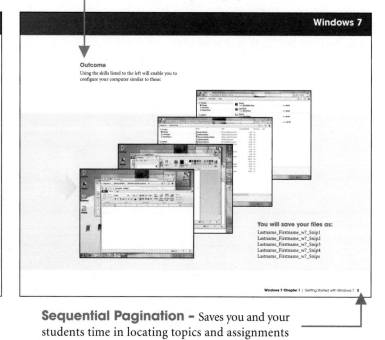

Skills List – A visual snapshot of what skills they will complete in the chapter

Sequential Pagination – Saves you and your students time in locating topics and assignments

Skills for Success

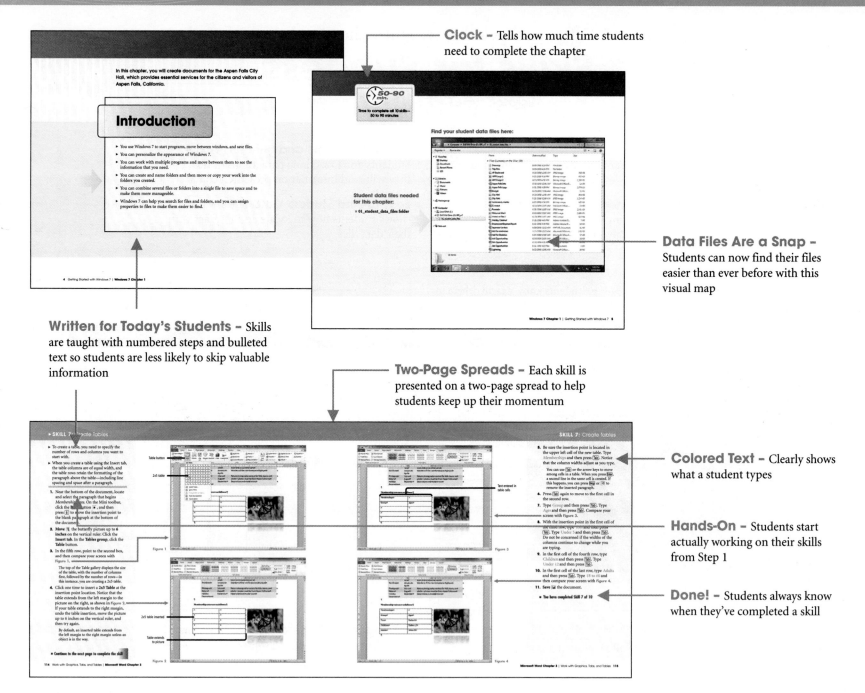

Clock – Tells how much time students need to complete the chapter

Data Files Are a Snap – Students can now find their files easier than ever before with this visual map

Written for Today's Students – Skills are taught with numbered steps and bulleted text so students are less likely to skip valuable information

Two-Page Spreads – Each skill is presented on a two-page spread to help students keep up their momentum

Colored Text – Clearly shows what a student types

Hands-On – Students start actually working on their skills from Step 1

Done! – Students always know when they've completed a skill

Skills for Success

More Skills – Additional skills included online

Online Project – Students practice using Microsoft Help online to help prepare them for using the applications on their own

End-of-Chapter Material – Several levels of assessment so you can assign the material that best fits your students' needs

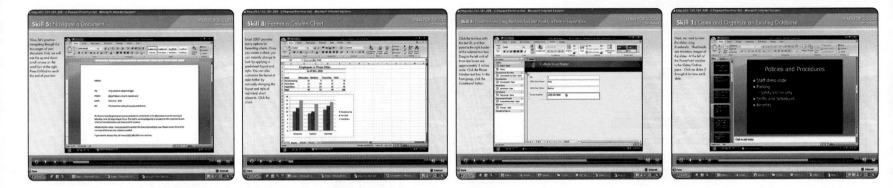

Videos! – Each skill within a chapter comes with a video that includes audio, which demonstrates the skill

NOTE: These videos are only available with *Skills for Success with Office 2010 Volume 1*

Instructor Materials

All Instructor materials available on the IRCD

Instructor's Manual – Teaching tips and additional resources for each chapter

Assignment Sheets – Lists all the assignments for the chapter, you just add in the course information, due dates, and points. Providing these to students ensures they will know what is due and when

Scripted Lectures – Classroom lectures prepared for you

Annotated Solution Files – Coupled with the scoring rubrics, these create a grading and scoring system that makes grading so much easier for you

Power Point Lectures – PowerPoint presentations for each chapter

Prepared Exams – Exams for each chapter

Scoring Rubrics – Can be used either by students to check their work or by you as a quick check-off for the items that need to be corrected

Syllabus Templates – For 8-week, 12-week, and 16-week courses

Test Bank – Includes a variety of test questions for each chapter

Companion Website – Online content such as the More Skills Projects, Online Study Guide, Glossary, and Student Data Files are all at www.pearsonhighered.com/skills

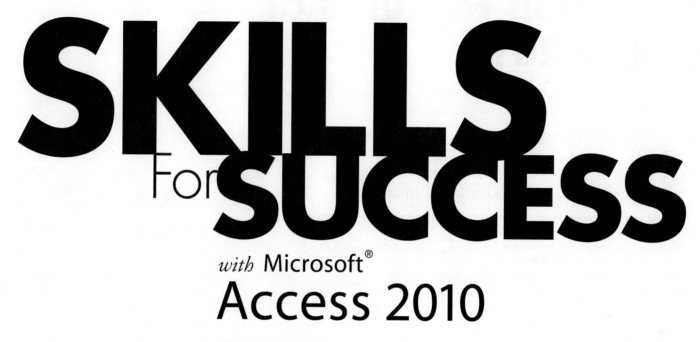

SKILLS For SUCCESS

with Microsoft®

Access 2010

COMPREHENSIVE

Common Features of Office 2010

▶ The programs in Microsoft Office 2010—Word, Excel, PowerPoint, and Access—share common tools that you use in a consistent, easy-to-learn manner.

▶ Common tasks include opening and saving files, entering and formatting text, and printing your work.

Your starting screen will look like this:

SKILLS

Skills 1-10 Training

At the end of this chapter, you will be able to:

Skill 1 Start Word and Navigate the Word Window

Skill 2 Start Excel and PowerPoint and Work with Multiple Windows

Skill 3 Save Files in New Folders

Skill 4 Print and Save Documents

Skill 5 Open Student Data Files and Save Copies Using Save As

Skill 6 Type and Edit Text

Skill 7 Cut, Copy, and Paste Text

Skill 8 Format Text and Paragraphs

Skill 9 Use the Ribbon

Skill 10 Use Shortcut Menus and Dialog Boxes

MORE SKILLS

More Skills 11 Capture Screens with the Snipping Tool

More Skills 12 Use Microsoft Office Help

More Skills 13 Organize Files

More Skills 14 Save Documents to Windows Live

Outcome

Using the skills listed to the left will enable you
to create documents similar to this:

Visit Aspen Falls!

Aspen Falls overlooks the Pacific Ocean
and is surrounded by many vineyards and
wineries. Ocean recreation is accessed
primarily at Durango County Park. The
Aspen Lake Recreation Area provides year
round fresh water recreation and is the
city's largest park.

Local Attractions
- Wine Country
  - Wine Tasting Tours
  - Wineries
- Wordsworth Fellowship Museum of Art
- Durango County Museum of History
- Convention Center
- Art Galleries
- Glider Tours

Aspen Falls Annual Events
- Annual Starving Artists Sidewalk Sale
- Annual Wine Festival
- Cinco de Mayo
- Vintage Car Show
- Heritage Day Parade
- Harvest Days
- Amateur Bike Races
- Farmer's Market
- Aspen Lake Nature Cruises
- Aspen Falls Triathlon
- Taste of Aspen Falls
- Winter Blues Festival

Contact Your Name for more information.

You will save your files as:

Lastname_Firstname_cf01_Visit1
Lastname_Firstname_cf01_Visit2
Lastname_Firstname_cf01_Visit3

In this chapter, you will create documents for the Aspen Falls City Hall, which provides essential services for the citizens and visitors of Aspen Falls, California.

Common Features of Office 2010

- ▶ Microsoft Office is the most common software used to create and share personal and business documents.

- ▶ Microsoft Office is a suite of several programs—Word, PowerPoint, Excel, Access, and others—that each have a special purpose.

- ▶ Because of the consistent design and layout of Microsoft Office, when you learn to use one Microsoft Office program, you can use most of those skills when working with the other Microsoft Office programs.

- ▶ The files you create with Microsoft Office need to be named and saved in locations where they can be easily found when you need them.

**Time to complete all
10 skills – 50 to 90 minutes**

Find your student data files here:

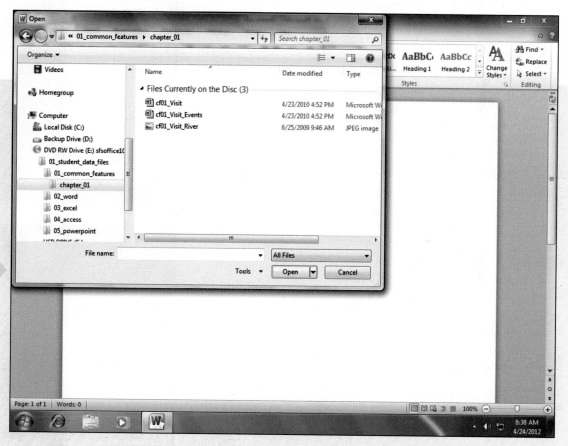

**Student data files needed
for this chapter:**

- cf01_Visit
- cf01_Visit_Events
- cf01_Visit_River

▶ The Word 2010 program can be launched by clicking the Start button, and then locating and clicking the *Microsoft Word 2010* command.

▶ When you start Word, a new blank document displays in which you can type text.

1. In the lower left corner of the desktop, click the **Start** button ⊕ .

2. In the lower left corner of the **Start** menu, click the **All Programs** command, and then compare your screen with **Figure 1**.

> The Microsoft Office folder is located in the All Programs folder. If you have several programs installed on your computer, you may need to scroll to see the Microsoft Office folder.

3. Click the **Microsoft Office** folder, and then compare your screen with **Figure 2**.

> Below the Microsoft Office folder, commands that open various Office 2010 programs display.

4. From the **Start** menu, under the **Microsoft Office** folder, click **Microsoft Word 2010**, and then wait a few moments for the Microsoft Word window to display.

5. If necessary, in the upper right corner of the Microsoft Word window, click the Maximize button .

■ **Continue to the next page to complete the skill** ▶

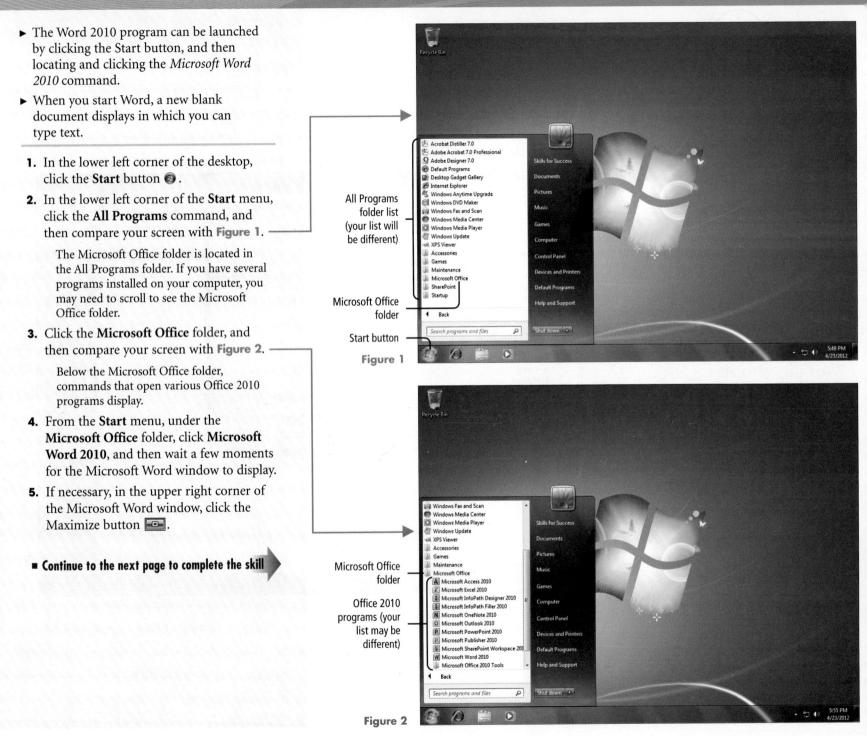

All Programs folder list (your list will be different)

Microsoft Office folder

Start button

Figure 1

Microsoft Office folder

Office 2010 programs (your list may be different)

Figure 2

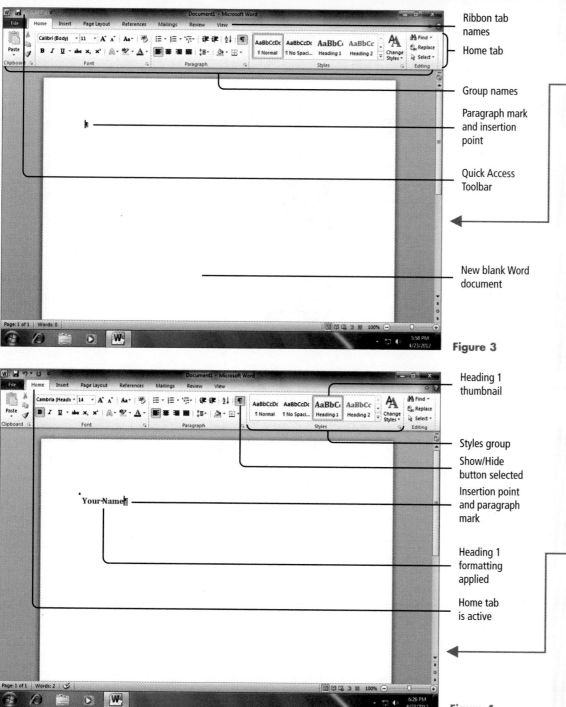

Ribbon tab names

Home tab

Group names

Paragraph mark and insertion point

Quick Access Toolbar

New blank Word document

Figure 3

Heading 1 thumbnail

Styles group

Show/Hide button selected

Insertion point and paragraph mark

Heading 1 formatting applied

Home tab is active

Figure 4

6. On the Ribbon's **Home tab**, in the **Paragraph group**, click the **Show/Hide** button ¶ until it displays in gold indicating that it is active. Compare your screen with **Figure 3**.

Above the blank Word document, the Quick Access Toolbar and Ribbon display. At the top of the Ribbon, a row of tab names display. Each Ribbon tab has buttons that you click to perform actions. The buttons are organized into groups that display their names along the bottom of the Ribbon.

In the document, the *insertion point*— a vertical line that indicates where text will be inserted when you start typing—flashes near the top left corner.

The Show/Hide button is a *toggle button*— a button used to turn a feature both on and off. The paragraph mark (¶) indicates the end of a paragraph and will not print.

7. In the document, type your first and last names. As you type, notice that the insertion point and paragraph mark move to the right.

8. On the **Home tab**, in the **Styles group**, point to—but do not click—the **Heading 1** thumbnail to show the *Live Preview*—a feature that displays the result of a formatting change if you select it.

9. Click the **Heading 1** thumbnail to apply the formatting change as shown in **Figure 4**. If the Word Navigation Pane displays on the left side of the Word window, click its Close ✕ button.

■ **You have completed Skill 1 of 10**

► When you open more than one Office program, each program displays in its own window.

► When you want to work with a program in a different window, you need to make it the active window.

1. Click the **Start** button ⬤, and then compare your screen with **Figure 1.**

   Your computer may be configured in such a way that you can open Office programs without opening the All Programs folder. The Office 2010 program commands may display as shortcuts in the Start menu's pinned programs area or the recently used programs area. Your computer's taskbar or desktop may also display icons that start each program.

2. From the **Start** menu, locate and then click **Microsoft Excel 2010.** Depending on your computer, you may need to double-click—not single click—to launch Excel. Compare your screen with **Figure 2.** If necessary, click the Maximize button 🔲.

   A new blank worksheet displays in a new window. The first *cell*—the box formed by the intersection of a row and column—is active as indicated by the thick, black border surrounding the cell. When you type in Excel, the text is entered into the active cell.

   The Quick Access Toolbar displays above the spreadsheet. The Excel Ribbon has its own tabs and groups that you use to work with an Excel spreadsheet. Many of these tabs, groups, and buttons are similar to those found in Word.

   On the taskbar, two buttons display—one for Word and one for Excel.

■ **Continue to the next page to complete the skill**

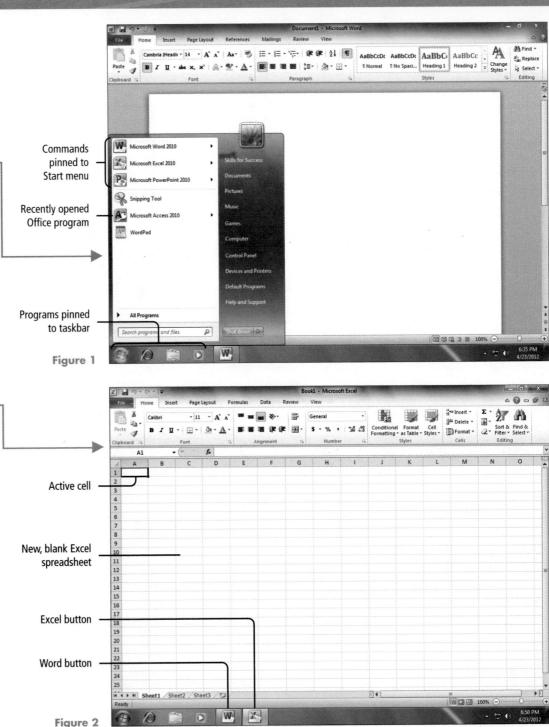

Commands pinned to Start menu

Recently opened Office program

Programs pinned to taskbar

Figure 1

Active cell

New, blank Excel spreadsheet

Excel button

Word button

Figure 2

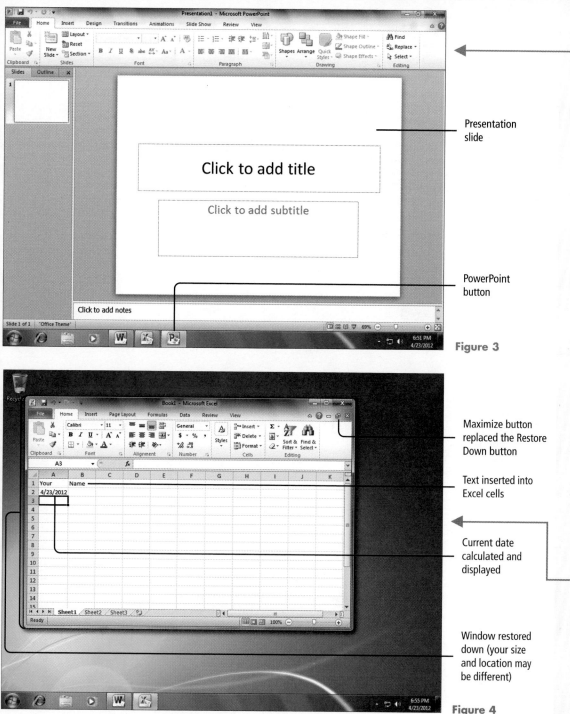

Presentation slide

PowerPoint button

Figure 3

Maximize button replaced the Restore Down button

Text inserted into Excel cells

Current date calculated and displayed

Window restored down (your size and location may be different)

Figure 4

3. From the **Start** menu ⊕, locate and then click **Microsoft PowerPoint 2010**. Compare your screen with **Figure 3**. If necessary, Maximize ▭ the Presentation1 - Microsoft PowerPoint window.

   A new, blank presentation opens in a new window. The PowerPoint window contains a slide in which you can type text. PowerPoint slides are designed to be displayed as you talk in front of a group of people.

4. In the upper right corner of the **PowerPoint** window, click the **Close** button ▭.

5. On the taskbar, click the **Word** button to make it the active window. With the insertion point flashing to the right of your name, press Enter, and then type Skills for Success Common Features Chapter

6. In the upper right corner of the **Document1 - Microsoft Word** window, click the **Minimize** button ▭.

   The Word window no longer displays, but its button is still available on the taskbar.

7. With the Excel window active, in the first cell—cell **A1**—type your first name. Press Tab, and then type your last name.

8. Press Enter, type =TODAY() and then press Enter to calculate the current date and to display it in the cell.

9. In the **Excel** window, click the **Restore Down** button ▭ and then compare your screen with **Figure 4**.

   The window remains open, but it no longer fills the entire screen. The Maximize button replaced the Restore Down button.

■ **You have completed Skill 2 of 10**

▶ A new document or spreadsheet is stored in the computer's temporary memory (*RAM*) until you save it to your hard drive or USB flash drive.

1. If you are saving your work on a USB flash drive, insert the USB flash drive into the computer now. If the Windows Explorer button 📁 flashes on the taskbar, right-click the button, and then on the Jump List, click Close window.

2. On the taskbar, click the **Word** button to make it the active window. On the **Quick Access Toolbar**, click the **Save** button 💾.

   For new documents, the first time you click the Save button, the Save As dialog box opens so that you can name the file.

3. If you are to save your work on a USB drive, in the Navigation pane scroll down to display the list of drives, and then click your USB flash drive as shown in **Figure 1**. If you are saving your work to another location, in the Navigation pane, locate and then click that folder or drive.

4. On the **Save As** dialog box toolbar, click the **New folder** button, and then immediately type Common Features Chapter 1

5. Press Enter to accept the folder name, and then press Enter again to open the new folder as shown in **Figure 2**.

   The new folder is created and then opened in the Save As dialog box file list.

■ **Continue to the next page to complete the skill**

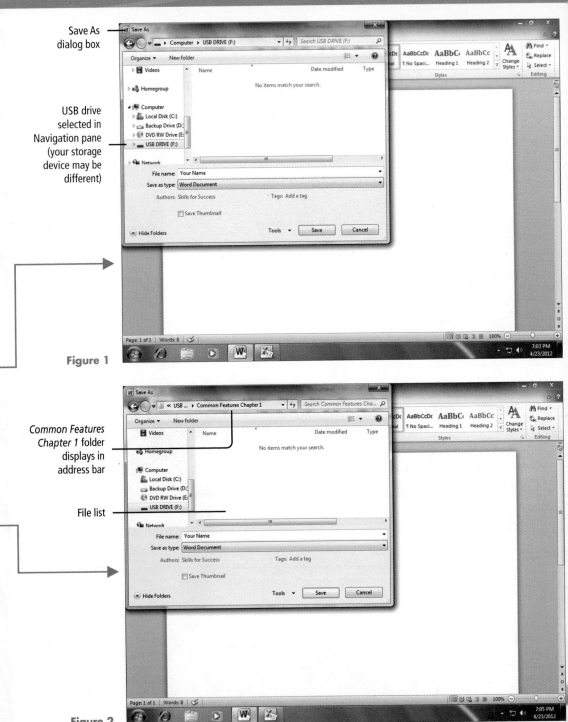

Save As dialog box

USB drive selected in Navigation pane (your storage device may be different)

Figure 1

Common Features Chapter 1 folder displays in address bar

File list

Figure 2

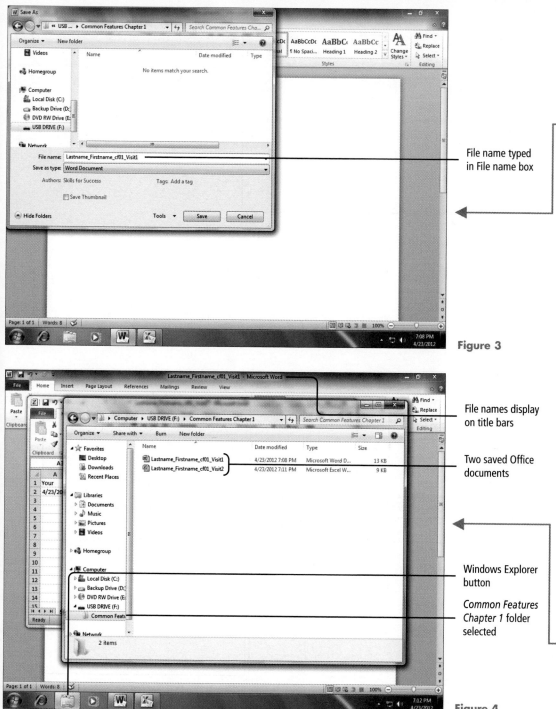

File name typed in File name box

Figure 3

File names display on title bars

Two saved Office documents

Windows Explorer button

Common Features Chapter 1 folder selected

Figure 4

6. In the **Save As** dialog box, click in the **File name** box one time to highlight all of the existing text.

7. With the text in the **File name** box still highlighted, type Lastname_Firstname_cf01_Visit1

8. Compare your screen with **Figure 3**, and then click **Save**.

    After the document is saved, the name of the file displays on the title bar at the top of the window.

9. On the taskbar, click the **Windows Explorer** button. In the folder window **Navigation** pane, open ▷ the drive on which you are saving your work, and then click the **Common Features Chapter 1** folder. Verify that *Lastname_Firstname_cf01_Visit1* displays in file list.

10. On the taskbar, click the **Excel** button to make it the active window. On the Excel **Quick Access Toolbar**, click the **Save** button.

11. In the **Save As** dialog box **Navigation** pane, open ▷ the drive where you are saving your work, and then click the **Common Features Chapter 1** folder to display its file list.

    The Word file may not display because the Save As box typically displays only files created by the program you are using. Here, only Excel files will typically display.

12. Click in the **File name** box, replace the existing value with Lastname_Firstname_cf01_Visit2 and then click the **Save** button.

13. On the taskbar, click the **Windows Explorer** button, and then compare your screen with **Figure 4**.

■ **You have completed Skill 3 of 10**

► Before printing, it is a good idea to work in *Page Layout view*—a view where you prepare your document or spreadsheet for printing.

1. On the taskbar, click the **Excel** button, and then click the **Maximize** button.

2. On the Ribbon, click the **View tab**, and then in the **Workbook Views group**, click the **Page Layout** button. Compare your screen with **Figure 1**.

   The worksheet displays the cells, the margins, and the edges of the paper as they will be positioned when you print. The *cell references*—the numbers on the left side and the letters across the top of a spreadsheet that address each cell—will not print.

3. On the Ribbon, click the **Page Layout tab**. In the **Page Setup group**, click the **Margins** button, and then in the **Margins** gallery, click **Wide**.

4. Click the **File tab**, and then on the left side of the Backstage, click **Print**. Compare your screen with **Figure 2**.

   The Print tab has commands that affect your print job and a preview of the printed page. Here, the cell references and *grid lines*—lines between the cells in a table or spreadsheet—do not display because they will not be printed.

5. In the **Print Settings**, under **Printer**, notice the name of the printer. You will need to retrieve your printout from this printer. If your instructor has directed you to print to a different printer, click the Printer arrow, and choose the assigned printer.

■ **Continue to the next page to complete the skill** ➤

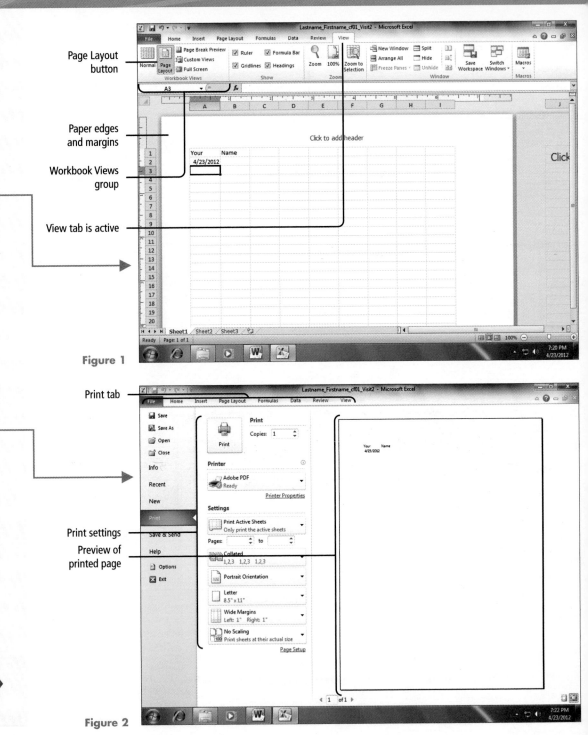

Page Layout button

Paper edges and margins

Workbook Views group

View tab is active

Figure 1

Print tab

Print settings

Preview of printed page

Figure 2

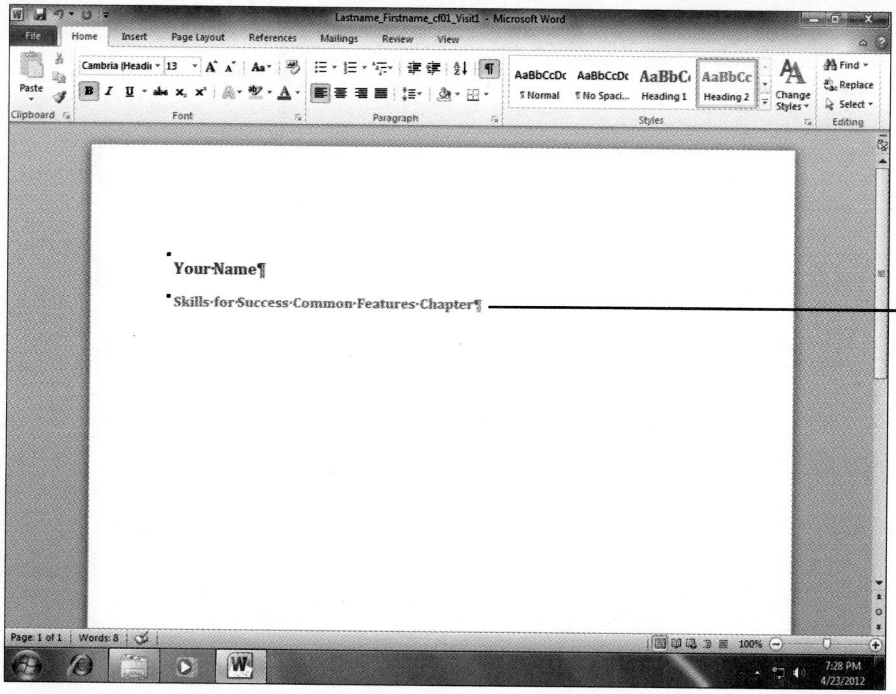

Heading 2 style applied

Figure 3

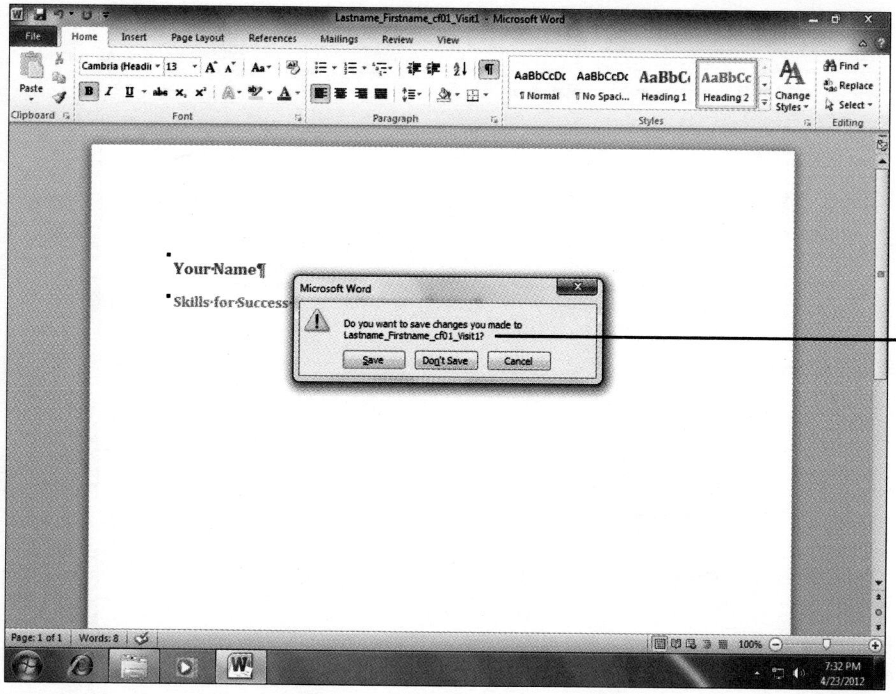

Message asks if you want to save changes

Figure 4

6. Check with your *Course Assignment Sheet* or *Course Syllabus*, or consult with your instructor to determine whether you are to print your work for this chapter. If you are to print your work, at the top left corner of the Print Settings section, click the Print button. If you printed the spreadsheet, retrieve the printout from the printer.

7. On the **File tab**, click **Save**.

> Because you have already named the file, the Save As dialog box does not display.

8. On the **File tab**, click **Exit** to close the spreadsheet and exit Excel.

9. In the Word document, verify that the insertion point is in the second line of text. If not, on the taskbar, click the Word button to make it the active window.

10. On the **Home tab**, in the **Styles group**, click the **Heading 2** thumbnail. Compare your screen with **Figure 3**.

11. On the **File tab**, click **Print** to display the Print tab. If you are printing your work for this chapter, click the Print button, and then retrieve your printout from the printer.

12. On the **File tab**, click **Exit**, and then compare your screen with **Figure 4**.

> When you close a window with changes that have not yet been saved, a message will remind you to save your work.

13. Read the displayed message, and then click **Save**.

- **You have completed Skill 4 of 10**

▶ This book often instructs you to open a student data file so that you do not need to start the project with a blank document.

▶ The student data files are located on the student CD that came with this book. Your instructor may have provided an alternate location.

▶ You use Save As to create a copy of the student data file onto your own storage device.

1. If necessary, insert the student CD that came with this text. If the AutoPlay dialog box displays, click Close.

2. Using the skills practiced earlier, start **Microsoft Word 2010**.

3. In the **Document1 - Microsoft Word** window, click the **File tab**, and then click **Open**.

4. In the **Open** dialog box **Navigation** pane, scroll down and then, if necessary, open Computer. In the list of drives, click the CD/DVD drive to display the contents of the student CD. If your instructor has provided a different location, navigate to that location instead of using the student CD.

5. In the file list, double-click the **01_ student_data_files** folder, double-click the **01_common_features** folder, and then double-click the **chapter_01** folder. Compare your screen with **Figure 1**.

6. In the file list, click **cf01_Visit**, and then click the **Open** button. Compare your screen with **Figure 2**.

   If you opened the file from the student CD, the title bar indicates that the document is in **read-only mode**—a mode where you cannot save your changes.

■ **Continue to the next page to complete the skill**

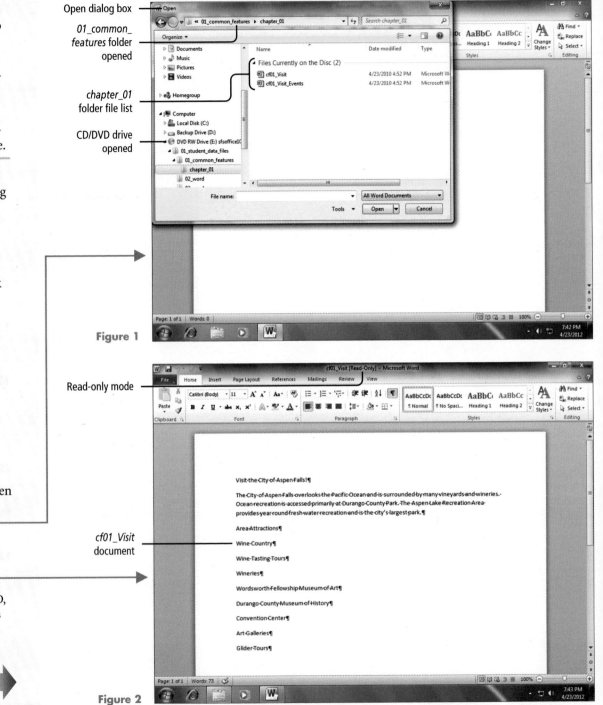

Open dialog box

01_common_ features folder opened

chapter_01 folder file list

CD/DVD drive opened

Figure 1

Read-only mode

cf01_Visit document

Figure 2

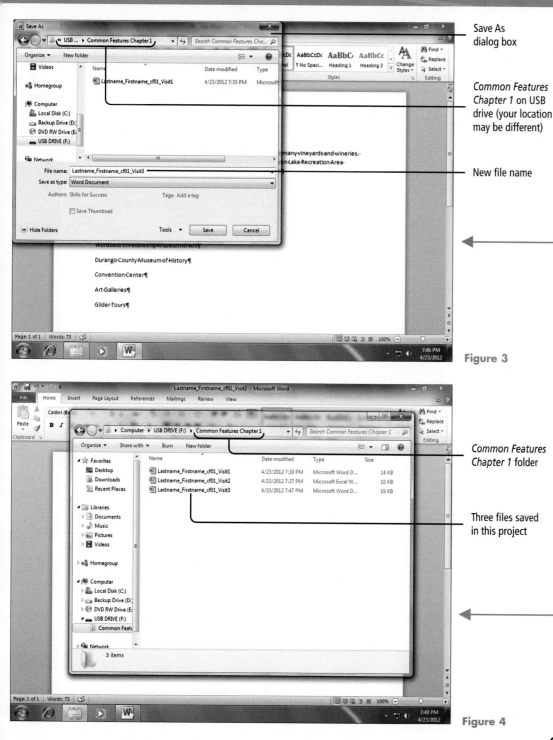

Save As
dialog box

*Common Features
Chapter 1* on USB
drive (your location
may be different)

New file name

*Common Features
Chapter 1* folder

Three files saved
in this project

Figure 3

Figure 4

7. If the document opens in Protected View, click the Enable Editing button.

> **Protected View** is a view applied to documents downloaded from the Internet that allows you to decide if the content is safe before working with the document.

8. Click the **File tab**, and then click **Save As**.

> Because this file has already been saved with a name in a specific location, you need to use Save As to create a copy with a new name and location.

9. In the **Save As** dialog box **Navigation** pane, navigate to the **Common Features Chapter 1** folder that you created previously—open ▷ the drive on which you are saving your work, and then click the **Common Features Chapter 1** folder.

10. In the **File name** box, replace the existing value with Lastname_Firstname_cf01_Visit3 Be sure to use your own first and last names.

11. Compare your screen with **Figure 3**, and then click the **Save** button.

12. On the title bar, notice the new file name displays and *[Read-Only]* no longer displays.

13. On the taskbar, click the **Windows Explorer** button. Verify that the three files you have saved in this chapter display as shown in **Figure 4**.

14. In the Windows Explorer window, navigate to the **student CD**, and then display the **chapter_01** file list.

15. Notice that the original student data file—*cf01_Visit*—is still located in the **chapter_01** folder, and then **Close** ⬛ the Windows Explorer window.

■ **You have completed Skill 5 of 10**

▶ To *edit* is to insert text, delete text, or replace text in an Office document, spreadsheet, or presentation.

▶ To edit text, you need to position the insertion point at the desired location or select the text you want to replace.

1. With the **Word** document as the active window, in the first line, click to the left of the word *Aspen*. Press Bksp 12 times to delete the words *the City of*. Be sure there is one space between each word as shown in **Figure 1**. ──────────

    The Backspace key deletes one letter at a time moving from right to left.

2. In the second line of the document, click to the left of the words *The City of Aspen Falls*. Press Delete 12 times to delete the phrase *The City of*.

    The Delete key deletes one letter at a time moving from left to right.

3. In the line *Area Attractions*, double-click the word *Area* to select it. Type Local and then compare your screen with **Figure 2**. ──────

    When a word is selected, it is replaced by whatever you type next.

■ **Continue to the next page to complete the skill** ▶

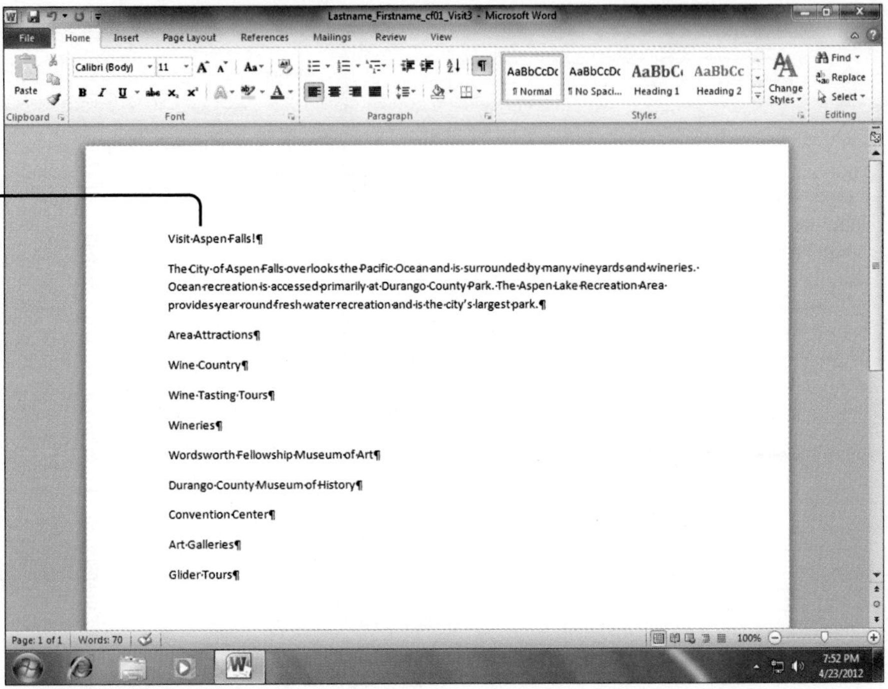

Text deleted

Figure 1

Text deleted

Word replaced

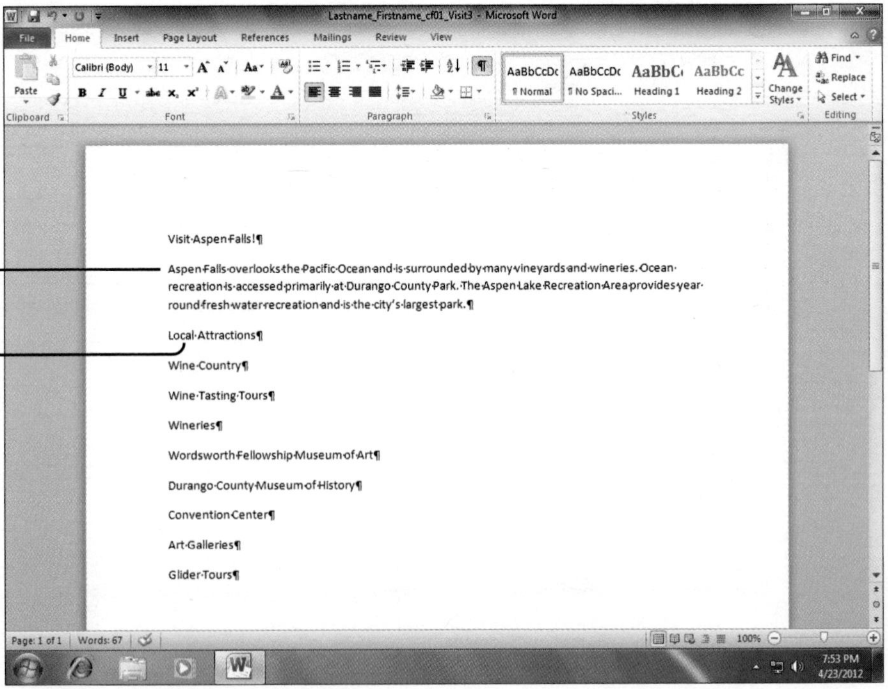

Figure 2

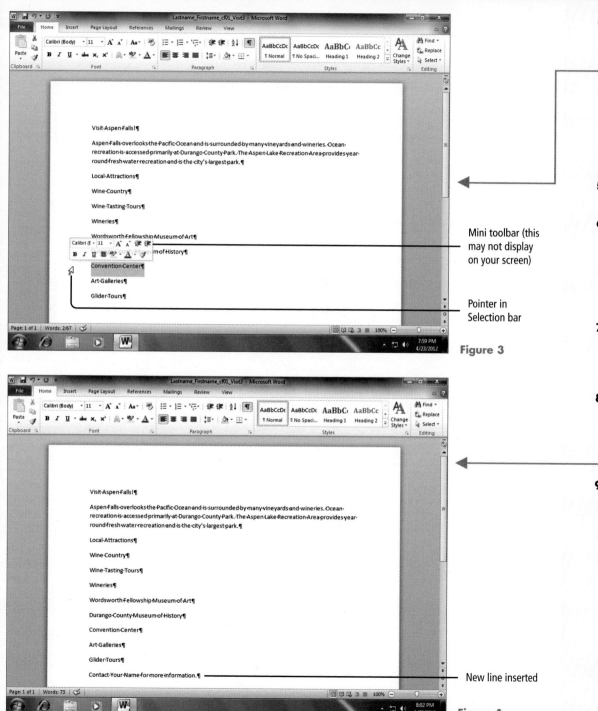

Mini toolbar (this may not display on your screen)

Pointer in Selection bar

Figure 3

New line inserted

Figure 4

4. Place the pointer approximately 1 inch to the left of the line *Convention Center*. When the ⟰ pointer displays as shown in **Figure 3**, click one time.

> Placing the pointer in the Selection bar and then clicking is a way to select an entire line with a single click. After selecting text, the ***Mini toolbar***—a toolbar with common formatting buttons—may display briefly as you move the mouse.

5. With the entire line still selected, press [Delete] to delete the line.

6. On the **Quick Access Toolbar**, click the **Undo** button ↻ one time. Notice the *Convention Center* line displays again.

> When you perform an incorrect action, clicking the Undo button often returns your document to its previous state.

7. At the end of the last line—*Glider Tours*—click between the last word and the paragraph formatting mark (¶). Press [Enter] to insert a new line.

8. With the insertion point in the new line, type Contact Your Name for more information. Be sure to use your first and last names in place of *Your* and *Name*. Compare your screen with **Figure 4**.

9. On the **Quick Access Toolbar**, click **Save** 🖫.

> When a document has already been saved with the desired name, click the Save button—the Save As dialog box is not needed.

■ **You have completed Skill 6 of 10**

► The *copy* command places a copy of the selected text or object in the *Clipboard*— a temporary storage area that holds text or an object that has been cut or copied.

► You can move text by moving it to and from the Clipboard or by dragging the text.

1. Click the **File tab**, and then click **Open**. In the **Open** dialog box, if necessary, navigate to the student files and display the contents of the chapter_01 folder. Click **cf01_Visit_Events**, and then click **Open**.

2. On the right side of the Ribbon's **Home tab**, in the **Editing group**, click the **Select** button, and then click **Select All**. Compare your screen with **Figure 1**.

3. With all of the document text selected, on the left side of the **Home tab**, in the **Clipboard group**, click the **Copy** button.

4. In the upper right corner of the Word window, click **Close**. You do not need to save changes—you will not turn in this student data file.

5. In **Lastname_Firstname_cf01_Visit3**, click to place the insertion point to the left of the line that starts *Contact Your Name.*

6. On the **Home tab**, in the **Clipboard group**, point to—but do not click—the **Paste** button. Compare your screen with **Figure 2**.

   The Paste button has two parts—the upper half is the Paste button, and the lower half is the Paste button arrow. When you click the Paste button arrow, a list of paste options display.

■ **Continue to the next page to complete the skill**

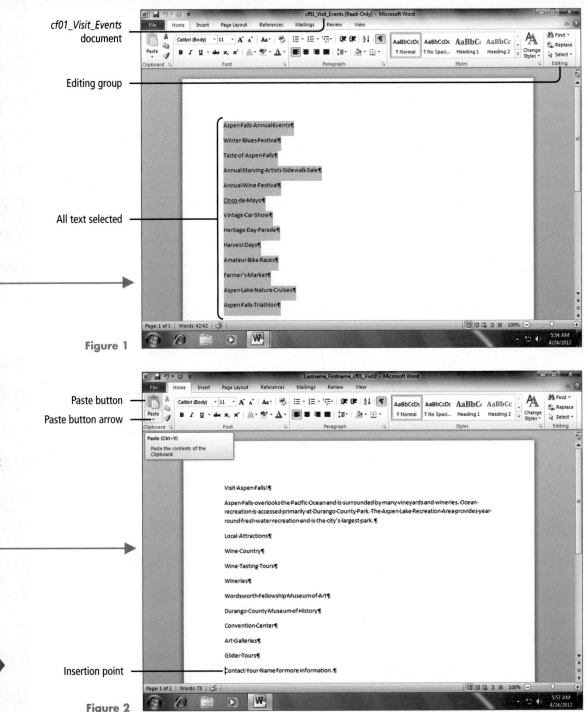

cf01_Visit_Events document

Editing group

All text selected

Figure 1

Paste button

Paste button arrow

Insertion point

Figure 2

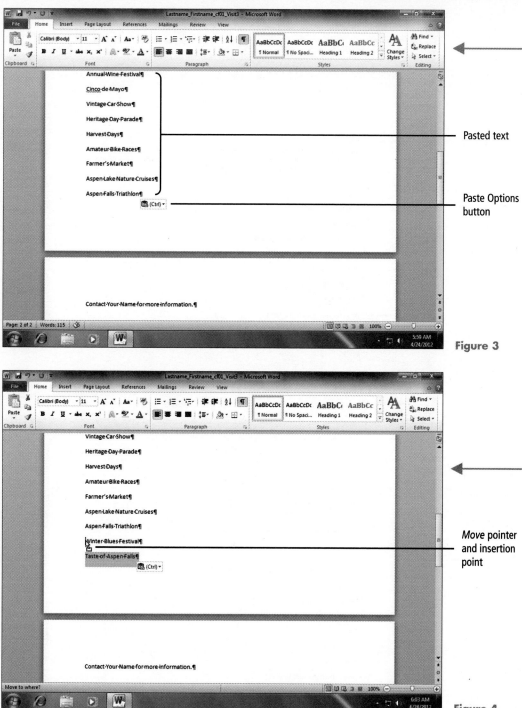

Pasted text

Paste Options button

Figure 3

Move pointer and insertion point

Figure 4

7. Click the upper half of the **Paste** button to paste the selected text. Compare your screen with **Figure 3**.

> When you *paste*, you insert a copy of the text or object stored in the Clipboard and the Paste Options button displays near the pasted text.

8. Press Esc to hide the Paste Options button.

9. Scroll up to display the line *Winter Blues Festival*. Place the I pointer to the left of the W, and then drag down and to the right to select two lines—*Winter Blues Festival* and *Taste of Aspen Falls*.

> To *drag* is to move the mouse while holding down the left mouse button and then to release it at the appropriate time.

10. On the **Home tab**, in the **Clipboard group**, click the **Cut** button.

> The *cut* command removes the selected text or object and stores it in the Clipboard.

11. Click to place the insertion point to the left of *Contact Your Name*, and then in the **Clipboard group**, click the **Paste** button to insert the text.

12. Drag to select the text *Taste of Aspen Falls*, including the paragraph mark.

13. With the pointer, drag the selected text to the left of *Winter Blues Festival*. When the pointer displays to the left of *Winter* as shown in **Figure 4**, release the mouse button.

14. On the **Quick Access Toolbar**, click **Save**.

> ■ **You have completed Skill 7 of 10**

▶ To *format* is to change the appearance of the text—for example, changing the text color to red.

▶ Before formatting text, you first need to select the text that will be formatted.

▶ Once text is selected, you can apply formatting using the Ribbon or the Mini toolbar.

1. Scroll to the top of the document, and then click anywhere in the first line, *Visit Aspen Falls*.

2. On the **Home tab**, in the **Styles group**, click the **Heading 1** thumbnail.

   When no text is selected, the Heading 1 style is applied to the entire paragraph.

3. Click in the paragraph, *Local Attractions*, and then in the **Styles group**, click the **Heading 2** thumbnail. Click in the paragraph, *Aspen Falls Annual Events*, and then apply the **Heading 2** style. Compare your screen with **Figure 1**.

4. Drag to select the text *Visit Aspen Falls!* Immediately point to—but do not click—the Mini toolbar to display it as shown in **Figure 2**. If necessary, right-click the selected text to display the Mini toolbar.

■ **Continue to the next page to complete the skill**

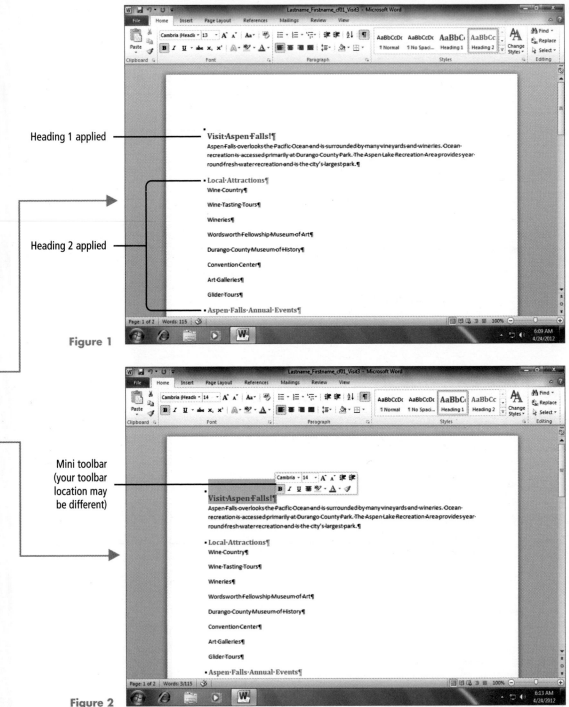

Heading 1 applied

Heading 2 applied

Figure 1

Mini toolbar (your toolbar location may be different)

Figure 2

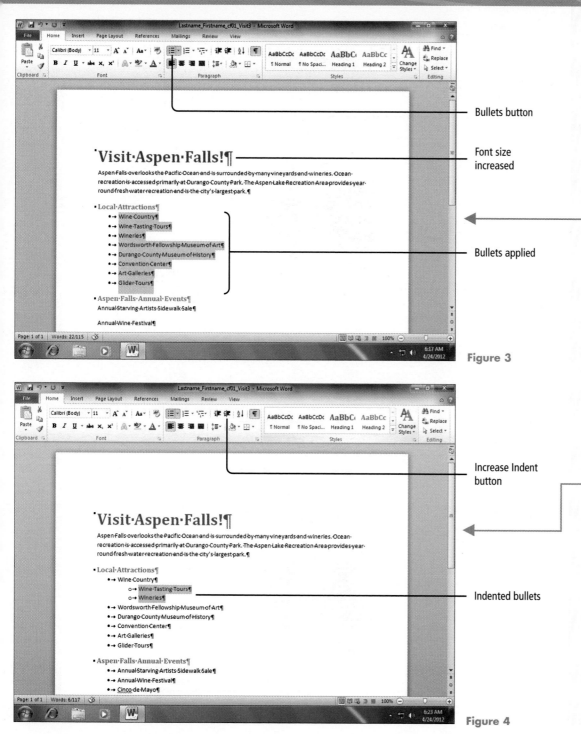

Figure 3

Figure 4

5. On the Mini toolbar, click the **Font Size arrow** ⬚, and then from the list, click **28** to increase the size of the selected text.

6. Place the pointer approximately 1 inch to the left of the line *Wine Country*. When the ⬚ pointer displays, drag straight down. When all the lines between and including *Wine Country* and *Glider Tours* are selected, release the left mouse button.

7. On the Ribbon, in the **Paragraph group**, click the **Bullets** button ⬚, and then compare your screen with **Figure 3**.

8. Click to the left of *Annual Starving Artists Sidewalk Sale*. Scroll down to display the bottom of the page. Press and hold ⬚Shift⬚ while clicking to the right of *Winter Blues Festival* to select all of the text between and including *Annual Starving Artists Sidewalk Sale* and *Winter Blues Festival*.

9. In the **Paragraph group**, click the **Bullets** button ⬚.

10. Scroll to the top of the document. Use either technique just practiced to select *Wine Tasting Tours* and *Wineries*.

11. In the **Paragraph group**, click the **Increase Indent** button ⬚ one time. Compare your screen with **Figure 4**.

12. On the **Quick Access Toolbar**, click **Save** ⬚.

■ **You have completed Skill 8 of 10**

Bullets button

Font size increased

Bullets applied

Increase Indent button

Indented bullets

► Each Ribbon tab contains commands organized into groups. Some tabs display only when a certain type of object is selected—a graphic, for example.

1. Press and hold ⌃Ctrl, and then press Home to place the insertion point at the beginning of the document.

2. On the **Ribbon,** to the right of the **Home tab**, click the **Insert tab**. In the **Illustrations group**, click the **Picture** button.

3. In the **Insert Picture** dialog box, navigate as needed to display the contents of the student files in the **chapter_01** folder. Click **cf01_Visit_River**, and then click the **Insert** button. Compare your screen with **Figure 1.**

   When a picture is selected, the Format tab displays below Picture Tools. On the Format tab, in the Picture Styles group, a *gallery*—a visual display of choices from which you can choose—displays thumbnails. The entire gallery can be seen by clicking the More button to the right and below the first row of thumbnails.

4. On the **Format tab**, in the **Picture Styles group**, click the **More** button ⤓ to display the **Picture Styles** gallery. In the gallery, point to the fourth thumbnail in the first row—**Drop Shadow Rectangle**—to display the ScreenTip as shown in **Figure 2.**

   A *ScreenTip* is informational text that displays when you point to commands or thumbnails on the Ribbon.

5. Click the **Drop Shadow Rectangle** thumbnail to apply the picture style.

■ **Continue to the next page to complete the skill**

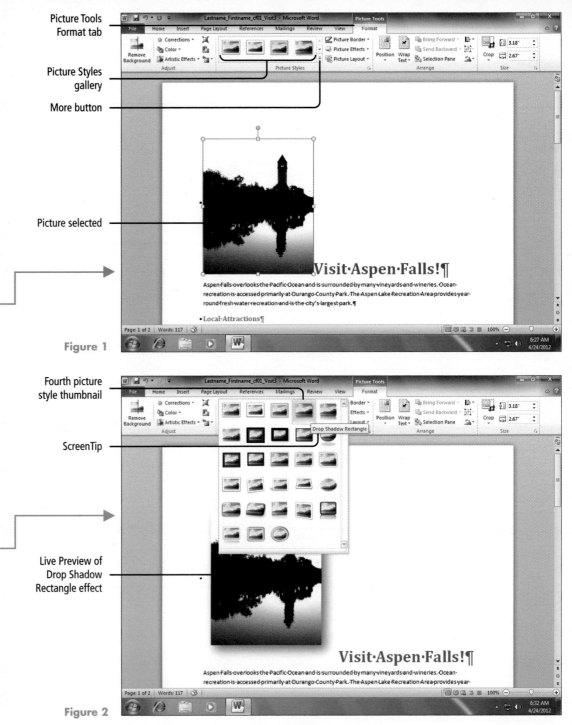

Picture Tools Format tab
Picture Styles gallery
More button
Picture selected

Figure 1

Fourth picture style thumbnail
ScreenTip
Live Preview of Drop Shadow Rectangle effect

Figure 2

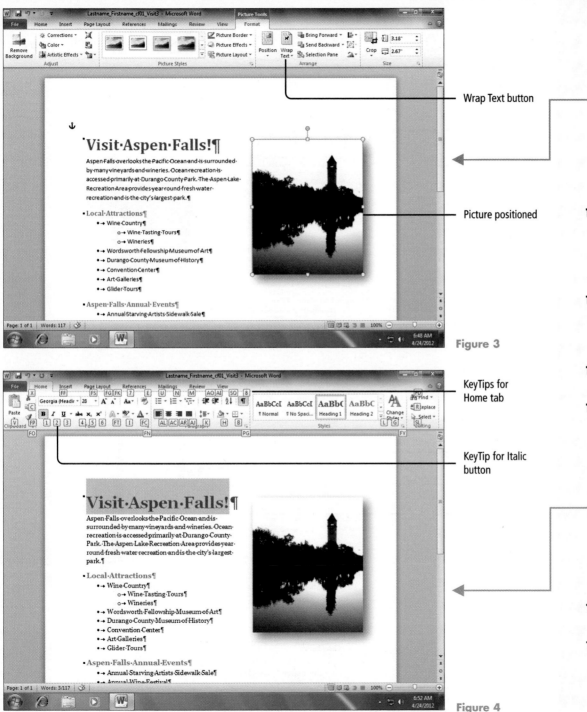

Wrap Text button

Picture positioned

Figure 3

KeyTips for Home tab

KeyTip for Italic button

Figure 4

6. On the **Format tab**, in the **Arrange group**, click the **Wrap Text** button, and then from the list of choices, click **Square**.

7. Point to the picture, and then with the pointer, drag the picture to the right side of the page as shown in **Figure 3**.

8. Click a blank area of the page, and then notice the Picture Tools Format tab no longer displays.

9. On the **Page Layout tab**, in the **Themes group**, click the **Themes** button.

10. In the **Themes** gallery, point to—but do not click—each of the thumbnails to display the Live Preview of each theme. When you are done, click the **Civic** thumbnail.

11. On the **View tab**, in the **Zoom group**, click the **One Page** button to display the entire page on the screen. If necessary, adjust the position of the picture.

12. On the **View tab**, in the **Zoom group**, click the **100%** button.

13. Select the text *Visit Aspen Falls!* without selecting the paragraph mark. Press Alt to display *KeyTips*—keys that you can press to access each Ribbon tab and most commands on each tab. Release Alt, and then press H one time to display the Home tab. Compare your screen with **Figure 4**.

   With KeyTips displayed on the Home tab, pressing 2 is the same as clicking the Italic button. In this manner, you select Ribbon commands without using the mouse.

14. Press 2 to apply the Italic format to the selected text.

15. **Save** the document.

■ **You have completed Skill 9 of 10**

► Commands can be accessed in *dialog boxes*—boxes where you can select multiple settings.

► You can also access commands by right-clicking objects in a document.

1. In the paragraph that starts *Aspen Falls overlooks the Pacific Ocean*, **triple-click**—click three times fairly quickly without moving the mouse—to highlight the entire paragraph.

2. On the **Home tab**, in the lower right corner of the **Font group**, point to the **Font Dialog Box Launcher** as shown in **Figure 1**. ──────────────

   The buttons at the lower right corner of most groups open a dialog box with choices that may not be available on the Ribbon.

3. Click the **Font Dialog Box Launcher** to open the Font dialog box.

4. In the **Font** dialog box, click the **Advanced tab**. Click the **Spacing arrow**, and then click **Expanded**.

5. To the right of the **Spacing** box, click the **By spin box up arrow** three times to display *1.3 pt*. Compare your screen with **Figure 2**, and then click **OK** to close the dialog box and apply the changes. ─────

■ **Continue to the next page to complete the skill**

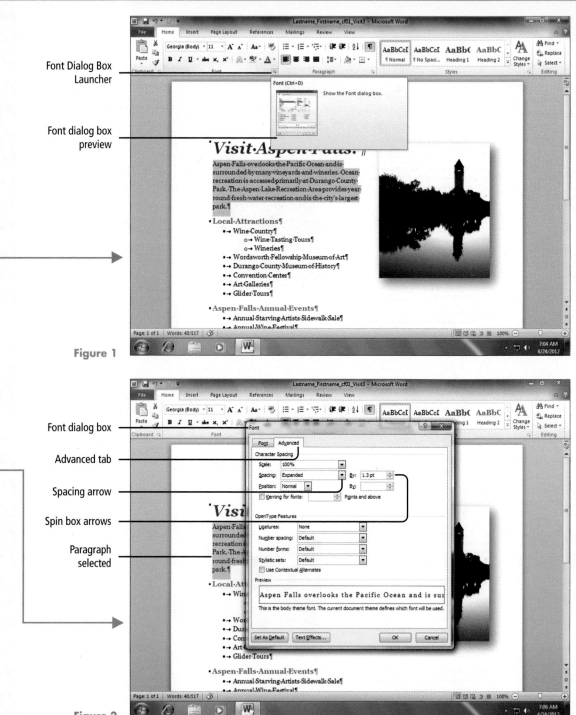

Font Dialog Box Launcher

Font dialog box preview

Figure 1

Font dialog box

Advanced tab

Spacing arrow

Spin box arrows

Paragraph selected

Figure 2

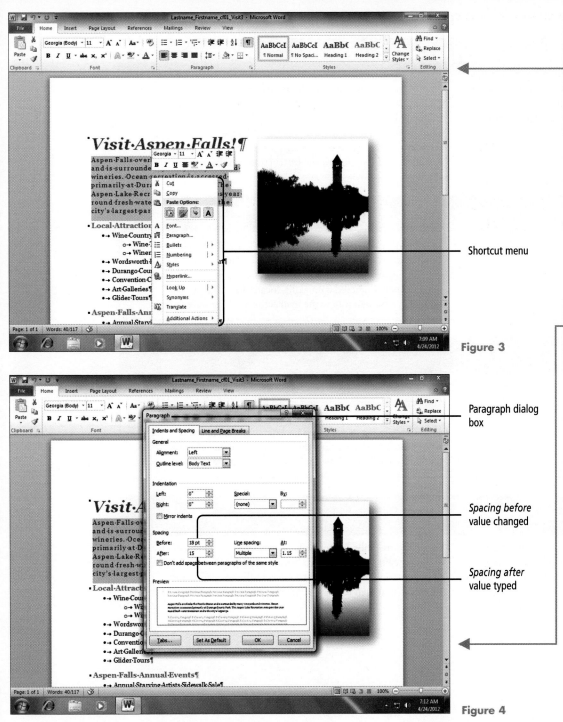

Shortcut menu

Figure 3

Paragraph dialog box

Spacing before value changed

Spacing after value typed

Figure 4

6. With the paragraph still selected, *right-click*—click the paragraph with the right mouse button—and then compare your screen with **Figure 3**.

   When you right-click selected text, the Mini toolbar and a shortcut menu display. A *shortcut menu* displays a list of commands related to the type of object that you right-click.

7. From the displayed shortcut menu, click the **Paragraph** command. Alternately, on the Home tab, click the Paragraph Dialog Box Launcher.

8. In the **Paragraph** dialog box, under **Spacing,** click the **Before spin up arrow** three times to display *18 pt.*

9. In the **After** box, highlight the existing value, and then type 15 Compare your screen with **Figure 4**, and then click **OK.**

10. If your instructor asks you to print your work, click the File tab, click Print, and then click the Print button.

11. Click **Save** 🖫, click the **File tab,** and then click **Exit.**

Done! You have completed Skill 10 of 10, and your document is complete!

More Skills

The following More Skills are located at **www.pearsonhighered.com/skills**

More Skills 11 Capture Screens with the Snipping Tool

Some of the work that you do in this book cannot be graded without showing your computer screens to the grader. You can use the Snipping Tool to create pictures of your screens. Snip files can be printed or submitted electronically.

In More Skills 11, you will use the Snipping Tool to create a picture of your screen and then copy the picture into a Word document.

To begin, open your web browser, navigate to www.pearsonhighered.com/skills, locate the name of your textbook, and then follow the instructions on the website.

More Skills 12 Use Microsoft Office Help

Microsoft Office 2010 has a Help system in which you can search for articles that show you how to accomplish tasks.

In More Skills 12, you will use the Office 2010 Help system to view an article on how to customize the Help window.

To begin, open your web browser, navigate to www.pearson highered.com/skills, locate the name of your textbook, and then follow the instructions on the website.

More Skills 13 Organize Files

Over time, you may create hundreds of files using Microsoft Office. To find your files when you need them, they need to be well-organized. You can organize your computer files by carefully naming them and by placing them into folders.

In More Skills 13, you will create, delete, and rename folders. You will then copy, delete, and move files into the folders that you created.

To begin, open your web browser, navigate to www.pearsonhighered.com/skills, locate the name of your textbook, and then follow the instructions on the website.

More Skills 14 Save Documents to Windows Live

If your computer is connected to the Internet, you can save your Office documents to a drive available to you free of charge through Windows Live. You can then open the files from other locations such as home, school, or work.

In More Skills 14, you will save a memo to Windows Live.

To begin, open your web browser, navigate to www.pearsonhighered.com/skills, locate the name of your textbook, and then follow the instructions on the website.

Key Terms

Online Help Skills

1. **Start** 🏵 Word. In the upper right corner of the Word window, click the **Help** button 📄. In the **Help** window, click the **Maximize** 🔲 button.

2. Click in the search box, type Create a document and then click the **Search** button. In the search results, click **Create a document**.

3. Read the article's introduction, and then below **What do you want to do**, click **Start a document from a template**. Compare your screen with **Figure 1**.

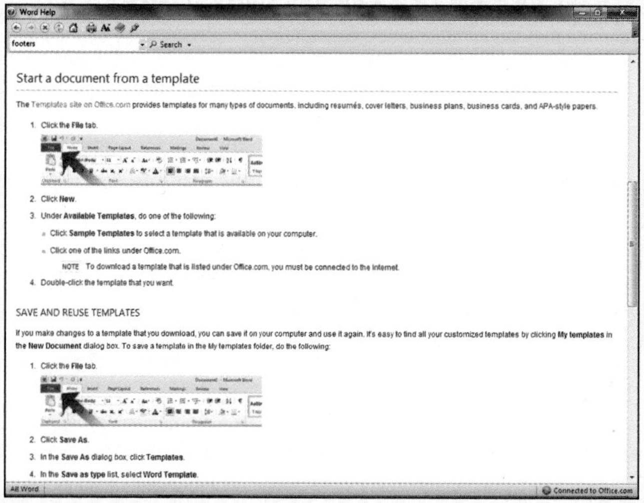

Figure 1

4. Read the Start a document from a template section to see if you can answer the following: What types of documents are available as templates? On the New tab, under Available Templates, what are the two general locations that you can find templates?

Matching

Match each term in the second column with its correct definition in the first column by writing the letter of the term on the blank line in front of the correct definition.

_____ **1.** A feature that displays the result of a formatting change if you select it.

_____ **2.** A line between the cells in a table or spreadsheet.

_____ **3.** A mode where you can open and view a file, but you cannot save your changes.

_____ **4.** A view where you prepare your document or spreadsheet for printing.

_____ **5.** Quickly click the left mouse button two times without moving the mouse.

_____ **6.** To insert text, delete text, or replace text in an Office document, spreadsheet, or presentation.

_____ **7.** A command that moves a copy of the selected text or object to the Clipboard.

_____ **8.** A command that removes the selected text or object and stores it in the Clipboard.

_____ **9.** To change the appearance of the text.

_____ **10.** A menu that displays a list of commands related to the type of object that you right-clicked on.

A Copy

B Cut

C Double-click

D Edit

E Format

F Grid line

G Live Preview

H Page Layout

I Read-only

J Shortcut

Multiple Choice

Choose the correct answer.

1. The flashing vertical line that indicates where text will be inserted when you start typing.
   - A. Cell reference
   - B. Insertion point
   - C. KeyTip

2. A button used to turn a feature both on and off.
   - A. Contextual button
   - B. On/Off button
   - C. Toggle button

3. The box formed by the intersection of a row and column.
   - A. Cell
   - B. Cell reference
   - C. Insertion point

4. Until you save a document, it is stored only here.
   - A. Clipboard
   - B. Live Preview
   - C. RAM

5. The combination of a number on the left side and a letter on the top of a spreadsheet that addresses a cell.
   - A. Coordinates
   - B. Cell reference
   - C. Insertion point

6. A temporary storage area that holds text or an object that has been cut or copied.
   - A. Clipboard
   - B. Dialog box
   - C. Live Preview

7. A toolbar with common formatting buttons that displays after you select text.
   - A. Gallery toolbar
   - B. Mini toolbar
   - C. Taskbar toolbar

8. Informational text that displays when you point to commands or thumbnails on the Ribbon.
   - A. Live Preview
   - B. ScreenTip
   - C. Shortcut menu

9. A visual display of choices from which you can choose.
   - A. Gallery
   - B. Options menu
   - C. Shortcut menu

10. An icon that displays on the Ribbon to indicate the key that you can press to access Ribbon commands.
    - A. KeyTip
    - B. ScreenTip
    - C. ToolTip

Topics for Discussion

1. You have briefly worked with three Microsoft Office programs: Word, Excel, and PowerPoint. Based on your experience, describe the overall purpose of each of these programs.

2. Many believe that computers enable offices to go paperless—that is, to share files electronically instead of printing and then distributing them. What are the advantages of sharing files electronically, and in what situations would it be best to print documents?

CHAPTER 1

Work with Databases and Create Tables

► Microsoft Access is an application used to store, organize, access, and update data.

► To build a database, you first save the database file and then create tables to store the information you need.

Your starting screen will look like this:

SKILLS  Skills 1-10 Training

At the end of this chapter, you will be able to:

Skill 1 Open and Organize Existing Databases

Skill 2 Enter and Edit Table Data

Skill 3 Create Forms and Enter Data

Skill 4 Filter Data in Queries

Skill 5 Create, Preview, and Print Reports

Skill 6 Create Databases and Tables

Skill 7 Change Data Types and Other Field Properties

Skill 8 Create Tables in Design View

Skill 9 Relate Tables

Skill 10 Enter Data in Related Tables

MORE SKILLS

More Skills 11 Compact and Repair Databases

More Skills 12 Import Data from Excel

More Skills 13 Work with the Attachment Data Type

More Skills 14 Work with the Hyperlink and Yes/No Data Types

Outcome

Using the skills listed to the left will enable you to create database objects like this:

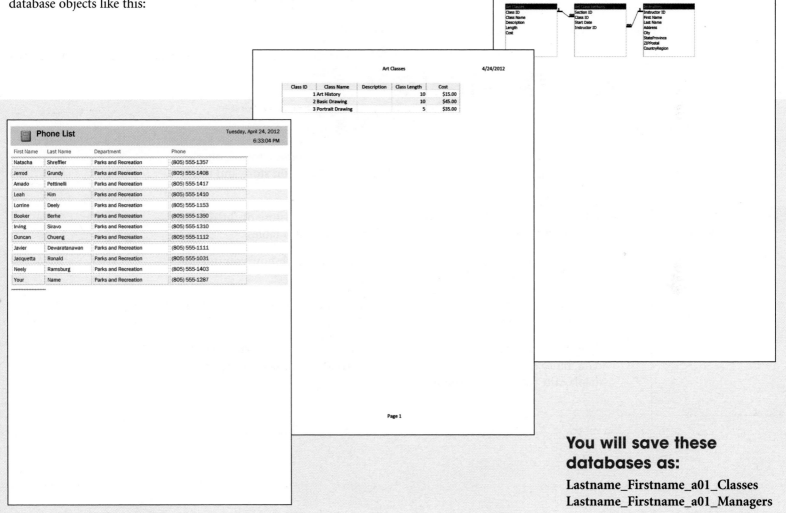

In this chapter, you will create documents for the Aspen Falls City Hall, which provides essential services for the citizens and visitors of Aspen Falls, California.

Introduction

- ▶ A single Access file contains many objects, including tables, forms, queries, and reports. Each object has a special purpose to help you store and track information.

- ▶ When you create a database, you first determine the purpose of the database. You can then plan how to organize the information into tables.

- ▶ When you create tables, you assign properties that match how you intend to enter data into the database.

- ▶ After creating tables, you establish the relationships between them and then test those relationships by adding sample data.

- ▶ After the table relationships are tested, you are ready to add forms to enter data, build queries to search for specific information, and create reports to display the information you need.

Time to complete all
10 skills – 50 to 75 minutes

Find your data files here:

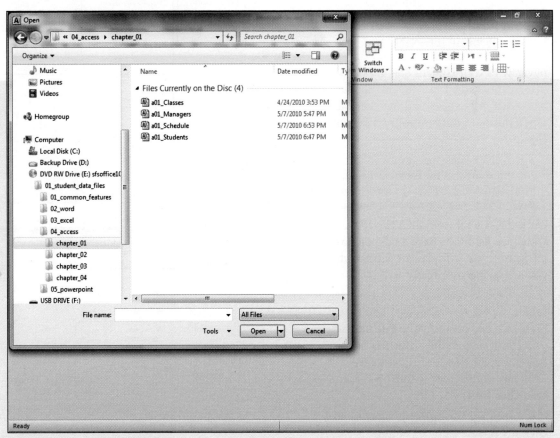

Student data file needed
for this chapter:

- a01_Managers

▶ A *database* is a structured collection of related information about people, events, and things.

1. Click the **Start** button 🌐. From the **Start** menu, locate and then click **Microsoft Access 2010**. If necessary, Maximize 🔲 the window.

2. If necessary, insert the Student CD that came with this book.

3. On the left side of the Backstage, click **Open**. In the **Open** dialog box, navigate to your student data files and display the student files for this chapter. Select **a01_Managers**, and then click the **Open** button. Compare your screen with **Figure 1**.

   A security warning may display so that you can verify that the database file came from a trusted source. In the Navigation Pane, several database objects are listed.

4. Click the **File tab**, and then click **Save Database As**. In the **Save As** dialog box navigation pane, display the file list where you are saving your files.

5. In the **Save As** dialog box, click **New folder**, type Access Chapter 1 and then press [Enter] two times. In the **File name** box, using your own name, name the file Lastname_Firstname_a01_Managers Compare your screen with **Figure 2**, and then click **Save**.

6. If the Security Warning message displays, click the Enable Content button.

■ **Continue to the next page to complete the skill**

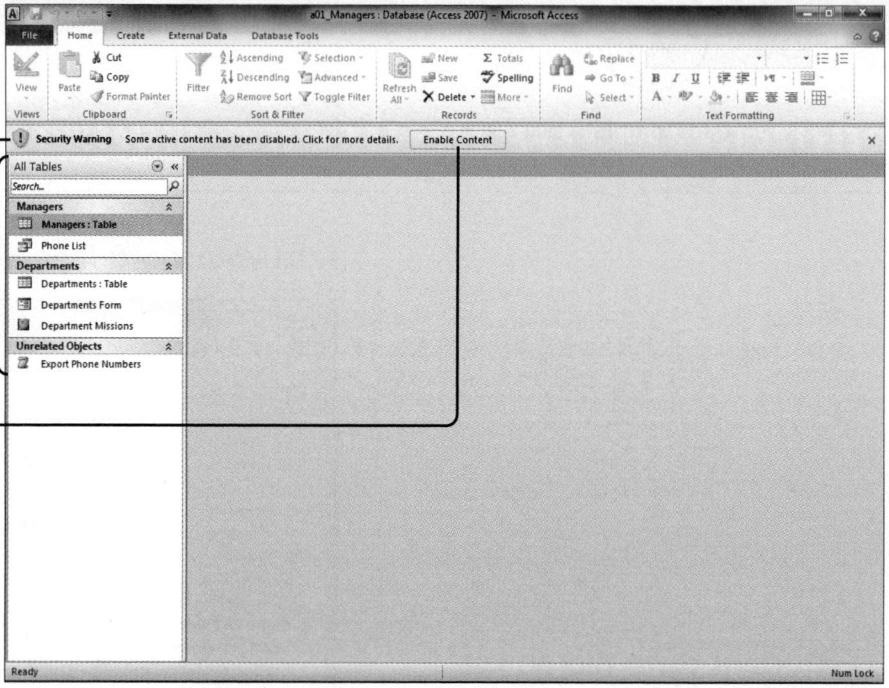

Security Warning message (yours may not display)

Objects in Navigation Pane

Enable Content button

Figure 1

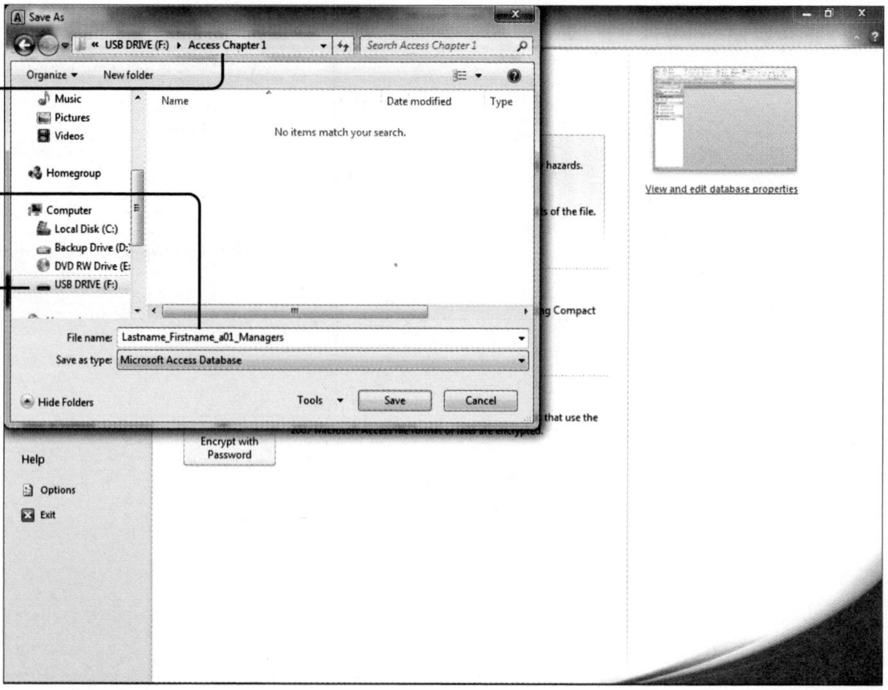

New folder created

File name changed

USB flash drive opened

Figure 2

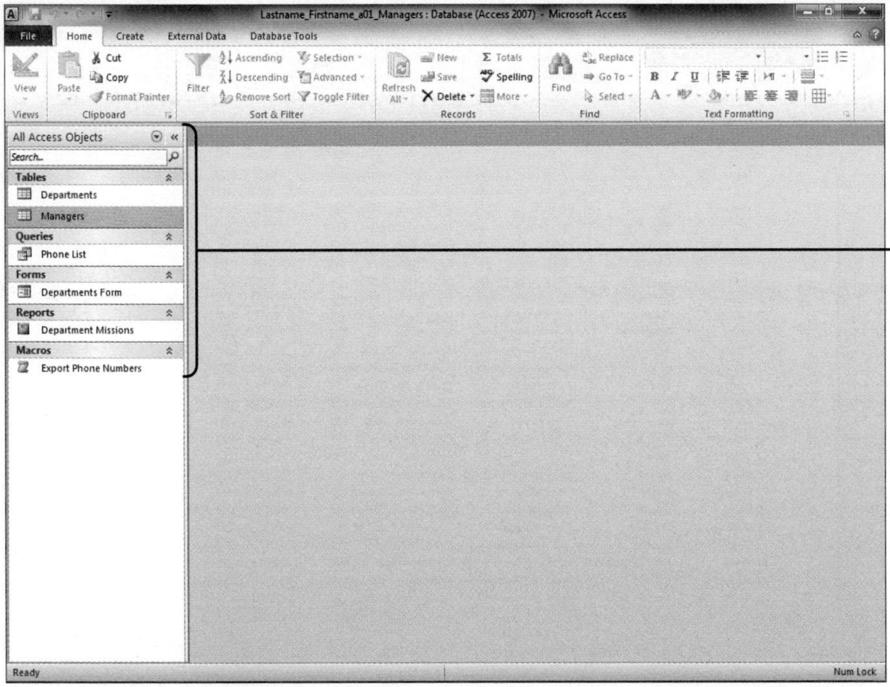

Navigation Pane organized by object type

Figure 3

Common Access Database Objects

Object	Purpose
Table	Store the data in rows and columns.
Form	Enter new records, delete records, or update existing records.
Query	Display a subset of the data in response to a specific question.
Report	Display table data or query results on the screen or in printed form.
Macro	Store a sequence of commands that can be performed as one task.

Figure 4

7. Click the **Navigation Pane arrow** ⊙, and then, in the list, click **Managers** to list only the objects related to the Managers data.

The Navigation Pane can display the objects by type. *Database objects*—or *objects*—are the basic parts of a database that you work with. Here, two tables, a query, a form, a report, and a macro are listed.

8. Click the **Navigation Pane arrow** ⊙, and then, in the list, click **Object Type**. Compare your screen with Figure 3.

Database objects work together to provide a *database management system (DBMS)*—software used to manage and interact with the database. The purpose of each database object is summarized in the table in Figure 4.

9. In the **Navigation Pane**, under **Forms**, double-click **Departments Form** to open the form.

10. In the **Navigation Pane**, under **Reports**, double-click **Department Missions** to open the report.

11. In the upper-right corner of the **Department Missions** report, click the **Close** ✕ button.

12. In the upper-right corner of **Departments Form**, click the **Close** ✕ button.

In this manner, database objects are opened and closed.

13. Leave the database open for the next skill.

■ **You have completed Skill 1 of 10**

▶ Databases store information in tables by organizing data into rows and columns.

▶ You can open tables to view the data that it stores and then make changes to that data.

1. In the **Navigation Pane**, under **Tables**, double-click the **Managers** table to open the table.

2. Click the **Shutter Bar Open/Close** button |«| to close the **Navigation Pane**, and then compare your screen with **Figure 1**.

> The *table*—the database object that stores the data—opens in Datasheet view. A *datasheet* displays records in rows and fields in columns similar to a Microsoft Excel spreadsheet. A *record* is the collection of related information that displays in a single row of a database table, and a *field* is a set of common characteristics around which a table is organized.

3. Point to the right of the **Position** column header. When the |✛| pointer displays, double-click to resize the column width automatically to fit its contents.

4. On the Quick Access Toolbar, click **Save** |💾|. Compare your screen with **Figure 2**.

> With Access objects, design changes should be saved. Here, the wider column settings are saved.

5. In the **First Name** column of the first row—the **First Name** field in the first record—double-click *Jake* to select the value, and then type Jack Press [Enter] to accept the change and move to the next field.

■ **Continue to the next page to complete the skill** ➤

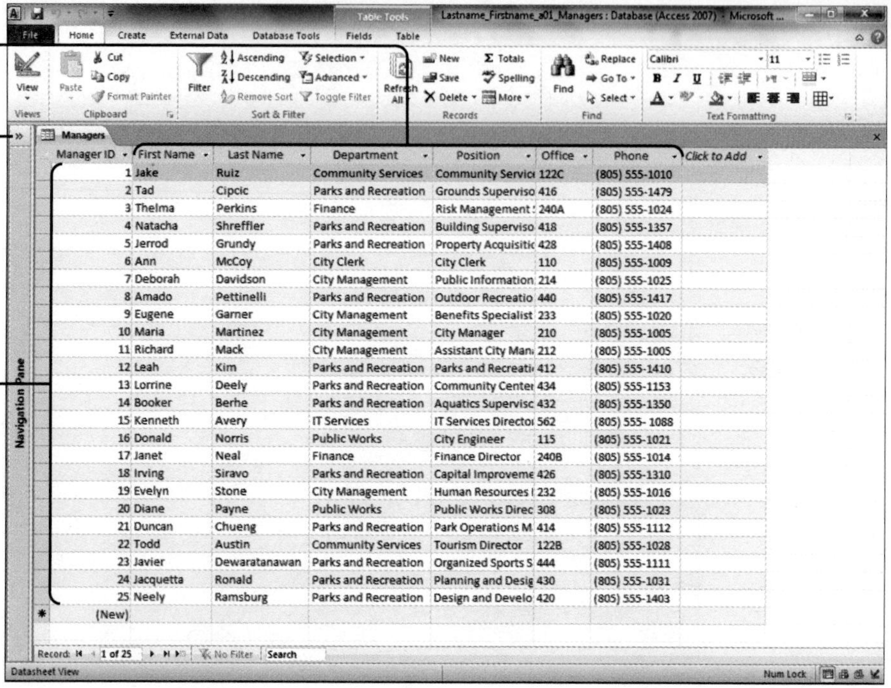

Figure 1

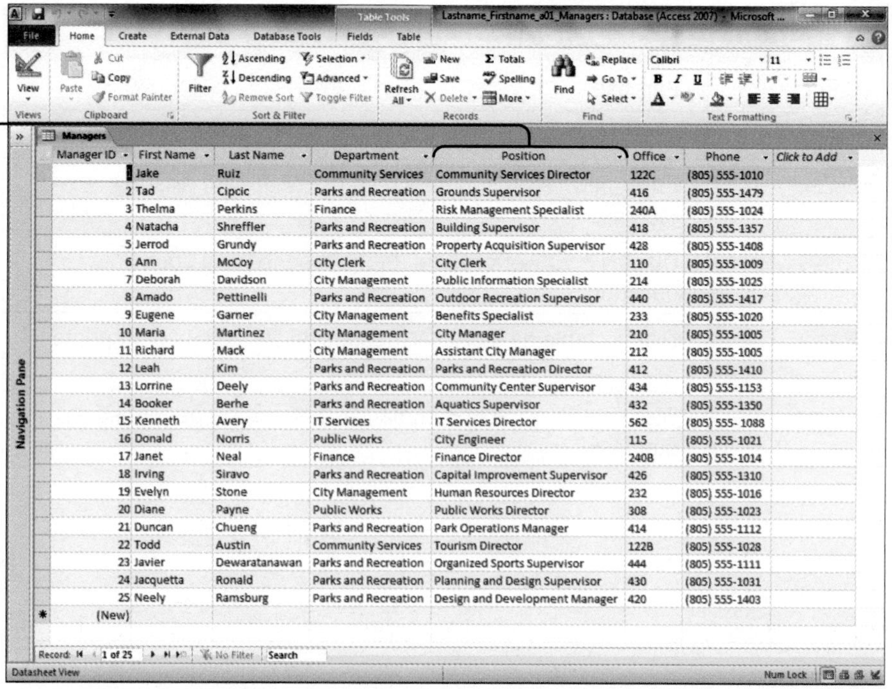

Field names
Navigation Pane Shutter Bar Open/Close button
Records in rows

Manager ID	First Name	Last Name	Department	Position	Office	Phone	Click to Add
1	Jake	Ruiz	Community Services	Community Servic	122C	(805) 555-1010	
2	Tad	Cipcic	Parks and Recreation	Grounds Superviso	416	(805) 555-1479	
3	Thelma	Perkins	Finance	Risk Management S	240A	(805) 555-1024	
4	Natacha	Shreffler	Parks and Recreation	Building Superviso	418	(805) 555-1357	
5	Jerrod	Grundy	Parks and Recreation	Property Acquisitio	428	(805) 555-1408	
6	Ann	McCoy	City Clerk	City Clerk	110	(805) 555-1009	
7	Deborah	Davidson	City Management	Public Information	214	(805) 555-1025	
8	Amado	Pettinelli	Parks and Recreation	Outdoor Recreatio	440	(805) 555-1417	
9	Eugene	Garner	City Management	Benefits Specialist	233	(805) 555-1020	
10	Maria	Martinez	City Management	City Manager	210	(805) 555-1005	
11	Richard	Mack	City Management	Assistant City Man	212	(805) 555-1005	
12	Leah	Kim	Parks and Recreation	Parks and Recreati	412	(805) 555-1410	
13	Lorrine	Deely	Parks and Recreation	Community Center	434	(805) 555-1153	
14	Booker	Berhe	Parks and Recreation	Aquatics Superviso	432	(805) 555-1350	
15	Kenneth	Avery	IT Services	IT Services Directo	562	(805) 555-1088	
16	Donald	Norris	Public Works	City Engineer	115	(805) 555-1021	
17	Janet	Neal	Finance	Finance Director	240B	(805) 555-1014	
18	Irving	Siravo	Parks and Recreation	Capital Improveme	426	(805) 555-1310	
19	Evelyn	Stone	City Management	Human Resources I	232	(805) 555-1016	
20	Diane	Payne	Public Works	Public Works Direc	308	(805) 555-1023	
21	Duncan	Chueng	Parks and Recreation	Park Operations M	414	(805) 555-1112	
22	Todd	Austin	Community Services	Tourism Director	122B	(805) 555-1028	
23	Javier	Dewaratanawan	Parks and Recreation	Organized Sports S	444	(805) 555-1111	
24	Jacquetta	Ronald	Parks and Recreation	Planning and Desig	430	(805) 555-1031	
25	Neely	Ramsburg	Parks and Recreation	Design and Develo	420	(805) 555-1403	
*	(New)						

Figure 2

Position column widened

Manager ID	First Name	Last Name	Department	Position	Office	Phone	Click to Add
1	Jake	Ruiz	Community Services	Community Services Director	122C	(805) 555-1010	
2	Tad	Cipcic	Parks and Recreation	Grounds Supervisor	416	(805) 555-1479	
3	Thelma	Perkins	Finance	Risk Management Specialist	240A	(805) 555-1024	
4	Natacha	Shreffler	Parks and Recreation	Building Supervisor	418	(805) 555-1357	
5	Jerrod	Grundy	Parks and Recreation	Property Acquisition Supervisor	428	(805) 555-1408	
6	Ann	McCoy	City Clerk	City Clerk	110	(805) 555-1009	
7	Deborah	Davidson	City Management	Public Information Specialist	214	(805) 555-1025	
8	Amado	Pettinelli	Parks and Recreation	Outdoor Recreation Supervisor	440	(805) 555-1417	
9	Eugene	Garner	City Management	Benefits Specialist	233	(805) 555-1020	
10	Maria	Martinez	City Management	City Manager	210	(805) 555-1005	
11	Richard	Mack	City Management	Assistant City Manager	212	(805) 555-1005	
12	Leah	Kim	Parks and Recreation	Parks and Recreation Director	412	(805) 555-1410	
13	Lorrine	Deely	Parks and Recreation	Community Center Supervisor	434	(805) 555-1153	
14	Booker	Berhe	Parks and Recreation	Aquatics Supervisor	432	(805) 555-1350	
15	Kenneth	Avery	IT Services	IT Services Director	562	(805) 555-1088	
16	Donald	Norris	Public Works	City Engineer	115	(805) 555-1021	
17	Janet	Neal	Finance	Finance Director	240B	(805) 555-1014	
18	Irving	Siravo	Parks and Recreation	Capital Improvement Supervisor	426	(805) 555-1310	
19	Evelyn	Stone	City Management	Human Resources Director	232	(805) 555-1016	
20	Diane	Payne	Public Works	Public Works Director	308	(805) 555-1023	
21	Duncan	Chueng	Parks and Recreation	Park Operations Manager	414	(805) 555-1112	
22	Todd	Austin	Community Services	Tourism Director	122B	(805) 555-1028	
23	Javier	Dewaratanawan	Parks and Recreation	Organized Sports Supervisor	444	(805) 555-1111	
24	Jacquetta	Ronald	Parks and Recreation	Planning and Design Supervisor	430	(805) 555-1031	
25	Neely	Ramsburg	Parks and Recreation	Design and Development Manager	420	(805) 555-1403	
*	(New)						

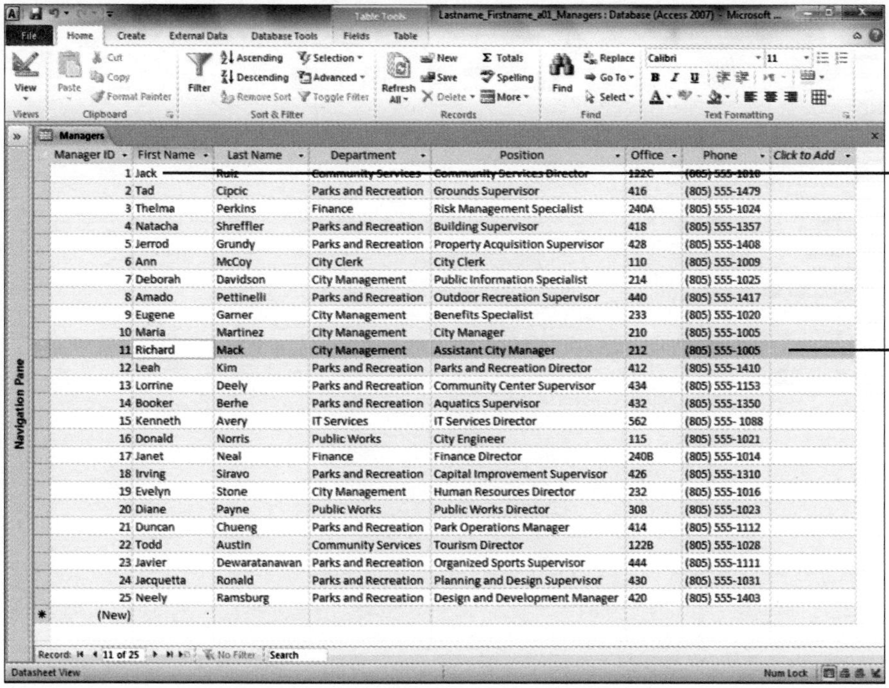

First Name value changed

Record for Richard Mack active

Figure 3

Department	Position	Office	Phone
Community Services	Development Director	122A	(805) 555-1015

Figure 4

6. Click anywhere in the 11th row—the record for Richard Mack. Compare your screen with **Figure 3**.

   When you change data, the new data is saved automatically when you click or navigate to a different record. Here, the new name entered in the previous step has been saved.

7. With the record for Richard Mack active, on the **Home tab**, in the **Records group**, click the **Delete button arrow**, and then click **Delete Record**. Read the message that displays, and then click **Yes**.

8. In the lower-left corner of the datasheet, click the **New (blank) record** button to move to the datasheet *append row*—a blank row in which a new record is entered.

9. Press Enter to move to the **First Name** column, and then watch the **Manager ID** column as you type Julia

   Manager ID is an *AutoNumber*—a field that automatically enters a unique, numeric value when a record is created. The number is assigned as soon as you begin adding data to a new record. Once an AutoNumber value has been assigned, it cannot be changed. When your AutoNumber values differ from the ones shown in figures, do not try to change yours to match.

10. Press Enter to move to the **Last Name** column, type Wagner and then press Enter. Repeat this technique to enter the data shown in **Figure 4**.

11. When you are done, press Enter to move to a new append row and to save the record. **Close** the table.

■ **You have completed Skill 2 of 10**

▶ Access *forms* are created so that you can modify or add to the data stored in tables.

1. **Open** » the **Navigation Pane**. If necessary, in the Navigation Pane, under **Tables**, click **Managers** one time to select it.

2. On the **Create tab**, in the **Forms group**, click the **Form** button to create a form for the **Managers** table. Compare your screen with **Figure 1**. If necessary, close the Property Sheet ✕.

   The Form tool creates a form for the table that you selected in the Navigation Pane.

3. Click **Save** 🖫, and then, in the **Save As** dialog box, accept the suggested name for the form by clicking **OK**. In the **Navigation Pane**, notice that the **Managers** form is listed under **Forms**.

4. On the **Design tab**, in the **Themes group**, click the **Themes** button. In the **Themes** gallery, point to—do not click—thumbnails to see their **Live Preview**. Under **Built-In**, click the third thumbnail—**Angles**—to apply the theme.

5. On the **Design tab**, in the **Views group**, click the **View button** to switch to **Form** view. Click **Save** 🖫 to save the design changes, and then compare your screen with **Figure 2**.

   Most forms use the *single form layout*, a layout that displays one record at a time. Here, the form shows the first record from the Managers table. The navigation bar in the lower-left corner of the form is used to move to other records.

▪ **Continue to the next page to complete the skill** ▶

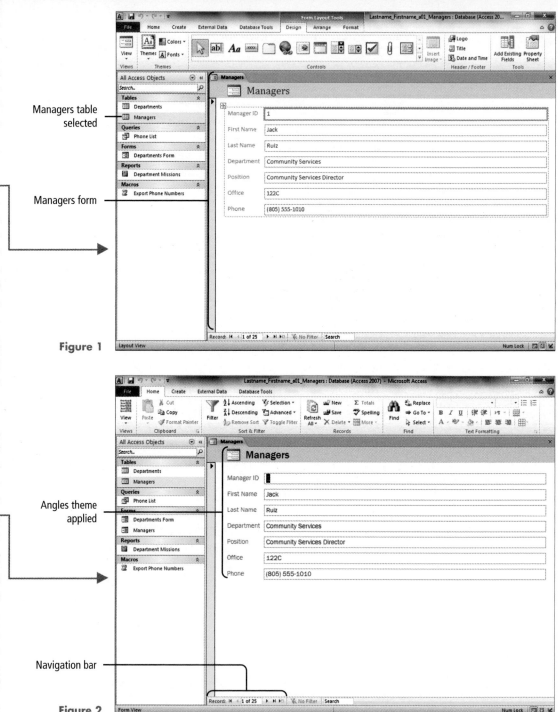

Managers table selected

Managers form

Figure 1

Angles theme applied

Navigation bar

Figure 2

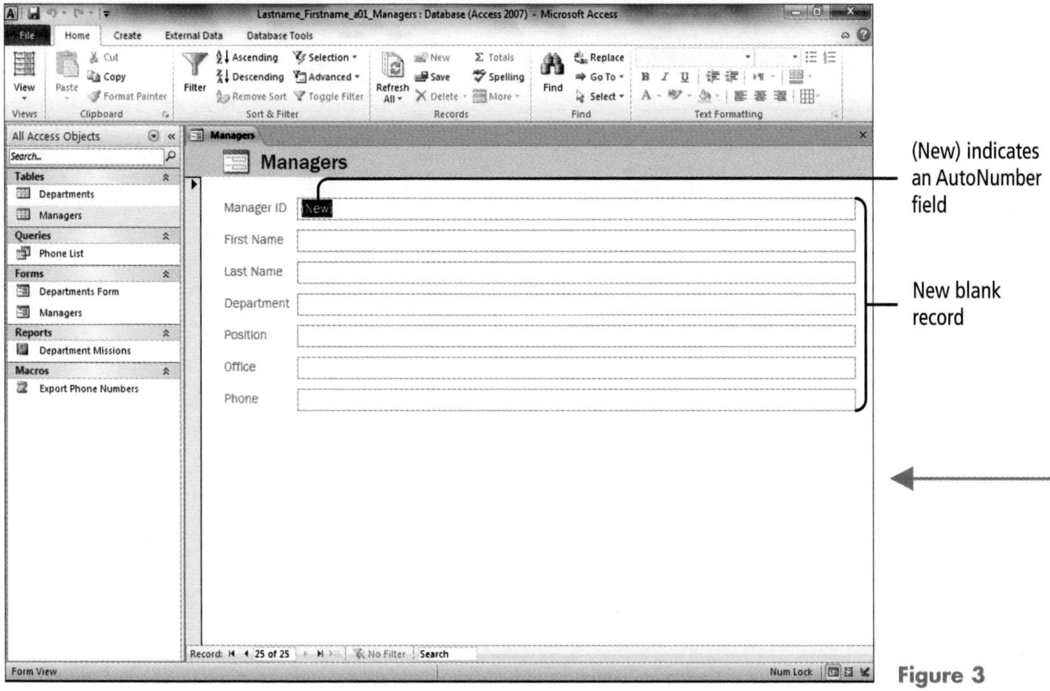

(New) indicates an AutoNumber field

New blank record

Figure 3

6. On the **Navigation bar**, click the **Next record** button ▶ to move to the second record—record 2 of 25.

7. In the **Records group**, click the **Delete button arrow**, and then click **Delete Record**. Read the message that displays, and then click **Yes** to remove the record for Tad Cipcic from the Managers table.

8. On the **Navigation bar**, click the **New (blank) record** button ▶* to create a new record. Compare your screen with **Figure 3**.

9. Click in the **First Name** text box, and then type your own first name. Using Enter to move to each field, enter the data shown in **Figure 4**.

10. With the insertion point still in the **Phone** field, press Tab.

    Pressing Enter or Tab when you are in the last field of the last record creates a new, blank record.

11. Press Enter, and then type Kevin Press Esc, and notice that the record returns to a blank record.

    You can cancel entering data into a new record by pressing Esc. This technique is helpful when you are entering data into a record, and you need to start over.

12. **Close** ☒ the **Managers** form.

    Recall that data is saved automatically as you complete each record. Access had already saved the data that you entered, and it did not ask you to save changes when you closed the form.

■ **You have completed Skill 3 of 10**

Field	Value
Manager ID	(Accept AutoNumber value)
First Name	Your first name
Last Name	Your last name
Department	Parks and Recreation
Position	Art School Supervisor
Office	442
Phone	(805) 555-1287

Figure 4

▶ A *query* displays a subset of the data in response to a specific question.

▶ Queries are modified in *Design view*—a view in which the structure and behavior of Access database objects are modified—and they display their results in Datasheet view.

1. In the **Navigation Pane**, under **Queries**, double-click **Phone List** to open the query datasheet. Compare your screen with **Figure 1**.

    Queries display the subset of data in Datasheet view. Here, the query displays the records of the four City Management Department managers from the Managers table.

2. In the **Views** group, click the upper half of the **View** button to switch to **Design** view. Compare your screen with **Figure 2**.

    The upper half of the Query tab—the *query design workspace*—lists the available tables and fields that the query should use. The lower half of the query tab—the *design grid*—lists the fields that will display in the query results.

    In Access, *criteria* are the conditions used to select the records that you are looking for. Here, the Department field must equal the text *City Management*.

■ **Continue to the next page to complete the skill**

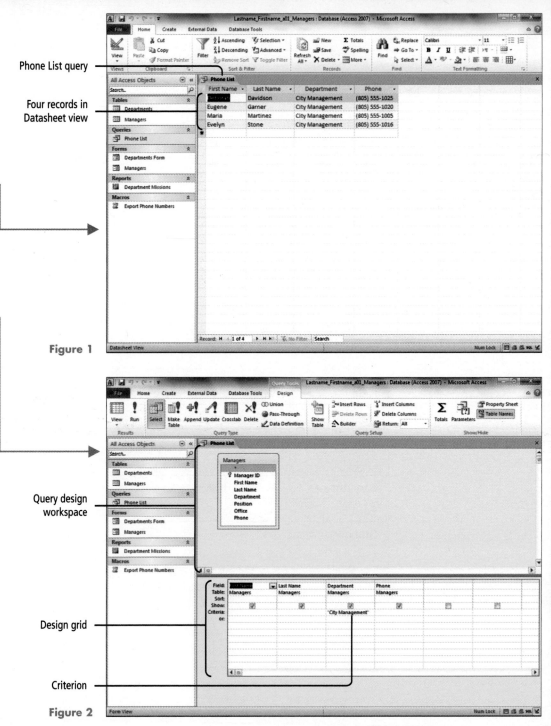

Phone List query

Four records in Datasheet view

Figure 1

Query design workspace

Design grid

Criterion

Figure 2

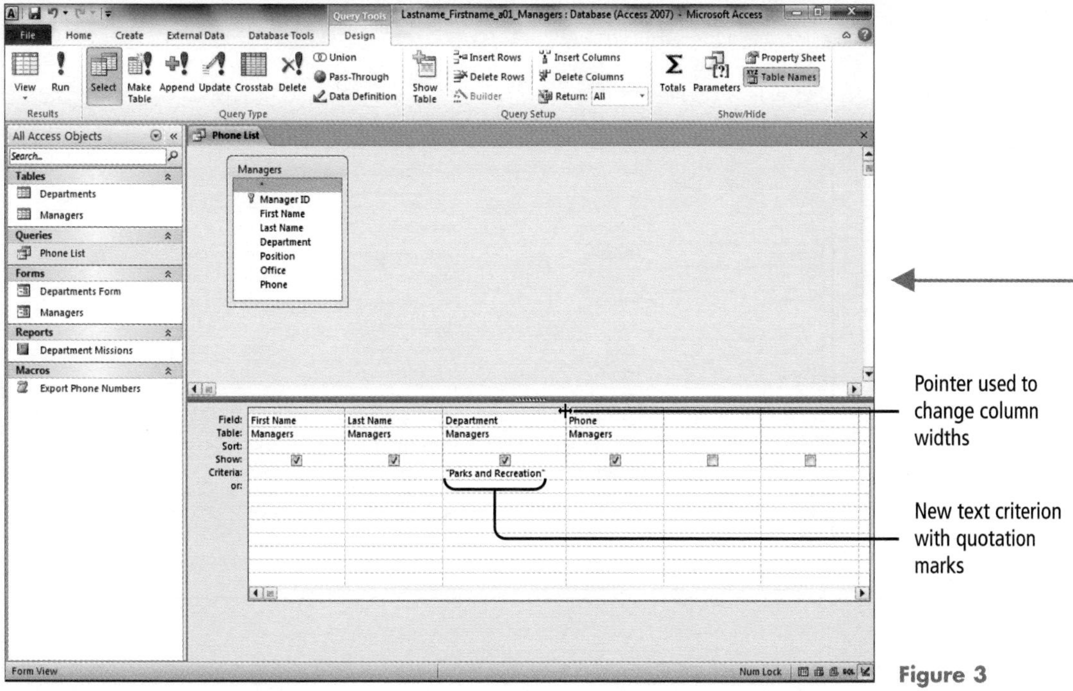

Pointer used to change column widths

New text criterion with quotation marks

Figure 3

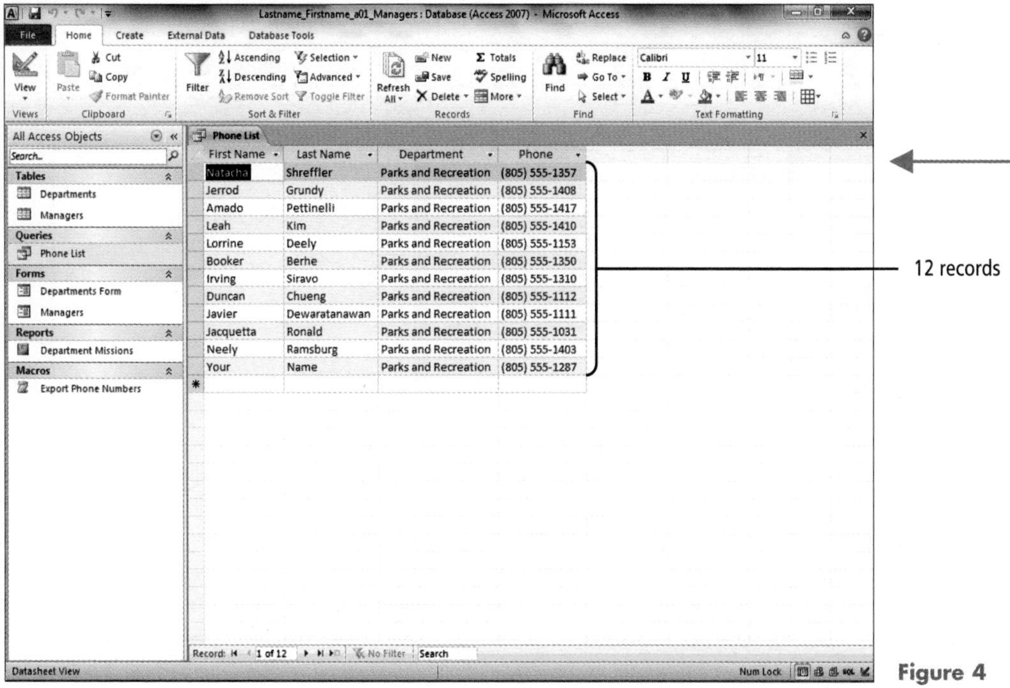

3. In the **Department** column, in the **Criteria** box, drag to select *"City Management"*, and then press Delete to remove the criterion.

4. In the **Results group**, click the **Run** button to display the phone numbers for all 25 city managers.

5. In the **Views group**, click the **View** button to switch to **Design** view. Click the **Department** column **Criteria** box, and then type "Parks and Recreation"

6. On the right of the **Department** column header, point to the line, and then, with the ⊞ pointer, drag to widen the column so that you can see the entire criterion just typed. Compare your screen with **Figure 3**.

   When a query criterion is a text value, the text value needs to be in quotation marks.

7. In the **Results group**, click the **Run** button to display the phone numbers for the 12 managers from the Parks and Recreation Department. Compare your screen with **Figure 4**.

8. On the **Quick Access Toolbar**, click the **Save** button 💾.

   When you widen datasheet columns or change query criteria, you need to save the changes.

9. **Close** ⊠ the Phone List query.

■ **You have completed Skill 4 of 10**

12 records

Figure 4

► *Reports* display the results of a query or the data in a table.

► Reports are often printed and cannot be used to change data.

1. If necessary, in the Navigation Pane, click the Phone List query one time to select it.

2. On the **Create tab**, in the **Reports** group, click the **Report** button to create a report for the selected query.

3. Click **Save** 🔲. In the **Save As** box, accept the name provided by clicking **OK**.

4. **Close** 🔳 the **Navigation Pane**, and then compare your screen with **Figure 1**.

   When you first create a report using the Report tool, it displays in *Layout view*—a view used to format a report or form while being able to view a sample of the data. Here, the report has the Angles theme because that was the theme last assigned in this database.

   The dashed line near the right edge of the report indicates when one printed page will end and another will begin.

5. On the **Home tab**, in the **Views group,** click the lower half of the **View** button— the **View button arrow**, and then click **Print Preview**.

6. On the **Print Preview tab**, in the **Zoom group**, click the **Two Pages** button, and then compare your screen with **Figure 2**.

   Print Preview is a view used to work with a report that will be printed. Here, the preview indicates that the phone numbers will be printed on two different pages.

■ **Continue to the next page to complete the skill** ▶

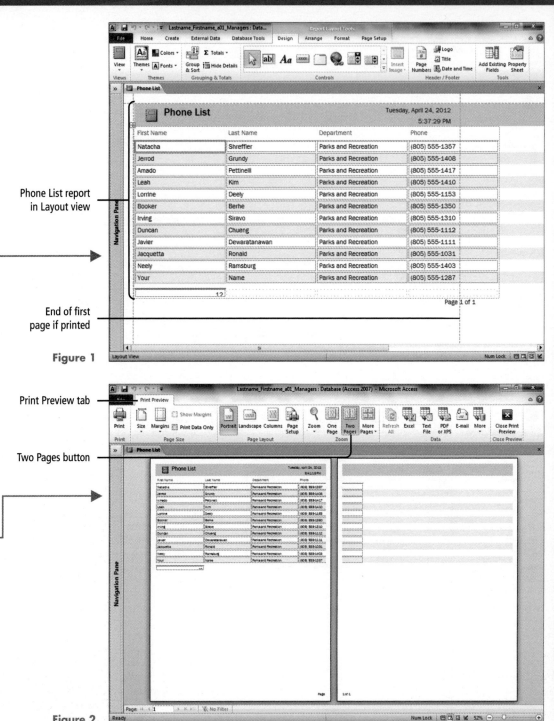

Phone List report in Layout view

End of first page if printed

Figure 1

Print Preview tab

Two Pages button

Figure 2

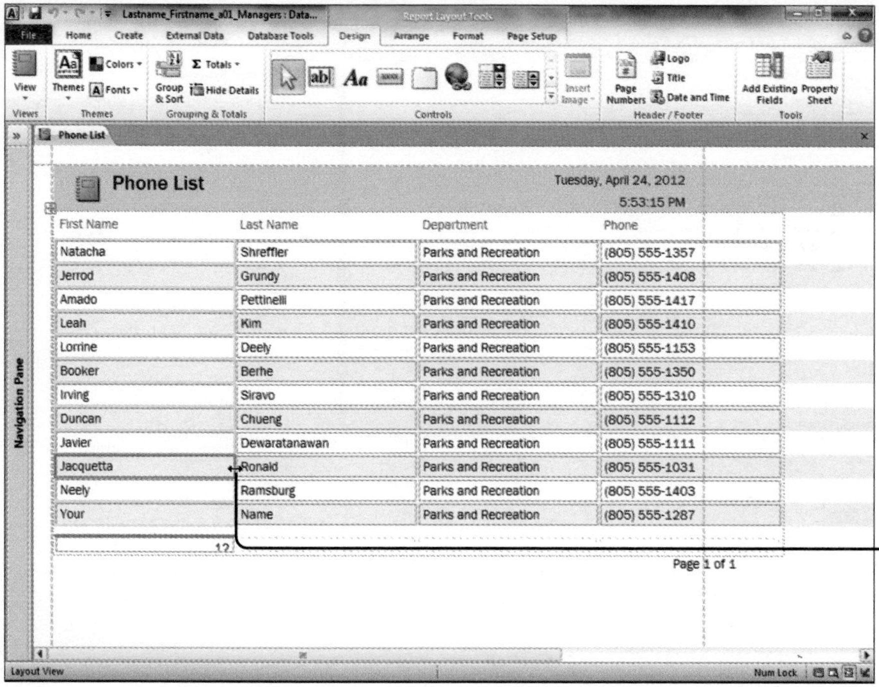

Change column
width pointer

Figure 3

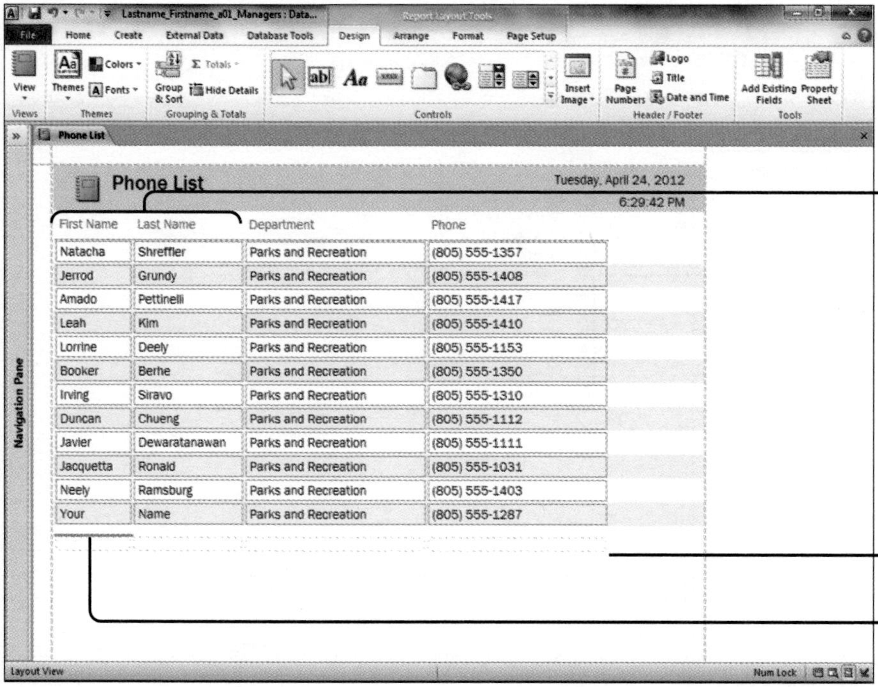

Column widths
decrease

Page number
deleted

Record count
deleted

Figure 4

7. Click the **Close Print Preview** button to return to **Layout** view. In the third to last record, click in the **First Name** field with the value *Jacquetta*. Point to the right edge of the selected field to display the ↔ pointer, as shown in **Figure 3**.

8. With the ↔ pointer, drag to the left to decrease the width of the **First Name** column so that it is slightly wider than the text *Jacquetta*.

9. Repeat the technique just practiced to decrease the width of the **Last Name** column so that it is slightly wider than the text *Dewaratanawan*.

10. Click a field in the **First Name** column. On the **Design tab**, in the **Grouping & Totals group**, click the **Totals** button, and click **Count Records** so that it is no longer selected.

11. At the lower-right edge of the report, click the text *Page 1 of 1*, and the press Delete to remove the page number. Compare your screen with **Figure 4**.

12. On the **Home tab**, in the **Views group**, click the **View button arrow**, and then click **Print Preview**.

13. On the **Print Preview tab**, in the **Page Layout group**, click the **Zoom** button to display the entire report.

14. In the **Print group**, click the **Print** button. If your instructor has asked you to print your work for this chapter, click OK. Otherwise, click Cancel.

15. Click **Save**, and then **Close** the **Phone List Report** tab. **Open** the **Navigation Pane**.

16. Click **File**, and then click **Exit**.

■ **You have completed Skill 5 of 10**

▶ Before you create a new database, you assign a name and location for the database file. You can then add objects such as tables, queries, forms, and reports.

▶ When you save design changes to the objects that you add to a database, they become part of the database file that you created.

1. **Start** 🔵 Access. On the right side of the **New tab**, click in the **File Name** box, and then type Lastname_Firstname_a01_Classes

2. Click the **Browse** button 📁, and then navigate to your **Access Chapter 1** folder. Compare your screen with **Figure 1.**

3. Click **OK**, and then on the right side of the **New tab**, click the **Create** button.

   When you create a blank database, a new table is automatically created. The table's ID field is an AutoNumber designated as the table's *primary key*—a field that uniquely identifies each record in a table.

4. Double-click the **ID** column header, and then type Instructor ID Press [Enter], and then compare your screen with **Figure 2.**

   When you move to the Click to Add column, a list of basic data types displays. The *Data Type* specifies the type of information that a field will hold; for example, text, number, date, and currency.

5. In the list of data types, click **Text**, and then type First Name

   The *Text data type* stores up to 255 characters of text.

6. Press [Enter]. In the list of data types, click **Text**, and then type Last Name

■ **Continue to the next page to complete the skill**

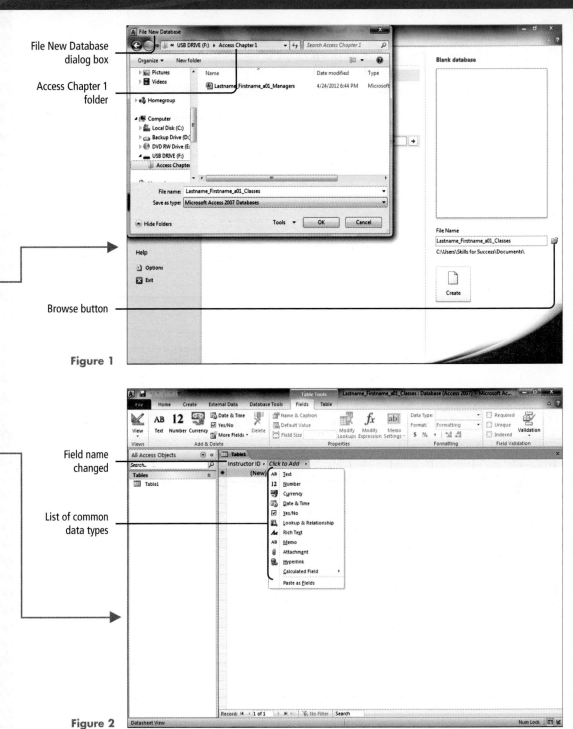

File New Database dialog box

Access Chapter 1 folder

Browse button

Figure 1

Field name changed

List of common data types

Figure 2

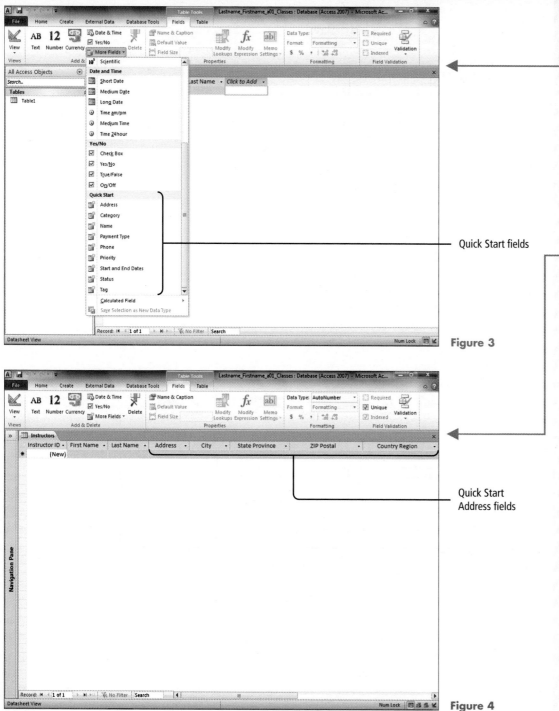

Quick Start fields

Figure 3

Quick Start
Address fields

Figure 4

7. Press Enter. On the **Fields tab**, in the **Add & Delete group**, click the **More Fields** button. Scroll to the bottom of the list of data types. Compare your screen with **Figure 3**.

> *Quick Start data types* are a set of fields that can be added with a single click. For example, the Address data type inserts five fields for storing postal addresses.

8. In the list of data types, under **Quick Start**, click **Address** to insert several address fields.

9. Click **Save** 🔲. In the **Save As** dialog box, type Instructors and then click **OK**. **Close** « the **Navigation Pane**, and compare your screen with **Figure 4**.

10. In the append row, click in the **First Name** field, and then type your first name. Press Enter, and then, in the **Last Name** column, type your last name. Continue in this manner to enter your address information in the remaining fields.

11. Click **File**, click **Print**, and then click **Print Preview**. On the **Print Preview tab**, in the **Page Layout group**, click **Landscape**.

12. On the **Print Preview tab**, in the **Page Size group**, click the **Margins** button, and then click **Narrow**. If you are printing your work, print the datasheet.

13. Click **Save**, and then **Close** ✕ the table. **Open** » the **Navigation Pane**.

- **You have completed Skill 6 of 10**

▶ Field properties define the characteristics of the data that can be added to a field.

▶ In addition to Data Type and Name, you can change several other field properties.

1. On the **Create tab**, in the **Tables group**, click the **Table** button to create a new table.

2. Click **Save** 🖫. In the **Save As** dialog box, type Art Classes and then press Enter. Compare your screen with **Figure 1.**

   Recall that when you create a table in Datasheet view, the first column is an AutoNumber that will be the table's primary key.

3. Double-click the **ID** column header to select the text *ID*, and then type Class ID

4. Press Enter, click **Text**, and then type Class Name

5. Press Enter, click **Memo**, and then type Description

   The *Memo data type* stores up to 65,535 characters of text data and the formatting assigned to that text.

6. Press Enter, click **Number**, and then type Length

   The *Number data type* stores numeric values.

7. Press Enter, click **Currency**, and then type Cost Compare your screen with **Figure 2.**

   The *Currency data type* stores numbers formatted as a monetary value.

■ **Continue to the next page to complete the skill**

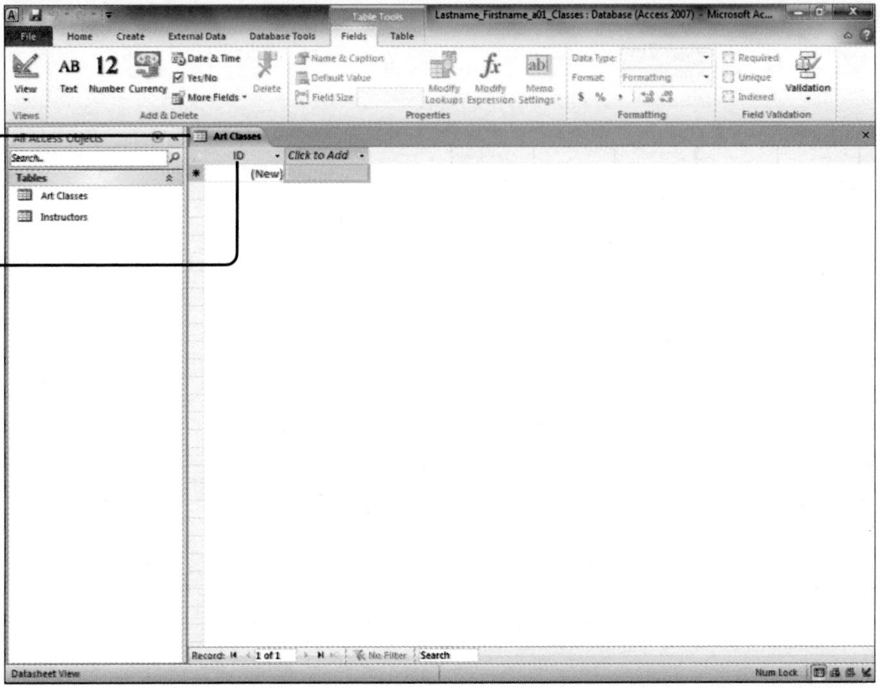

Table saved as Art Classes

Primary key AutoNumber

Figure 1

Fields added to table

Currency data type applied

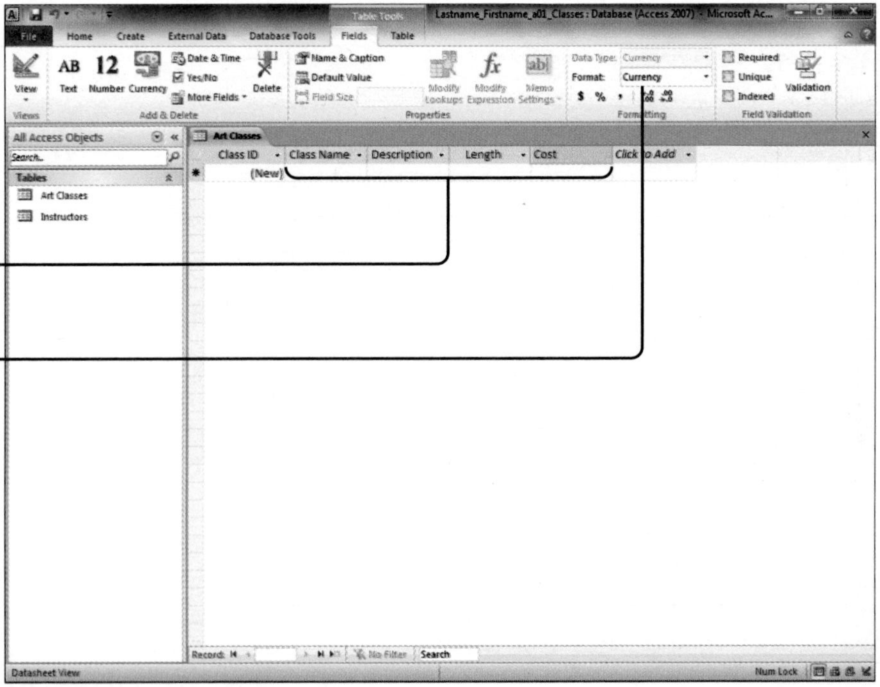

Figure 2

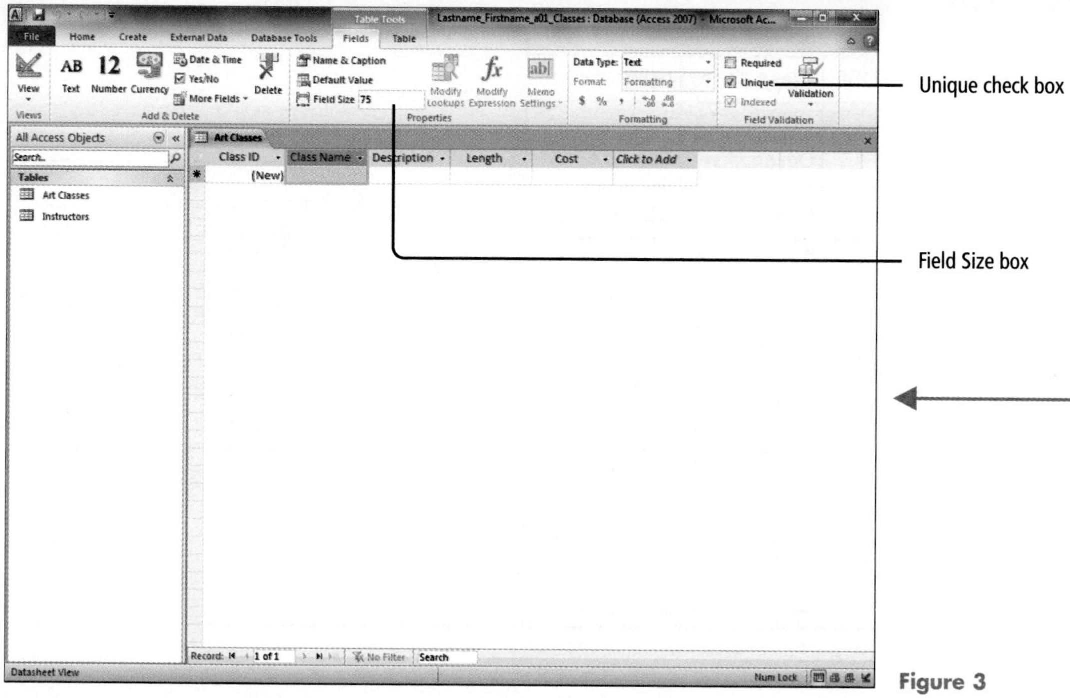

Unique check box

Field Size box

Figure 3

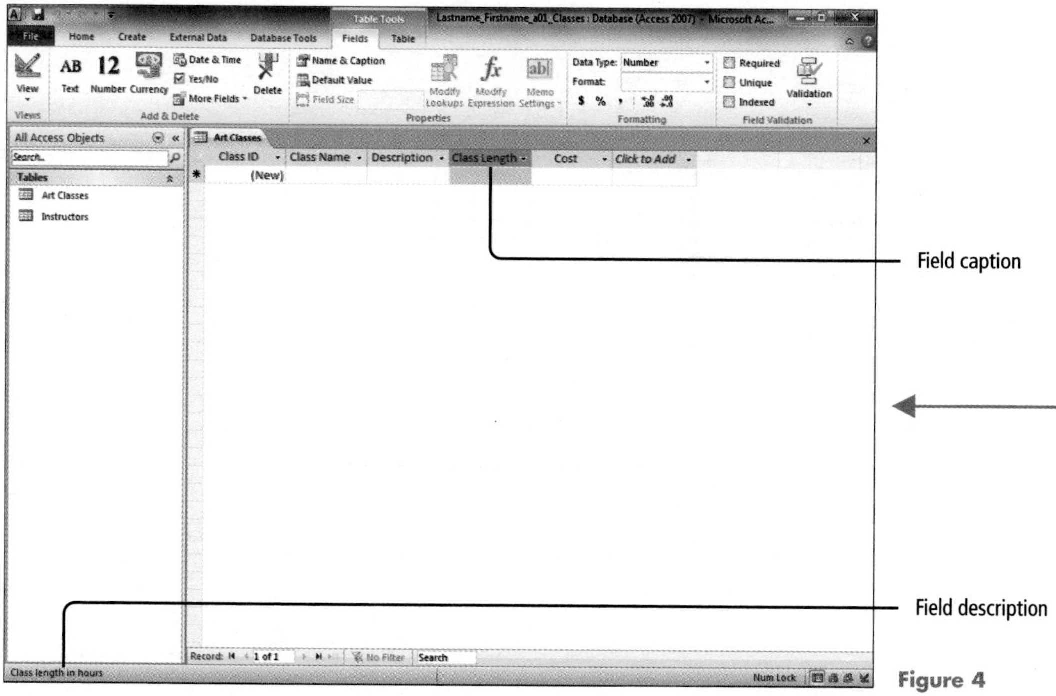

Field caption

Field description

Figure 4

8. Click the **Class Name** column header one time to select the column. On the **Fields tab**, in the **Properties group**, click in the **Field Size** box to select *255*. Type 75 and then press Enter.

> *Field Size* limits the number of characters that can be typed into a text or number field.

9. With the **Class Name** field still selected, on the **Fields tab**, in the **Field Validation group**, select the **Unique** check box. Compare your screen with **Figure 3**.

> When selected, the *Unique* field property requires that each record contain a unique value. Here, no two classes can share the same name.

10. Click the **Length** column header to select the column. On the **Fields tab**, in the **Properties group**, click the **Name & Caption** button.

11. In the **Enter Field Properties** dialog box, click in the **Caption** box, and then type Class Length Press Tab, and then with the insertion point in the **Description** box, type Class length in hours

12. Click **OK** to apply the changes, and then compare your screen with **Figure 4**.

> The *Caption* field property is the label that displays in datasheets, forms, and reports. The *Description* field property is used to document a field's purpose and displays in the lower-left corner of the datasheet when the field is active.

13. Click **Save** 🖫, and then **Close** ☒ the table.

■ **You have completed Skill 7 of 10**

▶ Database designers often sketch the database they need and then follow that plan to create tables.

▶ In a *relational database*, you can place the same field in two tables and then join the tables using the related fields. A *relationship* joins tables using common fields.

1. Take a few moments to study the entity relationship diagram in **Figure 1**.

   An *entity relationship diagram*, or *ERD*, is a visual model used to plan a database. An ERD shows the tables and their fields. Each field's data type is also displayed. The lines between the tables show how each table will be related.

2. On the **Create tab**, in the **Tables group**, click the **Table Design** button. With the insertion point in the first column of the first row, type Section ID

3. Press Enter. In the **Section ID** row, click the **Data Type** arrow, and then click **AutoNumber**.

4. With the **Data Type** box still selected, on the **Design tab**, in the **Tools group**, click the **Primary Key** button.

5. Click **Save** 💾, and then, in the **Save As** dialog box, type Art Class Sections and then press Enter. Compare your screen with **Figure 2**.

   When working with a table in Design view, the Field Name, Data Type, and Description data are entered in rows. Other field properties are entered in the Field Properties pane.

6. Click in the blank row below **Section ID**. Type Class ID

■ **Continue to the next page to complete the skill** ▶

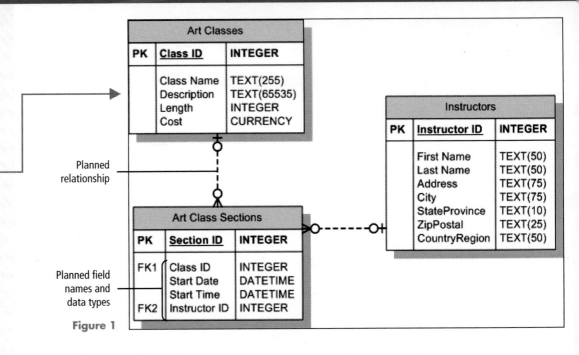

Figure 1

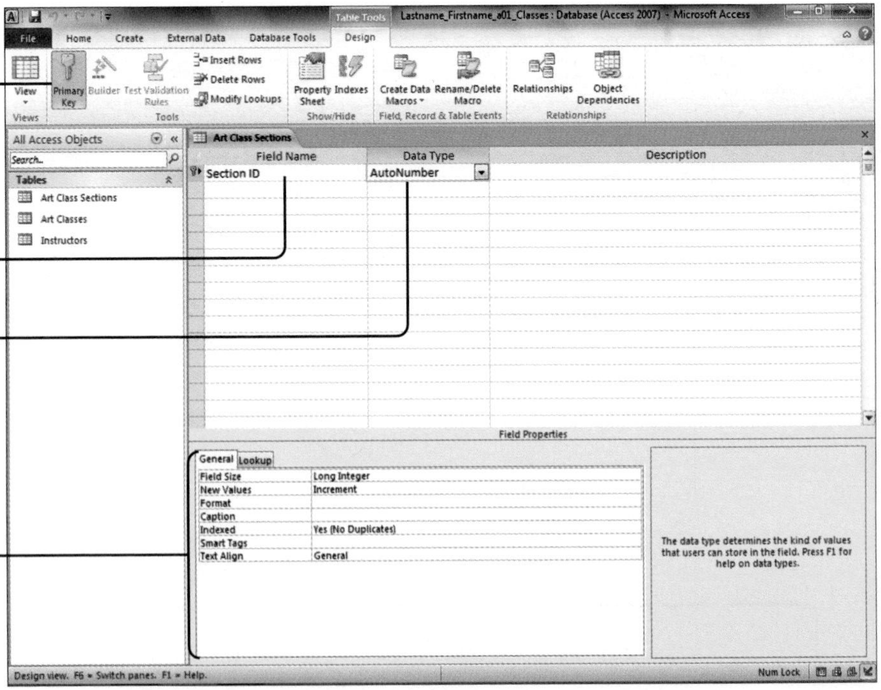

Figure 2

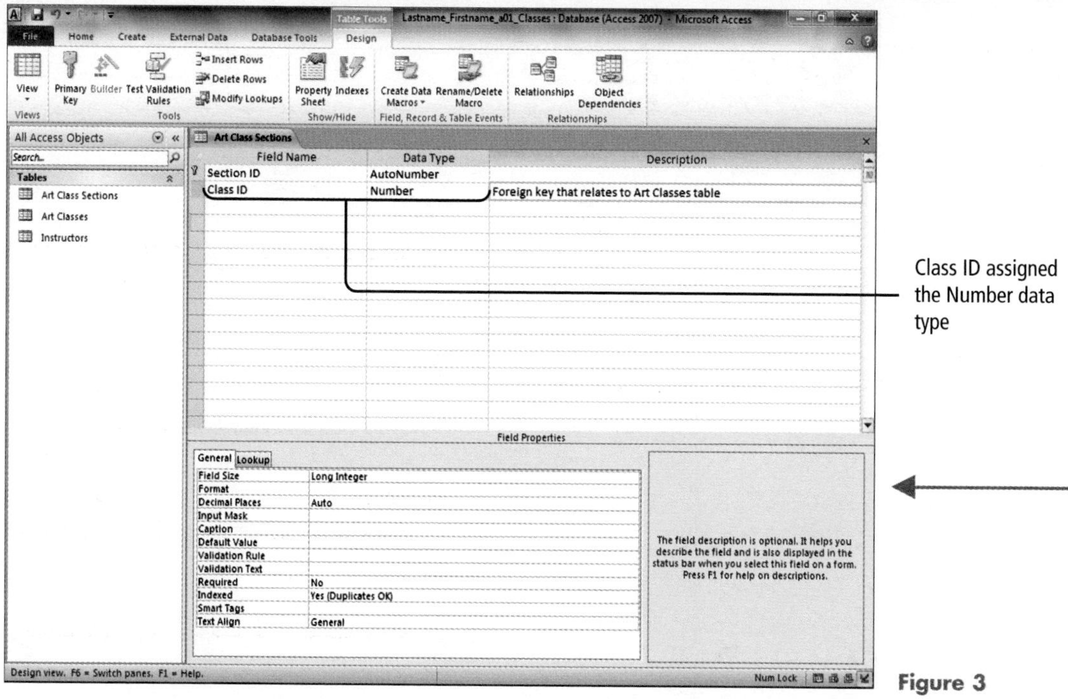

Class ID assigned the Number data type

Figure 3

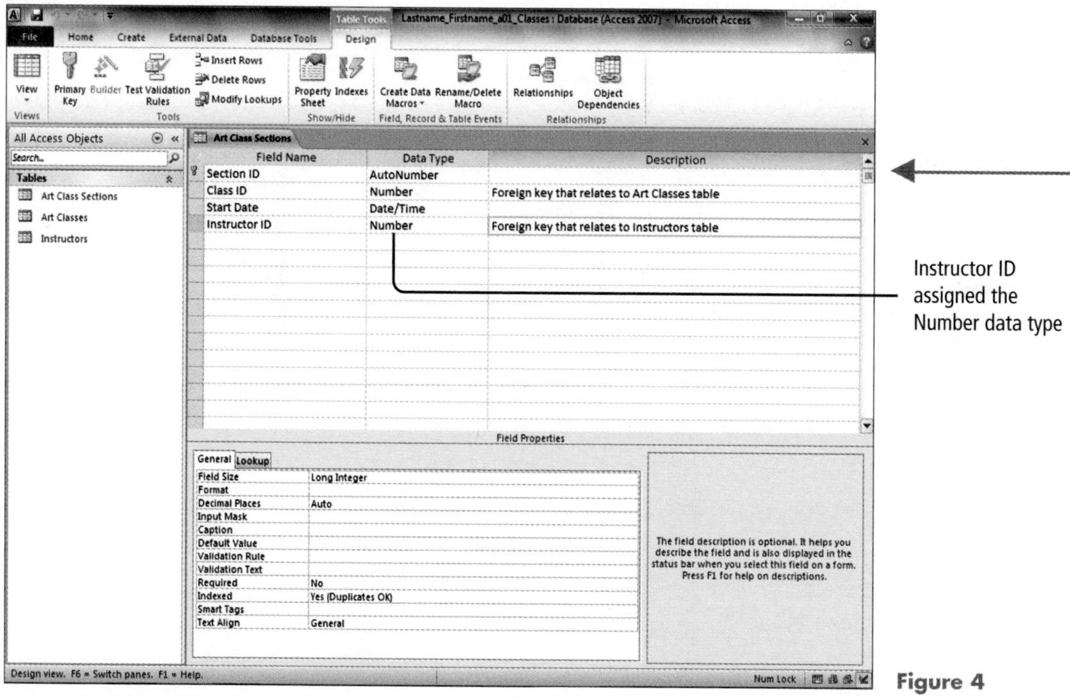

Instructor ID assigned the Number data type

Figure 4

7. Press [Enter], click the **Data Type arrow**, and then click **Number**.

8. Press [Enter]. In the **Description** box, type Foreign key that relates to Art Classes table Compare your screen with **Figure 3**.

> A **foreign key** is a field that is also in another related table. The field in the other table is usually that table's primary key. Here, Class ID is the primary key of the Art Classes table. The Class ID field will be used to join the Art Class Sections and Art Classes tables.

> When you join tables, the common fields must share the same data type. Because the Art Classes table automatically assigns a number to each record, the Class ID field should be assigned the Number data type.

9. Press [Enter] to move to a new row, and then type Start Date Press [Enter], and then type the letter D to assign the **Date/Time** data type.

> The **Date/Time data type** stores numbers in the date or time format.

10. Press [Enter] two times to move to a new row, and then type Instructor ID Press [Enter], and then assign the **Number** data type.

11. In the **Instructor ID Description** box, type Foreign key that relates to Instructors table Compare your screen with **Figure 4**.

> Instructor ID needs to be a number so that it can be joined to the Instructor ID AutoNumber values assigned to records in the Instructors table.

12. Click **Save** 🔲, and then **Close** ✖ the table.

■ **You have completed Skill 8 of 10**

► Tables are typically joined in a *one-to-many relationship*—a relationship where a record in the first table can have many associated records in the second table.

► One-to-many relationships enforce *referential integrity*—the principle that a rule keeps related values synchronized. For example, the foreign key value must match one of the primary key values in the other table.

1. On the **Database Tools tab**, in the **Relationships group**, click the **Relationships** button.

2. In the **Show Table** dialog box, double-click **Art Classes** to add it to the **Relationships** tab. In the **Show Table** dialog box, double-click **Art Class Sections**, double-click **Instructors**, and then click the **Close** button. Compare your screen with **Figure 1**.

3. From the **Art Classes** table, drag **Class ID** to the **Class ID** in the **Art Class Sections** table. When the 🖻 pointer displays, release the mouse button.

4. In the **Edit Relationships** dialog box, select the **Enforce Referential Integrity** check box. Select the **Cascade Update Related Fields** and **Cascade Delete Related Records** check boxes, and then compare your screen with **Figure 2**.

   With a *cascading update*, you can edit the primary key values in a table, and all the related records in the other table will update accordingly.

   With a *cascading delete*, you can delete a record on the *one* side of the relationship, and all the related records on the *many* side will also be deleted.

■ **Continue to the next page to complete the skill**

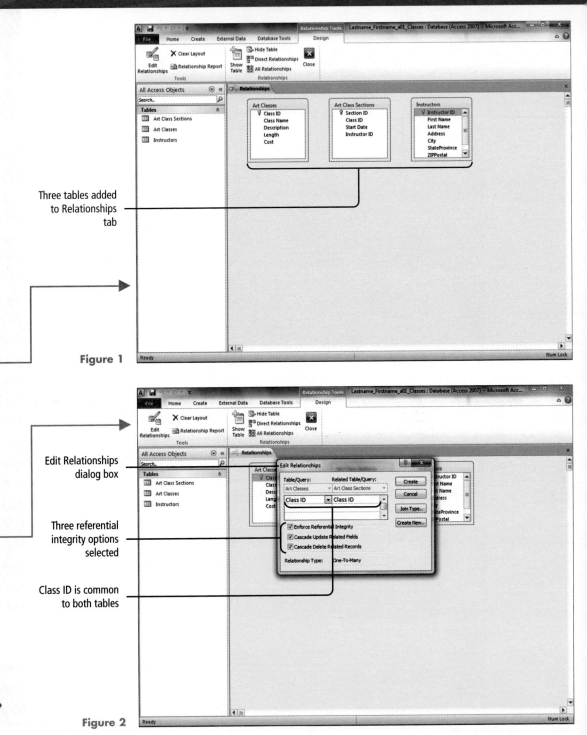

Three tables added to Relationships tab

Figure 1

Edit Relationships dialog box

Three referential integrity options selected

Class ID is common to both tables

Figure 2

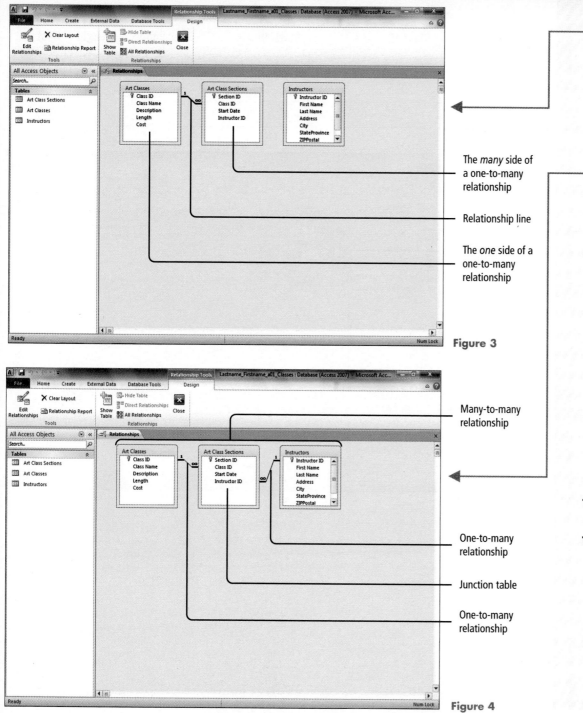

The *many* side of a one-to-many relationship

Relationship line

The *one* side of a one-to-many relationship

Figure 3

Many-to-many relationship

One-to-many relationship

Junction table

One-to-many relationship

Figure 4

5. Click **Create**, and then compare your screen with **Figure 3**.

6. From the **Instructors** table, drag **Instructor ID** to the **Instructor ID** in the **Art Class Sections** table. When the ⬚ pointer displays, release the mouse button.

7. In the **Edit Relationships** dialog box, select all three referential integrity options, and then click **Create**. Compare your screen with **Figure 4**.

   The three tables are joined to create a ***many-to-many relationship***—a relationship where one record in either of the outer tables can have many associated records in the other outer table.

   A many-to-many relationship is created by placing the primary keys from the outer tables into a middle table called a ***junction table***. Here, Art Class Sections is a junction table for Art Classes and Instructors. An art class can have several sections assigned and an instructor can be assigned to teach several different sections.

8. Click **Save** 🖫. On the **Design tab**, in the **Tools group**, click the **Relationship Report** button to create a report showing the database relationships.

9. If your instructor asks you to print your work for this chapter, print the report.

10. Click **Save** 🖫. In the **Save As** dialog box, accept the report name by clicking **OK**.

11. **Close** ⊠ the report, and then **Close** ⊠ the **Relationships tab**.

   ■ **You have completed Skill 9 of 10**

► After relating two tables, it is a good idea to enter sample data into both tables.

► When you enter data in related tables, referential integrity rules are applied. For example, a foreign key value must have a matching value in the related table.

1. In the **Navigation Pane**, double-click **Instructors** to open its datasheet.

2. Note the number assigned to the **Instructor ID** record with your name. Later in this skill, you will need to enter this value in another table.

3. **Close** ☒ the **Instructors** table. In the **Navigation Pane**, double-click **Art Classes** to open its datasheet. In the append row, enter the three records shown in **Figure 1**.

4. Point to the line to the right of the **Class Name** column header, and then with the ⊞ pointer, double-click to size the column automatically.

5. In the first record, click the **Expand** button ⊞, and then compare your screen with **Figure 2**.

    When a table is on the one side of a relationship, a subdatasheet is available. A *subdatasheet* displays related records from the table on the many side of the relationship.

6. In the subdatasheet append row for the **Art History** class, click in the **Start Date** column.

    Fields that have been assigned the Date/Time data type display the *Date Picker*—a feature used to enter dates by clicking dates on a calendar.

■ Continue to the next page to complete the skill ▶

Class ID	Class Name	Description	Class Length	Cost
Accept AutoNumbers	Art History	Leave blank	10	$15.00
	Basic Drawing		10	$45.00
	Portrait Drawing		5	$35.00

Figure 1

Subdatasheet expanded

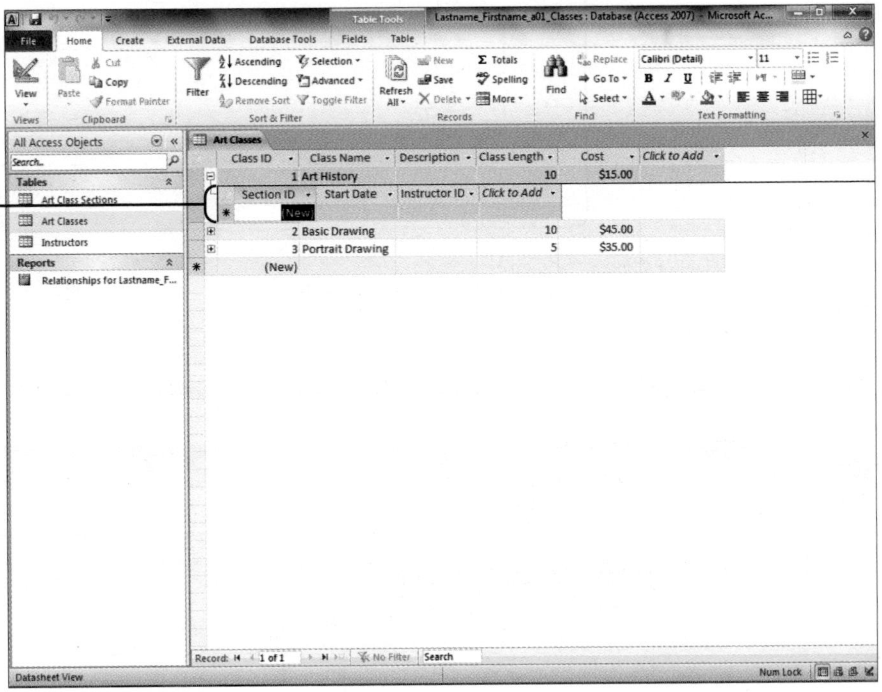

Figure 2

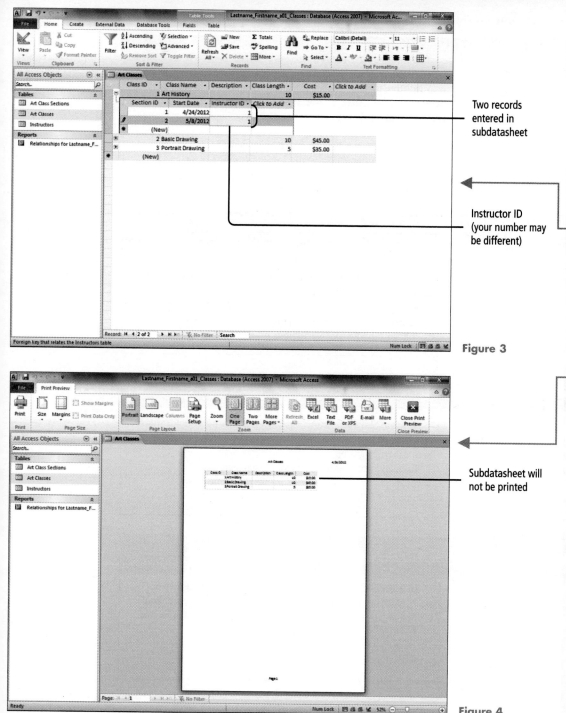

Two records
entered in
subdatasheet

Instructor ID
(your number may
be different)

Figure 3

Subdatasheet will
not be printed

Figure 4

7. Click the **Date Picker** button 🔲, and then click the **Today** button.

8. Press Enter. In the **Instructor ID** field, type 1 If necessary, use the number for your record, which you noted in step 2.

9. Press Enter two times to finish entering the record and to move to the **Start Date** field in the next row. Use the **Date Picker** to assign a date two weeks from today. In the **Instructor ID** field, type 1 If necessary, use the number for your record, as noted in step 2. Compare your screen with **Figure 3**.

   In this manner, records in a one-to-many relationship can be entered using a subdatasheet. Here, two sections of the Art History class have been created, and the same instructor has been assigned to teach both sections.

10. Click **File**, click **Print**, and then click **Print Preview**. Compare your screen with **Figure 4**. If you are printing your work, print the datasheet.

    When you print a datasheet, subdatasheets do not print.

11. Save 🔲, and then **Close** ⊠ the **Art Classes** table. In the **Navigation Pane**, double-click **Art Class Sections** to open the table. Notice that the data you entered in the subdatasheet is stored in this table. If you are printing your work for this project, print the datasheet.

12. **Close** ⊠ the table, and then **Exit** Access.

Done! You have completed Skill 10 of 10 and your databases are complete!

The following More Skills are located at **www.pearsonhighered.com/skills**

More Skills 11 Compact and Repair Databases

As tables, forms, queries, and reports are created and deleted, the size of the database file can grow quite large. Access provides a tool that rebuilds database files so that data and these objects are stored more efficiently. Applying the Compact and Repair tool decreases the size of a database file and improves database performance.

In More Skills 11, you will view the file size for a database before and after deleting several forms and reports. You will then compact and repair the database and observe the resulting change in file size.

To begin, open your web browser, navigate to www.pearsonhighered.com/skills, locate the name of your textbook, and follow the instructions on the website.

More Skills 12 Import Data from Excel

You can build Access tables by importing tables from Excel. You can also add data from Excel to an existing Access table. When you import data from Excel, the worksheet needs to be organized with records in rows and fields in columns.

In More Skills 12, you will import data from Excel into an existing Access table. You will then import a different Excel worksheet to create a new Access table.

To begin, open your web browser, navigate to www.pearsonhighered.com/skills, locate the name of your textbook, and follow the instructions on the website.

More Skills 13 Work with the Attachment Data Type

In Access, tables can store files such as Microsoft Word files, Excel files, or files created with a digital camera. Access provides a method to attach specific files to specific records. The attached files can then be opened and viewed in the application that created them.

In More Skills 13, you will create an Attachment field, attach several files to two records, and then open one of these attached files in other programs.

To begin, open your web browser, navigate to www.pearsonhighered.com/skills, locate the name of your textbook, and follow the instructions on the website.

More Skills 14 Work with the Hyperlink and Yes/No Data Types

In Access, a field can be used to store a hyperlink to a web page or file. These fields use the Hyperlink data type. Another data type, called Yes/No, can be assigned to a field that will have only two possible values, such as Yes or No.

In More Skills 14, you will create a new field, assign it the Hyperlink data type, and enter a web address into a record. You will then create a Yes/No field and enter a Yes value into a record.

To begin, open your web browser, navigate to www.pearsonhighered.com/skills, locate the name of your textbook, and follow the instructions on the website.

Key Terms

Online Help Skills

1. **Start** 🪟 Access. In the upper right corner of the Access window, click the **Help** button 🔘. In the **Help** window, click the **Maximize** 🔲 button.

2. Click in the search box, type templates and then click the **Search** button. In the search results, click **Where do I find templates**. Compare your screen with **Figure 1**.

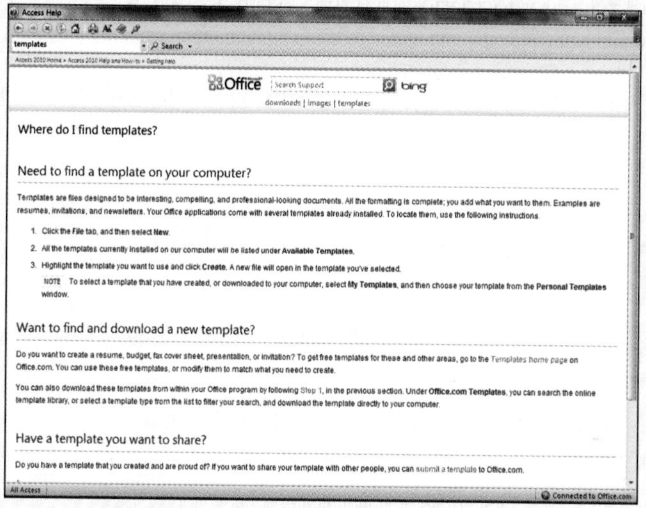

Figure 1

3. Read the article to see if you can answer the following: What is a template and where can you find them?

Matching

Match each term in the second column with its correct definition in the first column by writing the letter of the term on the blank line in front of the correct definition.

___ **1.** The basic part of a database that you work with; for example, tables, queries, forms, and reports.

___ **2.** The collection of related information that displays in a single row of a database table.

___ **3.** A form that displays one record at a time uses this type of layout.

___ **4.** A data type that automatically assigns a unique, numeric value to a field.

___ **5.** A database object used to enter new records, delete records, or update existing records.

___ **6.** The conditions used in a query to select the records that you are looking for.

___ **7.** This specifies the kind of information that a field will hold; for example, text or numbers.

___ **8.** A set of fields that can be added with a single click. For example, the Address data type inserts five fields for storing postal addresses.

___ **9.** An Access field property that prevents a field in a table from having two of the same values.

___ **10.** A database that consists of two or more tables that are related by sharing a field common to both tables.

A AutoNumber

B Criteria

C Data type

D Database object

E Form

F Quick Start

G Record

H Relational database

I Single Form

J Unique

Multiple Choice

Choose the correct answer.

1. A structured collection of related information about people, events, and things.
   - A. Database
   - B. Database management system
   - C. Database object

2. The computer software that allows people to interact with a database.
   - A. Database
   - B. Database management system
   - C. Database object

3. An Access view that displays records in rows and fields in columns.
   - A. Database
   - B. Data grid
   - C. Datasheet

4. Each individual characteristic in a record that displays as a single column in a datasheet.
   - A. Field
   - B. Record
   - C. Subset

5. A database object that displays a subset of data in response to a specific question.
   - A. Form
   - B. Query
   - C. Table

6. A database object used to display the results of a query or the contents of a table on the screen or in printed form.
   - A. Form
   - B. Macro
   - C. Report

7. The blank row at the end of a datasheet used to add records to a table.
   - A. Append
   - B. Data entry
   - C. New record

8. An Access field property that limits the number of characters that can be typed into a text or number field.
   - A. Character Limit
   - B. Character Size
   - C. Field Size

9. A rule that keeps related values synchronized.
   - A. Data duplication
   - B. Data redundancy
   - C. Referential integrity

10. An Access view that displays tools to modify the format of a report or form while being able to view the data that it is intended to display.
    - A. Layout
    - B. Print Preview
    - C. Report

Topics for Discussion

1. What kind of information do you think a small business or organization would organize into a database?

2. Each database object has a special purpose. For example, a query is used to filter and sort records. Why do you think that the filter and sort tools are also available when you work with tables, forms, and reports?

Skill Check

To complete this database, you will need the following file:

- a01_Students

You will save your databases as:

- Lastname_Firstname_a01_Councils
- Lastname_Firstname_a01_Students

1. **Start** Access, and then click **Open**. In the **Open** dialog box, navigate to the student files for this chapter, and then open **a01_Students**.

2. Click the **File tab**, and then click **Save Database As**. In the **Save As** dialog box, navigate to your **Access Chapter 1** folder and then, using your own name, save the database as Lastname_Firstname_a01_Students If the Security Warning displays, click the Enable Content button.

3. In the **Navigation Pane**, double-click **Student Data Entry Form**. In the Navigation bar, click the **New (blank) record** button. In the new blank record, enter the information shown in **Figure 1**. Use [Enter] to move to each text box, and be sure to use your own name where indicated. **Close** the form.

4. In the **Navigation Pane**, under **Queries**, double-click **Central Neighborhood**. In the **Views group**, click the **View** button to switch to **Design** view.

5. In the **Neighborhood** column, in the **Criteria** box, change the criteria to "Central"

6. In the **Results group**, click the **Run** button to display 10 records. **Save** the query design, and then **Close** the query.

7. In the **Navigation Pane**, double-click **Central Students Report**. In the **Views group**, click the **View button arrow**, and then click **Print Preview**. Compare your screen with **Figure 2**.

8. If your instructor asks you to print your work for this project, print the report. **Close** the report, and then **Exit** Access.

9. **Start** Access. On the **New tab**, in the **File Name** box, type Lastname_Firstname_a01_Councils

10. Click the **Browse** button, and then navigate to your **Access Chapter 1** folder. Click **OK** and then click **Create**.

11. In **Table1**, double-click the **ID** field, type Member ID and then press [Enter].

Student ID:	(Accept AutoNumber value)
First Name:	First name
Last Name:	Last name
Street:	8446 W Marvelo St
City:	Aspen Falls
State:	CA
Zip:	93464
Neighborhood:	Central

Figure 1

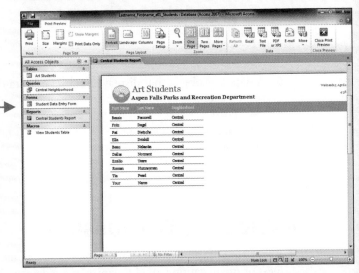

Figure 2

 Continue to the next page to complete this Skill Check ▶

12. In the list of fields, click **Text**, type First Name and then press ⏎. Click **Text**, and then type Last Name Press ⏎, click **Number**, and then type Council ID

13. Click the **First Name** column. In the **Properties group**, click the **Field Size** box, type 50 and then press ⏎. Repeat this technique to change the **Last Name** field size to 50

14. Click **Save**, type Members and then press ⏎. Compare your screen with **Figure 3**.

15. Close the table. On the **Create tab**, in the **Tables group**, click **Table Design**.

16. In the first **Field Name** box, type Council ID Press ⏎, and then set the **Data Type** to **AutoNumber**. With the first row still active, on the **Tools** group, click the **Primary Key** button.

17. In the second **Field Name** box, type Council Name Press ⏎ two times, and then click **Save**. In the **Save As** dialog box, type Councils and then press ⏎. **Close** the table.

18. On the **Database Tools tab**, click the **Relationships** button. In the **Show Table** dialog box, double-click to add each table to the **Relationships tab**, and then click **Close**.

19. Drag **Council ID** from the **Councils** table to **Council ID** in the **Members** table. In the **Edit Relationships** dialog box, select **Enforce Referential Integrity**, and then click **Create**. Compare your screen with **Figure 4**.

20. On the **Design tab**, in the **Tools group**, click **Relationship Report**. If you are printing this project, print the report. Click **Save**, and then click **OK**. **Close** the report, and then **Close** the **Relationships tab**.

21. In the **Navigation Pane**, double-click **Councils** to open the table. In the **Council Name** column, type Parks & Recreation Council Double-click the line to the right of the **Council Name** column header to resize the column.

22. Press ⏎ two times, and then type City Council Repeat this technique to add the Planning Council and Public Works Commission

23. Expand the **Public Works Commission** subdatasheet. In the subdatasheet append row, click in the **First Name** column, and then type your own first name. Press ⏎, and then type your last name.

24. If you are printing this project, print the datasheet. **Save**, and then **Close** the table.

25. In the **Navigation Pane**, double-click the **Members** table. If you are printing this project, print the datasheet. **Close** the table.

26. Exit Access. Submit your printouts or database files as directed by your instructor.

Done! You have completed the Skill Check

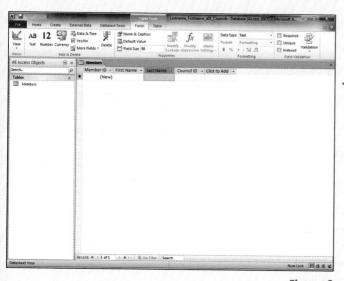

Figure 3

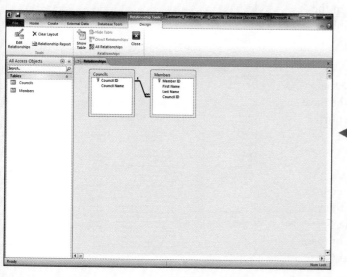

Figure 4

Assess Your Skills 1

To complete this database, you will need the following file:

- a01_Schedule

You will save your database as:

- Lastname_Firstname_a01_Schedule

1. **Start** Access, and then open the student data file **a01_Schedule**. Save the database in your **Access Chapter 1** folder with the name Lastname_Firstname_a01_Schedule

2. Open the **Outings Form**, and then add a new record. Accept the **AutoNumber** value, and then type the **Outing Name**, Rattlesnake Snowshoe The **Ages** field is 18 & over and the **Fee** is 20 **Close** the form.

3. Open the **Adult Outings** query to display 12 records, and then **Close** the query.

4. Open the **Adult Outings Report**, and then switch to **Print Preview**. If asked by your instructor, print the report. **Close** the report.

5. Create a new table in datasheet view. Rename the **ID** field Leader ID Add two new **Text** fields named First Name and Last Name

6. Click the **Click to Add** column, and then add the **Address Quick Start** fields. **Save** the table with the name Leaders

7. In the append row, enter a record using your own name and contact information. Note the **AutoNumber** value that is assigned to your record, and then **Close** the table.

8. Create a new table in **Design** view. Name the first field Schedule ID Assign it the **AutoNumber** data type, and then make it the **Primary Key**. Name the second field Outing ID and assign the **Number** data type. Name the third field Leader ID and assign

the **Number** data type. Name the fourth field Outing Date and assign the **Date/Time** data type.

9. **Save** the table as Scheduled Outings and then **Close** the table.

10. Open the **Relationships tab** and then add all three tables to the tab. Create a relationship that enforces referential integrity between the **Outings** and **Scheduled Outings** tables using the fields common to both tables. Create a similar relationship between the **Leaders** and **Scheduled Outings** tables.

11. Arrange the tables as shown in **Figure 1**, and then click **Save**.

12. Create a **Relationship Report**. **Save** the report with the name provided in the **Save As** dialog box. If asked, print the report. **Close** the report, and then **Close** the **Relationships tab**.

13. Open the **Outings** table, and then expand **Family Fun Canoe Paddle**. In the record's subdatasheet, set the **Leader ID** to the value assigned to you in the Leaders table. Set **Outing Date** to the current date. Compare your screen with **Figure 2**, and then **Close** the table.

14. If asked, print the Scheduled Outings datasheet. **Exit** Access. Submit your printouts or database file as directed.

Done! You have completed Assess Your Skills 1

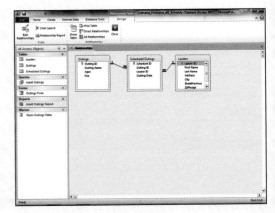

Figure 1

Figure 2

Assessment

Assess Your Skills 3 and 4 can be found at
www.pearsonhighered.com/skills.

Assess Your Skills 2

To complete this database, you will need the following file:

- New blank Access database

You will save your database as:

- Lastname_Firstname_a01_Camps

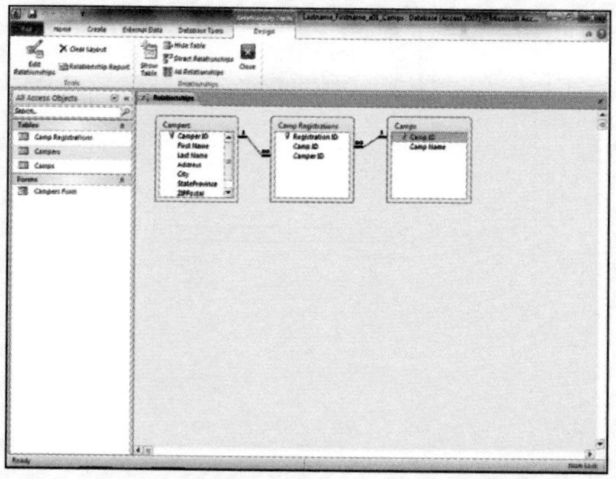

Figure 1

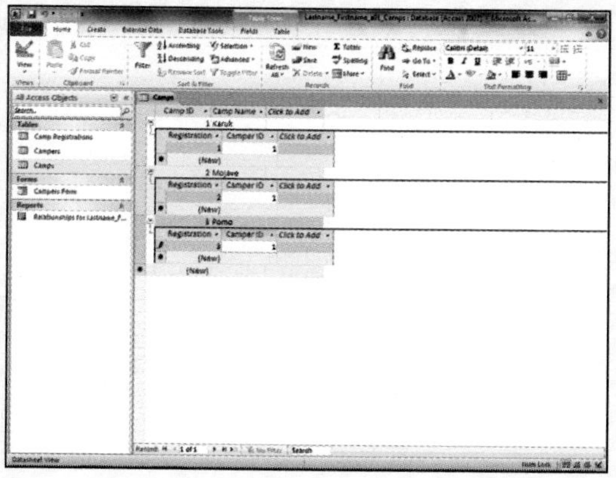

Figure 2

1. **Start** Access. Create a new database with the name Lastname_Firstname_a01_Camps and save it in your **Access Chapter 1** folder.

2. In the new table, rename the **ID** field Camper ID Add two new **Text** fields named First Name and Last Name

3. Click the **Click to Add** column, and then add the **Address Quick Start** fields. For all fields except **Camper ID**, change the **Field Size** to 50 **Save** the table with the name Campers and then **Close** the table.

4. Select the **Campers** table, and then, on the **Create tab**, in the **Forms group**, click the **Form** button. Use the form to add yourself as a camper. Include your own contact information. **Save** the form as Campers Form Note the **Camper ID** value, and then **Close** the form.

5. Create a new table in **Datasheet** view. Rename the **ID** field Camp ID Add a new **Text** field named Camp Name **Save** the table as **Camps** and then **Close** the table.

6. Create a new table in **Design** view. Name the first field Registration ID Assign it the **AutoNumber** data type, and then make it the **Primary Key**. Name the second field Camp ID and assign the **Number** data type. Name the third field Camper ID and assign the **Number** data type.

7. **Save** the table as Camp Registrations and then **Close** the table.

8. Open the **Relationships tab**, and then add all three tables to the tab. Create a relationship that enforces referential integrity between the **Camps** and **Camp Registrations** tables using their common field. Create a similar relationship between the **Campers** and **Camp Registrations** tables.

9. Arrange the tables as shown in **Figure 1**, and then click **Save**.

10. Create a **Relationship Report**. **Save** the report with the name provided in the **Save As** dialog box. If asked, print the report. **Close** the report and **Close** the **Relationships tab**.

11. Open the **Camps** table, and add these three camps: Karuk and Mojave and Pomo Open each record's subdatasheet, and then enter your **Camper ID** value to add yourself as a registered camper in all three camps. Compare your screen with **Figure 2**.

12. **Close** the table. With the **Camps** table still selected, on the **Create tab**, in the **Reports group**, click the **Report** button to create a report for the table. In the **Grouping & Totals group**, click **Totals**, and then click **Count Records**. **Save** the report as Camps Report If asked, print the report. **Close** the report.

13. If asked, print the Camp Registrations datasheet. **Exit** Access. Submit your printouts or database file as directed.

Done! You have completed Assess Your Skills 2

Assess Your Skills Visually

To complete this database, you will need the following file:

- New blank Access database

You will save your database as:

- Lastname_Firstname_a01_Race

Create a new, blank database and **Save** it in your **Access Chapter 1** folder with the name Lastname_Firstname_a01_Race Create the tables shown in **Figure 1**. For each table, assign the primary key as indicated. For each table, rename the primary key, and then add the fields shown in **Figure 1**. For any field that will be on the many side of a one-to-many relationship, assign the **Number** data type. For the **Year** field, assign the **Number** data type. For the remaining fields, assign the data type appropriate for the type of data it will store. Create the many-to-many relationship shown in **Figure 1**. Create a relationships report and then **Save** the report using the name suggested by Access.

Print the report or submit the database file as directed by your instructor.

Done! You have completed Assess Your Skills Visually

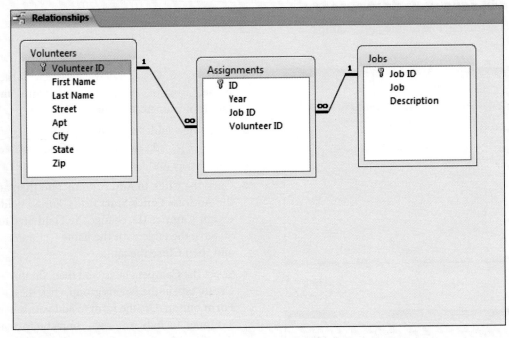

Figure 1

Skills in Context

To complete this database, you will need the following file:

- New blank Access database

You will save your database as:

- Lastname_Firstname_a01_Volunteers

Create a new database named Lastname_Firstname_a01_Volunteers and save it in your **Access Chapter 1** folder. Create a table to store the data in the table to the right. Add an AutoNumber primary key and assign appropriate field names. Consider the type of data that is being stored, and then assign appropriate data types and field sizes. Name the table Volunteers

Create a form for the table and then apply the theme of your choice. Use the form to enter the following contacts:

Your First Name	Virginia	Nancy
Your Last Name	Pipe	Warns
3924 S Williams St	9218 NE North St	53893 SE Park St
Aspen Falls	Marshall	Paulden
CA	CA	AZ
93464	94940	86334
Your phone number	(992) 555-2259	(928) 555-9512
Your date of birth	2/15/1986	8/6/1954

Print the table datasheet or submit the database file as directed by your instructor.

Done! You have completed Skills in Context

Skills and You

To complete this database, you will need the following file:

- New blank Access database

You will save your database as:

- Lastname_Firstname_a01_Contacts

Using the skills you have practiced in this chapter, create a database named Lastname_Firstname_a01_Contacts Create a table that can be used to store personal contacts. Include fields for names, addresses, e-mail addresses, and phone numbers. Use the table to enter at least 10 contacts, and include your own contact information. Print the datasheet or submit the database file electronically as directed by your instructor.

Done! You have completed Skills and You

CHAPTER 2

Manage Datasheets and Create Queries

▶ Filtering, sorting, and formatting tables or queries are techniques used to present data in more meaningful ways.

▶ Queries are used to display fields from several tables, apply complex filters, or calculate new values based on the data in the query.

Your starting screen will look similar to this:

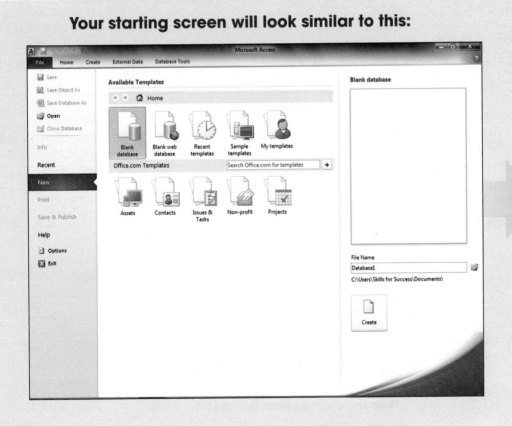

SKILLS

Skills 1-10 Training

At the end of this chapter, you will be able to:

Skill 1 Find and Replace Data

Skill 2 Filter and Sort Datasheets

Skill 3 Use the Simple Query Wizard

Skill 4 Format Datasheets

Skill 5 Add Date and Time Criteria

Skill 6 Create Queries in Design View

Skill 7 Add Calculated Fields to Queries

Skill 8 Work with Logical Criteria

Skill 9 Add Wildcards to Query Criteria

Skill 10 Group and Total Queries

MORE SKILLS

More Skills 11 Export Queries to Other File Formats

More Skills 12 Find Duplicate Records

More Skills 13 Find Unmatched Records

More Skills 14 Create Crosstab Queries

Outcome

Using the skills listed to the left will enable you to create database objects like these:

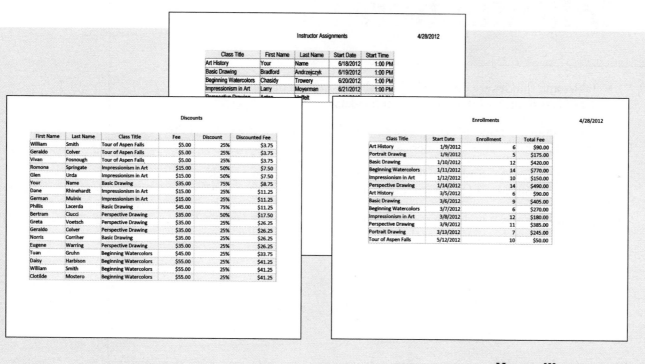

Instructor Assignments 4/28/2012

Class Title	First Name	Last Name	Start Date	Start Time
Art History	Your	Name	6/18/2012	1:00 PM
Basic Drawing	Bradford	Andrzejczyk	6/19/2012	1:00 PM
Beginning Watercolors	Chasidy	Trowery	6/20/2012	1:00 PM
Impressionism in Art	Larry	Moyerman	6/21/2012	1:00 PM
Perspective Drawing	Arlen	Moffelt		

Discounts

First Name	Last Name	Class Title	Fee	Discount	Discounted Fee
William	Smith	Tour of Aspen Falls	$5.00	25%	$3.75
Geraldo	Colver	Tour of Aspen Falls	$5.00	25%	$3.75
Vivan	Fosnough	Tour of Aspen Falls	$5.00	25%	$3.75
Romona	Springate	Impressionism in Art	$15.00	50%	$7.50
Glen	Urda	Impressionism in Art	$15.00	50%	$7.50
Your	Name	Basic Drawing	$35.00	75%	$8.75
Dane	Rhinehardt	Impressionism in Art	$15.00	25%	$11.25
German	Mulnix	Impressionism in Art	$15.00	25%	$11.25
Phillis	Lacerda	Basic Drawing	$45.00	75%	$11.25
Bertram	Ciucci	Perspective Drawing	$35.00	50%	$17.50
Greta	Voetsch	Perspective Drawing	$35.00	25%	$26.25
Geraldo	Colver	Perspective Drawing	$35.00	25%	$26.25
Norris	Corriher	Basic Drawing	$35.00	25%	$26.25
Eugene	Warring	Perspective Drawing	$35.00	25%	$26.25
Tuan	Gruhn	Beginning Watercolors	$45.00	25%	$33.75
Daisy	Harbison	Beginning Watercolors	$55.00	25%	$41.25
William	Smith	Beginning Watercolors	$55.00	25%	$41.25
Clotilde	Mostero	Beginning Watercolors	$55.00	25%	$41.25

Enrollments 4/28/2012

Class Title	Start Date	Enrollment	Total Fee
Art History	1/9/2012	6	$90.00
Portrait Drawing	1/9/2012	5	$175.00
Basic Drawing	1/10/2012	12	$420.00
Beginning Watercolors	1/11/2012	14	$770.00
Impressionism in Art	1/12/2012	10	$150.00
Perspective Drawing	1/14/2012	14	$490.00
Art History	3/5/2012	6	$90.00
Basic Drawing	3/6/2012	9	$405.00
Beginning Watercolors	3/7/2012	6	$270.00
Impressionism in Art	3/8/2012	12	$180.00
Perspective Drawing	3/9/2012	11	$385.00
Portrait Drawing	3/13/2012	7	$245.00
Tour of Aspen Falls	5/12/2012	10	$50.00

You will save your database as:

Lastname_Firstname_a02_Classes

In this chapter, you will create documents for the Aspen Falls City Hall, which provides essential services for the citizens and visitors of Aspen Falls, California.

Introduction

▶ Tables and queries are displayed in datasheets. You can organize these datasheets to derive information from the data.

▶ You can filter datasheets to display a subset of the data, and you can sort the records in alphabetical or numeric order.

▶ When you need to display fields from more than one table in a single datasheet, you can add those fields to a query.

▶ In queries, you can write expressions to filter the information you need, calculate values based on other fields, and provide statistics that summarize your data.

Time to complete all
10 skills – 50 to 75 minutes

Find your student data files here:

**Student data files needed
for this chapter:**

- a02_Classes

▶ Specific information can be located using the Find tool, and data can be searched and changed using Find and Replace.

1. **Start** ⊕ Access. If necessary, **Maximize** ▭ the window.

2. If necessary, insert the Student CD that came with this book.

3. On the **File tab**, click **Open**. In the **Open** dialog box, navigate to your student data files and display the student files for this chapter. Select **a02_Classes**, and then click the **Open** button.

4. Click the **File tab**, and then click **Save Database As**. In the **Save As** dialog box navigation pane, display the file list where you are saving your files.

5. In the **Save As** dialog box, click **New folder**, type Access Chapter 2 and then press Enter two times. In the **File name** box, using your own name, name the file Lastname_Firstname_a02_Classes Compare your screen with **Figure 1**, and then click **Save**.

6. If the Security Warning message displays, click the Enable Content button.

7. In the **Navigation Pane**, double-click **Students** to open the table. Click anywhere in the **Last Name** column to make it the active column.

8. On the **Home tab**, in the **Find group**, click the **Find** button. In the **Find and Replace** dialog box, in the **Find What** box, type Brennan and then press Enter. Compare your screen with **Figure 2**.

Access searches the Last Name field for the text *Brennan*. The record for Eliseo Brennan displays with the text *Brennan* selected.

■ **Continue to the next page to complete the skill**

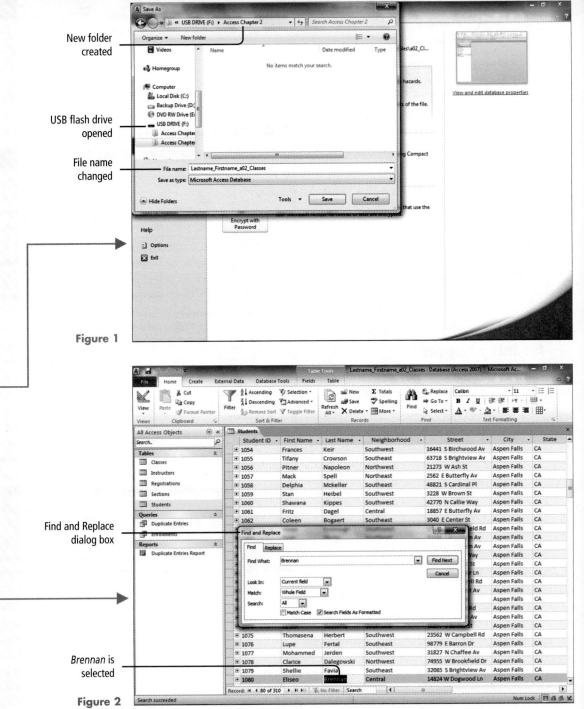

New folder created

USB flash drive opened

File name changed

Figure 1

Find and Replace dialog box

Brennan is selected

Figure 2

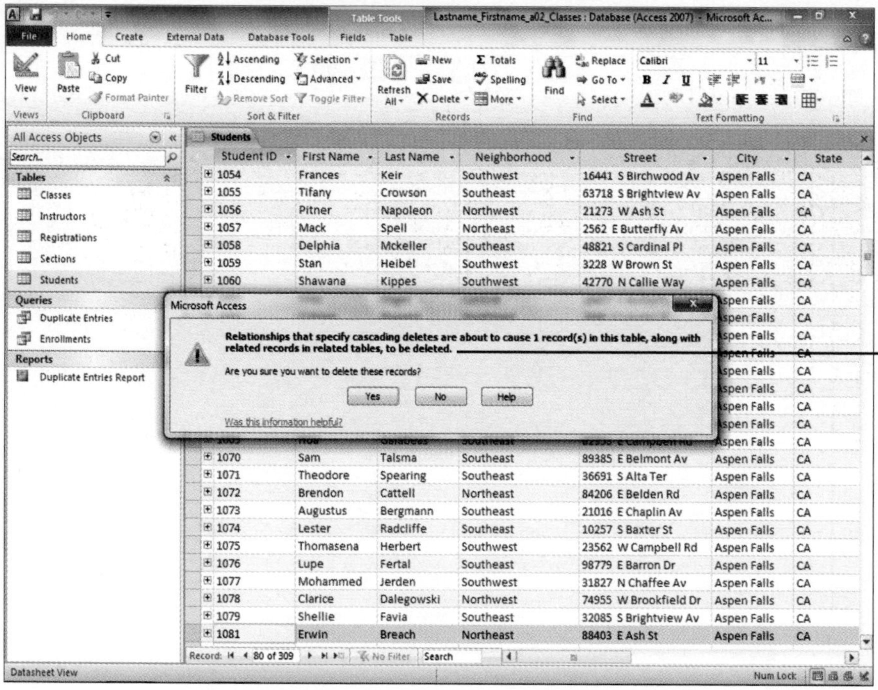

Cascading delete will be performed

Figure 3

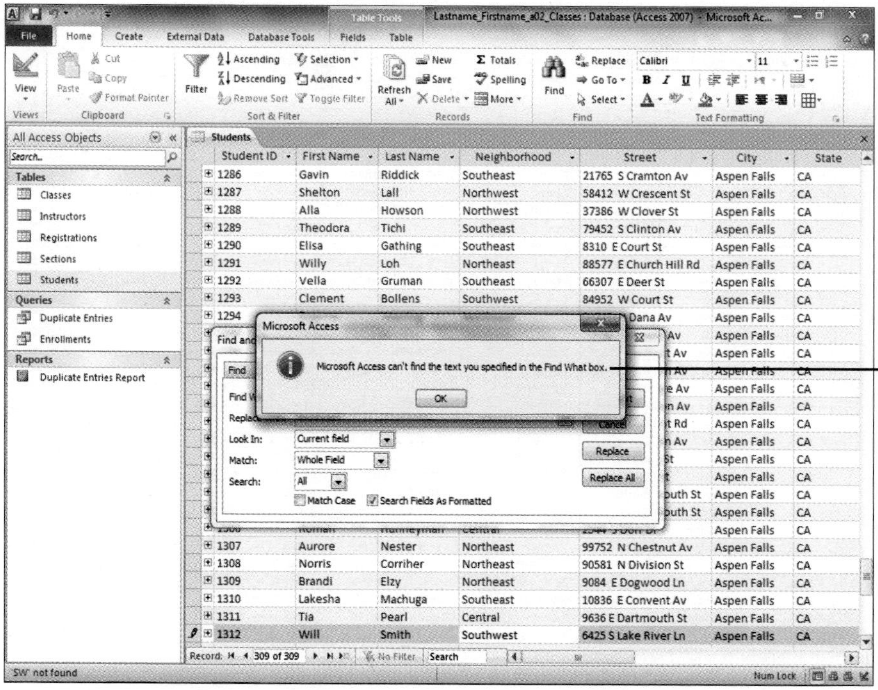

Search item not found

Figure 4

9. **Close** the **Find and Replace** dialog box. Be sure that the text *Brennan* is still selected. In the **Records group**, click the **Delete button arrow**, and then click **Delete Record**. Compare your screen with **Figure 3**, and then click **Yes**.

   The Students table is related to other tables with the cascading delete referential integrity option. Here, any records for Eliseo Brennan in related tables will also be deleted.

10. Click anywhere in the **Neighborhood** column, and then, in the **Find group**, click the **Replace** button.

11. In the **Find What** box, type SW In the **Replace With** box, type Southwest

12. In the **Find and Replace** dialog box, click the **Find Next** button. Notice that the first instance of *SW* is selected, and then click the **Replace** button.

    When you click the Replace button, the old value is replaced and the next instance of the old value is located.

13. Continue clicking the **Replace** button until the message shown in **Figure 4** displays.

14. Read the message, and then click **OK**. **Close** the **Find and Replace** dialog box.

15. Repeat the techniques just practiced to **Find** the record for *Kisha Algeo*, and then change that record's first and last name to your own first and last name.

16. Leave the table open for the next skill.

    Recall that the data you changed was saved automatically as you made changes. The table does not need to be saved.

■ **You have completed Skill 1 of 10**

► Information can be sorted by one or more columns. Sorting arranges data in ways that make it more useful.

► The Filter tool displays a list of all values for the active column. In the filter list, you can display or hide that value by clicking its check box.

1. **Close** ◄ the **Navigation Pane** to make more room for the **Students** datasheet.

2. Scroll to the top of the datasheet, and then compare your screen with **Figure 1.**

   By default, the records are sorted by the **Student ID** field.

3. Scroll the datasheet to the right, and click the **Birth Date** column header to select the column. In the **Sort & Filter group**, click the **Ascending** button to sort the records by date.

4. Scroll down to display the last four records. Notice that the records are sorted by birth date in chronological order and that students born in the same year are grouped together.

5. In the **Sort & Filter group**, click the **Remove Sort** button to return the datasheet to its original sort order.

6. Select the **Last Name** column. In the **Sort & Filter group**, click the **Ascending** button.

7. Select the **Neighborhood** column. In the **Sort & Filter group**, click the **Ascending** button. Compare your screen with **Figure 2.**

   The records are now sorted by Neighborhood, and within each group of neighborhoods, the records remain sorted by Last Name.

■ **Continue to the next page to complete the skill**

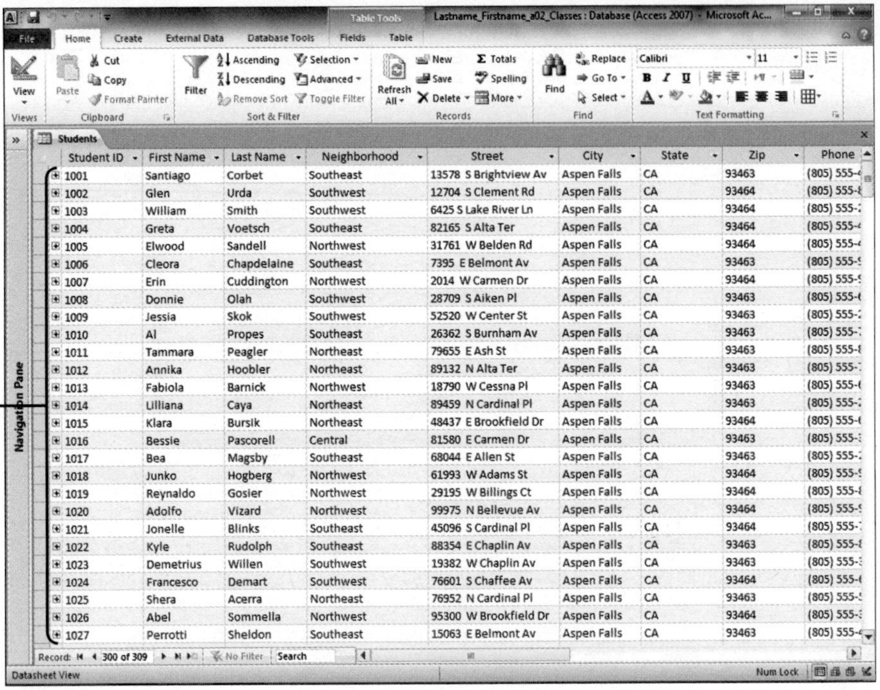

Records sorted by Student ID

Figure 1

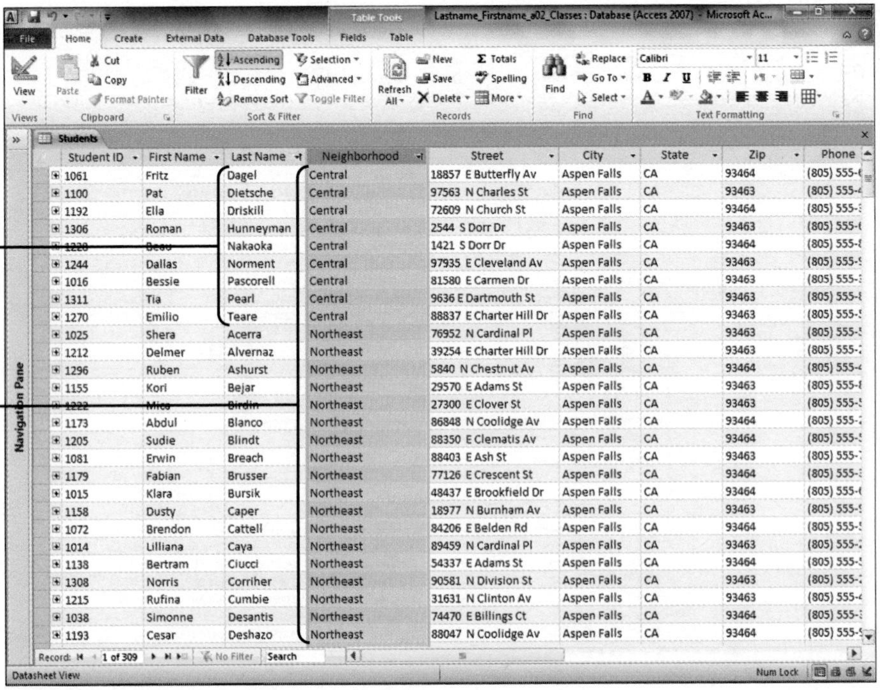

Records sorted by Last Name within Neighborhood

Records sorted by Neighborhood

Figure 2

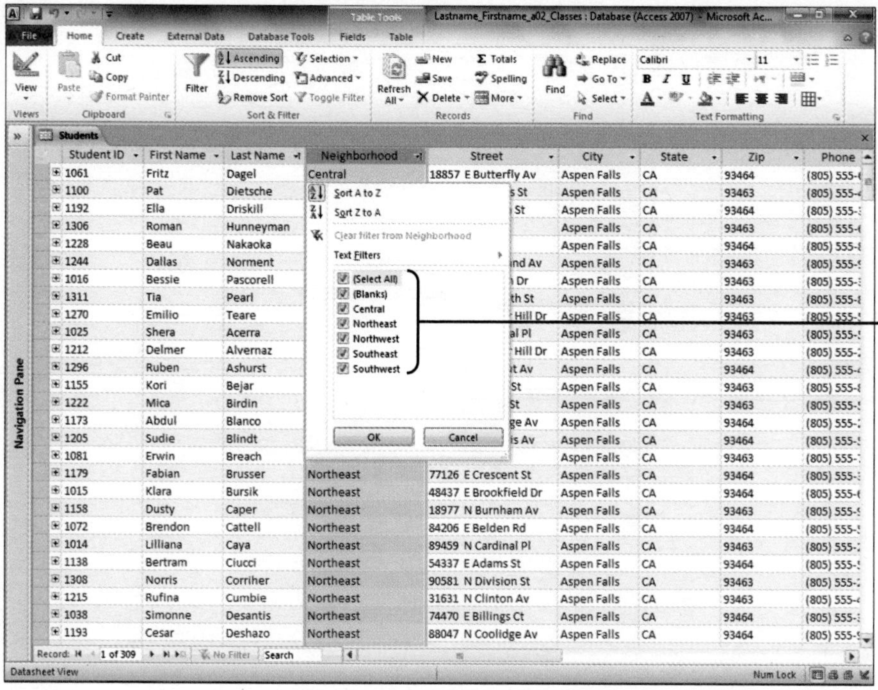

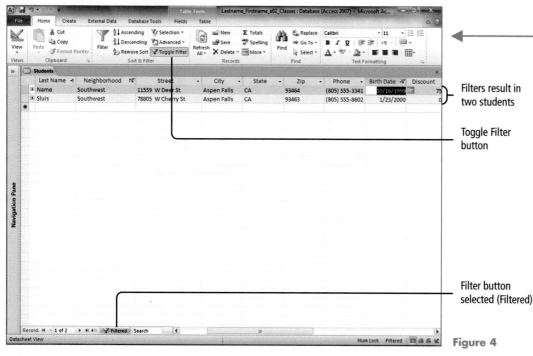

List of unique values in the Neighborhood field

Figure 3

Filters result in two students

Toggle Filter button

Filter button selected (Filtered)

Figure 4

8. With the **Neighborhood** column still selected, in the **Sort & Filter group**, click the **Filter** button, and then compare your screen with **Figure 3**.

   The Filter menu displays each unique value stored in the Neighborhood field. By default, each value is selected.

9. From the **Filter** menu, clear the **(Select All)** check box to clear all the check boxes. Select the **Southwest** check box, and then click **OK** to display the 68 students from the Southwest neighborhood.

10. Find the record with your name. Click in the **Birth Date** field, which has the value *10/16/1999*.

11. In the **Sort & Filter group**, click the **Selection** button, and then click **On or After 10/16/1999**. Compare your screen with **Figure 4**.

12. In the **Sort & Filter group**, click the **Toggle Filter** button.

    The filter is no longer applied to the datasheet and the Filter button displays the text *Unfiltered*. Turning a filter off does not delete the filter.

13. In the **Filter** status bar, click the **Unfiltered** button to reapply the filter.

14. On the **File** tab, click **Print**, and then click the **Print** button. In the **Print** dialog box, under **Print Range**, click in the **From** box, and then type 1 Click in the **To** box, and then type 1 If your instructor asks you to print your work, click OK to print the first page of the datasheet. Otherwise, click **Cancel**.

15. Click **Save**, and then **Close** the table. **Open** the **Navigation Pane**.

■ **You have completed Skill 2 of 10**

▶ The *Simple Query Wizard* quickly adds fields to a new query.

▶ You can include fields from related tables and all the fields will display in a single datasheet.

1. On the **Create tab**, in the **Queries group**, click the **Query Wizard** button.

2. In the **New Query** dialog box, with **Simple Query Wizard** selected, click **OK**.

3. Click the **Tables/Queries arrow**, and then click **Table: Classes**. Click **Class Title**, click the **Move** button, and then compare your screen with **Figure 1**.

4. Click the **Tables/Queries arrow**, and then click **Table: Instructors**. Click **First Name**, and then click the **Move** button. Repeat this technique to move the **Last Name** field into **Selected Fields**.

5. Click the **Tables/Queries arrow**, and then click **Table: Sections**. Move the **Start Date** and **Start Time** fields into **Selected Fields**.

6. Compare your screen with **Figure 2**, and then click **Next** two times.

7. In the **What title do you want for your query** box, replace the existing text with Instructor Assignments

8. Select the **Modify the query design** option button, and then click **Finish**.

▪ **Continue to the next page to complete the skill**

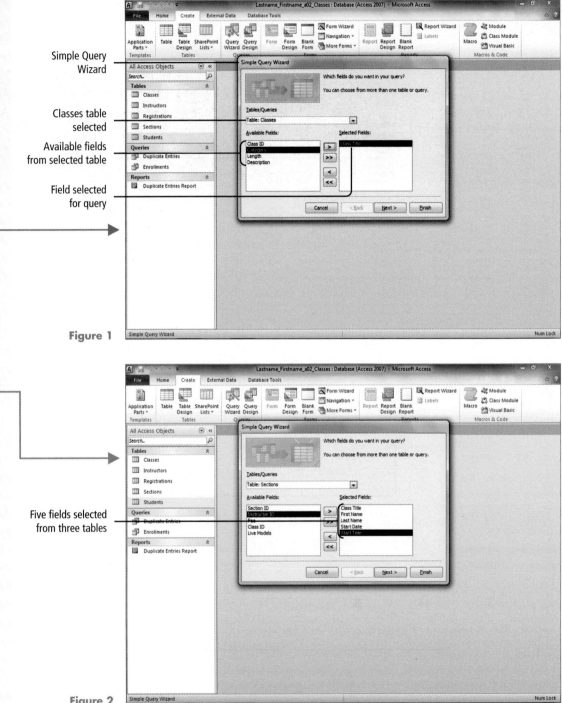

Simple Query Wizard

Classes table selected

Available fields from selected table

Field selected for query

Figure 1

Five fields selected from three tables

Figure 2

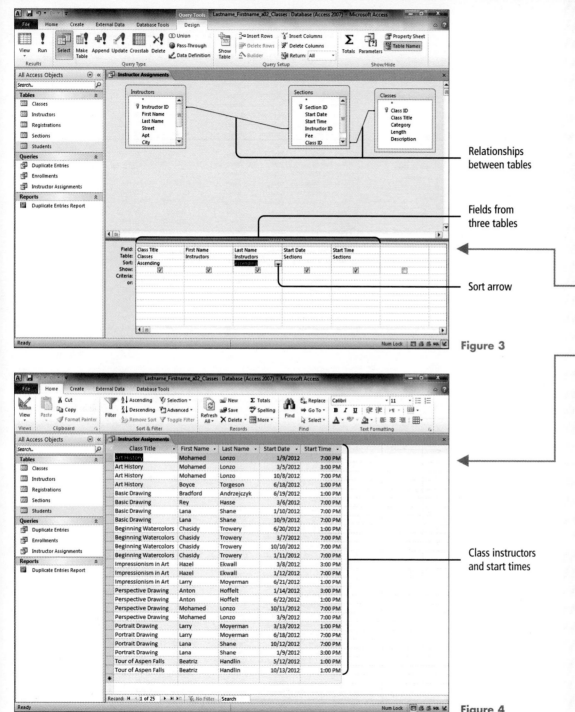

Relationships
between tables

Fields from
three tables

Sort arrow

Figure 3

Class instructors
and start times

Figure 4

9. In the query design workspace, point to the **Classes** table title bar and then drag it to the right of the **Sections** table.

When you choose fields from multiple tables in a query, the relationships defined in the Relationships tab will also apply to the query. Here, an instructor can be assigned to teach many sections, and a class can be assigned to many sections.

10. Click the **Class Title** column **Sort** box to display its arrow. Click the **Class Title** column **Sort arrow**, and then click **Ascending**.

11. Repeat the technique just practiced so that the **Last Name** column is sorted in **Ascending** order. Compare your screen with **Figure 3**.

12. On the **Design tab**, in the **Results group**, click the **Run** button. Alternately, click the View button. Compare your screen with **Figure 4**.

Recall that queries show subsets of the data to answer a question. Here, the query shows fields from three related tables and answers the question: *When do classes start and who is assigned to teach them?*

13. Click **Save** 🖫, and leave the query open for the next skill.

■ **You have completed Skill 3 of 10**

► Datasheets—for tables or for queries—can be formatted to make the data easier to read.

1. If necessary, open the Instructor Assignments query datasheet.

2. On the **Home tab**, in the **Text Formatting group**, click the **Font arrow**. Scroll to the top of the list of fonts, and then click **Arial Narrow**.

3. On the **Home tab**, in the **Text Formatting group**, click the **Font Size arrow**, and then click **12**. Compare your screen with Figure 1.

   When you change the font size or font, the changes are applied to the entire datasheet.

4. In the upper-left corner of the datasheet, click the **Select All** button ▢. Place the pointer on the line between any two column headers. With the ⊞ pointer, double-click to resize all the columns automatically.

5. Click in any cell to deselect the datasheet, and then compare your screen with Figure 2.

■ **Continue to the next page to complete the skill**

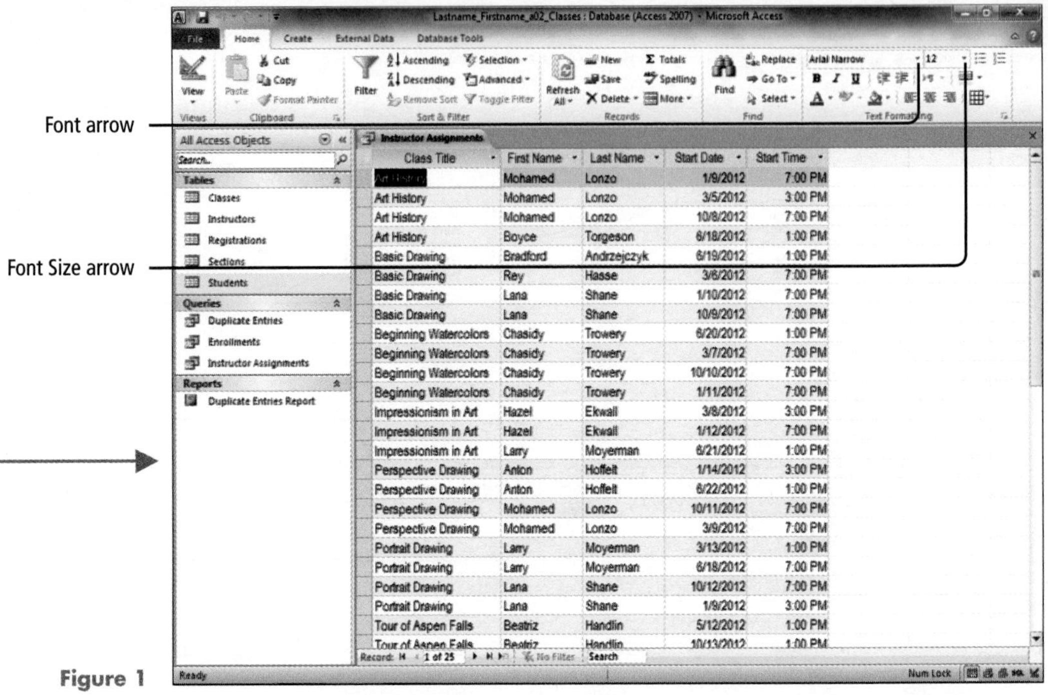

Font arrow

Font Size arrow

Figure 1

Columns resized

Select All button

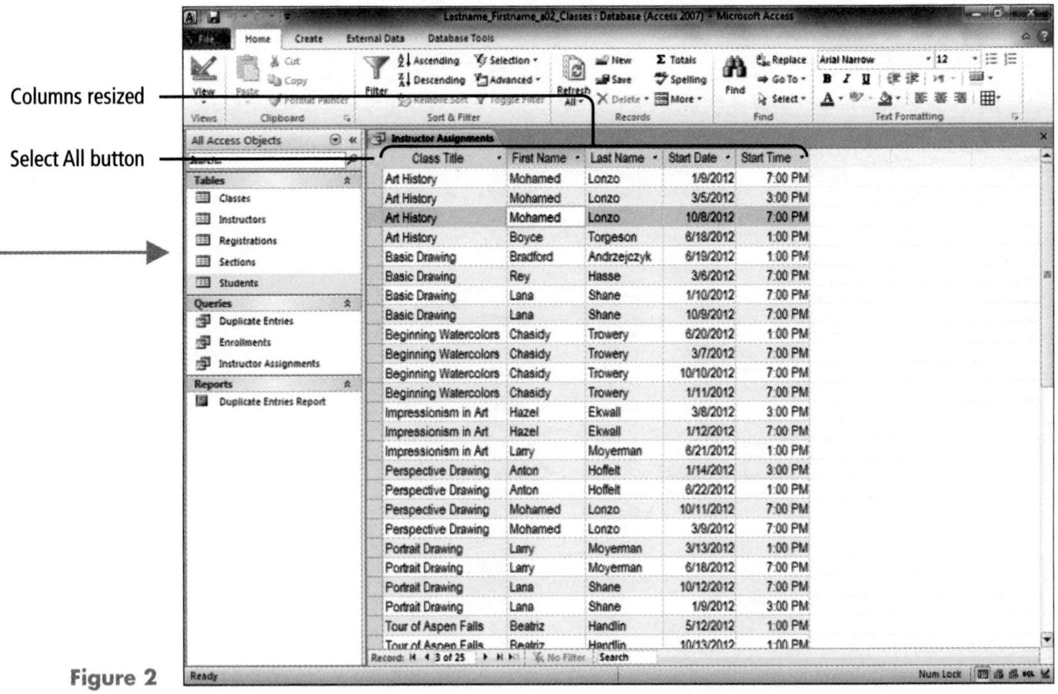

Figure 2

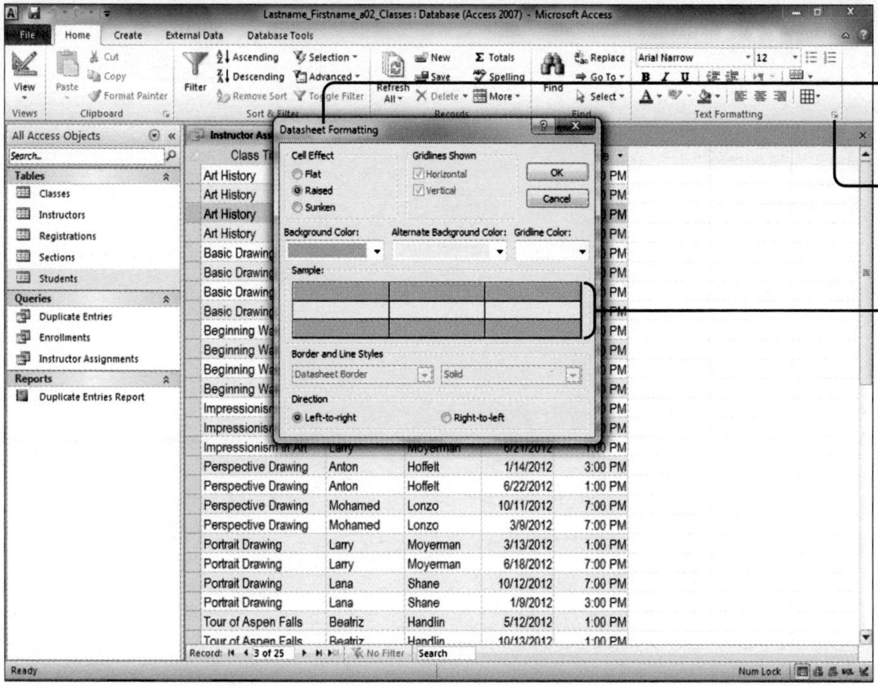

Datasheet Formatting dialog box

Datasheet Formatting Dialog Box Launcher

Sample of selected formatting

Figure 3

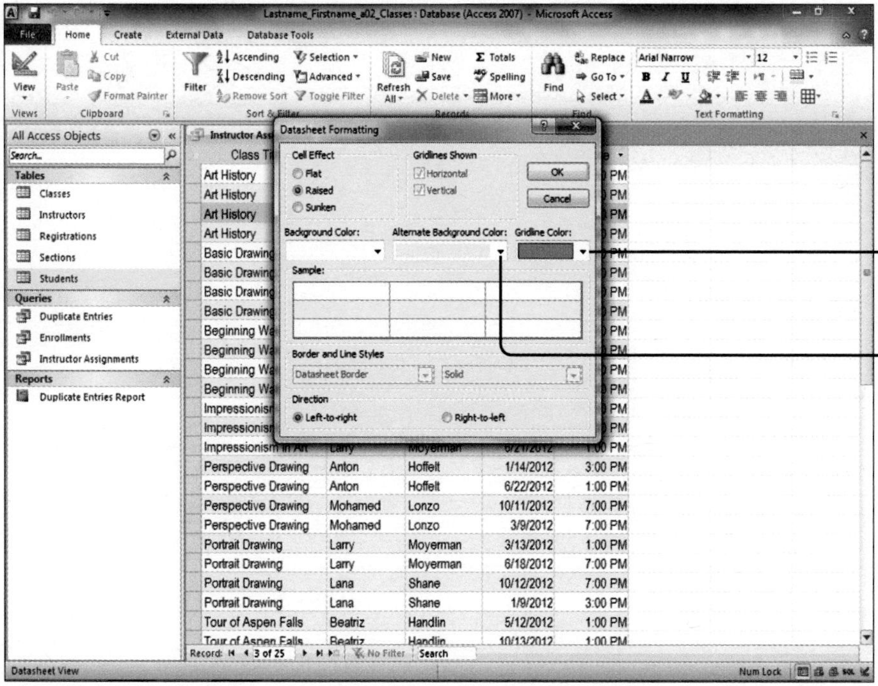

Gridline Color arrow

Alternate Background Color arrow

Figure 4

6. In the **Text Formatting group**, click the **Datasheet Formatting Dialog Box Launcher** 🔽.

7. In the **Datasheet Formatting** dialog box, under **Cell Effect**, select the **Raised** option button. Compare your screen with **Figure 3**.

   In the Datasheet Formatting dialog box, a sample of the selected formatting displays.

8. In the **Datasheet Formatting** dialog box, click the **Background Color arrow**. In the gallery, click **Automatic**.

9. In the **Datasheet Formatting** dialog box, click the **Alternate Background Color arrow**. In the gallery, under **Theme Colors**, click the sixth color in the second row—**Aqua, Accent 2, Lighter 80%**.

10. Click the **Gridline Color arrow**. In the gallery, under **Theme Colors**, click the eighth color in the first row—**Gray-50%, Accent 4**. Compare your screen with **Figure 4**.

11. Click **OK** to apply the changes and to close the dialog box.

12. Click the **Save** 🔲 button to save the design changes that you made. Leave the query open for the next skill.

■ **You have completed Skill 4 of 10**

▶ In Access, dates and times are stored as numbers. The underlying numbers display as dates in database objects. For example, the number 37979 displays as *12/24/2003* if the Short Date format is assigned to the Date/Time field.

▶ When dates are used as query criteria, they are surrounded by number signs (#).

1. With the **Instructor Assignments** query still open, click the **View** button to switch to Design view.

2. Click in the **Start Time** column **Criteria** box, and then type 1:00 PM Compare your screen with **Figure 1**. ──────

   As you type in a date criteria box, ***IntelliSense***—Quick Info, ToolTips, and AutoComplete—display. ***AutoComplete*** is a menu of commands that match the characters you type. The ***Quick Info*** box explains the purpose of the selected AutoComplete. Here, the suggested command—Pmt—is not needed and should be ignored.

3. On the **Design tab**, in the **Results group**, click the **Run** button. Verify that the eight classes that start at 1:00 PM display, and then switch to Design view. Compare your screen with **Figure 2**. ──────

   When you do not type the number symbols that surround dates or times, Access inserts them before running the query.

■ **Continue to the next page to complete the skill** ▶

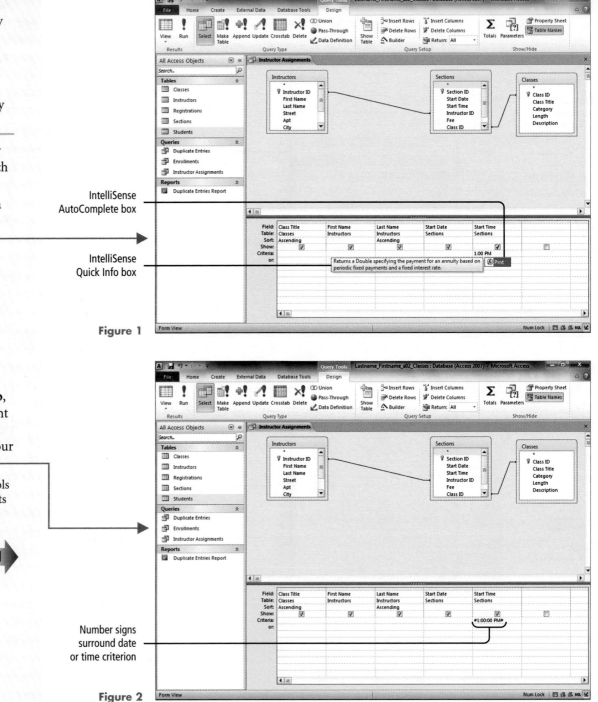

IntelliSense
AutoComplete box

IntelliSense
Quick Info box

Figure 1

Number signs
surround date
or time criterion

Figure 2

Common Comparison Operators

Operator	Purpose
=	Is true when the field's value is equal to the specified value
<>	Is true when the field's value does not equal the specified value
<	Is true when the field's value is less than the specified value
<=	Is true when the field's value is less than or equal to the specified value
>	Is true when the field's value is greater than the specified value
>=	Is true when the field's value is greater than or equal to the specified value

Figure 3

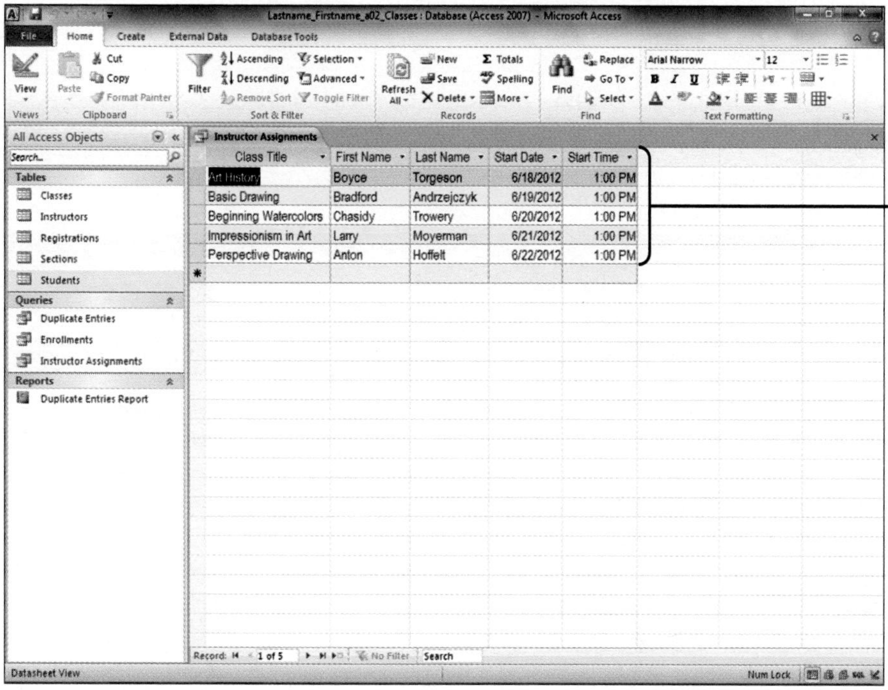

June classes that start at 1 PM

Figure 4

4. In the **Start Date** column **Criteria** box, type >4/1/2012 **Run** the query to display the seven classes that start after April 1, 2012 and start at 1:00 PM.

   Dates, times, and other numeric criteria often use *comparison operators*—operators used to compare two values—for example, = (equal to) and < (less than). Common comparison operators are listed in the table in **Figure 3**.

5. Switch to Design view. In the **Start Date** column **Criteria** box, replace the existing criterion with Between 6/1/2012 And 6/30/2012 With the ⊞ pointer, increase the width of the **Start Date** column to display all its criteria.

   The *Between...And operator* finds all numbers or dates between and including two values. Here, all the June classes that start at 1:00 PM will display in the query.

   When you widen a query column in the design grid, the column will return to its original width when the query is closed.

6. **Save** 🖫, and then **Run** the query to display the June classes that start at 1:00 PM. Compare your screen with **Figure 4**.

7. In the first record, change the name *Boyce Torgeson* to your own first and last name. If you are printing your work, print the datasheet.

8. **Close** ✕ the query.

- **You have completed Skill 5 of 10**

▶ To create a query in Design view, you first add the tables you will need to the query design workspace. You then add the fields you want to use to the design grid. Finally, you add criteria and run the query.

1. On the **Create tab**, in the **Queries group**, click the **Query Design** button.

2. In the **Show Table** dialog box, double-click **Classes** to add the table to the query design workspace. Alternately, select the table in the dialog box, and then click the Add button.

3. Repeat the technique just practiced to add the **Sections** and **Registrations** tables. Compare your screen with **Figure 1**, and then **Close** the **Show Table** dialog box.

4. In the **Navigation Pane**, point to the **Students** table. Drag the table from the **Navigation Pane** to the right of the **Registrations** table in the query design workspace. Compare your screen with **Figure 2**.

Tables can be added to the query design workspace using the Show Table dialog box or by dragging them from the Navigation Pane.

This query needs to ask the question: *Which students receive a discount?* To answer this question, fields from three tables are needed. The Registrations table has been added to the query to join Sections and Students in a many-to-many relationship.

■ **Continue to the next page to complete the skill**

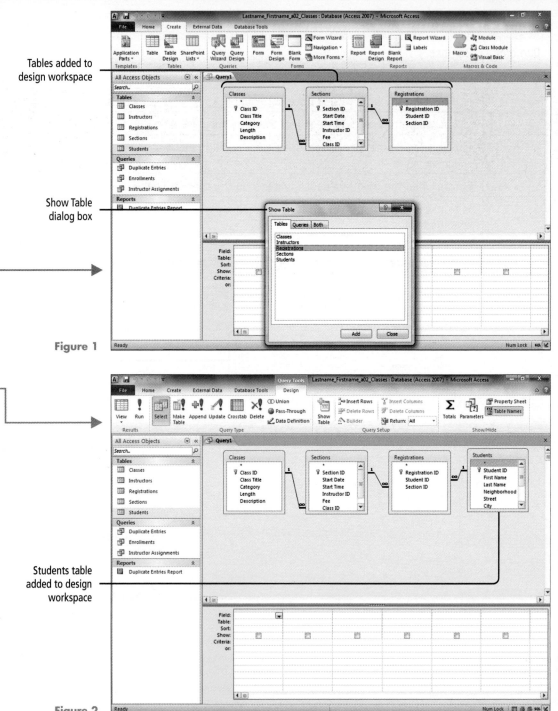

Tables added to design workspace

Show Table dialog box

Figure 1

Students table added to design workspace

Figure 2

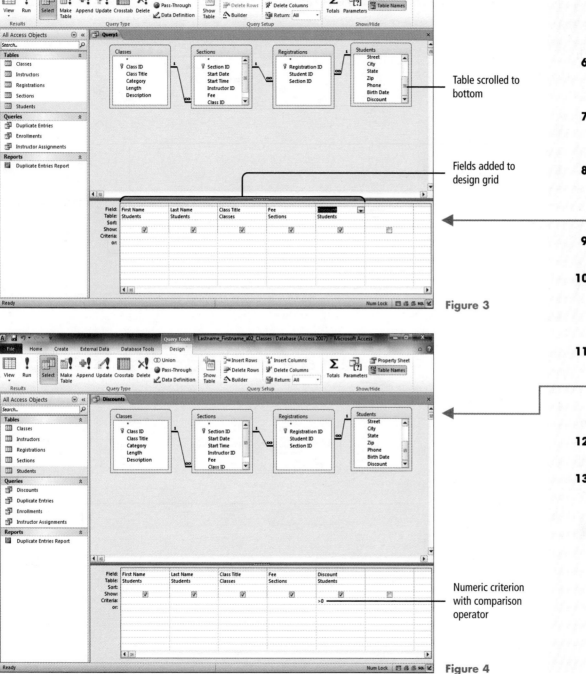

Table scrolled to bottom

Fields added to design grid

Figure 3

Numeric criterion with comparison operator

Figure 4

5. In the query design workspace, in the **Students** table, double-click the **First Name** field to add it to the first column of the design grid. Alternately, drag the field into the first column Field box.

6. In the **Students** table, double-click **Last Name** to add it to the second column of the design grid.

7. From the **Classes** table, add the **Class Title** field. From the **Sections** table, add the **Fee** field.

8. In the **Students** table, scroll down to display the **Discount** field, and then add the **Discount** field to the design grid. Compare your screen with **Figure 3**.

9. Click **Save** 🔲. In the **Save As** dialog box, type Discounts and then press Enter.

10. On the **Design tab**, in the **Results group**, click **Run**.

    The query displays all students registered for Art Center classes.

11. Switch to Design view. In the **Discount** column **Criteria** box, type >0 Compare your screen with **Figure 4**.

    Here, only the students with a discount greater than zero will display.

12. Run the query to display the 18 students with discounts, and then click **Save** 🔲.

13. Leave the query open for the next skill.

    ■ **You have completed Skill 6 of 10**

► A *calculated field* is a column added to a query that derives its value from other fields.

1. If necessary, open the Discounts query datasheet. Click the **View** button to switch to Design view.

2. **Close** ⟪ the **Navigation Pane**. Click in the first empty **Field** box to the right of the **Discount** column. Click the **Field arrow** to display the field list.

   Clicking fields in the Field list is an alternate method of selecting fields in queries.

3. Press Esc to close the field list.

   In this Field box, you will create a new field that derives its value from two different fields—Fee and Discount.

4. With the insertion point in the first blank field box, type Discounted Fee followed by a colon (:). Compare your screen with **Figure 1**.

   In a query, calculated fields begin with a descriptive label that ends with a colon. Here, Discounted Fee will be the column label when the query is run.

5. Point to the line to the right and slightly above the **Discounted Fee** column. When the ⊞ pointer displays, drag to the right to the middle of the second blank column and then release the mouse button. Compare your screen with **Figure 2**.

   ■ **Continue to the next page to complete the skill**

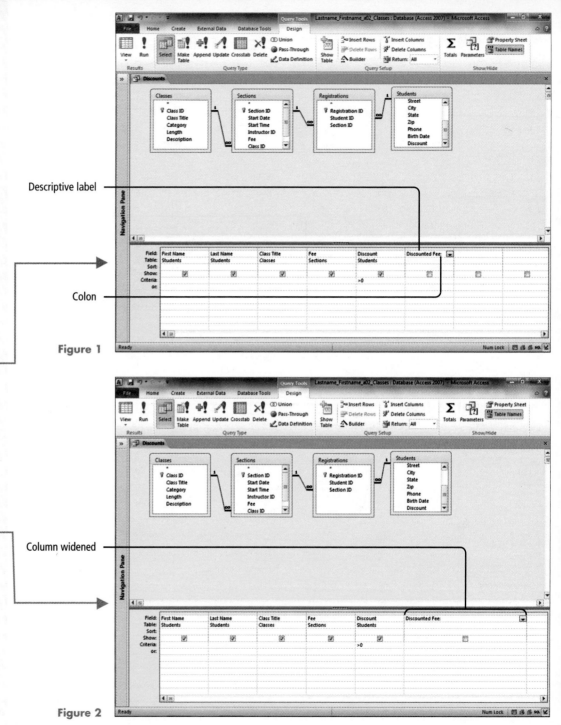

Descriptive label

Colon

Figure 1

Column widened

Figure 2

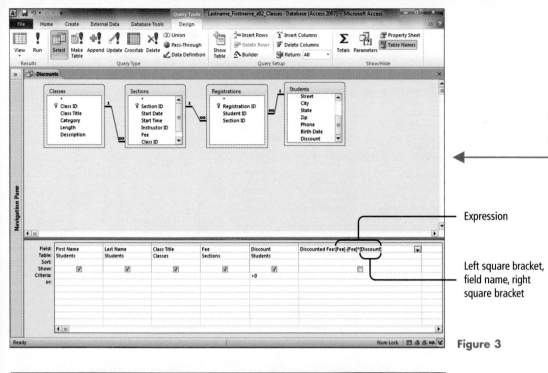

Figure 3

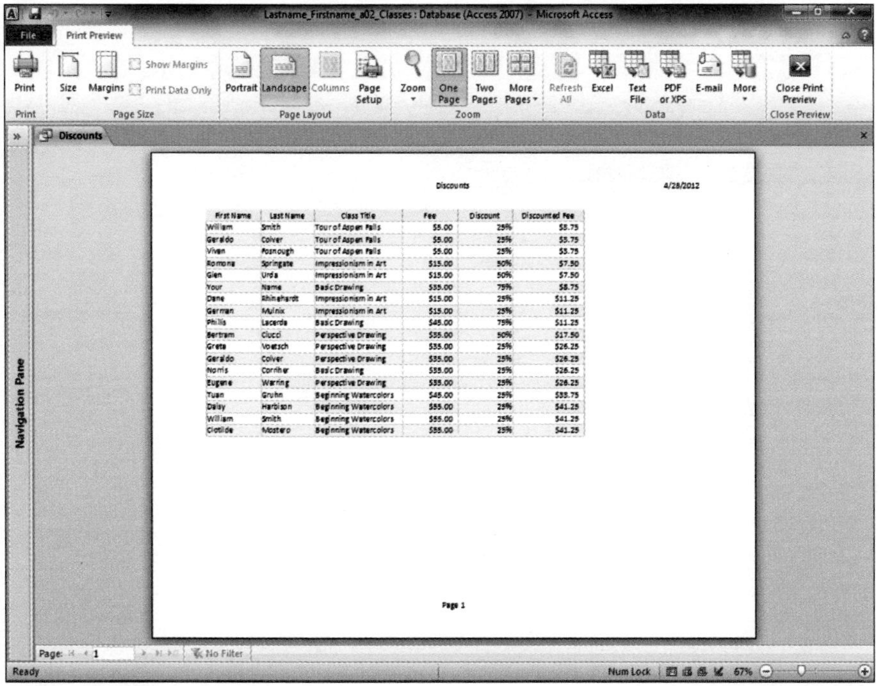

Expression

Left square bracket,
field name, right
square bracket

Figure 4

6. With the insertion point to the right of the colon, type the following expression: [Fee]-[Fee]*[Discount] Compare your screen with **Figure 3**.

> An *expression* is a combination of fields, mathematical operators, and prebuilt functions that calculates values in tables, forms, queries, and reports.

> In expressions, field names are always enclosed between a left square bracket and a right square bracket. Here, the expression multiplies the fee by the discount to determine the discount amount. To determine the discounted fee, the discount amount is subtracted from the original fee.

7. In the **Results group**, click **Run**. If the Enter Parameter Value dialog box or any other dialog box displays, close the dialog box, and then carefully check the placement of the colon and square brackets, and check that you spelled the field names correctly. Then run the query again.

8. With the ⊞ pointer, double-click to resize the **Discounted Fee** column automatically.

9. Click anywhere in the **Discounted Fee** column, and then, on the **Home tab**, in the **Sort & Filter group**, click the **Ascending** button.

10. Click **File**, click **Print**, and then click **Print Preview**. In the **Page Layout group**, click **Landscape**. Compare your screen with **Figure 4**.

11. Click **Save** 🖫. If you are printing this project, print the datasheet.

12. **Close** ☒ the datasheet, and then **Open** ⟫ the **Navigation Pane**.

■ **You have completed Skill 7 of 10**

▶ When criteria are in more than one column, the placement of the criteria in the design grid rows determines if one or both of the criteria must be true for the record to display.

1. On the **Create tab**, in the **Queries group**, click the **Query Design** button. In the **Show Table** dialog box, add the **Classes** table, add the **Sections** table, and then **Close** the dialog box.

2. In the design workspace, point to the bottom edge of the **Sections** table. With the ⬍ pointer, drag down so that all the table fields display, and then release the mouse button.

3. From the **Classes** table, add the **Class Title** field to the design grid. From the **Sections** table, add the **Start Date** and **Live Models** fields to the design grid.

4. Click **Save** 🖫, type Adults Only Classes and then click **OK**.

5. In the **Results group**, click the **Run** button, and then compare your screen with **Figure 1**.

   The Live Models field has been assigned the *Yes/No data type*—a data type used to store values that can have one of two possible values—for example, yes and no, or true and false.

6. Click the **View** button to switch to Design view. In the **Live Models** column **Criteria** box, type =Yes **Run** the query, and then compare your results with **Figure 2**.

   When a check box in a Yes/No field is selected, the value *Yes* is stored in the field. When the check box is cleared, the value *No* is stored in that field.

■ **Continue to the next page to complete the skill**

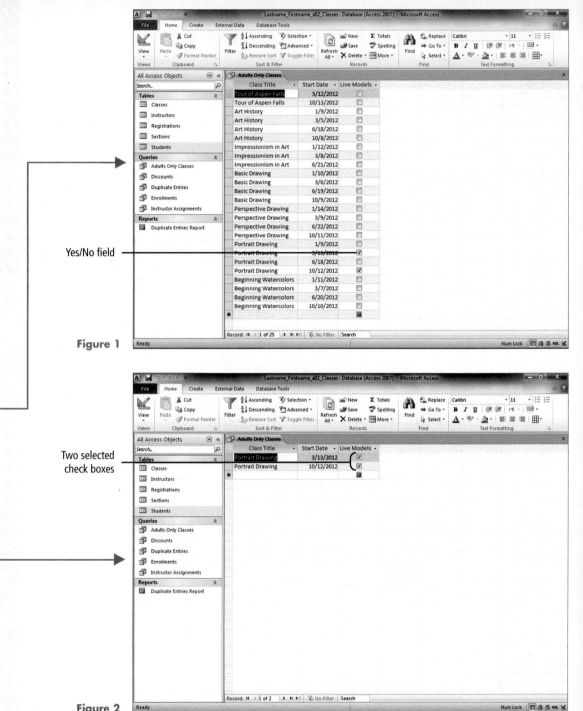

Yes/No field

Figure 1

Two selected check boxes

Figure 2

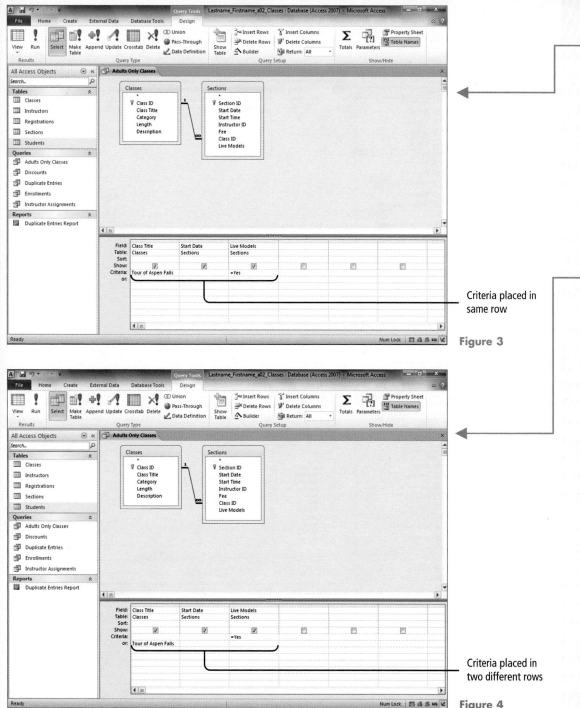

Criteria placed in
same row

Figure 3

Criteria placed in
two different rows

Figure 4

7. Switch to Design view. In the **Class Title** column **Criteria** box, type Tour of Aspen Falls Compare your screen with **Figure 3**.

When two criteria are placed in the same row, the **And logical operator**—a logical comparison of two criteria that is true only when both criteria outcomes are true—applies. Here, the Class Title must be Tour of Aspen Falls *and* Live Models must equal Yes for the record to display.

8. **Run** the query. Notice that no records match both criteria, and then switch to Design view.

9. In the **Class Title** column **Criteria** box, delete the criterion. In the **Class Title** column **or** box, type Tour of Aspen Falls Compare your screen with **Figure 4**.

When two criteria are placed in *different* rows in the design grid, the **Or logical operator**—a logical comparison of two criteria that is true if either of the criteria outcomes are true—applies. Here, the Class Title can be Tour of Aspen Falls or Live Models can equal Yes for the record to display.

10. **Run** the query to display four records that match the criteria. If you are printing your work for this project, print the datasheet.

11. **Save** 🔲 and then **Close** ☒ the query.

■ **You have completed Skill 8 of 10**

► A *wildcard* is a special character, such as an asterisk, used in query criteria to allow matches for any combination of letters or characters.

► Using wildcards, you can expand your search criteria to find a more accurate subset of the data.

1. In the **Navigation Pane**, under **Queries**, right-click **Duplicate Entries**, and then, from the shortcut menu, click **Design View**.

2. In the **First Name** column **Criteria** box, type William In the **Last Name** column **Criteria** box, type Smith **Run** the query to display the record for William Smith.

   William Smith reports that he receives four copies of every Art Center flyer. With the current criteria, his record is listed one time.

3. Switch to Design view. In the **First Name** column **Criteria** box, replace the existing criterion with Will* **Run** the query, and then compare your screen with **Figure 1**.

   The *asterisk (*) wildcard* character matches any combination of characters. Here, the first names all begin with *Will* but end differently.

4. Switch to Design view, and then compare your screen with **Figure 2**.

   When you include wildcards, the criterion needs to start with the Like operator. If you don't type the Like operator, it will be inserted automatically when the query is run.

■ **Continue to the next page to complete the skill** ➡

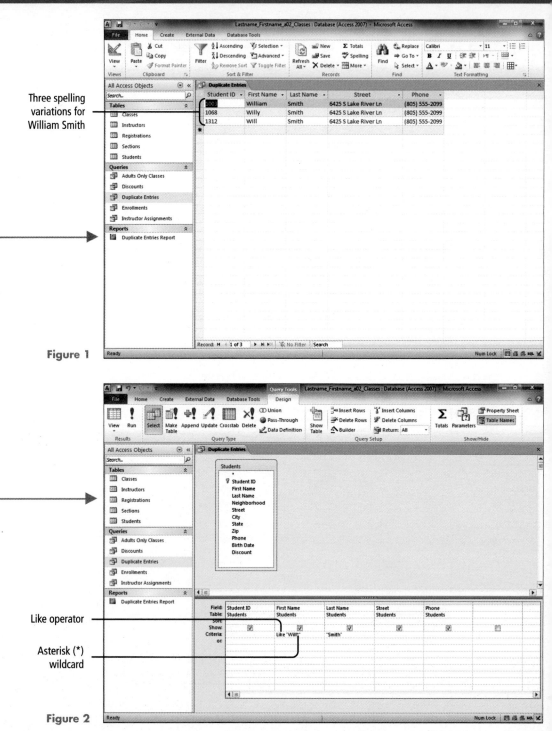

Three spelling variations for William Smith

Figure 1

Like operator

Asterisk (*) wildcard

Figure 2

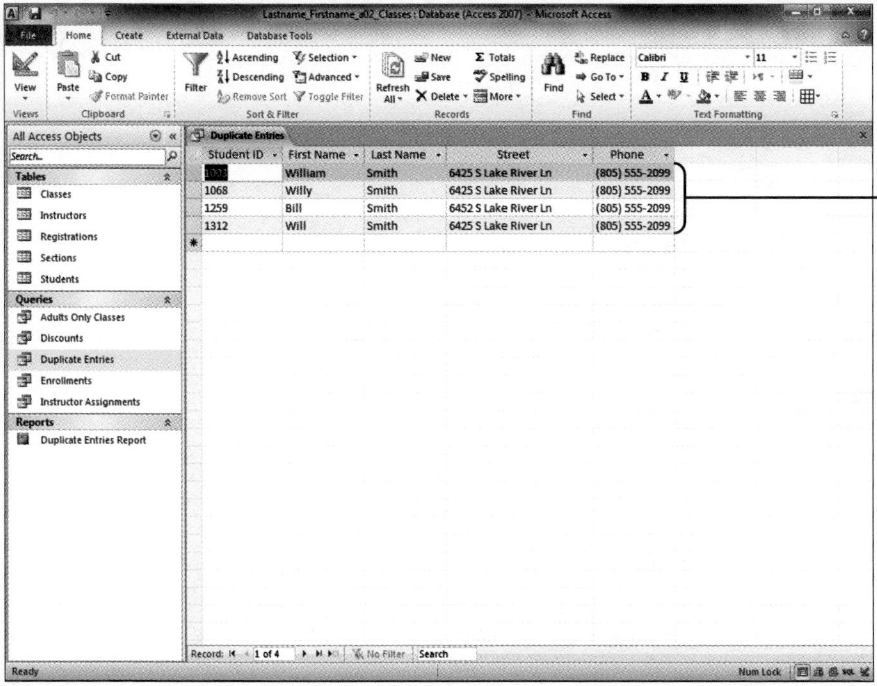

Four spelling variations for William Smith

Figure 3

5. In the **First Name** column **Criteria** box, replace the existing criterion with Like "?ill*" **Run** the query to display the four duplicate records for William Smith. Compare your screen with **Figure 3**.

 The *question mark (?) wildcard* character matches any single character. Common wildcard characters supported by Access are summarized in the table in **Figure 4**.

6. **Save** 🖫, and then **Close** ✕ the query.

7. In the **Navigation Pane**, under **Reports**, double-click **Duplicate Entries Report**. If you are printing this project, print the report.

 Recall that reports are often used to display the results of queries. Here, the report displays the results of the Duplicate Entries query.

8. **Close** ✕ the report.

 Because you did not make any design changes to the report, you do not need to save it.

■ **You have completed Skill 9 of 10**

Common Access Wildcard Characters

Character	Description	Example
*	Matches any number of characters.	Don* matches Don and Donna, but not Adonna.
?	Matches any single alphabetic character.	D?n matches Don and Dan, but not Dean.
[ ]	Matches any single character in the brackets.	D[ao]n matches Dan and Don, but not Den.
#	Matches any single numeric character.	C-#PO matches C-3PO, but not C-DPO.

Figure 4

▶ A *summary statistic* is a calculation for a group of data such as a total, an average, or a count.

▶ When summary statistics are added to a query, the query calculates statistics for a group of data.

1. In the **Navigation Pane**, under **Queries**, right-click **Enrollments**, and then, from the shortcut menu, click **Design View**.

2. In the query design workspace, in the **Classes** table, double-click **Class Title** to add it to the design grid. Repeat this technique to insert the **Start Date, Student ID**, and **Fee** fields.

3. Change the **Start Date** column **Sort** box to **Ascending**. **Run** the query, and then compare your screen with **Figure 1**.

   The query lists each class and its starting date, the Student ID of each student enrolled in the class, and the normal Fee charged to each student.

4. Switch to Design view. On the **Design tab**, in the **Show/Hide group**, click the **Totals** button to insert the **Total** row in the design grid.

5. Click in the **Student ID** column **Total** box to display its arrow. Click the **Student ID** column **Total arrow**, and then click **Count**. Repeat this technique to change the **Fee** column **Total** box to **Sum**. Compare your screen with **Figure 2**.

   The Total row is used to determine how queries should be grouped and summarized. Here, two columns have been designated as columns to group by and the other two columns have been designated to calculate statistics—count and sum.

■ **Continue to the next page to complete the skill**

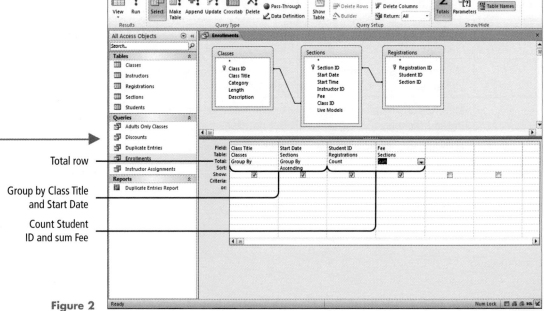

All students enrolled in classes and normal fees

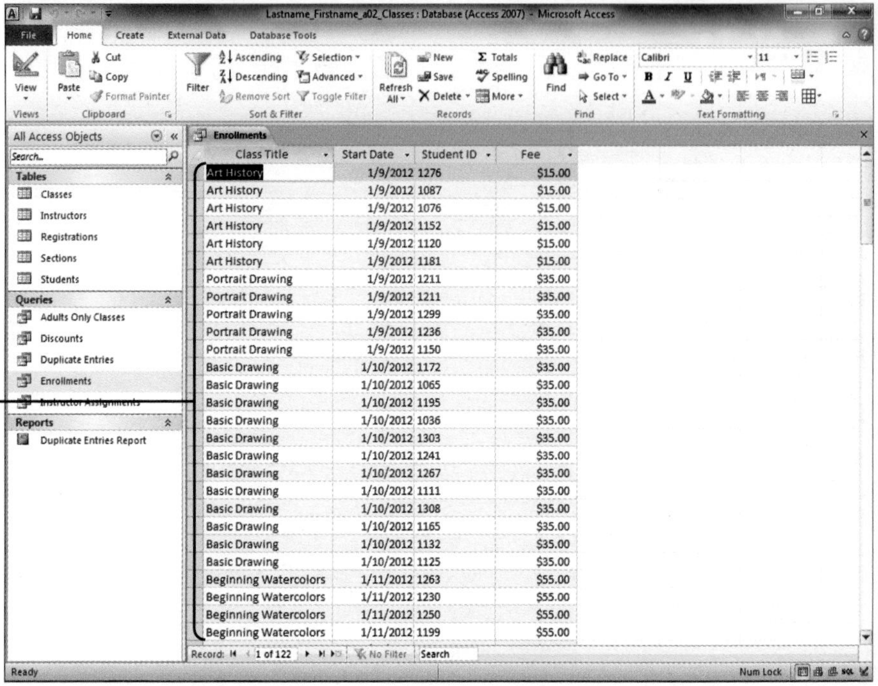

Figure 1

Total row

Group by Class Title and Start Date

Count Student ID and sum Fee

Figure 2

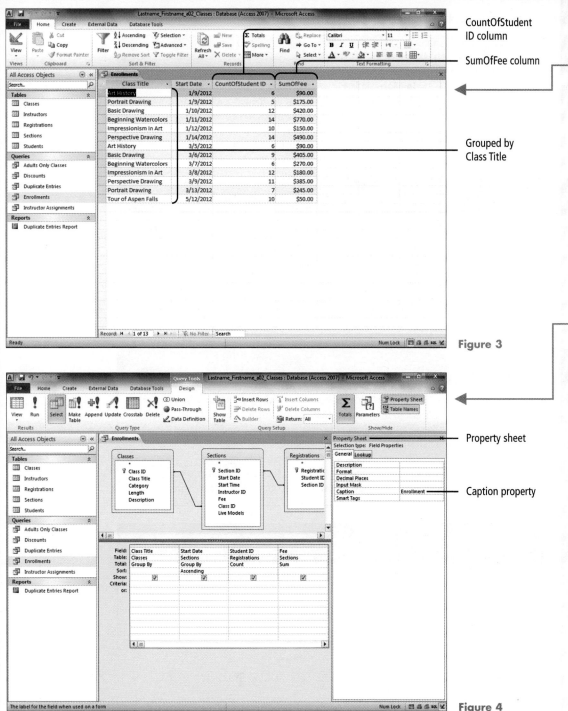

Figure 3

Figure 4

CountOfStudent ID column

SumOfFee column

Grouped by Class Title

Property sheet

Caption property

6. Run the query. Widen the **CountOfStudent ID** column to display its entire name, and then compare your screen with **Figure 3**.

When you include summary statistics, the column names change. Here, Student ID changes to CountOfStudent ID and Fee changes to SumOfFee. Summary queries display a single row for each group. Here, instead of showing the individual students within each class, the query shows the number of students in that class and the total fees.

7. Switch to Design view. Click anywhere in the **Student ID** column. On the **Design tab**, in the **Show/Hide group**, click the **Property Sheet** button. On the property sheet **General tab**, click in the **Caption** box, and then type Enrollment Compare your screen with **Figure 4**.

Recall that a caption is the value that displays in place of actual field names in datasheets, forms, and reports.

8. In the design grid, click anywhere in the **Fee** column to display its properties in the property sheet. Change the **Caption** property to Total Fee

9. Close ✕ the property sheet, and then click **Save** 💾.

10. Run the query to verify that the **Enrollment** and **Total Fee** captions display in the column headers.

11. If you are printing your work, print the datasheet.

12. Close ✕ the query, and then **Exit** Access. Submit your printouts or database file as directed by your instructor.

Done! You have completed Skill 10 of 10 and your databases are complete!

More Skills

The following More Skills are located at **www.pearsonhighered.com/skills**

More Skills 11 Export Queries to Other File Formats

There are times when you need to work with data in a table or query using another application. Access can export database tables and queries into several file formats that are used by other applications. For example, you can export a table to a Word document or an Excel spreadsheet, or to a web page.

In More Skills 11, you will export a query to an Excel spreadsheet and to a file that can be opened with a web browser.

To begin, open your web browser, navigate to www.pearsonhighered.com/skills, locate the name of your textbook, and then follow the instructions on the website.

More Skills 12 Find Duplicate Records

The purpose of a relational database is to avoid duplicate data. When tables contain many records, it is often difficult to discover when duplicate data exists. The Find Duplicates Query Wizard is used to find duplicate data quickly.

In More Skills 12, you will use the Find Duplicates Query Wizard to locate duplicate data and then correct the records with duplicate values. You will then run the query again to test your changes.

To begin, open your web browser, navigate to www.pearsonhighered.com/skills, locate the name of your textbook, and then follow the instructions on the website.

More Skills 13 Find Unmatched Records

When two tables are related, each record in the table on the *many* side of the relationship must have a corresponding value in the table on the *one* side of the relationship. The Find Unmatched Query Wizard compares the values from two tables and then lists the records that do not have corresponding values.

In More Skills 13, you will use the Find Unmatched Query Wizard to find records that are missing a value in a related table. You will then correct the data and create a one-to-many relationship between the two tables.

To begin, open your web browser, navigate to www.pearsonhighered.com/skills, locate the name of your textbook, and then follow the instructions on the website.

More Skills 14 Create Crosstab Queries

The Crosstab Query Wizard creates a special query that calculates the results of two groupings. One group displays down the left column and the other group displays across the top. Each remaining cell in the query displays a total, average, or other summary statistic for each pair of groupings.

In More Skills 14, you will create a crosstab query.

To begin, open your web browser, navigate to www.pearsonhighered.com/skills, locate the name of your textbook, and then follow the instructions on the website.

Key Terms

Online Help Skills

1. **Start** 🅐 Access. In the upper-right corner of the Access window, click the **Help** button 🔳. In the **Help** window, click the **Maximize** 🔳 button.

2. Click in the search box, type query criteria and then click the **Search** button. In the search results, click **Examples of query criteria**.

3. Read the article's introduction, and then, below **In this topic**, click **Overview**. Compare your screen with **Figure 1**.

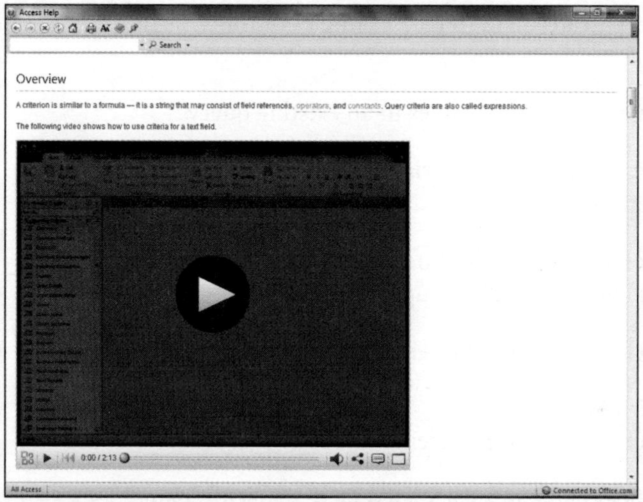

Figure 1

4. Read the Overview section and watch the video to see if you can answer the following: What expression would you use to find all students who are over 30 years old? How would you change this expression to find students who are 18 or over?

Matching

Match each term in the second column with its correct definition in the first column by writing the letter of the term on the blank line in front of the correct definition.

___ **1.** A wizard that quickly adds fields to a new query.

___ **2.** A technology that displays Quick Info, ToolTips, and AutoComplete as you type expressions.

___ **3.** Equal to (=) and greater than (>) are examples of this type of operator.

___ **4.** This dialog box is used to add tables to an existing query.

___ **5.** In the query design grid, two criteria placed in the same row use this logical operator.

___ **6.** When two criteria are placed in different rows in the query design grid, this logical operator will be applied.

___ **7.** This wildcard character can represent any combination of characters.

___ **8.** This wildcard character can represent any single character.

___ **9.** When using a field name in a calculated field, the field's name must start and end with this character.

___ **10.** To add summary statistics to a query, this row must be added to the query.

A And

B Asterisk (*)

C Comparison

D IntelliSense

E Or

F Question mark (?)

G Show Table

H Simple Query

I Square bracket

J Total

Multiple Choice

Choose the correct answer.

1. In a query, criteria is added in this view.
   A. Datasheet
   B. Design
   C. Workspace

2. In a query, results are displayed in this view.
   A. Datasheet
   B. Design
   C. Design grid

3. An IntelliSense menu of commands that match the characters you are typing.
   A. AutoComplete
   B. Quick Info
   C. ToolTips

4. An IntelliSense box that explains the purpose of the selected AutoComplete.
   A. AutoComplete
   B. Quick Info
   C. ToolTips

5. In query criteria, dates are surrounded by this character.
   A. >
   B. !
   C. #

6. An operator that finds all numbers or dates between and including two values.
   A. And...Between
   B. Between...And
   C. In...Between

7. A combination of fields, mathematical operators, and pre-built functions that calculates values.
   A. Comparison operator
   B. Expression
   C. Quick Info

8. A data type used to store values that can have one of two possible values.
   A. Byte
   B. Switch
   C. Yes/No

9. The operator that is placed at the beginning of criteria that use wildcards.
   A. Like
   B. Similar
   C. Wildcard

10. A calculation for a group of data such as a total, an average, or a count.
    A. Calculated column
    B. Group formula
    C. Summary statistic

Topics for Discussion

1. You have created queries using the Simple Query Wizard and using Design view. Which method do you prefer, and why? What situations may be better suited to using the Simple Query Wizard? What situations may be better suited to using Design view?

2. Data that can be calculated from existing fields can be entered manually into its own field, or it can be included as a calculated field in a query. Which method would produce the most accurate results, and why?

Skill Check

To complete this database, you will need the following file:

- a02_Outings

You will save your database as:

- Lastname_Firstname_a02_Outings

1. **Start** Access, and then open the student data file **a02_Outings**. Save the database in your **Access Chapter 2** folder with the name Lastname_Firstname_a02_Outings If necessary, enable the content.

2. Open the **Participants** table. Click the **Last Name** column. In the **Find group**, click the **Find** button. In the **Find What** box, type Binder and then click the **Find Next** button. **Close** the dialog box, and then change *Freddie Binder* to your own first and last name.

3. With the **Last Name** column active, in the **Sort & Filter group**, click the **Ascending** button.

4. Select the **Neighborhood** column, and then, in the **Sort & Filter** group, click the **Filter** button. In the **Filter** pane, clear the (**Select All**) check box, and then select the **Southeast** check box. Click **OK** to apply the filter.

5. **Close** the **Navigation Pane**. In the **Text Formatting group**, click the **Font Size arrow**, and then click **9**.

6. Select all the columns, and then double-click to resize their widths automatically.

7. On the **File tab**, click **Print**, and then click **Print Preview**. In the **Page Layout group**, click the **Landscape** button. Compare your screen with **Figure 1**. If you are printing this project, print the datasheet.

8. **Save**, and then **Close** the table. On the **Create tab**, in the **Queries group**, click **Query Wizard**. In the **New Query** dialog box, click **OK**.

9. In the **Simple Query Wizard**, click the **Tables/Queries arrow**, and then click **Table: Outings**.

10. Click **Outing Name** and then click the **Move** button. Repeat the procedure to move **Outing Date** into **Selected Fields**, and then click **Finish**.

11. On the **Home tab**, click the **View** button, and then, in the **Outing Date** column **Criteria** box, type >10/1/2012

12. **Run** the query, double-click to resize the **Outing Name** column automatically, and then compare your screen with **Figure 2**.

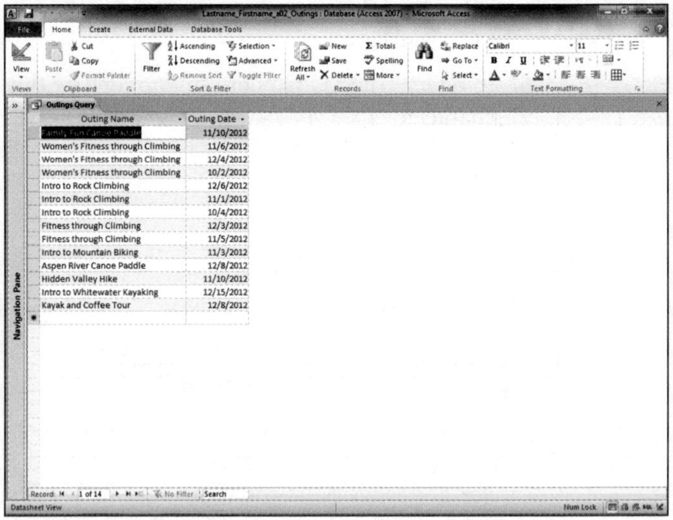

- ▶ Continue to the next page to complete this Skill Check

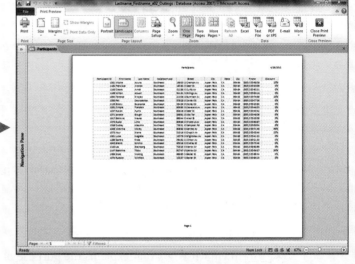

Figure 1

Figure 2

13. If you are printing your work, print the Outings Query datasheet. **Save**, and then **Close** the query.

14. On the **Create tab**, in the **Queries group**, click **Query Design**. Use the displayed **Show Table** dialog box to add the following tables in this order: **Outings, Registrations**, and **Participants**. **Close** the dialog box.

15. Double-click to add the following fields in this order: **Outing Name, First Name, Last Name, Fee**, and, from the bottom of the **Participants** table, **Discount**.

16. In the **Last Name** column **Criteria** box, type Sorens?n to show records for Sorensen or Sorenson. In the **Last Name** column **or** box, type your own last name.

17. In the first blank column, type the following label and expression: Discounted Fee:[Fee]-[Fee]*[Discount] If necessary, widen the column for the calculated field.

18. In the **Last Name** column, click the **Sort** box. Click the displayed **Sort arrow**, and then click **Ascending**.

19. Click **Save**. In the **Save As** dialog box, type Duplicate Records and then press ⏎.

20. **Run** the query, and then compare your screen with **Figure 3**. If the Enter Parameter Value dialog box displays, return to Design view and then repeat step 17, taking care to spell field names correctly and to include the square brackets.

21. If you are printing your work, print the datasheet. **Close** the **Duplicate Records** query.

22. **Open** the **Navigation Pane**. In the **Navigation Pane**, under **Queries**, right-click **Counts by Category**, and then click **Design View**.

23. On the **Design tab**, in the **Show/Hide group**, click the **Totals** button. Click in the **Registration ID** column **Total** box, click the displayed **Total arrow**, and then click **Count**.

24. With the **Registration ID** column still active, in the **Show/Hide group**, click the **Property Sheet** button. Click in the property sheet **Caption** box, type Category Count and then **Close** the property sheet.

25. Click **Save**, and then **Run** the query. Widen the **Category Count** column so that the entire label displays, and then compare your screen with **Figure 4**.

26. If you are printing your work, print the datasheet. **Save**, and then **Close** the **Counts by Category** query.

27. **Exit** Access. Submit your printouts or database file as directed by your instructor.

Done! You have completed the Skill Check

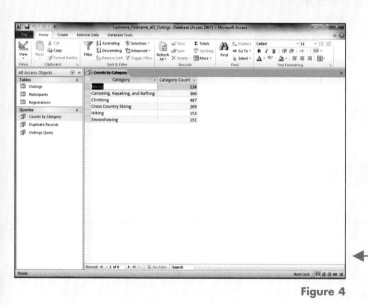

Figure 3

Figure 4

Assess Your Skills 1

To complete this database, you will need the following file:

- a02_Reviews

You will save your database as:

- Lastname_Firstname_a02_Reviews

1. **Start** Access, and then open **a02_Reviews**. Save the database in your **Access Chapter 2** folder as Lastname_Firstname_a02_Reviews If necessary, enable the content.

2. Open the **Employees** table. **Find** the record for *Cyril Calta* and replace his name with your own first and last name.

3. Filter the **Department** column so only the nine **Art Center** employees display, and then sort the datasheet in alphabetical order by **Last Name**. Change the datasheet's font size to **10**.

4. In **Print Preview**, change orientation to **Landscape**, and then **Save** the table. If you are printing your work, print the datasheet. **Close** the table.

5. Start the **Simple Query Wizard**. From the **Employees** table, add **First Name** and **Last Name**. From the **Reviews** table, add **Review Date, Attendance**, and **Customer Relations**. Use the wizard to name the query Employee Reviews and accept all other wizard defaults.

6. Switch to Design view. In the **Last Name** column **Criteria** box, add a criterion with a wildcard that accepts all last names starting with B and ending with thin Use a wildcard character that accepts any number of characters.

7. In the **Last Name** column **or** box, type your own last name.

8. Set the query to sort in alphabetical order by **Last Name**. Add a criterion to the **Review Date** column so that reviews after 12/31/2009 display.

9. In the first blank column, add a calculated field with the label Review Total Have the calculated field add the Attendance field to the Customer Relations field.

10. In the **Review Total** column just created, add a criterion so that only totals that are greater than or equal to 7 display. **Save**, and then **Run** the query. Verify that four records result as shown in **Figure 1**.

11. If asked, print the datasheet. **Close** the query.

12. Create a new query in Design view. From the **Employees** table, add **Departments**, and from the **Reviews** table add **Employee ID**. Add the **Total** row, group by **Department**, and **Count Employee ID**.

13. For the **Employee ID** column, set the **Caption** property to Number of Employees **Save** the query with the name Department Counts

14. **Run** the query, widen the **Number of Employees** column to display the entire caption, and then compare your screen with **Figure 2**.

15. If you are printing your work, print the datasheet. **Save**, and then **Close** the query.

16. **Exit** Access, and then submit your printouts or database file as directed by your instructor.

Done! You have completed Assess Your Skills 1

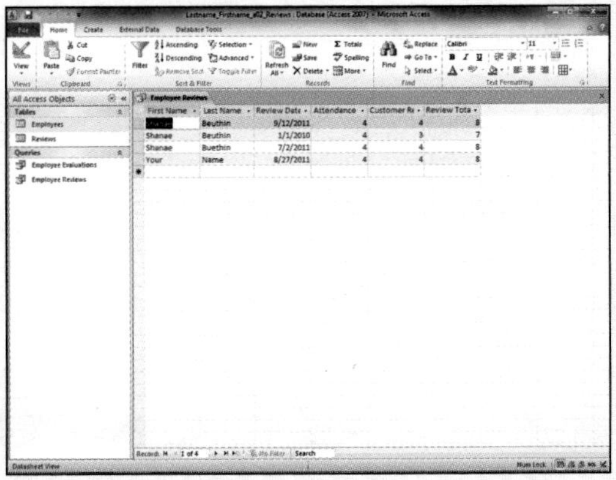

Figure 1

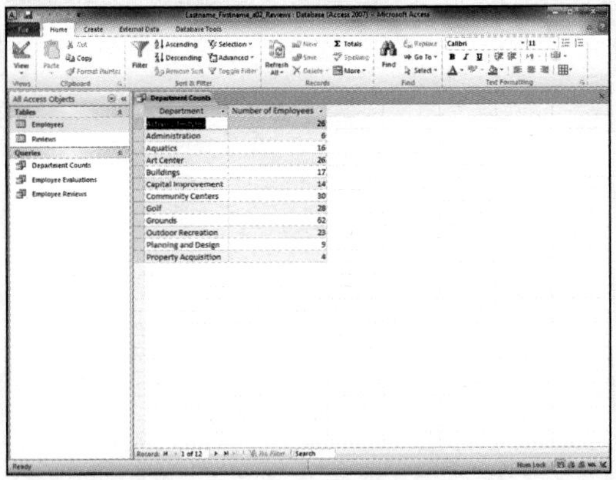

Figure 2

Assessment

Assess Your Skills 3 and 4 can be found at
www.pearsonhighered.com/skills.

Assess Your Skills 2

To complete this database, you will need the following file:

- a02_Camps

You will save your database as:

- **Lastname_Firstname_a02_Camps**

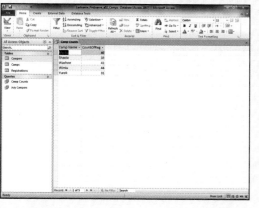

Figure 1

Figure 2

1. **Start** Access, and then open **a02_Camps**. Save the database in your **Access Chapter 2** folder as Lastname_Firstname_a02_Camps

2. Open the **Campers** table. **Find** the record for *Kurt Davion* and replace his name with your own first and last name.

3. **Filter** the **Parent/Guardian** column so that only **(Blanks)** display, and then sort the datasheet in alphabetical order by **Last Name**. Change the datasheet's font size to **10**.

4. In **Print Preview**, change orientation to **Landscape**, and then **Save** the table. If you are printing your work, print the datasheet. **Close** the table.

5. Start the **Simple Query Wizard**. From the **Camps** table, add **Camp Name** and **Start Date**. From the **Campers** table, add **First Name** and **Last Name**. Use the wizard to name the query July Campers and accept all other wizard defaults.

6. Switch to Design view. In the **Start Date** column **Criteria** box, enter an expression that will result in dates between 7/1/2012 and 7/31/2012.

7. In the **First Name** column **Criteria** box, add a criterion with a wildcard that accepts all first names starting with Carl

8. In the **Last Name** column **or** box, type your own last name.

9. Set the query to sort in alphabetical order by **Last Name**.

10. In the first blank column, add a calculated field with the label Discount Amount Calculate the amount by multiplying the Discount field by 75.

11. Click in the **Discount Amount** column **or** box, and then open the property sheet. On the property sheet **General** tab, click the **Format** box, click the displayed **Format arrow**, and, from the list, click **Currency**. **Close** the property sheet.

12. **Save**, and then **Run** the query. Widen the **Discount Amount** column to display the entire caption. Verify that three records result, as shown in **Figure 1**.

13. If asked, print the datasheet. **Save**, and then **Close** the query.

14. Create a new query in Design view. From the **Camps** table, add **Camp Name**, and from the **Registrations** table, add **Registration Number**. Add the **Total** row, and group by **Camp Name** and **Count** by **Registration Number**.

15. **Save** the query with the name Camp Counts **Run** the query, and then compare your screen with **Figure 2**.

16. If you are printing your work, print the datasheet. **Close** the query.

17. **Exit** Access, and then submit your printouts or database file as directed by your instructor.

Done! You have completed Assess Your Skills 2

Assess Your Skills Visually

To complete this database, you will need the following file:

- a02_Instructors

You will save your database as:

- Lastname_Firstname_a02_Instructors

Open the database **a02_Instructors**, and then using your own name, **Save** the database as Lastname_Firstname_a02_Instructors

Format the **Art Instructors** table as shown in **Figure 1**. Change the datasheet's font size to **10**, and then resize the columns to fit their data. Apply the **Raised** cell effect with each row color alternating between **White, Background 1** and the standard color **Green 2**. Format the grid line color to the standard color **Green 5**.

Sort the datasheet by **Last Name**. In the first record of the **Art Instructors** table, replace *Kacey Alkbsh* with your own name.

Save the datasheet changes. Print the datasheet or submit the database file as directed by your instructor.

Done! You have completed Assess Your Skills Visually

Art Instructors

Instructor ID	First Name	Last Name	Street	City	State	Zip	Phone	Click to Add
A106	Your	Name	82522 E Madison St	Aspen Falls	CA	93463	(805) 555-7170	
A121	Bradford	Andrzejczyk	63734 W Meadow St	Aspen Falls	CA	93464	(805) 555-7316	
A107	Carrol	Chicharello	63471 S High St	Aspen Falls	CA	93463	(805) 555-6131	
A113	Faustino	Cummisky	44705 S Earle St	Aspen Falls	CA	93463	(805) 555-7475	
A105	Hazel	Ekwall	82075 N Mahoney St	Aspen Falls	CA	93463	(805) 555-5713	
A116	Brant	Floerke	23812 E Eastview Ct	Aspen Falls	CA	93463	(805) 555-4683	
A103	Beatriz	Handlin	23926 S Harrington Av	Aspen Falls	CA	93464	(805) 555-3580	
A117	Rey	Hasse	38789 E East St	Aspen Falls	CA	93464	(805) 555-4704	
A111	Cortez	Herke	58065 N Templewood Ct	Aspen Falls	CA	93464	(805) 555-8010	
A112	Anton	Hoffelt	19199 W Field Av	Aspen Falls	CA	93463	(805) 555-4937	
A102	Carlie	Litzenberg	75732 S Porter Pl	Aspen Falls	CA	93463	(805) 555-3997	
A114	Mohamed	Lonzo	83721 N Mayfield Rd	Aspen Falls	CA	93463	(805) 555-9831	
A119	Ron	Morey	70416 S Nelson Pl	Aspen Falls	CA	93464	(805) 555-2287	
A109	Larry	Moyerman	62877 N Strongs Av	Aspen Falls	CA	93463	(805) 555-9205	
A108	Macie	Ryhal	60034 W Meadow Brook Rd	Aspen Falls	CA	93464	(805) 555-5281	
A104	Mitchell	Screen	76117 W Second St	Aspen Falls	CA	93463	(805) 555-3976	
A101	Lana	Shane	5396 S West St	Aspen Falls	CA	93463	(805) 555-3817	
A118	Sherman	Stobb	8121 S Plain St	Aspen Falls	CA	93463	(805) 555-4462	
A100	Carolyne	Teeple	42018 N Horton St	Aspen Falls	CA	93464	(805) 555-6684	
A115	Dustin	Termilus	33533 S Lafayette St	Aspen Falls	CA	93463	(805) 555-4134	
A120	Boyce	Torgeson	38431 S Mayfield Rd	Aspen Falls	CA	93463	(805) 555-2202	
A110	Chasidy	Trowery	81976 W E Washington St	Aspen Falls	CA	93463	(805) 555-8726	

Figure 1

Skills in Context

To complete this database, you will need the following file:

- a02_Neighborhoods

You will save your database as:

- Lastname_Firstname_a02_Neighborhoods

Open **a02_Neighborhoods** and save the database in your **Access Chapter 2** folder as Lastname_Firstname_a02_Neighborhoods Create a summary query named Neighborhood Counts that counts the number of registrations from each neighborhood. The Neighborhood field is in the Students table, and the Registration ID field is in the Registrations table. The query will have five rows, one for each neighborhood. In the first column, display the neighborhood name, and in the second column, display the

number of registered students. For the second column, change the caption to Number of Students In the datasheet, widen the Number of Students column to display the entire caption.

Print the datasheet or submit the database file as directed by your instructor.

Done! You have completed Skills in Context

Skills and You

To complete this database, you will need the following file:

- a02_Contacts

You will save your database as:

- Lastname_Firstname_a02_Contacts

Open a02_Contacts, and then save the database as Lastname_Firstname_a02_Contacts Open the Contacts table, and then add at least 12 personal contacts to the table. In the Contact Type field, enter either *Family, Friend,* or *Business* for each contact. Create a query that displays all the fields from the Contacts table. Add criteria to display only the contacts that you

assigned as *Family*. Format the query datasheet as desired and assign the Landscape orientation. Print or submit the file as directed by your instructor.

Done! You have completed Skills and You

CHAPTER 3

Create Forms

▶ Forms are typically used to edit, delete, and add the records stored in database tables.

▶ Most forms show one record at a time so that you can work with just that data.

Your starting screen will look similar to this:

SKILLS

myitlab
Skills 1-10 Training

At the end of this chapter, you will be able to:

Skill 1   Use the Form Wizard

Skill 2   Format Forms in Layout View

Skill 3   Use Forms to Modify Data

Skill 4   Use the Blank Form Tool

Skill 5   Customize Form Layouts

Skill 6   Add Input Masks

Skill 7   Apply Conditional Formatting

Skill 8   Create One-to-Many Forms

Skill 9   Enter Data Using One-to-Many Forms

Skill 10   Create Forms from Queries

MORE SKILLS

More Skills 11 Validate Fields

More Skills 12 Add Combo Boxes to Forms

More Skills 13 Create Multiple Item Forms

More Skills 14 Create Macros

Outcome

Using the skills listed to the left will enable you to create forms like these:

Student Entry Form

Student ID	1001
Last Name	Corbet
First Name	Santiago
Neighborhood	Southeast
Street	13578 S Brightview Av
City/State/Zip	Aspen Falls	CA	93463
Phone	(804) 555-6894
Birth Date	9/26/1940
Discount	0%

Class Schedule

Class ID	1001
Class Title	Tour of Aspen Falls
Category	Art History
Length	1 day

Sections

Section ID	Start Date	Start Time	Instructor ID	Fee
20121	5/12/2012	1:00 PM	A103	$5.00
20141	10/13/2012	1:00 PM	A103	$5.00
20147	12/4/2012	1:00 PM	A101	$5.00

Record: 1 of 3   No Filter   Search

You will save your files as:

Lastname_Firstname_a03_Classes
Lastname_Firstname_a03_Classes_Snip1
Lastname_Firstname_a03_Classes_Snip2
Lastname_Firstname_a03_Classes_Snip3
Lastname_Firstname_a03_Classes_Snip4

In this chapter, you will create documents for the Aspen Falls City Hall, which provides essential services for the citizens and visitors of Aspen Falls, California.

Introduction

- ► Forms are often designed to enter data for specific needs of the database. For example, one form is used to manage student records, another to manage class records, and another to register students into classes.

- ► Access has many methods for building forms so that you can choose the method that best creates the form you need.

- ► Forms can display the records from a single table or display records from two related tables.

- ► Forms are designed to be viewed on a computer screen and are rarely printed.

- ► Forms can be based on queries so that you can work with a subset of the data from a single table or several related tables.

Time to complete all
10 skills – 60 to 90 minutes

Find your student data files here:

Student data files needed for this chapter:

- a03_Classes
- a03_Classes_Logo
- a03_Classes_Picture

Open

◀ 04_access ▶ chapter_03   Search chapter_03

Organize ▾

Music
Pictures
Videos

Homegroup

Computer
Local Disk (C:)
Backup Drive (D:)
DVD RW Drive (E:) sfsoffice10
01_student_data_files
01_common_features
02_word
03_excel
04_access
chapter_01
chapter_02
chapter_03
chapter_04
05_powerpoint
USB DRIVE (F:)

Name	Date modified	Ty
▲ Files Currently on the Disc (12)		
a03_Camps	5/8/2010 2:34 PM	M
a03_Camps_Logo	12/16/2009 10:31 ...	Pl
a03_Classes	5/8/2010 7:44 PM	M
a03_Classes_Logo	5/8/2010 11:21 AM	JP
a03_Classes_Picture	5/1/2010 1:08 PM	JP
a03_Contacts	5/5/2010 7:22 PM	M
a03_Councils	5/5/2010 6:03 PM	M
a03_Councils_Logo	5/8/2010 1:09 PM	JP
a03_Managers	5/8/2010 3:37 PM	M
a03_Outings	5/2/2010 1:17 PM	M
a03_Outings_Logo	5/8/2010 1:07 PM	JP
a03_Reviews	5/16/2010 4:09 PM	M

File name: All Files

Tools ▾   Open ▾   Cancel

Switch
Windows ▾
Window

B I U
A ▾
Text Formatting

Ready   Num Lock

► Access has several tools for creating forms. The Form Wizard is used to select multiple tables and specific fields for your form.

1. **Start** 🌐 Access. If necessary, Maximize 🔲 the window.

2. From the student files that came with this book, open **a03_Classes**.

3. Click the **File tab**, and then click **Save Database As**. In the **Save As** dialog box, display the file list where you are saving your files. Click **New folder**, type Access Chapter 3 and then press Enter two times. Name the file Lastname_Firstname_a03_Classes and then click **Save**.

4. If the Security Warning message displays, click the Enable Content button.

5. On the **Create tab**, in the **Forms group**, click the **Form Wizard** button. Click the **Tables/Queries arrow**, and then click **Instructors**. Compare your screen with **Figure 1**.

   The first screen of the Form Wizard is used to select the fields that you want your form to display.

6. With **Instructor ID** selected under **Available Fields**, click the **Move** button ▶ so that the field will be included in the form.

7. Use the **Move** button ▶ to move **First Name** and **Last Name** into **Selected Fields**.

8. Use either technique just practiced to move the following fields into **Selected Fields** in this order: **Street**, **City**, **State**, **Zip**, and **Phone**. Do not move the Current W-4 field. Compare your screen with **Figure 2**.

■ Continue to the next page to complete the skill ▶

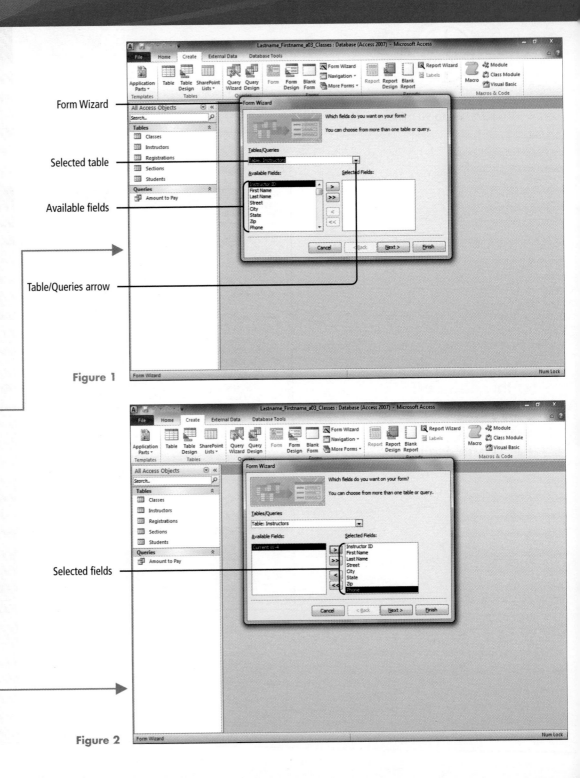

Form Wizard

Selected table

Available fields

Table/Queries arrow

Figure 1

Selected fields

Figure 2

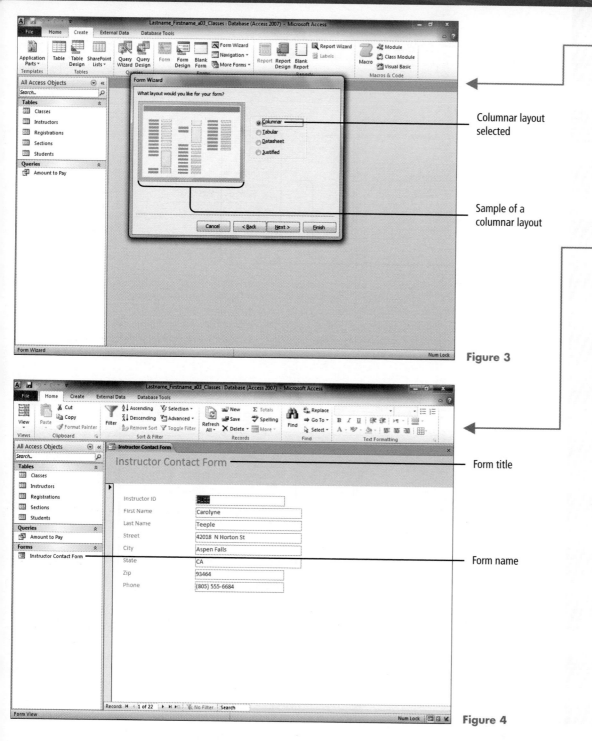

Columnar layout selected

Sample of a columnar layout

Figure 3

Form title

Form name

Figure 4

9. In the **Form Wizard**, click **Next**, and then compare your screen with **Figure 3**.

> You can use the Form Wizard to pick different layouts for your form. A *layout* determines how data and labels are arranged in a form or report. For example, the *columnar layout* places labels in the first column and data in the second column.

10. With **Columnar layout** selected, click **Next**. Under **What title do you want for your form**, replace *Instructors* with Instructor Contact Form

11. In the **Form Wizard**, click **Finish**, and then compare your screen with **Figure 4**.

> The title that you type in the last screen of the Form Wizard becomes the name of the form in the Navigation Pane and the theme last used in the database is applied. Here, the Adjacency theme has been applied.

12. Leave the form open for the next skill.

■ **You have completed Skill 1 of 10**

▶ *Layout view* is used to format a form or report while viewing a sample of the data.

1. With the **Instructor Contact Form** still open, on the **Home tab**, in the **Views group**, click the **View** button to switch to Layout view. Compare your screen with **Figure 1**.

   In Layout view, you can select individual labels and text boxes. A *label* is an object on a form or report that describes other objects on the report or form. Here, the Instructor ID text box is selected. A *text box* is an object on a form or report that displays the data from a field in a table or query.

2. On the **Design tab**, in the **Themes group**, click the **Themes** button. Scroll to the bottom of the **Themes** gallery, and then, in the third to last row, click the second theme—**Paper**.

3. In the **Header/Footer group**, click the **Date and Time** button. Compare your screen with **Figure 2**.

4. In the **Date and Time** dialog box, accept the default settings by clicking **OK** to insert the date and time into the form's header.

   ■ **Continue to the next page to complete the skill**

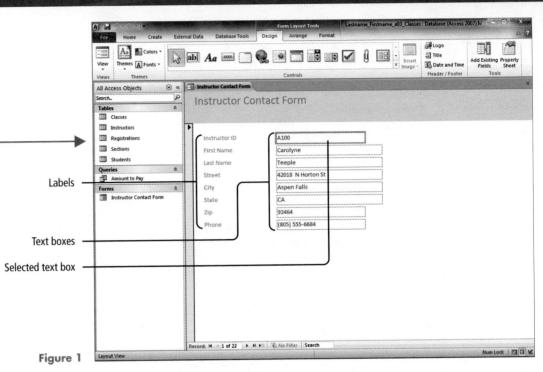

Labels

Text boxes

Selected text box

Figure 1

Date and Time dialog box

Date and Time button

Figure 2

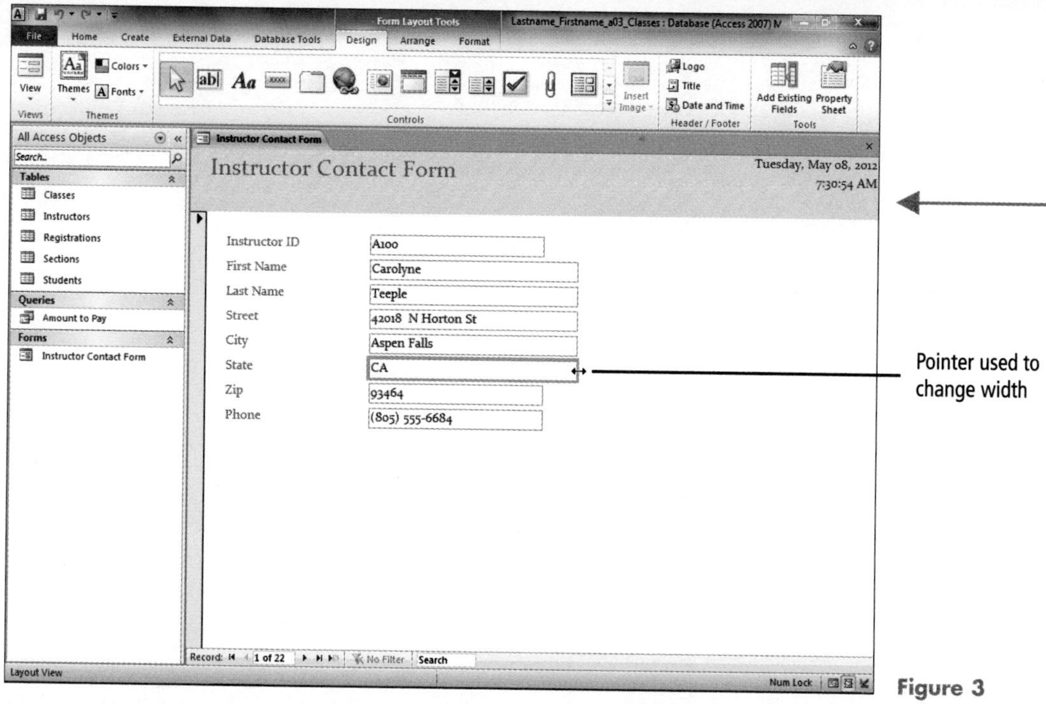

Pointer used to change width

Figure 3

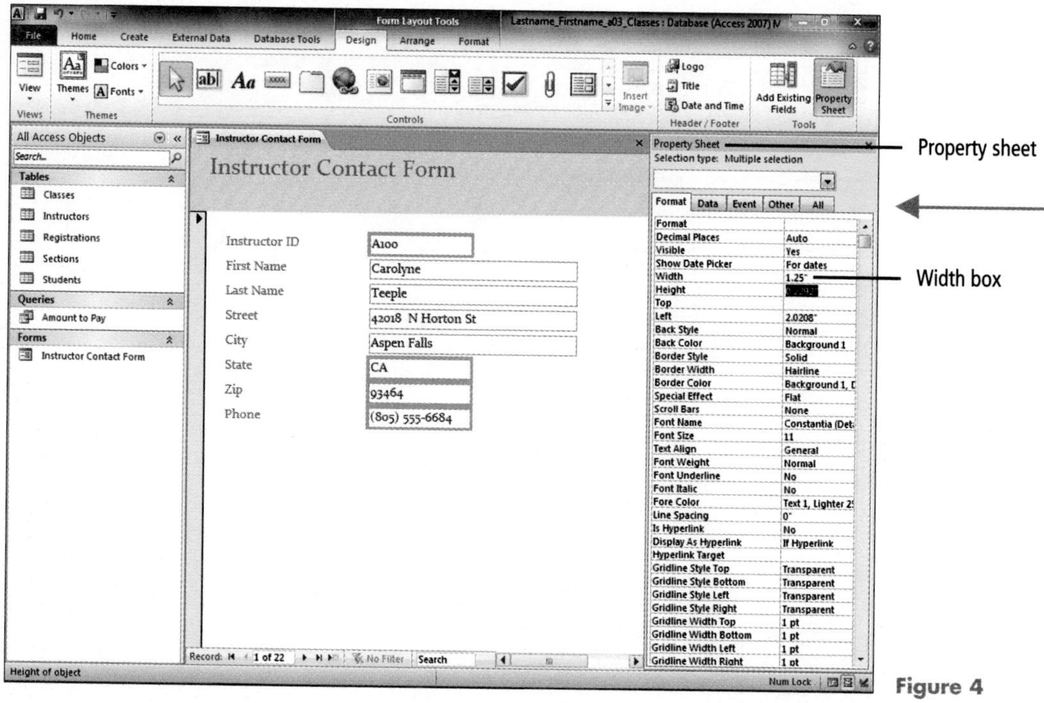

Property sheet

Width box

Figure 4

5. Click the **State** text box to select the *control*—an object in a form or report such as a label or text box.

6. Point to the middle of the control's right border to display the ↔ pointer, and then compare your screen with **Figure 3**.

7. With the ↔ pointer, drag to the left so that the **State** text box is approximately the same width as the **Zip** text box.

8. Click the **Instructor ID** text box. Press and hold Ctrl while clicking the **State**, **Zip**, and **Phone** text boxes. Be careful not to move the mouse while clicking.

9. With the four controls selected, on the **Design tab**, in the **Tools group**, click the **Property Sheet** button.

10. If necessary, in the property sheet, click the **Format tab**. In the **Width** box, replace the existing value with 1.25 and then press Enter. Compare your screen with **Figure 4**.

    In this manner, you can select multiple controls and then format them the same.

11. **Close** × the **Property Sheet**, and then **Save** 🖫 the design changes. Leave the form open for the next skill.

■ **You have completed Skill 2 of 10**

► Recall that forms are designed to input data into tables. You do not need to use the mouse as you key data into forms, and the changes are stored automatically in the underlying table.

1. With the **Instructor Contact Form** open, click the **View** button to switch to Form view.

2. On the Navigation bar, click the **Next record** button ▶ to display record 2 of 22—Lana Shane.

3. Press Enter to select the value in the **First Name** text box. Replace *Lana* with your own first name.

4. Press Enter, and then compare your screen with **Figure 1**. ────────

> Recall that you can move to the next text box in a form by pressing Enter or Tab. In this way, you can continue typing values without having to use the mouse. Keeping your hands over the keyboard speeds data entry and increases accuracy.

5. In the **Last Name** text box, replace *Shane* with your own last name.

6. Press Enter, to accept the change, and then click in the **Last Name** text box to select it. On the **Home** tab, in the **Find group**, click the **Find** button.

7. In the **Find and Replace** dialog box **Find What** box, type Moyerman and then press Enter. With the record for Celia Moyerman displayed, **Close** ✕ the **Find and Replace** dialog box.

8. With the **Last Name** *Moyerman* selected, type Stock Compare your screen with **Figure 2**. ────────

■ **Continue to the next page to complete the skill**

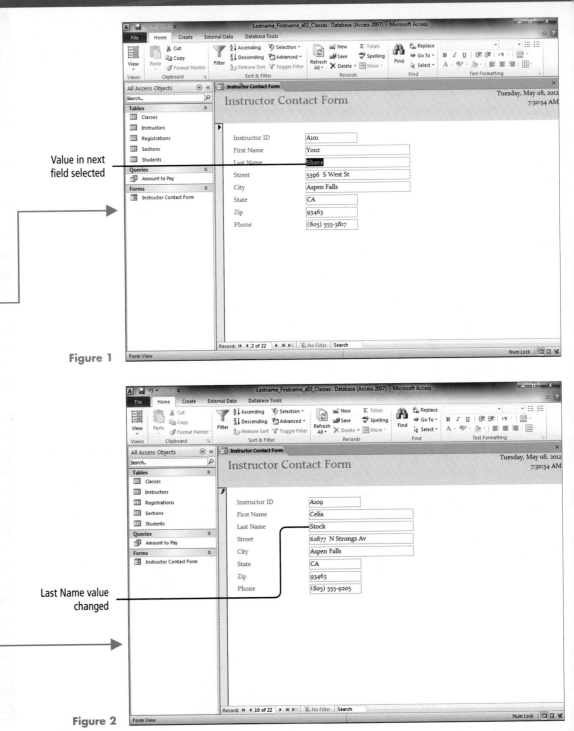

Value in next field selected

Figure 1

Last Name value changed

Figure 2

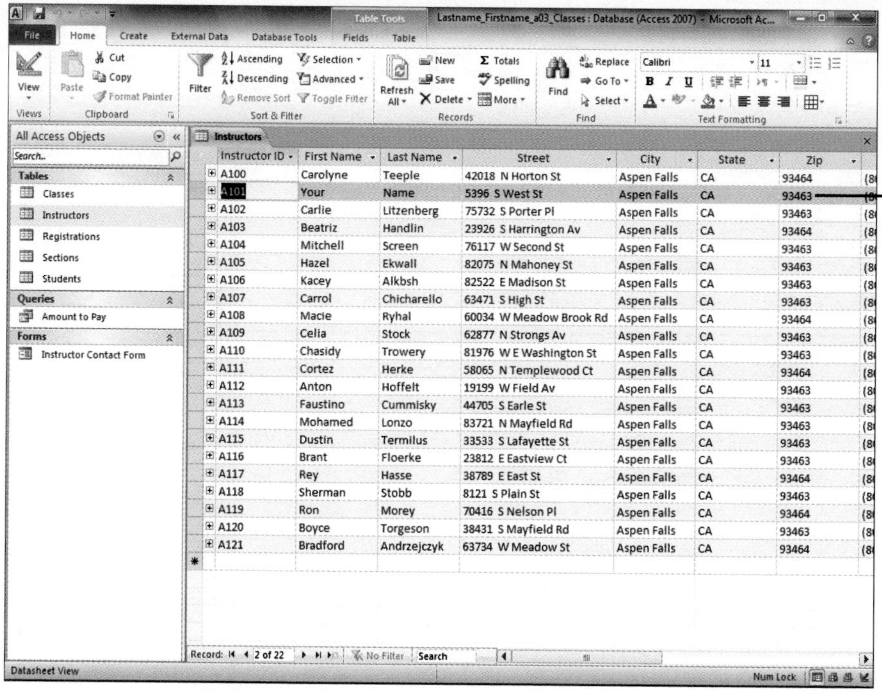

Record changed
using a form

Figure 3

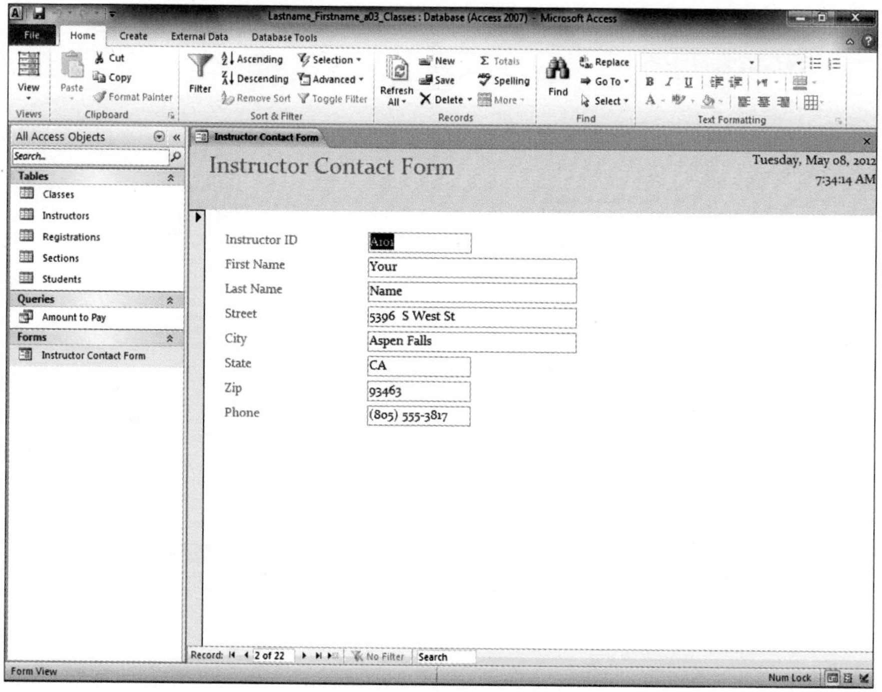

Figure 4

9. **Close** ☒ the form. In the **Navigation Pane**, double-click **Instructors** to open the table. In the Navigation bar, click the **Next record** button ▶ to select the second row, and then compare your screen with **Figure 3**.

As you enter data in a form, it is stored automatically in the table that the form is based on. Here, records 2 and 10 reflect the changes you made using the form.

10. **Close** ☒ the table. In the **Navigation Pane**, double-click **Instructor Contact Form** to open the form. Navigate to the second record—the record with your name. Compare your screen with **Figure 4**.

11. **Start** 🕐 the **Snipping Tool**. In the **Snipping Tool** dialog box, click the **New button arrow**, and then click **Full-screen Snip**.

12. Click the **Save Snip** button 💾. In the **Save As** dialog box, navigate to your **Access Chapter 3** folder, **Save** the file as Lastname_Firstname_a03_Classes_Snip1 and then **Close** ☒ the **Snipping Tool** window.

13. **Close** ☒ the form.

■ **You have completed Skill 3 of 10**

▶ The Blank Form tool is used when you want to build a form by adding fields one at a time or arrange them in a different layout.

1. On the **Create tab**, in the **Forms group**, click the **Blank Form** button.

2. In the **Field List**, click **Show all tables**. In the **Field List**, to the left of **Students**, click the **Expand** button ⊞. Compare your screen with **Figure 1**.

3. In the **Field List**, double-click **Student ID** to add the field to the form. Double-click **First Name** to add the field to the form.

4. Continue to double-click to add the nine remaining fields starting with **Last Name** and ending with **Discount**. Compare your screen with **Figure 2**.

When you add a field to the form, the other tables move to the lower sections of the Field List pane. Here, Registrations is a related table, and the other three tables are available, but they are not related to the Students table.

■ **Continue to the next page to complete the skill**

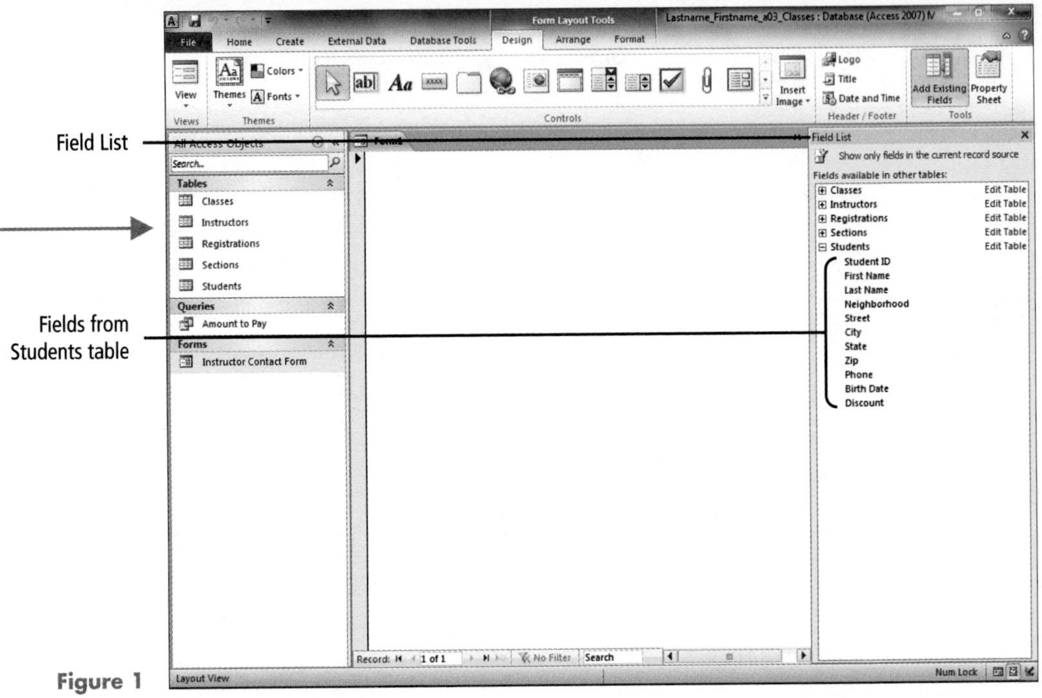

Field List

Fields from Students table

Figure 1

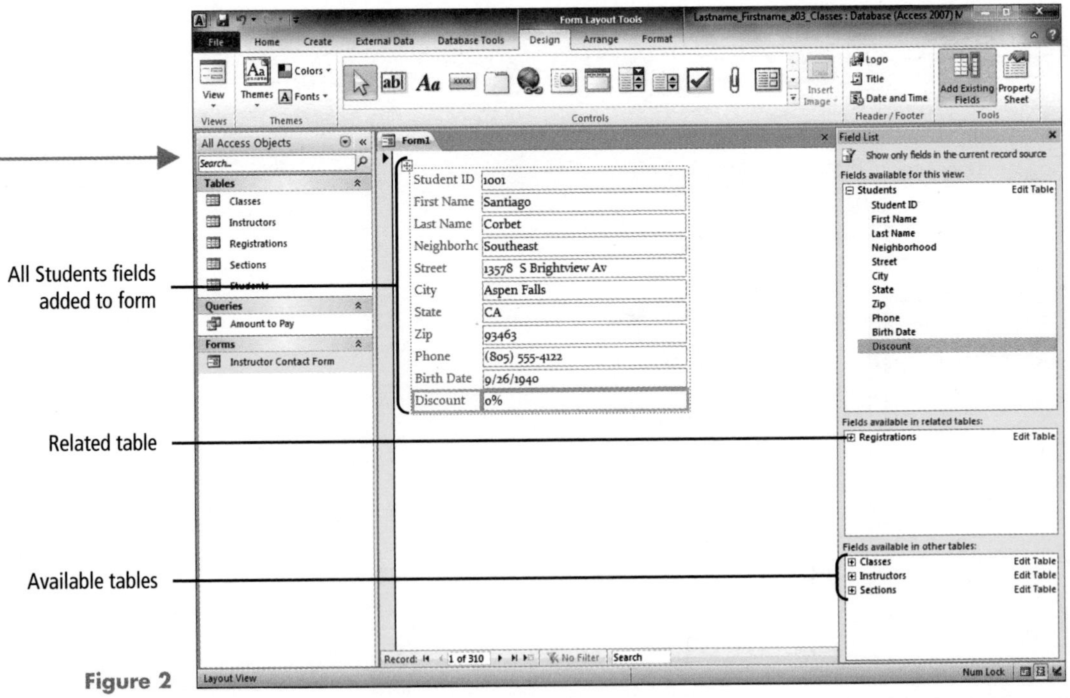

All Students fields added to form

Related table

Available tables

Figure 2

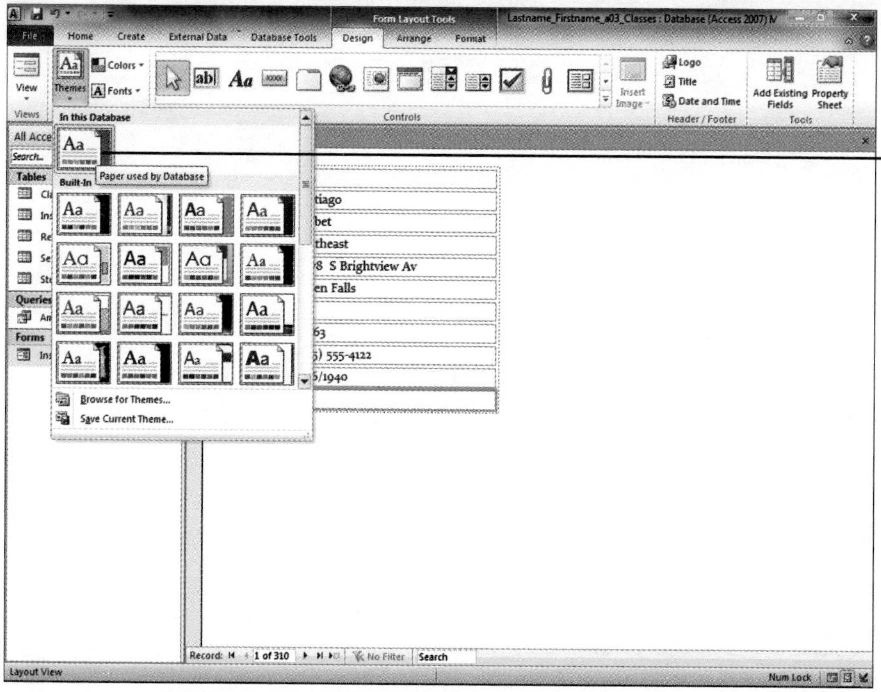

Paper theme is the current theme

Figure 3

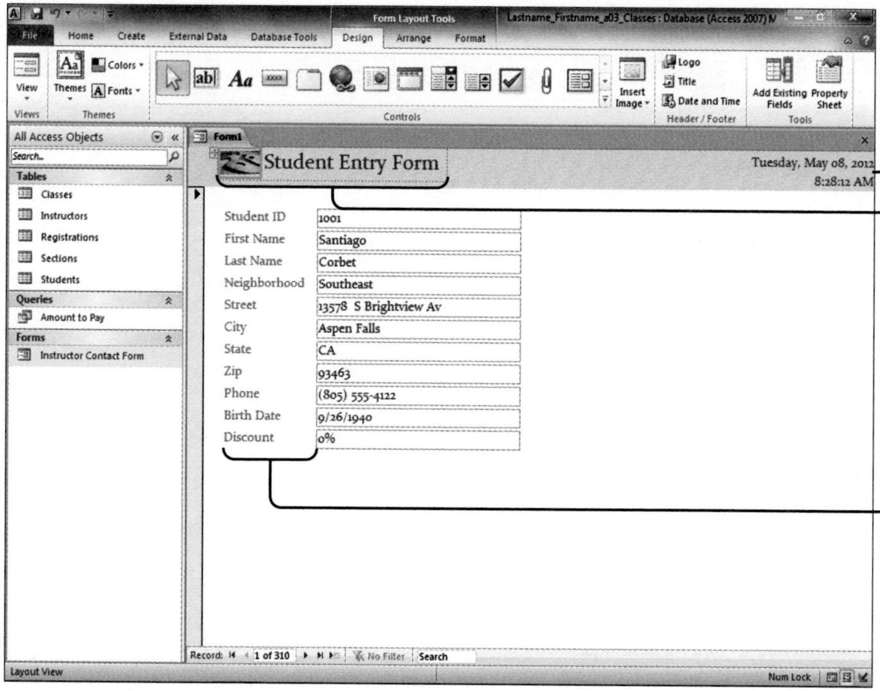

Date and time

Title and logo

Label column widened

Figure 4

5. **Close** ☒ the **Field List**. In the **Themes group**, click the **Themes** button. In the **Themes** gallery, under **In this Database**, point to the thumbnail, and then compare your screen with **Figure 3**.

   The ScreenTip should display *Paper used by Database*—the theme applied to the previous form.

6. Press [Esc] to close the gallery.

7. Click the **Neighborhood** label, and then with the ↔ pointer, drag to increase the column's width so that the entire label text displays.

8. On the **Design tab**, in the **Header/Footer group**, click the **Title** button, and then type Student Entry Form

9. In the **Header/Footer group**, click the **Logo** button. In the **Insert Picture** dialog box, navigate to the student files, select **a03_Classes_Logo**, and then click **OK**.

10. In the **Header/Footer group**, click the **Date and Time** button. In the **Date and Time** dialog box, click **OK**. Compare your screen with **Figure 4**.

11. Click **Save** 🖫. In the **Save As** dialog box, type Student Entry Form and then press [Enter]. Leave the form open for the next skill.

   ■ **You have completed Skill 4 of 10**

▶ Form and report layouts use *control grids*—cells arranged in rows and columns into which controls are placed.

▶ Control grids work much like tables. You can arrange several fields in a single row and merge multiple cells across rows and columns.

1. **Close** « the **Navigation Pane**. With the **Student Entry Form** open, click the **State** text box to select the control.

2. Point to the **State** text box, and then with the pointer, drag the control up and to the right. When the orange line displays to the right of the **City** text box, as shown in **Figure 1**, release the mouse button. —

3. Point to the **Zip** text box, and then with the pointer, drag the control to the right of the **State** text box, and then release the mouse button to move the text box and create a new column.

4. Select the **State** text box, point to the right border, and then with the ↔ pointer, drag to resize the column approximately as shown in **Figure 2**. Repeat to resize the **Zip** text box as shown in the figure.

5. Double-click in the **City** label, select the text *City*, and then type City/State/Zip

6. In the **First Name** row, click the **First Name** text box, press and hold Shift while clicking the last empty cell in the row. With the three cells selected, on the **Arrange tab**, in the **Merge/Split group**, click the **Merge** button.

■ **Continue to the next page to complete the skill** ▶

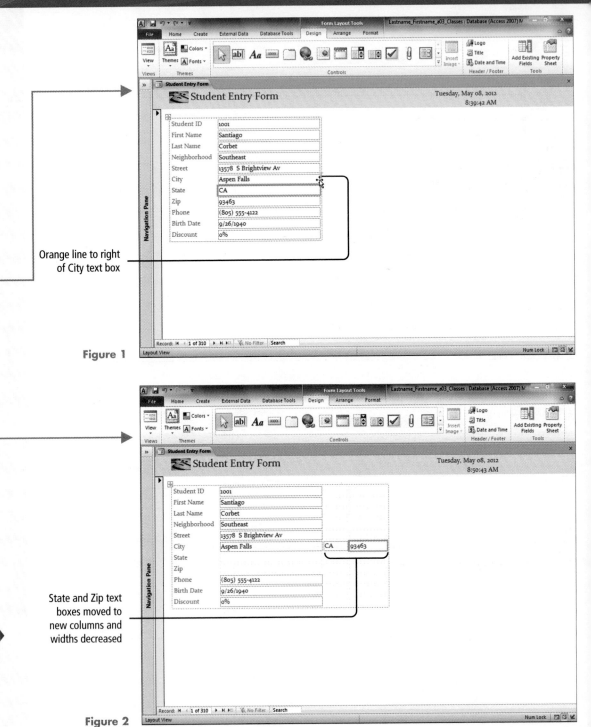

Orange line to right of City text box

Figure 1

State and Zip text boxes moved to new columns and widths decreased

Figure 2

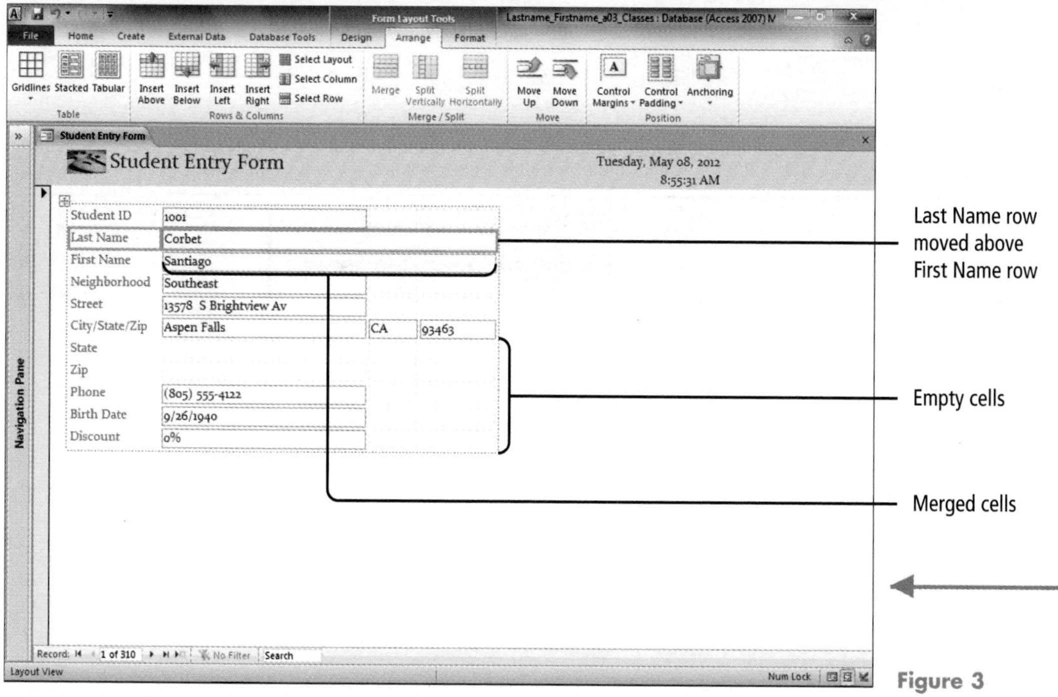

Figure 3

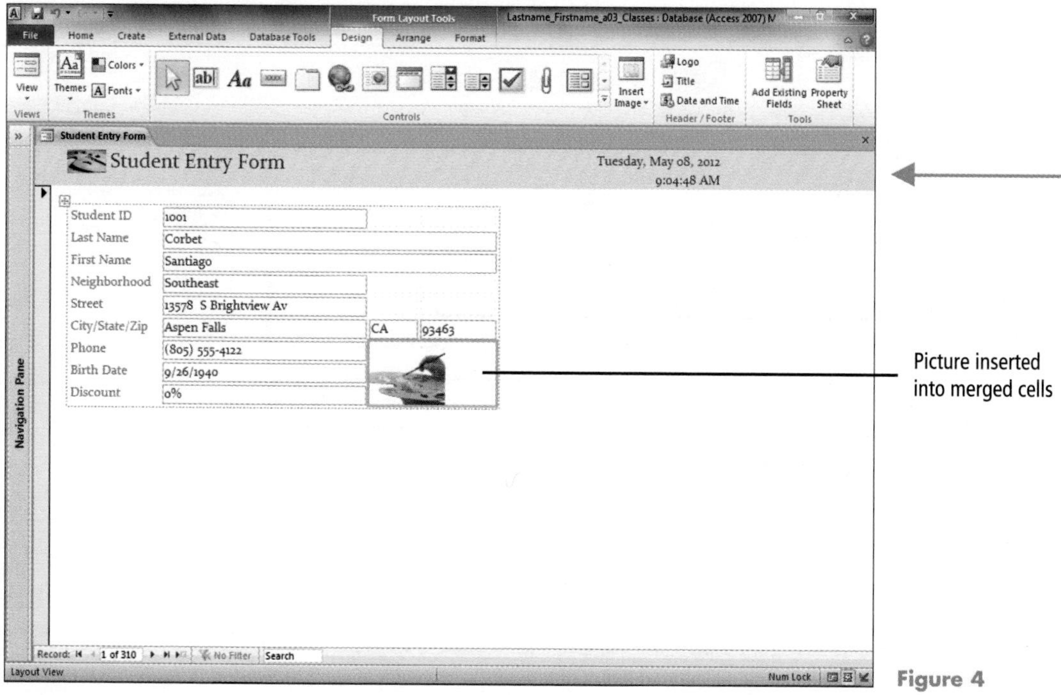

Figure 4

7. In the **Last Name** row, repeat the technique just practiced to merge the last three cells in the row, and then merge the last three cells in the **Neighborhood** and **Street** rows.

8. Click the **Last Name** label to select it. Press and hold [Shift] while clicking the **Last Name** text box.

9. On the **Arrange tab**, in the **Move group**, click the **Move Up** button one time to move the **Last Name** row above the **First Name** row. Compare your screen with Figure 3.

10. Click the **State** label. Press and hold [Shift], while clicking the last empty cell in the **Zip** row. With the eight cells selected, press [Delete] to remove the two empty rows from the layout.

11. In the **Phone** row, click the first empty cell. Press and hold [Shift], and then click the last cell in the **Discount** row. With the six cells selected, in the **Merge/Split group**, click the **Merge** button.

12. On the **Design tab**, in the **Controls group**, click the **Insert Image** button, and then click **Browse**. In the **Insert Picture** dialog box, navigate to your student files. Click **a03_Classes_Picture**, and then click **OK**. Point 🖼 to the cell in the lower-right corner of the layout, and then click to insert the picture. Compare your screen with Figure 4.

13. Save 🖫 the form. Leave the form open for the next skill.

■ **You have completed Skill 5 of 10**

▶ An *Input mask* is a set of special characters that control what can and cannot be entered in a field.

1. With **Student Entry Form** open in Layout view, click the **Phone** text box. On the **Design tab**, in the **Tools group**, click the **Property Sheet** button.

2. In the **Property Sheet**, click the **Data tab**. On the **Property Sheet Data tab**, click the **Input Mask** box, and then click the displayed **Build** button ⬜ to start the **Input Mask Wizard**. Compare your screen with **Figure 1**.

3. With **Phone Number** selected in the **Input Mask Wizard**, click **Next**. Click the **Placeholder character arrow**, and then click the number sign (#). Click in the **Try It** box, and then compare your screen with **Figure 2**.

   The Try It box displays a sample of the input mask in which you can try entering sample data. *Placeholder characters* are the symbols in an input mask that are replaced as you type data into the field. Here, the parentheses, space, and hyphen are in place, and number signs display where each number can be typed.

4. In the **Try It** box, click the first number sign, and then watch the box as you type 10 digits.

■ **Continue to the next page to complete the skill**

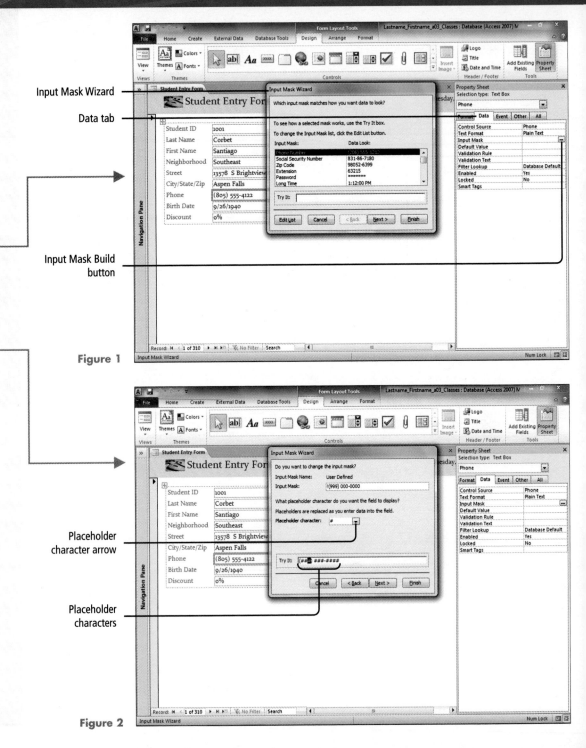

Input Mask Wizard

Data tab

Input Mask Build button

Figure 1

Placeholder character arrow

Placeholder characters

Figure 2

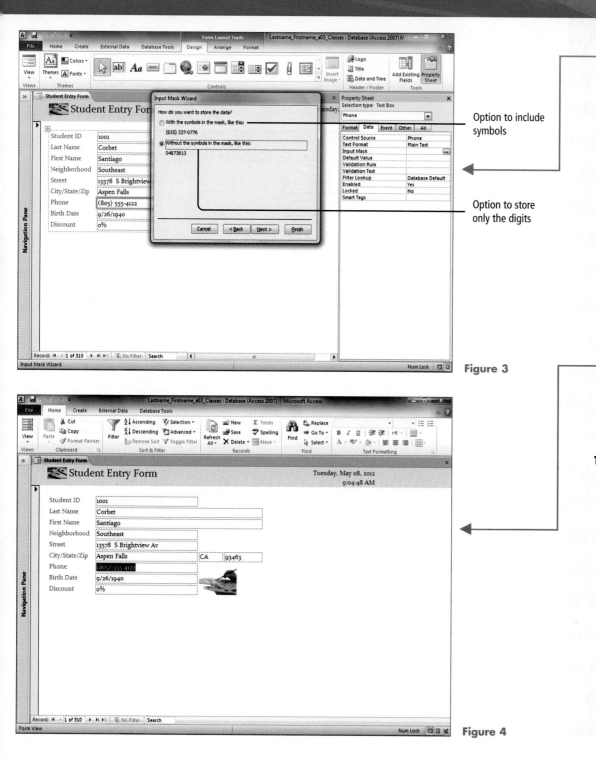

Figure 3

Figure 4

5. Click **Next**, and then compare your screen with **Figure 3**.

> The Phone Number input mask has one option that stores the parentheses, space, and hyphen in the table; the other option stores only the digits in the phone number.

6. Select the **With the symbols in the mask** option button, click **Next**, and then click **Finish**.

> In the Property Sheet Input Mask box, special characters have been inserted. These characters are needed for the input mask to perform correctly.

7. **Close** ⊠ the Property Sheet, and then Save 🖫 the form.

8. Click the **View** button to switch to Form view. If necessary, in the record for Santiago Corbet, press Tab to select the Phone value. Compare your screen with **Figure 4**.

9. Watch the **Phone** field as you type the following phone number: 8045556894

> The input mask converts the digits to *(804) 555-6894* and stores that value in the table.

10. Click **Save** 🖫, and then leave the form open for the next skill.

■ **You have completed Skill 6 of 10**

Option to include symbols

Option to store only the digits

► You can format values so that when a condition is true, the value will be formatted differently than when the condition is false.

1. With the **Student Entry Form** open, click the **View** button to switch to Layout view.

2. Click the **Discount** text box, and then, on the **Format tab**, in the **Control Formatting group**, click the **Conditional Formatting** button.

3. In the **Conditional Formatting Rules Manager**, click the **New Rule** button. In the **New Formatting Rule** dialog box, under **Format only cells where the**, click the second **arrow**. Compare your screen with **Figure 1**.

4. In the conditions list, click **greater than**. Click in the third box, and then type 0

5. In the **New Formatting Rule** dialog box, click the **Font Color button arrow**, and then click the sixth color in the last row—**Green**. Preview the conditional formatting, as shown in **Figure 2**.

■ **Continue to the next page to complete the skill**

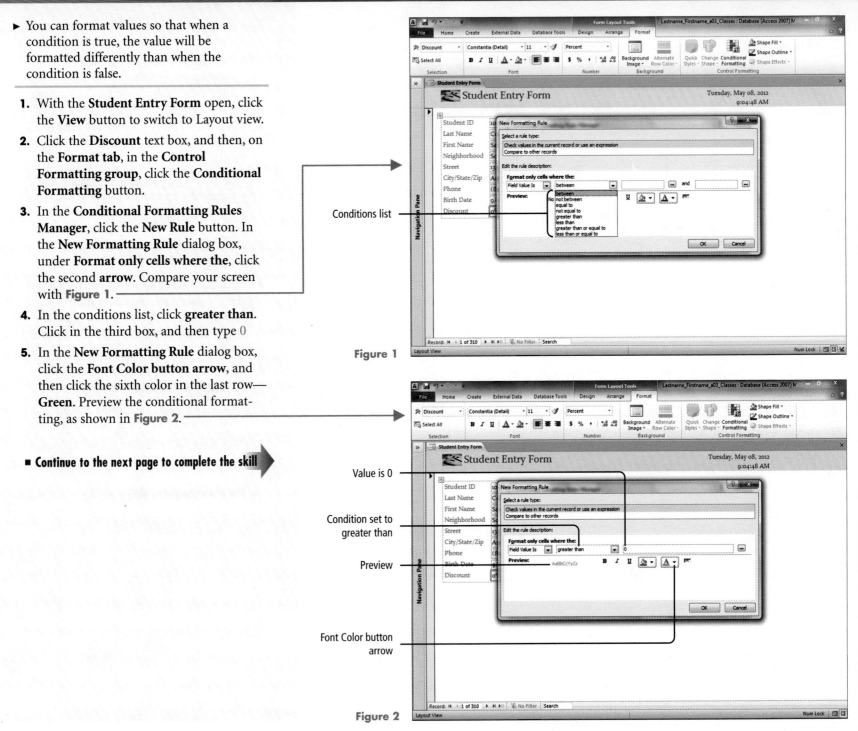

Conditions list

Figure 1

Value is 0

Condition set to greater than

Preview

Font Color button arrow

Figure 2

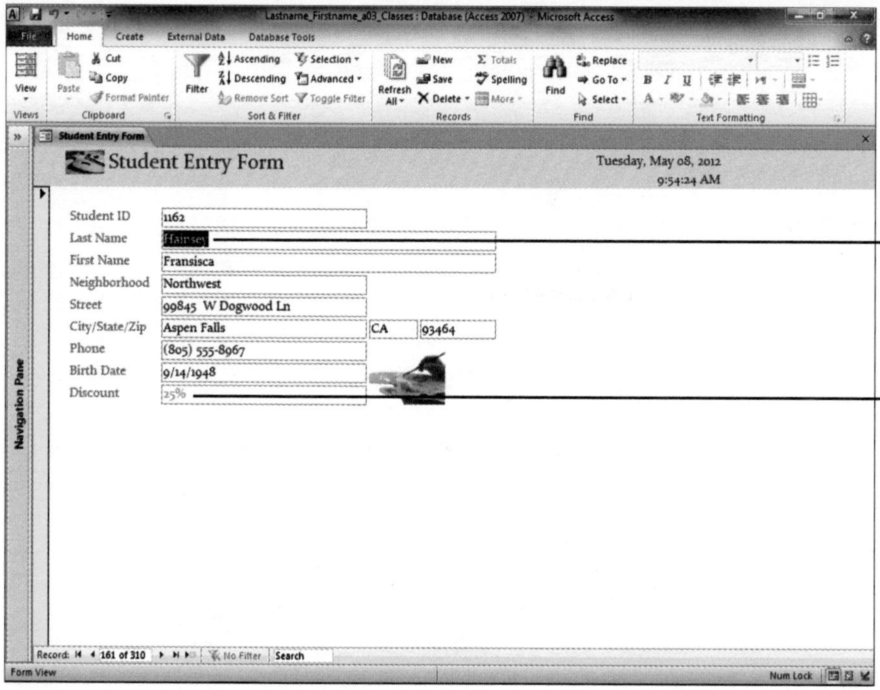

Last name is
Hainsey

Conditional
formatting applied

Figure 3

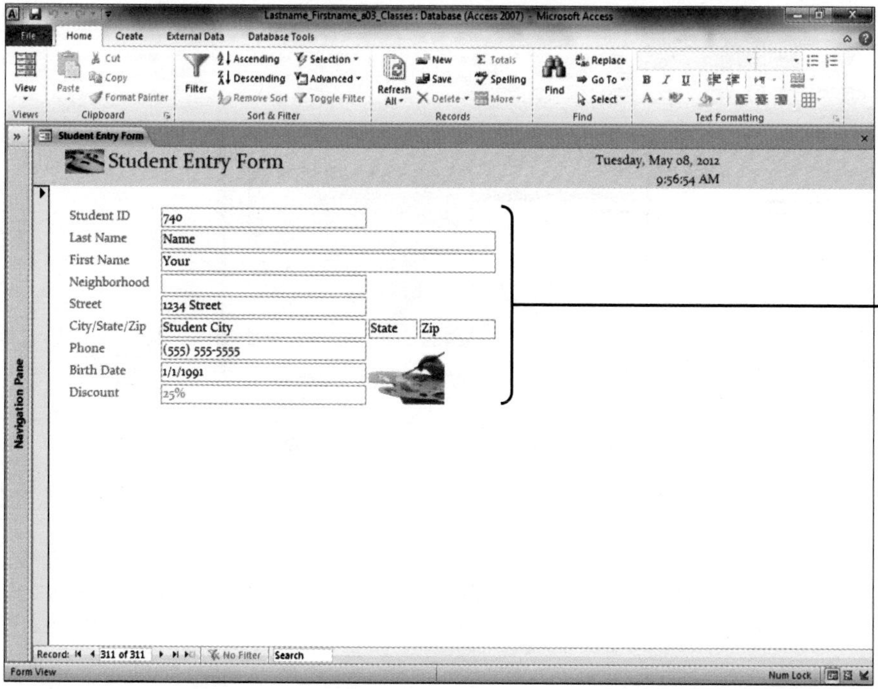

New record

Figure 4

6. Click **OK** two times, and then **Save** 🖫 the
   form. On the **Home tab**, click the **View**
   button to switch to Form view.

7. Click in the **Last Name** text box. On the
   Home tab, in the **Find group**, click the
   Find button. In the **Find What** box, type
   Hainsey and then press Enter.

8. **Close** ❎ the **Find and Replace** dialog
   box, and notice the conditional
   formatting, as shown in **Figure 3**.

9. In the Navigation bar, click the **New
   (blank) record** button ▶. In the **Student
   ID** text box, type 740 and then, in **Last
   Name** and **First Name**, enter your own
   last and first name. Leave **Neighborhood**
   blank, and then enter your own contact
   data and birth date. In the **Discount** text
   box, type 25%

10. Click in the **Neighborhood** text box, and
    then compare your screen with **Figure 4**.

11. **Start** ⊙ the **Snipping Tool**, click the **New
    button arrow**, and then click **Full-screen
    Snip**.

12. Click the **Save Snip** button 🖫. In the **Save
    As** dialog box, navigate to your **Access
    Chapter 3** folder, **Save** the snip as
    Lastname_Firstname_a03_Classes_Snip2
    and then **Close** ❎ the **Snipping Tool**
    window.

13. **Close** ❎ the form.

- **You have completed Skill 7 of 10**

► The Form Wizard can be used to create forms with fields from more than one table.

► When the data in a form has records that are also in a related table, the related data can be displayed in a *subform*—a form contained within another form.

► A *one-to-many form* is a main form and a subform that displays the related records for the record displayed in the main form.

1. **Open** ›› the **Navigation Pane**. On the **Create tab**, in the **Forms group**, click the **Form Wizard** button.

2. Click the **Tables/Queries arrow**, and then click **Table: Classes** to display the fields from that table.

3. Click the **Move All** button ›› to move all the fields into the **Selected Fields** list.

4. Click the **Tables/Queries arrow**, and then click **Table: Sections**.

5. Move the following fields to the **Selected Fields** list in this order: **Section ID**, **Start Date**, **Start Time**, **Instructor ID**, and **Fee**.

6. Compare your screen with **Figure 1**, and then click **Next**.

7. In the **Form Wizard**, compare your preview of the form and subform with **Figure 2**.

■ **Continue to the next page to complete the skill**

Fields from two tables

Figure 1

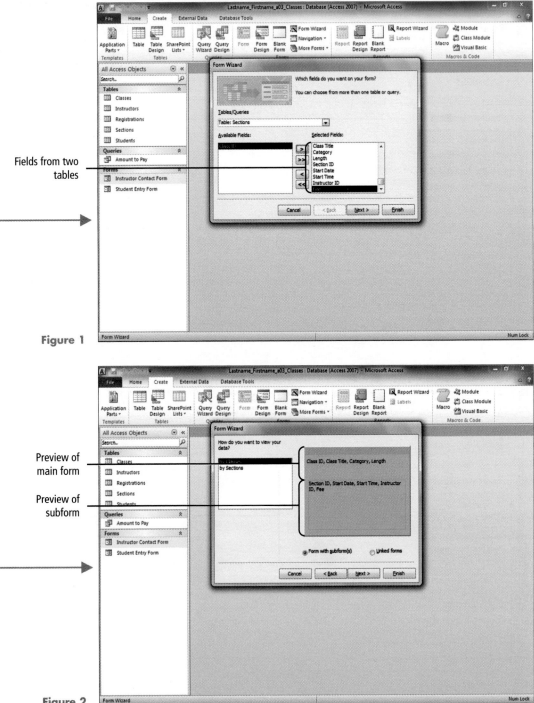

Preview of main form

Preview of subform

Figure 2

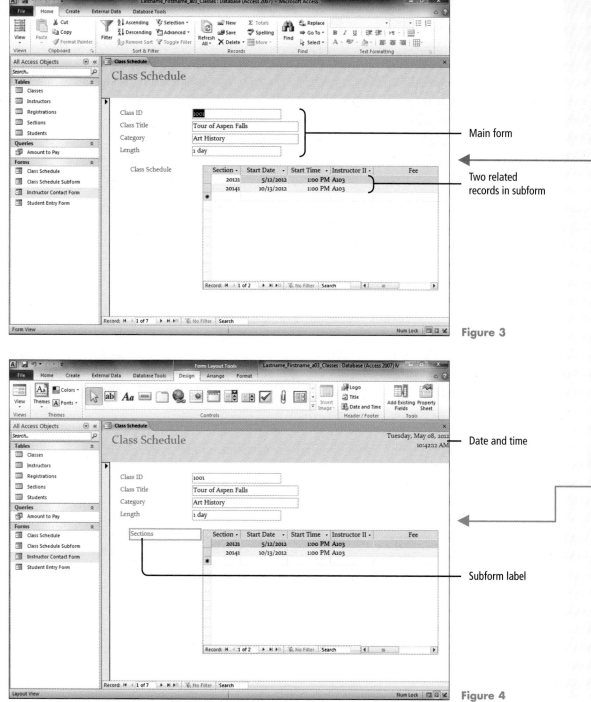

Figure 3

Figure 4

Main form

Two related records in subform

Date and time

Subform label

8. Click **Next**. Under **What layout would you like for your subform**, be sure that **Datasheet** is selected, and then click **Next**.

9. Under **What titles do you want for your forms**, replace the value in the **Form** box with Class Schedule Press Tab, and then replace the value in the **Subform** box, with Class Schedule Subform

10. Click **Finish**, and then compare your screen with **Figure 3**.

The main form displays the data for one record at a time, and all the related records display in the subform datasheet. Here, the Tour of Aspen Falls record has two sections scheduled.

A form and subform are saved as two separate forms. Here, both the main form—Class Schedule—and the subform—Class Schedule Subform—are listed in the Navigation Pane.

11. In the **Views group**, click the **View** button to switch to Layout view.

12. On the **Design tab**, in the **Header/Footer group**, click the **Date and Time** button, and click **OK**.

13. Click the subform label, and then replace the label text *Class Schedule* with Sections

14. **Save** ▢ the design changes, and then compare your screen with **Figure 4**.

■ **You have completed Skill 8 of 10**

► In a one-to-many form, you can work with the data from two tables on a single screen.

1. With the **Class Schedule** form open, click the **View** button to switch to Form view.

2. In the **Sections** subform datasheet, click the **Select All** button ▢. In the datasheet header row, point to a line between two columns, and then with the ⊞ pointer, double-click to resize the column widths automatically.

3. Click in the **Start Date** column, and then on the **Home tab**, in the **Sort & Filter group**, click the **Ascending** button. Save ▤ the changes to the datasheet, and then compare your screen with **Figure 1**. ──

4. With the Tour of Aspen Falls class displayed in the main form, click the subform's **New (blank) record** button ▷* to move to the subform's append row.

5. Type 20147 Press Enter, and then type 12/4/2012 Assign a **Time** of 1:00 PM an **Instructor ID** of A101 and a **Fee** of $5.00 Press Enter, and then compare your screen with **Figure 2**. ──

■ **Continue to the next page to complete the skill** ▶

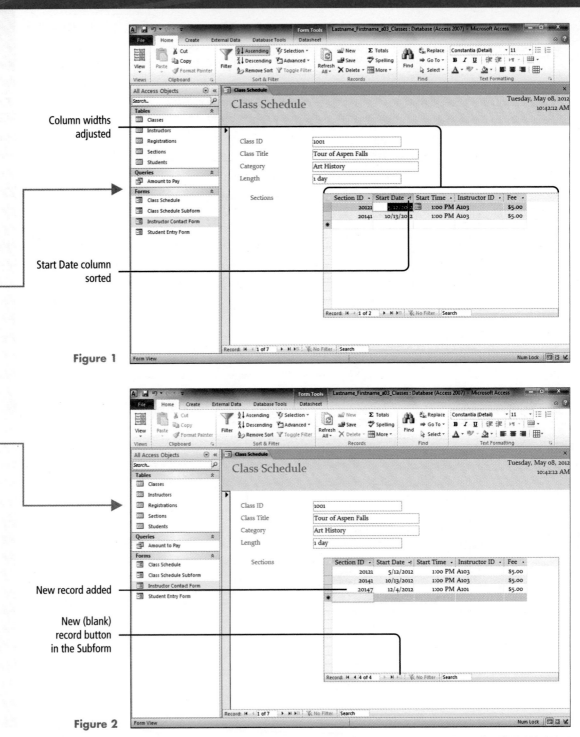

Column widths adjusted

Start Date column sorted

Figure 1

New record added

New (blank) record button in the Subform

Figure 2

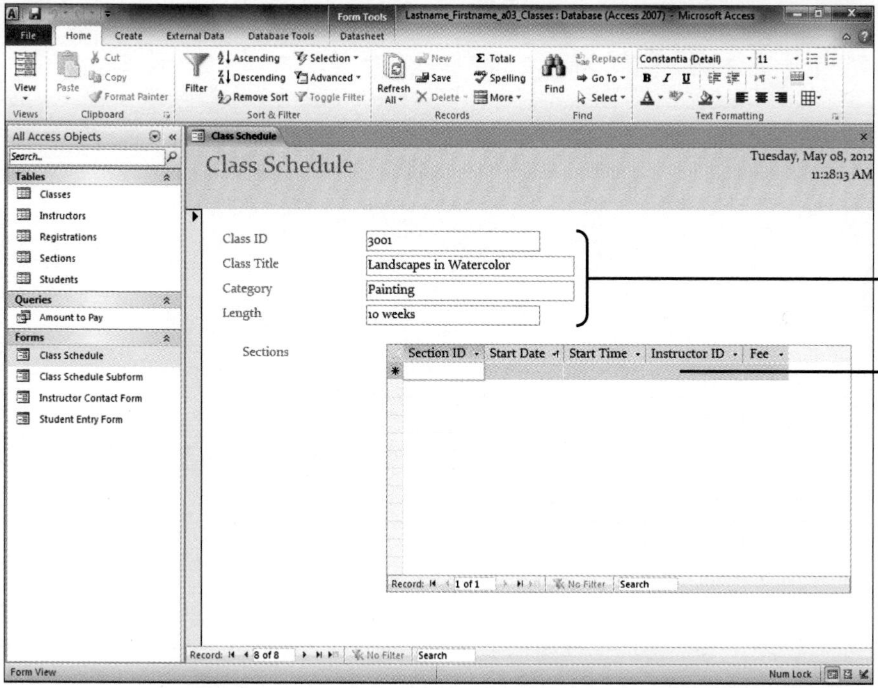

New class data

Subform append row active

Figure 3

Section ID	Start Date	Start Time	Instructor ID	Fee
20148	2/1/2012	1:00 PM	A101	25
20149	3/7/2012	7:00 PM	A114	25
20150	4/4/2012	1:00 PM	A120	25

Figure 4

6. In the main form's Navigation bar, click the **New (blank) record** button ▸ to create a new class.

7. Use the form to add the following class data: **Class ID** is 3001 **Class Title** is Landscapes in Watercolor **Category** is Painting and **Length** is 10 weeks Press ⏎ to move to the subform append row. Compare your screen with **Figure 3**.

8. In the subform, enter the sections shown in **Figure 4**.

9. **Start** ⊙ the **Snipping Tool**, click the **New button arrow**, and then click **Full-screen Snip**.

10. Click the **Save Snip** button 🖫. In the **Save As** dialog box, navigate to your **Access Chapter 3** folder, **Save** the snip as Lastname_Firstname_a03_Classes_Snip3 and then **Close** 🞫 the **Snipping Tool** window.

11. **Close** 🞩 the form.

■ **You have completed Skill 9 of 10**

▶ When you need to edit data for a specific subset of data, you can base the form on a query.

▶ A form based on a query displays only the records returned by the query's criteria.

1. In the **Navigation Pane**, under **Queries**, right-click **Amount to Pay**, and then, from the shortcut menu, click **Design View**.

2. In the **Discount** column **Criteria** box, type >0 **Close** « the **Navigation Pane**, and then compare your screen with **Figure 1.**

   The query displays records from four related tables and calculates the fee charged to students who have a discount.

3. Click **Save** 💾. **Run** the query to display 18 records, and then **Close** ✕ the query.

4. **Open** » the **Navigation Pane**. If necessary, under **Queries**, click one time to select **Amount to Pay**.

5. On the **Create tab**, in the **Forms group**, click the **Form** button. **Close** « the **Navigation Pane**, and then decrease the width of the text box columns approximately, as shown in **Figure 2.**

■ **Continue to the next page to complete the skill**

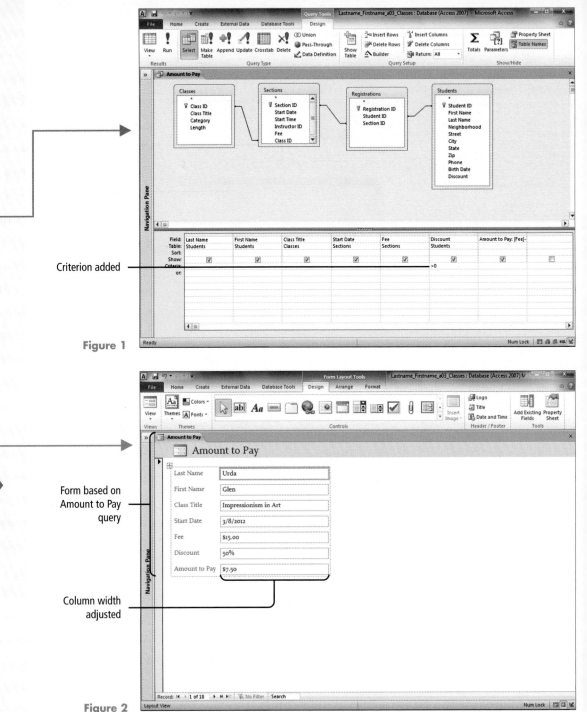

Criterion added

Figure 1

Form based on Amount to Pay query

Column width adjusted

Figure 2

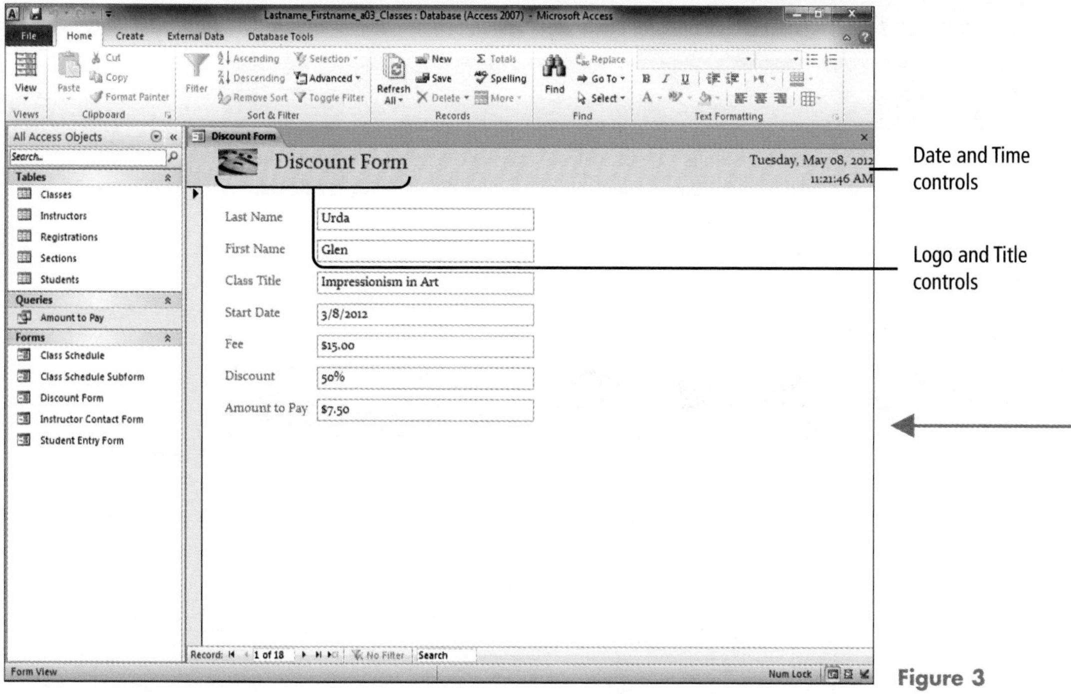

Date and Time controls

Logo and Title controls

Figure 3

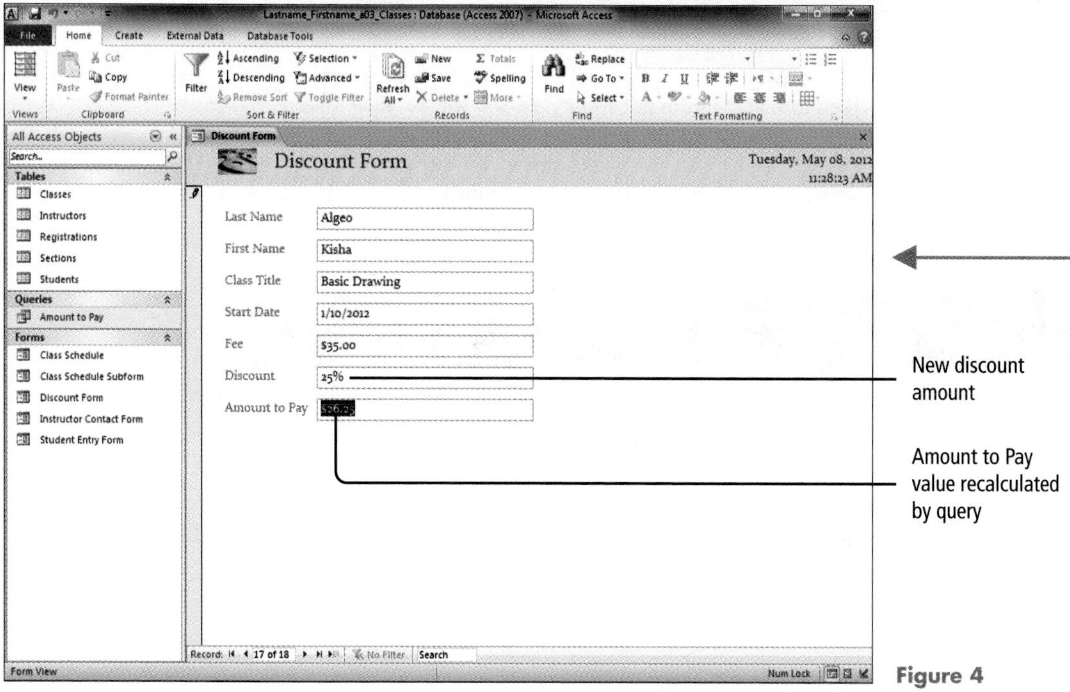

6. **Open** [»] the **Navigation Pane**. On the **Design tab**, in the **Header/Footer group**, click the **Date and Time** button, and then click **OK**.

7. Double-click the form's **Title** control, select the text *Amount to Pay*, and then type Discount Form

8. In the **Header/Footer group**, click the **Logo** button. In the **Insert Picture** dialog box, navigate to the student files for this chapter, click **a03_Classes_Logo**, and then click **OK**.

9. Click **Save** [🖫]. In the **Save As** box, type Discount Form and then press [Enter].

10. Click the **View** button to switch to Form view, and then compare your screen with **Figure 3**.

11. **Find** the record for Kisha Algeo, select the **Discount** 75%, type 25 and then press [Enter]. Compare your screen with **Figure 4**.

12. **Start** ⊙ the **Snipping Tool**, click the **New button arrow**, and then click **Full-screen Snip**.

13. Click the **Save Snip** button [🖫]. In the **Save As** dialog box, navigate to your **Access Chapter 3** folder, **Save** the snip as Lastname_Firstname_a03_Classes_Snip4 and then **Close** [❌] the **Snipping Tool** window.

14. **Close** [❌] the form, and then **Exit** Access. Print the snips or submit the database and snip files as directed by your instructor.

Done! You have completed Skill 10 of 10 and your database is complete!

New discount amount

Amount to Pay value recalculated by query

Figure 4

More Skills

The following More Skills are located at **www.pearsonhighered.com/skills**

More Skills 11 Validate Fields

Designing databases involves setting field properties so that those who use the database enter data correctly. For example, the data type, field size, and input mask properties all limit the types of data that can be entered into a field. Validation rules are also written so that the desired values are entered into fields.

In More Skills 11, you will set the Field Size and Format field properties to validate data. You will then add a validation rule that limits what can be typed into the field.

To begin, open your web browser, navigate to www.pearsonhighered.com/skills, locate the name of your textbook, and then follow the instructions on the website.

More Skills 12 Add Combo Boxes to Forms

When you need to enter ID fields in forms, you can change the ID text box to a combo box that displays more information than just an ID number. For example, when you need to enter a Student ID, you can use a combo box to show the numbers and the student names.

In More Skills 12, you will view a form with a Student ID text box, and then replace that text box with a combo box that displays the student's name. You will then use the combo box to add a student to a class.

To begin, open your web browser, navigate to www.pearsonhighered.com/skills, locate the name of your textbook, and then follow the instructions on the website.

More Skills 13 Create Multiple Item Forms

A multiple items form displays records in rows so that several records may be viewed on a single screen. Multiple item forms appear similar to a datasheet, but offer the formatting and layout options of forms.

In More Skills 13, you will create a multiple item form and then format the form in Layout view. You will use the property sheet to change control width and height of the controls.

To begin, open your web browser, navigate to www.pearsonhighered.com/skills, locate the name of your textbook, and then follow the instructions on the website.

More Skills 14 Create Macros

Macros are used to perform a sequence of steps with a single click of the mouse. Using macros in forms and reports saves time and automates common tasks.

In More Skills 14, you will create two macros using two different methods, and then use the macros to update a report that is based on a query.

To begin, open your web browser, navigate to www.pearsonhighered.com/skills, locate the name of your textbook, and then follow the instructions on the website.

Key Terms

Online Help Skills

1. **Start** 🌐 Access. In the upper-right corner of the Access window, click the **Help** button 🔘. In the **Help** window, click the **Maximize** button ⬜⬜.

2. Click in the search box, type Introduction to Forms and then click the **Search** button. In the search results, click **Introduction to Forms**.

3. Read the article's introduction, and then below **In this article**, click **Understand Layout view and Design view**. Compare your screen with **Figure 1**.

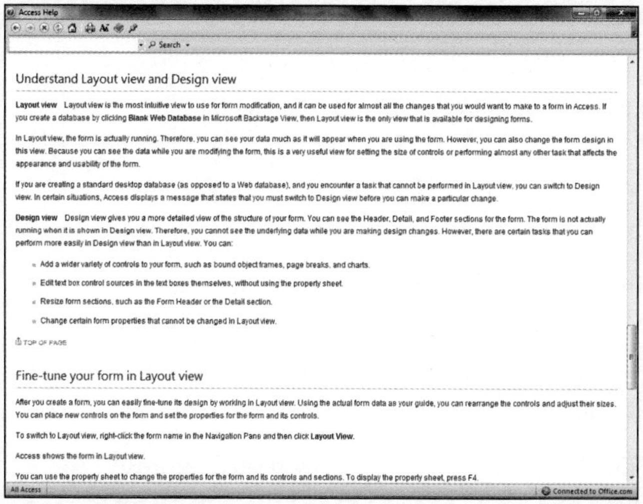

Figure 1

4. Read the Understand Layout view and Design view section to see if you can answer the following: What is the main advantage of using Layout view? What are the reasons for using Design view instead of Layout view?

Matching

Match each term in the second column with its correct definition in the first column by writing the letter of the term on the blank line in front of the correct definition.

____ **1.** The arrangement of data and labels in a form or report.

____ **2.** A tool used to create a form where the desired fields are selected before they are added to the form.

____ **3.** An Access feature that adds fields to the form when you double-click them in the Field List.

____ **4.** A small picture that can be added to a form header, typically to the left of the title.

____ **5.** A form control that displays the name of a form by default; the actual text can be edited later.

____ **6.** Cells arranged in rows and columns into which controls are placed.

____ **7.** A set of special characters that control what can and cannot be entered in a field.

____ **8.** A type of form that has a subform that displays related records from another table.

____ **9.** This name is often applied to the form that has a subform.

____ **10.** By default, subforms display in this view.

A Blank Form tool

B Control grid

C Datasheet

D Form Wizard

E Input mask

F Layout

G Logo

H Main form

I One-to-many form

J Title

Multiple Choice

Choose the correct answer.

1. An Access view used to format a form or report while viewing a sample of the data.
   - A. Design view
   - B. Form view
   - C. Layout view

2. A layout that places labels in the first column and data in the second column.
   - A. Columnar
   - B. Datasheet
   - C. Tabular

3. An Access view used to enter data in a form.
   - A. Data view
   - B. Form view
   - C. Layout view

4. Objects on a form or report that describe each field.
   - A. IntelliSense Quick Info boxes
   - B. Labels
   - C. Text boxes

5. Objects on a form or report that display the data from fields.
   - A. Labels
   - B. Text boxes
   - C. Titles

6. This property sheet tab contains the Input Mask property.
   - A. Data
   - B. Format
   - C. Other

7. The symbol in an input mask that is replaced as you type data into the field.
   - A. Data character
   - B. Input character
   - C. Placeholder character

8. Formatting that evaluates the values in a field and formats that data according to the rules you specify; for example, only values over 1000 will have bold applied.
   - A. Conditional formatting
   - B. Logical formatting
   - C. Rules-based formatting

9. A form contained within another form that displays records related to the other form.
   - A. Parent form
   - B. Relationship form
   - C. Subform

10. When you want to build a form for a subset of data, you can base the form on this.
   - A. Blank Form tool
   - B. Filtered table Query
   - C. Query

Topics for Discussion

1. You have created forms using three different methods: the Form tool, the Form Wizard, and the Blank Form tool. Which method do you prefer and why? What are the primary advantages of each method?

2. Recall that forms are used to enter data into a database. Consider the types of data businesses might store in a database. For example, a school needs a class registration form to enter students into classes. What type of forms might other businesses need to enter data?

Skill Check

To complete this database, you will need the following files:

- a03_Outings
- a03_Outings_Logo

You will save your files as:

- Lastname_Firstname_a03_Outings
- Lastname_Firstname_a03_Outings_Snip1
- Lastname_Firstname_a03_Outings_Snip2
- Lastname_Firstname_a03_Outings_Snip3

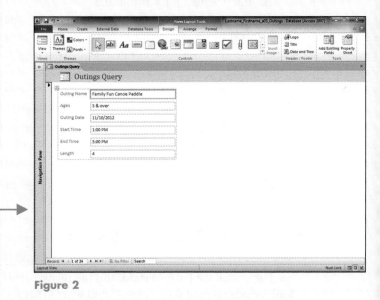

Figure 1

Figure 2

1. **Start** Access, and then open the student data file **a03_Outings**. Save the database in your **Access Chapter 3** folder with the name Lastname_Firstname_a03_Outings If necessary, enable the content.

2. On the **Create tab**, in the **Forms group**, click the **Form Wizard** button. In the **Form Wizard**, select the **Participants** table, and then move **Participant ID**, **First Name**, and **Last Name** into **Selected Fields**.

3. In the **Form Wizard**, select the **Registrations** table, and then move the **Registration ID** and **Outing ID** fields into **Selected Fields**. Click **Next** three times. Name the **Form** Registrants Accept the **Subform** name by clicking **Finish**.

4. In the subform, double-click to adjust the width of both columns automatically, and then click **Save**.

5. In the main form Navigation bar, click the **Last record** button. In the subform for Julia Saxton, enter a **Registration ID** of 1501 and an **Outing ID** of 100 Enter another record with a **Registration ID** of 1502 and an **Outing ID** of 101 Compare your screen with **Figure 1**.

6. Create a **Full-screen Snip**, and then save it in your **Access Chapter 3** folder as Lastname_Firstname_a03_Outings_Snip1 **Close** the **Snipping Tool** window.

7. **Close** the form. In the **Navigation Pane**, right-click **Outings Query**, and then click **Design View**. In the **Outing Date** column **Criteria** box, type >9/1/2012 **Save**, **Run**, and then **Close** the query.

8. With the query selected in the **Navigation Pane**, on the **Create tab**, in the **Forms group**, click the **Form** button.

9. **Close** the **Navigation Pane**, and then decrease the width of the right column approximately, as shown in **Figure 2**.

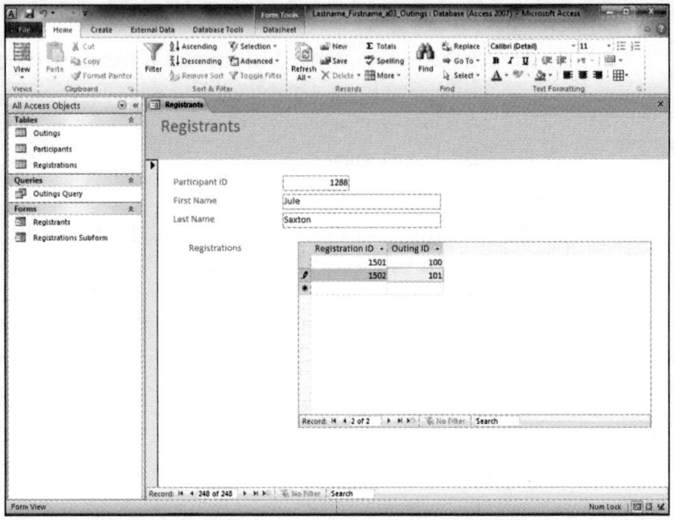

▪ Continue to the next page to complete this Skill Check ▶

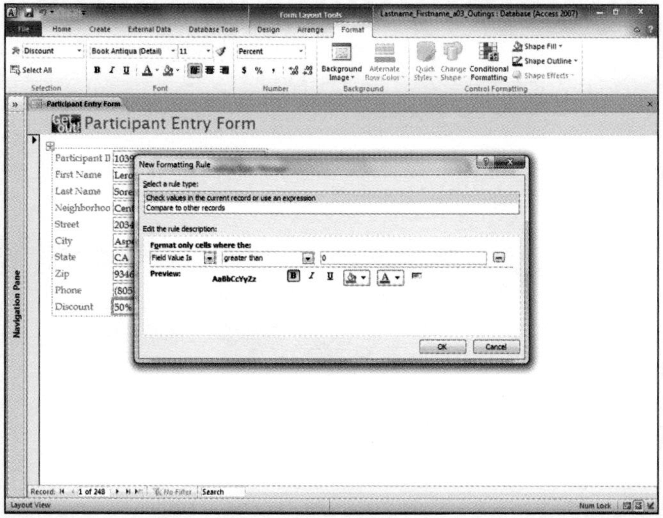

Figure 3

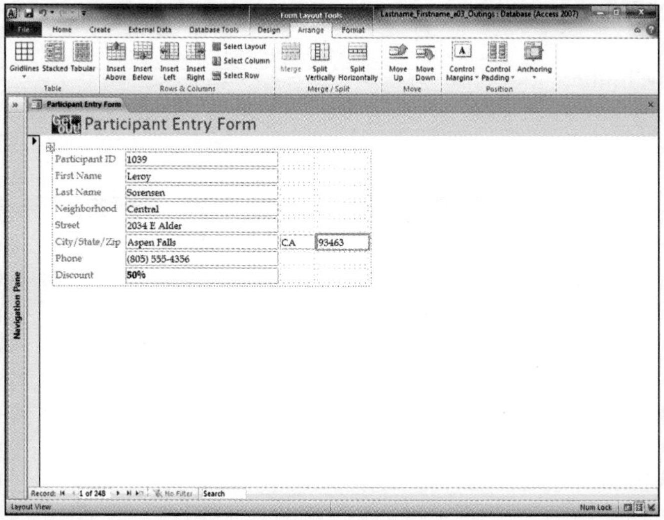

Figure 4

10. Create a **Full-screen Snip**, and then save it in your **Access Chapter 3** folder as Lastname_Firstname_a03_Outings_Snip2 **Close** the **Snipping Tool** window.

11. Click **Save**, type Fall Outings and then click **OK**. **Close** the form.

12. On the **Create tab**, in the **Forms group**, click the **Blank Form** button. In the **Field List**, show all tables, and then expand the **Participants** table.

13. In the **Field List**, double-click to add the 10 fields from the **Participants** table, starting with **Participant ID** and ending with **Discount**. Close the **Field List** pane.

14. Click **Save**, type Participant Entry Form and then click **OK**.

15. On the **Design tab**, click the **Themes** button, and then click the fourth thumbnail—**Apex**.

16. In the **Header/Footer group**, click the **Logo** button. In the **Insert Picture** dialog box, navigate to the student files for this chapter and then double-click **a03_Outings_Logo**. In the **Header/Footer group**, click the **Title** button.

17. Click the **Phone** text box, and then, in the **Tools group**, click the **Property Sheet** button. On the Property Sheet **Data tab**, click the **Input Mask** box, and click the displayed **Build** button. In the **Input Mask Wizard**, be sure that **Phone Number** is selected, and then click **Finish**. **Close** the **Property Sheet**.

18. Click the **Discount** text box, and then, on the **Format tab**, in the **Control Formatting group**, click **Conditional Formatting**. In the dialog box, click the **New Rule** button. Change the condition to **greater than** and then type 0 Click the **Bold** button and then compare your screen with **Figure 3**.

19. Click **OK** two times. Click the **State** text box, and then drag it to the right of the **City** text box to create a new column. Drag the **Zip** text box to the right of the **State** text box to create a new column.

20. Click the **State** label. Press and hold (Shift), and then click the last empty cell in the **Zip** row. Press (Delete) to delete the two empty rows.

21. Double-click the **City** label, and then change the text to City/State/Zip

22. Drag to decrease the width of the **State** text box, and then decrease the width of the **Zip** text box approximately, as shown in **Figure 4**.

23. Switch to Form view. Create a **Full-screen Snip**, and then save it in your **Access Chapter 3** folder as Lastname_Firstname_a03_Outings_Snip3 **Close** the **Snipping Tool** window.

24. Click **Save**, and then **Exit** Access. Print the snips or submit the files as directed by your instructor.

Done! You have completed the Skill Check

Assess Your Skills 1

To complete this database, you will need the following files:

- a03_Camps
- a03_Camps_Logo

You will save your files as:

- Lastname_Firstname_a03_Camps
- Lastname_Firstname_a03_Camps_Snip1
- Lastname_Firstname_a03_Camps_Snip2
- Lastname_Firstname_a03_Camps_Snip3

1. **Start** Access, and then open **a03_Camps**. **Save** the database in your **Access Chapter 3** folder as Lastname_Firstname_a03_Camps If necessary, enable the content.

2. Start the **Blank Form** tool, and then add the eight fields from the **Directors** table in the order that they are listed in the **Field List** pane. **Save** the form as Director Entry Form

3. Apply the **Aspect** theme, add a logo using **a03_Camps_Logo**, and then add a **Title** with the name of the form.

4. Add a **Phone Number** input mask to the **Phone** text box using the default wizard settings.

5. Move the **State** text box in a new column to the right of the **City** text box, and then move the **Zip** text box into a new column to the right of the **State** text box. Delete the two empty rows, and then change the **City** label to City/State/Zip

6. Decrease the width of the **State** and **Zip** text boxes approximately, as shown in **Figure 1**.

7. Switch to Form view, and then add yourself as a new camp director.

8. Create a **Full-screen snip**, and then save it in your **Access Chapter 3** folder as Lastname_Firstname_a03_Camps_Snip1

9. **Save**, and then **Close** the form. Start the **Form Wizard**. From the **Directors** table, add the **First Name** and **Last Name** fields, and then,

from the **Camps** table, add all but the **Director ID** field. Accept all other **Form Wizard** defaults.

10. In Form view, navigate to the last record. Use the subform to add the following camps:

Camp ID	Camp Name	Start Date
8	Hoopa	8/13/2012
9	Paiute	8/20/2012

11. Create a **Full-screen snip**, and then save it in your **Access Chapter 3** folder as Lastname_Firstname_a03_Outings_Snip2

12. **Close** the form, and then open the **Discounted Fees** query in Design view. In the **Discount** column **Criteria** box, type >0 **Save**, **Run**, and then **Close** the query.

13. Use the **Form** tool to create a form based on the **Discounted Fees** query.

14. Apply conditional formatting to the **Discounted Fee** text box so that the text will be **Red** when the field value is **greater than** 100

15. Decrease the width of the text box column to approximately 3 inches. Switch to Form view, and then compare your screen with **Figure 2**.

16. Create a **Full-screen snip**. **Save** the snip in your **Access Chapter 3** folder as Lastname_Firstname_a03_Camps_Snip3

17. **Save** the form as Discounted Fees **Close** the form, and then **Exit** Access. Print the snips or submit the files as directed by your instructor.

Done! You have completed Assess Your Skills 1

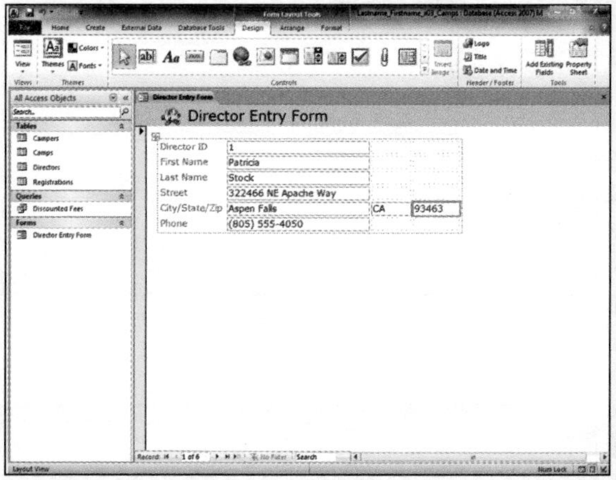

Figure 1

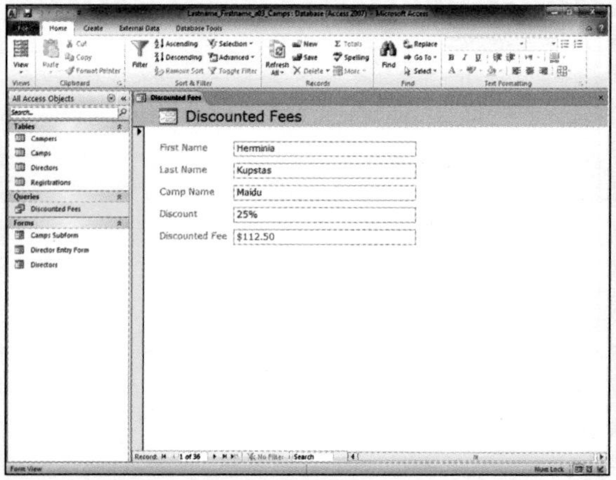

Figure 2

Assessment

Assess Your Skills 3 and 4 can be found at **www.pearsonhighered.com/skills**.

Assess Your Skills 2

To complete this database, you will need the following file:

- a03_Reviews

You will save your files as:

- **Lastname_Firstname_a03_Reviews**
- **Lastname_Firstname_a03_Reviews_Snip1**
- **Lastname_Firstname_a03_Reviews_Snip2**
- **Lastname_Firstname_a03_Reviews_Snip3**

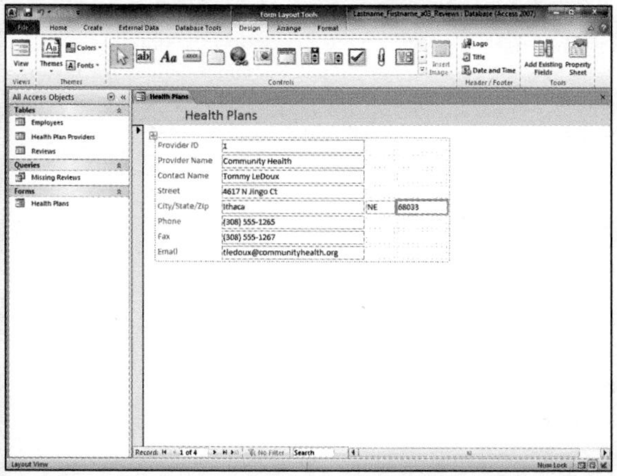

Figure 1

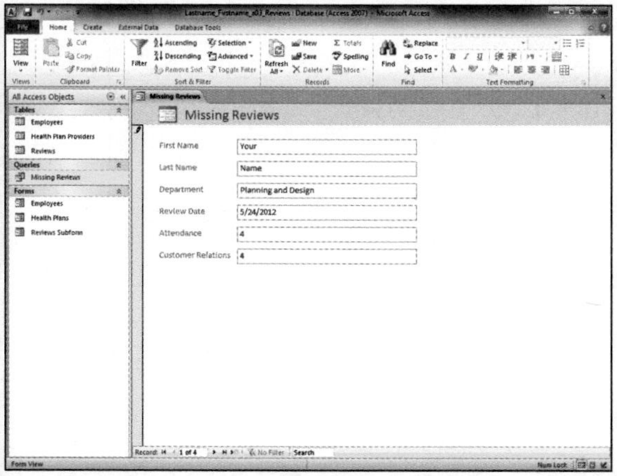

Figure 2

1. **Start** Access, and then open **a03_Reviews**. Save the database in your **Access Chapter 3** folder as Lastname_Firstname_a03_Reviews If necessary, enable the content.

2. Start the **Blank Form** tool, and then add the 10 fields from the **Health Plan Providers** table in the order that they are listed in the **Field List** pane. **Save** the form as Health Plans

3. Apply the **Composite** theme, and then add a **Title** with the name of the form. Increase the width of the label column so **Provider Name** displays in its label control.

4. Add **Phone Number** input masks to the **Phone** and **Fax** text boxes using the default wizard settings.

5. Move the **State** text box in a new column to the right of the **City** text box, and then move the **Zip** text box into a new column to the right of the **State** text box. Delete the two empty rows, and then change the **City** label to City/State/Zip

6. Decrease the width of the **State** and **Zip** text boxes approximately, as shown in **Figure 1**.

7. Switch to Form view, and then change the Community Health **Contact Name** to your name.

8. Create a **Full-screen snip**, and then save it in your **Access Chapter 3** folder as Lastname_Firstname_a03_Reviews_Snip1

9. **Save**, and then **Close** the form. Start the **Form Wizard**. From the **Employees** table, add the **First Name**, **Last Name**, and **Department** fields. From the **Reviews** table, add all but the **Employee ID** field. Accept all other Form Wizard defaults.

10. In the first record, change the name fields to your own first and last name. In the subform, automatically resize the column widths.

11. Create a **Full-screen Snip**, and then save it in your **Access Chapter 3** folder as Lastname_Firstname_a03_Reviews_Snip2

12. **Save**, and then **Close** the form. Open the **Missing Reviews** query in Design view. In the **Attendance** column **Or** box, below the existing Is Null criterion, type Is Null **Save**, **Run**, and then **Close** the query.

13. Use the **Form** tool to create a form based on the **Missing Reviews** query.

14. Decrease the width of the text box column to approximately 3 inches. In Form view, change the first record's **Attendance** value to 4 and the **Customer Relations** value to 4 Compare your screen with **Figure 2**.

15. Create a **Full-screen Snip**. **Save** the snip in your **Access Chapter 3** folder as Lastname_Firstname_a03_Reviews_Snip3

16. **Save** the form as Missing Reviews **Close** the form, and then **Exit** Access. Print the snips or submit the files as directed by your instructor.

Done! You have completed Assess Your Skills 2

Assess Your Skills Visually

To complete this database, you will need the following files:

- a03_Councils
- a03_Councils_Logo

You will save your database as:

- Lastname_Firstname_a03_Councils
- Lastname_Firstname_a03_Councils_Snip

Open the database **a03_Councils**, and then using your own name, save the database in your **Access Chapter 3** folder as Lastname_Firstname_a03_Councils

Use the Form Wizard to create the form shown in **Figure 1**. Include the **Council Name** field, and from the **Members** table, include the **First Name** and **Last Name** fields. The form uses the **Metro** theme. The title provided by the Form Wizard has been deleted and a new title inserted with the text Council Members The logo is from the student file **a03_Councils_Logo**. Arrange the subform and controls approximately as shown in the figure.

Use the form to enter the following members to the Planning Council:

Cyril Shore
Richie Bona
Hisako Lavoy
Octavio Coogan
Barton Bierschbach
Jung Ortolano
Jerrold Calhaun
Gwyneth Rondeau
Tammi Markewich

Save the form and subform. Create a **Full-Screen Snip** named a03_Councils_Snip Print the snip or submit the files as directed by your instructor.

Done! You have completed Assess Your Skills Visually

Councils

CITY HALL **Council Members**

Council Name | Planning Council |

Members

First Name ▾	Last Name ▾
Cyril	Shore
Richie	Bona
Hisako	Lavoy
Octavio	Coogan
Barton	Bierschbach
Jung	Ortolano
Jerrold	Calhaun
Gwyneth	Rondeau
Tammi	Markewich
*	

Record: I◀ ◀ 9 of 9 ▶ ▶I ▶⊞ No Filter Search

Figure 1

Skills in Context

To complete this database, you will need the following file:
- a03_Managers

You will save your files as:
- Lastname_Firstname_a03_Managers
- Lastname_Firstname_a03_Managers_Snip

Open **a03_Managers** and save the database in your **Access Chapter 3** folder as Lastname_Firstname_a03_Managers Create a form that displays all the records from the Managers table, but only those managers from the Parks and Recreation Department. Base the form on a query, and in the query criterion, type "Parks and Recreation" Be sure to include the quotation marks in the criterion. Apply an appropriate theme and a title with the text Parks and Recreation Managers Use the form to add yourself as a manager with the position of Health and Wellness Coordinator and an office number of 424 and a phone number of (805) 555-8492

Create a full-screen snip of the record with your name. Save the snip in your **Access Chapter 3** folder as a03_Managers_Snip Print the snip or submit the database file as directed by your instructor.

Done! You have completed Skills in Context

Skills and You

To complete this database, you will need the following file:
- a03_Contacts

You will save your files as:
- Lastname_Firstname_a03_Contacts
- Lastname_Firstname_a03_Contacts_Snip

Open **a03_Contacts**, and then save the database as Lastname_Firstname_a03_Contacts Create a form to enter contacts into the Contacts table. Format the form as appropriate, and then use the form to enter at least 10 personal contacts. Create a full-screen snip of the form. Save the snip in your **Access Chapter 3** folder as a03_Contacts_Snip Print or submit the file as directed by your instructor.

Done! You have completed Skills and You

CHAPTER 4

Create Reports

► Access reports are designed to present information on the screen or to be printed on paper.

► There are several methods that you can use to add fields to reports. You can then format and arrange the fields to make the information more meaningful.

Your starting screen will look similar to this:

SKILLS

Skills 1-10 Training

At the end of this chapter, you will be able to:

Skill 1 Create Reports and Apply Themes

Skill 2 Modify Report Layouts

Skill 3 Prepare Reports for Printing

Skill 4 Use the Blank Report Tool

Skill 5 Group and Sort Reports

Skill 6 Format and Filter Reports

Skill 7 Create Label Reports

Skill 8 Use the Report Wizard

Skill 9 Modify Layouts in Design View

Skill 10 Add Totals and Labels to Reports

MORE SKILLS

More Skills 11 Export Reports to Word

More Skills 12 Export Reports as HTML Documents

More Skills 13 Create Parameter Queries

More Skills 14 Create Reports for Parameter Queries

Outcome

Using the skills listed to the left will enable you to create reports like these:

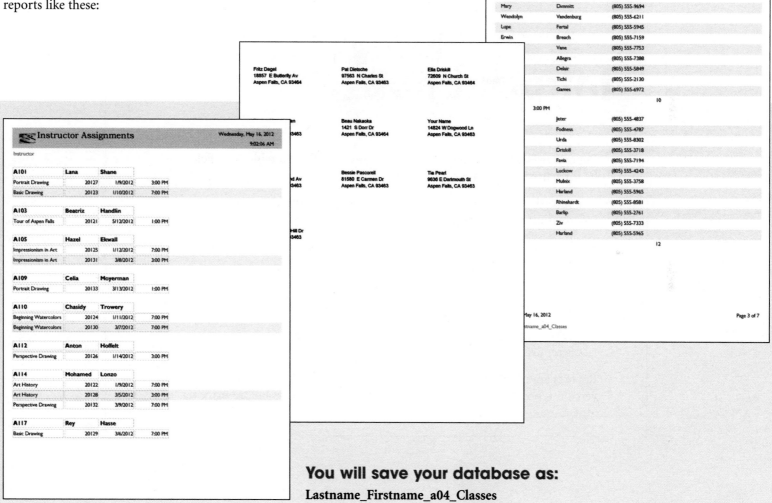

You will save your database as:

Lastname_Firstname_a04_Classes

In this chapter, you will create documents for the Aspen Falls City Hall, which provides essential services for the citizens and visitors of Aspen Falls, California.

Introduction

- ▶ Reports present the results of a query or the data from a table. The fields can be formatted and arranged in a variety of ways.

- ▶ The records in reports can be grouped, sorted, and filtered to make the information more meaningful.

- ▶ You can build a report with fields from an entire table or query using the Report tool.

- ▶ When you want to select certain fields from one or more tables, you can create the report using the Report Wizard or Blank Report tool.

- ▶ When you need to print addresses on self-adhesive labels, you can create a labels report.

- ▶ Reports are modified in Layout or Design view. Report view shows the screen version reports, and Print Preview is used to view reports before printing.

**Time to complete all
10 skills – 60 to 90 minutes**

Find your student data files here:

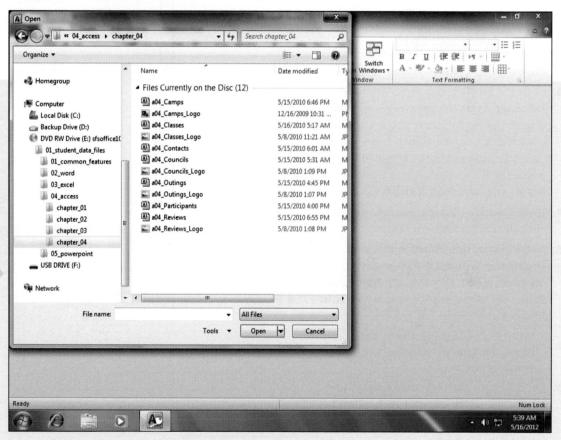

Student data files needed for this chapter:

- a04_Classes
- a04_Classes_Logo

► Reports are often based on queries. You can add the fields that you need to the query, add criteria, and then use the Report tool to create a report to display the results of the query.

► After selecting a theme for your database, you can apply fonts or colors from a different theme.

1. **Start** ⊙ Access. If necessary, **Maximize** ◻ the window.

2. From the student files that came with this book, open **a04_Classes**.

3. Click the **File tab**, and then click **Save Database As**. In the **Save As** dialog box, display the file list where you are saving your files. Click **New folder**, type Access Chapter 4 and then press Enter two times. Name the file Lastname_Firstname_ a04_Classes and then click **Save**.

4. If the Security Warning message displays, click the Enable Content button.

5. In the **Navigation Pane**, double-click **Instructors without a W-4** to view the query datasheet. **Close** « the **Navigation Pane**, and then compare your screen with **Figure 1**.

   When you are working with an Access object, the status bar contains buttons for switching views.

6. On the status bar, click the **Design View** button ◪. In the **Current W-4** column **Criteria** box, type No Compare your screen with **Figure 2**.

7. **Save** ◻, **Run**, and then **Close** ⊠ the query.

■ **Continue to the next page to complete the skill**

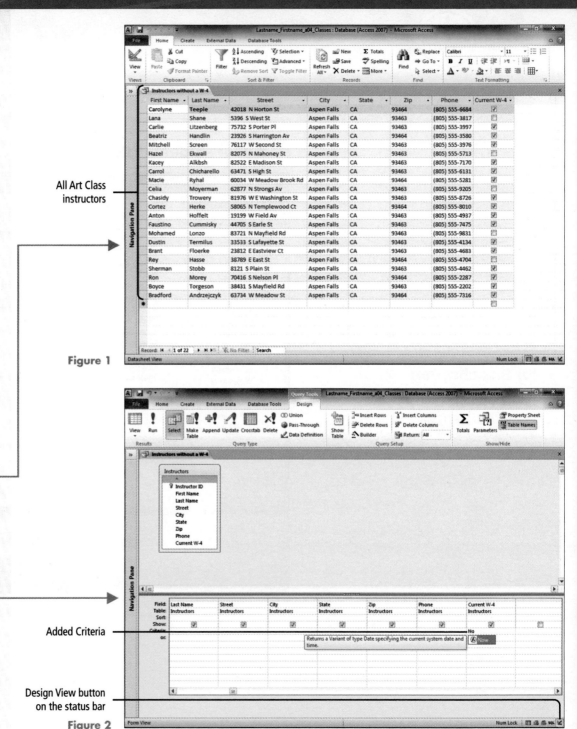

All Art Class instructors

Figure 1

Added Criteria

Design View button on the status bar

Figure 2

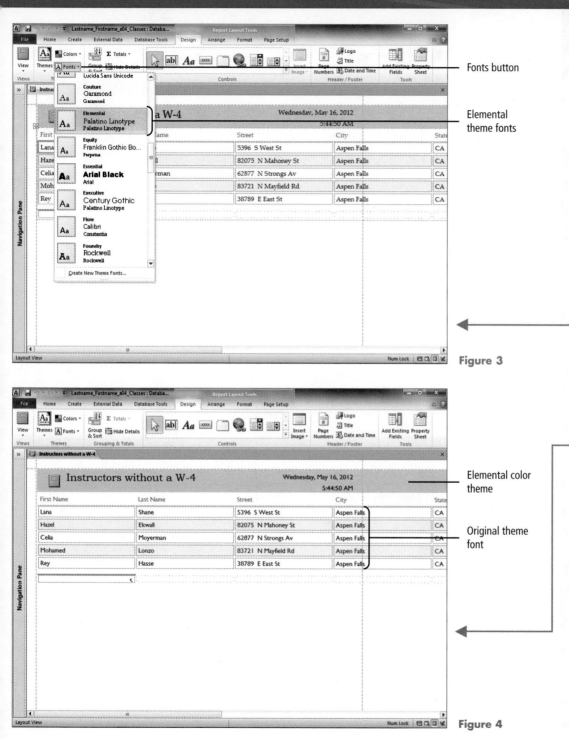

Fonts button

Elemental
theme fonts

Figure 3

Elemental color
theme

Original theme
font

Figure 4

8. **Open** 〉〉 the **Navigation Pane**. In the **Navigation Pane**, be sure the **Instructors without a W-4** is selected. On the **Create tab**, in the **Reports group**, click the **Report** button.

   When a report is based on a query, the query criteria are applied to the report. Here, only the five instructors without a W-4 form on file are listed.

9. **Close** 〈〈 the **Navigation Pane**. On the **Design tab**, in the **Themes group**, click the **Themes** button, and then click the second thumbnail in the fourth row—**Elemental**.

10. In the **Themes group**, click the **Fonts** button. Scroll down the list to display the **Elemental** font set, and then compare your screen with **Figure 3**.

   When you select a theme, you are applying a set of fonts and a set of colors. Here, the Elemental font set includes Palatino Linotype for both labels and text boxes.

11. In the list of font sets, scroll down to locate and then click **Origin**. Compare your screen with **Figure 4**.

   In this manner, you can combine your current theme with a color or font set from a different theme. Here, the report's fonts have changed to Bookman Old Style for the report header controls and Gill Sans MT for the values in the text boxes. The colors from the Elemental theme are still applied.

12. Click **Save** 🖫. In the **Save As** dialog box, click **OK** to save the report as Instructors without a W-4. Leave the report open for the next skill.

   ■ **You have completed Skill 1 of 10**

▶ Recall that forms and reports use layouts—cells arranged in rows and columns into which controls are placed. You can resize, delete, and merge these rows and columns so the report can be viewed on a screen without scrolling.

First Name column width decreased

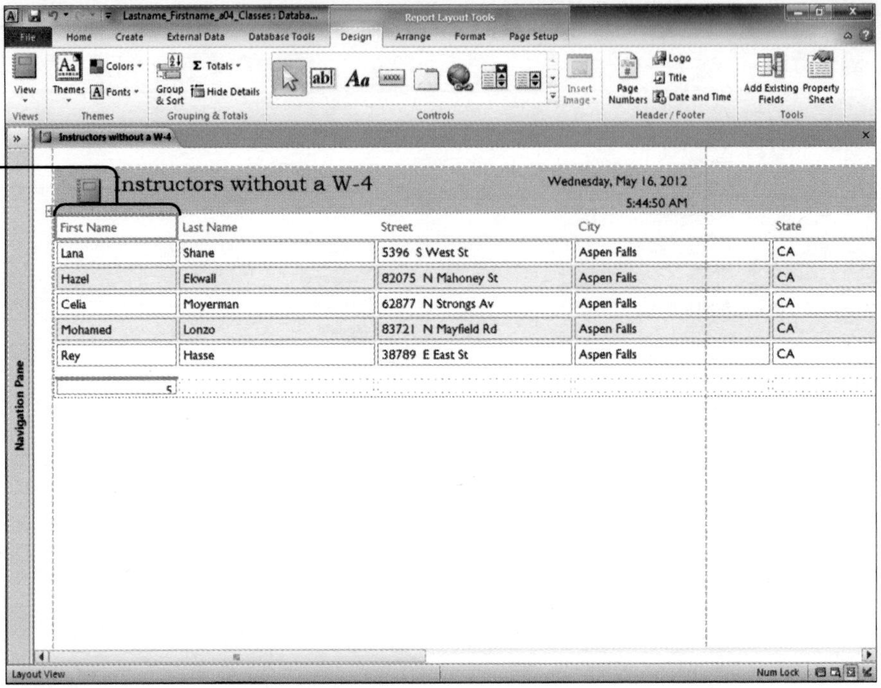

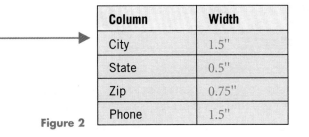

1. With the **Instructors without a W-4** report still open in Layout view, click the **First Name** label. With the ↔ pointer over the right border of the label, drag to the left to resize the column, approximately as shown in **Figure 1**.

   When you resize one text box or label in a report's layout, all the label text boxes in that column are also resized. In this report, the First Name text box repeats five times—one row for each record in the query.

2. Click the **Last Name** label. On the **Design tab**, in the **Tools group**, click the **Property Sheet** button. On the property sheet **Format tab**, replace the **Width** value with 1.5".

Figure 1

3. Click the **Street** column to display its properties, and then change the column's **Width** to 2" Continue in this manner to set the remaining column widths using the values in **Figure 2**. Scroll as needed to select each column.

Column	Width
City	1.5"
State	0.5"
Zip	0.75"
Phone	1.5"

Figure 2

4. Click the **Current W-4 label**. On the **Arrange tab**, in the **Rows & Columns group**, click **Select Column**. Press Delete to remove the column from the report.

■ **Continue to the next page to complete the skill**

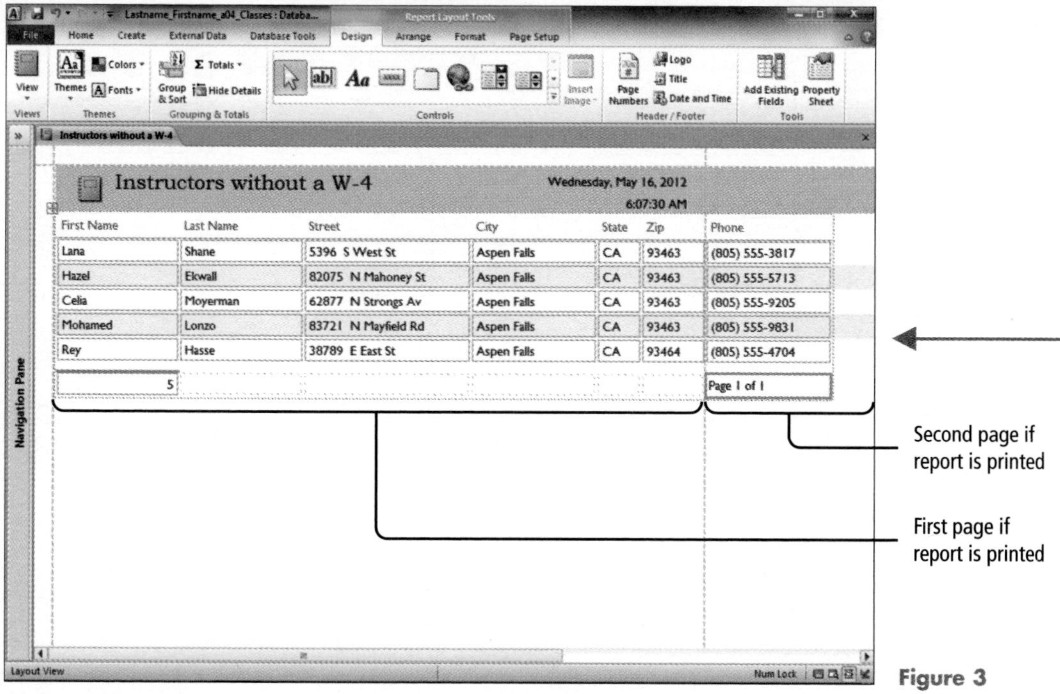

Second page if
report is printed

First page if
report is printed

Figure 3

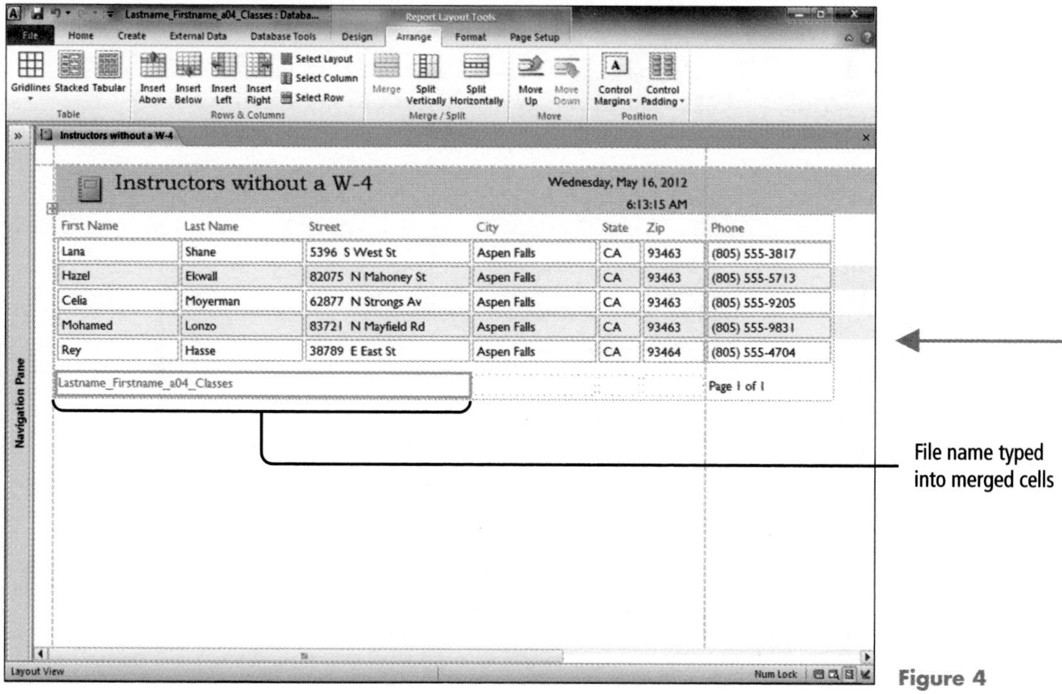

File name typed
into merged cells

Figure 4

5. Scroll to the right as needed to display the text box with the value *Page 1 of 1*. With the ☼ pointer, drag the control into the empty cell below the **Phone** column.

6. With the *Page 1 of 1* text box still selected, on the property sheet **Format tab**, change the Height value to .25".

7. **Close** ⊠ the property sheet, scroll the report all the way to the left, and then compare your screen with **Figure 3**.

   The entire report now displays within the width of a typical computer screen. The report is wider than a single sheet of paper, as indicated by the dashed vertical line.

8. On the layout's bottom row—the **Totals** row—click the text box that displays the value *5*. On the **Design tab**, in the **Grouping & Totals group**, click the **Totals** button, and then click **Count Records** to remove the Count Records control from the report.

9. In the **Totals** row, click the first empty cell. Press and hold Shift while clicking the third empty cell in the row.

10. With the three cells selected, on the **Arrange tab**, in the **Merge/Split group**, click the **Merge** button.

11. Click the cell just merged, and then using your own name, type Lastname_Firstname_a04_Classes Press Enter, and then compare your screen with **Figure 4**.

12. Click **Save** 🖫. Leave the report open for the next skill.

■ **You have completed Skill 2 of 10**

► When you need to print a report, you can adjust its margins and orientation to fit the size of a sheet of paper. You may also need to remove extra space from the report to prevent printing blank pages.

1. With the **Instructors without a W-4** report still open in Layout view, double-click the report title to enter Edit mode. To the right of *W-4*, add a space and then type Form

2. Click a blank area below the layout to leave Edit mode. On the **Design tab**, in the **Header / Footer group**, click the **Logo** button. In the **Insert Picture** dialog box, navigate to the student files, select **a04_Classes_Logo**, and then click **OK**.

3. On the status bar, click the **Print Preview** button. In the **Zoom group**, click the **Two Pages** button, and then compare your screen with **Figure 1**.

   The first column is very close to the edge of the paper and the Phone column is on another sheet of paper.

4. In the **Page Size group**, click the **Margins** button, and then click **Normal**.

5. In the **Page Layout group**, click the **Landscape** button, and then compare your screen with **Figure 2**.

   When you modify a report so that all the controls fit within a single sheet of paper, some report elements may still extend to a second sheet of paper. When this happens, a warning displays that the second sheet will be empty.

■ **Continue to the next page to complete the skill**

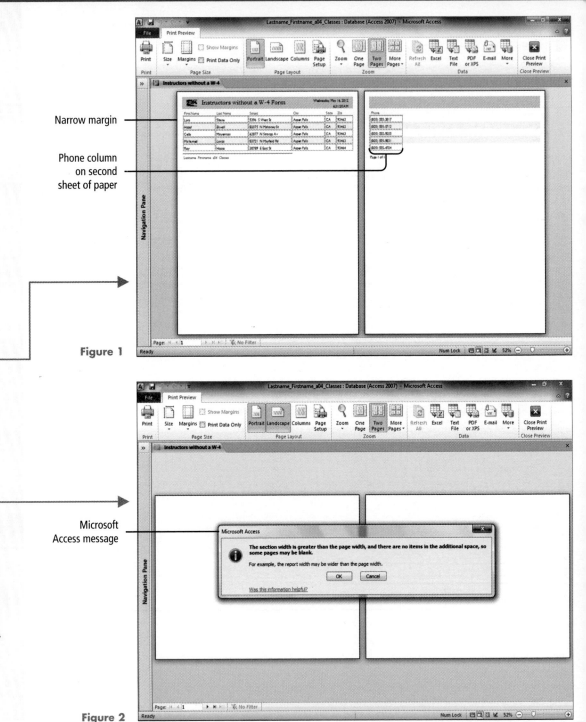

Narrow margin

Phone column on second sheet of paper

Figure 1

Microsoft Access message

Figure 2

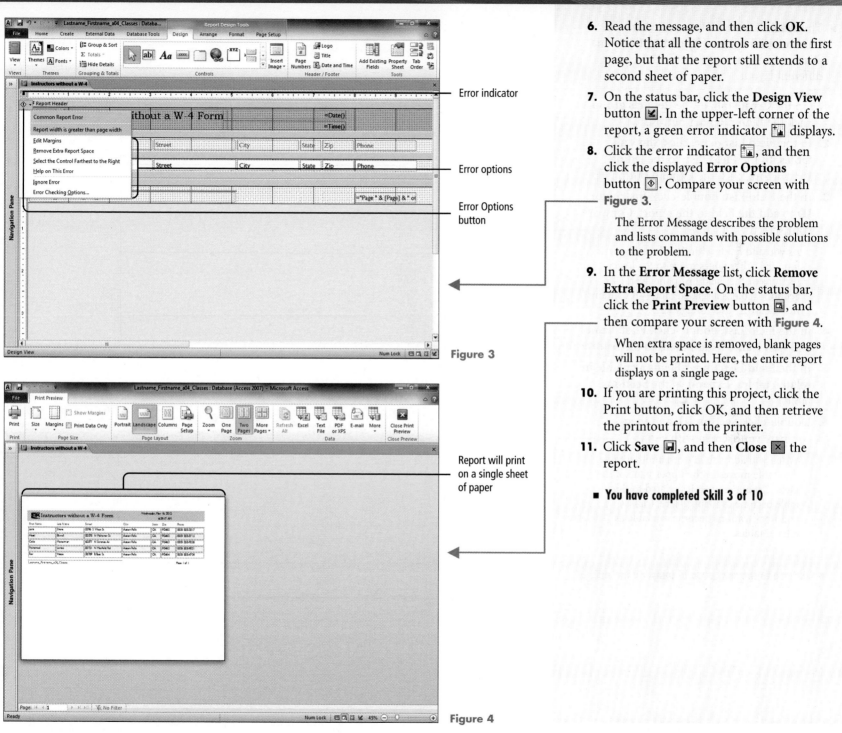

Error indicator

Error options

Error Options button

Figure 3

Report will print on a single sheet of paper

Figure 4

6. Read the message, and then click **OK**. Notice that all the controls are on the first page, but that the report still extends to a second sheet of paper.

7. On the status bar, click the **Design View** button 🖳. In the upper-left corner of the report, a green error indicator 🖬 displays.

8. Click the error indicator 🖬, and then click the displayed **Error Options** button ⬦. Compare your screen with **Figure 3**.

   The Error Message describes the problem and lists commands with possible solutions to the problem.

9. In the **Error Message** list, click **Remove Extra Report Space**. On the status bar, click the **Print Preview** button 🔍, and then compare your screen with **Figure 4**.

   When extra space is removed, blank pages will not be printed. Here, the entire report displays on a single page.

10. If you are printing this project, click the Print button, click OK, and then retrieve the printout from the printer.

11. Click **Save** 🖬, and then **Close** ⊠ the report.

   ■ **You have completed Skill 3 of 10**

▶ The Blank Report tool is used when you want to build a report by adding fields one at a time or to arrange the fields in a different layout.

1. On the **Create tab**, in the **Reports group**, click the **Blank Report** button.

2. In the **Field List pane**, click **Show all tables**. In the **Field List**, to the left of **Instructors**, click the **Expand** button ⊞.

3. In the **Field List**, double-click **Instructor ID** to add the field to the report. Compare your screen with **Figure 1**.

> As you add fields with the Blank Report tool, the other tables move to the lower sections of the Field List pane. Here, the Sections table is a related table—it contains Instructor ID as a foreign key.

4. In the **Field List**, double-click **First Name** and **Last Name** to add them to the report.

5. In the **Field List**, under **Fields available in related tables**, **Expand** ⊞ the **Sections** table.

6. Double-click **Section ID**, and then compare your screen with **Figure 2**.

> When you add a field from another table, that table moves to the upper pane of the Field List and any tables related to this table become available. Here, Classes and Registrations become available as related tables.

■ **Continue to the next page to complete the skill** ➤

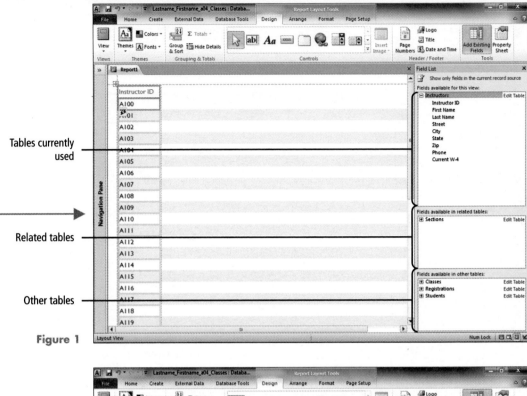

Tables currently used

Related tables

Other tables

Figure 1

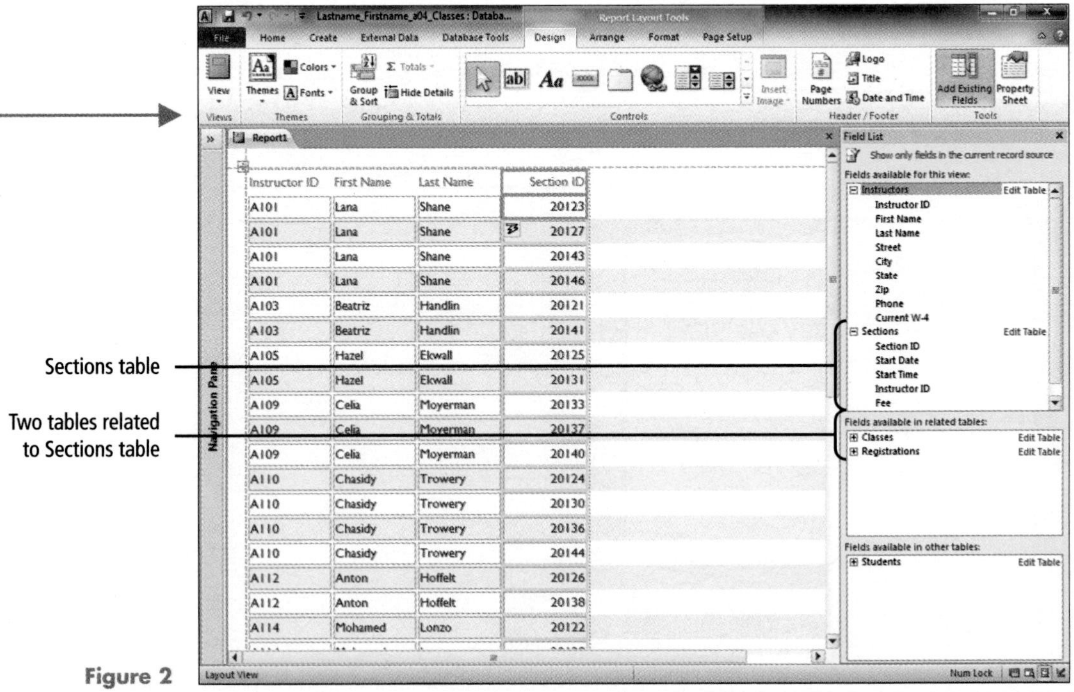

Sections table

Two tables related to Sections table

Figure 2

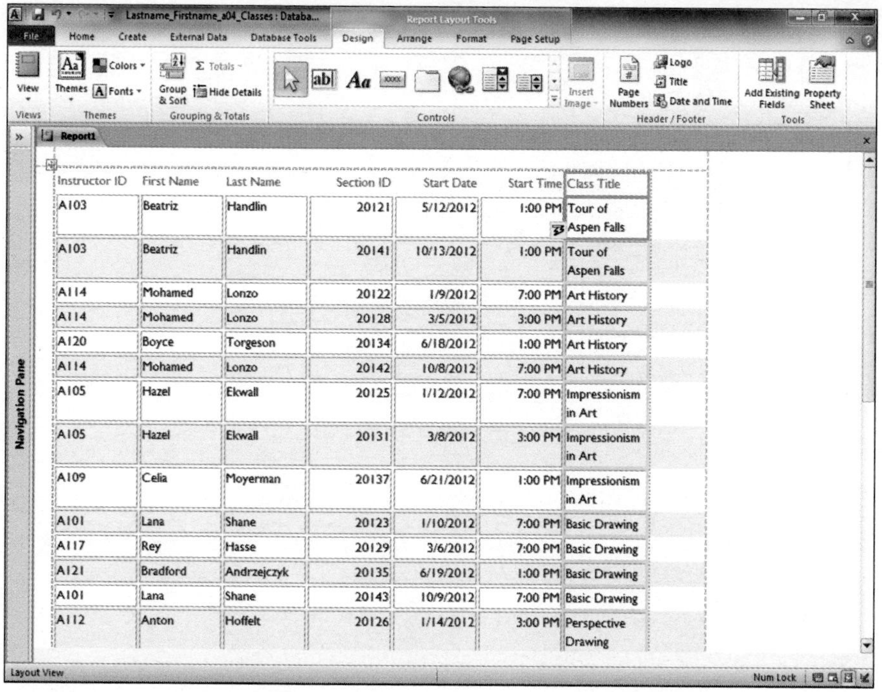

Figure 3

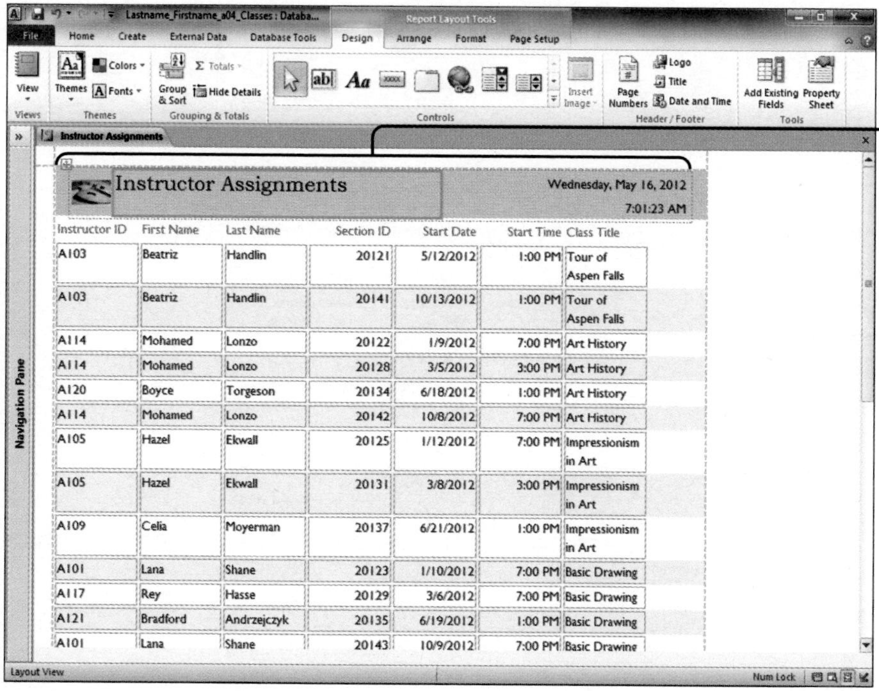

Controls added to report header

Figure 4

7. In the **Field List**, under **Sections**, double-click **Start Date** and **Start Time** to add the two fields to the report.

8. In the **Field List**, under **Fields available in related tables**, **Expand** ⊞ the **Classes** table. Double-click **Class Title** to add it to the report.

9. **Close** ⊠ the **Field List**, and then compare your screen with **Figure 3**.

10. In the **Header/Footer group**, click the **Logo** button. In the **Insert Picture** dialog box, navigate to the student files, select **a04_Classes_Logo**, and then click **OK**.

11. On the **Design tab**, in the **Header / Footer group**, click the **Title** button, type Instructor Assignments and then press Enter.

12. In the **Header/Footer group**, click the **Date and Time** button. In the **Date and Time** dialog box, click **OK**.

13. Click **Save** 🔲. In the **Save As** dialog box, type Instructor Assignments and then press Enter. Compare your screen with **Figure 4**.

14. Leave the report open for the next skill.

■ **You have completed Skill 4 of 10**

► Report data can be grouped and sorted to add meaning to it.

1. If necessary, open the Instructor Assignments report in Layout view. In the **Grouping & Totals group**, click the **Group & Sort** button to display the **Group, Sort, and Total** pane.

2. In the **Group, Sort, and Total** pane, click the **Add a group** button. In the list of fields, click the **Instructor ID** field to group the classes by instructor.

3. Click one of the **First Name** text boxes, and then, with the 🔭 pointer, drag the control up to the empty cell to the right of the **Instructor ID** text box.

4. Repeat the technique just practiced to move the **Last Name** text box to the empty cell to the right of the **First Name** text box. Compare your screen with **Figure 1**.

Because the instructor names do not change within each group of Instructor IDs, they can be in the same row as the Instructor ID. In this way, the instructor name is not repeated in each section row.

5. At the top of the **Instructor ID** column, double-click the **Instructor ID** label to enter Edit mode. Change the label text to Instructor and then press Enter.

6. Click the **First Name** label, and then press Delete to remove the label from the report. Repeat this technique to delete the **Last Name** and **Section ID** labels. Compare your screen with **Figure 2**.

■ **Continue to the next page to complete the skill**

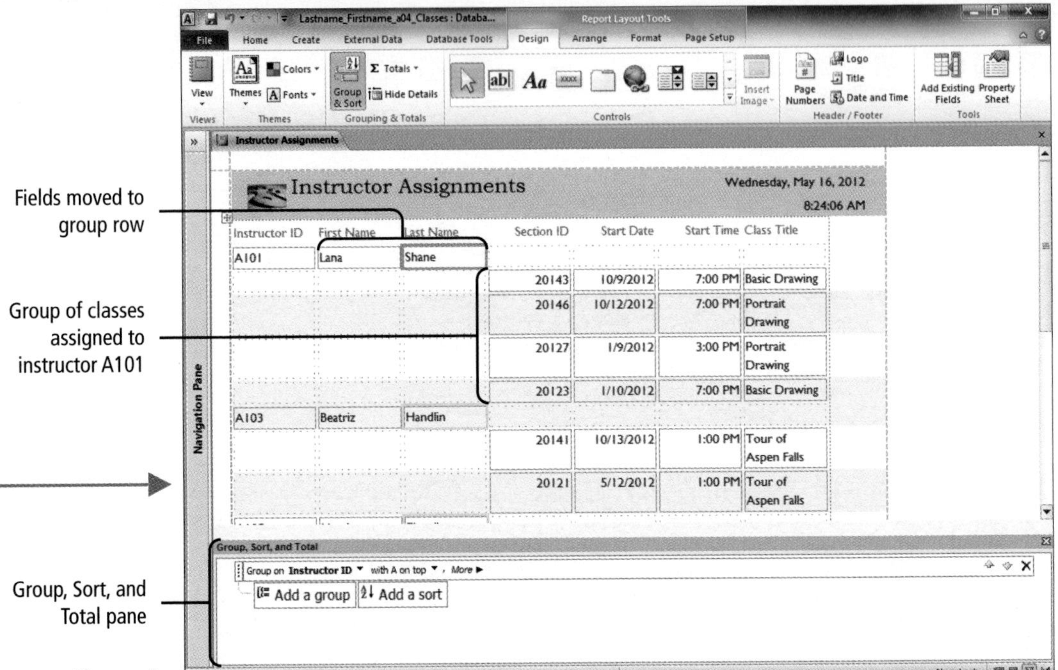

Fields moved to group row

Group of classes assigned to instructor A101

Group, Sort, and Total pane

Figure 1

Label text edited

Labels removed

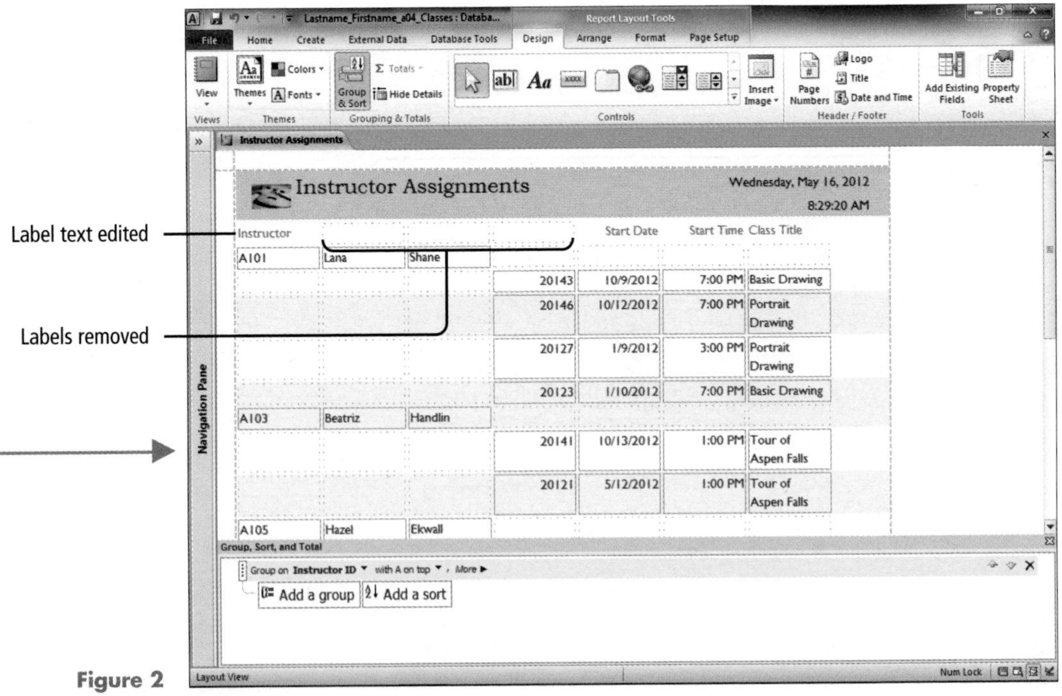

Figure 2

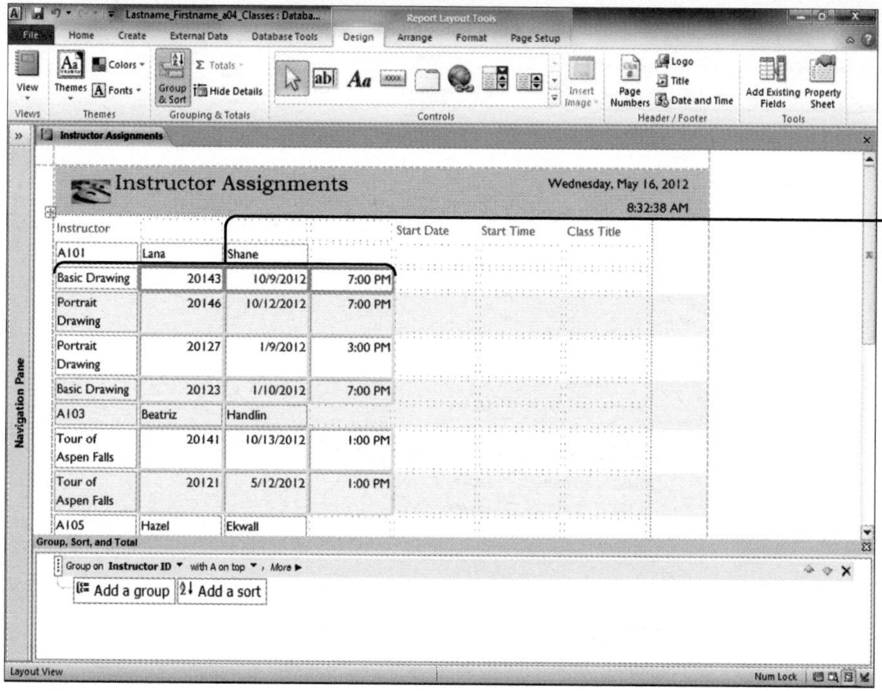

Columns rearranged

Figure 3

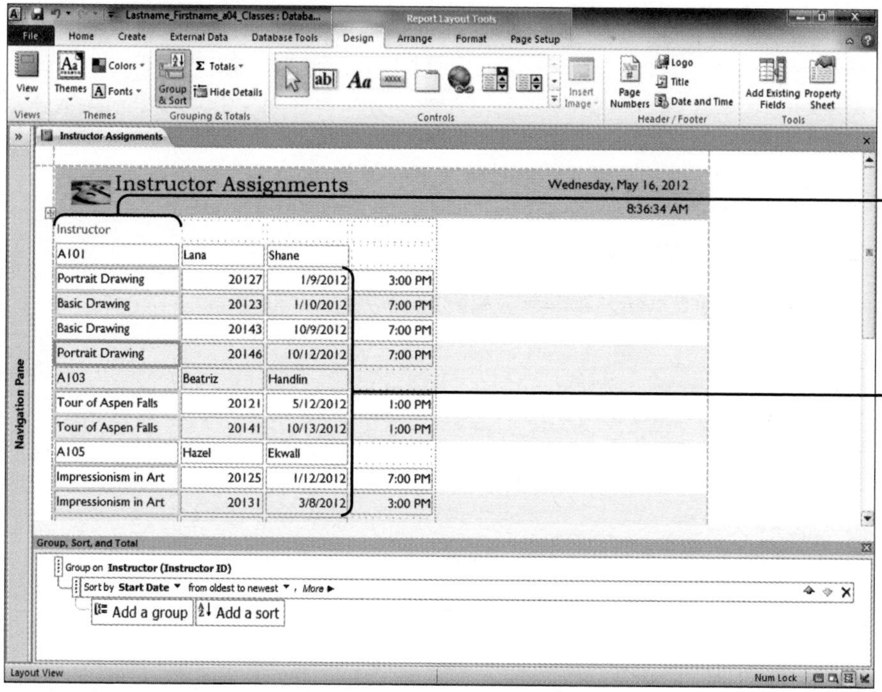

Column widened

Groups sorted by Start Date

Figure 4

7. Click one of the **Class Title** text boxes. With the ⬚ pointer, drag the text box into the left-most empty cell in that row.

8. Click one of the **Section ID** text boxes, press and hold Shift, and then click one of the **Start Time** text boxes. With the three columns selected, drag the selected **Section ID** text box into the left-most empty cell in that row. Compare your screen with **Figure 3**.

9. Click an empty cell below the **Start Date** label. On the **Arrange tab**, in the **Rows & Columns group**, click the **Select Column** button. Press Delete to remove the column from the report.

10. Repeat the technique just practiced to delete the two empty columns on the right side of the layout.

11. Select one of the **Class Title** text boxes, and then, on the **Design tab**, in the **Tools group**, click the **Property Sheet** button. Set the control's **Width** property to 1.5″

12. **Close** ⊠ the property sheet. In the **Group, Sort, and Total** pane, click the **Add a sort** button. In the list of fields, click **Start Date**. Compare your screen with **Figure 4**.

13. On the **Design tab**, in the **Grouping & Totals group**, click the **Group & Sort** button to close the pane.

14. **Save** 🖫 the report. Leave the report open for the next skill.

■ **You have completed Skill 5 of 10**

- Reports can be formatted to clarify the information that they contain. For example, group headings should be formatted to stand out from the details within each group.

- You can filter a report to show a subset of the data.

1. With the **Instructor Assignments** report open in Layout view, click the **Instructor ID** text box with the value *A101*. On the **Format tab**, in the **Font group**, click the **Bold** button $\boxed{B}$.

2. With the **Instructor ID** text box still selected, in the **Font group**, click the **Font Size arrow**, and then click **12**.

3. With the **Instructor ID** text box still selected, in the **Font group**, double-click the **Format Painter** button $\boxed{\mathscr{J}}$. With the $\boxed{\mathbb{k}_\mathbb{A}}$ pointer, click the **First Name** text box with the value *Lana*. With the $\boxed{\mathbb{k}_\mathbb{A}}$ pointer, click the **Last Name** text box with the value *Shane*. Compare your screen with **Figure 1**.

   In this manner, the Format Painter can be used to copy all the formatting of one control to other controls. When the Format Painter is on, its button displays in gold on the Ribbon.

4. In the **Font group**, click the **Format Painter** button $\boxed{\mathscr{J}}$ one time to turn it off.

5. On the **Format tab**, in the **Selection group**, click the **Object arrow**, and then click **Group Header0**. Compare your screen with **Figure 2**.

   You can use the Selection group to select different objects in your report. Here, the entire header row for each group of instructors is selected.

■ **Continue to the next page to complete the skill**

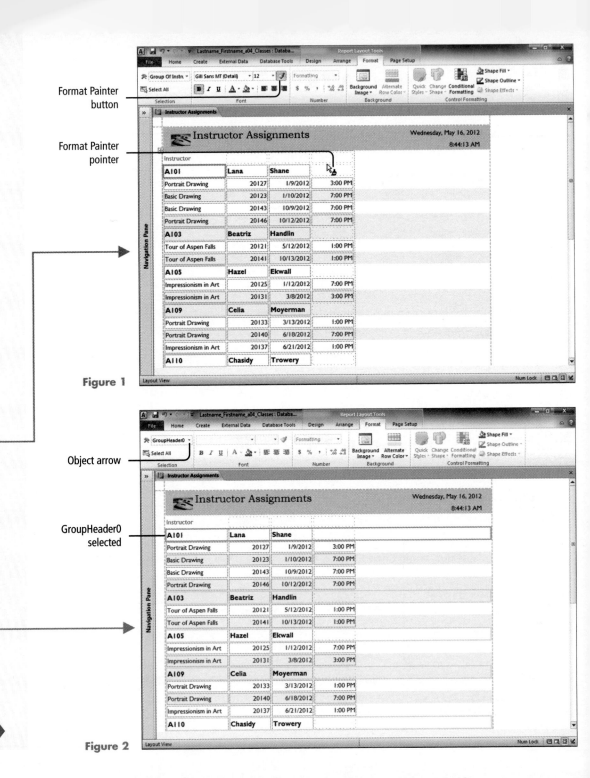

Format Painter button

Format Painter pointer

Figure 1

Object arrow

GroupHeader0 selected

Figure 2

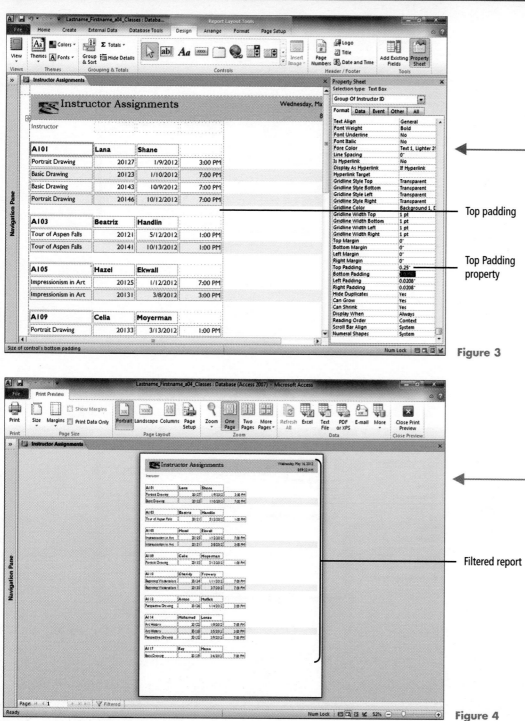

Figure 3

Figure 4

6. On the **Format tab**, in the **Background group**, click the **Alternate Row Color button arrow**, and then click **No Color**.

7. Click the **Instructor ID** text box with the value *A101*. On the **Design tab**, in the **Tools group**, click the **Property Sheet** button.

8. Scroll to the bottom of the property sheet **Format tab**. Change the **Top Padding** property to .25" Press Enter, and then compare your screen with **Figure 3**.

   Padding is the amount of space between a control's border and other controls on the form or report.

9. **Close** ☒ the property sheet. On the status bar, click the **Report View** button 🗔. Scroll down to view the list of instructors and their assigned classes.

10. Scroll to the top of the report. In the classes for Beatriz Handlin, click the text box with the value *5/12/2012*.

11. In the **Sort & Filter group**, click the **Selection** button, and then click **On or Before 5/12/2012** to filter the report.

12. On the status bar, click the **Print Preview** button 🗔. Compare your screen with **Figure 4**. If necessary, click the One Page button.

13. If you are printing your work, print the report.

14. Click **Save** 🗗, and then **Close** ☒ the report. **Open** ⏩ the **Navigation Pane**.

   ■ **You have completed Skill 6 of 10**

▶ A ***label report*** is a report formatted so that the data can be printed on a sheet of labels.

1. In the **Navigation Pane**, under **Queries**, double-click **Central Students** to display the records for students from the Central neighborhood.
2. In the first record, change *Eliseo* and *Brennan* to your own first and last names.
3. **Close** [×] the query, and then on the **Create tab**, in the **Reports group**, click the **Labels** button.
4. In the **Label Wizard**, be sure that the **Filter by manufacturer** box displays the text **Avery**. Under **What label size would you like**, select the label size where **Product number** is **C2160**, as shown in **Figure 1**.

   Each manufacturer identifies its label sheets using a product number. Access formats the report to match the dimensions of the selected sheet.
5. Click **Next**. If necessary, change the Font name to Arial and the Font weight to Light. Change the **Font size** to **10**.
6. Click **Next**. Under **Available fields**, click **First Name**, and then click the **Move** [>] button to add the field to the Prototype label.
7. With the insertion point in the **Prototype label** and to the right of *{First Name}*, add a space, and then **Move** [>] the **Last Name** field into the first line of the **Prototype label**.
8. Press Enter, and then **Move** [>] the **Street** field into the second line of the **Prototype label**. Compare your screen with **Figure 2**.

■ **Continue to the next page to complete the skill**

Label Wizard

Product number is C2160

Manufacturer is Avery

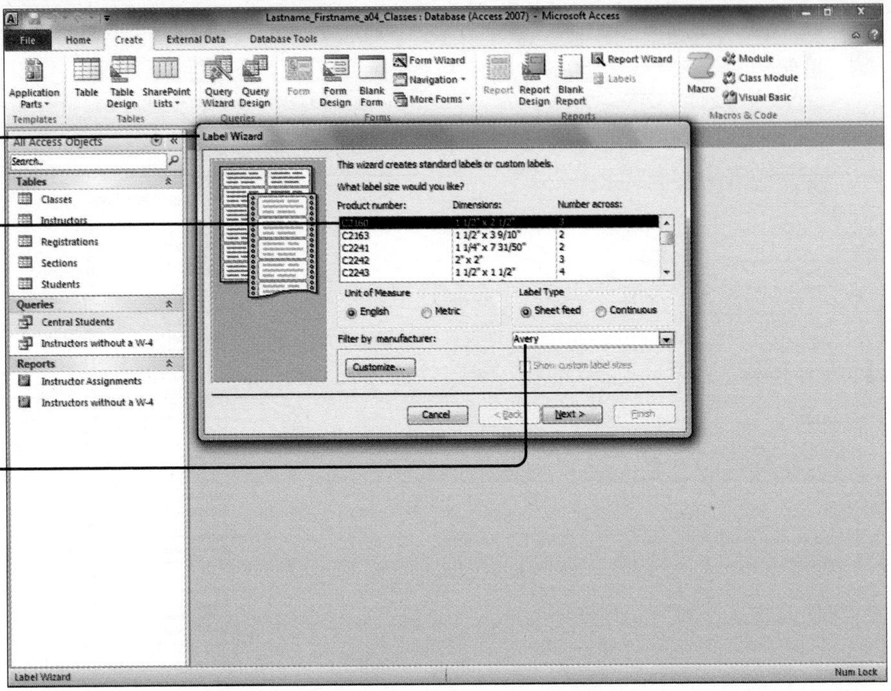

Figure 1

Fields added to Prototype label

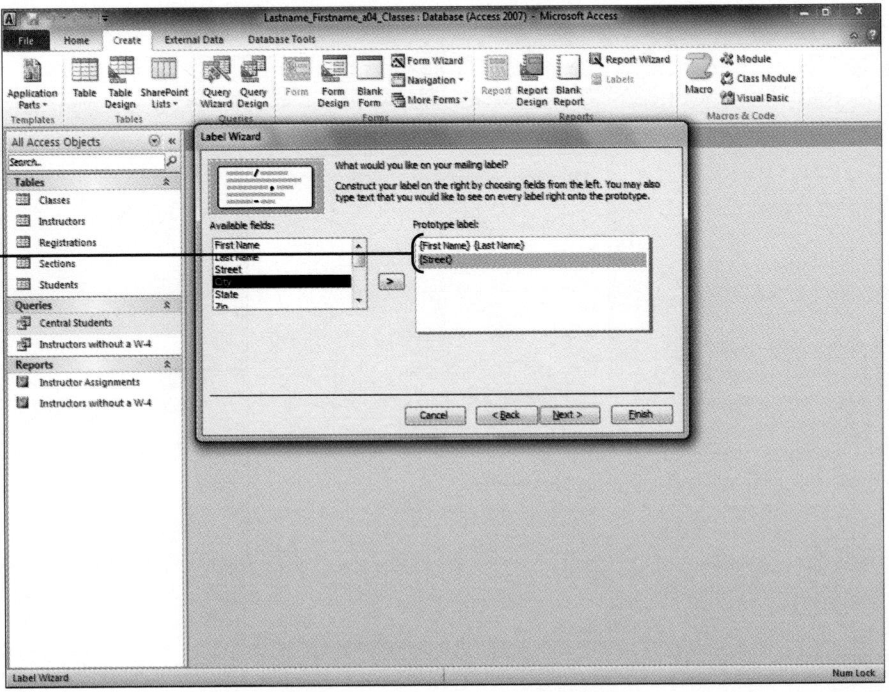

Figure 2

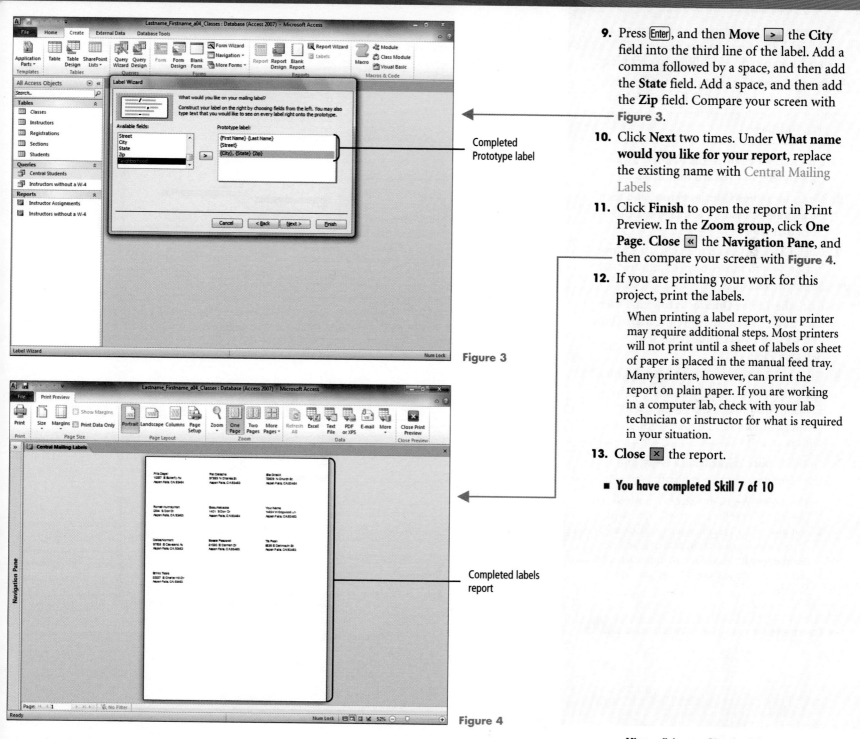

Completed
Prototype label

Figure 3

Completed labels
report

Figure 4

9. Press Enter, and then **Move** ▶ the **City** field into the third line of the label. Add a comma followed by a space, and then add the **State** field. Add a space, and then add the **Zip** field. Compare your screen with **Figure 3**.

10. Click **Next** two times. Under **What name would you like for your report**, replace the existing name with Central Mailing Labels

11. Click **Finish** to open the report in Print Preview. In the **Zoom group**, click **One Page. Close** « the **Navigation Pane**, and then compare your screen with **Figure 4**.

12. If you are printing your work for this project, print the labels.

> When printing a label report, your printer may require additional steps. Most printers will not print until a sheet of labels or sheet of paper is placed in the manual feed tray. Many printers, however, can print the report on plain paper. If you are working in a computer lab, check with your lab technician or instructor for what is required in your situation.

13. **Close** ✕ the report.

■ **You have completed Skill 7 of 10**

▶ The Report Wizard can be used when you need fields from multiple tables. In the wizard, you can preview different groupings.

▶ After you create a report using the Report Wizard, it displays in Print Preview. When you close Print Preview, the report displays in Design view.

1. On the **Create tab**, in the **Reports group**, click the **Report Wizard** button.

2. Click the **Tables/Queries arrow**, and then click **Table: Classes** to display the fields from that table.

3. Click **Class Title**, and then click the **Move** button ▷ to move the field into the **Selected Fields** list.

4. Click the **Tables/Queries arrow**, and then click **Table: Sections**. Move the **Start Date**, and then the **Start Time** fields into **Selected Fields**.

5. Click the **Tables/Queries arrow**, and then click **Table: Students**. Move the following fields in this order: **First Name**, **Last Name**, and **Phone**. Compare your screen with **Figure 1**.

6. In the **Report Wizard**, click **Next**, and then compare your screen with **Figure 2**.

   The Report Wizard has screens in which you can change how the report will be viewed and grouped. Here, the report is grouped by Class Title—each section of a class will be listed under its Class Title. Within each section, the students in that section will be listed.

■ **Continue to the next page to complete the skill**

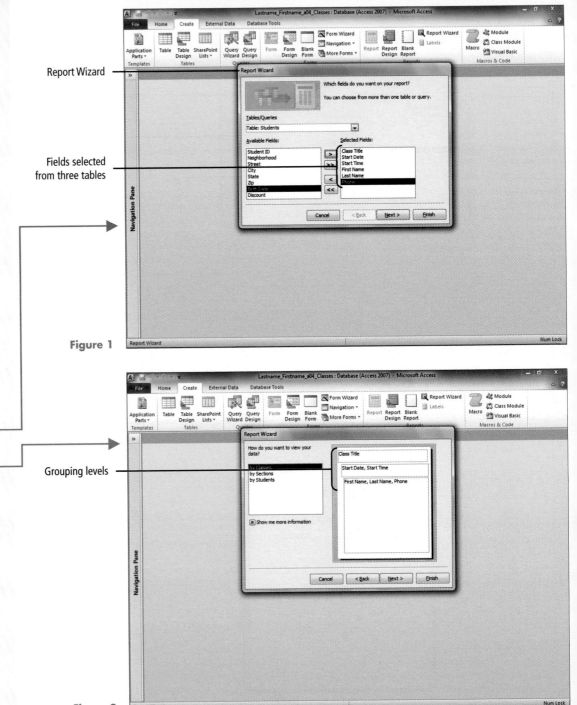

Report Wizard

Fields selected from three tables

Figure 1

Grouping levels

Figure 2

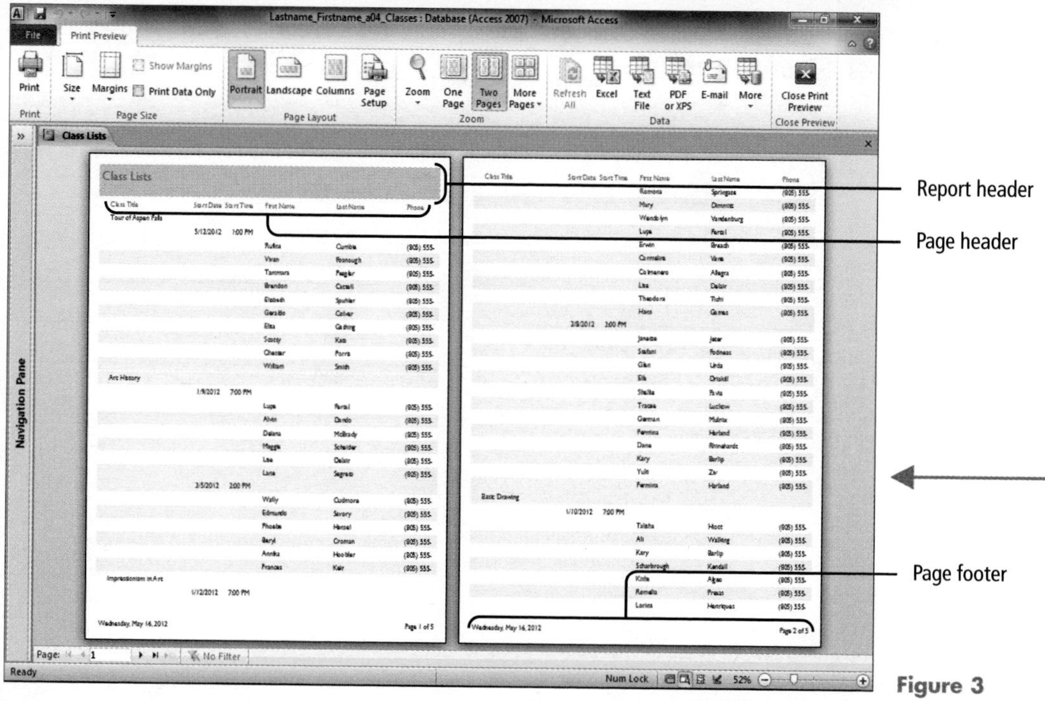

Figure 3

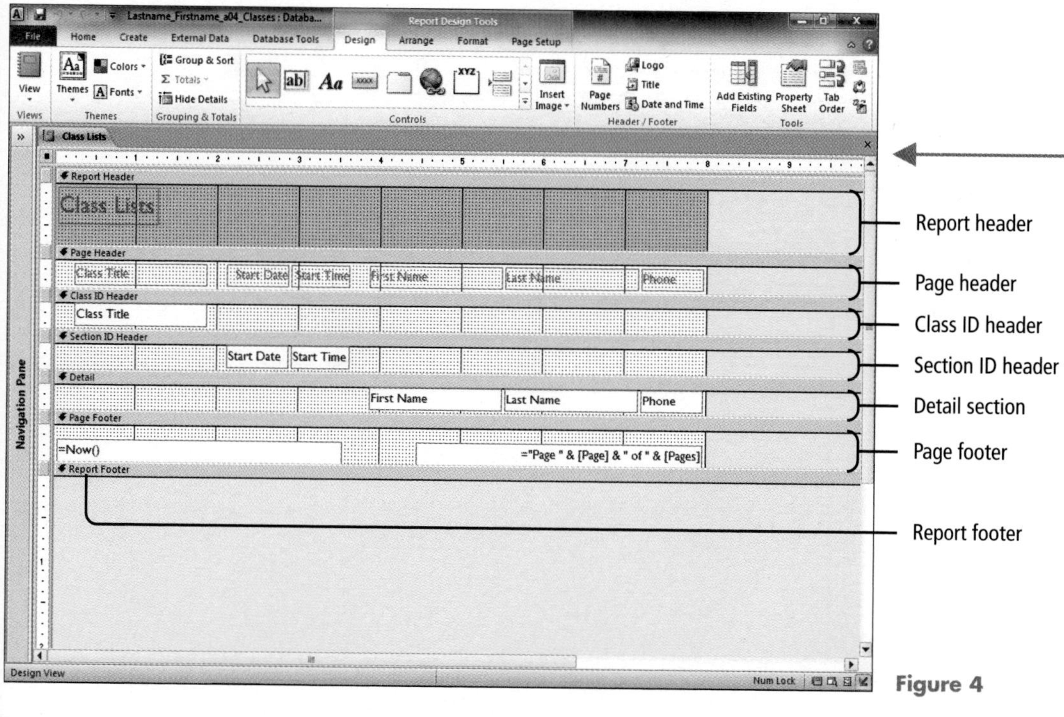

Figure 4

7. Click **Next** four times to accept the default Report Wizard settings for grouping, sorting, and layout.

8. Under **What title do you want for your report**, replace the value with Class Lists

9. Click **Finish**. In the **Zoom group**, click the **Two Pages** button. Compare your screen with **Figure 3**.

   A **report header** is an area at the beginning of a report that contains labels, text boxes, and other controls. Here, the report title, *Class Lists*, is in the report header.

   Page headers are areas at the top of each page that contain labels, text boxes, and other controls. Here, the labels for each column are in the page header.

   Page footers are areas at the bottom of each page that contain labels, text boxes, and other controls. Here, the date and page number text boxes are in the page footer.

10. Click the **Close Print Preview** button, and then compare your screen with **Figure 4**.

   In Design view, each report section has a bar above it with that section's name, and each group has its own header.

   In the Detail section, text boxes display in one row, and a sample of the data is not displayed or repeated for each record.

   A **report footer** is an area at the end of a report that contains labels, text boxes, and other controls. Here, the report has no report footer and the area below its bar is collapsed.

11. Leave the report open for the next skill.

- **You have completed Skill 8 of 10**

► Design view can be used when you want more control over your layout.

1. If necessary, open the Class Lists report in Design view. In the **Report Header**, click the **Title** control one time, and then press Delete.

2. Just above the **Page Header** bar, point to the lower edge of the **Report Header**. When the ⊞ pointer displays, drag up, as shown in **Figure 1**.

   You can remove report headers and footers by deleting their controls and decreasing the section's height to zero.

3. In the **Page Header**, click the **Class Title** label. Press and hold Shift and then, in the **Page Header**, click each of the remaining labels. With the six labels selected, press Delete to remove the labels.

4. Point to the lower edge of the **Page Header**, and then with the ⊞ pointer, drag up to set the **Page Header** height to zero.

5. In the **Class ID Header**, click the **Class Title** text box. Press ← approximately five times to move the control one grid dot from the left edge of the report.

6. With the **Class Title** text box still selected, on the **Format** tab, in the **Font group**, click the **Bold** button. In the **Font group**, click the **Font Size arrow**, and then click **14**.

7. With the ↔ pointer, increase the width of the **Class Title** text box so that the control's right edge is on the **4 inch** vertical grid line. Compare your screen with **Figure 2**.

■ **Continue to the next page to complete the skill** ➤

Report Header height set to zero

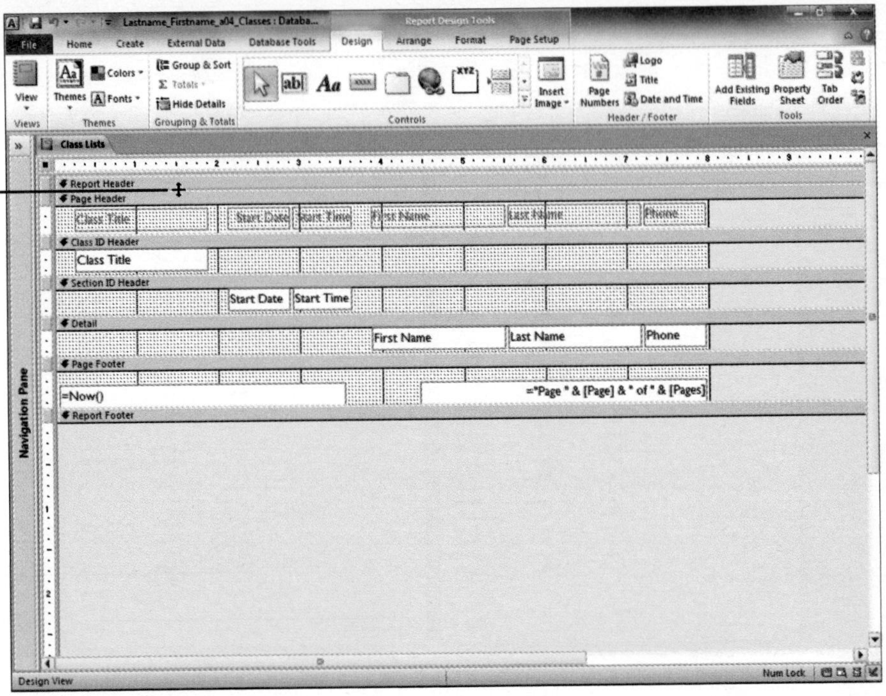

Figure 1

Page Header height set to zero

Class Title text box moved, formatted, and resized

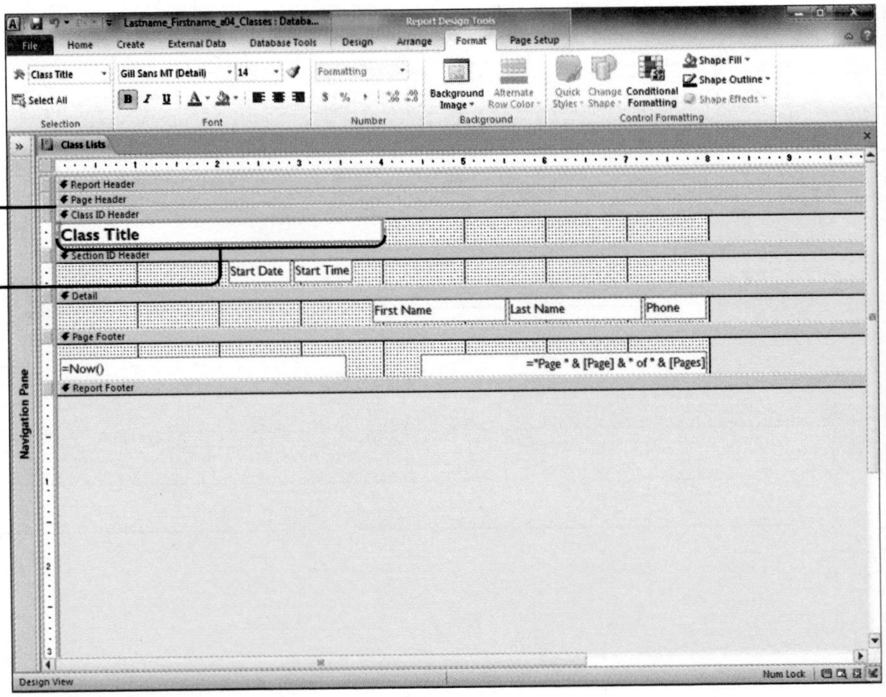

Figure 2

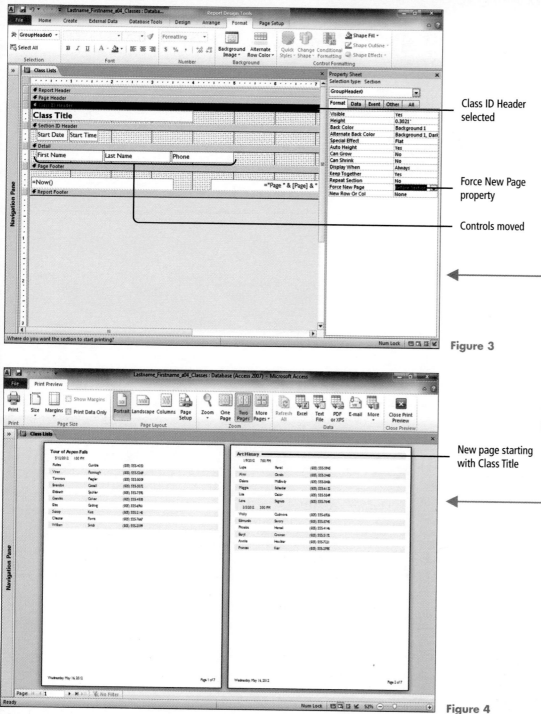

Class ID Header selected

Force New Page property

Controls moved

Figure 3

New page starting with Class Title

Figure 4

8. In the **Section ID Header**, click the **Start Date** text box. Press and hold Shift while clicking the **Start Time** text box. With the two controls selected, repeatedly press ← until the left edge of the **Start Date** control is four grid dots from the left edge of the report.

9. In the **Detail** section, repeat the technique just practiced to select all three controls. Move the three selected controls so that the left edge of the **First Name** control is four grid dots from the left edge of the report.

10. Click a blank area of the report to deselect the controls. With the ↔ pointer, increase the width of the **Phone** text box so that the control's right edge is on the **5 inch** vertical grid line.

11. Double-click the **Class ID Header** bar to select the section and to display its properties.

12. In the property sheet **Format tab**, click the **Force New Page** box. Click the displayed **arrow**, and then click **Before Section**. Compare your screen with **Figure 3**.

13. **Close** ☒ the property sheet. On the status bar, click the **Print Preview** button 🔍, and then compare your screen with **Figure 4**.

    Forcing a new page before a report header starts a new page for each new value in the header. Here, a new page starts with each class title.

14. Click **Save** 💾, and then click the **Close Print Preview** button. Leave the report open for the next skill.

■ **You have completed Skill 9 of 10**

► In Design view, you can work directly with *calculated controls*—text boxes that display the results of expressions.

1. If necessary, open the Class Lists report in Design view. Point to the lower edge of the **Page Footer**. When the ⊞ pointer displays, use the vertical ruler to drag the bar down approximately half an inch. Compare your screen with **Figure 1**.

2. On the **Design tab**, in the **Controls group**, click the **Label** button Aa. Position the ⁺A pointer approximately two grid dots below the =**Now()** text box and approximately 1 grid dot from the left edge of the report. Click one time to insert the label.

3. In the label just inserted, using your own name, type Lastname_Firstname_a04_Classes and then press Enter. Click the **Error Options** button ◈ that displays, and then compare your screen with **Figure 2**.

    When you insert a label in a page footer that does not describe a text box, an error message displays.

4. In the **Error Options** list, click **Ignore Error**.

5. In the **Detail** section, click the **Phone** text box. On the **Design tab**, in the **Grouping & Totals group**, click the **Totals** button, and then click **Count Records**.

    When you add a summary statistic, a calculated control is inserted for each group. Here, the expression =*Count(*)* counts the number of phone numbers within each section, within each class, and for the entire report.

■ **Continue to the next page to complete the skill** ▶

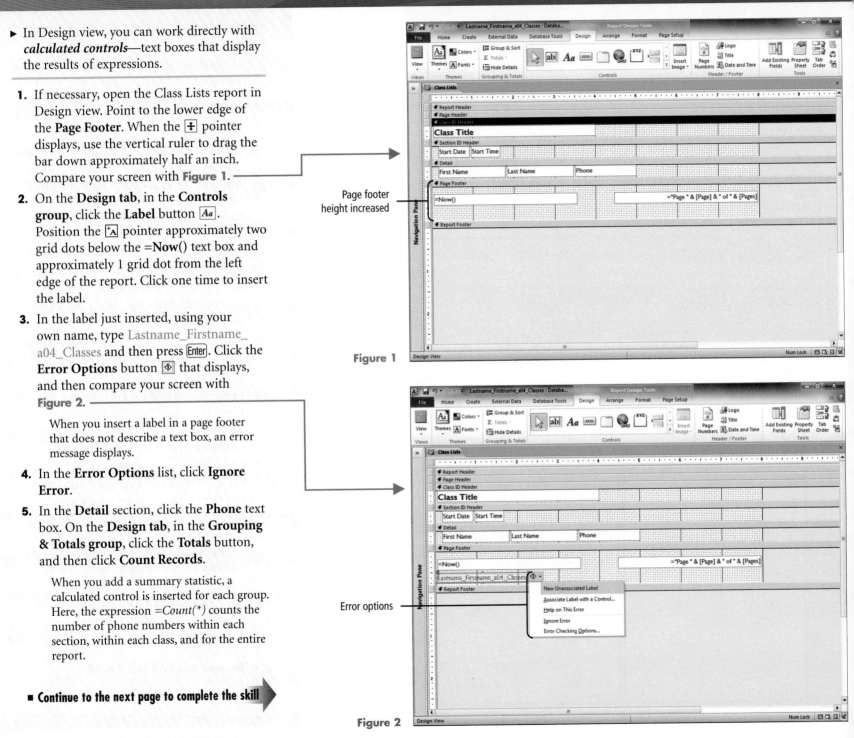

Page footer height increased

Figure 1

Error options

Figure 2

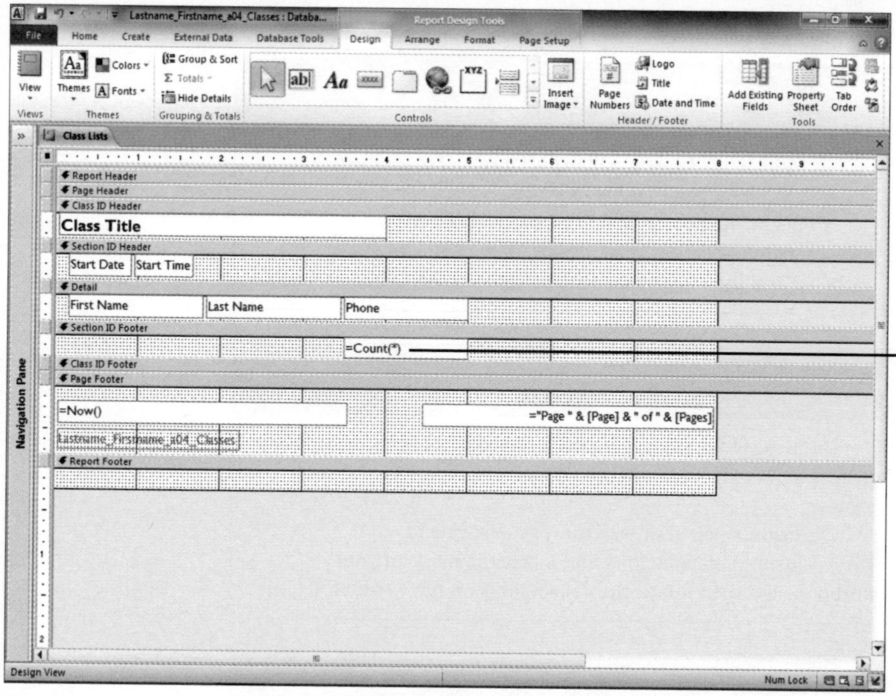

Count Records calculated control

Figure 3

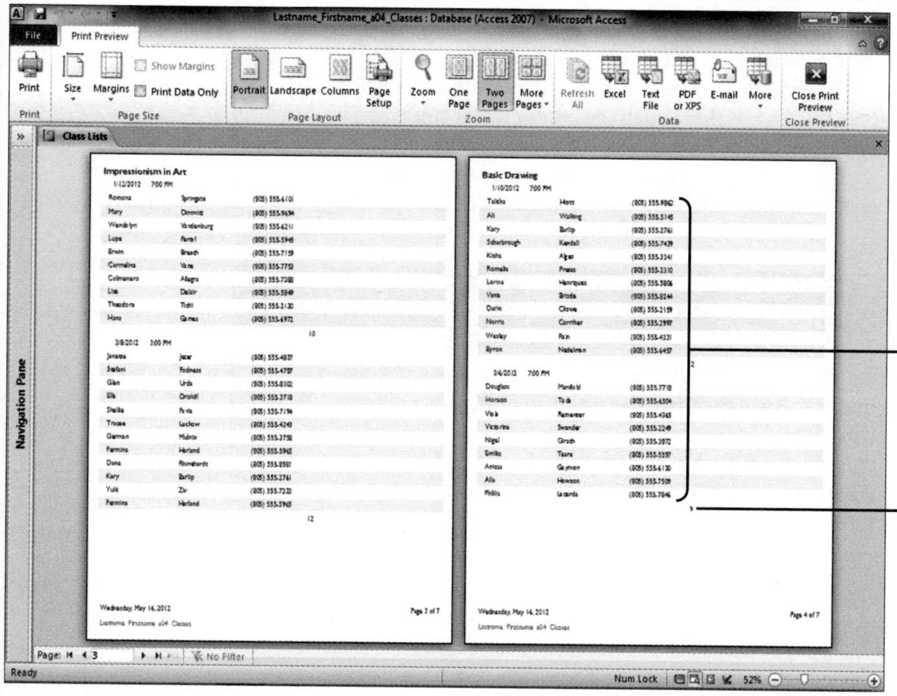

Students in two sections of Basic Drawing class

Class count

Figure 4

6. In the **Class ID Footer**, click the **=Count(*)** text box, and then press Delete. Drag to set the **Class ID Footer** height to zero. In the **Report Footer**, delete the **=Count(*)** text box. Compare your screen with **Figure 3**.

7. Click the **Class ID Header** bar to select the header. On the **Format tab**, in the **Background group**, click the **Alternate Row Color button arrow**, and then click **No Color**.

8. Click the **Section ID Header** bar, and then repeat the technique just practiced to set the **Alternate Row Color** to **No Color**. Repeat to remove the alternating row color from the **Section ID Footer**.

9. On the status bar, click the **Print Preview** button . On the Navigation bar, click the **Next Page** button to display page three and four. Compare your screen with **Figure 4**.

10. Click the **Print** button. In the **Print** dialog box, under **Print Range**, click in the **From** box, and then type 3 Click in the **To** box, and then type 3 If you are printing this project, click OK. Otherwise, click Cancel.

11. Click **Save** , and then **Close** the report.

12. **Open** the **Navigation Pane**, and then **Exit** Access. Submit your printouts or the database file as directed by your instructor.

Done! You have completed Skill 10 of 10 and your database is complete.

More Skills

The following More Skills are located at **www.pearsonhighered.com/skills**

More Skills 11   Export Reports to Word

You can export reports to other file formats so that you can work with the data in other applications. For example, you can export a report so that it can be opened in Word or sent as an email attachment.

In More Skills 11, you will export a report to another file format and then open that file in Word.

To begin, open your web browser, navigate to www.pearsonhighered.com/skills, locate the name of your textbook, and then follow the instructions on the website.

More Skills 12   Export Reports as HTML Documents

You can export reports so that they can be opened in a web browser. In this manner, reports can be published and shared on the World Wide Web.

In More Skills 12, you export a report as a Hypertext Markup Language (HTML) document and view the report in your web browser.

To begin, open your web browser, navigate to www.pearsonhighered.com/skills, locate the name of your textbook, and then follow the instructions on the website.

More Skills 13   Create Parameter Queries

You can build a query that asks you to type the criterion that should be applied. In this way, a single query can return several different data subsets depending on the values you type when the query is run.

In More Skills 13, you will create a parameter query that asks for a criterion. You will then run the query several times and type a different criterion each time. Each time, the query will display only the records that match the criterion that you type.

To begin, open your web browser, navigate to www.pearsonhighered.com/skills, locate the name of your textbook, and then follow the instructions on the website.

More Skills 14   Create Reports for Parameter Queries

You can use reports based on parameter queries. When the report is opened, it asks for a criterion and the report will display a subset of the data based on the value you type. In this manner, you can use a single report to display a variety of results without having to create multiple queries and reports.

In More Skills 14, create a report based on a parameter query. You will then run the report to display two different sets of data.

To begin, open your web browser, navigate to www.pearsonhighered.com/skills, locate the name of your textbook, and then follow the instructions on the website.

Key Terms

Online Help Skills

1. **Start** Access. In the upper-right corner of the Access window, click the **Help** button . In the **Help** window, click the **Maximize** button.

2. Click in the search box, type Introduction to Controls and then click the **Search** button. In the search results, click **Introduction to controls**.

3. Read the article's introduction, and then below **In this article**, click **Understand layouts**. Compare your screen with **Figure 1**.

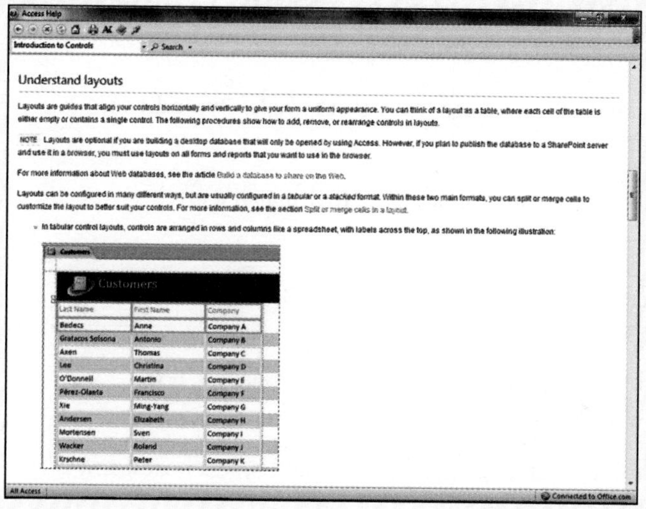

Figure 1

4. Read the **Understand layouts** section to see if you can answer the following: How are tabular control layouts different than stacked control layouts? How are they the same?

Matching

Match each term in the second column with its correct definition in the first column by writing the letter of the term on the blank line in front of the correct definition.

_____ **1.** Cells arranged in rows and columns into which controls are placed.

_____ **2.** To combine two or more cells in a tabular layout.

_____ **3.** This is used when you want to build a report by adding fields one at a time or arrange them in a different layout.

_____ **4.** A small picture that can be added to a report header, typically to the left of the title.

_____ **5.** To display a subset of records on a report that match a given criterion.

_____ **6.** The amount of space between a control's border and other controls on the form or report.

_____ **7.** An area at the beginning of a report that contains labels, text boxes, and other controls.

_____ **8.** An area at the top of each page that contains labels, text boxes, and other controls.

_____ **9.** An area at the bottom of each page that contains labels, text boxes, and other controls.

_____ **10.** An area at the end of a report that contains labels, text boxes, and other controls.

A Blank Report tool

B Filter

C Layout

D Logo

E Merge

F Padding

G Page Footer

H Page Header

I Report Footer

J Report Header

Multiple Choice

Choose the correct answer.

1. A tool that can create a report with a single click.
   A. Blank Report tool
   B. Report tool
   C. Report Wizard

2. A page orientation where the page is wider than it is tall.
   A. Landscape
   B. Portrait
   C. Wide

3. This can be removed from a report to prevent printing blank pages.
   A. Alternating row colors
   B. Extra space
   C. White space

4. This pane is used to add fields to a report in Layout view.
   A. Add Fields
   B. Blank Report
   C. Field List

5. This pane is used to group and sort reports.
   A. Group pane
   B. Group and Sort pane
   C. Group, Sort, and Total pane

6. A report formatted so that the data can be printed on a sheet of labels.
   A. Label report
   B. Mail report
   C. Merge report

7. This view is used when you want the most control over your report layout.
   A. Design view
   B. Layout view
   C. Print Preview

8. This property is changed when you need to add page breaks before report headers.
   A. Force New Page
   B. Padding
   C. Page Break

9. A text box that displays the result of an expression.
   A. Calculated control
   B. Expression box
   C. Label

10. When no alternating row color is desired, select this value.
    A. Blank
    B. None
    C. No Color

Topics for Discussion

1. You have created reports using three different methods: the Report tool, the Report Wizard, and the Blank Report tool. Which method do you prefer and why? What are the primary advantages of each method?

2. Consider the types of data that businesses might store in a database. For example, each instructor at a school needs a class roster listing each student in the class. What type of reports might other businesses need?

Skill Check

To complete this database, you will need the following files:

- a04_Outings
- a04_Outings_Logo

You will save your database as:

- Lastname_Firstname_a04_Outings

1. **Start** Access, and then open the student data file **a04_Outings**. Save the database in your **Access Chapter 4** folder with the name Lastname_Firstname_a04_Outings If necessary, enable the content.

2. On the **Create tab**, in the **Reports group**, click the **Blank Report** button. In the **Field List pane**, click **Show all tables**, and then expand the **Participants** table. Double-click to add the following fields: **First Name**, **Last Name**, and **Neighborhood**. Compare your screen with **Figure 1**. ────────

3. **Close** the **Field List** pane. In the **Themes group**, click the **Fonts** button, and then click the first theme font—**Office**.

4. In the **Header / Footer group**, click the **Logo** button. In the **Insert Picture** dialog box, navigate to the student files for this chapter, click **a04_Outings_Logo**, and then click **OK**.

5. In the **Header / Footer group**, click the **Title** button, type Central Neighborhood Participants and then press Enter.

6. In the **Grouping & Totals group**, click the **Group & Sort** button. In the **Group, Sort, and Total** pane, click **Add a group**, and then click **Neighborhood**.

7. Click the **Report View** button. In the **Sort & Filter group**, click the **Selection** button, and then click **Equals "Central"**.

8. Click **Save**, type Central Report and then click **OK**. Click the **Print Preview** button, and then compare your screen with **Figure 2**. If necessary, click the ──── One Page button.

9. If you are printing this project, print the report. **Close** the report.

10. On the **Create tab**, in the **Reports group**, click the **Report Wizard** button. If necessary, in the Report Wizard, click the Tables/Queries button, and click Table: Outings. Move the **Outing Name** and **Outing Date** fields into **Selected Fields**. Select the **Participants** table, move **First Name** and **Last Name**, and then click **Finish**.

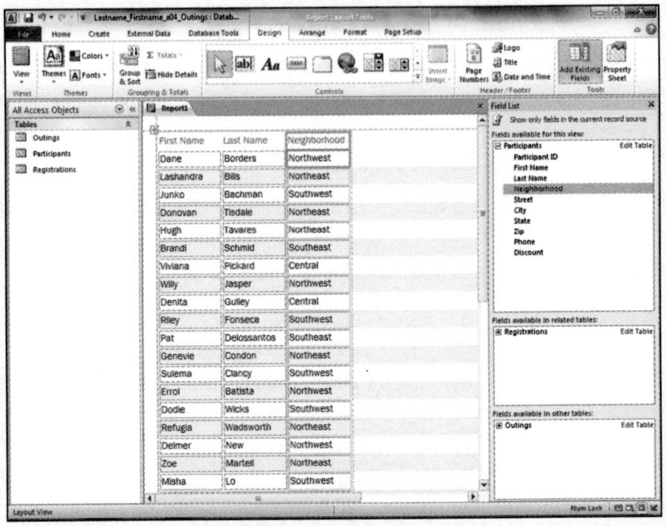

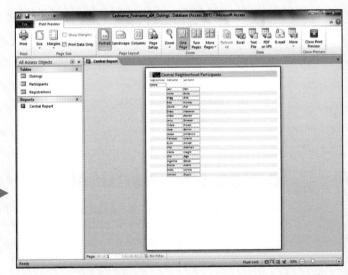

Figure 1

Figure 2

- Continue to the next page to complete this Skill Check

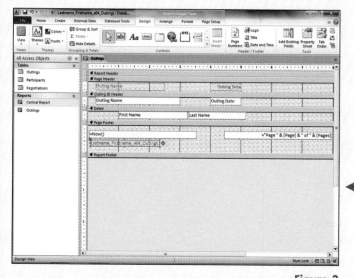

Figure 3

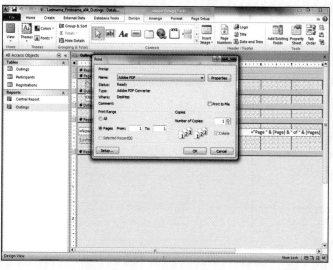

Figure 4

11. Click the **Close Print Preview** button. In the **Report Header**, click the **Title** control, and then press Delete. Drag the lower edge of the **Report Header** to set the section's height to zero.

12. In the **Page Header**, click the **First Name** label. Press and hold Shift, while clicking the **Last Name** label, and then press Delete.

13. In the **Page Header**, click the **Outing Date** label. In the **Outing ID Header**, press Shift while clicking the **Outing Date** text box. Press → repeatedly to place the right edge of the two controls on the **5 inch** vertical grid line.

14. In the **Outing ID Header**, click the **Outing Name** text box. Drag to increase the width of the text box so that its right edge is on the **3 inch** vertical grid line.

15. Click the **Outing ID Header**. On the **Format tab**, in the **Background group**, click the **Alternate Row Color button arrow**, and then click **No Color**.

16. Double-click the **Outing ID Header**, and then, in the property sheet **Format tab**, change the **Force New Page** property to **Before Section**. **Close** the property sheet.

17. Click the **Outing Name** text box, and then, on the **Format tab**, in the **Font group**, click the **Bold** button. In the **Font group**, click the **Font Color button arrow**, and then click the last color in the first row—**Blue-Gray, Accent 6**.

18. In the **Font group**, click the **Format Painter** button one time, and then, in the **Outing ID Header**, click the **Outing Date** text box to apply the formatting.

19. In the **Detail** section, click the **First Name** text box. Press Shift while clicking the **Last Name** text box. Press ← to place the left edge of the **First Name** field on the **1 inch** vertical grid line.

20. Point to the lower edge of the **Page Footer**, and then drag down to increase its height by approximately half an inch.

21. On the **Design tab**, in the **Controls group**, click the **Label** button. In the **Page Footer**, click approximately 1 grid dot below the **=Now()** calculated control and 1 grid dot from the left edge of the report. Using your own name, type Lastname_Firstname_a04_Outings Click **Save**, and then compare your screen with **Figure 3**.

22. On the **File tab**, click **Print**, and then click the **Print** button. Under **Print Range**, in the **From** box, type 1 In the **To** box, type 1 Compare your screen with **Figure 4**. If you are printing this project, click OK. Otherwise, click Cancel.

23. Click **Save, Close** the report, and then **Exit** Access. Submit as directed.

Done! You have completed the Skill Check

Assess Your Skills 1

To complete this database, you will need the following files:

- a04_Camps
- a04_Camps_Logo

You will save your file as:

- Lastname_Firstname_a04_Camps

1. **Start** Access, and then open the student data file **a04_Camps**. Save the database in your **Access Chapter 4** folder with the name Lastname_Firstname_a04_Camps

2. Use the **Blank Report** button to add these fields from the **Directors** table: **Director ID**, **First Name**, and **Last Name**. From the **Camps** table, add **Camp Name** and then **Start Date**.

3. Apply the **Equity** theme, and then apply the **Angles** theme font.

4. Add a logo using the file **a04_Camps_Logo**, and then add a title with the text Camp Directors

5. Group the report by **Director ID**, and then sort by **Start Date**.

6. Move the **First Name** text box up one row in the layout, and then move the **Last Name** text box up one row. Move the **Camp Name** text box to the row's first cell and the **Start Date** text box to the row's second cell.

7. Use the **Ribbon** to select **GroupHeader0**, and then remove the header's alternate row color.

8. Delete the two empty columns on the right of the report. Select the Director ID label, and then change its Top Padding property to 0.25" **Close** the property sheet, and then compare your screen with **Figure 1**.

9. **Save** the report as Camp Directors and then **Close** the report.

10. Use the **Report Wizard** button to add these fields from the **Camps** table: **Camp Name** and

Start Date. From the **Campers** table, add the **First Name**, **Last Name**, and **Parent/Guardian** fields. Accept all other wizard defaults.

11. In Design view, delete the report title, and then set the height of the **Report Header** to zero.

12. In the **Page Header**, delete the **First Name**, **Last Name**, and **Parent/Guardian** labels.

13. Increase the width of the **Start Date** text box so that its right edge is on the **3 inch** vertical grid line.

14. In the **Detail** section, select the three text boxes, and then move the **First Name** text box approximately six grid dots from the left edge of the report.

15. Select the **Camp ID Header**, remove the alternate row color, and then change its property to start a new page before each section.

16. Increase the height of the **Page Footer** by approximately half an inch. Below the =**Now()** calculated control, add a label with the file name as its text.

17. Filter the report to display only the campers registered in the **Yurok** camp. Click **Save**, and then compare your screen with **Figure 2**.

18. **Close** the report. If you are printing this project, print the two reports.

19. Click **Save**, and then **Exit** Access. Submit as directed by your instructor.

Done! You have completed Assess Your Skills 1

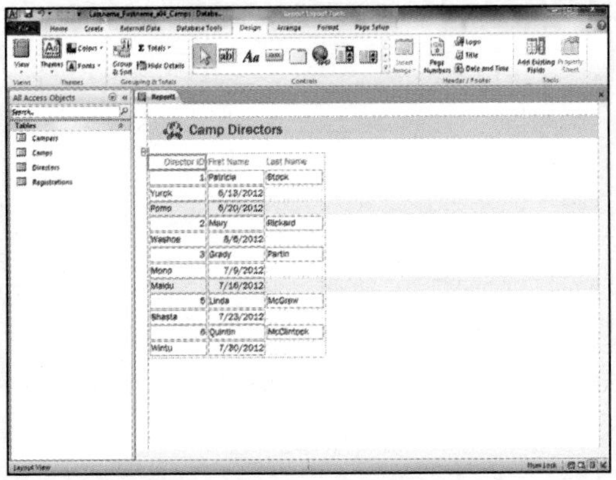

Figure 1

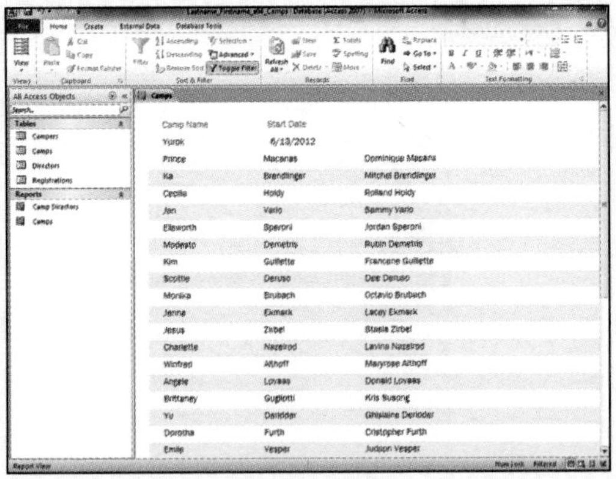

Figure 2

Assess Your Skills 2

Assess Your Skills 3 and 4 can be found at www.pearsonhighered.com/skills.

To complete this database, you will need the following files:

- a04_Reviews
- a04_Reviews_Logo

You will save your file as:

- Lastname_Firstname_a04_Reviews

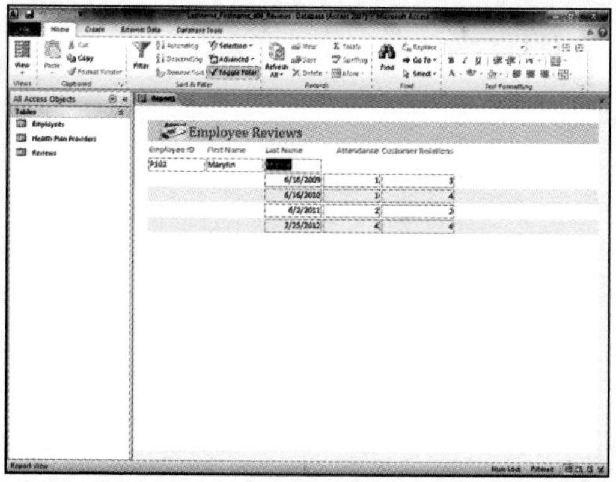

Figure 1

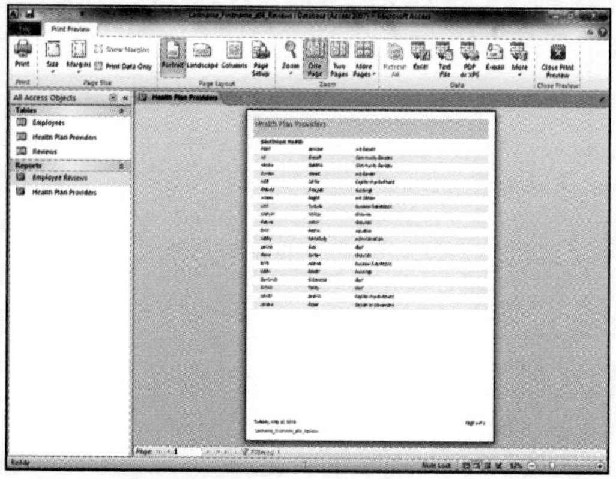

Figure 2

1. **Start** Access, and then open the student data file **a04_Reviews**. Save the database in your **Access Chapter 4** folder with the name Lastname_Firstname_a04_Reviews

2. Use the **Blank Report** button to add these fields from the **Employees** table: **Employee ID**, **First Name**, and **Last Name**. From the **Reviews** table, add **Review Date**, **Attendance**, and **Customer Relations**.

3. Apply the **Apex** theme, and then apply the **Office** theme font.

4. Add a logo using the file **a04_Reviews_Logo**, and then add a title with the text Employee Reviews

5. Group the report by **Employee ID**, and then sort by **Review Date**.

6. Move the **First Name** text box up one row in the layout, and then move the **Last Name** text box up one row. Move the **Review Date** text box one cell to the left, and then delete the empty column.

7. Filter the report so that only the records for *Marylin Mintor* display. Compare your screen with **Figure 1**.

8. **Save** the report as Employee Reviews If you are printing this project, print the report. **Close** the report.

9. Use the **Report Wizard** button to add the **Provider Name** field from the **Health Plan Providers** table: From the **Employees** table,

add the **First Name**, **Last Name**, and **Department** fields. Accept all other wizard defaults.

10. In the **Page Header**, delete all four labels, and then decrease the section height to zero.

11. In the **Detail** section, select the three text boxes, and then move the **First Name** text box approximately six grid dots from the left edge of the report.

12. Increase the width of the **Department** text box so that the right border is on the **6 inch** vertical grid line.

13. For the **Provider ID Header**, remove the alternate row color. Select the **Provider Name** text box, apply **Bold**, and then set the **Font Size** to 14.

14. Increase the height of the **Page Footer** by approximately half an inch. Below the =**Now()** calculated control, add a label with the file name as its text.

15. Filter the report to show only the employees enrolled in *Southwest Health*.

16. **Save**, and then switch to Print Preview, and then compare your screen with **Figure 2**. If you are printing this project, print the report.

17. **Close** the report. Click **Save**, and then **Exit** Access. Submit as directed by your instructor.

Done! You have completed Assess Your Skills 2

Assess Your Skills Visually

To complete this database, you will need the following files:

- a04_Councils
- a04_Councils_Logo

You will save your database as:

- Lastname_Firstname_a04_Councils

Open the database **a04_Councils**, and then, using your own name, save the database in your **Access Chapter 4** folder as Lastname_Firstname_a04_Councils

Use the Blank Report tool to create the report shown in **Figure 1**. Include three fields: **Council Name**, **First Name**, and **Last Name**, and group by **Council Name**. Arrange the fields as shown. The **Page Header** has been removed. The three cells in the **Council Name** row have been merged and the top padding has been set to 0.25" The **Council Name** has been formatted bold and size 14. The logo uses the file **a04_Councils_Logo** and the title has the text City Councils The report has the **Clarity** theme and the **Apex** theme font.

Save the report as City Council List Print the report or submit the database file as directed by your instructor.

Done! You have completed Assess Your Skills Visually

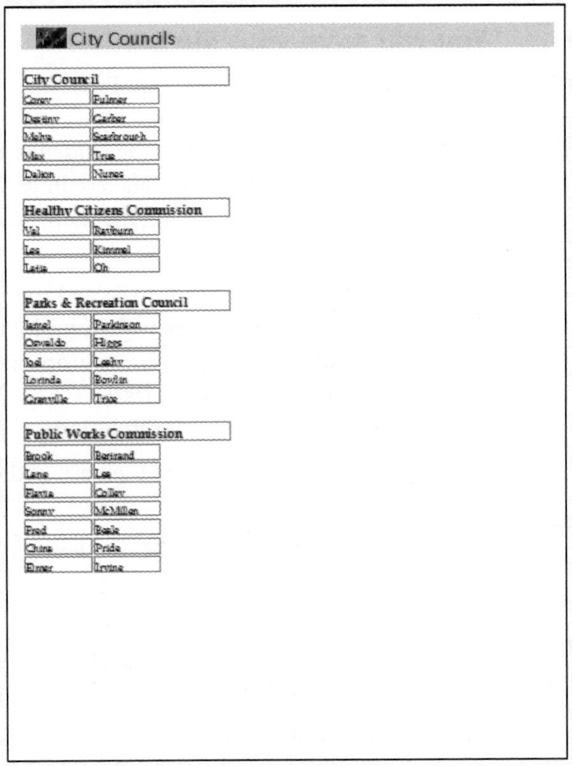

Figure 1

Skills in Context

To complete this database, you will need the following file:

- a04_Participants

You will save your database as:

- Lastname_Firstname_a04_Participants

Open **a04_Participants** and save the database in your **Access Chapter 4** folder as Lastname_Firstname_a04_Participants Create a query that can be used to create a mailing labels report. In the query, include the necessary name and address fields from the **Participants** table, and then filter the query so that only participants from the Central neighborhood display. Use the **Label Wizard** to create a label report. Arrange the fields in the

standard mailing address format. Include space and punctuation where appropriate. Do not include the Neighborhood field.

Print the report or submit the database file as directed by your instructor.

Done! You have completed Skills in Context

Skills and You

To complete this database, you will need the following file:

- a04_Contacts

You will save your database as:

- Lastname_Firstname_a04_Contacts

Open **Lastname_Firstname_a03_Contacts** that you created in a previous chapter. If you do not have this database, open **a04_Contacts**, and then add at least 10 personal contacts to the **Contacts** table. Save the database as Lastname_Fistname_a04_Contacts Create a report for the **Contacts** table. Format and

arrange the report as appropriate. Print the report or submit the database file as directed by your instructor.

Done! You have completed Skills and You

CHAPTER 5

Add Advanced Report Features

▶ In Access, you can add features to your report to make it look more professional and informative.

▶ Adding Subreports, Charts, and Queries to your report enables you to present data in meaningful and useful ways.

Your starting screen will look like this:

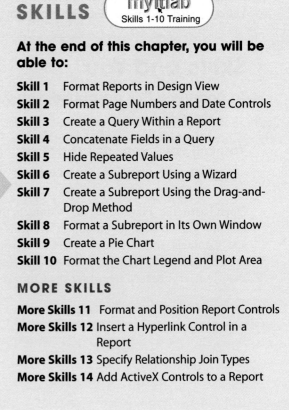

SKILLS

myitlab
Skills 1-10 Training

At the end of this chapter, you will be able to:

Skill 1 Format Reports in Design View

Skill 2 Format Page Numbers and Date Controls

Skill 3 Create a Query Within a Report

Skill 4 Concatenate Fields in a Query

Skill 5 Hide Repeated Values

Skill 6 Create a Subreport Using a Wizard

Skill 7 Create a Subreport Using the Drag-and-Drop Method

Skill 8 Format a Subreport in Its Own Window

Skill 9 Create a Pie Chart

Skill 10 Format the Chart Legend and Plot Area

MORE SKILLS

More Skills 11 Format and Position Report Controls

More Skills 12 Insert a Hyperlink Control in a Report

More Skills 13 Specify Relationship Join Types

More Skills 14 Add ActiveX Controls to a Report

Outcome

Using the skills listed to the left will enable you to create documents like these:

Section Enrollments

11% 11%
22% 19%
19% 18%

☐ Art History   ■ Basic Drawing   ☐ Beginning Watercolors
☐ Impressionism in Art   ■ Perspective Drawing   ■ Portrait Drawing

Art Instructor

First Name   Last Name
Lana   Shane

	20123	Basic Drawing	A101	$35.00
	20127	Portrait Drawing	A101	$35.00
	20143	Basic Drawing	A101	$45.00

Section ID	Class Title	Instructor ID	Fee
20123	Basic Drawing	A101	$35.00
20124	Beginning Watercolors	A110	$55.00
20126	Perspective Drawing	A112	$35.00
20127	Portrait Drawing	A101	$35.00

Student Classes   Thursday, February 09, 2012
                                                       9:34:22 PM

Full Name	Class Title
Agnus Manuele	Beginning Watercolors
Ali Walking	Basic Drawing
Alla Howson	Basic Drawing
Alvin Dando	Art History
Anusia Gaymon	Basic Drawing
	Beginning Watercolors
Annika Hoobler	Art History
Argentina Dibello	Perspective Drawing

Art Class Categories   Sunday, December 13, 2009
                                        5:44:42 PM

Category   Description
Art History   Classes focus on art appreciation grouped by genre,
                artist, or geographic area.

Art Classes   12/13/2009
                                              5:44 PM

Architectural Tour of Aspen Falls	Art History	A walking tour of historic Aspen Falls homes and commercial buildings. Vans will transport participants between sites, but expect to walk about 5 miles.
Art History	Art History	A survey of medieval, renaissance, baroque, classical, impressionists, and modern art. Includes tour of Wordsworth Fellowship Museum of Art.
Impressionism in Art	Art History	A survey of impressionist painters and their work including Monet, Manet, Degas, Renoir, and Cézanne.

Lastname Firstname a05 Art Center

Drawing   Classes focus on perspective and proportion using
                        pencil, charcoal, or chalk.

Art Classes   12/13/2009
                                              5:44 PM

Basic Drawing	Drawing	For beginners wishing to improve their drawing skills. Concepts include freehand drawing, light, shadow, form, composition, texture, and perspective.
Perspective Drawing	Drawing	Learn to draw objects with one, two, and three-point perspective using the mechanics of perspective drawing. Previous drawing experience recommended.
Portrait Drawing	Drawing	Learn to draw portraits using pencil and charcoal. Previous drawing experience recommended.

Lastname Firstname a05 Art Center

Art Classes   2/9/2012
                                              7:40 PM

Class Title	Category	Description
Architectural Tour of Aspen Falls	Art History	A walking tour of historic Aspen Falls homes and commercial buildings. Vans will transport participants between sites, but expect to walk about 5 miles.
Art History	Art History	A survey of medieval, renaissance, baroque, classical, impressionists, and modern art. Includes tour of Wordsworth Fellowship Museum of Art.
Basic Drawing	Drawing	For beginners wishing to improve their drawing skills. Concepts include freehand drawing, light, shadow, form, composition, texture, and perspective.
Beginning Watercolors	Painting	Beginning level class covers washes, wet-in-wet, dry brush, and lifting colors.
Impressionism in Art	Art History	A survey of impressionist painters and their work including Monet, Manet, Degas, Renoir, and Cézanne.
Perspective Drawing	Drawing	Learn to draw objects with one, two, and three-point perspective using the mechanics of perspective drawing. Previous drawing experience recommended.
Portrait Drawing	Drawing	Learn to draw portraits using pencil and charcoal. Previous drawing experience recommended.

Lastname Firstname a05 Art Center

You will save your files as:

Lastname_Firstname_a05_Art_Center

In this chapter, you will create documents for the Aspen Falls City Hall, which provides essential services for the citizens and visitors of Aspen Falls, California.

Introduction

▶ Access 2010 provides numerous ways to modify reports, such as positioning and modifying controls.

▶ A query can be embedded in a report so that the desired data from multiple tables can be presented.

▶ A subreport allows you to view data from multiple reports.

▶ Once a subreport is created, it can be modified in its own window.

▶ You can create numerous types of charts and then modify their designs using different colors and patterns.

Time to complete all
10 skills – 50 to 90 minutes

Find your student data files here:

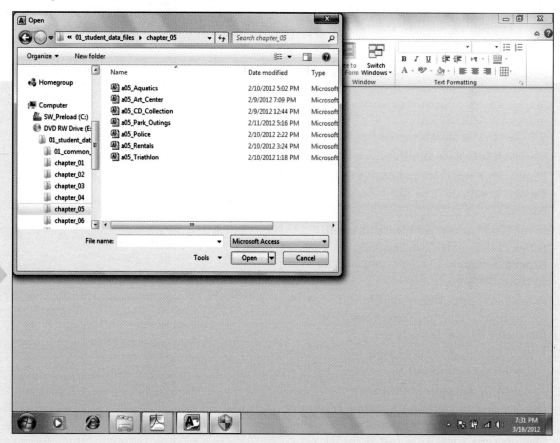

Student data files needed for this chapter:

- a05_Art_Center

► When working with reports, Design view provides more tools and more precision than Layout view.

► When a report is created, calculated controls that display dates, times, and page numbers are automatically placed in the report headers and footers. These controls can be deleted.

► Changing the layout and applying theme colors can make the report more presentable.

1. **Start** ☻ Access, and then open **a05_Art_Center**. Use the **Save As** dialog box to create a **New folder** named Access Chapter 5 **Save** the database in the new folder as Lastname_Firstname_ a05_Art_Center and then press Enter. If necessary, enable the content.

2. Display the **Create tab**, and then in the **Reports group**, click the **Blank Report** button.

3. In the Field List task pane, click **Show all tables**, click the **Art Class Sections Expand** ⊞ button, and then compare your screen with **Figure 1**. ─────

4. In the Field List task pane, double-click the **Section ID**, **Starting Date**, **Class Title**, **Instructor ID**, and **Fee** fields.

   The fields from the table have now been added to the report template.

5. Switch to Design view. In the **Page Header**, click the **Section ID** control. Press and hold the Shift key, and then click the **Starting Date**, **Class Title**, **Instructor ID**, and **Fee** controls. Compare your screen with **Figure 2**. ─────

■ **Continue to the next page to complete the skill**

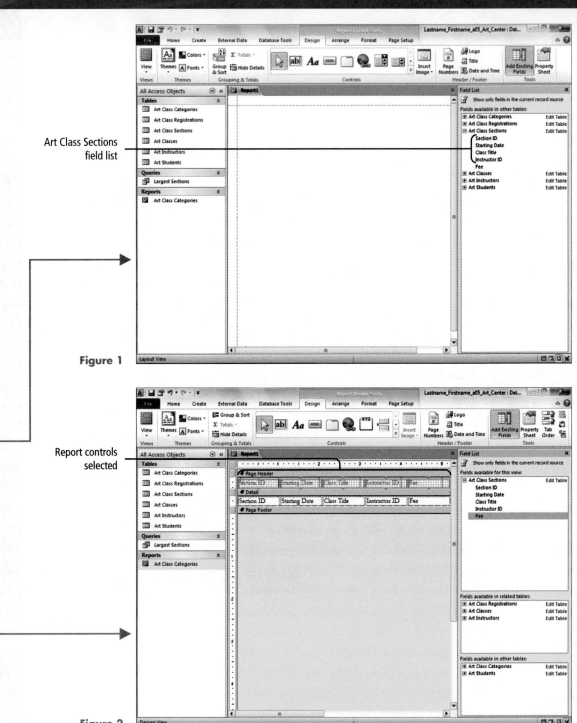

Art Class Sections field list

Figure 1

Report controls selected

Figure 2

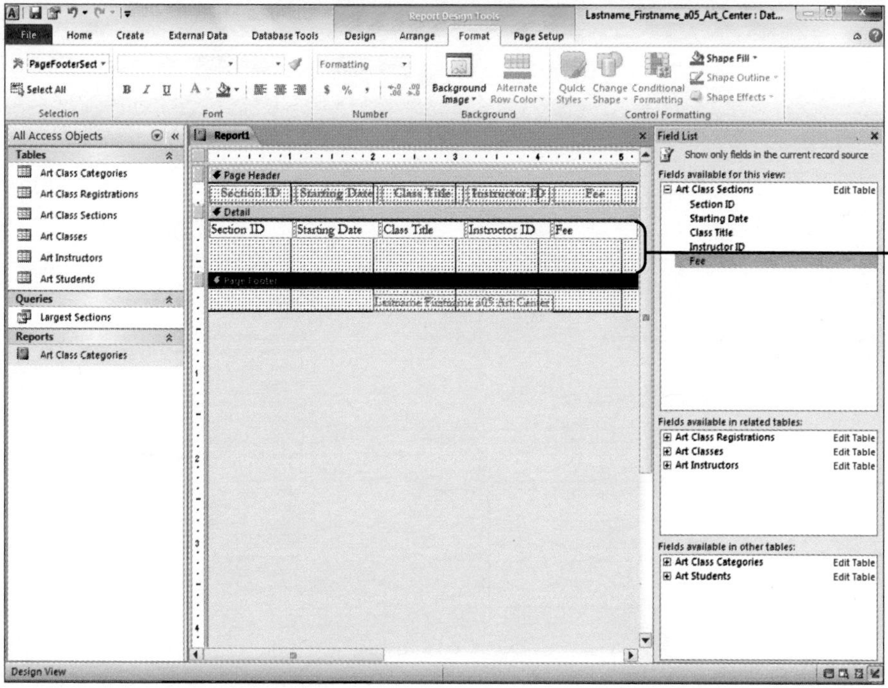

Detail section increased

Figure 3

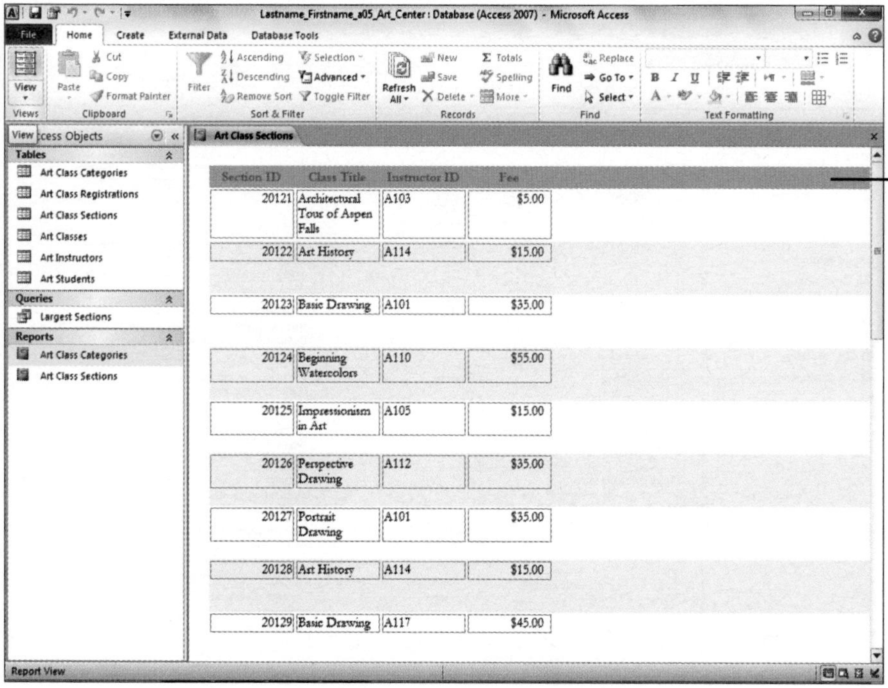

Access Theme 5 applied

Figure 4

6. Display the **Format tab**. In the **Font group**, click the **Center** button ▤, and then click the **Bold** button Ⓑ.

7. On the **Design tab**, in the **Controls group**, click the **Label** button 𝐴𝑎. Position the ⁺𝐴 pointer one grid dot below the top of the **Page Footer** and on the **2 inch** horizontal grid line, and then click the left mouse button. Type Lastname Firstname a05 Art Center

8. Point to the top edge of the **Page Footer** bar, and then, with the 𝕀 pointer, drag down about **0.5 inches**. Compare your screen with **Figure 3**.

9. Click the **Page Header** bar. Display the **Design tab** and then in the **Tools group**, click the **Property Sheet** button.

   The property sheet might already be displayed.

10. On the **Format tab** of the property sheet, click the **Back Color** box. Click the down arrow, and then click **Access Theme 5**.

11. Click **Save** ▤. In the **Save As** dialog box, type Art Class Sections and then click **OK**.

12. Switch to **Layout View**. Click the **Starting Date** column heading. Display the **Arrange tab**. In the **Rows and Columns group**, click **Select Column** and then press 〔Delete〕.

13. **Close** ⊠ the property sheet, switch to Report view, and then compare your screen with **Figure 4**.

14. Click **Save** ▤, and then **Close** ⊠ the report.

   ▪ **You have completed Skill 1 of 10**

► The date controls added by the Report Tool or Report Wizard can be modified.

► In any report, page numbers can be added, formatted, and positioned.

1. In the **Navigation Pane**, select the **Art Classes** table. Display the **Create tab**, and then, in the **Reports group**, click the **Report** button.

   Notice that the Page Header formatting from the previous layout was used as the default design.

2. On the **Design tab**, in the **Views group**, click the **View button arrow**. From the displayed list, click **Design View**. In the **Page Footer**, click the calculated control with the text = "Page " & [Page] & " of " & [Pages], and then press Delete.

   In this report, the Footer sections display text boxes that calculate values. A text box that derives its value from an expression is called a *calculated control*.

3. Click in the **Page Footer**. On the **Design tab**, in the **Header/Footer group**, click **Page Numbers**.

4. In the **Page Numbers** dialog box, under **Format**, choose **Page N of M**. Under **Position**, choose **Bottom of Page [Footer]**. Click the **Alignment** arrow, and then click **Left**. Click **OK** to close the dialog box.

5. Switch to Layout view. Scroll to the bottom of the report and then compare your screen with **Figure 1**.

6. Scroll to the top of the report, and then click the control that displays the current date.

7. On the **Format tab**, in the **Number group**, click the **Format arrow**, and then click **Short Date**, as shown in **Figure 2**.

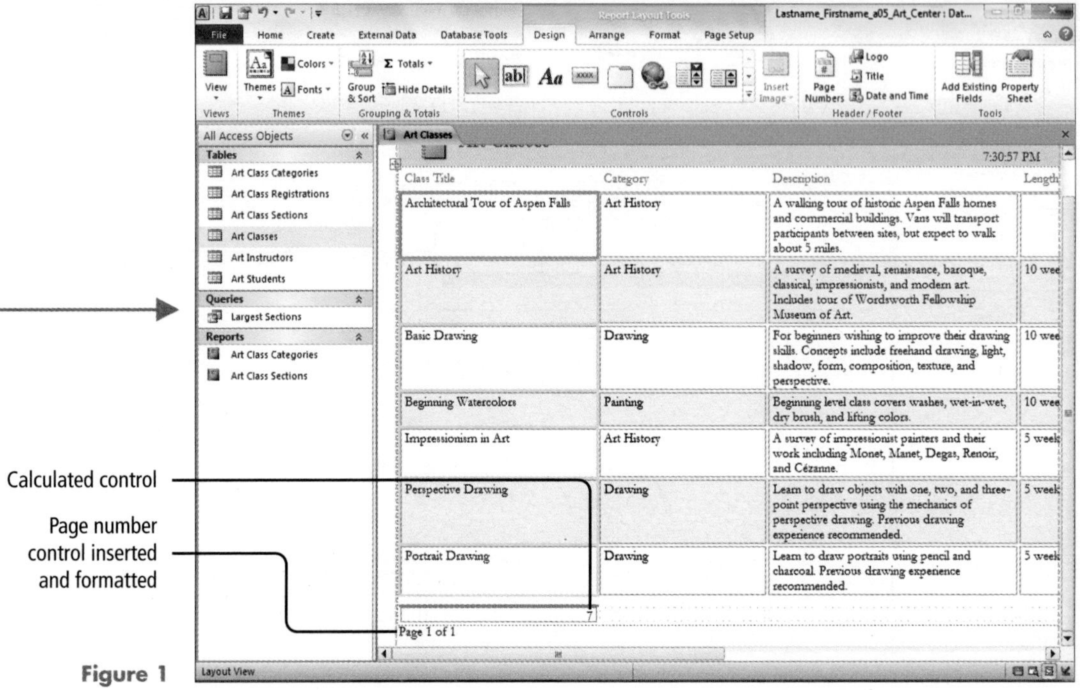

■ **Continue to the next page to complete the skill**

Calculated control
Page number control inserted and formatted
Figure 1

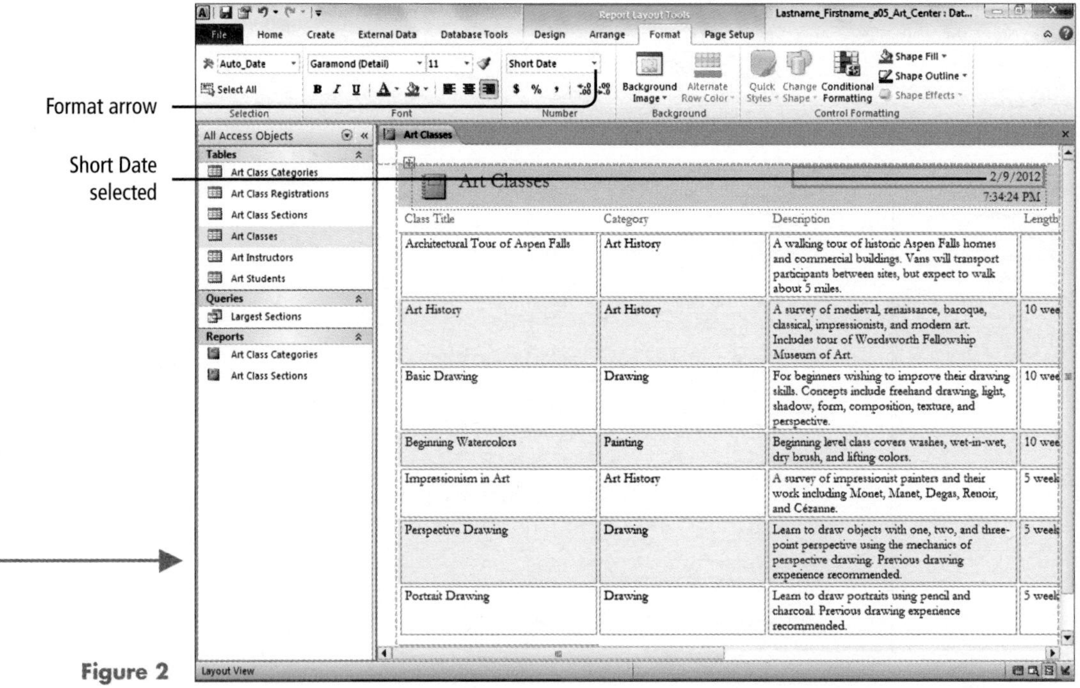

Format arrow
Short Date selected
Figure 2

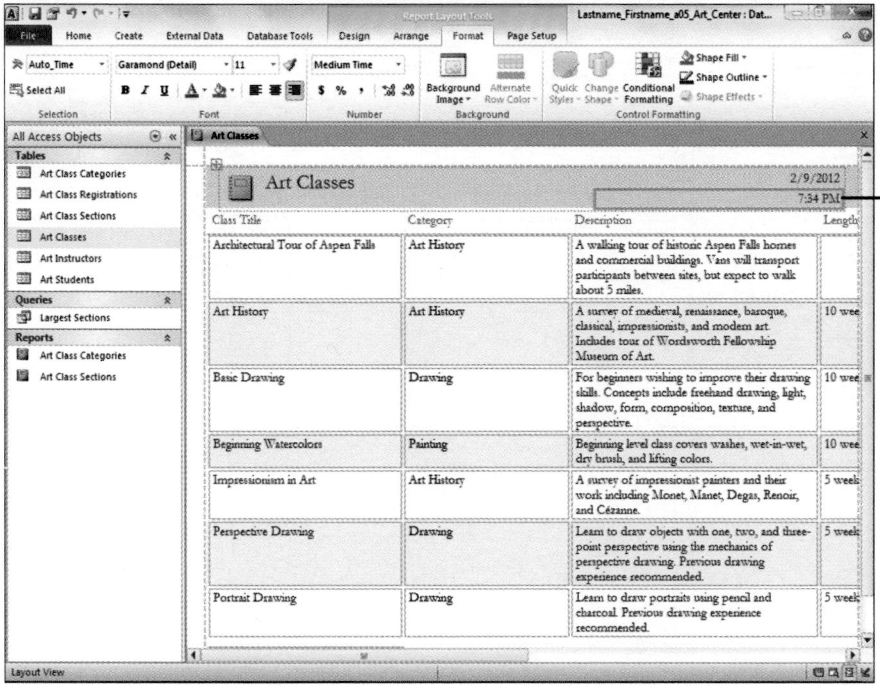

Medium Time
format applied

Figure 3

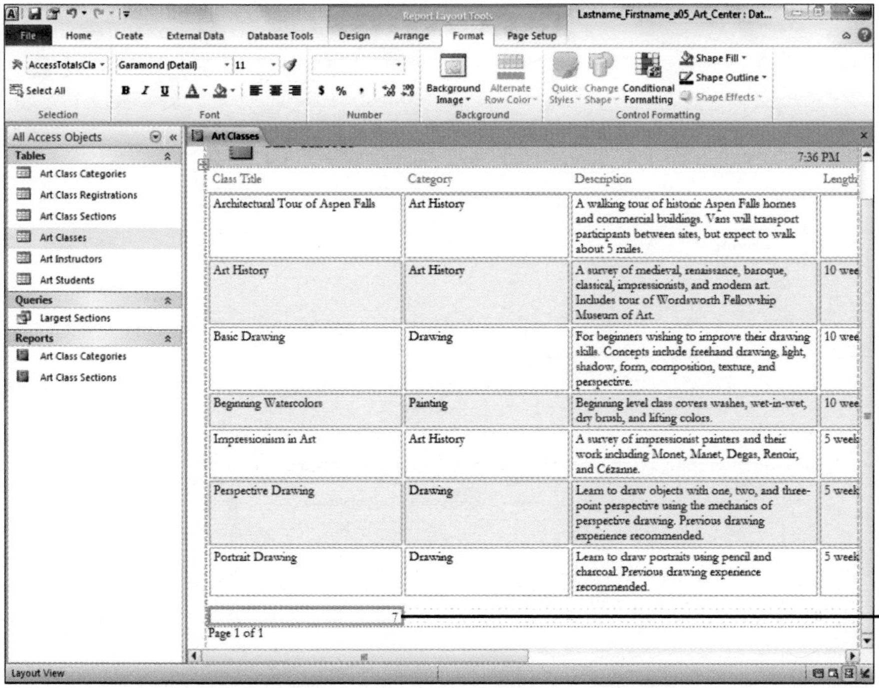

Record Count
control

Figure 4

8. In the report, click the text box control that displays the time.

9. In the **Number group**, click the **Format arrow**, and then click **Medium Time**. Compare your screen with **Figure 3**.

10. Scroll to the bottom of the report, click the **Record Count** control with the text *7*, and then compare your screen with **Figure 4**.

   Record Count is a calculated control.

11. Press Delete to remove the **Record Count** control from the report.

12. Switch to Design view, and then, in the **Controls group**, click the **Label** button Aa. Position the A pointer in the upper left corner of the **Report Footer**, click, and then immediately type Lastname Firstname a05 Art Center

13. In the **Page Header**, click the **Length** control. Press Shift, and then, in the **Detail** section, click the **Length** control. Press Delete.

14. Display the **Page Setup tab**, and then, in the **Page Layout group**, click **Landscape**. Scroll to the right, and then with the ✛ pointer drag the right edge of the report to the **8 inch** horizontal grid line.

15. Click **Save**, and then, in the **Save As** dialog box, click **OK**.

16. If instructed, print the report.

17. **Close** the report.

■ **You have completed Skill 2 of 10**

► When creating a report that uses data from tables in a many-to-many relationship, it is helpful to create a query within the report to display the information.

► The *Query Builder* creates queries within database objects such as forms and reports.

1. In the **Navigation Pane**, under **Reports**, double-click the **Art Class Sections** report.

2. Switch to **Design** view, and then open the property sheet.

3. If necessary, click the **Selection type arrow**, and then select **Report**. On the **Data tab** of the property sheet, click the **Record Source** box, and then compare your screen to **Figure 1**. ────────────

4. Click the **Build** button 📖, and then compare your screen with **Figure 2**. ────

   The Query Builder screen displays with all of the fields from the Art Class Sections table.

■ **Continue to the next page to complete the skill** ▶

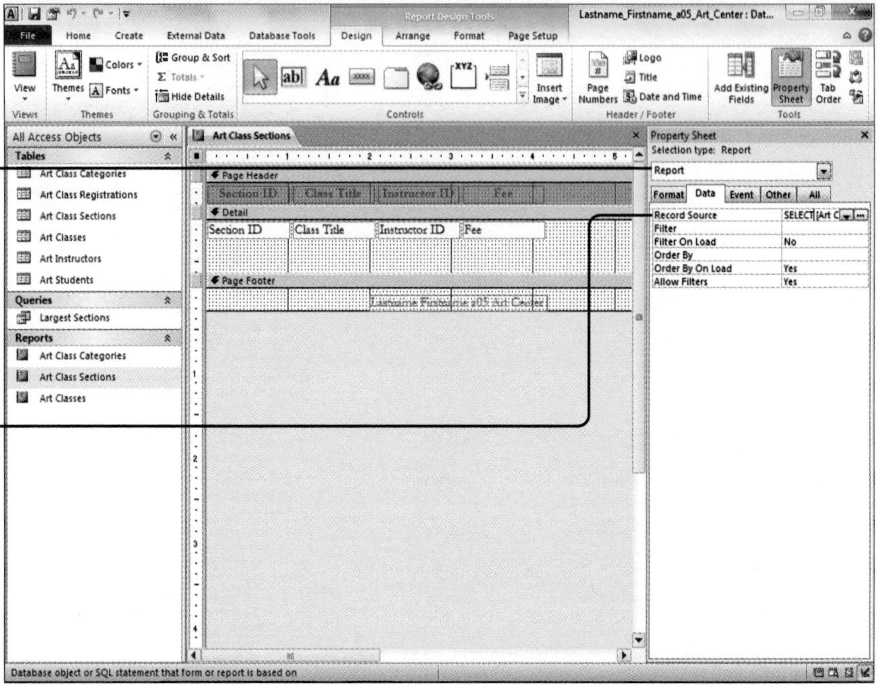

Report selected

Record Source box

Figure 1

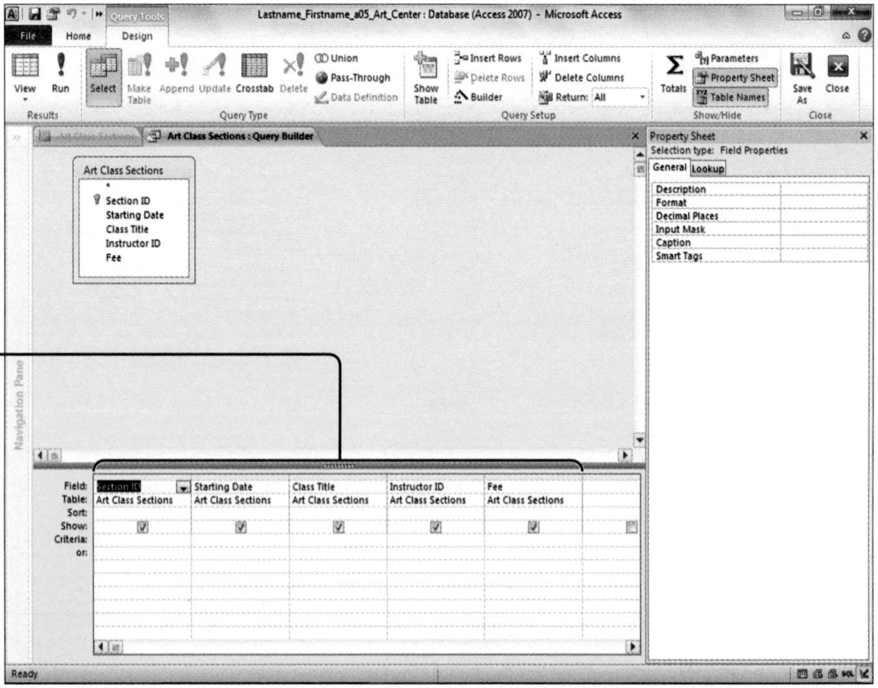

All fields added to design grid

Figure 2

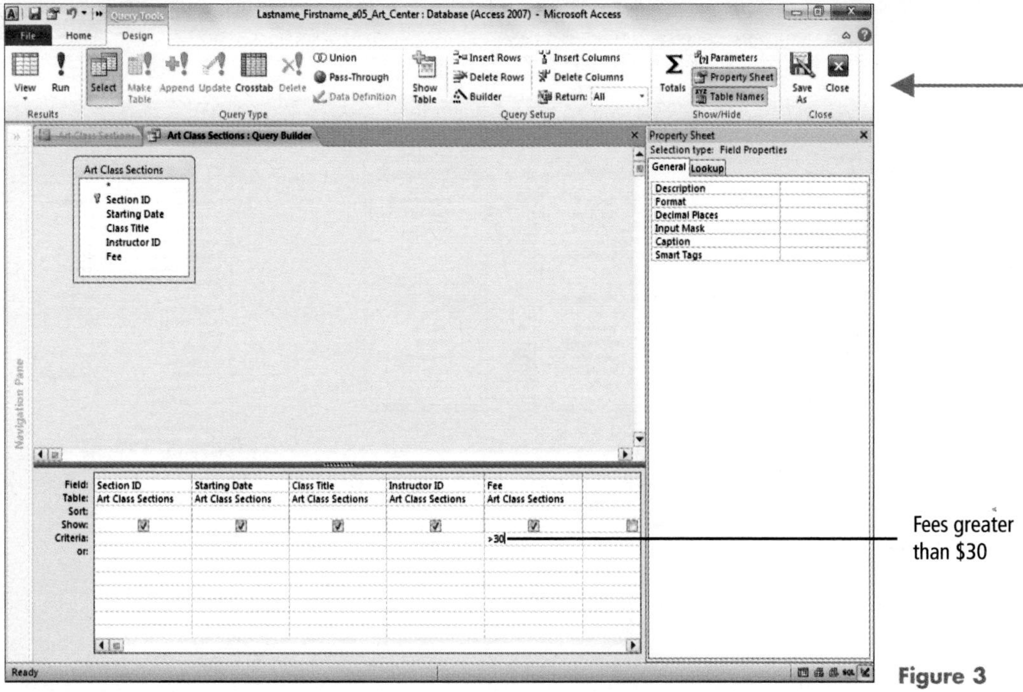

Fees greater
than $30

Figure 3

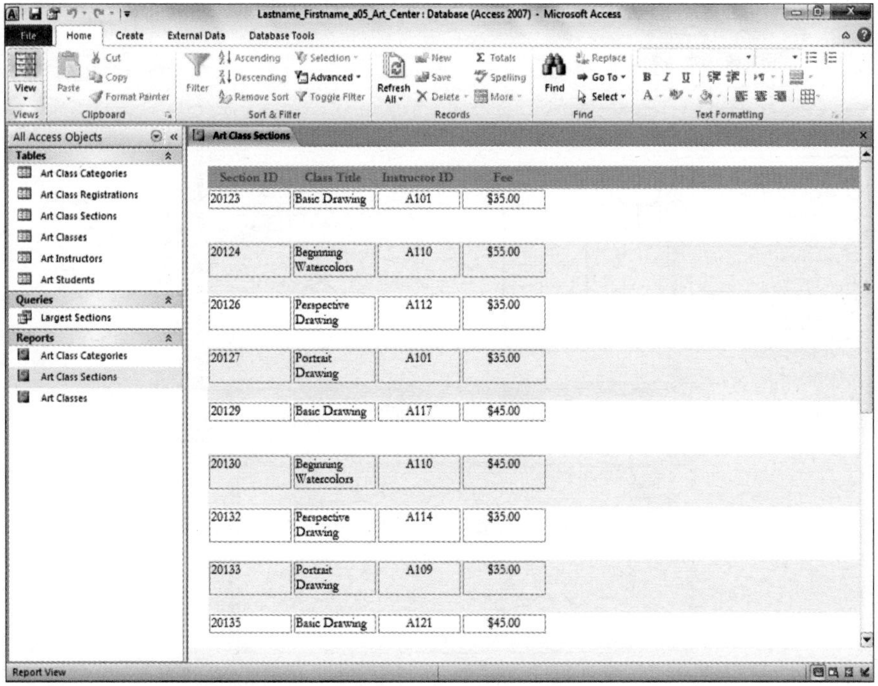

Figure 4

5. In the **Fee** column **Criteria** box, type >30 and then compare your screen with **Figure 3**.

6. On the **Design tab**, in the **Results group**, click **Run**. Verify that 16 records display in the query datasheet—only the classes that have a fee greater than $30.

7. Click **Save** 🖫, and then **Close** ✖ the Art Class Sections Report: Query Builder window.

8. In the **Detail** section, click the **Section ID** control. Display the **Format tab**, and then in the **Font group**, click **Align Text Left** 📧.

9. In the **Detail** section, click the **Instructor ID** control. Press and hold the Shift key, and then click the **Fee** control. On the **Format tab**, in the **Font group**, click **Center** 📧.

10. Click **Save** 🖫, switch to Report view, and then verify that the report displays only classes with fees that are greater than $30. Compare your screen with **Figure 4**.

11. If your instructor has asked you to print your work for this chapter, print the report.

12. **Save** 🖫 the report design changes, and then **Close** ✖ the report.

■ **You have completed Skill 3 of 10**

▶ **Concatenation** is the process of combining two or more text values to create one text value. The text value can be a space, a word, phrases, or sentences.

▶ Access can concatenate the values from more than one field into a *calculated field*—a single field that displays both the first and last names with a space between them, for example.

1. On the **Create tab**, in the **Queries group**, click **Query Design**.

2. In the **Show Table** dialog box, double-click the **Art Students**, **Art Class Registrations**, **Art Class Sections**, and **Art Classes** tables. Click **Close**, and then compare your screen with **Figure 1**.

3. Right-click the first **Field** row of the first column, and then click **Zoom**. In the **Zoom** dialog box, type Full Name: [First Name] + " " + [Last Name] Be sure to include a space between the two quote marks. Compare your screen with **Figure 2**, and then click **OK**.

> This field creates a calculated field labeled *Full Name*. The *Full Name* field concatenates the *First Name* value, and then the *Last Name* value.

4. In the design grid, drag to widen the first column so that the entire expression displays including the *Full Name* label.

5. Select the **Full Name** column **Sort** box, select the displayed arrow, and then click **Ascending**.

■ **Continue to the next page to complete the skill**

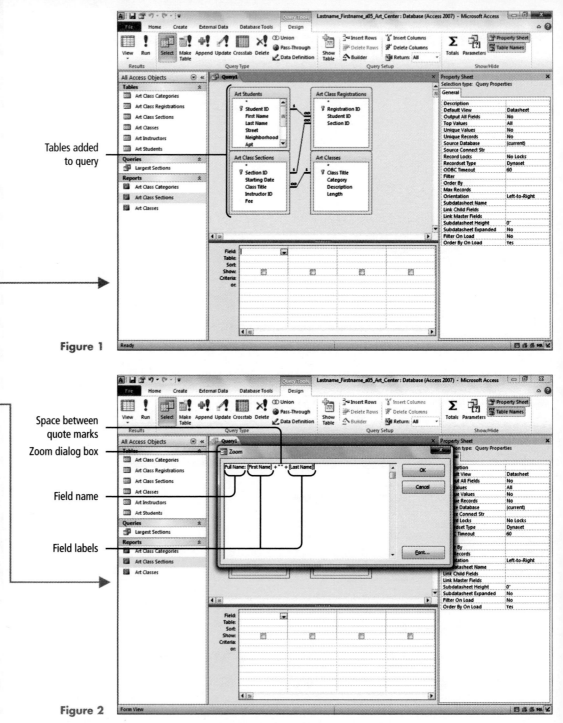

Tables added to query

Figure 1

Space between quote marks

Zoom dialog box

Field name

Field labels

Figure 2

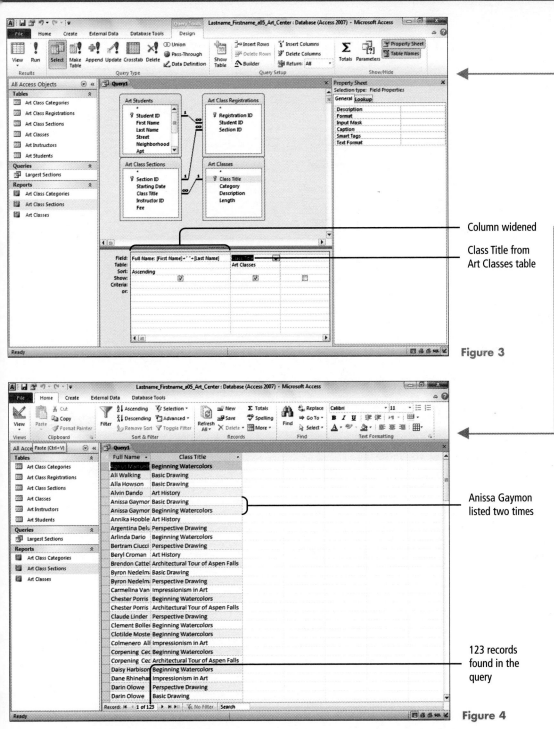

Column widened

Class Title from
Art Classes table

Figure 3

Anissa Gaymon
listed two times

123 records
found in the
query

Figure 4

6. In the query workspace, in the **Art Classes** table, double-click the **Class Title** field to add it to the query design grid. Compare your screen with **Figure 3**.

7. On the **Design tab**, in the **Results group**, click the **Run** button. If the Enter Parameter Value dialog box displays, click Cancel, and then repeat steps 1–6, carefully checking your typing. In the datasheet, notice that Anissa Gaymon's name is displayed two times—one time for each art class that she has taken—as shown in **Figure 4**.

8. Click **Save** 🔲, and in the **Save As** dialog box, type Student Classes Click **OK**, and then **Close** ⊠ the query.

■ **You have completed Skill 4 of 10**

► In a query or report that displays fields from tables in a one-to-many or many-to-many relationship, the values from the "one" side of the relationship are often repeated on each row.

► In a report, repeated values can be hidden so that only one unique value displays.

1. In the **Navigation Pane**, select the **Student Classes** query. On the **Create tab**, in the **Reports group**, click **Report**.

2. On the **Design tab**, in the **Grouping & Totals group**, click the **Group & Sort** button.

3. In the **Group, Sort, and Total** pane, click the **Add a Sort** button, and then, from the displayed list, click **Full Name**. Notice that Anissa Gaymon's name is repeated, as shown in **Figure 1**.

4. **Close** ☒ the **Grouping** dialog box. Be careful not to delete the sort. Switch to Design view.

5. Click a blank area of the report and then, in the **Detail** section, click the **Full Name** text box. Display the property sheet. On the **Format tab** of the property sheet, scroll down to locate the **Hide Duplicates** property, and then change the **Hide Duplicates** value to **Yes**.

6. **Close** ☒ the property sheet, and then switch to Report view. Notice that a blank value displays where a student name would repeat, as shown in **Figure 2**.

7. Switch to Design view. In the **Page Footer**, click the calculated control with the text =*"Page " & [Page] & " of " & [Pages]*, and then press [Delete].

■ **Continue to the next page to complete the skill** ▶

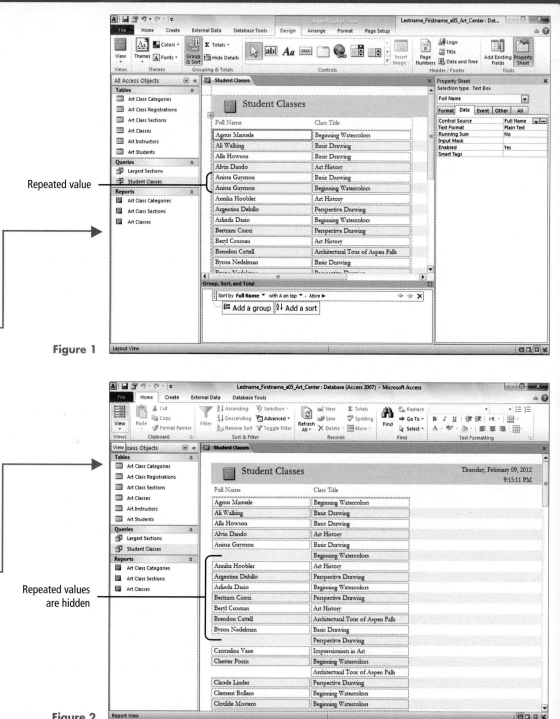

Repeated value

Figure 1

Repeated values are hidden

Figure 2

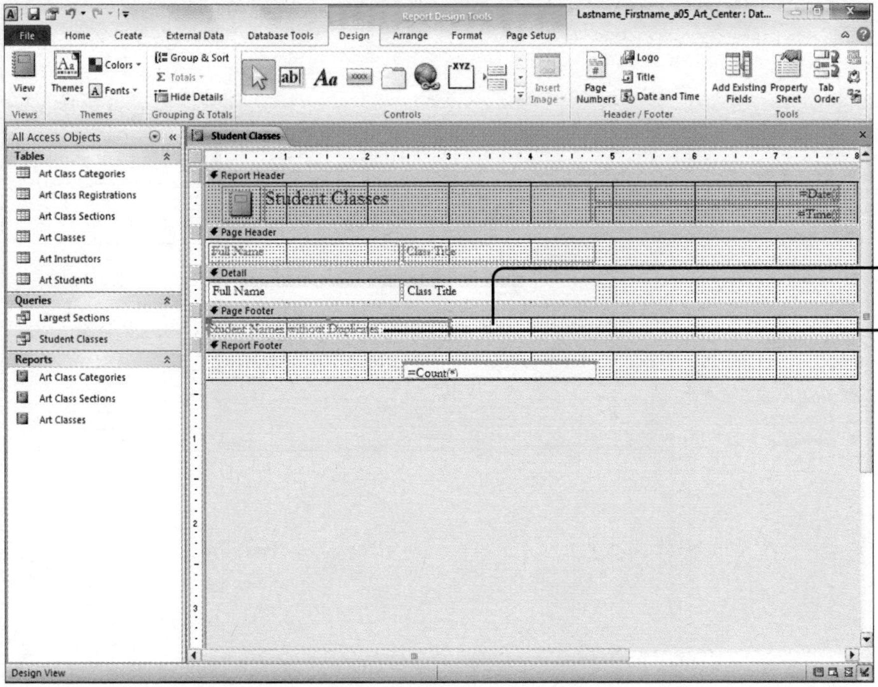

Page number
control deleted

Label inserted

Figure 3

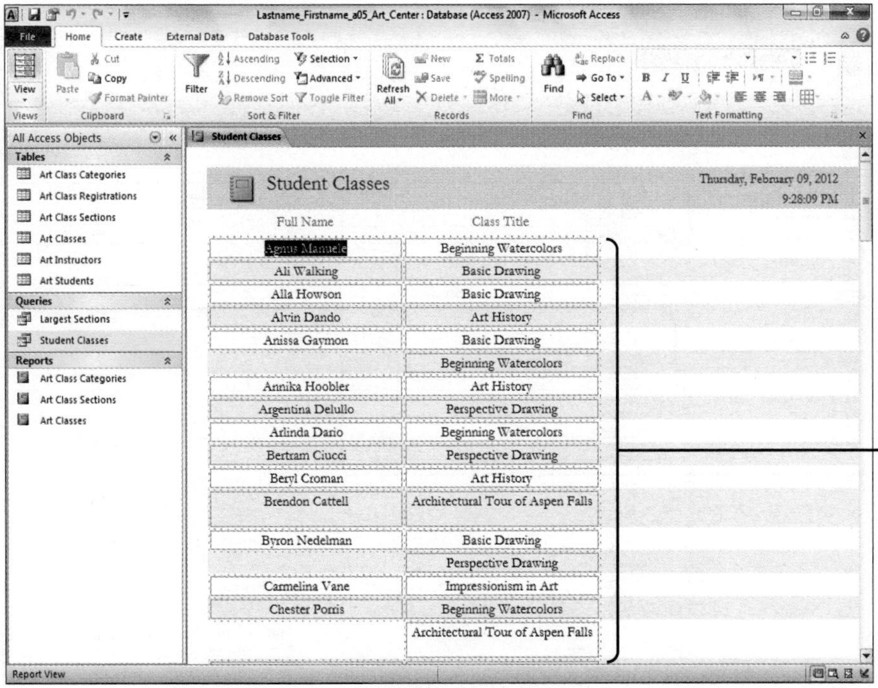

Column labels
formatted

Figure 4

8. On the **Design tab**, in the **Controls group**, click the **Label** button. Position the pointer in the upper left corner of the **Page Footer**, and then click the left mouse button. Immediately type Student Names without Duplicates Click outside the control, and then click the **Label** control. Position the pointer over the right sizing handle, and then drag to the **3 inch** horizontal grid line. Compare your screen with **Figure 3**.

9. Switch to Layout view. Click the **Full Name** column label. Press Shift, and then click the **Class Title** column label. Display the **Arrange tab**, and then, in the **Rows & Columns group**, click **Select Column**.

10. On the **Arrange tab**, in the **Table group**, click the **Gridlines** button. From the displayed menu, click **Border**, and then click **Sparse Dots**, the sixth choice in the list.

11. On the **Format tab**, in the **Font group**, click the **Font Size** arrow, and then click **12**. In the **Font group**, click the **Center** button.

12. Switch to Report view, and then compare your screen with **Figure 4**.

13. Switch to Layout view, and then display the **Page Setup tab**. In the **Page Layout group**, click **Landscape**.

14. Click **Save**. In the **Save As** dialog box, click **OK**.

15. If your instructor has asked you to print your work for this chapter, print the report.

16. **Close** the report.

■ **You have completed Skill 5 of 10**

▶ A *subreport* is a report that is inserted into another report.

▶ Typically, the main report is linked to a subreport using a common field.

▶ Reports and subreports are commonly used to show related records from tables in a one-to-many relationship.

1. Open the **Art Class Categories** report in Design view. Point to the lower edge of the **Detail** section and then, with the ⊞ pointer, drag down about 1 inch.

2. On the **Design tab**, in the **Controls group**, click the **More** button ⊡. From the displayed menu, click the **Subform/Subreport** button ▣. Position the 🔲 pointer in the upper left corner of the **Detail** section, just below the **Category** control, and then click the left mouse button.

3. In the **SubReport Wizard**, click to select **Use an existing report or form**, click **Art Classes**. Click **Next**, and then compare your screen with **Figure 1**. ────────

4. Under **Would you like to define which fields link your main form to this subform yourself, or choose from the list below?**, be sure that the **Choose from a list** option button is selected, and then click **Next**.

5. Under **What name would you like for your subform or subreport?**, notice the name provided by the displayed wizard, and then click **Finish**. Compare your screen with **Figure 2**. ────────

■ **Continue to the next page to complete the skill** ▶

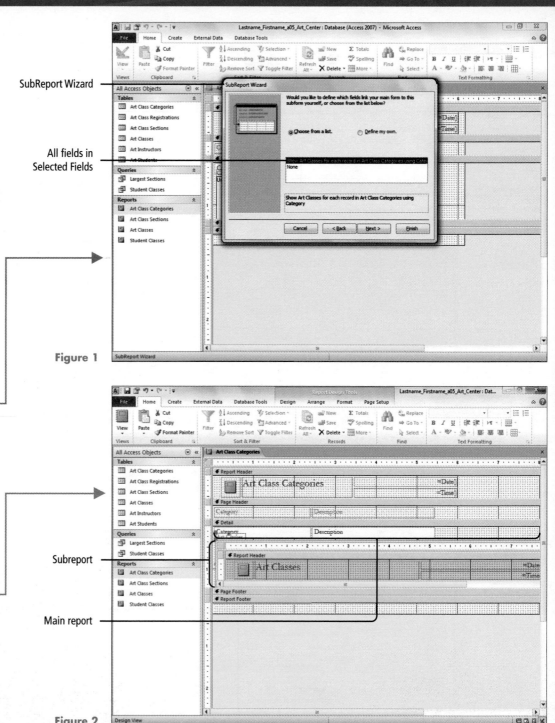

SubReport Wizard

All fields in Selected Fields

Figure 1

Subreport

Main report

Figure 2

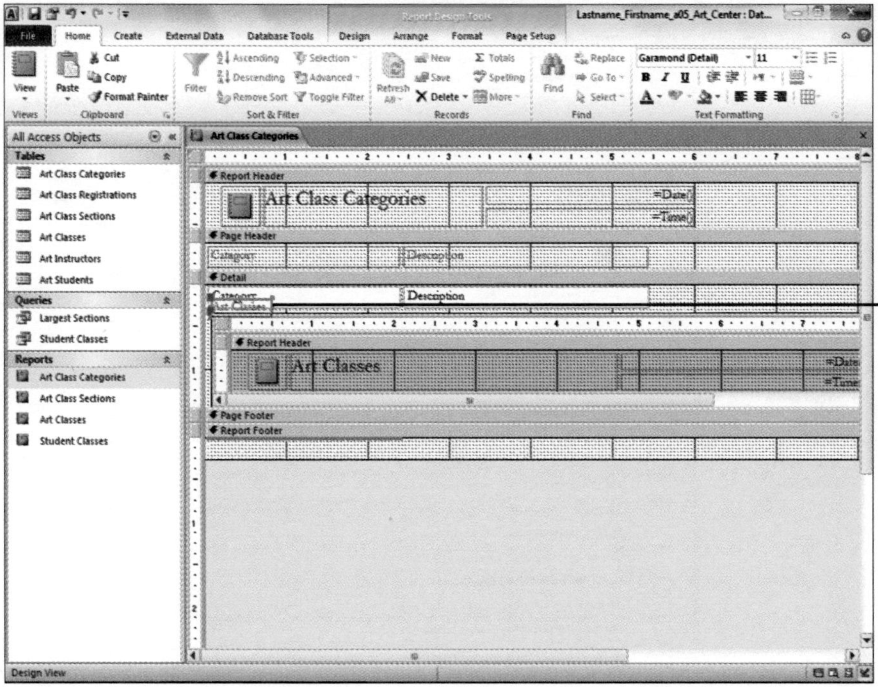

Subreport label
selected

Figure 3

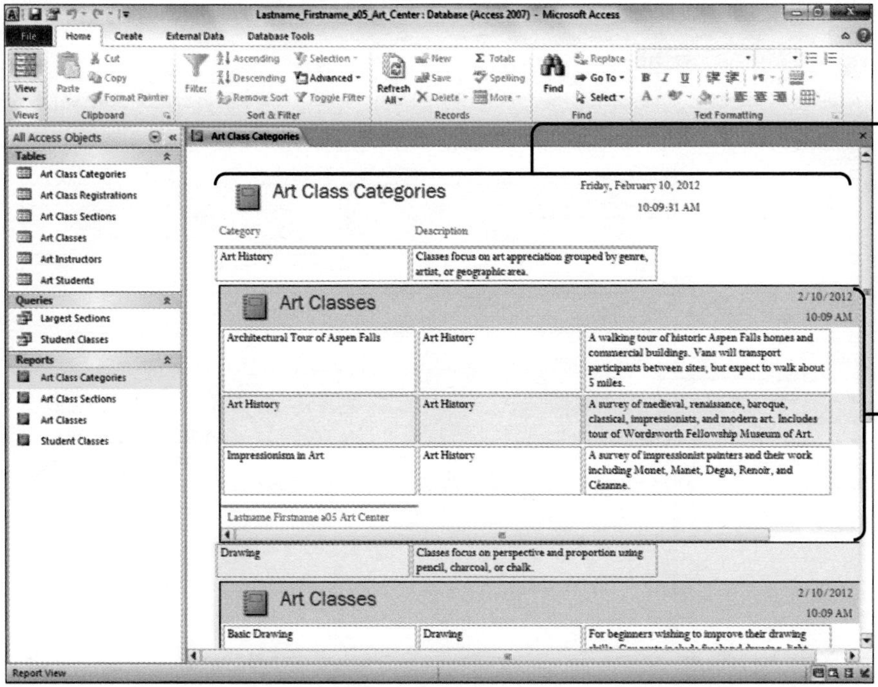

Main report

Subreport

Figure 4

6. In the **Detail** section, select the control labeled **Art Classes**. Compare your screen with **Figure 3**, and then press Delete.

7. Display the **Design tab**. In the **Controls group**, click the **Label** button [Aa]. In the upper left corner of the **Report Footer**, insert a label with the text Lastname Firstname a05 Art Center Click outside the label, and then click the label. Position the ↔ pointer over the right sizing handle, and then drag to the **3 inch** horizontal grid line. Display the **Format tab**. In the **Font group**, click **Font Size arrow** [u ·], and then click **10**.

8. Switch to Layout view. On the **Design tab**, in the **Themes group**, select **Themes**, and then click **Equity**, the fourth choice in the third row under **Built-In**.

9. Switch to Design view. Select the subreport and then scroll to the right. With the ↔ pointer over the right border, click and then drag to the left until the border reaches the **Date** and **Time** controls in the **Art Classes** subreport.

10. Scroll to the right. Position the ↔ pointer over the right edge of the main report border, click, and then drag to the left until the border meets the **8.5 inch** horizontal grid line.

11. Display the **Page Setup tab**, and then in the **Page Layout group**, click **Landscape**.

12. Click **Save** 🔲. Scroll to the left. Switch to Report view, and then compare your screen to **Figure 4**.

13. If your instructor has asked you to print your work for this chapter, print the first page of the report.

14. **Close** ✖ the report.

▪ **You have completed Skill 6 of 10**

▶ A report can be added to another report as a subreport by dragging the report from the Navigation Pane into the open report.

▶ Using the drag-and-drop method to add a subreport enables you to create and work with the subreport before adding it to the main report.

1. Display the **Create tab**, and then in the **Reports group**, click the **Report Wizard** button.

2. In the **Report Wizard**, select the **Tables/Queries arrow**, and then click **Table: Art Instructors. Move** `>` the **First Name** and **Last Name** fields into **Selected Fields**, and then click **Finish**. Click **Close Print Preview**.

3. In the **Navigation Pane**, select the **Art Class Sections** table. Display the **Create tab**, and then in the **Reports group**, click the **Report** button.

4. Click **Save** 🖫, type Sections Subreport and then click **OK**. Switch to Report view. Compare your screen with **Figure 1**, and then **Close** ✖ the report.

5. With the **Art Instructors** report open in Design view, expand the **Detail** section by about 1 inch.

6. From the **Navigation Pane**, drag the **Sections Subreport** to the **Detail** section of the open report. Position the 🔳 pointer about four grid dots below the bottom edge of the **First Name** text box, and then release the left mouse button. Compare your screen with **Figure 2**.

   The Sections Report becomes a subreport in the main report.

■ **Continue to the next page to complete the skill**

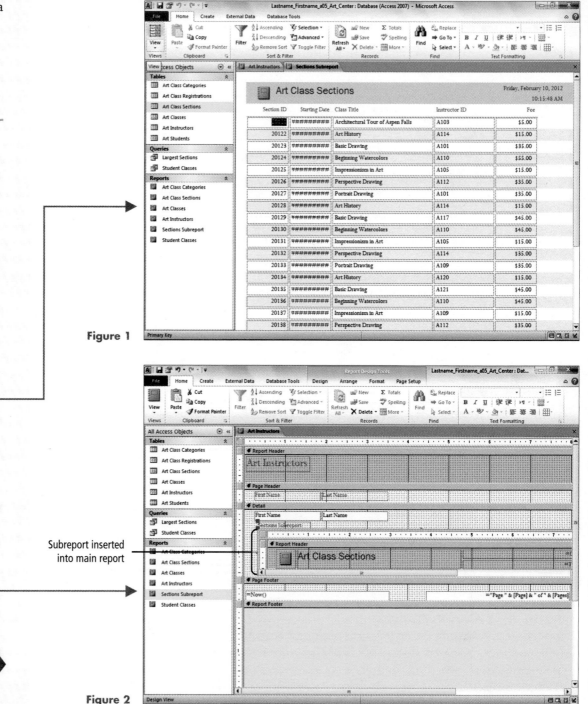

Figure 1

Subreport inserted
into main report

Figure 2

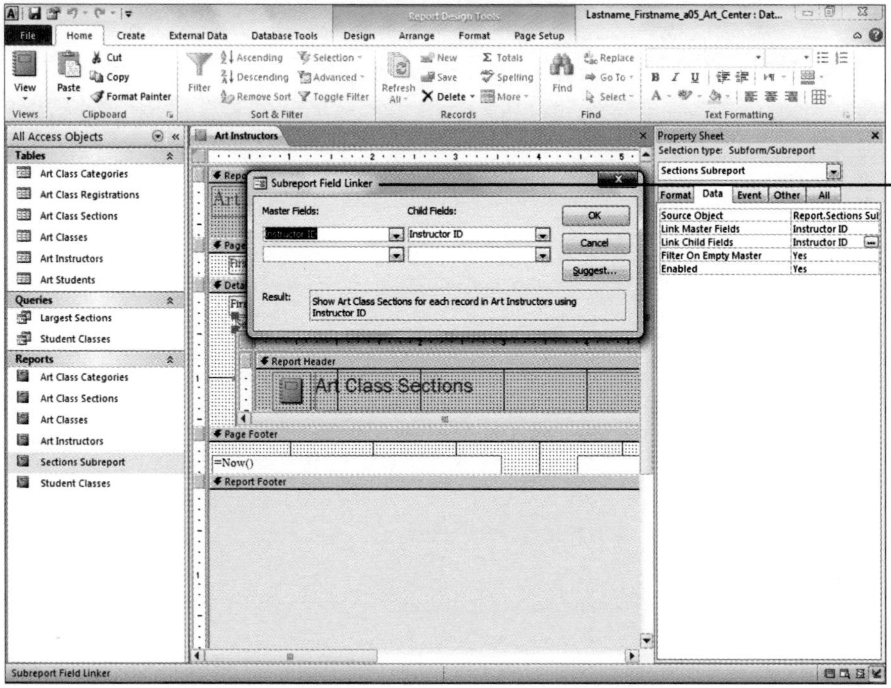

Subreport Field
Linker dialog box

Figure 3

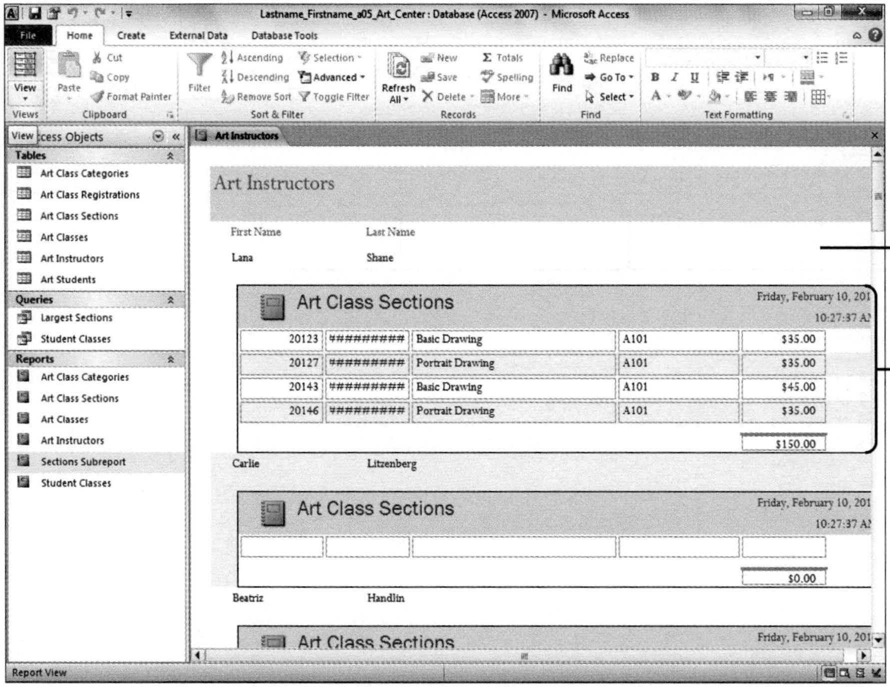

Main report

Formatted
subreport

Figure 4

7. On the **Design tab**, in the **Tools group**, click the **Property Sheet** button. Alternately, press [F4]. If necessary, in the property sheet, click the **Selection type arrow**, scroll as needed, and then click **Sections Subreport**.

8. On the **Data tab** of the property sheet, select the **Link Child Fields** box, and then click the **Build** button ⬚. Compare your screen with **Figure 3**.

> The Subreport Field Linker dialog box is used to set the link between a report and its subreport. A *child field* is the field in a subreport that links the report to its subreport. A *parent field* is the field to which a child field is linked. A *master field* is a field in a report that is used to link the report to its subreport.

9. Click **OK** to accept the suggested master and child fields.

10. **Close** ☒ the property sheet. In the **Detail** section, if the label with the text *Sections Subreport* displays, then press [Delete].

11. On the **Design tab**, in the **Controls group**, click the **Label** button [Aa]. In the upper left corner of the **Report Footer**, insert a label with the text Lastname Firstname a05 Art Center

12. Switch to Report view. Notice that the subreport still needs to be formatted, as shown in **Figure 4**.

13. Click **Save** 🖫, and then **Close** ☒ the report.

■ **You have completed Skill 7 of 10**

▶ Formatting a subreport in its own window provides more options and control over the design of the subreport.

1. In the **Navigation Pane**, under **Reports**, double-click the **Sections Subreport**.

2. Switch to Design view, and then increase the height of the **Detail** section by about 1 inch.

3. Switch to Layout view. Use Shift to select the **Logo**, **Title**, **Date**, and **Time** controls, and then press Delete. Compare your screen with **Figure 1**.

4. Switch to Design view. In the **Detail** section, select the **Section ID** text box, press and hold Shift, and then click the **Starting Date**, **Class Title**, **Instructor ID**, and **Fee** controls. On the **Design tab**, in the **Themes group**, click **Fonts**, scroll down, and then from the displayed menu click **Black Tie**—Garamond. Switch to Layout view, and then compare your screen with **Figure 2**.

5. Scroll to the bottom of the report, and then delete the text box displaying the sum of *$755.00*. Scroll to the bottom of the report, and delete the control displaying the page numbers.

■ **Continue to the next page to complete the skill**

Controls removed

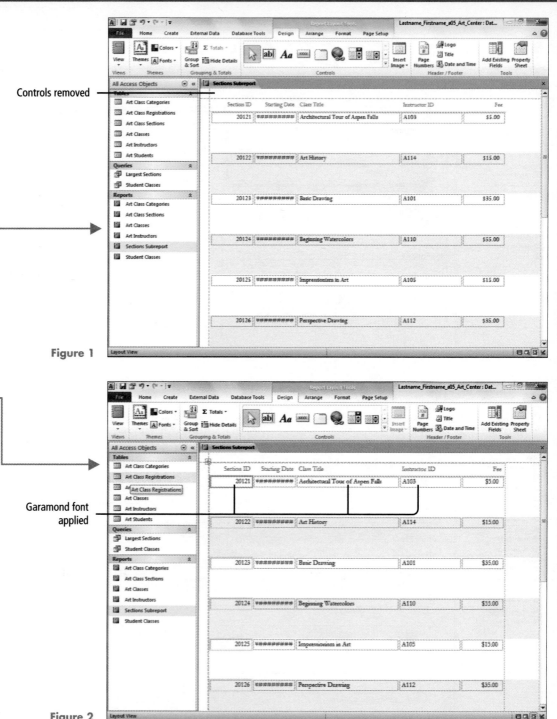

Figure 1

Garamond font applied

Figure 2

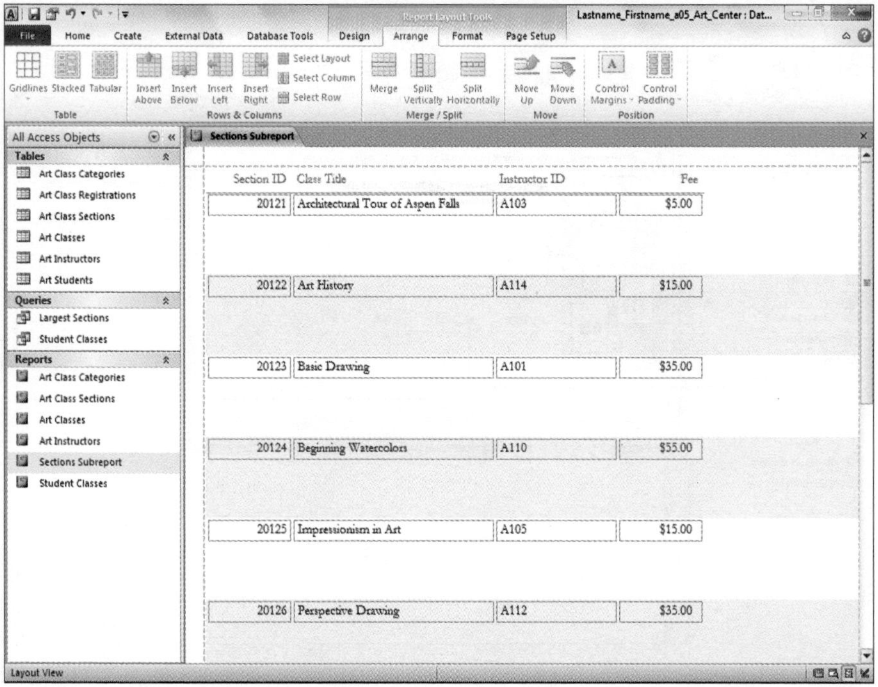

Figure 3

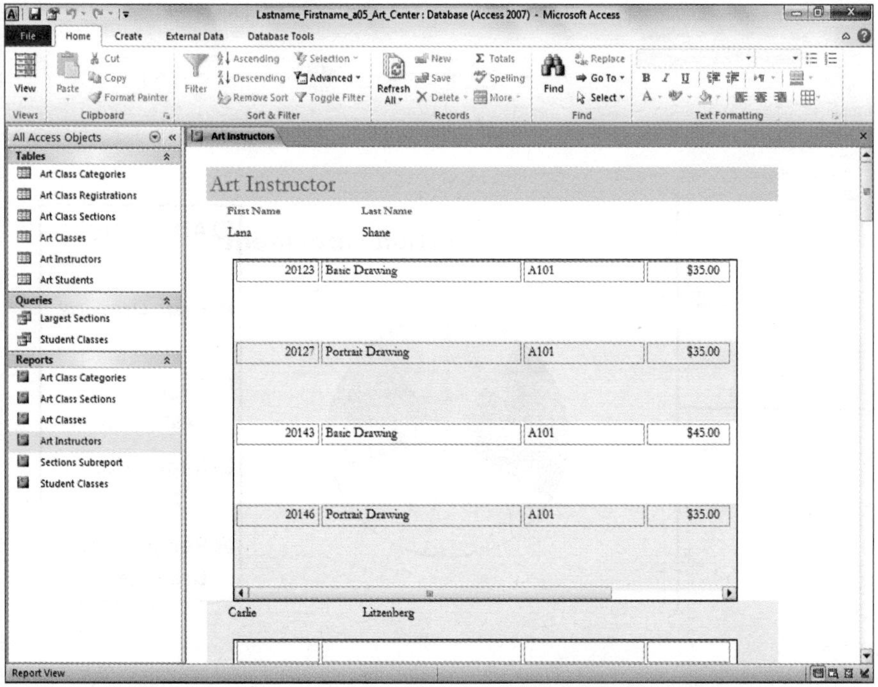

Figure 4

6. Click anywhere in the **Starting Date** column, and then on the **Arrange tab**, in the **Rows & Columns group**, click **Select Column**. Press Delete. Compare your screen to **Figure 3**.

7. **Save** 🖫, and then **Close** ☒ the report.

8. In the **Navigation Pane**, under **Reports**, open **Art Instructors** in Layout view. Select the **First Name** and **Last Name** text boxes, and then apply **Font Size 10** and **Bold**.

9. Switch to Design view. Delete the control displaying the page numbers.

10. In the **Detail** section, click to select the subreport. Scroll to the right, and then with the ↔ pointer over the right border, drag to the left until the right border meets the **6.5 inch** horizontal grid line of the main report.

11. Scroll to the right. Position the ↔ pointer over the right edge of the main report, click, and then drag to the left until the border meets the **7 inch** horizontal grid line.

12. Scroll to the left. In the **Report Footer**, click the file name label. Position the ↔ pointer over the right edge of the label, and then drag to the right until the right border meets the **3 inch** horizontal grid line.

13. Switch to Report view and compare your screen with **Figure 4**. If your instructor has asked you to print your work for this chapter, print the report.

14. **Save** 🖫, and then **Close** ☒ the report.

- **You have completed Skill 8 of 10**

► Report charts are an effective method of visually displaying data in reports.

► Charts can display data from a table, a query, or both.

1. Display the **Create tab**, and then, in the **Reports group**, click the **Report Design** button.

2. Position the crosshairs of the ↔ pointer over the right edge of the **Detail** section, and then drag to the right so that the **Detail** section reaches the **8 inch** horizontal grid line.

3. In the **Controls group**, click the **More** button ⊟, and then click the **Chart** button 📊. Position the crosshairs of the ⬚ pointer in the upper left corner of the **Detail** section, and then drag down and to the right so that the ⬚ pointer is two grid dots to the left of the **5 inch** vertical grid line and **8 inch** horizontal grid line, and then release the mouse button.

4. In the **Chart Wizard**, under **View**, select the **Queries** option button. With **Query: Largest Sections** selected, compare your screen with **Figure 1**.

5. Click **Next** and then click the **Move All** button ⏩. Click **Next** and then click the **Pie Chart** button—the first chart in the last row.

6. Click **Next** two times. In the **What title would you like for your chart?** box, replace the existing text with Section Enrollments Click **Finish**, switch to Report view, and then compare your screen to **Figure 2**.

■ Continue to the next page to complete the skill ▶

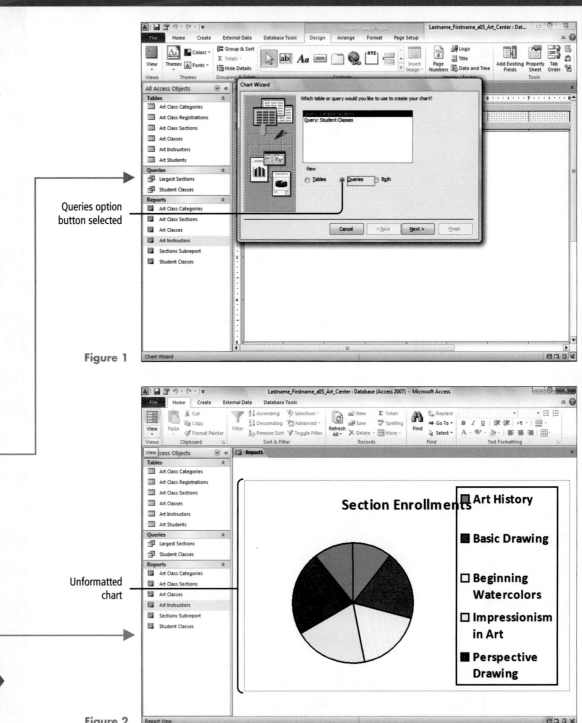

Queries option button selected

Figure 1

Unformatted chart

Figure 2

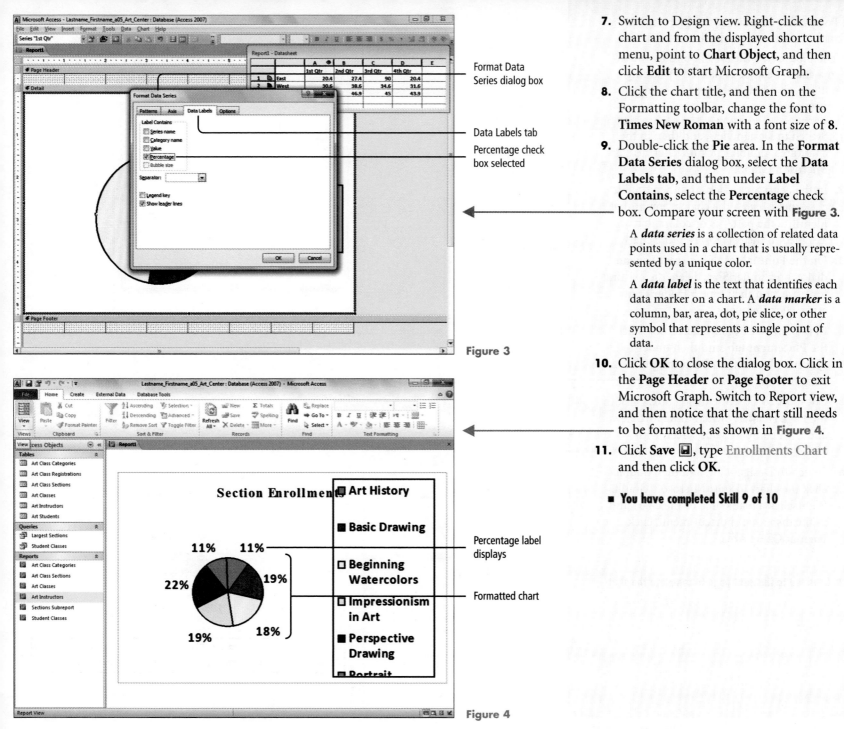

Format Data
Series dialog box

Data Labels tab

Percentage check
box selected

Figure 3

Percentage label
displays

Formatted chart

Figure 4

7. Switch to Design view. Right-click the chart and from the displayed shortcut menu, point to **Chart Object**, and then click **Edit** to start Microsoft Graph.

8. Click the chart title, and then on the Formatting toolbar, change the font to **Times New Roman** with a font size of **8**.

9. Double-click the **Pie** area. In the **Format Data Series** dialog box, select the **Data Labels tab**, and then under **Label Contains**, select the **Percentage** check box. Compare your screen with **Figure 3**.

   A ***data series*** is a collection of related data points used in a chart that is usually represented by a unique color.

   A ***data label*** is the text that identifies each data marker on a chart. A ***data marker*** is a column, bar, area, dot, pie slice, or other symbol that represents a single point of data.

10. Click **OK** to close the dialog box. Click in the **Page Header** or **Page Footer** to exit Microsoft Graph. Switch to Report view, and then notice that the chart still needs to be formatted, as shown in **Figure 4**.

11. Click **Save** 🔲, type Enrollments Chart and then click **OK**.

   ■ **You have completed Skill 9 of 10**

▶ Positioning or resizing the chart legend can make more space available for a chart.

▶ The *plot area*—the area bound by the axes in a chart—can be enhanced by adding a pattern, changing colors, or inserting an image.

1. Switch to Design view, and then in the chart area, double-click the chart to start Microsoft Graph.

2. In the chart area, click, and then double-click the *legend*—the chart element that identifies the patterns or colors that are assigned to the categories in the chart.

3. On the **Font tab** of the **Format Legend** dialog box, under **Size**, delete the existing font size, and then type 5 Under **Font style**, click **Regular**.

4. In the **Format Legend** dialog box, click the **Placement tab**, and then under **Placement**, select the **Bottom** option button. Compare with **Figure 1**.

5. Click **OK** to close the dialog box. Click in the **Page Header**. Switch to Report view, and then compare your screen with **Figure 2**.

6. Switch to Design view, and then double-click the chart to start Microsoft Graph. Right-click a blank area of the chart and in the displayed shortcut menu, click **Format Chart Area**.

■ Continue to the next page to complete the skill

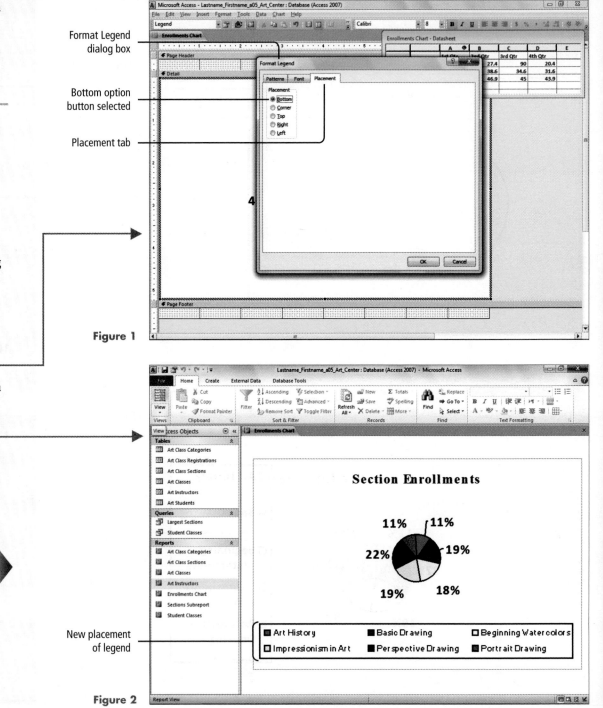

Format Legend dialog box

Bottom option button selected

Placement tab

Figure 1

New placement of legend

Figure 2

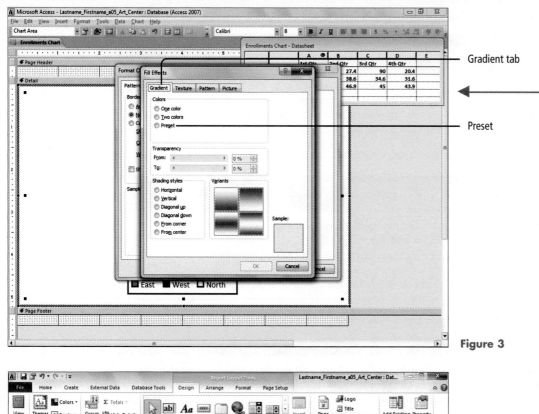

Gradient tab

Preset

Figure 3

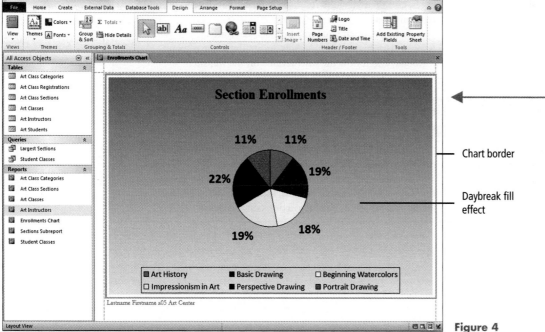

Chart border

Daybreak fill effect

Figure 4

7. In the **Format Chart Area** dialog box, on the **Patterns tab**, click the **Fill Effects** button, and then compare your screen with **Figure 3**.

> The Fill Effects dialog box provides design options for your plot area. These options include gradients, textures, patterns, and background images.

8. On the **Gradient tab** of the **Fill Effects** dialog box, under **Colors**, select the **Preset** option button. Click the **Preset colors arrow**, and then select **Daybreak**.

> A *gradient* is not a single color but rather it is a range of position-dependent colors typically ranging from lighter to darker. A *gradient fill* is an effect where one color fades into another.

9. Click **OK** to close the **Fill Effects** dialog box.

10. Click **OK** to close the **Format Chart Area** dialog box.

11. Click in the **Page Header** section to exit Microsoft Graph.

12. On the **Design tab**, in the **Controls group**, click the **Label** button [Aa]. Scroll down, position the [A] pointer in the upper left corner of the **Page Footer**, and then click the left mouse button. Immediately type Lastname Firstname a05 Art Center

13. Switch to Layout view. Click in the chart area, and then with the [↕] pointer, drag the bottom border down until the border meets the **Page Footer** label. Compare your screen with **Figure 4**.

14. If your instructor has asked you to print your work for this chapter, print the report.

15. Save [💾], and then **Close** [✖] the report. **Exit** Access.

Done! You have completed Skill 10 of 10 and your document is complete!

More Skills

The following More Skills are located at **www.pearsonhighered.com/skills**

More Skills ⑪ Format and Position Report Controls

Proper alignment and spacing of controls improves the professional look and feel of a form or report. The Access alignment and position tools enable you to position controls efficiently and precisely in a report or form.

In More Skills 11, you will align and position controls in a report to make it look more professional.

To begin, open your web browser, navigate to www.pearsonhighered.com/skills, locate the name of your textbook, and follow the instructions on the website.

More Skills ⑫ Insert a Hyperlink Control in a Report

Hyperlinks are inserted into forms or reports. When a hyperlink control is clicked, the corresponding web page or file displays in an web browser.

In More Skills 12, you will add a hyperlink control to a report and then test the link.

To begin, open your web browser, navigate to www.pearsonhighered.com/skills, locate the name of your textbook, and follow the instructions on the website.

More Skills ⑬ Specify Relationship Join Types

When a database object displays data from two related tables, it joins the two tables by matching the values in the field common to both tables. The relationship between the two tables can be modified so that all of the records from one of the tables can be displayed even when there is no match in the other table.

In More Skills 13, you will specify different relationship join types, and then view the results in queries that depend on those relationships.

To begin, open your web browser, navigate to www.pearsonhighered.com/skills, locate the name of your textbook, and follow the instructions on the website.

More Skills ⑭ Add ActiveX Controls to a Report

When working with forms or reports, you can use ActiveX controls to enhance your reports with advanced features from other applications.

In More Skills 14, you will embed a Windows Media Player into your report to play a media file.

To begin, open your web browser, navigate to www.pearsonhighered.com/skills, locate the name of your textbook, and follow the instructions on the website.

Key Terms

Online Help Skills

1. **Start** ⊕ Access. In the upper right corner of the Access window, click the **Help** button ⊙. In the **Help** window, click the **Maximize** ⬜ button.

2. Click in the search box, type report and then click the **Search** button 🔍. In the search results, click **Create a grouped or summary report**. Compare your screen with **Figure 1**.

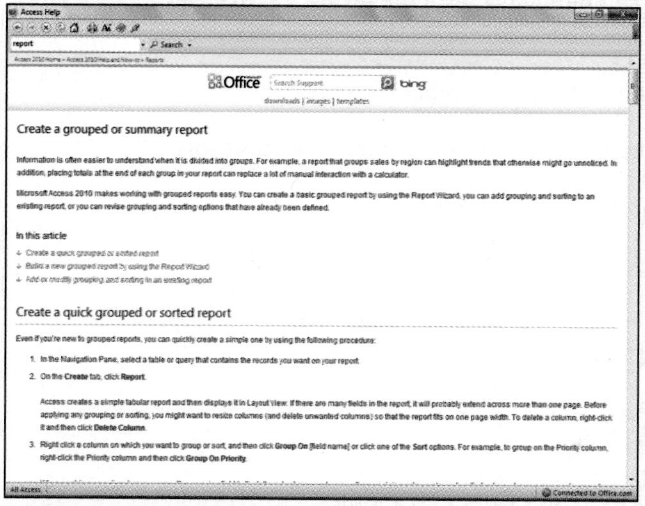

Figure 1

3. Read the section to see if you can answer the following: When could you use a grouped report? What tool in Access can be used to create a grouped report?

Matching

Match each term in the second column with its correct definition in the first column by writing the letter of the term on the blank line in front of the correct definition.

____ **1.** A tool used to create queries within database objects such as forms and reports.

____ **2.** The process of combining two or more text values to create one text value.

____ **3.** A report that is inserted into another report.

____ **4.** A field in a subreport that links the report to its subreport.

____ **5.** A field in a report that is used to link the report to its subreport.

____ **6.** The text that identifies each data marker on a chart.

____ **7.** A column, bar, area, dot, pie slice, or other symbol that represents a single point of data.

____ **8.** A collection of related data points used in a chart that is usually represented by a unique color.

____ **9.** An effect where one color fades into another.

____ **10.** A chart element that identifies the patterns or colors that are assigned to the categories in a chart.

A Child field

B Concatenation

C Data label

D Data marker

E Data series

F Gradient fill

G Legend

H Master field

I Query Builder

J Subreport

Multiple Choice

Choose the correct answer.

1. A text box that derives its value from an expression.
   A. Field control
   B. Calculated control
   C. Query control

2. The process of combining two or more text values to create one text value.
   A. Concatenation
   B. Conjunction
   C. Linking

3. A report that is inserted into another report.
   A. Secondary report
   B. Linked report
   C. Subreport

4. A field in a report that is used to link the report to its subreport.
   A. Master field
   B. Primary field
   C. Secondary field

5. The field to which a child field is linked.
   A. Master field
   B. Parent field
   C. Orphan field

6. The text that identifies each data marker on a chart.
   A. Title
   B. Data label
   C. Legend

7. A range of position-dependent colors typically ranging from lighter to darker.
   A. Gradient
   B. Montage
   C. Spectrum

8. An effect where one color fades into another.
   A. Impressionism
   B. Color scheme
   C. Gradient fill

9. A chart element that identifies the patterns or colors that are assigned to the categories in the chart.
   A. Axis
   B. Legend
   C. Plot area

10. The area bound by the axes in a chart.
    A. Plot area
    B. Legend
    C. Title

Topics for Discussion

1. When creating a report based on a query, which method would be best: creating a query and then building the report from the query or creating a report and then embedding a query in the report? State the reasons for your answer.

2. When creating a subreport, which method would be best: using the SubReport Wizard or using the drag-and-drop method? State the reasons for your answer.

Skill Check

To complete this database, you will need the following file:

- a05_Triathlon

You will save your database as:

- Lastname_Firstname_a05_Triathlon

1. **Start** Access. Open **a05_Triathlon**, and then save the database in your **Access Chapter 5** folder as Lastname_Firstname_a05_Triathlon If necessary, enable the content.

2. Open the **Largest Sponsors in 2011** report in Layout view. On the **Design tab**, in the **Tools group**, click **Add Existing Fields**. From the **Field List** task pane, drag the **Race Year** and **Amount** fields from the pane and then drop them to the right of the **Sponsor Name** column to create two new report columns. **Close** the **Field List**.

3. Switch to Design view, and then open the property sheet. On the **Data tab** of the property sheet, in the **Record Source** box, click the **Build** button. For the **Amount** criterion, type >3000 and for the **Race Year** criterion, type =2011 Compare your screen with **Figure 1**. ──────────

4. **Run** the query, click **Save**, and then **Close** the Query Builder window. Scroll to view the **Date** and **Time** controls, and then select the **Date** control. On the **Format tab**, change its **Format** property box to **Medium Date**.

5. Click in the **Page Footer**. On the **Design tab**, in the **Header/Footer group**, click **Page Numbers**. In the **Page Numbers** dialog box, under **Format**, select **Page N of M**, select **Bottom of Page [Footer]**, and then click **OK**. Switch to Report view, and then compare with **Figure 2**. ──────────

6. Switch to Design view, and then in the **Report Footer**, insert a label with text Lastname Firstname a05 Triathlon Switch to Report view. **Save** and **Close** the report.

7. On the **Create tab**, click **Query Design**. Double-click to add the **Racers**, **Results**, and **Brackets** tables, and then **Close** the **Show Table** dialog box.

 Continue to the next page to complete this Skill Check

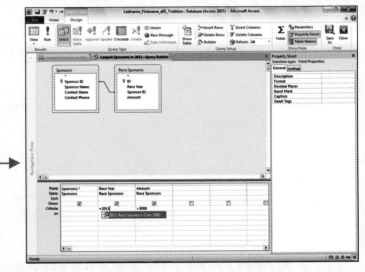

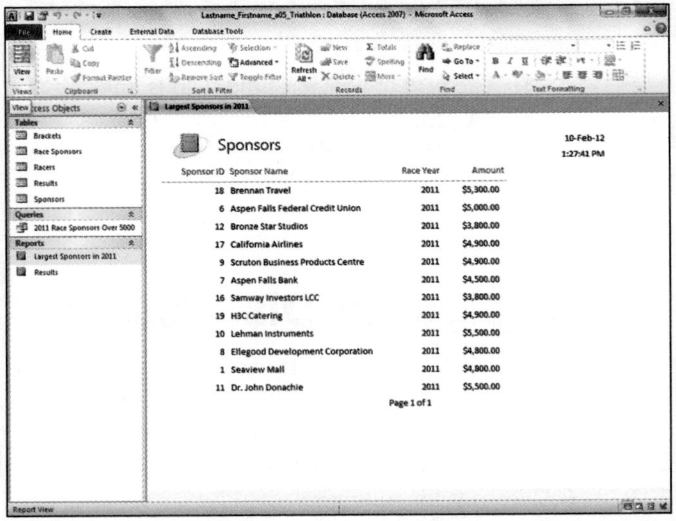

Figure 1

Figure 2

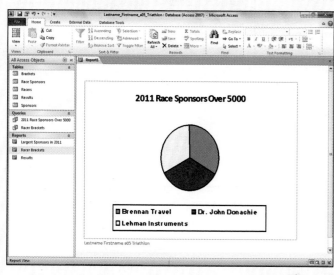

Figure 3

Figure 4

8. Right-click the **Field** box in the first column, and then click **Zoom**. Type Full Name: [First Name] + " " + [Last Name] and then click **OK**. Change the **Full Name** column **Sort** box to **Ascending**. In the **Brackets** table, double-click the **Bracket ID** and **Description** fields, and then **Run** the query. **Save** the query as Racer Brackets and then **Close** the query.

9. With the **Racer Brackets** query selected, on the **Create tab**, click **Report**. In Design view, in the **Detail** section, click in a blank area of the report. Click the first **Full Name** text box. On the **Format tab** of the property sheet, scroll down to locate the **Hide Duplicates** property, and then change the property to **Yes**.

10. With the pointer, drag the **Page Footer** bar down about 1 inch. In the **Navigation Pane**, drag the **Results** report to the **Detail** section just below **Full Name**. Delete the subreport label, and then in the **Report Footer**, delete the **Count** control. In the **Report Footer**, insert a label with text Lastname Firstname a05 Triathlon

11. **Save** the report as Racer Brackets Switch to Report view, wait a few seconds, compare your screen with **Figure 3**, and then **Close** the report.

12. On the **Create tab**, in the **Reports group**, click **Report Design**. In the **Controls group**, click **Chart**. In the **Detail** section, position the crosshairs of the pointer in the upper left corner of the **Detail** section, drag down and to the right to the **5 inch** vertical grid line and the **7 inch** horizontal grid line.

13. In the **Chart Wizard**, under **View**, select **Queries**, and then choose **Query: 2011 Race Sponsors Over 5000**. Click **Next**, and then **Move all** the query's fields to the **Fields for Chart** list. Click **Next**, and then click **Pie Chart**. Click **Finish**.

14. Double-click a blank area of the chart, click, and then double-click the **Legend** to display the **Format Legend** dialog box. Change the **Font Size** to **5**. Click the **Placement tab**, and then select **Bottom**. Click **OK**. Double-click the **Chart Title**. In the displayed dialog box, under **Size**, select **8**, and then click **OK**. Click in the **Page Footer**. Scroll to the left.

15. In the **Detail** section, just below the chart, add a label with the text Lastname Firstname a05 Triathlon Switch to Report view and compare with **Figure 4**.

16. Click **Save**, type 2011 Sponsors and then click **OK**. Print or submit electronically as directed by your instructor, and then **Exit** Access.

Done! You have completed the Skill Check

Assess Your Skills 1

To complete this database, you will need the following file:

- a05_Police

You will save your database as:

- Lastname_Firstname_a05_Police

1. **Start** Access and open the student data file **a05_Police. Save** the file in your **Access Chapter 5** folder with the name Lastname_Firstname_a05_Police

2. Create a new query in Design view. Add the **Employees** and **Police Awards** tables to the query design. In the first column, write an expression that joins the **First Name** and **Last Name** fields from the **Employees** table with a space between the two fields. Label the column Name Sort the column in ascending order.

3. In the query's second column, add the **Award** field from the **Police Awards** table. Add the **Employee ID** from the **Employees** table. **Save** the query as Employees with Awards

4. Create a report based on the **Employees with Awards** query. Hide the duplicate records within the report, and then delete the **Count** calculated control.

5. Switch to Report view. **Save** the report as Employees with Awards and then **Close** the report.

6. Create a **Blank Report**. From the Field List for the **Employees** table, add the **First Name**, Last Name, and **Home Phone** fields. **Save** the report as Employee Contact Information

7. Create a report for the **Police Awards** table. Reduce the width of the columns to fit the report on one page. **Save** the report as Police Awards and then **Close** the report.

8. Use the drag-and-drop method to add the **Police Awards** report to the **Employees with Awards** report as a subreport. Link the reports using the **Employee ID** field. Delete the subreport label. **Save**, and then **Close** the **Employees with Awards** report.

9. **Open** the **Police Awards** subreport, and then switch to Design view. Delete the controls that display the logo, title, count, date, and time.

10. **Save** and then **Close** the subreport.

11. **Open** the **Employees with Awards** report in Design view. Reduce the width of the report. In the **Report Footer**, using your own name, insert a label with the text Lastname Firstname a05 Police Switch to Report view and compare your work with **Figure 1**.

12. **Save**, and then **Close** the report, and then **Exit** Access. Submit your work as directed by your instructor.

   Done! You have completed Assess Your Skills 1

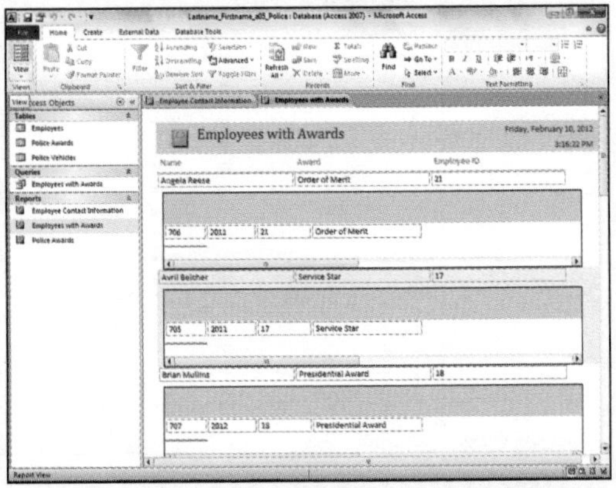

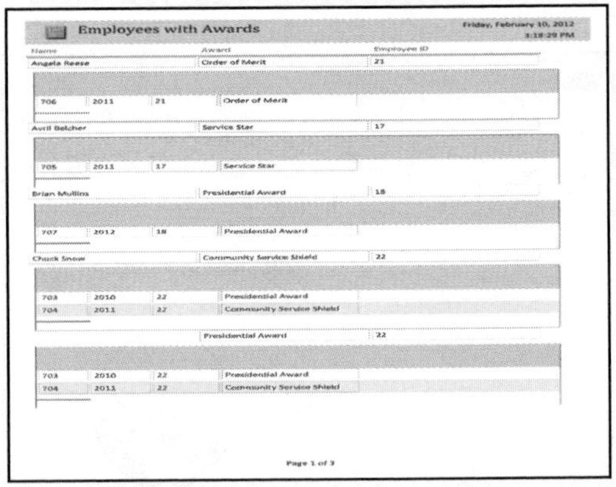

Figure 1

Assess Your Skills 2

To complete this database, you will need the following file:

- a05_Rentals

You will save your database as:

- Lastname_Firstname_a05_Rentals

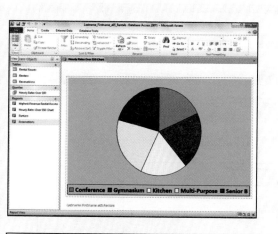

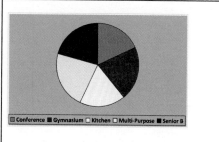

Figure 1

1. **Start** Access and open **a05_Rentals**. **Save** the file in your **Access Chapter 5** folder with the name Lastname_Firstname_a05_Rentals

2. Use the **Report** tool to create a new report based on the **Rental Rooms** table, and then **Save** the report with the name Highest Revenue Rental Rooms In the report, use the **Query Builder** tool to add the **Room Number, Room Type, Hourly Rate, Deposit,** and **Description** fields from the **Rental Rooms** table. Add criteria to the query that will display the records where the **Hourly Rate** is greater than $50

3. Run the query, and then verify that five records display. **Save**, and then **Close** the **Query Builder** window.

4. Switch to Layout view, and adjust the column widths so that the report will be no more than one page wide. Delete the **Page** and **Count** controls. **Save** and **Close** the report.

5. Open the **Renters** report in Design view. In the **Detail** section, use the **SubReport Wizard** to add the **Reservations** report as a subreport.

6. In the **Renters** report, change the **Date** control to **Medium Date** format. Remove the **Page** control, and then remove the **Count** control.

7. In the **Report Footer**, using your own name, insert a label with the text

Lastname_Firstname_a05_Rentals **Save**, and then **Close** the report.

8. Open the **Reservations** subreport in its own window and remove the **Logo, Title, Date, Time, Page,** and **Count** controls. Reduce the size of the **Report Header** so that it no longer displays. Reduce the width of the report. **Save**, and then **Close** the report.

9. Create a blank report, and then insert a **Pie Chart** based on the **Hourly Rates Over $50** query. Use the **Room Type** and **Hourly Rate** for the Data Series. Place the **Legend** below the chart axis, and then change its **Font Size** to **7**. Format the **Plot Area** with light green—the third color in the third row—and then delete the **Chart Title**.

10. Switch to Design view, and then drag the right border of the chart to the **8 inch** horizontal grid line. Change the **Page Layout** to **Landscape**. In the **Page Footer**, insert a label with the text Lastname Firstname a05 Rentals

11. **Save** the report as Hourly Rates Over $50 Chart Switch to Report view, and then compare your screen with **Figure 1**.

12. **Close** the report, and then **Exit** Access. Submit your work as directed by your instructor.

Done! You have completed Assess Your Skills 2

Assess Your Skills Visually

To complete this database, you will need the following file:

■ a05_Park_Outings

You will save your database as:

■ Lastname_Firstname_a05_Park_Outings

Open the database **a05_Park_Outings** and save the database in your **Access Chapter 5** folder as Lastname_Firstname_a05_Park_Outings

Create the report and subreport shown in **Figure 1**. The main report displays fields from the **Outings** table and the subreport displays fields from the **Schedule Outings** table. The report layout is **Landscape**. Using the **Report** tool, create an **Outings** report, from the **Outings** table. In the **Navigation Pane**, select the **Scheduled Outings** table. Using the **Report** tool, create a **Scheduled Outings** report from the **Scheduled Outings** table. **Close** the **Scheduled Outings** report. Add the **Scheduled Outings** report to the **Outings** report as a subreport, and then format the subreport as shown in **Figure 1**.

Done! You have completed Assess Your Skills Visually

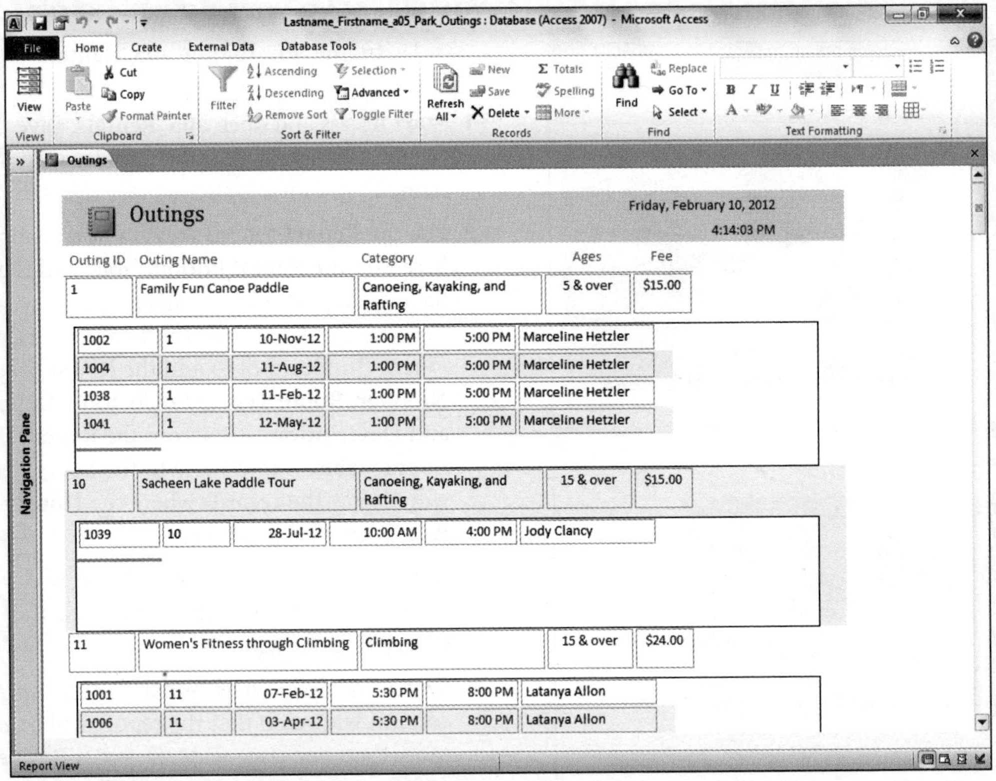

Figure 1

Skills in Context

To complete this database, you will need the following file:

- a05_Aquatics

You will save your database as:

- Lastname_Firstname_a05_Aquatics

Open **a05_Aquatics** and save the database in your **Access Chapter 5** folder as Lastname_Firstname_a05_Aquatics Create a report named Classes with Low Enrollment Within the report, build a query that shows the swimming classes with enrollments of less than eight people. The query should show all fields from the **Swimming Classes** table. Remove the **Count** control and

format the **Date** control with the **Short Date** format. Add the file name to the report **Page Footer**, apply a **Theme** of your choice, and then format the report to create an effective display.

Submit the report as directed by your instructor.

Done! You have completed Skills in Context

Skills and You

To complete this database, you will need the following file:

- a05_CD_Collection

You will save your database as:

- Lastname_Firstname_a05_CD_Collection

Using the skills you have practiced in this chapter, open the database **a05_CD_Collection**, which tracks compact disc (CD) music collections. Using the **Album** form provided, enter five of your favorite CDs. If you do not own any CDs, use data from CDs listed at an online store. Create a report based on the **Album**

table. In the main report, add a subreport based on the **Tracks** table, which you have populated. In the subreport, be sure that the tracks display for each album listed in the main report.

Done! You have completed Skills and You

CHAPTER 6

Add Advanced Form Features

▶ Access 2010 enables the user to create a form that can access and edit multiple tables.

▶ The controls in forms can be modified to produce a superior layout than the default layout.

Your starting screen will look like this:

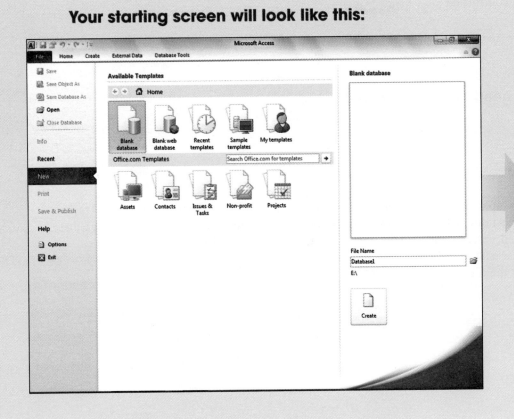

SKILLS

Skills 1-10 Training

At the end of this chapter, you will be able to:

Skill 1 Create Forms in Design View

Skill 2 Position Controls in Forms

Skill 3 Use Lookup Fields in Forms

Skill 4 Create Pop Up Forms

Skill 5 Add Button Controls to Forms

Skill 6 Create PivotChart Forms

Skill 7 Create PivotTable Forms

Skill 8 Create Navigation Forms

Skill 9 Modify Navigation Forms

Skill 10 Add Pages to Navigation Forms

MORE SKILLS

More Skills 11 Add Option Groups to Forms

More Skills 12 Create Switchboards

More Skills 13 Apply Special Effects to Form Controls

More Skills 14 Position and Size Controls in Design View

Outcome

Using the skills listed to the left will enable you to create documents like these:

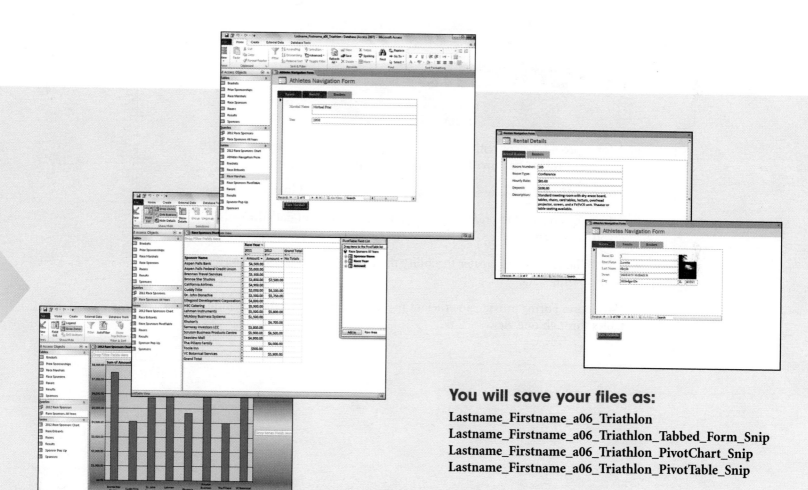

You will save your files as:

Lastname_Firstname_a06_Triathlon
Lastname_Firstname_a06_Triathlon_Tabbed_Form_Snip
Lastname_Firstname_a06_Triathlon_PivotChart_Snip
Lastname_Firstname_a06_Triathlon_PivotTable_Snip

In this chapter, you will create documents for the Aspen Falls City Hall, which provides essential services for the citizens and visitors of Aspen Falls, California.

Introduction

- ▶ A form provides a convenient way of entering data into a table. Access 2010 allows controls to be moved with ease in Layout view.

- ▶ Access 2010 allows the user to add functional buttons and images to forms.

- ▶ A form can be used to create a graphical representation of data through a PivotChart form.

- ▶ A PivotTable provides greater flexibility than a table when it comes to summarizing data.

- ▶ Navigation Forms provide an efficient method for entering data into multiple tables through one view.

Find your student data files here:

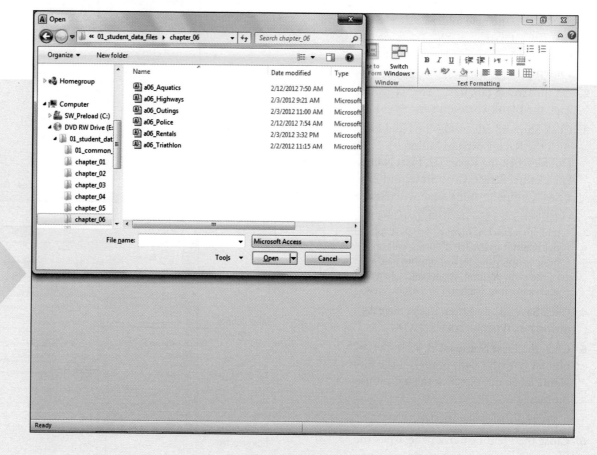

Student data files needed for this chapter:

- a06_Triathlon

- Creating a form for data entry is very simple using the Blank Form tool.
- Working with forms in Design View enables advanced editing.

1. **Start** ● Access, and then open **a06_Triathlon**. Use the **Save As** dialog box to create a **New folder** named Access Chapter 6 Save the database in the new folder as Lastname_Firstname_a06_Triathlon and then press Enter. If necessary, enable the content.

2. On the **Create tab**, in the **Forms group**, click the **Blank Form** button.

3. Click Show all tables. On the **Field List**, click the **Racers** expand button ⊞. Double-click the **Racer ID, First Name, Last Name, Street, City, State,** and **Zip** fields. Compare your screen with **Figure 1**.

   The form displays the fields from the *Racers* table in a ***stacked layout***—labels display the field names in the left column, and text boxes display the corresponding field values in the right column. By default, when a form is created, it is displayed in Layout View.

4. Click **Save** 🖫, and then in the **Save As** dialog box type Racers Click **OK**.

5. Click the **First Name** label. With the pointer over the right border of the **First Name** label, double-click the left mouse button.

   The entire label now displays.

6. **Close** the **Field List** task pane. Click the **State** text box, and then compare your screen with **Figure 2**.

■ **Continue to the next page to complete the skill**

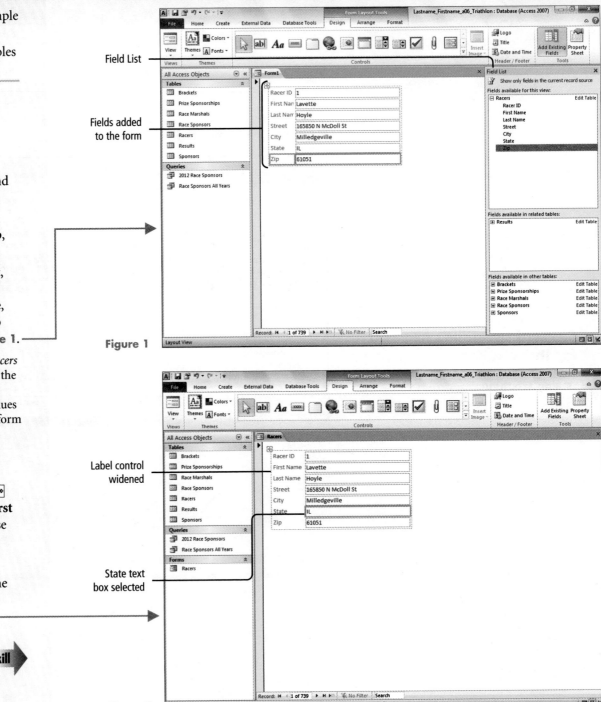

Field List

Fields added to the form

Figure 1

Label control widened

State text box selected

Figure 2

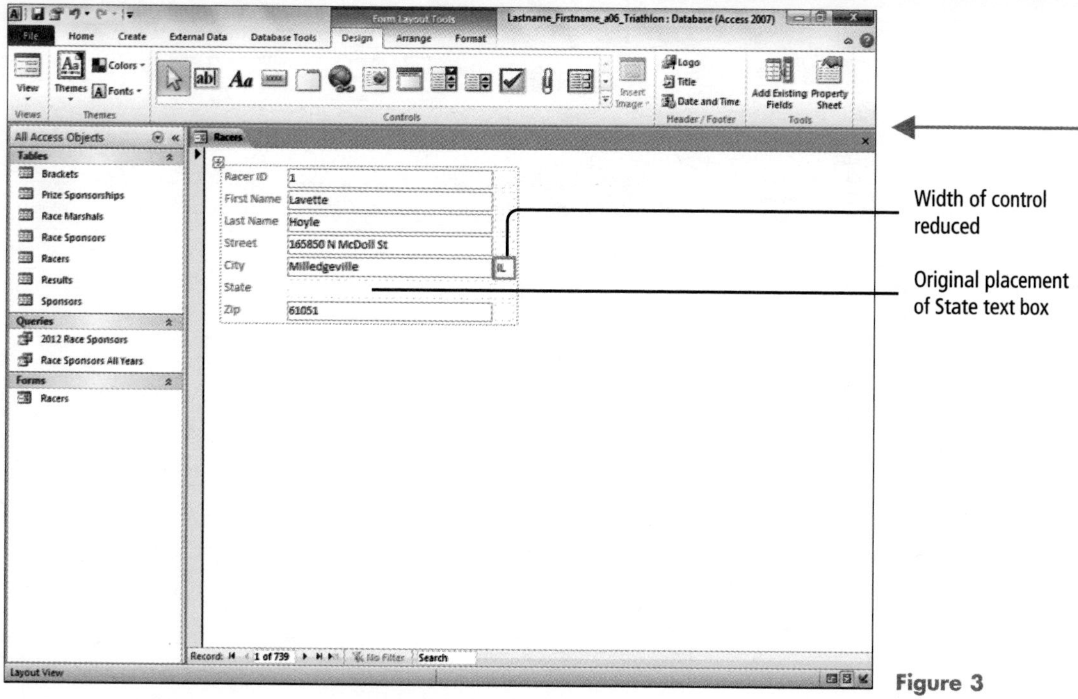

Width of control reduced

Original placement of State text box

Figure 3

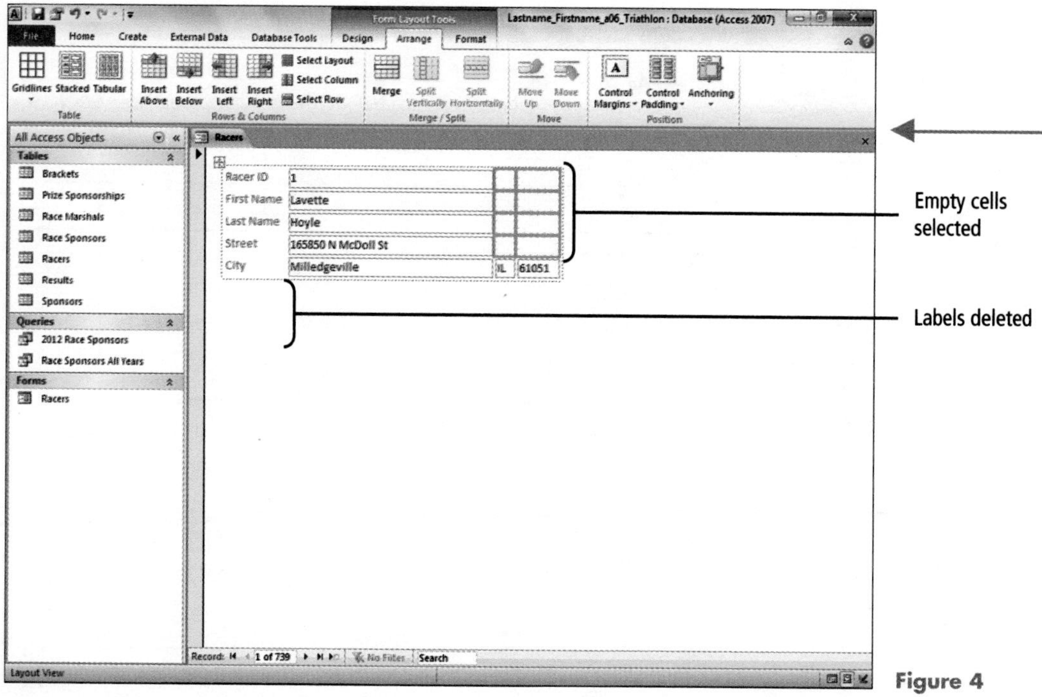

Empty cells selected

Labels deleted

Figure 4

7. With the ↔ pointer displayed, drag the **State** text box to the right of the **City** text box just before the dotted line. When a vertical orange line displays to the right of the **City** text box, release the left mouse button.

8. With the ↔ pointer displayed, drag the right border of the **State** text box to the left, as shown in **Figure 3**.

9. Click the **Zip** text box, and then drag the text box to the right of the **State** text box. Reduce the width of the **Zip** text box.

10. Click the **State** label. Press (Shift), and then click the **Zip** label. On the **Arrange tab**, in the **Rows & Columns group**, click **Select Row**, and then press (Delete).

11. Click the empty cell to the right of the **Racer ID** text box. Press (Shift), and then click the remaining empty cells, as shown in **Figure 4**.

12. On the **Arrange tab**, in the **Merge/Split group**, click **Merge**.

    The eight empty cells have now been merged to create one cell.

13. Display the **Design tab**, and then, in the **Controls group**, click the **More** button. From the displayed list, click the **Image** button. Click in the merged cell.

    An Insert Picture dialog box displays.

14. Navigate to your **Access Chapter 6** student data files, and then click **a06_Aspen_River**. Click **OK**.

15. Click **Save**, and then **Close** the form.

- **You have completed Skill 1 of 10**

▶ Access provides a number of tools to change easily the position of controls in a form.

▶ Using positioning tools in Access can allow for greater accuracy when repositioning controls.

1. In the **Navigation Pane**, select the **Racers** table. Display the **Create tab**, and then in the **Forms group**, click the **Form** button.

2. Click **Save** 🖫, and then type Race Entrants Click **OK**.

3. Switch to Design view, click the **Table.Results** subform, and then press ⌈Delete⌉ to remove the subform. Compare your screen with **Figure 1**.

   The Form tool is included in the Results table as a subform because it is related to the Racers table. The subform is not needed because it will be included later in a Navigation control.

4. In the **Detail** section, click the **Racer ID** text box. Press ⌈Shift⌉, and then click the **First Name**, **Last Name**, **Street**, **City**, **State**, and **Zip** text boxes.

5. If necessary, close the **Field List** pane. Scroll to the right. Point to the right border of one of the selected text boxes. With the ⬌ pointer, drag to the left until the right border reaches the **3 inch** horizontal grid line. Compare your screen with **Figure 2**.

6. Display the **Arrange tab**, and then in the **Table group**, click **Remove Layout**.

   The stacked control layout is removed, and each control can now be positioned independent of the others.

■ **Continue to the next page to complete the skill**

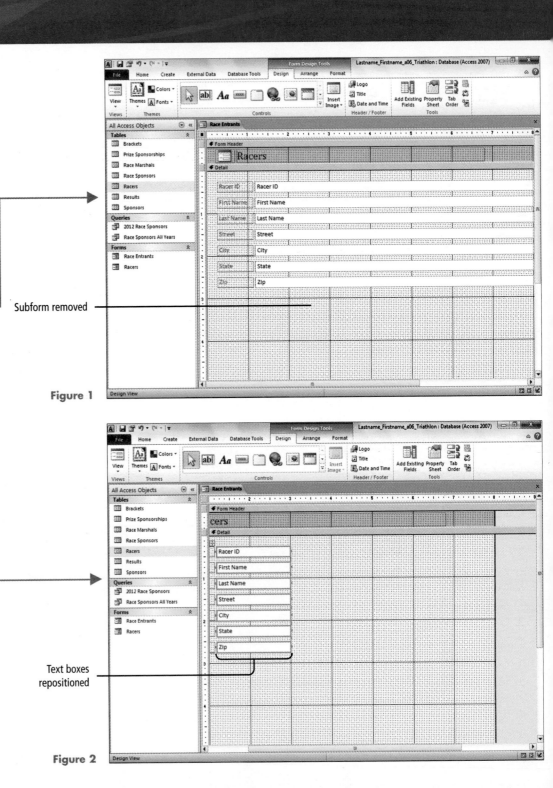

Subform removed

Figure 1

Text boxes repositioned

Figure 2

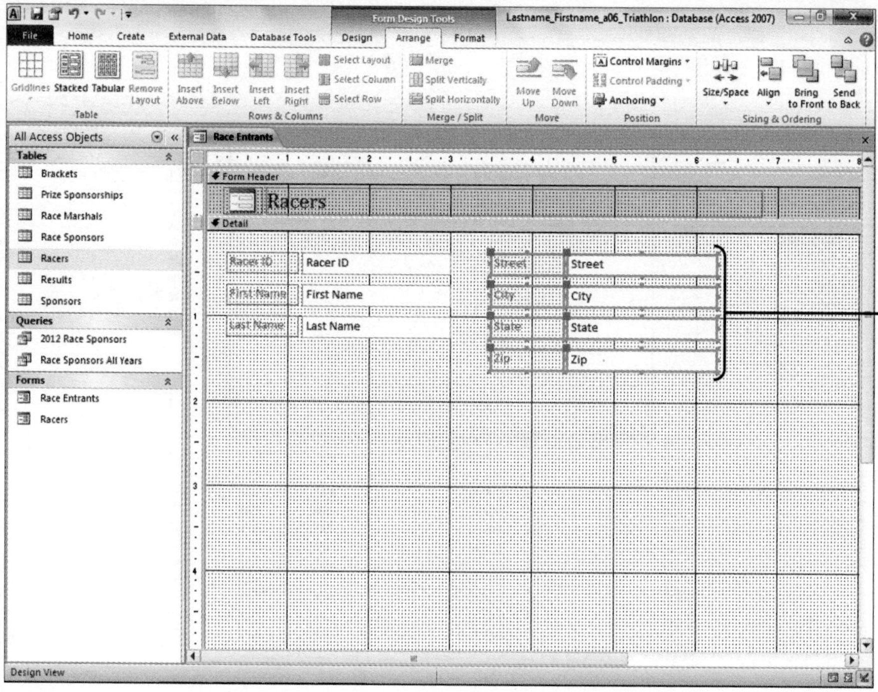

Repositioned
controls

Figure 3

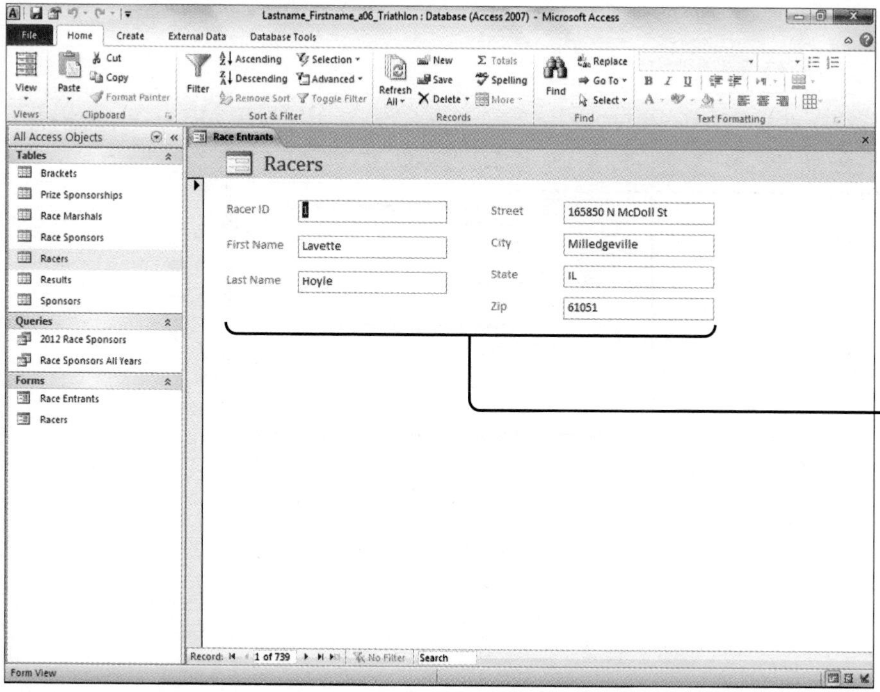

Controls in two
columns

Figure 4

7. Click a blank area of the form so that no controls are selected. Click the **Street** label, press [Shift], and then click the **Street** text box, the **City** label, the **City** text box, the **State** label, the **State** text box, the **Zip** label, and then the **Zip** text box.

   The four address labels and four text boxes are now selected.

8. With the pointer over the center of the **City** label, hold down the left mouse button and drag all of the controls and labels up and to the right so that the controls are placed on the **3.5 inch** horizontal grid line and the top edge of the **Street** controls are vertically aligned with the top edge of the **Racer ID** controls. Compare your screen with **Figure 3**.

9. Click the **Racer ID** label. Press [Shift], and then click the **Racer ID** text box, the two **First Name** controls, and the two **Last Name** controls.

10. With the six controls still selected, on the **Arrange tab**, in the **Sizing & Ordering group**, click **Size/Space**. From the displayed menu, click **Increase Vertical**.

11. With the six controls still selected, on the **Arrange tab**, in the **Sizing & Ordering group**, click **Align**, and then click **To Grid**.

12. Switch to Form view, and then compare your screen with **Figure 4**.

13. Click **Save** , and then **Close** the form.

▪ **You have completed Skill 2 of 10**

► A *lookup field* is a field whose values are retrieved from another table or from a list.

► The Lookup Wizard simplifies the steps for creating a lookup field.

1. Open the **Results** table, and then click in the last column.

2. Display the **Fields tab**. In the **Add & Delete group**, click the **More Fields** button, and then under **Basic Types**, click **Lookup & Relationship** to start the Lookup Wizard as shown in **Figure 1**.

   A lookup field can retrieve values from a table, a query, or from a list that you type.

3. Be sure that the **I want the lookup field to get the values from another table or query** option button is selected, and then click **Next**.

4. In the list of available tables, be sure that **Table: Brackets** is selected, and then click **Next**.

5. In the list of **Available Fields**, be sure that **Bracket ID** is selected, and then click the **Move** button ▸.

6. Click **Next** three times. In the **What label would you like for your lookup field** box, replace the existing text with Bracket Compare your screen with **Figure 2**, and then click **Finish**.

■ **Continue to the next page to complete the skill** ▸

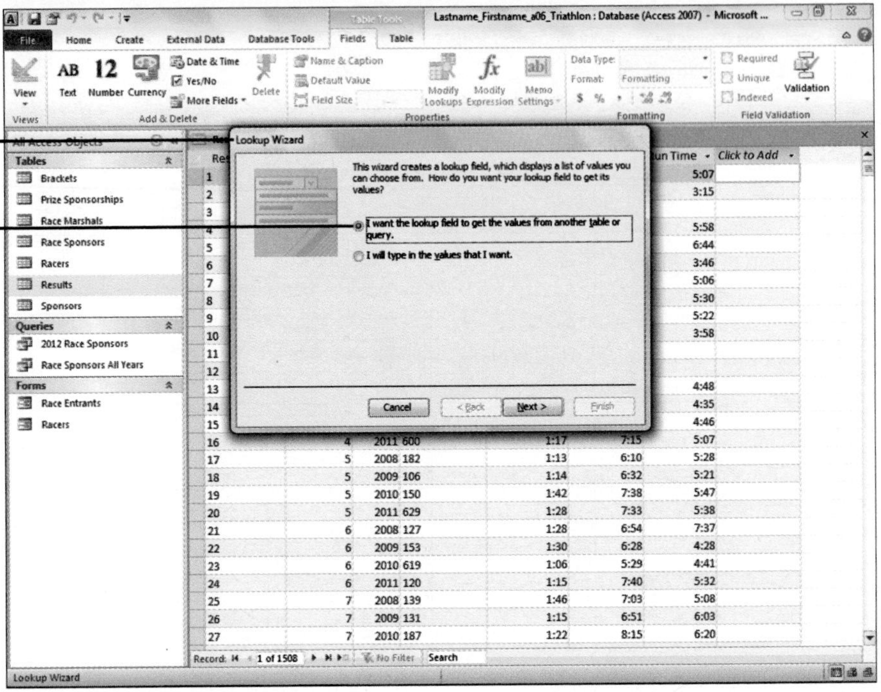

Lookup Wizard dialog box

Option selected

Figure 1

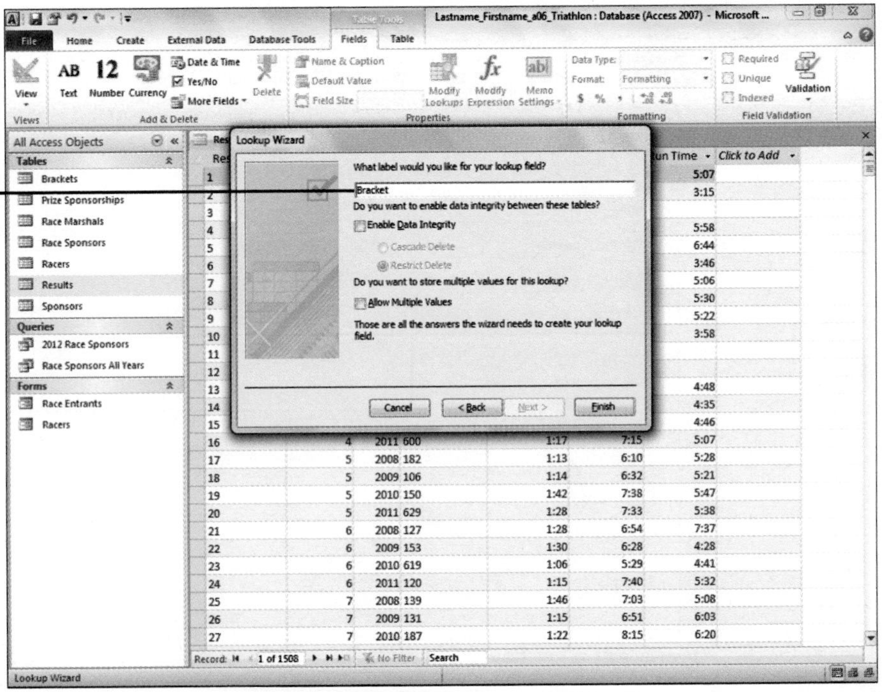

Value assigned to lookup field

Figure 2

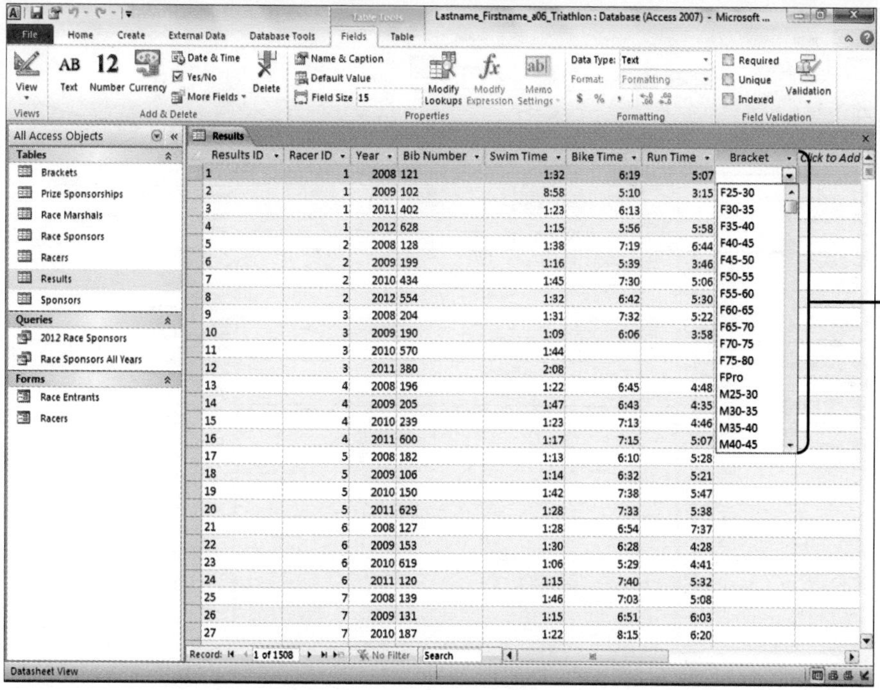

Combo box

Figure 3

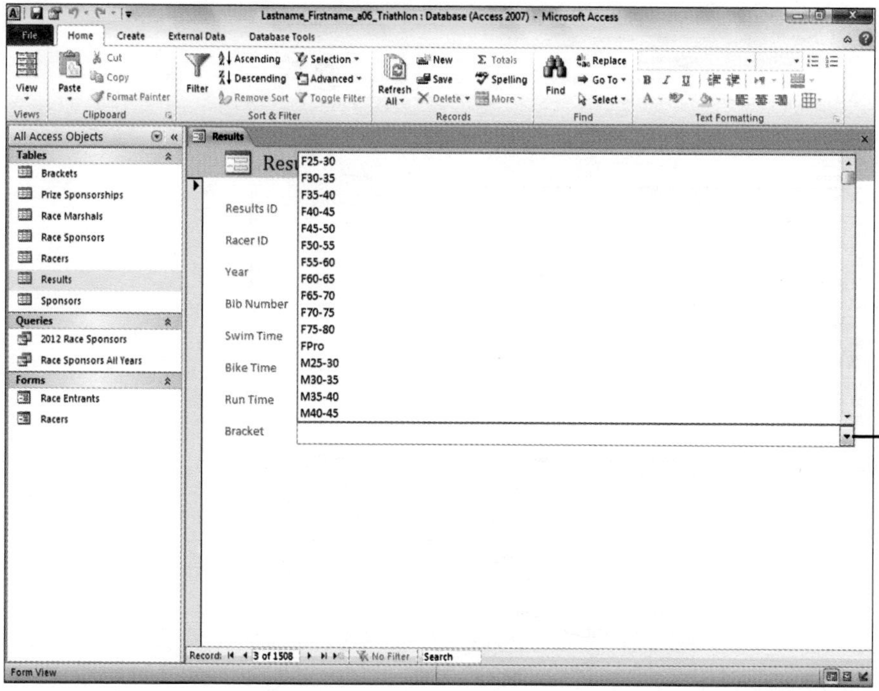

Bracket combo box

Figure 4

7. Click **Save**. If necessary, in the first record, click the Bracket field to select it. Click the displayed **Bracket arrow**. Compare your screen with Figure 3, and then from the list, click **F25-30**.

> The values from the Brackets table display in a *combo box*—a text box and a list that is hidden until you click its arrow. Lookup fields display as combo boxes in datasheets and forms.

8. In the second record, click the **Bracket** field. Type fp and notice that the first choice in the combo box list that starts with the letter *FP* displays. Press Tab to assign *FPro* the Bracket field.

> In this manner, a lookup field increases speed and accuracy when data is entered into tables.

9. Close ☒ the **Results** table. With the **Results** table selected in the **Navigation Pane**, on the **Create tab**, in the **Forms group**, click **Form**.

10. Switch to Form view, and then in the Navigation bar, click the **Next record** ▶ button two times.

11. Click the **Bracket box arrow**, compare your screen with Figure 4, and then click **FPro**.

12. Click **Save**, and then press Enter.

13. Close ☒ the table.

■ **You have completed Skill 3 of 10**

► A *pop up form* is a form that when opened remains on top, even when it is not the active form.

1. In the **Navigation Pane**, select the **Sponsors** table. On the **Create tab**, in the **Forms group**, click **More Forms**, and then click **Split Form**.

    The Race Sponsors form displays with Form view in the top half of the form and Datasheet view in the lower half of the form. Recall that a split form displays two synchronized views of the same form where the lower view displays as a datasheet.

2. Click **Save** 💾. In the **Save As** dialog box, type Sponsor Pop Up and then click **OK**.

3. Switch to Design view, and then open the property sheet. In the displayed property sheet, select the **Selection type** box arrow, and then click **Form**. On the **Other tab**, click in the **Pop Up** box. Click the displayed **Pop Up** arrow, and then click **Yes**. Compare your screen with **Figure 1**.

4. Switch to Form view. In the **Navigation Pane**, double-click the **Racers** form, and then compare your screen with **Figure 2**.

    Notice that the pop up form remains over the active Racers form. It is generally a good idea to reduce the size of the pop up form so that an active form is partially visible.

■ **Continue to the next page to complete the skill**

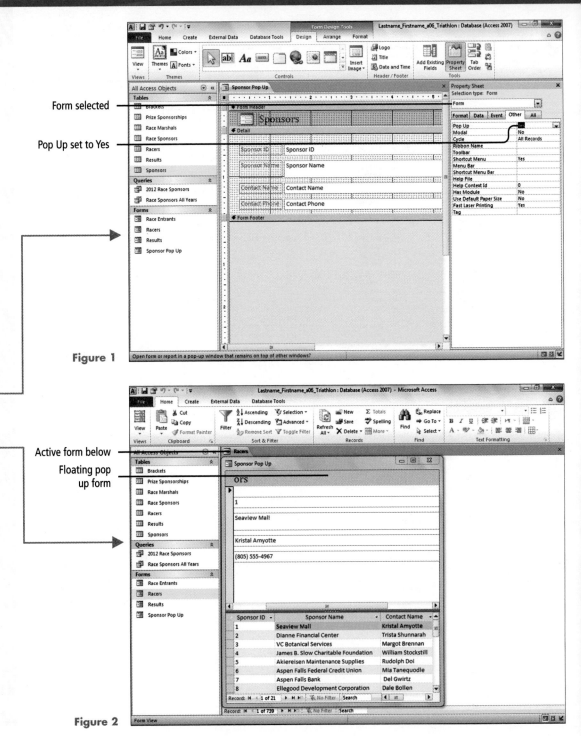

Form selected

Pop Up set to Yes

Figure 1

Active form below

Floating pop up form

Figure 2

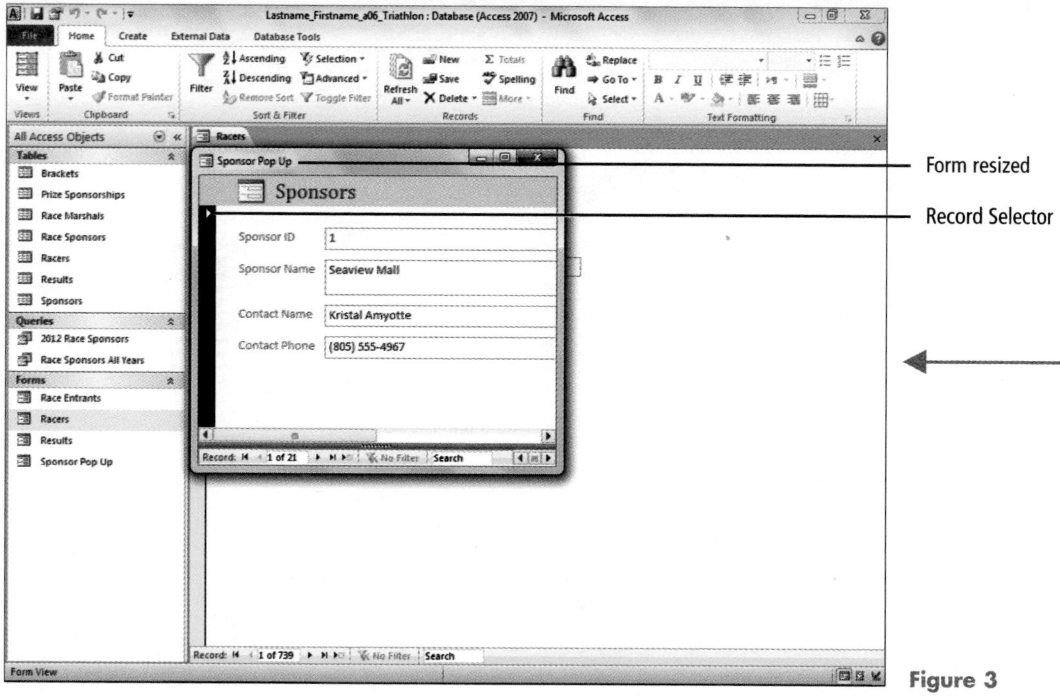

Form resized

Record Selector

Figure 3

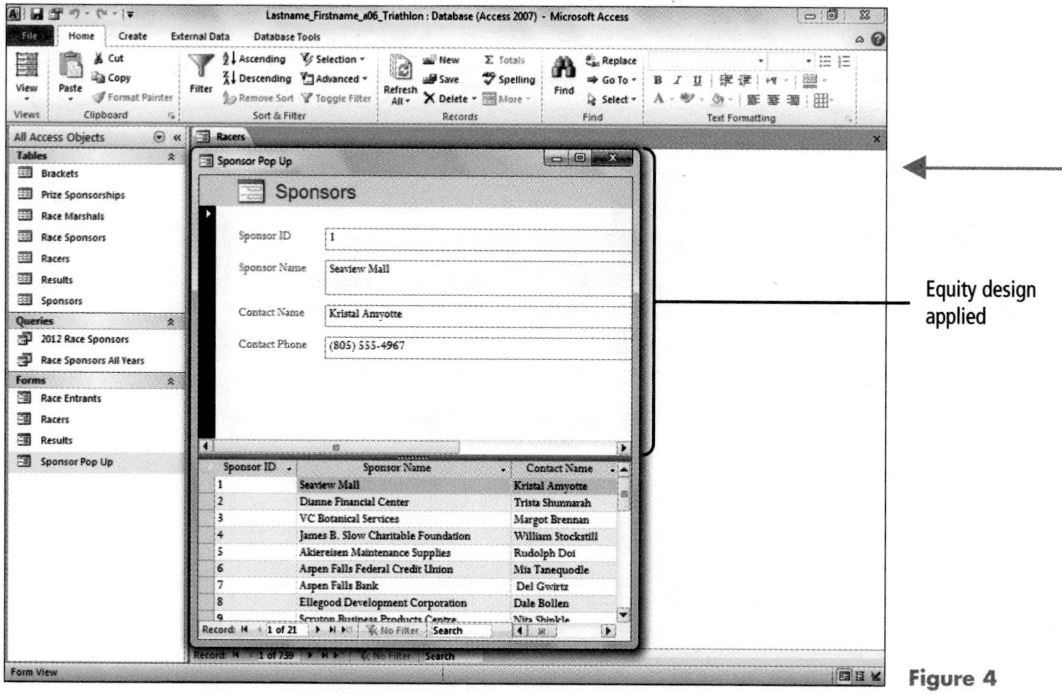

Equity design applied

Figure 4

5. Move the pointer over the lower right corner of the pop up form until the ⬉ displays. Click the left mouse button, and then drag the edge of the form up and to the left until the form is approximately two-thirds its original size and the subform is no longer visible.

6. On the displayed pop up form, click the **Record Selector** ▶ to display the **Sponsor Pop Up** form fields, and then compare your screen with **Figure 3**.

7. Click **Save** 🖫, and then **Close** ✖ the **Sponsor Pop Up** form.

8. In the **Navigation Pane**, select the **Sponsor Pop Up** form. Right-click, and then click **Design View**.

9. On the **Design tab**, in the **Themes group**, click **Themes**. From the displayed gallery, click **Equity**—third choice in the fourth row.

10. Switch to Form view, click the **Record Selector** arrow ▶, and then compare your screen with **Figure 4**.

   Notice that the form has been resized back to its original size.

11. Click **Save** 🖫, and then **Close** ✖ the **Sponsor Pop Up** form. **Close** ✖ the **Racers** form.

■ **You have completed Skill 4 of 10**

► A ***Command button*** is a control that performs an action or sequence of actions when it is clicked.

► Buttons can perform a variety of tasks when clicked such as opening other objects—forms, queries, or reports—or starting the printing process.

1. In the **Navigation Pane**, select the **Sponsors** table. Display the **Create tab**, and then in the **Forms group**, click the **Form** button.

2. Click **Save** 🖫, and then click **OK**.

3. Switch to Design view, click the **Table.Race Sponsors** subform control, and then press Delete. Compare your screen with **Figure 1**.

4. On the **Design tab**, in the **Controls group**, click the **Button** button ▭.

5. In the **Detail** area, position the ⊞ pointer where the **2 inch** vertical grid line and **2 inch** horizontal grid line meet, and then click one time.

    A button displays in the Detail section, and the Command Button Wizard displays a list of actions that the button can perform when clicked in Form view.

6. In the **Command Button Wizard**, under **Categories**, click **Form Operations**. Under **Actions**, click **Open Form**, and then compare your screen with **Figure 2**.

7. Click **Next**, and then under **What form would you like the command button to open**, verify that **Race Entrants** is selected.

■ **Continue to the next page to complete the skill** ▶

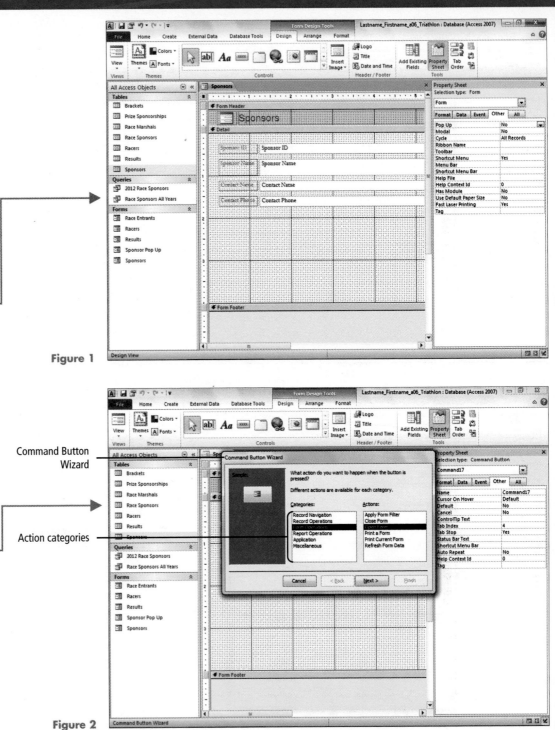

Figure 1

Command Button Wizard

Action categories

Figure 2

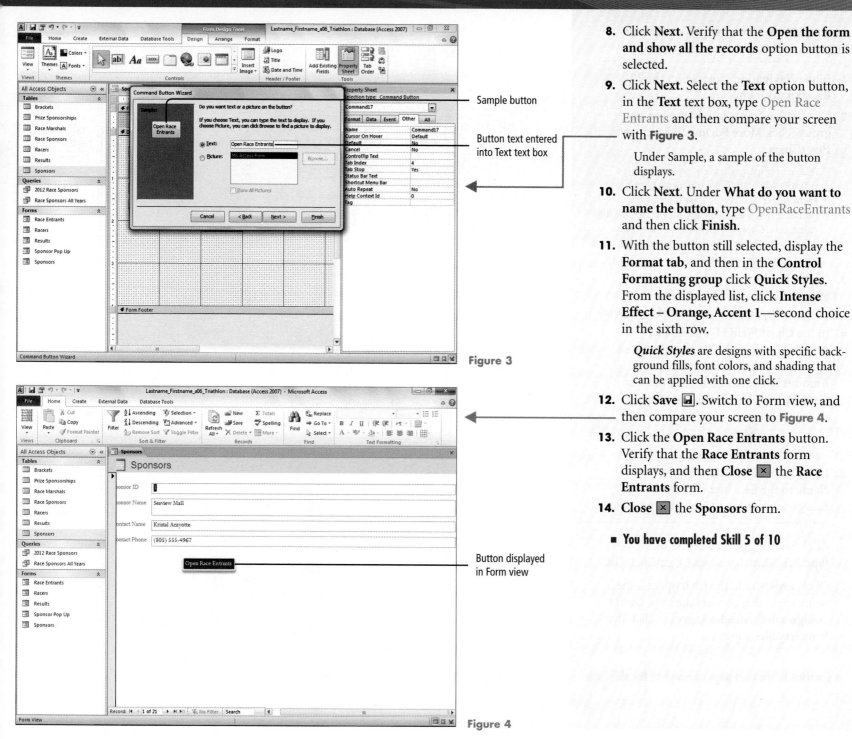

Sample button

Button text entered
into Text text box

Figure 3

Button displayed
in Form view

Figure 4

8. Click **Next.** Verify that the **Open the form and show all the records** option button is selected.

9. Click **Next.** Select the **Text** option button, in the **Text** text box, type Open Race Entrants and then compare your screen with **Figure 3.**

   Under Sample, a sample of the button displays.

10. Click **Next.** Under **What do you want to name the button**, type OpenRaceEntrants and then click **Finish.**

11. With the button still selected, display the **Format tab**, and then in the **Control Formatting group** click **Quick Styles.** From the displayed list, click **Intense Effect – Orange, Accent 1**—second choice in the sixth row.

    Quick Styles are designs with specific background fills, font colors, and shading that can be applied with one click.

12. Click **Save**. Switch to Form view, and then compare your screen to **Figure 4.**

13. Click the **Open Race Entrants** button. Verify that the **Race Entrants** form displays, and then **Close** the **Race Entrants** form.

14. **Close** the **Sponsors** form.

    ■ **You have completed Skill 5 of 10**

▶ A *PivotChart* is an interactive graphical representation of summarized data.

1. In the **Navigation Pane**, select the **2012 Race Sponsors** query.

2. Display the **Create tab**. In the **Forms group**, click **More Forms**, and then click **PivotChart**.

   A chart template displays, which requires you to add a data field and a category field. *Data fields* in a PivotChart refer to the numeric fields that will appear on the chart's value axis. *Category fields* in a PivotChart refer to the fields that will appear on the chart's category axis as labels.

3. On the **Design tab**, in the **Show/Hide group**, click the **Field List** button two times to display the **Chart Field List** pane.

4. In the **Chart Field List** pane, click **Amount**. Press and hold the left mouse button, and then drag and drop the **Amount** to the field box with the text *Drop Data Fields Here*. Compare your screen with **Figure 1**.

   The chart displays the total of the largest donations in 2012.

5. In the **Chart Field List**, drag **Sponsor Name** to the field box with the text *Drop Category Fields Here*. Compare your screen with **Figure 2**.

6. Click **Save** 🖫. In the **Save As** dialog box, type 2012 Race Sponsors Chart Click **OK**.

7. Click anywhere in the Chartspace—the white space that borders the axes. On the **Design tab**, in the **Tools group**, click the **Property Sheet** button.

■ **Continue to the next page to complete the skill**

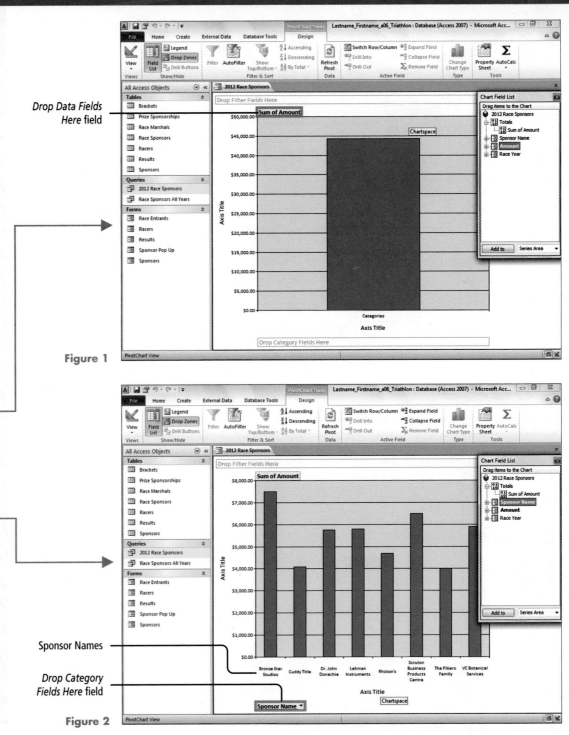

Drop Data Fields Here field

Figure 1

Sponsor Names

Drop Category Fields Here field

Figure 2

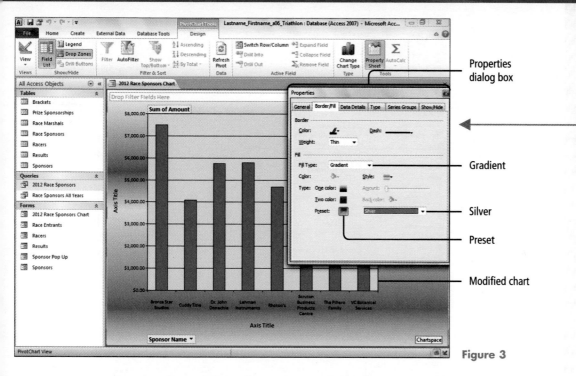

Properties
dialog box

Gradient

Silver

Preset

Modified chart

Figure 3

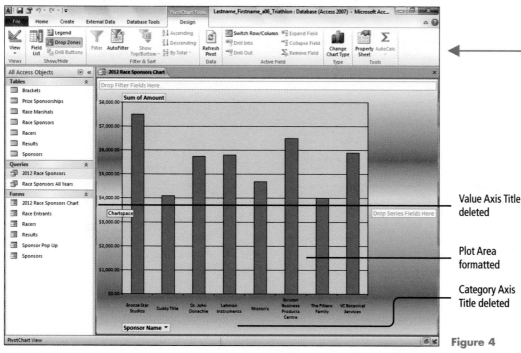

Value Axis Title
deleted

Plot Area
formatted

Category Axis
Title deleted

Figure 4

8. Click the **Properties Border/Fill tab**. Under **Fill**, click the **Fill Type arrow**, and then click the **Preset Gradient** button. Under **Type**, click the **Preset** button. Click the displayed **Preset arrow**, and then click **Silver**. Compare your screen with **Figure 3**.

9. Select the Properties **General tab**, click the **Select arrow**, and then click **Plot Area**.

   With Plot Area selected, the options and tabs in the Properties dialog box changes.

10. Click the **Border/Fill tab**. In the **Fill** area, in **Color**, select the **Fill Color** button [icon], and then click **Gainsboro**—the third choice in the last row. **Close** [icon] the **Properties** dialog box. **Close** [icon] the **Chart Field List**.

11. Under the category axis, click the control with the text *Axis Title*, and then press Delete.

12. To the left of the value axis, click the control with the text *Axis Title*, press Delete, and then compare your screen with **Figure 4**.

13. Click **Start** [icon], click **All Programs**, and then open the **Accessories** folder. Click **Snipping Tool**, click the **New button arrow**, and then click **Full-screen Snip**.

14. Click the **Save Snip** button [icon]. In the **Save As** dialog box, navigate to your **Access Chapter 6** folder, **Save** the file as Lastname_Firstname_a06_Triathlon_PivotChart_Snip and then **Close** [icon] the **Snipping Tool** window.

15. **Save** [icon], and then **Close** [icon] the PivotChart.

■ **You have completed Skill 6 of 10**

▶ A *PivotTable* provides an interactive way to summarize quickly large amounts of data.

▶ Once created, a single PivotTable can be manipulated to display and summarize the data in numerous views.

▶ A PivotTable provides summary statistics for each row or column.

1. In the **Navigation Pane**, select the **Race Sponsors All Years** query.

2. On the **Create tab**, in the **Forms group**, click the **More Forms** button, and then click **PivotTable**.

3. On the **Design tab**, in the **Show/Hide group**, click the **Field List** button two times to display the **PivotTable Field List** pane.

4. In the **PivotTable Field List** pane, drag **Sponsor Name** to the *Drop Row Fields Here* field box.

5. In the **PivotTable Field List** pane, drag **Race Year** to the *Drop Column Fields Here* field box, and then compare your screen with **Figure 1**.

6. In the **PivotTable Field List** pane, drag **Amount** to the *Drop Totals or Details Fields Here* field box, and then compare your screen with **Figure 2**.

■ **Continue to the next page to complete the skill**

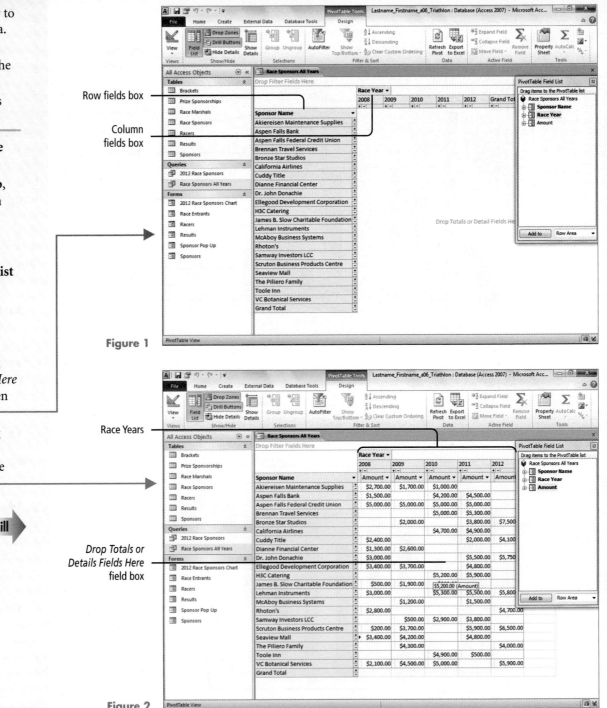

Row fields box

Column fields box

Figure 1

Race Years

Drop Totals or Details Fields Here field box

Figure 2

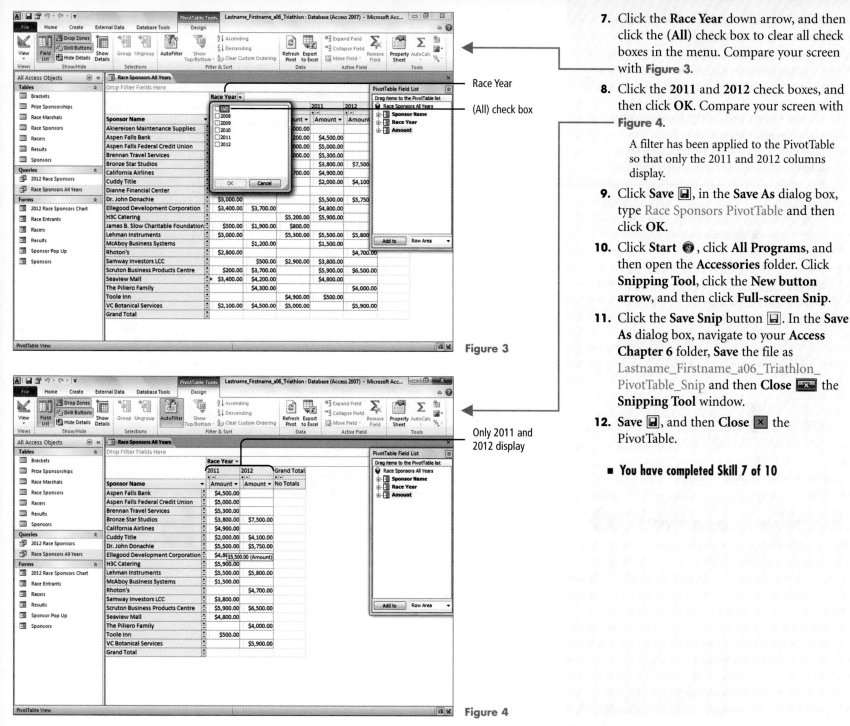

Race Year

(All) check box

Figure 3

Only 2011 and 2012 display

Figure 4

7. Click the **Race Year** down arrow, and then click the **(All)** check box to clear all check boxes in the menu. Compare your screen with **Figure 3**.

8. Click the **2011** and **2012** check boxes, and then click **OK**. Compare your screen with **Figure 4**.

   A filter has been applied to the PivotTable so that only the 2011 and 2012 columns display.

9. Click **Save** ⊞, in the **Save As** dialog box, type Race Sponsors PivotTable and then click **OK**.

10. Click **Start** ⚉, click **All Programs**, and then open the **Accessories** folder. Click **Snipping Tool**, click the **New button arrow**, and then click **Full-screen Snip**.

11. Click the **Save Snip** button ⊞. In the **Save As** dialog box, navigate to your **Access Chapter 6** folder, **Save** the file as Lastname_Firstname_a06_Triathlon_PivotTable_Snip and then **Close** ✕ the **Snipping Tool** window.

12. **Save** ⊞, and then **Close** ✕ the PivotTable.

   ■ **You have completed Skill 7 of 10**

▶ *Navigation forms* enable you to add several forms or reports to a single form.

▶ Navigation forms enable you to enter data into multiple tables while only opening one form.

1. On the **Create tab**, in the **Forms group**, click **Navigation**, and then from the displayed menu click **Horizontal Tabs, 2 Levels**. Compare your screen with **Figure 1**.

   A Navigation Form displays with two *[Add New]* sections. Note that the colors in your form may be different from the figure shown here.

2. From the **Navigation Pane**, drag the **Racers** form to the uppermost area of the Navigation Form with text *[Add New]*. Compare your screen with **Figure 2**.

   The *Racers* form is now displayed in the Navigation Form, and an *[Add New]* field now appears to the right of Racers, as well as below Racers.

3. In the **Navigation Pane**, select the **Brackets** table. Display the **Create tab**, and then in the **Forms group**, click the **Form** button.

4. Click **Save** 🔲, and then click **OK**.

■ Continue to the next page to complete the skill

Navigation Form

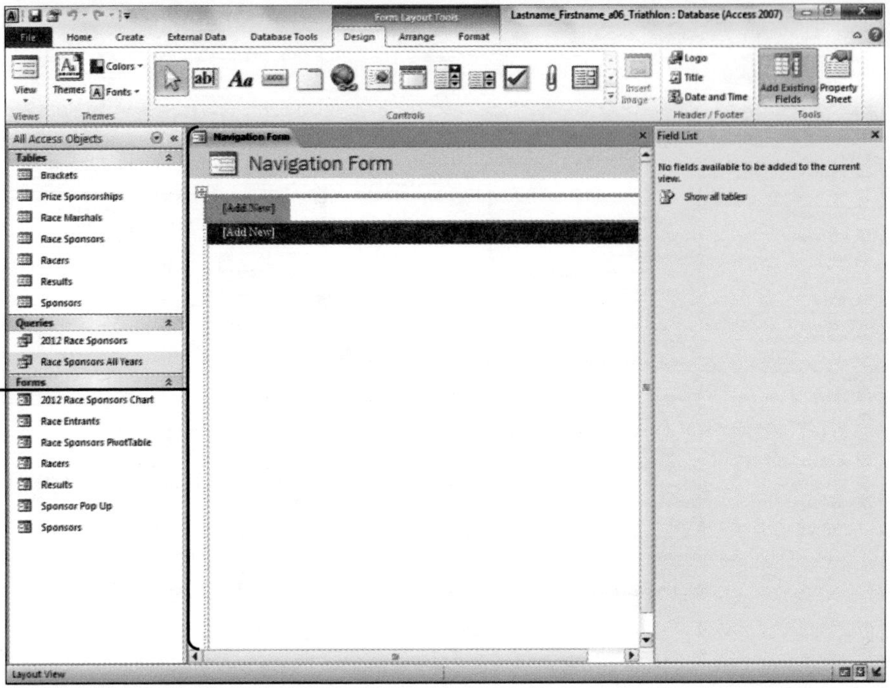

Figure 1

Navigation Control button

Navigation control

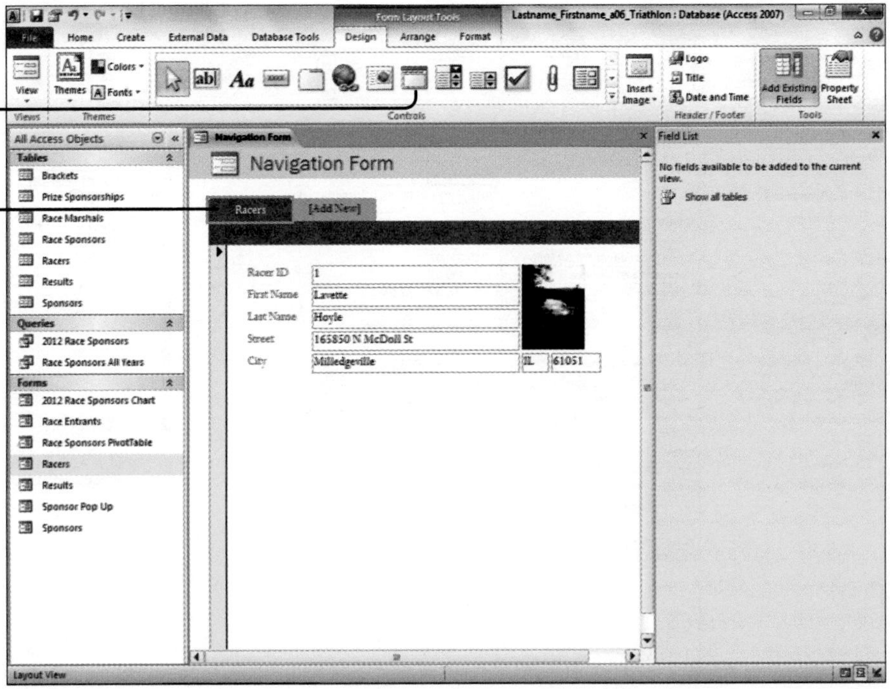

Figure 2

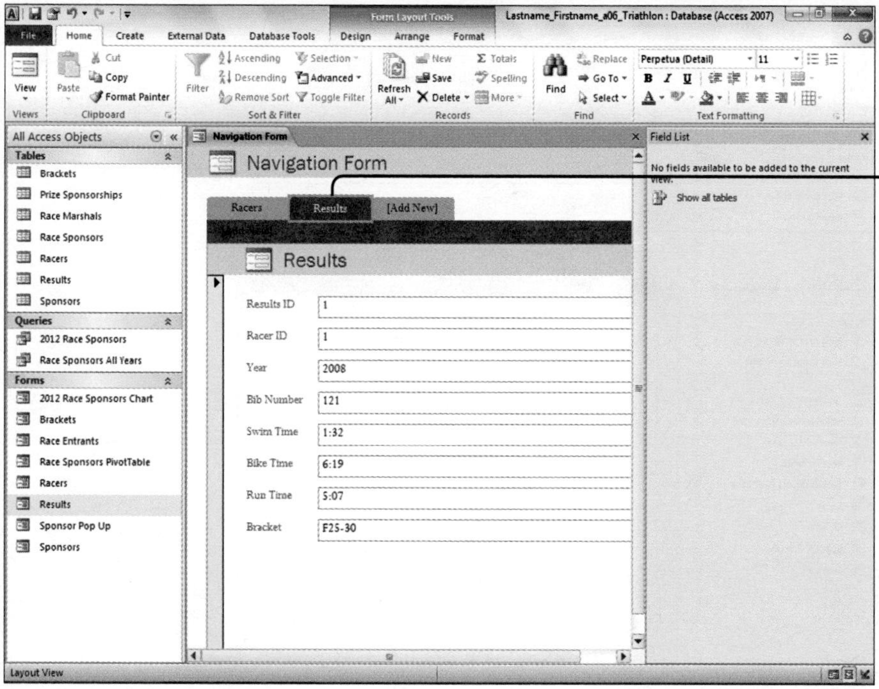

Results form
added to
Navigation Form

Figure 3

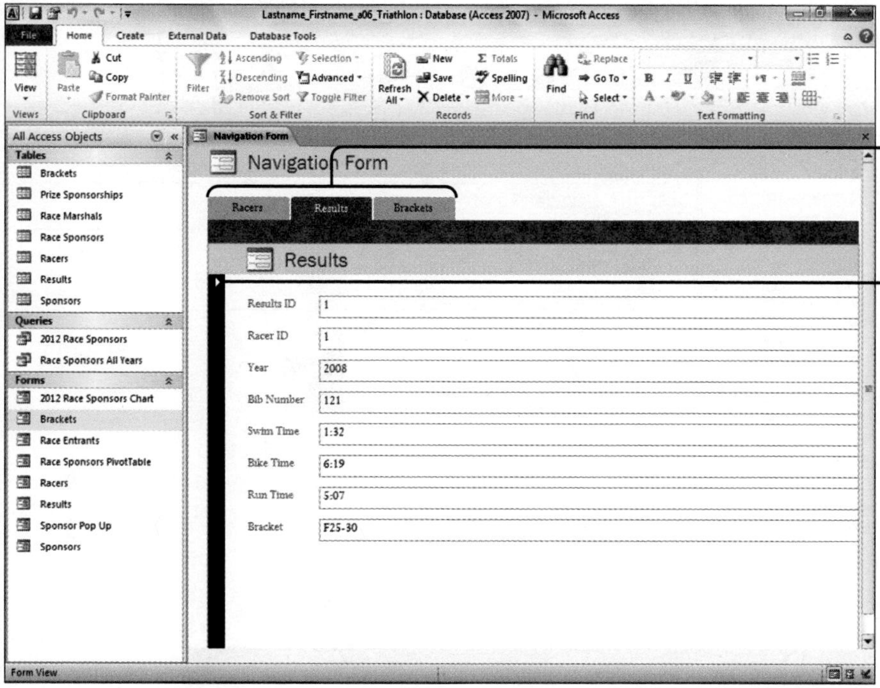

Forms added

Record Selector
arrow

Figure 4

5. Switch to Design view, click the **Table.Results** subform, and then press Delete to remove the subform. **Save** 🔲, and then **Close** ☒ the **Brackets** form.

6. From the **Navigation Pane**, drag the **Results** form and drop it in the *[Add New]* field to the right of the **Racers** form, and then compare your screen with **Figure 3**.

7. From the **Navigation Pane**, drag the **Brackets** form and drop it in the *[Add New]* field to the right of the **Results** form.

8. Switch to Form view, and then click each form to view. Click the **Record Selector** ▶ on the form, and then compare your screen with **Figure 4**.

9. Click **Save** 🔲, and then in the **Save As** dialog box type Athletes Navigation Form

■ **You have completed Skill 8 of 10**

▶ Navigation Forms require adjustments after being created, especially if they ever need to be printed.

1. With the **Athletes Navigation Form** open, switch to Design view.

2. Click in the second row of the Navigation Form with the text *[Add New]*, as shown in **Figure 1**.

3. Press Delete, and then switch to Form view.

4. Switch to Design view, and then **Close** ☒ the **Field List**.

5. With the **Racers** form active, click in the active form in the center of the page to select the *Unbound* area. Scroll to the bottom of the page. Position the crosshairs of the ⊕ pointer to the bottom edge of the form and then drag the edge of the form up to the **3.5 inch** vertical grid line of the **Athletes Navigation Form**, as shown in **Figure 2**.

■ **Continue to the next page to complete the skill**

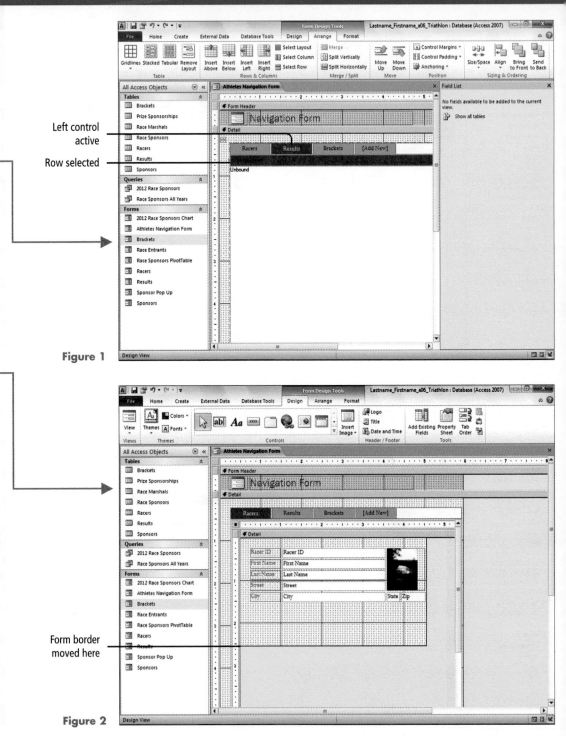

Left control active

Row selected

Figure 1

Form border moved here

Figure 2

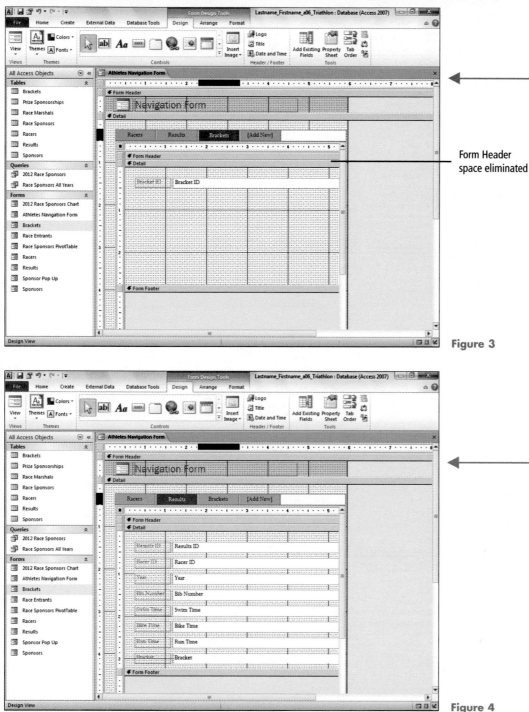

Form Header space eliminated

Figure 3

Figure 4

6. Click **Save** 🖫. Click to select the **Brackets** form, and then click the **Logo** control. Press and hold the Shift key, click the **Title** control, and then press Delete.

7. In the **Brackets** form, drag the **Detail** bar up until it touches the **Form Header** bar and then compare your screen with **Figure 3**.

8. Click **Save** 🖫. Click the **Results** form control, click in the **Logo** control. Press and hold the Shift key, click in the **Title** control, and then press Delete.

9. Drag the **Detail** bar up until it meets the **Form Header** bar, and then compare your screen to **Figure 4**.

10. On the **Athletes Navigation Form**, click in the **Title** control. Replace the existing text with Athletes Navigation Form

11. Click **Save** 🖫.

■ **You have completed Skill 9 of 10**

► Additional forms can be added to a Navigation Form.

1. With the **Athletes Navigation Form** open in Design view, click the **Results** form, and then click in the **Form Footer**. Scroll down, and then with the ⬍ pointer, drag the bottom edge of the form up to the **4.5 inch** vertical grid line.

2. On the **Design tab**, in the **Controls group**, click the **Navigation Control** button.

3. In the **Detail** area, position the 📱 pointer where the **4.5 inch** vertical grid line and **0.5 inch** horizontal grid line meet, and then click one time. Compare your screen to **Figure 1**.

   A new control is added, which allows the user to drag and drop a form to this location.

4. Click just outside the control to deselect the new control. In the **Navigation Pane**, select the **Race Marshals** table.

5. Display the **Create tab**, and then in the **Forms group**, click the **Form** button.

6. Click **Save** 🖫, and then click **OK**.

7. Switch to Design view, click the **Table.Results** control, press ⌦, and then compare your screen to **Figure 2**.

8. Click in the **Logo** control. Press and hold the ⇧ key, click in the **Title** control, and then press ⌦.

9. Drag the **Detail** bar up until it meets the **Form Header** bar. Click **Save** 🖫, and then **Close** ✕ the **Race Marshalls** form.

■ **Continue to the next page to complete the skill**

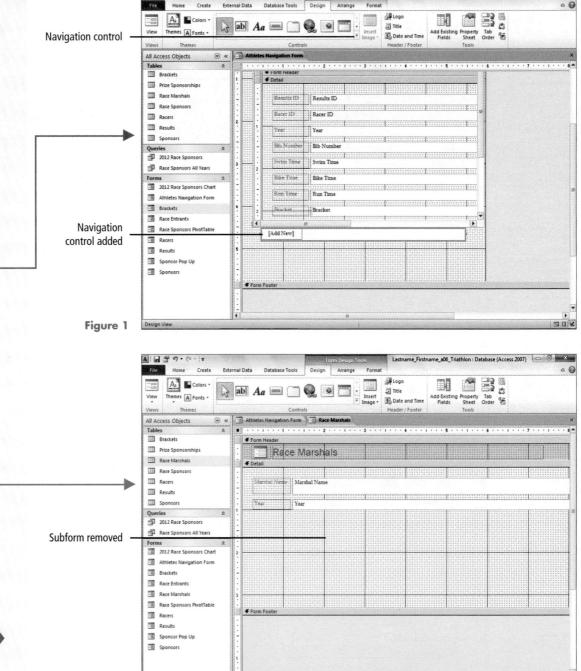

Figure 1

Figure 2

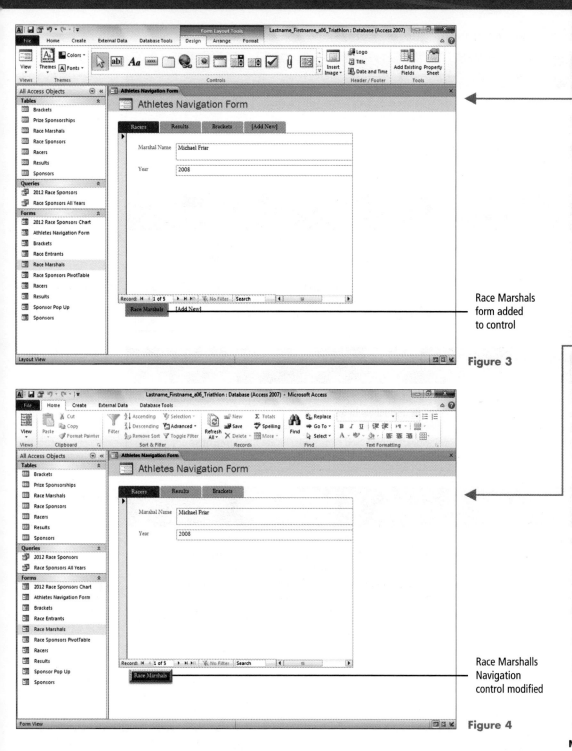

Race Marshals
form added
to control

Figure 3

Race Marshals
Navigation
control modified

Figure 4

10. Switch to Layout view, and then click in the new Navigation control. From the **Navigation Pane**, drag the **Race Marshalls** form to the new Navigation control. Compare your screen with **Figure 3**.

 The Race Marshalls Navigation control now displays.

11. With the **Race Marshalls** Navigation control selected, display the **Format tab**. In the **Control Formatting group**, click **Quick Styles**, and then from the displayed list click **Light 1 Outline, Colored Fill - Orange**—second choice in the third row.

12. On the **Format tab**, in the **Control Formatting group**, click **Shape Effects**, click **Bevel**, and then click **Cool Slant**— fourth choice in the first row.

13. Switch to Form view, and then compare your screen with **Figure 4**.

14. Click **Start** 🔵, click **All Programs**, and then open the **Accessories** folder. Click **Snipping Tool**, click the **New button arrow**, and then click **Full-screen Snip**.

15. Click the **Save Snip** button 🔲. In the **Save As** dialog box, navigate to your **Access Chapter 6** folder, **Save** the file as Lastname_Firstname_a06_Triathlon_ Tabbed_Form_Snip and then **Close** ❎ the **Snipping Tool** window.

16. Click **Save** 🔲, and then **Close** ❎ the **Athletes Navigation Form. Exit** Access.

Done! You have completed Skill 10 of 10 and your document is complete!

The following More Skills are located at **www.pearsonhighered.com/skills**

More Skills (11) Add Option Groups to Forms

Sometimes adding an option group is a more efficient method of choosing options for a single field. An option group consists of a set of check boxes, toggle buttons, or option buttons, which can be either bound or unbound to a field.

In More Skills 11, you will create an option group, which is bound to a field in a table.

To begin, open your web browser, navigate to www.pearsonhighered.com/skills, locate the name of your textbook, and follow the instructions on the website.

More Skills (12) Create Switchboards

Switchboards are often created to provide users with a customized user interface; very often tables in the Navigation Pane are hidden from the user.

In More Skills 12, you will create a customized user interface, called a switchboard, within which the user will be provided with forms for data input as well as reports.

To begin, open your web browser, navigate to www.pearsonhighered.com/skills, locate the name of your textbook, and follow the instructions on the website.

More Skills (13) Apply Special Effects to Form Controls

Labels and controls can be made more prominent or less prominent through the use of special effects. Special effects also make forms look more professional. Special effects include the Raised, Shadowed, Chiseled, and Sunken effects.

In More Skills 13, you will apply special effects to both controls and labels in a form.

To begin, open your web browser, navigate to www.pearsonhighered.com/skills, locate the name of your textbook, and follow the instructions on the website.

More Skills (14) Position and Size Controls in Design View

Controls in a form can be positioned and resized using anchoring.

In More Skills 14, you will use anchoring to stretch controls in a form to allow the controls to maximize the available space.

To begin, open your web browser, navigate to www.pearsonhighered.com/skills, locate the name of your textbook, and follow the instructions on the website.

Key Terms

Online Help Skills

1. Start 🌐 Access. In the upper right corner of the Access window, click the **Help** button 🔵. In the **Help** window, click the **Maximize** ▭ button.

2. Click in the search box, type introduction to forms and then click the **Search** button 🔎. In the search results, click **Introduction to forms**.

3. Scroll down, and then below **In this article**, click **Understand Layout view and Design view**. Compare your screen with **Figure 1**.

Figure 1

4. Read the section to see if you can answer the following: What are the benefits of working in Layout view? What tasks are easier to perform in Design view?

Matching

Match each term in the second column with its correct definition in the first column by writing the letter of the term on the blank line in front of the correct definition.

____ **1.** An arrangement where the labels display the field names in the left column, and text boxes display the corresponding field values in the right column.

____ **2.** A field whose values are retrieved from another table or from a list.

____ **3.** A form that when opened remains on top, even when it is not the active form.

____ **4.** The control that performs an action or sequence of actions when it is clicked.

____ **5.** Designs with specific background fills, font colors, and shading that can be applied with one click.

____ **6.** An interactive graphical representation of summarized data.

____ **7.** In a PivotChart, this refers to the numeric fields that will appear on the chart's value axis.

____ **8.** In a PivotChart, this refers to the fields that will appear on the chart's category axis as labels.

____ **9.** This provides an interactive way to summarize quickly large amounts of data.

____ **10.** This enables you to add several forms or reports into a single form that contains several pages, each with its own tab.

A Category field

B Command button

C Data field

D PivotChart

E PivotTable

F Pop Up form

G Navigation form

H Quick Styles

I Stacked layout

J Lookup field

Multiple Choice

Choose the correct answer.

1. When the left column labels display the field names and the right column text boxes display the field values, this is referred to as:
   A. Layout view
   B. Stacked layout
   C. Column layout

2. A text box connected to a list is referred to as which of the following?
   A. Combo box
   B. List box
   C. Lookup box

3. This control can be added to a form to perform operations such as printing a form with a single click:
   A. Quick Style
   B. Pop Up form
   C. Command button

4. This function provides numerous designs with specific background fills, font colors, and shading, which can be applied with a single click:
   A. Quick Style
   B. Design tool
   C. Command button

5. When this form is opened it remains on top, even when it is not the active form:
   A. Tabbed form
   B. Navigation form
   C. Pop Up form

6. This interactive graph displays summarized data:
   A. Scattered graph
   B. PivotChart
   C. PivotTable

7. The numeric fields that will appear on the chart's value axis are called:
   A. Data fields
   B. Category fields
   C. Rich text fields

8. The fields that will appear on the chart's axis as labels are called:
   A. Data fields
   B. Category fields
   C. Rich text fields

9. Large amounts of data can be summarized quickly using this type of form:
   A. PivotChart
   B. PivotTable
   C. Navigation form

10. The form that enables you to add several forms or reports into a single form with several pages:
    A. Web form
    B. PivotTable
    C. Navigation form

Topics for Discussion

1. What are the advantages and disadvantages of using a Navigation form instead of several single forms?

2. What are the advantages of using a PivotTable to summarize data instead of using a query to summarize data?

Assessment

Skill Check

To complete this database, you will need the following file:

- a06_Rentals

You will save your files as:

- Lastname_Firstname_a06_Rentals
- Lastname_Firstname_a06_PivotChart_Snip
- Lastname_Firstname_a06_Rental_Rooms_Snip

1. **Start** Access. Open **a06_Rentals**, and then save the database in your **Access Chapter 6** folder as Lastname_Firstname_a06_Rentals If necessary, enable the content.

2. Select the **Rental Rooms** table, display the **Create tab**, in the **Forms group**, click **More Forms**, and then click **PivotChart**.

3. On the **Design tab**, in the **Show/Hide group**, click the **Field List** button until the **Chart Field List** dialog box displays. On the **Chart Field List**, drag **Room Type** to the **Category** area, and then drag **Hourly Rate** to the **Data** area. **Save** the form as Rental Rooms PivotChart and then compare your screen with **Figure 1**.

4. **Start** the **Snipping Tool**, and then create a **Full-screen Snip**. **Save** the Snip as Lastname_Firstname_a06_PivotChart_Snip and then **Close** the **Snipping Tool** window. **Close** the form.

5. On the **Create tab**, in the **Forms group**, click **Navigation**, and then from the displayed menu click **Horizontal Tabs, 2 Levels**.

6. From the **Navigation Pane**, drag the **Rental Rooms** form to the uppermost area of the Navigation Form.

7. From the **Navigation Pane**, drag the **Renters** form to the uppermost area of the Navigation Form to the right of **Rental Rooms**. Compare your screen with **Figure 2**.

8. Click the Navigation Form control in the second row, and then press Delete.

9. Click the **Title** control in the main form, and then replace the existing title with Rental Details

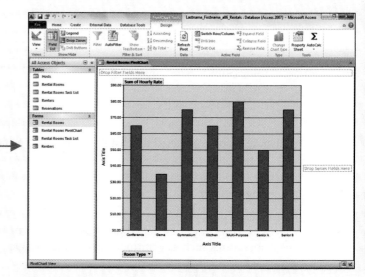

Figure 1

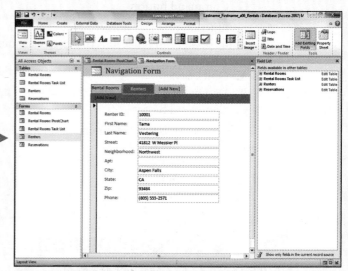

Figure 2

■ Continue to the next page to complete this Skill Check

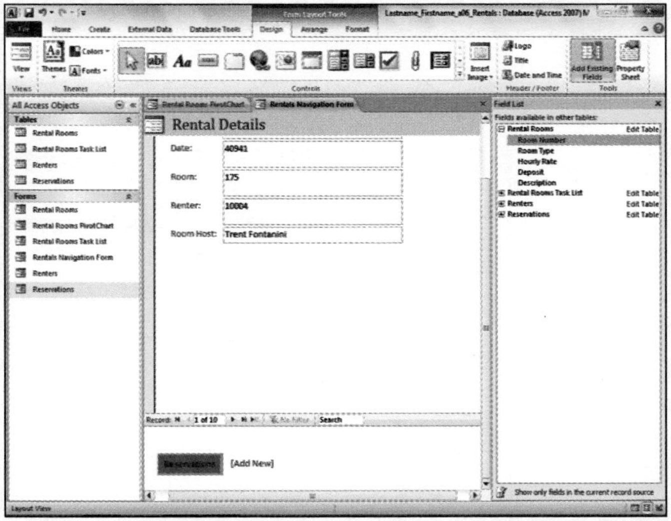

Figure 3

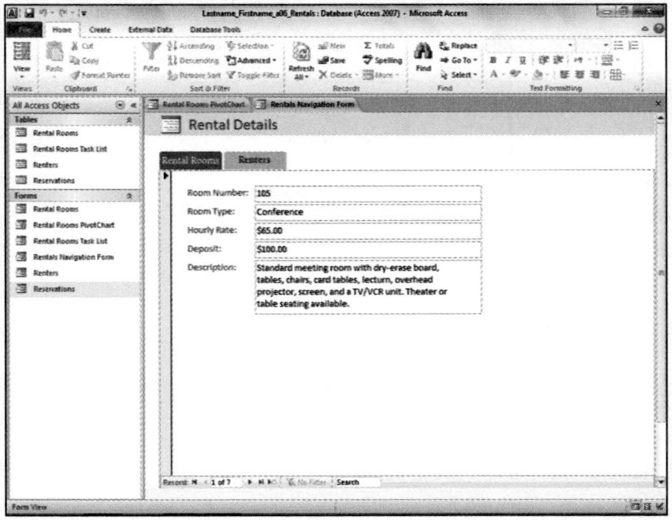

Figure 4

10. In the Navigation Form, drag the **Form Footer** bar down 1 inch. On the **Design tab**, in the **Controls group**, click the **Navigation Control** button. Position the pointer where the **6 inch** vertical grid line and **0.5 inch** horizontal grid line meet, and then click one time.

11. Open the **Reservations** table, and then in the first row click in the **Renter** column. Display the **Fields tab**, and then in the **Add & Delete group**, click **More Fields**. From the list, click **Lookup & Relationship**. Click **Next**, and then with the **Hosts** table selected click **Next**. Click to add the **Host** field to **Selected Fields**. Click **Next** three times, and then type Host Click **Finish**, and then **Close** the table.

12. On the **Create tab**, in the **Forms group**, click **Blank Form**. In the **Field List**, click **Show all tables**, and then click the **Reservations** expand button. Add all of the fields to the form. Click the **Renter** label, and then, with the pointer over the right edge of the control, double-click the left mouse button. Click **Save**, and then type Reservations Click **OK**, and then **Close** the form.

13. With the Navigation Form in Layout view, scroll down, click the new navigation control, and then drag the **Reservations** form to the new control, and then compare your screen to **Figure 3**.

14. With the new control selected, on the **Format tab**, in the **Control Formatting group**, click **Quick Styles**. From the displayed menu, click **Moderate Effect - Blue, Accent 1**—second choice in the fifth row.

15. Click **Save**, type Rentals and then click **OK**. Scroll up, and then click the **Renters tab**. Switch to Design view.

16. On the **Design tab**, in the **Controls group**, click the **Button** button. In the **Detail** section, position the pointer on the **1 inch** horizontal grid line just below the **Phone** label, and then click the left mouse button. In the **Command Button Wizard**, under **Categories**, click **Form Operations**, and then under **Actions**, click **Open Form**. Use the button to open the **Rental Rooms PivotChart**. Add a label to the button with text Open PivotChart and then click **Finish**.

17. On the property sheet, in **Selection type**, click **Form**. On the **Other tab**, click **Pop Up**. Select the displayed arrow, and then click **Yes**. Switch to Form view, click the **Rental Rooms tab**, and then compare your screen with **Figure 4**.

18. **Start** the **Snipping Tool**, and then create a **Full-screen Snip**. **Save** the Snip as Lastname_Firstname_a06_Rental_Rooms_Snip and then **Close** the **Snipping Tool** window. **Close** and **Save** the form.

19. **Exit** Access and submit as directed by your instructor.

Done! You have completed the Skill Check

Assess Your Skills 1

To complete this database, you will need the following file:

- a06_Outings

You will save your files as:

- Lastname_Firstname_a06_Outings
- Lastname_Firstname_a06_Outings_Form_Snip
- Lastname_Firstname_a06_Outings_Snip

1. **Start** Access, and then open the student data file **a06_Outings**. **Save** the database in your **Access Chapter 6** folder with the name Lastname_Firstname_a06_Outings

2. Open the **Volunteers** table, and then in the append row, enter your name. **Close** the table.

3. Open the **Scheduled Outings** table, and then add a lookup field after the **Leader** column. In the **Lookup Wizard**, select the **Volunteers** table, add the **Volunteer** field to **Selected Fields**, and then name the lookup field Volunteer **Close** the table.

4. Create a **Blank Form**. Add all of the fields from the **Scheduled Outings** to the form. **Save** the form as Scheduled Outings

5. In Form view, use the **Volunteer** lookup to add **Your Name** to the first record. Compare your screen to **Figure 1**. **Close** the **Scheduled Outings** form.

6. Create a new Navigation Form, with a layout of **Horizontal Tabs, 2 Levels**.

7. Add the **Scheduled Outings** and **Outing Leaders** forms to the first row of the Navigation Form. Delete the second tab row from the Navigation Form. Insert a **Navigation Control** into the bottom of the Navigation Form and then add **Outing Categories** to the new control bar.

8. **Save** the Navigation Form as Outings Navigation Form Switch to Form view.

9. Use the **Snipping Tool** to create a **Full-screen Snip**. Name the snip Lastname_Firstname_ a06_Outings_Form_Snip and **Save** it in your **Access Chapter 6** folder. **Close** the Snipping Tool. **Close** the form.

10. Create an **Outing Leader Contact Listing** form, based on the **Outing Leader Contact Listing** table. In Design view, reduce the width of the controls and the form.

11. In the **Detail** section of the **Outing Leader Contact Listing** form, insert a command button that opens the **Scheduled Outings** form. Label the button Open Scheduled Outings Apply the **Light 1 Outline, Colored Fill - Blue, Accent 1** Quick Style format to the button.

12. Switch to Form view, and then compare with **Figure 2**.

13. Use the **Snipping Tool** to create a **Full-screen Snip**. Name the snip Lastname_Firstname_ a06_Outings_Snip and **Save** it in your **Access Chapter 6** folder.

14. **Close** the **Snipping Tool**. Click **Save**, click **OK**, and then **Close** the form. **Exit** Access.

Done! You have completed Assess Your Skills 1

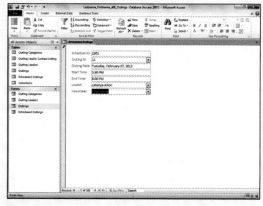

Figure 1

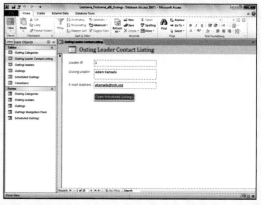

Figure 2

Assess Your Skills 2

To complete this database, you will need the following file:

- a06_Highways

You will save your files as:

- Lastname_Firstname_a06_Highways
- Lastname_Firstname_a06_Highways_PivotChart_Snip
- Lastname_Firstname_a06_Highways_PivotTable_Snip
- Lastname_Firstname_a06_Sponsors_Snip

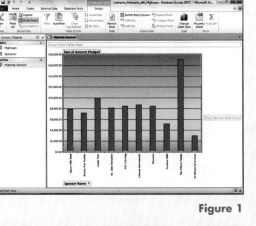

Figure 1

Figure 2

1. **Start** Access, and then open **a06_Highways**. **Save** the file in your **Access Chapter 6** folder with the name Lastname_Firstname_a06_Highways

2. Use the **Highway Sponsor** query to create a PivotChart. For the **Data** field, use **Amount Pledged** and for the **Category** field, use **Sponsor Name**. Delete both axis titles.

3. Open the property sheet, and then format the Plot Area with the **Gradient** and **Preset** design of **Fog**. Compare your screen with **Figure 1**.

4. **Save** the form as Highway Sponsor PivotChart

5. Use the **Snipping Tool** to create a **Full-screen Snip**. Name the snip Lastname_Firstname_a06_Highways_PivotChart_Snip and **Save** it in your **Access Chapter 6** folder. **Close** the Snipping Tool. **Save**, and then **Close** the form.

6. Select the **Highways** table, and then create a PivotTable form. From the **Field List** pane, add **Highway Name** to the Row Fields, and then add **Sponsor ID** to the Column Fields. Finally add the **Amount Pledged** to the Totals Fields. **Save** the form as Highways PivotTable

7. Use the **Snipping Tool** to create a **Full-screen Snip**. Name the snip Lastname_Firstname_a06_Highways_PivotTable_Snip and **Save** it in your **Access Chapter 6** folder. **Close** the Snipping Tool, and then **Close** the form.

8. Using the **Blank Form** tool, create a form called Sponsors Add all of the fields from the **Sponsors** table. Adjust the **Sponsor Name** label so that the entire label displays.

9. Switch to Design view. In the **Detail** section, insert a command button that opens the **Highway Sponsor PivotChart** form. Label the button Open Highway Sponsor PivotChart Apply a Quick Style of **Intense Effect – Blue, Accent 1**. Format the form as a pop up form. Switch to Form view, and then compare your screen with **Figure 2**.

10. Use the **Snipping Tool** to create a **Full-screen Snip**. Name the snip Lastname_Firstname_a06_Sponsors_Snip and **Save** it in your **Access Chapter 6** folder.

11. **Close** the Snipping Tool. Click **Save**, and then **Close** the form. **Exit** Access.

Done! You have completed Assess Your Skills 2

Assess Your Skills Visually

To complete this database, you will need the following file:

- a06_Aquatics

You will save your file as:

- Lastname_Firstname_a06_Aquatics

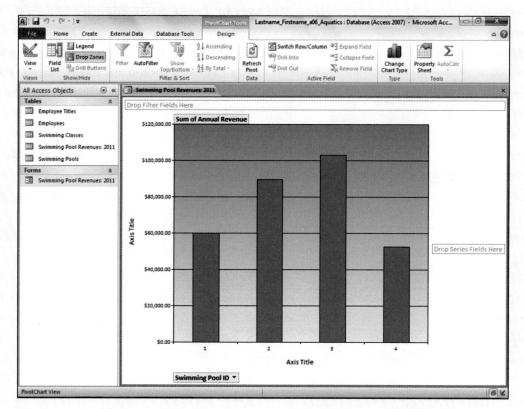

Open the database **a06_Aquatics** and **Save** the database in your **Access Chapter 6** folder as Lastname_Firstname_a06_Aquatics

Using the **Swimming Pool Revenues: 2011** table as a data source, create and format the PivotChart form as shown in **Figure 1**. Use *Annual Revenue* as the **Data** field and *Swimming Pool ID* as the **Category** field. For the **Plot Area** background, apply the **Preset Fill** color of **Daybreak**. **Save** and then submit as directed by your instructor.

Done! You have completed Assess Your Skills Visually

Figure 1

Skills in Context

To complete this database, you will need the following file:

- a06_Police

You will save your file as:

- Lastname_Firstname_a06_Police

Open **a06_Police** and **Save** the database in your **Access Chapter 6** folder as Lastname_Firstname_a06_Police Create a form from the **Employees**, **Police Awards**, and **Police Vehicles** tables. Create a new Navigation Form with the **Horizontal Tabs, 2 Levels** format, and then add all three forms to the Navigation Form. Format the form tabs with a suitable Quick Style and then format the Navigation Form with the **Civic** theme. Save the form as Police Navigation Form

Submit the form as directed by your instructor.

Done! You have completed Skills in Context

Skills and You

To complete this database, you will need the following file:

- New blank Access database

You will save your file as:

- Lastname_Firstname_a06_Dinner

Create an **Event** table that contains the details for two dinner parties that you would like to host for two different events. Provide details about the two events in the table, including **Event ID**, **Location**, **Event Date**, and **Start Time**. Create two new tables, one with a list of 10 of your friends and the other with a list of 10 of your relations. Then decide who you would like to have at each party; a friend or relation can only be invited to one party. Link the **Friends** table, as well as the **Relations** table, to the **Events** table through the **Event ID** foreign key. Create a form for each of the tables. Create a new Navigation Form and **Save** as Event Navigation Form Add the **Events**, **Friends**, and **Family** forms to the Navigation Form. Remove the logo and title from each tab of the Navigation Form. Format each of the tab buttons with an appropriate Quick Style. Add a suitable theme to the form. Change the Navigation Form title to 2012 Events

Submit as directed by your instructor.

Done! You have completed Skills and You

CHAPTER 7

Optimize Tables and Create Macros

▶ Tables and relationships should be designed and created to increase database performance and accuracy.

▶ The date and time that each record is created can be automatically entered and stored in a table.

Your starting screen will look like this:

SKILLS

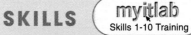

Skills 1-10 Training

At the end of this chapter, you will be able to:

Skill 1 Analyze Tables to Improve Performance

Skill 2 Adapt Tables Created by the Table Analyzer

Skill 3 Create Indexes and Establish One-to-One Relationships

Skill 4 Format Field Properties

Skill 5 Work with the Date Data Type

Skill 6 Create Tables Using Queries

Skill 7 Format Table Datasheets

Skill 8 Create Tables from Application Parts

Skill 9 Work with Table Events

Skill 10 Work with Calculated Fields

MORE SKILLS

More Skills 11 Create New Field Data Types

More Skills 12 Create Custom Input Masks

More Skills 13 Insert Quick Start Fields

More Skills 14 Check for Spelling Errors

Outcome

Using the skills listed to the left will enable you to create documents like these:

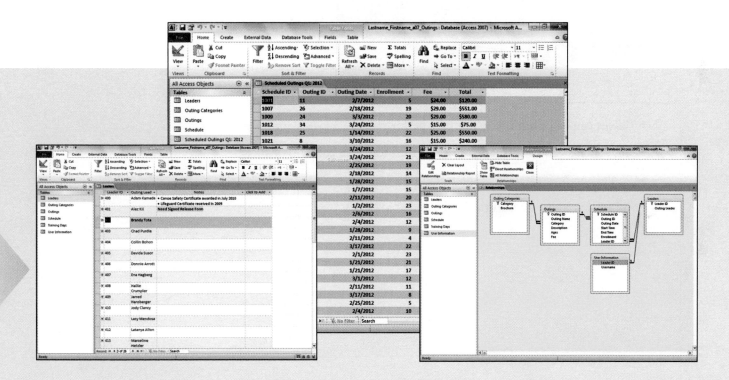

You will save your files as:

Lastname_Firstname_a07_Outings_Snip
Lastname_Firstname_a07_Outings_Snip1
Lastname_Firstname_a07_Outings_Snip2
Lastname_Firstname_a07_Outings_Snip3

In this chapter, you will create documents for the Aspen Falls City Hall, which provides essential services for the citizens and visitors of Aspen Falls, California.

Introduction

- ▶ Tables can be optimized to improve performance.
- ▶ Table fields can be formatted to allow for more rich content.
- ▶ Tables can be created from queries.
- ▶ Important auditing features can be added to tables.

**Time to complete all
10 skills – 50 to 90 minutes**

Find your student data files here:

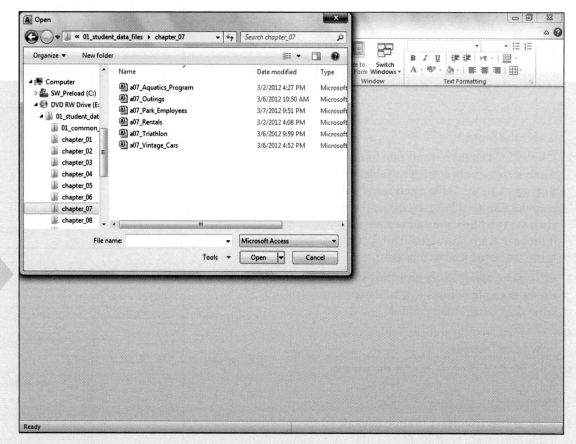

**Student data file needed
for this chapter:**

- a07_Outings

► ***Redundant data*** is data duplicated in more than one location within a database.

► Redundant data can be avoided by organizing data into tables with one-to-many relationships.

► ***Table Analyzer*** searches a table for redundant data and when found, suggests how to split the table into two or more related tables.

1. **Start** ● Access, and then open **a07_ Outings**. Use the **Save As** dialog box to create a **New folder** named Access Chapter 7 **Save** the database in the new folder as Lastname_Firstname_a07_ Outings and then press Enter. If necessary, enable the content.

2. Display the **Database Tools tab**. In the **Analyze group**, click **Analyze Table**. In the first screen of the **Table Analyzer Wizard**, read the displayed information, and then click the two **Show me an example** buttons to learn how redundant data can waste space and lead to mistakes.

3. Click **Next**, and then click the two **Show me an example** buttons to learn how redundant data can be avoided.

4. Click **Next**, and then under **Tables**, click **Scheduled Outings**.

5. Click **Next**. Verify that **Yes, let the wizard decide** is selected, and then click **Next**. Compare your screen with **Figure 1**. ──────

6. Click to select **Table1**. Click the **Rename Table** button 📝, type Schedule and then click **OK**.

7. Click **Table2**, and then repeat the technique just practiced to name the table Leaders Compare your screen with **Figure 2**. ──────

■ **Continue to the next page to complete the skill** ▶

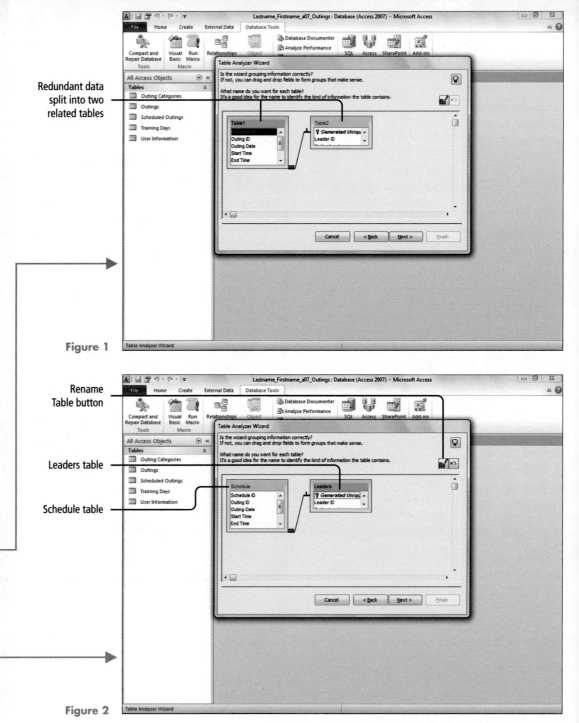

Redundant data split into two related tables

Figure 1

Rename Table button

Leaders table

Schedule table

Figure 2

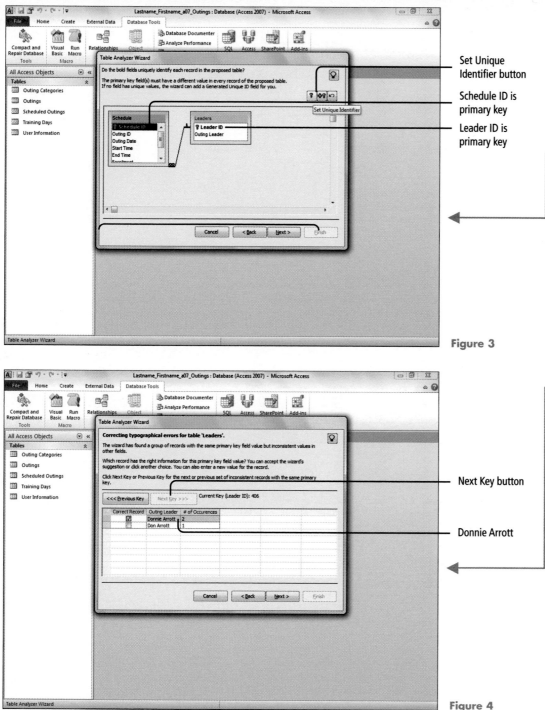

Figure 3

Set Unique Identifier button

Schedule ID is primary key

Leader ID is primary key

Next Key button

Donnie Arrott

Figure 4

8. Click **Next**. In the **Leaders** table, click **Leader ID**, and then click the **Set Unique Identifier** button 🔑.

> Leader ID will be the primary key in the Leaders table. *Unique identifier* is another term for *primary key*.

9. In the **Schedule** table, set **Schedule ID** as the unique identifier. Compare your screen with **Figure 3**.

> Schedule ID will be the primary key in the Schedule table.

10. Click **Next**.

> The Table Analyzer has identified potential typographical errors in the new Leaders table. *Typographical errors* are errors created during data entry. Access identifies potential typographical errors by comparing inconsistent values. Here, Collin Bohon's name has been spelled two different ways.

11. With *Collin Bohon* selected as the correct entry, click the **Next Key** button. Verify that *Donnie Arrott* is selected as shown in **Figure 4**.

12. Click **Next**. If a message box displays then click **Yes**, and then select the **No, don't create the query** option button. Click **Finish**. If a message displays, click **OK**.

> The new Schedule and Leaders tables are created and the Navigation Pane has been closed.

13. With the **Leaders** table displayed, in the Navigation bar, click the **New (blank) record** navigation button ▶*.

14. Under **Leader ID**, type 425 Press ⊤ab, and then type Your Name

15. **Close** ☒ the **Schedule** and **Leaders** tables.

■ **You have completed Skill 1 of 10**

▶ Table Analyzer creates new tables and copies the original data without deleting the original table and its data. Storing the same data in two tables creates redundant data. During data entry, the wrong table could be used, which would lead to errors in the data.

▶ If you plan to use the tables created by the Table Analyzer, you should delete the original table. Otherwise, you should delete the new tables.

1. On the **Database Tools tab**, in the **Relationships group**, click **Relationships**. On the displayed **Design tab**, in the **Relationships group**, click **Show Table**.

   A list of the database's tables displays in the Show Table dialog box.

2. With the **Leaders** table selected, click **Add**. Click the **Schedule** table, click **Add**, and then click **Close**. Compare your screen with **Figure 1**. ─────────

   Notice that a one-to-many join between the Leaders and Schedule tables displays.

3. Click the one-to-many relationship line between **Scheduled Outings** and **Outings**, and then compare your screen with **Figure 2**. ─────────

   The relationship (or join) line is highlighted when selected.

4. Press ⌦ Delete . Read the displayed message, and then click **Yes**.

   The relationship between the two tables has been removed.

■ **Continue to the next page to complete the skill** ▶

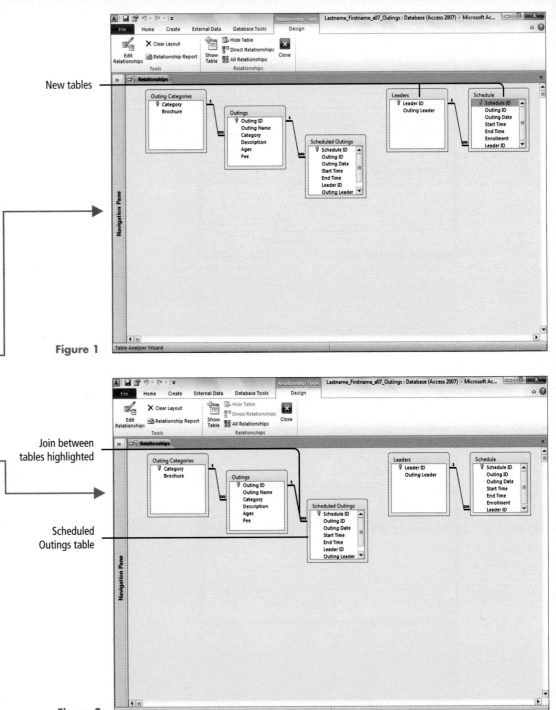

New tables

Figure 1

Join between tables highlighted

Scheduled Outings table

Figure 2

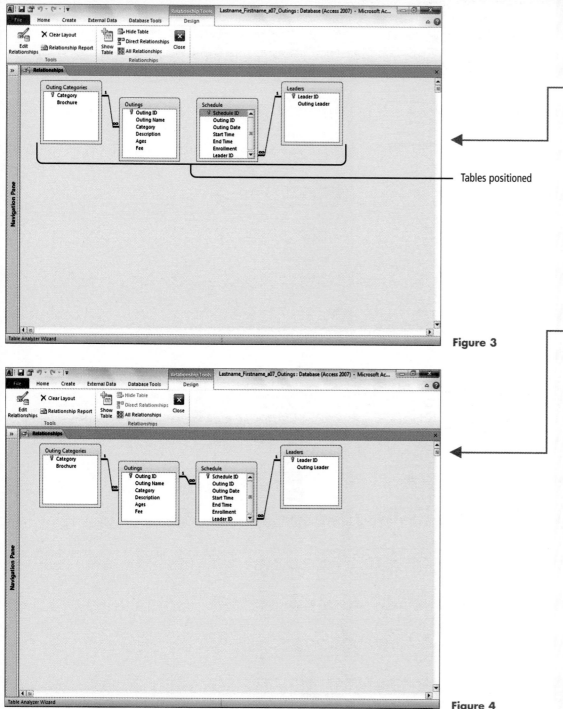

Figure 3

Figure 4

5. Click the border of the **Scheduled Outings** table, and then press Delete to remove it from the Relationships window.

6. Position the **Schedule** and **Leaders** tables, as shown in **Figure 3**.

7. Drag **Outing ID** from the **Outings** table and drop it on the **Outing ID** field in the **Schedule** table.

8. In the **Edit Relationships** dialog box, verify that **Outing ID** from each table is displayed. In the **Edit Relationships** dialog box, click the **Enforce Referential Integrity** check box, and then select both the **Cascade Update Related Fields** and **Cascade Delete Related Records** check boxes.

9. Click **Create**, and notice that a one-to-many relationship now joins the two tables as shown in **Figure 4**.

10. Verify that there is a one-to-many relationship between the **Schedule** table and the **Leaders** table with the **Enforce Referential Integrity**, **Cascade Update Related Fields**, and **Cascade Delete Related Records** check boxes selected.

11. Click **Save** 🔲, and then, in the **Relationships group**, click the **Close** button.

12. **Open** 》 the **Navigation Pane**, and then delete the **Scheduled Outings** table.

■ **You have completed Skill 2 of 10**

▶ An *index* stores the location of records based on the values in a field. An index improves performance when the field is searched or sorted.

▶ A *one-to-one relationship* is a relationship where each record in one table can have only one corresponding record in the other table. In both tables, the field that relates the two tables must contain a unique value.

▶ One-to-one relationships are used to split tables with numerous fields into two related tables, or to store sensitive data such as Social Security numbers and passwords in a separate table.

1. In the **Navigation Pane**, open the **User Information** table.

2. Click to select the **Leader ID** field. On the **Fields tab**, in the **Field Validation group**, select the **Indexed** check box. Compare your screen with **Figure 1**.

   By default, only a table's primary key, fields with unique values, and foreign keys have indexes. A foreign key is a field in a table that is also the primary key of a second table; it creates a relationship with that table.

3. Click to select the **Username** column. In the **Field Validation group**, select the **Unique** check box. Compare your screen with **Figure 2**.

   When a field is assigned the Unique property, an index is automatically created. Thus, the Indexed button is dimmed.

   In a one-to-one relationship, the foreign key must contain unique values. Here, Username will be used as a foreign key.

4. Switch to Design view. With **Leader ID** selected, in the **Field Properties** pane, display and click the **Indexed arrow**. From the displayed list click **Yes (No Duplicates)**.

■ **Continue to the next page to complete the skill**

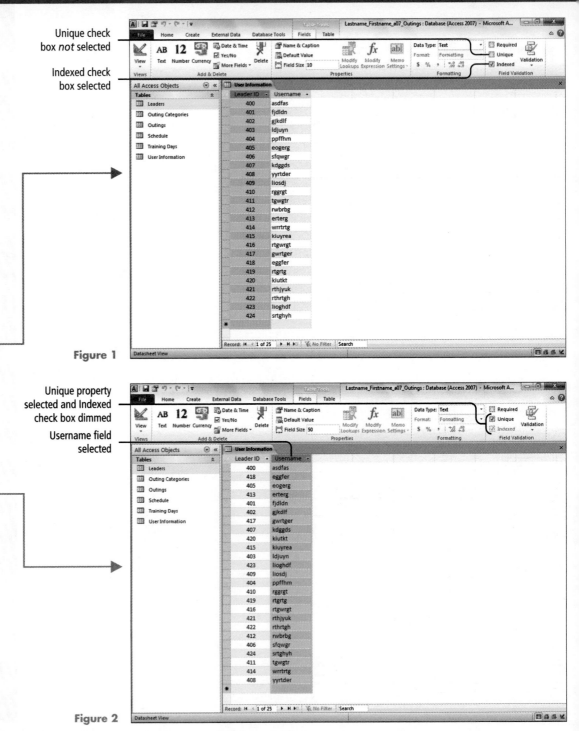

Unique check box *not* selected
Indexed check box selected

Figure 1

Unique property selected and Indexed check box dimmed
Username field selected

Figure 2

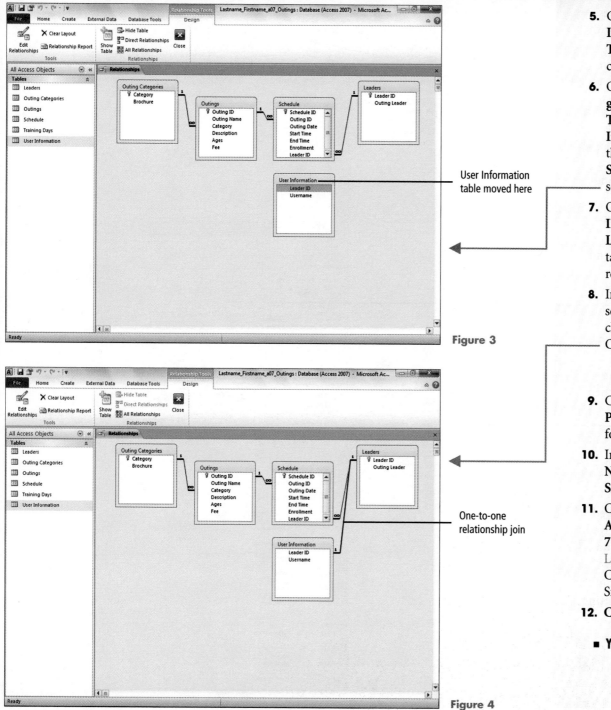

User Information
table moved here

Figure 3

One-to-one
relationship join

Figure 4

5. Click **Save** ☐. **Close** ☒ the **User Information** table. Display the **Database Tools tab**. In the **Relationships group** click the **Relationships** button.

6. On the **Design tab**, in the **Relationships group**, click **Show Table**. In the **Show Table** dialog box, double-click **User Information** and then click **Close**. Move the **User Information** table below the **Schedule** table, and then compare your screen with **Figure 3**.

7. On the **Relationships tab**, drag the **Leader ID** field from the **Leaders** table to the **Leader ID** field in the **User Information** table. When the pointer displays, release the mouse button.

8. In the **Edit Relationships** dialog box, select the **Enforce Referential Integrity** check box. Click the **Create** button. Compare your screen with **Figure 4**.

   A one-to-one relationship between Outing Leader and Username has been created.

9. Click **Start** , and then click **All Programs**. Click to open the **Accessories** folder, and then click **Snipping Tool**.

10. In the **Snipping Tool** dialog box, click the **New button arrow**. Click **Full-screen Snip**.

11. Click the **Save Snip** button ☐. In the **Save As** dialog box, go to your **Access Chapter 7** folder. In the **File name** box, type Lastname_Firstname_a07_Outings_Snip Click the **Save Snip** button. **Close** the Snipping Tool. Click **Save** ☐.

12. **Close** the **Relationships** tab.

■ **You have completed Skill 3 of 10**

► By default, the Text and Memo data types store values in *Plain Text*—characters with no formatting capabilities.

► Memo fields can also store values in *Rich Text*—text that can be formatted—for example, bold, italics, and bulleted lists.

1. In the **Navigation Pane**, right-click the **Leaders** table, and then click **Design View**.

2. Click the **Field Name** box below **Outing Leader**, and then type Notes

3. Press Tab, click the displayed **Data Type arrow**, and then click **Memo**.

4. In the **Field Properties** pane, display and click the **Text Format arrow**, and then from the displayed list, click **Rich Text**. Compare your screen with **Figure 1**.

5. Click **Save** 🖫, and then switch to Datasheet view. Click to highlight the first row, right-click, and then from the displayed menu, click **Row Height**. In the **Row Height** dialog box, type 25 and then click **OK**. Compare your screen with **Figure 2**.

   On the Ribbon, the Rich Text group is enabled only when a field with the Rich Text data type is active.

6. Click to highlight the **Notes** column. Right-click, and then from the displayed menu, click **Field Width**. In the displayed **Column Width** dialog box, type 40 and then click **OK**.

7. On the first row, click in the **Notes** field. On the **Home tab**, in the **Text Formatting group**, click the **Bullets** button 📋▾.

■ **Continue to the next page to complete the skill** ▶

Data Type as Memo

Rich Text selected

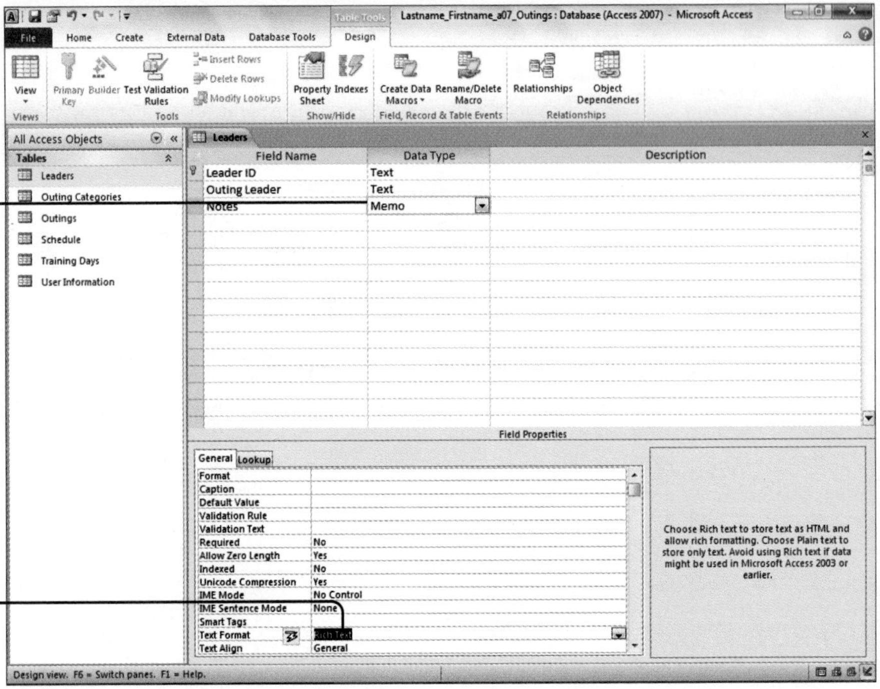

Figure 1

Row height adjusted

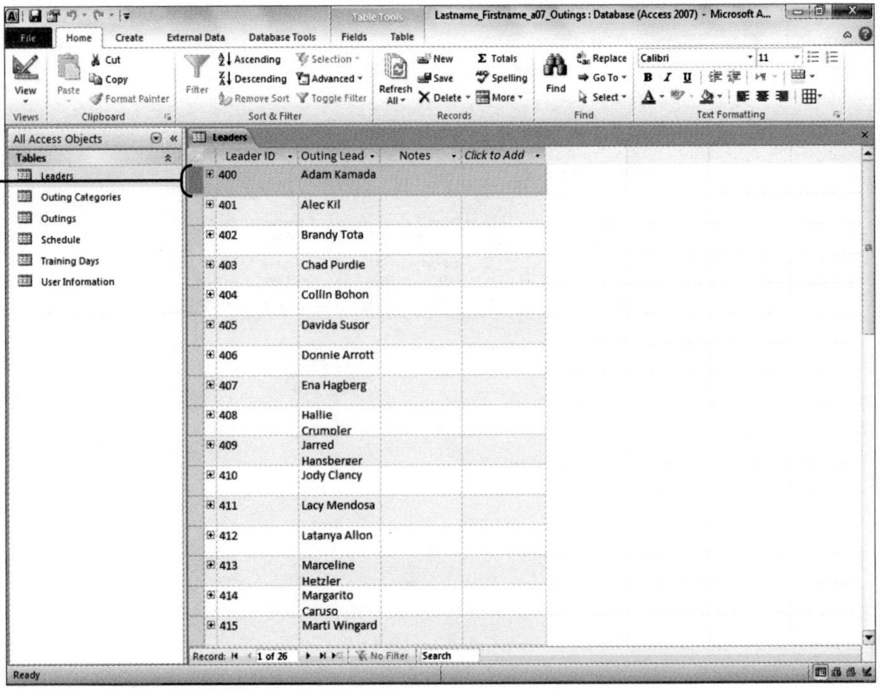

Figure 2

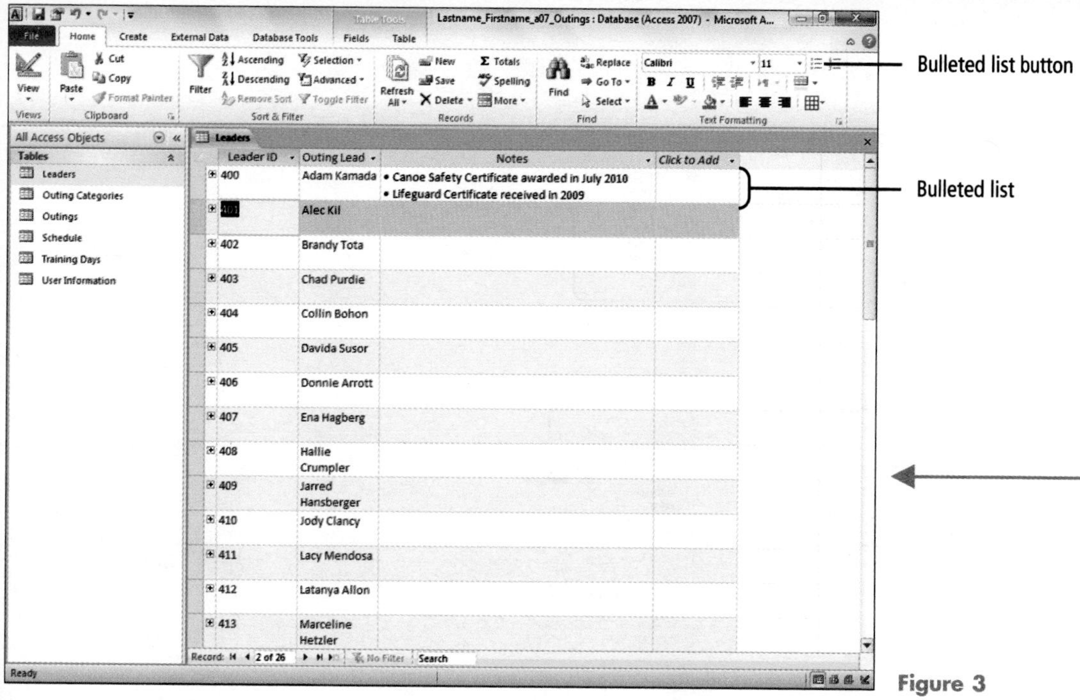

Bulleted list button

Bulleted list

Figure 3

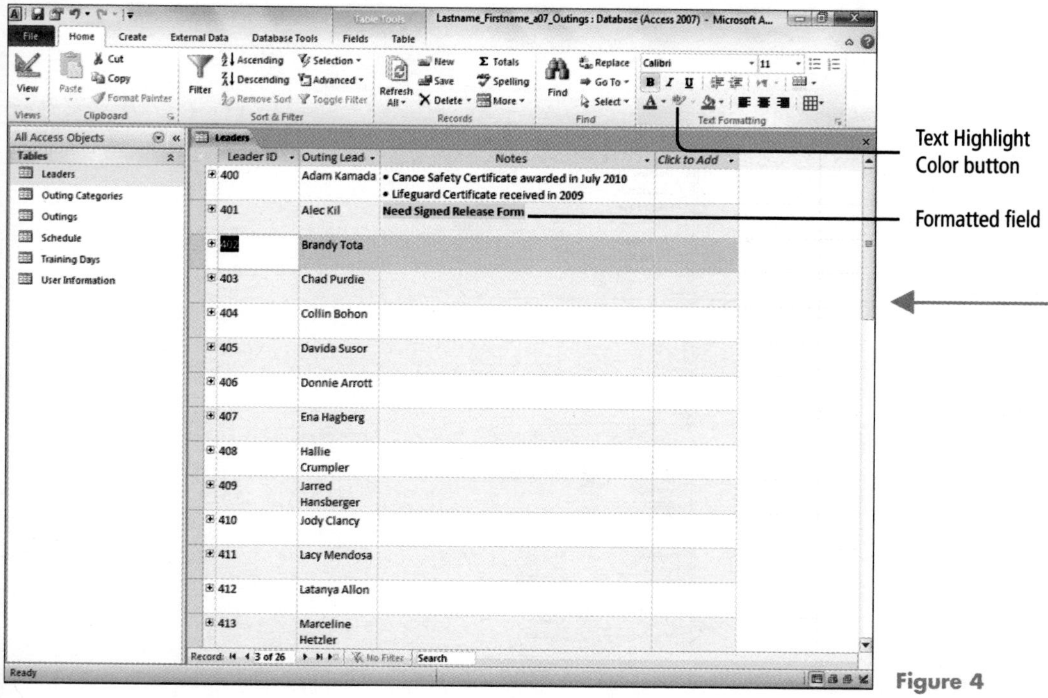

Text Highlight Color button

Formatted field

Figure 4

8. In the **Notes** column, in the first record, type Canoe Safety Certificate awarded in July 2010 Hold down the Ctrl key and then press Enter.

   The pointer moves to a new bullet in the list.

9. Type Lifeguard Certificate received in 2009 as a new bullet in the first record. Press Tab.

10. With the ⊞ pointer between the first row and the second row on the left of the datasheet, drag down until the second bullet displays. Compare your screen with **Figure 3**.

11. In the **Notes** column, in the second record, type Need Signed Release Form Select the text you just typed. In the **Text Formatting group**, click the **Text Highlight Color button arrow** ✍▾, and then click **Yellow**. In the **Text Formatting group**, click the **Bold** button **B**, press Tab, and then compare your screen with **Figure 4**.

12. Click **Start** ⊛, and then click **All Programs**. Click to open the **Accessories** folder, and then click **Snipping Tool**.

13. In the **Snipping Tool** dialog box, click the **New button arrow**, and then click **Full-screen Snip**.

14. Click the **Save Snip** button 🖫. In the **Save As** dialog box, navigate to your **Access Chapter 7** folder. In the **File name** box, type Lastname_Firstname_a07_ Outings_Snip1 and then click the **Save Snip** button. **Close** ✖ the Snipping Tool window.

15. Click **Save** 🖫, and then **Close** ✖ the table.

■ **You have completed Skill 4 of 10**

► The Date/Time data type stores dates as *serial dates*—the number of days since December 30, 1899, and the fraction of 24 hours that has expired for the day. For example, the serial date 37979.875—9:00 p.m. on December 24, 2003—is 37,979 days from December 30, 1899, and 21 hours into that day.

► Serial dates can be displayed in several date formats, including European—24.12.2003— and American—12/24/2003 or December 24, 2003.

1. Open the **Training Days** table in Design view. Notice that the data types for every field are set to Text.

2. For the **Event Date** field, display and click the **Data Type arrow**, and then from the displayed list of data types, click **Date/Time**.

3. In the **Field Properties** pane, display and then click the **Format arrow**. Notice the list of date formats, and then click **Long Date**. Compare with **Figure 1**. ─────

4. Change the **Start Time** data type to **Date/Time**. In the **Field Properties** pane, display and click the **Format arrow**, and then click **Medium Time**.

5. Change the **End Time** data type to **Date/Time**, and then set the **Format** property to **Medium Time**. Compare your screen with **Figure 2**. ─────

■ **Continue to the next page to complete the skill**

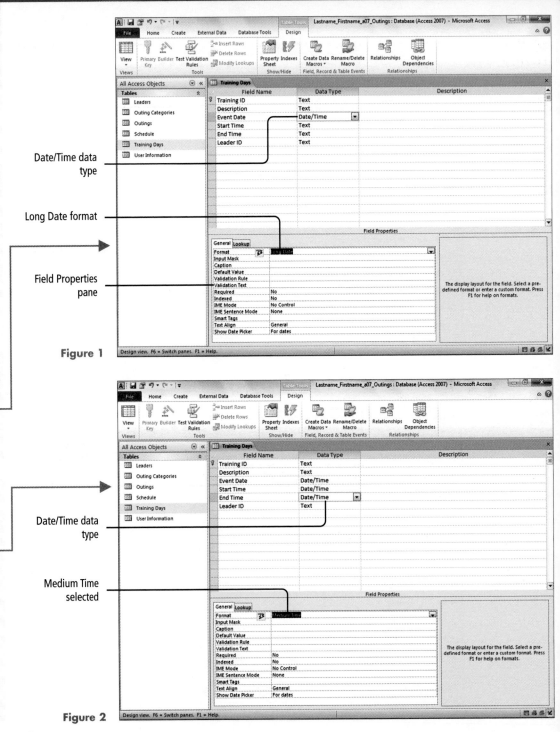

Date/Time data type

Long Date format

Field Properties pane

Figure 1

Date/Time data type

Medium Time selected

Figure 2

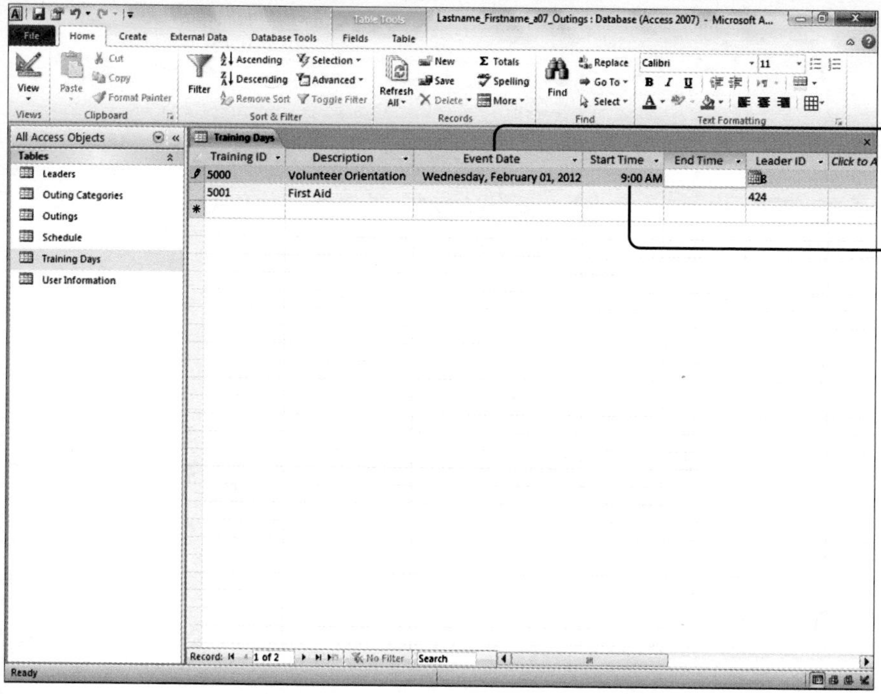

Event Date
displayed

Start Time
entered

Figure 3

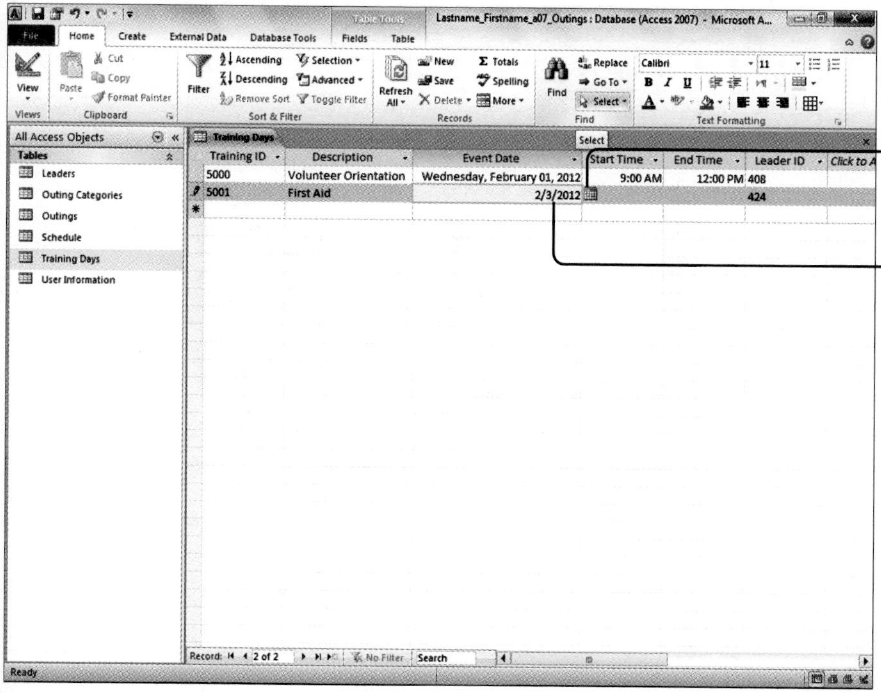

6. Click **Save** 🔲, and then switch to Datasheet view. With the **Training ID** value in the first record selected, press Tab two times, and then type 2/1/12 Press Enter.

   The date is stored as a serial date and displayed in the Long Date format. The date may be obscured.

7. If the **Event Date** field is obscured, then position the ⊞ pointer between the **Event Date** and the **Start Time** column headings and then double-click the left mouse button.

   The entire date now displays.

8. In the **Start Time** field of the first record, type 9:00am and then press Enter. Compare your screen with **Figure 3**.

9. In the **End Time** field of the first record, type 12:00 and then press Enter. Notice that *12:00 PM* is automatically entered into the field.

10. Click the **Event Date** column for the second record. Notice that the calendar icon 🗓 displays.

    The *Date Picker* is a control that enables you to navigate a calendar and then click the desired date.

11. Click the calendar icon 🗓. In the displayed **Date Picker** control, scroll through the months until you reach *February 2012*. Click *February 3, 2012*, and then compare your screen with **Figure 4**.

12. Press Enter, and then type 10:00 am Press Enter, and then type 1:00 pm

    The Date Picker is used to enter dates and cannot be used to enter the Start Time and the End Time, which are hours.

13. Click **Save** 🔲, and then **Close** ❌ the table.

   ▪ **You have completed Skill 5 of 10**

Calendar icon

Date selected

Figure 4

► Creating a table from a query is an efficient way to capture and store a subset of data at a particular point in time.

► A table created by a query is a historical record or snapshot of the database, and the table is often saved in a separate database to avoid confusion with the original table.

1. Display the **Create tab**, and then in the **Queries group**, click **Query Design**.

2. In the **Show Table** dialog box, double-click the **Schedule** table, double-click the **Outings** table, and then click **Close**.

3. In the **Schedule** table, double-click **Schedule ID**, **Outing ID**, **Outing Date**, **Enrollment**, and then from the **Outings** table, double-click **Fee**. Compare your screen with **Figure 1**.

   All of the fields from the Schedule table have been added to the query design grid.

4. Right-click the **Outing Date** column **Criteria** box, and then from the displayed shortcut menu click **Zoom**. In the **Zoom** dialog box, type Between 1/1/2012 and 3/31/2012 Compare your screen with **Figure 2**.

   The Zoom box is a helpful tool for making longer entries in the macro design grid.

5. Click **OK**, and then press Tab.

   Notice how the dates are automatically enclosed by pound symbols (#).

6. On the **Design tab**, in the **Results group**, click **Run**.

■ **Continue to the next page to complete the skill**

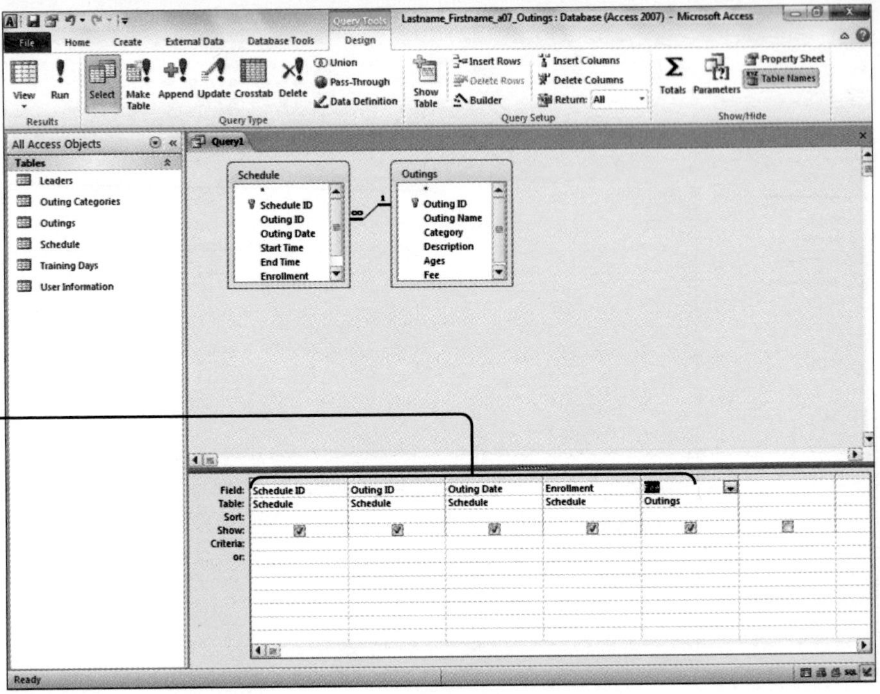

Fields added to query design grid

Figure 1

Zoom dialog box

Type criteria here

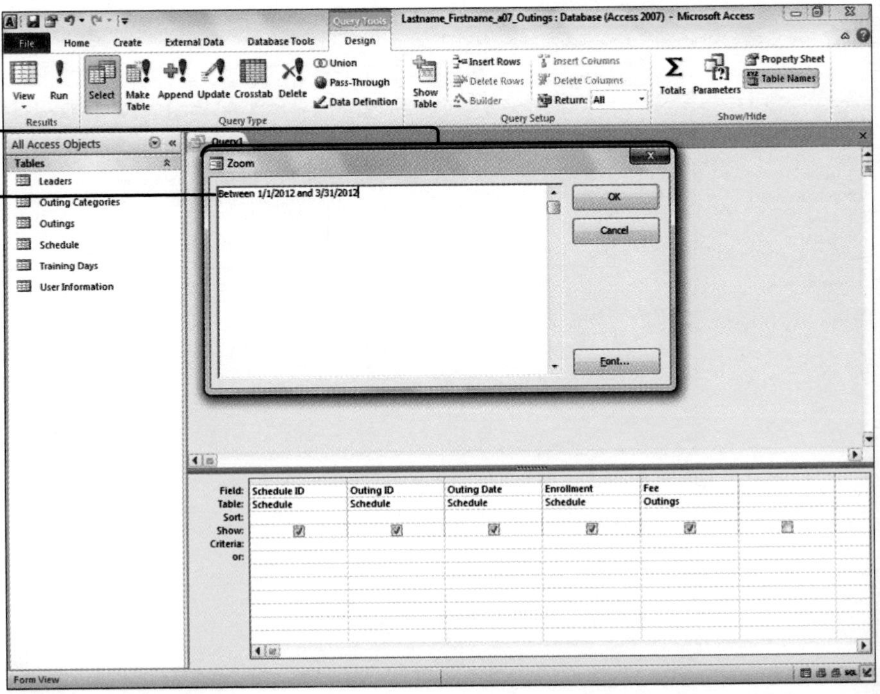

Figure 2

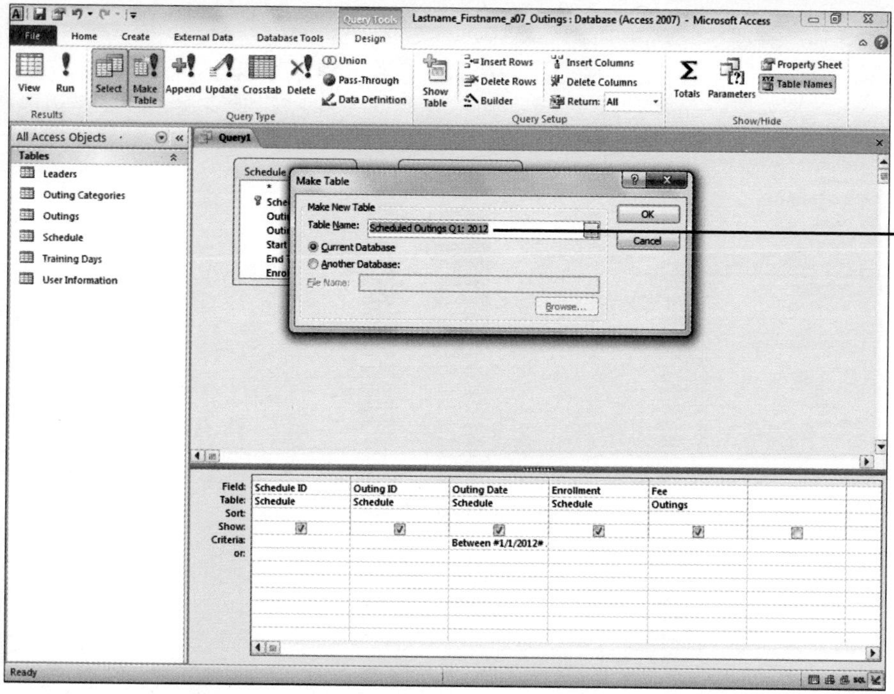

New table name entered

Figure 3

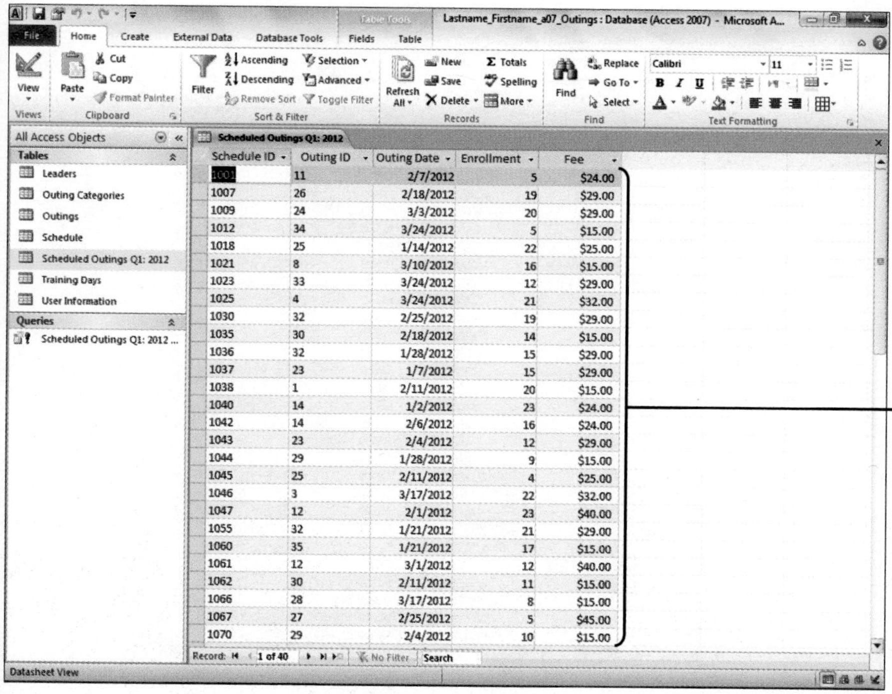

Scheduled Outings Q1: 2012 in Datasheet view

Figure 4

7. Switch to Design view. On the **Design tab**, in the **Query Type group**, click **Make Table**.

8. In the **Make Table** dialog box, type Scheduled Outings Q1: 2012 Compare your screen with **Figure 3**, and then click **OK**.

9. On the **Design tab**, in the **Results group**, click **Run**.

   The Microsoft Office Access dialog box displays and notifies that you are about to paste 40 rows into a new table.

10. Read the displayed message, and then click **Yes**.

    The new table displays in the Navigation Pane.

11. Click **Save**, type Scheduled Outings Q1: 2012 Query and then click **OK**. **Close** the query, and then in the Navigation Pane, notice that the Make Table icon displays next to the query name.

12. In the Navigation Pane, double-click the **Scheduled Outings Q1: 2012** table to view the datasheet, as shown in **Figure 4**.

■ **You have completed Skill 6 of 10**

▶ A table datasheet can be formatted with many of the same features used in forms and reports.

▶ A datasheet's grid lines, font color, font face, font size, text alignment, and fill color can be modified using tools found in the Font group.

1. With the **Scheduled Outings Q1: 2012** table open in Datasheet view, on the **Home tab**, in the **Text Formatting group**, click the **Gridlines** ⊞ button. From the displayed list, click **Gridlines: None**.

    The default horizontal and vertical grid lines are removed.

2. On the **Home tab**, in the **Text Formatting group**, click the **Gridlines** ⊞ button, and then click **Gridlines: Horizontal**. Compare your screen with **Figure 1**.

    Removing the vertical grid lines emphasizes the data as rows. Conversely, removing only the horizontal grid lines emphasizes the data as columns.

3. On the **Home tab**, in the **Text Formatting group**, click the **Background Color button arrow**. From the displayed gallery, click the third color in the second row, under **Theme Colors—Tan, Background 2, Darker 10%**. Compare your screen with **Figure 2**.

    The alternating fill color helps the reader track the data one row at a time.

■ **Continue to the next page to complete the skill**

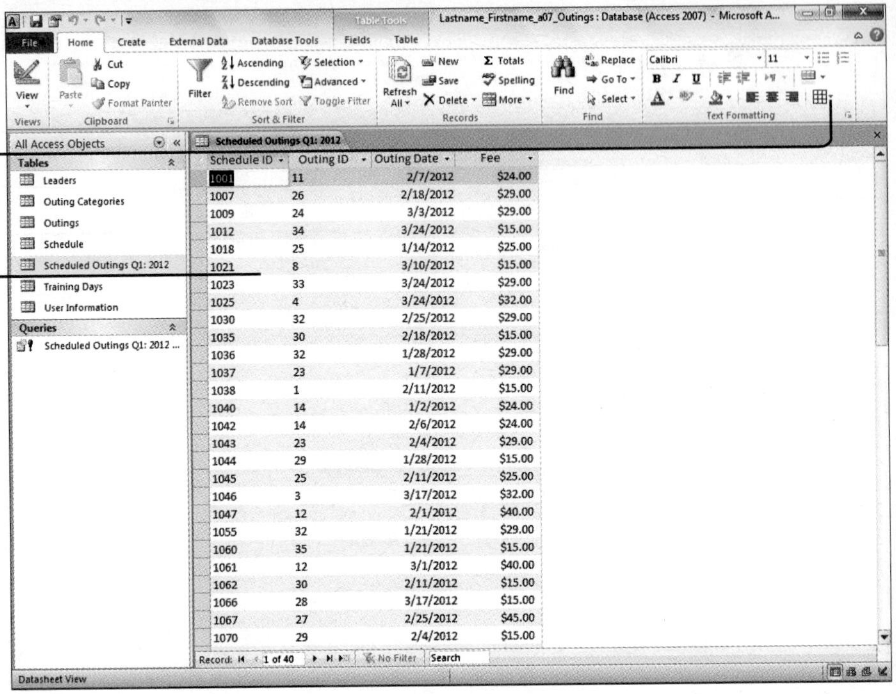

Gridlines button

Horizontal grid line

Figure 1

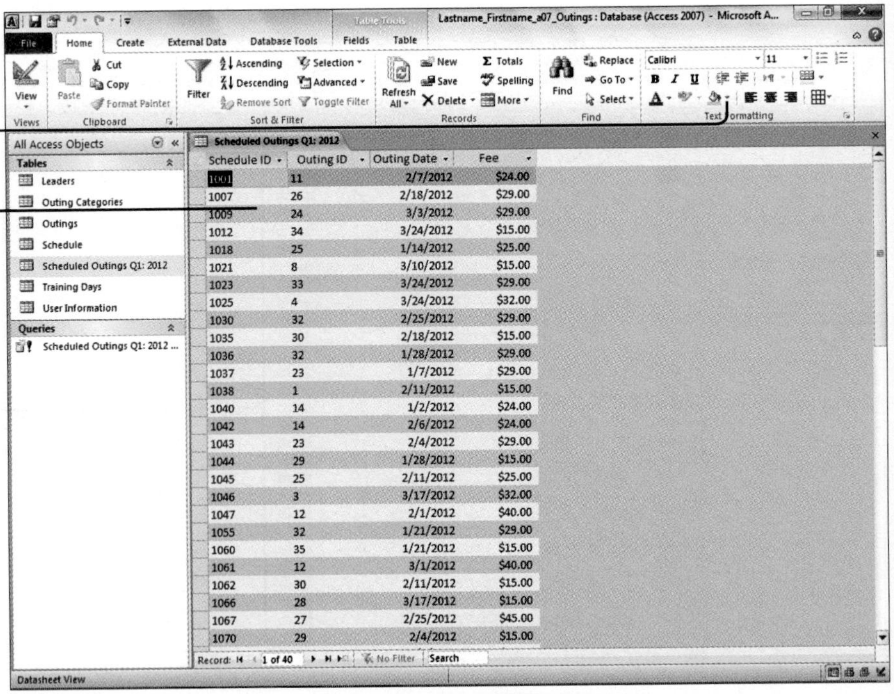

Fill/Back Color button arrow

Tan fill color

Figure 2

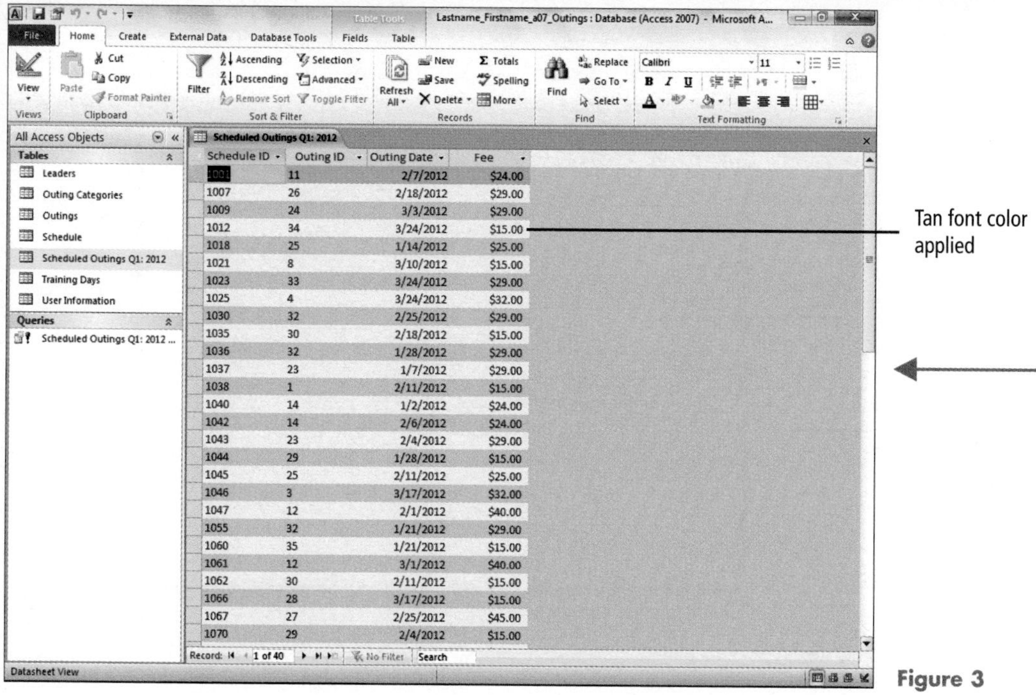

Tan font color applied

Figure 3

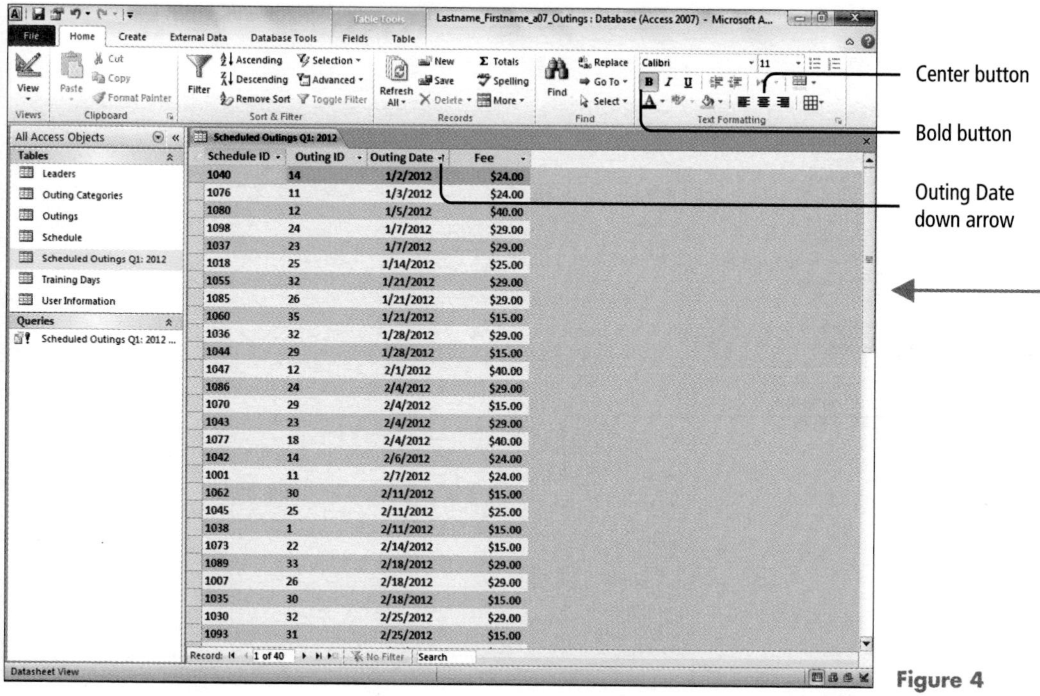

Center button

Bold button

Outing Date down arrow

Figure 4

4. On the **Home tab**, in the **Text Formatting group**, click the **Font Color button arrow**. From the displayed gallery, click the third color, in the last row, under **Theme Colors—Tan Background 2, Darker 90%**. Compare your screen with **Figure 3**.

> The font color is applied to the entire datasheet.

5. With the pointer, click the **Outing Date down arrow**. In the displayed menu, click **Sort Oldest to Newest**.

> The first record displays an Outing Date of *1/2/2012*.

6. On the **Home tab**, in the **Text Formatting group**, click the **Center** button.

> The center alignment is applied to just the selected column.

7. Click anywhere in the datasheet. On the **Home tab**, in the **Text Formatting group**, click the **Bold** button, and then compare your screen with **Figure 4**.

> Bold is applied to all fields in the datasheet.

8. If requested, print the datasheet.

9. Save, and then **Close** the **Scheduled Outings Q1: 2012** table.

■ **You have completed Skill 7 of 10**

▶ **Application Parts** is an Access tool that contains pre-built tables with fields for common information needs—for example, Notes and Tasks.

1. On the **Create tab**, in the **Templates group**, click **Application Parts**. From the displayed list of table templates, click **Users**. In the displayed message, c.ick **Yes**.

2. In the **Create Relationship** dialog box, verify that the **Leaders** table is highlighted and the **One 'Leaders' to many 'Users'** option is selected.

   The first option ensures that only one login can be created for each *Leader*.

3. Click **Next**. Verify that in **Field from 'Leaders'** that **Leader ID** is selected. Click the **Sort this field arrow**, and then click **Sort Ascending**. Press Tab, and then in **What name would you like for your lookup column?** type Leader ID Compare with **Figure 1**.

4. Click the **Create** button.

   Notice the *Users* table that was created. *UserDetails* and *UsersMain* forms also display in the Navigation Pane.

5. Open the **Users** table in Design view. Click in the field below **Login**, and then type Department In **Field Properties**, click in **Field Size**, and then replace the existing value with 20 Compare with **Figure 2**.

■ **Continue to the next page to complete the skill** ▶

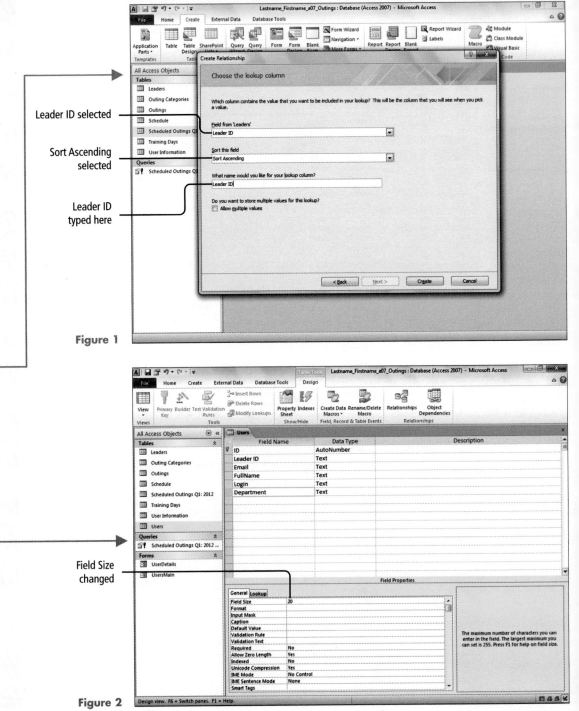

Leader ID selected

Sort Ascending selected

Leader ID typed here

Figure 1

Field Size changed

Figure 2

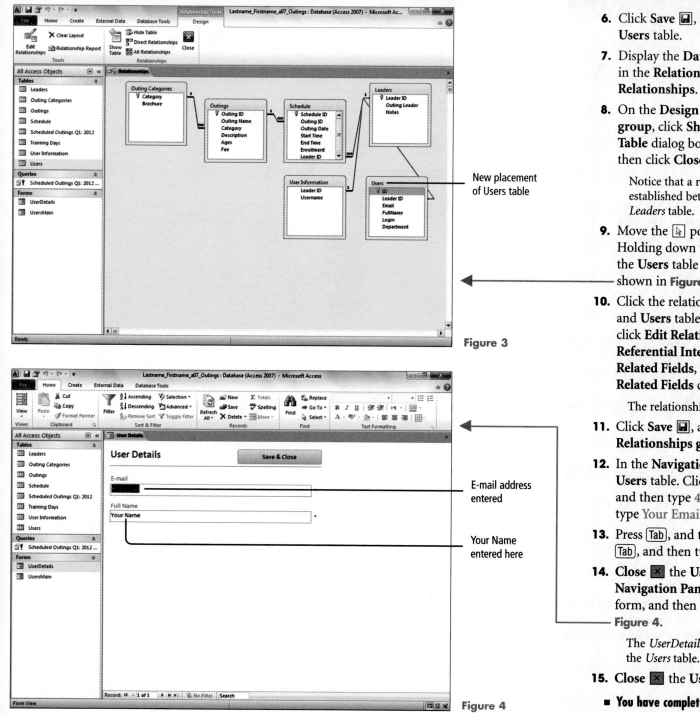

New placement
of Users table

Figure 3

E-mail address
entered

Your Name
entered here

Figure 4

6. Click **Save** 🖫, and then **Close** ☒ the Users table.

7. Display the **Database Tools tab**, and then in the **Relationships group**, click **Relationships**.

8. On the **Design tab**, in the **Relationships group**, click **Show Table**. In the **Show Table** dialog box, double-click **Users**, and then click **Close**.

> Notice that a relationship has been established between the *Users* table and the *Leaders* table.

9. Move the 🔓 pointer over the **Users** table. Holding down the left mouse button, drag the **Users** table below the **Leaders** table, as shown in **Figure 3**.

10. Click the relationship between the **Leaders** and **Users** tables. Right-click, and then click **Edit Relationship**. Select the **Enforce Referential Integrity, Cascade Update Related Fields**, and **Cascade Delete Related Fields** check boxes. Click **OK**.

> The relationship changes to one-to-many.

11. Click **Save** 🖫, and then, in the **Relationships group**, click **Close**.

12. In the **Navigation Pane**, double-click the **Users** table. Click in the **Leader ID** field, and then type 424 Press ⎆Tab, and then type Your Email

13. Press ⎆Tab, and then type Your Name Press ⎆Tab, and then type username

14. **Close** ☒ the **Users** table. From the **Navigation Pane**, open the **UserDetails** form, and then compare your screen with **Figure 4**.

> The *UserDetails* form can be used to update the *Users* table.

15. **Close** ☒ the **UserDetails** form.

■ **You have completed Skill 8 of 10**

► Recall that a macro is a set of saved actions that you can use to automate tasks.

► *Table Events* are used to register changes to records through the use of macros. A macro can be created to record the date and time a record is changed.

1. Open the **Training Days** table in Design view.

2. Add a new field named Date Modified and then assign it the **Date/Time** data type.

3. Add a new field named Time Modified and then assign it the **Date/Time** data type. Press (Enter), click **Save** 🖫, and then compare your screen with **Figure 1**.

4. **Close** ☒ the table. Display the **Create tab**, and then in the **Macros & Code group** click **Macro**.

5. On the **Design tab**, in the **Show/Hide group**, click **Show All Actions**. On the macro workspace, click the **Add New Action** arrow, and then click **SetValue**.

   SetValue is a macro action used to enter a value into a field or control. SetValue is a macro action that is hidden by default because it is considered to possibly be unsafe.

6. Click in the **Item** box, and then type [Date Modified] Press (Tab) two times, and then type Date()

7. On the macro workspace, click the **Add New Action** arrow, and then click **SetValue**.

8. Click in the **Item** box, and then type [Time Modified] Press (Tab) two times, and then type Time() Compare your screen with **Figure 2**.

■ Continue to the next page to complete the skill

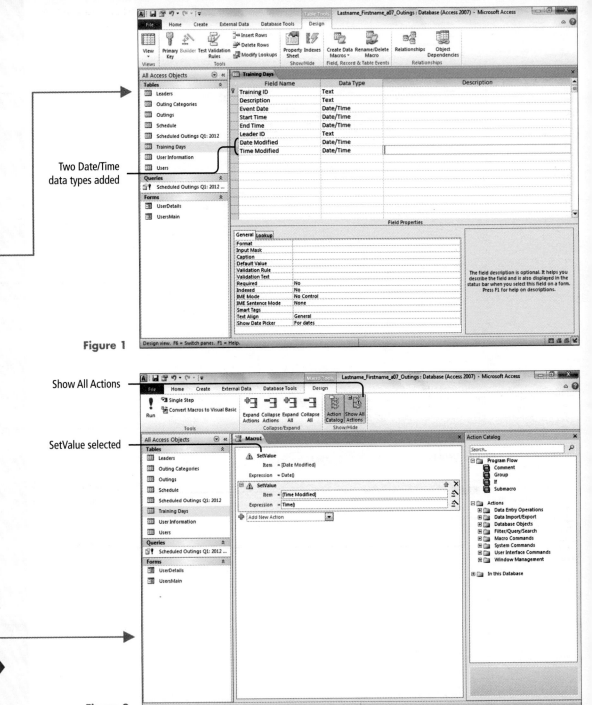

Two Date/Time data types added

Figure 1

Show All Actions

SetValue selected

Figure 2

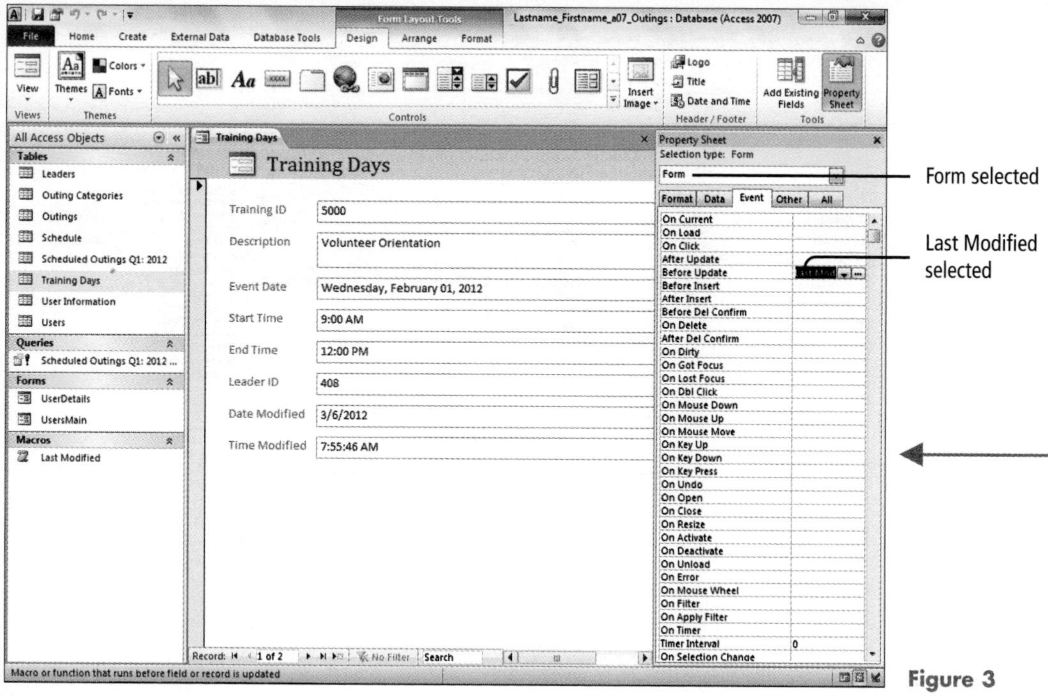

Form selected

Last Modified selected

Figure 3

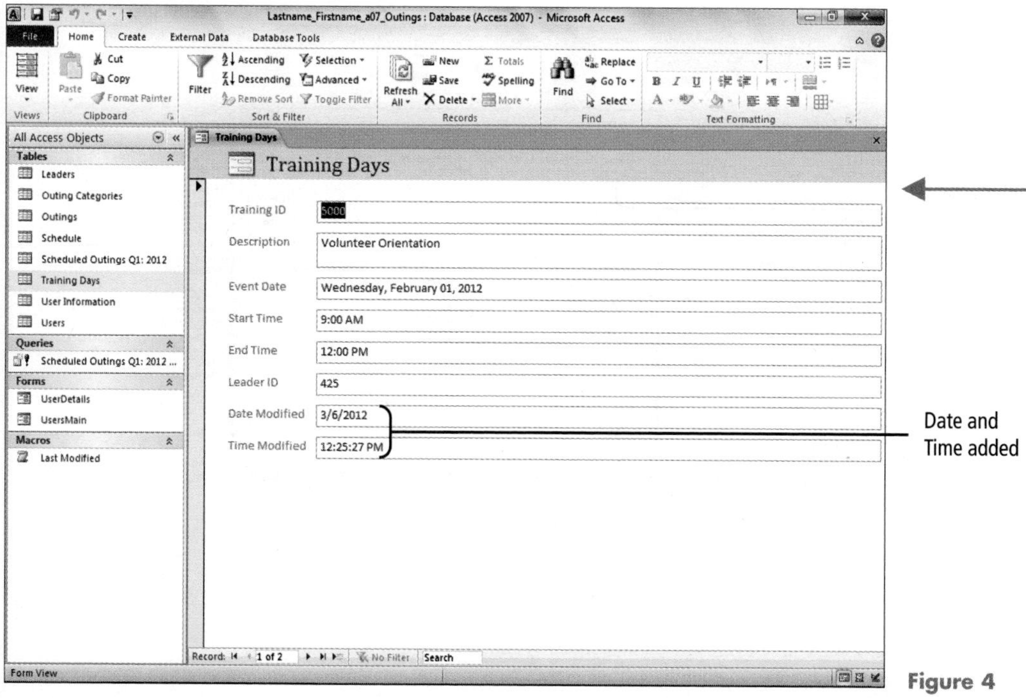

Date and Time added

Figure 4

9. Click **Save** 🖫, and then type Last Modified Click **OK**, and then **Close** ⊠ the macro.

10. In the **Navigation Pane**, select the **Training Days** table. On the **Create tab**, in the **Forms** group, click **Form**.

11. On the property sheet, click the **Selection type arrow**, and then from the displayed list click **Form**.

12. On the **Event tab**, click in the **Before Update** box. Click the down arrow, and then click **Last Modified**. Compare your screen with **Figure 3**.

13. Switch to Form view. In the first record, click in the **Leader ID** field and replace 408 with 425 Press and hold (Shift), and then press (F9) to save and update the record. Compare your screen with **Figure 4**.

14. Click **Start** ⊛, and then click **All Programs**. Click to open the **Accessories** folder, and then click **Snipping Tool**.

15. In the **Snipping Tool** dialog box, click the **New button arrow**, and then click **Full-screen Snip**.

16. Click the **Save Snip** button 🖫. In the **Save As** dialog box, navigate to your **Access Chapter 7** folder. In the **File name** box, type Lastname_Firstname_a07_Outings_ Snip2 and then click the **Save Snip** button. **Close** ⊠ the Snipping Tool window.

17. Click **Save** 🖫, and then click **OK**. **Close** ⊠ the **Training Days** form.

■ **You have completed Skill 9 of 10**

► A *calculated field* is a column added to a datasheet that derives its value from an expression.

► Access 2010 allows the user to enter a calculated field directly into a table. However, when the required fields for an expression exist in multiple tables then a query is used.

1. Open the **Scheduled Outings Q1: 2012** table in Design view.

2. Click in the **Field Name** box under **Fee**, and then type Total

3. Press Tab, click the **Data Type box arrow**, and then from the displayed list click **Calculated**. Compare your screen with **Figure 1.**

   The Expression Builder dialog box displays. Here is where you will enter the fields to be calculated.

4. In the **Expression Builder** dialog box, under **Expression Categories**, double-click **Enrollment**.

   [Enrollment] is added to the expression.

5. Click to the right of *[Enrollment]*, and then type * as shown in **Figure 2.**

   In Access, an "*" is used to multiply two numbers in a calculated fields.

6. In the **Expression Builder** dialog box, under **Expression Categories**, double-click **Fee**.

■ **Continue to the next page to complete the skill**

Expression Builder

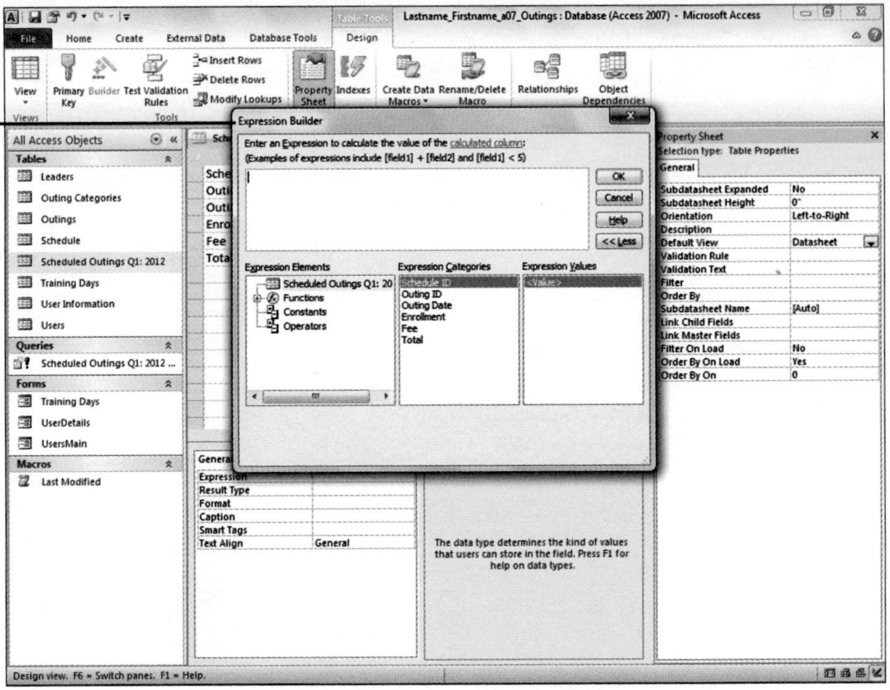

Figure 1

Enrollment field
added

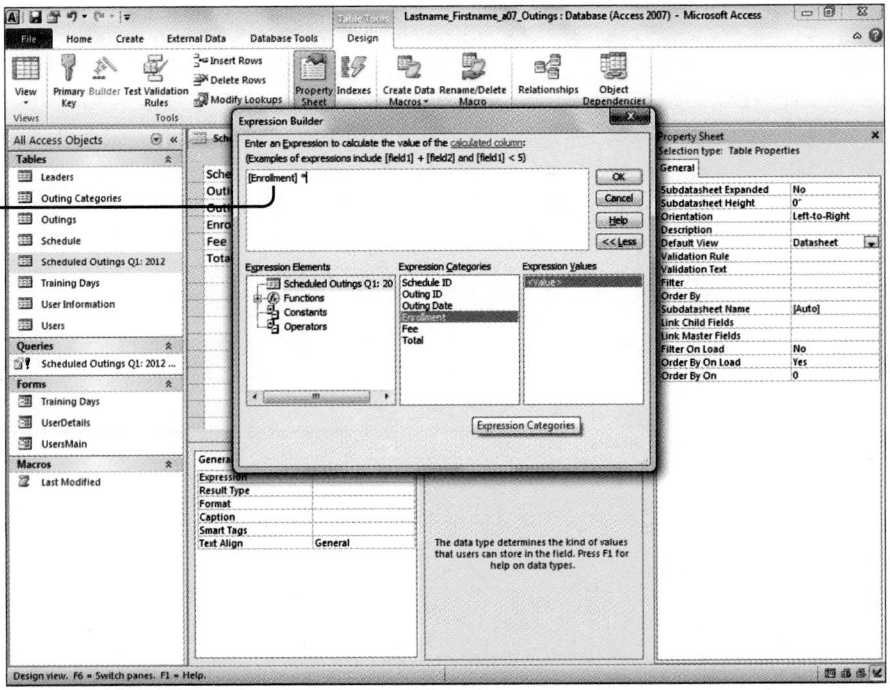

Figure 2

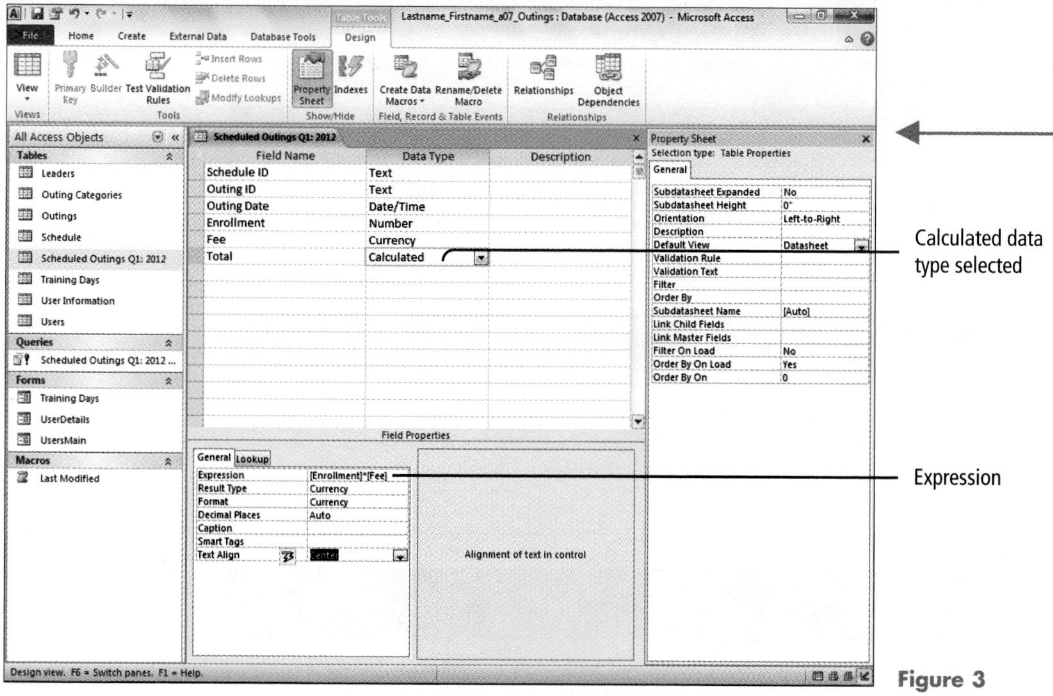

Calculated data type selected

Expression

Figure 3

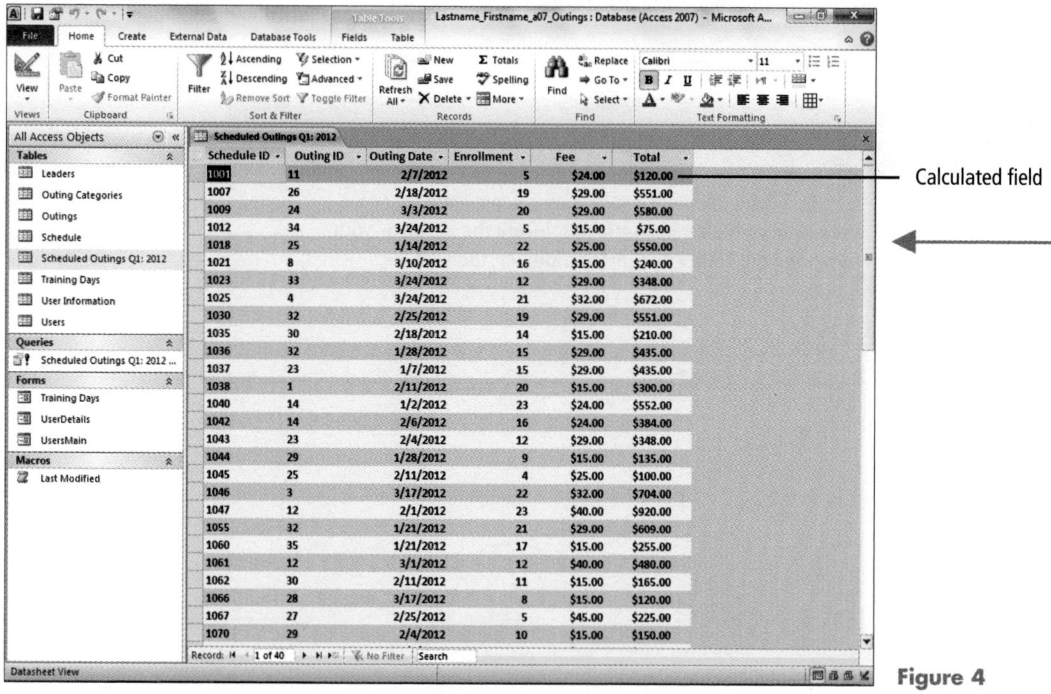

Calculated field

Figure 4

7. Click **OK**.

The expression is now displayed in Field Properties.

8. In the **Field Properties** pane, click in the **Result Type** box. Click the down arrow, and then from the list click **Currency**.

9. In the **Field Properties** pane, click in the **Text Align** box. Click the down arrow, and then from the list click **Center**. Compare your screen with **Figure 3**.

10. Click **Save**, and then switch to Datasheet view.

The Total column displays the Enrollment multiplied by the Fee.

11. On the **Home tab**, in the **Text Formatting group**, click the **Font Color arrow**, and then click **Black**—the first color. Compare your screen with **Figure 4.**

12. Click **Start**, and then click **All Programs**. Click to open the **Accessories** folder, and then click **Snipping Tool**.

13. In the **Snipping Tool** dialog box, click the **New button arrow**, and then click **Full-screen Snip**.

14. Click the **Save Snip** button. In the **Save As** dialog box, navigate to your **Access Chapter 7** folder. In the **File name** box, type Lastname_Firstname_a07_Outings_Snip3 and then click the **Save Snip** button. **Close** the Snipping Tool window.

15. Click **Save**, and then **Close** the table.

16. **Exit** Access.

Done! You have completed Skill 10 of 10 and your document is complete!

More Skills

The following More Skills are located at **www.pearsonhighered.com/skills**

More Skills ⑪ Create New Field Data Types

With Access 2010, you can add an attachment field, where you can store links to multiple files.

In More Skills 11, you will create an attachment field to store photos.

To begin, open your web browser, navigate to www.pearsonhighered.com/skills, locate the name of your textbook, and follow the instructions on the website.

More Skills ⑫ Create Custom Input Masks

When multiple users enter into a database, you may want to control the way that data is entered and formatted.

In More Skills 12, you will create an input mask for users to enter states in a specific format.

To begin, open your web browser, navigate to www.pearsonhighered.com/skills, locate the name of your textbook, and follow the instructions on the website.

More Skills ⑬ Insert Quick Start Fields

Quick Start fields allow you to quickly add a group of related fields, such as address fields, to a table.

In More Skills 13, you will work with a Category Quick Start field, which will categorize different classes.

To begin, open your web browser, navigate to www.pearsonhighered.com/skills, locate the name of your textbook, and follow the instructions on the website.

More Skills ⑭ Check for Spelling Errors

Table data can sometimes have spelling mistakes. Access 2010 has a spelling tool, which searches a table for potential spelling mistakes and provides suggestions for correcting them.

In More Skills 14, you will check a table for spelling mistakes and use the Spelling dialog box to correct or ignore the words that it flags.

To begin, open your web browser, navigate to www.pearsonhighered.com/skills, locate the name of your textbook, and follow the instructions on the website.

Key Terms

Online Help Skills

1. **Start** ● Access. In the upper-right corner of the Access window, click the **Help** button ⊙. In the **Help** window, click the **Maximize** ⬜ button.

2. Click in the search box, type tables and then click the **Search** button ⌕. In the search results, click **Introduction to tables**.

3. Scroll down to **Keys**. Compare your screen with **Figure 1**.

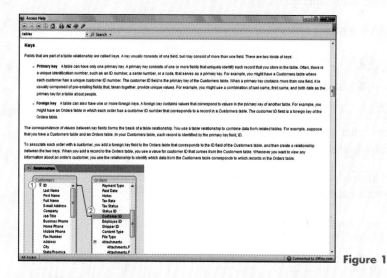

Figure 1

4. Read the section to see if you can answer the following questions: Can more than one foreign key exist in a database? The foreign key in one table is linked to what type of key in another table?

Matching

Match each term in the second column with its correct definition in the first column by writing the letter of the term on the blank line in front of the correct definition.

____ **1.** These values repeat themselves by being stored in more than one location in a database.

____ **2.** A mistake made during data entry.

____ **3.** Characters with no formatting capabilities.

____ **4.** Characters that have formatting capabilities.

____ **5.** The number of days since December 30, 1899, and the fraction of 24 hours that has expired for the day.

____ **6.** A control that enables you to navigate a calendar and then click the desired value.

____ **7.** Tool that produces pre-built tables with fields for common information needs.

____ **8.** This tool is used to register changes to records through the use of macros.

____ **9.** A macro action used to add a value to a field or control.

____ **10.** A field that derives its value from an expression.

A Application Parts

B Calculated field

C Date Picker

D Plain Text

E Redundant data

F Rich Text

G Serial dates

H SetValue

I Table Events

J Typographical error

Multiple Choice

Choose the correct answer.

1. This refers to text that cannot be formatted.
   - **A.** Plain Text
   - **B.** Smart Text
   - **C.** Rich Text

2. The name assigned to duplicated data in a database.
   - **A.** Redundant data
   - **B.** Linked data
   - **C.** Data copies

3. This tool is used to identify whether a table should be divided into two or more tables.
   - **A.** Database Documenter
   - **B.** Application Parts
   - **C.** Table Analyzer

4. This is an alternative name for a table's primary key.
   - **A.** Foreign key
   - **B.** Unique identifier
   - **C.** SetValue

5. This term is used to describe inaccurate data entered into a database.
   - **A.** Typographical error
   - **B.** Database misinformation
   - **C.** Critical error

6. This stores the location of records based on the values in a field.
   - **A.** Date Picker
   - **B.** Application Parts
   - **C.** Index

7. This join states that a record in one table can have only one corresponding record in the other table.
   - **A.** Quick Start fields
   - **B.** One-to-one relationship
   - **C.** Table Analyzer

8. This refers to text that can be formatted.
   - **A.** Plain Text
   - **B.** Smart Text
   - **C.** Rich Text

9. This control enables you to use a calendar to select a date.
   - **A.** Date selector
   - **B.** Date Picker
   - **C.** Date chooser

10. This tool can be used to create a table from a template.
    - **A.** Table Analyzer
    - **B.** Table Events
    - **C.** Application Parts

Topics for Discussion

1. What is the purpose of using the Table Analyzer tool?

2. Under what circumstances would you use Rich Text in a field instead of Plain Text?

Skill Check

To complete this database, you will need the following file:

- a07_Vintage_Cars

You will save your database as:

- Lastname_Firstname_a07_Vintage_Cars

1. **Start** Access. Open **a07_Vintage_Cars**, and then save the database in your **Access Chapter 7** folder as Lastname_Firstname_a07_Vintage_Cars If necessary, enable the content.

2. Display the **Database Tools tab**, and then in the **Analyze group**, click **Analyze Table**.

3. In the **Table Analyzer Wizard**, click **Next** two times. Under **Tables**, with **Vintage Cars** selected, click **Next**. Verify that **Yes, let the wizard decide** is selected, and then click **Next**.

4. Click **Table1**, and then click the **Rename Table** button. In **Table Name:** type Vintage Car Detail and then click **OK**. Rename **Table2** as Volunteers Click **Next**. In the **Vintage Car Detail** table, click **License Plate**, and then click the **Set Unique Identifier** button. Compare your screen with **Figure 1**. ⎯⎯⎯

5. Click **Next**, and then with **No, don't create the query** selected, click **Finish**. Click **OK**.

6. **Close** all tables, and then open the **Navigation Pane**. Delete the **Vintage Cars** table. In the displayed message box, click **Yes**.

7. On the **Database Tools tab**, in the **Relationships group**, click **Relationships**. On the **Design tab**, in the **Relationships group**, click **Show Table**. Double-click the **Vintage Car Detail** and **Volunteers** tables, and then **Close** the **Show Table** dialog box.

8. In the **Event Details** table, drag the **License Plate** field and drop it on the **License Plate** field in the **Vintage Car Detail** table.

9. In the **Edit Relationships** dialog box, select the **Enforce Referential Integrity**, **Cascade Update Related Fields**, and the **Cascade Delete Related Records** check boxes. Click **Create**. Compare your screen with **Figure 2**, **Save**, and then **Close** ⎯⎯⎯ the Relationships window.

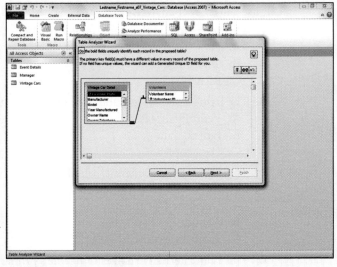

Figure 1

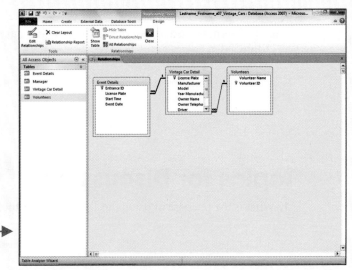

Figure 2

 Continue to the next page to complete this Skill Check

10. Open the **Volunteers** table in Design view. Add two fields named Date Modified and Time Modified with Date/Time data types. **Save**, and then switch to Datasheet view.

11. On the **Create tab**, in the **Macros & Code group**, click **Macro**.

12. Click **Show All Actions**. Click the **Add New Action arrow**, and then click **SetValue**. In the **Item** box, type [Date Modified] Press ⎇Tab⎇ two times, and then in the **Expression** box, type Date() Click the **Add New Action arrow**, and then click **SetValue**. Click in the **Item** box, and then type [Time Modified] Press ⎇Tab⎇ two times, and then in **Value** type Time() Click **Save**, type Last Modified click **OK**, and then **Close** the macro.

13. Add a new record with Your Name as the **Volunteer Name** and 7 as the **Volunteer ID**. On the **Home tab**, in the **Text Formatting group**, click the **Gridlines** button, and then from the displayed list click **Gridlines: Horizontal**. Click the **Background Color** button, and then click **Tan, Background 2. Save**, and then **Close** the table.

14. With the **Volunteers** table selected, on the **Create tab**, click **Form**. On the property sheet, in **Selection type**, click **Form**. On the **Event tab**, click in the **Before Update** box. Click the down arrow, and then click **Last Modified**. Click **Save**, press ⎇Enter⎇, and then **Close** the form.

15. On the **Create tab**, in the **Queries group**, click **Query Design**. Add the **Event Details** table, and then add all the fields from the table to the design grid. In the **Start Time** column **Criteria** box, type Between 10:00 AM and 11:00 AM Under **Event Date** in the **Criteria** box, type =6/9/2012

16. On the **Design tab**, in the **Query Type group**, click **Make Table**. In the **Make Table** dialog box, in the **Table Name** box, type Opening Ceremony 2012 and then click **OK**. Click **Run**, click **Yes**, and then compare with **Figure 3**.

17. **Save** the query as Opening Ceremony 2012 Query **Close** the query.

18. On the **Create tab**, in the **Templates group**, click **Application Parts**, and then click **Tasks**. Click **Yes**. Click **Next**, and then click **Create**. Open the **Tasks** table. In the **Task Title** column, on the first row, type Opening Ceremony 2012 Purchase balloons

19. Open the **Manager** table. Click the *Click to Add* column arrow, and then click **Calculated Field**, and then click **Currency**. Type [Hourly Rate] * [Weekly Hours] Click **OK**, type Weekly Total and then compare with **Figure 4. Exit** Access.

Done! You have completed the Skill Check

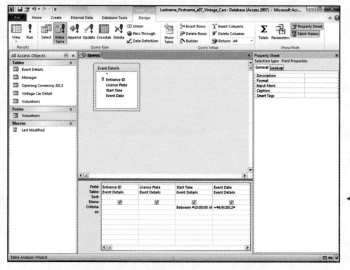

Figure 3

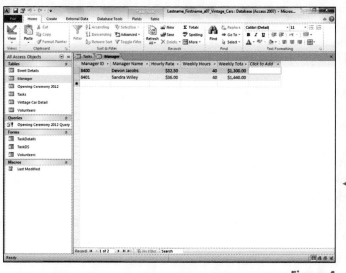

Figure 4

Assess Your Skills 1

To complete this database, you will need the following file:

- a07_Triathlon

You will save your files as:

- Lastname_Firstname_a07_Triathlon
- Lastname_Firstname_a07_Triathlon_Snip
- Lastname_Firstname_a07_Triathlon_Snip1

1. **Start** Access, and then open **a07_Triathlon**. **Save** the file in your **Access Chapter 7** folder as Lastname_Firstname_a07_Triathlon

2. Create a new query in Design view. Add all of the fields from the **Race Sponsors** table. Under **Amount**, in **Criteria**, type >5000 Under **Race Year**, in **Criteria**, type =2012 Use the query to make a table named Sponsors Contributing more than 5000 Run the query to make the table. **Save** the query as Sponsors Contributing >$5000 and then **Close** the query.

3. Create a new **Users** table from **Application Parts**. In the **Create Relationship** dialog box, select the **There is no relationship** option. Format the table to display only the horizontal grid lines and the **Blue Accent 1** as the **Alternate Row Color**.

4. Add the following columns to the **Racers** table: Date Modified and Time Modified

5. Create a **Racers** form. Create a new macro that will insert the date and time into fields named Date Modified and Time Modified whenever a record is modified in the **Racers** form. Enter Your Name in the first row. **Save** the macro as Last Modified Update the record, and then compare with **Figure 1**. Create a Full-screen Snip and **Save** as Lastname_Firstname_a07_Triathlon_Snip

6. Create a new table, add Guest ID as the primary key, and add Guest Name as the second column heading. Change the **Field Size** for **Guest ID** and **Guest Name** to 50 **Save** the table as Guests

7. In Design view, add a new field named Comments to the **Guests** table. Change the **Comments** field data type to **Memo**, and then change its **Text Format** property to **Rich Text**.

8. **Save**, and then switch to Datasheet view. On the first row, in **Guest ID** type 400 in the **Guest Name** column enter Your Name and then in the **Comments** column, add two bullets detailing your favorite foods. Adjust the column width and row height to display both bullets. Compare your screen with **Figure 2**. Create a Full-screen Snip and **Save** as Lastname_Firstname_a07_Triathlon_Snip1

9. Create a one-to-one relationship between the **Sponsor Contact** table and the **Sponsors** table. **Save**, and then **Close** the **Relationships** window.

10. **Save** the **Guests** table. **Save** the form as Racers and then **Exit** Access.

   Done! You have completed Assess Your Skills 1

Figure 1

Figure 2

Assess Your Skills 2

To complete this database, you will need the following file:

- a07_Park_Employees

You will save your files as:

- Lastname_Firstname_a07_Park_Employees
- Lastname_Firstname_a07_Park_Employees_Snip

Figure 1

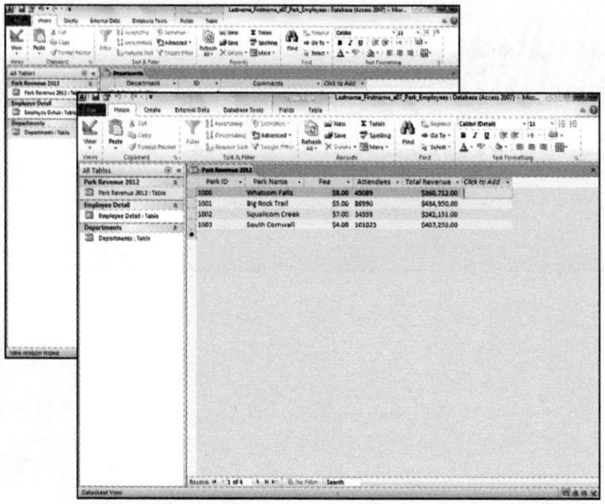

Figure 2

1. **Start** Access, and then open **a07_Park_Employees**. **Save** the file in your **Access Chapter 7** folder as Lastname_Firstname_a07_Park_Employees

2. Use the **Table Analyzer** to analyze the **Employees** table. Let the **Table Analyzer** decide how to split the tables. Name **Table1** Employee Detail and name **Table2** Departments Accept the primary key suggested by the wizard for **Departments**. Use **Employee ID** as the primary key for the **Employee Detail** table. When prompted about correcting typographical errors, select **Leave as is** and do not create a query.

3. For the **Departments** and **Employee Detail** tables, adjust the column widths. **Save** and **Close** the tables. Expand the Navigation Pane, and then delete the **Employees** table.

4. Edit the relationship between the **Departments** and **Employee Detail** tables so that it enforces referential integrity, cascade updates related fields, and cascade deletes related records. **Close** the **Relationships** window.

5. Open the **Departments** table in Design view, and then add a column named Comments with the **Memo** data type. Change its **Text Format** property to **Rich Text**.

6. In Datasheet view, add the following as numbered bullets in the **Comments** column for **Aquatics**: 1. Employees located at City Hall 2. Need to hire two interns

7. Adjust the **Comments** column width and row height so that the field's content displays. Compare your screen with **Figure 1**. **Save**, and then **Close** the **Departments** table.

8. Open the **Park Revenue 2012** table. Add a new calculated field called Total Revenue The **Total Revenue** column will multiply the **Fees** column by the **Attendees** column.

9. Adjust the **Total Revenue** column width. Apply a background color of **Tan, Background 2**. Compare your screen with **Figure 2**.

10. Create a Full-screen Snip and **Save** as Lastname_Firstname_a07_Park_Employees_Snip

11. **Save** and **Close** the **Park Revenue 2012** table, and then **Exit** Access.

Done! You have completed Assess Your Skills 2

Assess Your Skills Visually

To complete this database, you will need the following file:

- a07_Rentals

You will save your database as:

- Lastname_Firstname_a07_Rentals

Open the database **a07_Rentals** and save the database in your **Access Chapter 7** folder as Lastname_Firstname_a07_Rentals

Format the **Rental Rooms** table as shown in **Figure 1**. **Blue, Accent 1, Lighter 80%** has been selected as the **Background color**. Increase the **Font Size** to 12, and then change the font style to **Bold** and **Italic**. Add horizontal grid lines. Format the **Description** field to a Text Format of **Rich Text**, and then add a numbered list for each feature of each room. Adjust the row height to display the contents of the **Description** column.

Save the datasheet changes. **Print** the datasheet or submit the database file as directed by your instructor.

Done! You have completed Assess Your Skills Visually

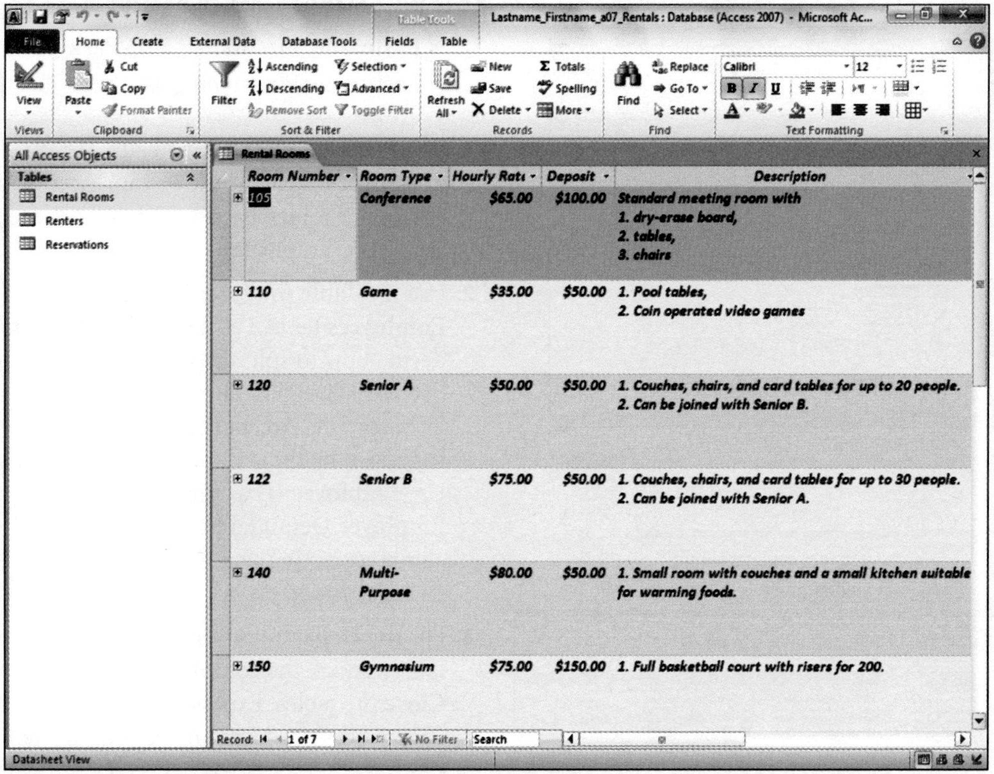

Figure 1

Skills in Context

To complete this database, you will need the following file:

- a07_Aquatics_Program

You will save your database as:

- Lastname_Firstname_a07_Aquatics_Program

Open **a07_Aquatics_Program** and save the database in your **Access Chapter 7** folder as Lastname_Firstname_a07_Aquatics_Program Use a query to create a table, which displays all of the events from **June 1 – 15, 2012**, at **Franklin Lowe Sports Multiplex**. Save the query as June 1-15 2012 Franklin Lowe Events Query Save the table as June 1-15 2012 Franklin Lowe Events Add a new **Total** field, which calculates the revenue for each swimming

class. Format the table with horizontal grid lines and apply **Blue, Accent 1, Lighter 80%** background color. Adjust the width of the **Event Name** column.

Submit as directed by your instructor.

Done! You have completed Skills in Context

Skills and You

To complete this database, you will need the following file:

- New blank database

You will save your database as:

- Lastname_Firstname_a07_Assignments

Using the skills you have practiced in this chapter, create a database named Lastname_Firstname_a07_Assignments Create a new table named Assignments Add the following columns: Work ID, Subject, Description, Instructor, Due Date, Date Modified, and Time Modified Create a new macro, which will record the date and time of when records are changed. Create an **Assignments** form to enter at least two of your school

assignments. Test the form to see if the **Date Modified** and **Time Modified** fields are updated. Finally, format the font color and background color of the table with your own professional design.

Submit as directed by your instructor.

Done! You have completed Skills and You

CHAPTER **8**

Integrate Data with Other Applications

▶ Data can be moved between Access and other applications. For example, an Access table can be exported as a table in Microsoft Word or exported as a table that displays on a web page.

▶ Data organized into tables in other programs like Excel can be imported into Access to create new tables.

Your starting screen will look like this:

SKILLS

myitlab
Skills 1-10 Training

At the end of this chapter, you will be able to:

Skill 1 Import Data from Text Files

Skill 2 Export Data to Excel

Skill 3 Link to External Data Sources

Skill 4 Prepare Worksheet Data for Importing in Access

Skill 5 Import Data from Excel

Skill 6 Export Tables into Word

Skill 7 Import XML Data

Skill 8 Export XML Data

Skill 9 Export Data to HTML Documents

Skill 10 Merge Data into Word Documents

MORE SKILLS

More Skills 11 Save Tables as PDF Documents

More Skills 12 Save Export Steps

More Skills 13 Import Objects from External Databases

More Skills 14 Update a Database through E-Mail

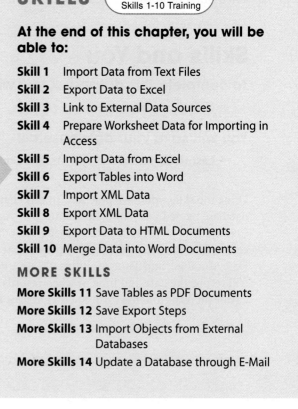

Outcome

Using the skills listed to the left will enable you to create documents like these:

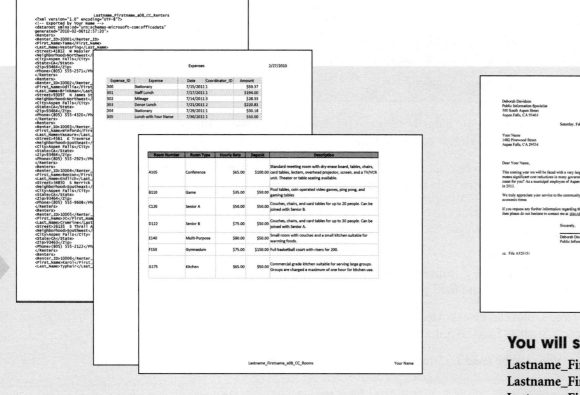

You will save your files as:

Lastname_Firstname_a08_CC_Employees

Lastname_Firstname_a08_CC_Letter

Lastname_Firstname_a08_CC_Rooms

Lastname_Firstname_a08_CC_Rentals

Lastname_Firstname_a08_Renters_HTML

Lastname_Firstname_a08_CC_Renters

Lastname_Firstname_a08_CC_Rooms.rtf

Lastname_Firstname_a08_CC_Rooms.xlsx

In this chapter, you will create databases for the Aspen Falls City Hall, which provides essential services for the citizens and visitors of Aspen Falls, California.

Introduction

- ► Before data is inserted into a database, it can be viewed and worked with in other programs, such as a text editor or Excel.

- ► Imported data needs to be organized so that each row is a record, each column is a field, and duplicate records are deleted.

- ► Data from other programs can be imported to create a new Access table or linked so that Access can use the data while storing it in the other program's file.

- ► After creating a new table from imported data, the table can be joined to other tables in the database and field properties may need to be changed.

- ► Data from tables can be exported into file formats that can be opened in other programs, such as Excel, Word, or a web browser.

- ► Access tables can be used as data sources for Word mail merge documents.

Time to complete all
10 skills – 50 to 90 minutes

Find your student data files here:

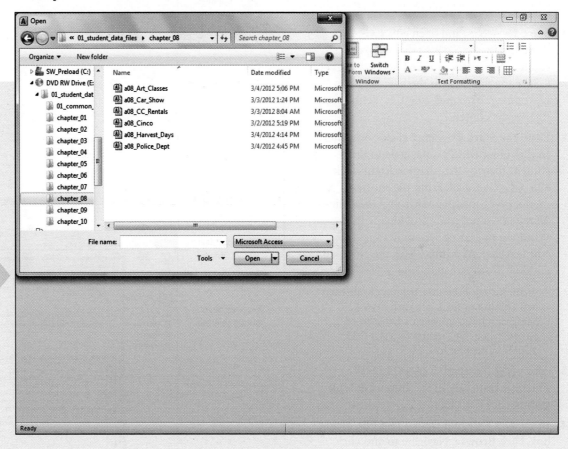

Student data files needed for this chapter:

- a08_CC_Rentals
- a08_CC_Contacts
- a08_CC_Employees
- a08_CC_Renters
- a08_CC_Expenses
- a08_CC_Letter

▶ *Text files*—files that store only the text characters but not the formatting, tab stops, or tables—are often used to move data from databases made by other programs into Access databases.

▶ Access can import data from a *delimited text file*—a text file where the data in each column is separated by an identifying character such as a comma, a space, or a tab.

1. **Start** ⦿ Access, and open **a08_CC_Rentals**. Use the **Save As** dialog box to create a **New folder** named Access Chapter 8 **Save** the database in the new folder as Lastname_Firstname_a08_CC_Rentals Enable the content.

2. From the **Start** ⦿ menu, click **Computer**. In the folder window, navigate to the student files for this chapter. Right-click **a08_CC_Contacts**. From the shortcut menu, point to **Open with**, and then click *Notepad*—a program provided with the Windows operating system designed to edit text files. **Maximize** 🔲 the Notepad window. Compare with **Figure 1**.

   A comma has been inserted to indicate each new column or field, and each new paragraph indicates when a new row or record begins. The names for each field display in the first row.

3. Close 🗙 Notepad. In Access, on the **External Data tab**, in the **Import & Link group**, click **Text File**.

4. In the **Get External Data - Text File** dialog box, click **Browse**. Navigate to and click **a08_CC_Contacts**, and then click **Open**. With the **Import the source data into a new table in the current database** option button selected, click **OK**. Compare with **Figure 2**.

■ **Continue to the next page to complete the skill**

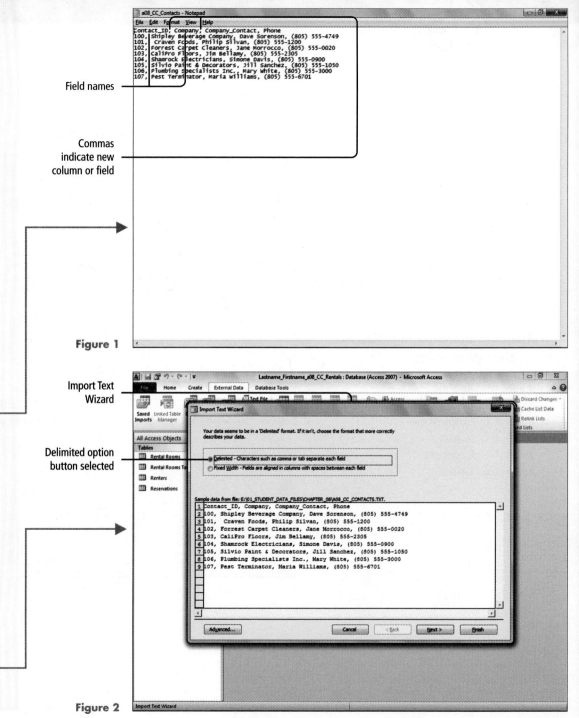

Field names

Commas indicate new column or field

Figure 1

Import Text Wizard

Delimited option button selected

Figure 2

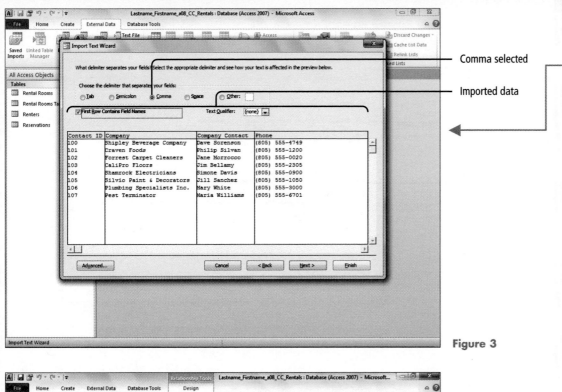

Comma selected

Imported data

Figure 3

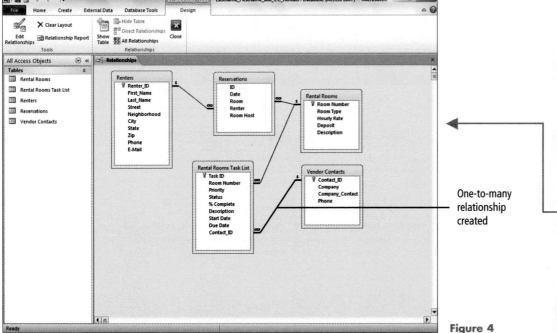

One-to-many relationship created

Figure 4

5. With the **Delimited** option button selected, click **Next**. Select the **First Row Contains Field Names** check box, as shown in **Figure 3**.

   The wizard identified the comma as the *delimiter*—the character used to separate fields in a delimited text file.

6. Click **Next**. Under **Field Options**, click the **Indexed arrow**, and then click **Yes (No Duplicates)**.

7. Click **Next**, and then select the **Choose my own primary key** option button. With **Contact_ID** displayed in the primary key box, click **Next**.

8. In the **Import to Table** box, replace the existing text with Vendor Contacts and then click **Finish**. **Close** the **Get External Data – Text File** dialog box.

9. **Open** the **Vendor Contacts** table. Verify the data imported.

10. **Close** ☒ the **Vendor Contacts** table. Display the **Database Tools tab**, and then in the **Relationships group**, click **Relationships**.

    Notice that the *Vendor Contacts* table has been added to the Relationships window.

11. Use the **Contact_ID** field to create a one-to-many relationship between **Rental Rooms Task List** and **Vendor Contacts**. For the relationship, select the options to **Enforce Referential Integrity, Cascade Update Related Fields**, and **Cascade Delete Related Records**. Compare your screen to **Figure 4**.

12. Click **Save** 🖫, and then in the **Relationships group**, click the **Close** button.

■ **You have completed Skill 1 of 10**

► Data in Access tables can be exported into Excel spreadsheets. In Excel, the data can be summarized or charts can be created to represent the data.

1. In the **Navigation Pane**, click the **Rental Rooms** table. Display the **External Data tab**, and then in the **Export group**, click the **Excel** button.

2. In the **Export - Excel Spreadsheet** dialog box, click the **Browse** button, and then in the **File Save** dialog box, navigate to your **Access Chapter 8** folder. In the **File name** box, name the file Lastname_Firstname_a08_CC_Rooms and then click **Save**.

3. Under **Specify export options**, select the **Export data with formatting and layout** check box.

4. Select the **Open the destination file after the export operation is complete** check box, as shown in **Figure 1.**

5. Click **OK**, and then compare your screen with **Figure 2.**

The data displays in an Excel spreadsheet with each field in a column and each record in a row. On the taskbar, the Access button will be flashing.

■ **Continue to the next page to complete the skill**

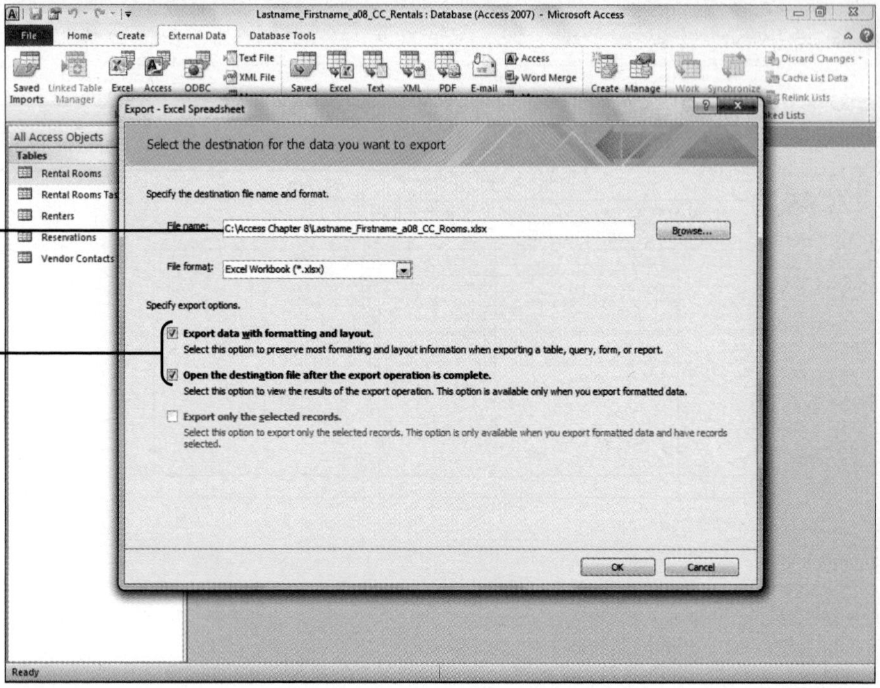

File path and name changed

Export options selected

Figure 1

Rental Rooms data exported to Excel

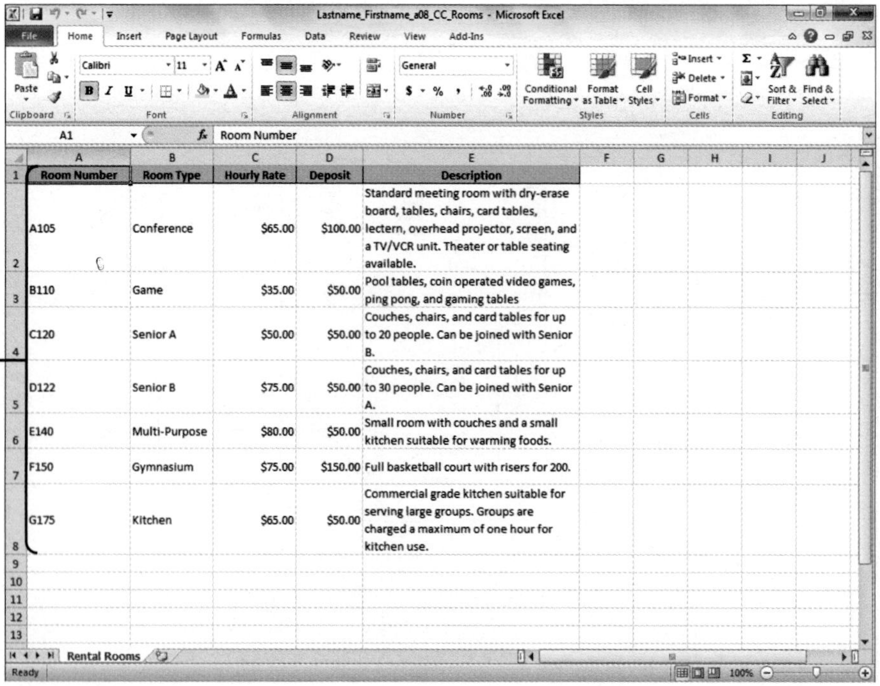

Figure 2

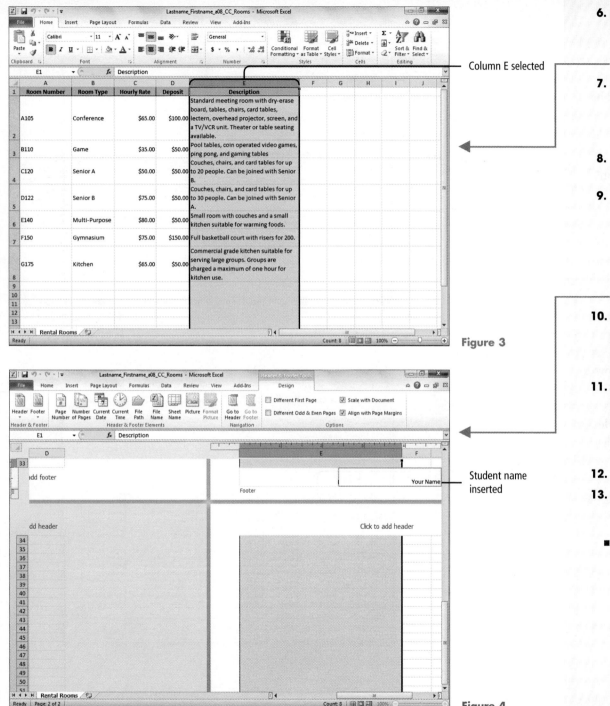

Column E selected

Figure 3

Student name inserted

Figure 4

6. In the displayed spreadsheet, point to the top of column **E**, and then with the ↓ pointer, click to select the column, as shown in **Figure 3**.

7. On the **Home tab**, in the **Cells group**, click the **Format** button. In the displayed list, click **Column Width**.

   The Column Width dialog box displays.

8. In the **Column Width** dialog box, type 50 and then click **OK**.

9. Display the **Insert tab**, and then in the **Text group**, click **Header & Footer**. On the **Design tab**, in the **Navigation group**, click **Go to Footer**. In the **Header & Footer Elements group**, click the **File Name** button. Press Tab, type Your Name and then compare with **Figure 4**.

10. Click in any cell above or below the footer. On the **View tab**, in the **Workbook Views group**, click the **Normal** button. Scroll up and click in cell **A1**.

11. On the **Page Layout tab**, in the **Page Setup group**, click the **Orientation** button, and then click **Landscape**. If you are printing your work for this chapter, print the worksheet.

12. Click **Save** 🖫, and then **Close** ✕ Excel.

13. In Access, in the **Export - Excel Spreadsheet** dialog box, click **Close**.

■ **You have completed Skill 2 of 10**

► Access can use data stored in *linked tables*—tables that exist in a different file created by an application such as Access, Excel, or Microsoft SQL Server.

► Once a linked table is inserted, it can be joined to other tables in the database and be used to create queries and reports. To update the data, the file must be opened in the application that created it.

1. With the **External Data tab** displayed, in the **Import & Link group**, click **Excel**.

2. In the **Get External Data – Excel Spreadsheet** dialog box, click **Browse**. Navigate to your **Access Chapter 8** student files, and then double-click **a08_CC_Employees**.

3. Select the **Link to the data source by creating a linked table** option button, as shown in **Figure 1**.

4. Click **OK**. In the displayed **Link Spreadsheet Wizard**, select the **First Row Contains Column Headings** check box, as shown in **Figure 2**.

5. Click **Next**, and then in the **Linked Table Name** box, replace the existing text with
   Employees

■ **Continue to the next page to complete the skill**

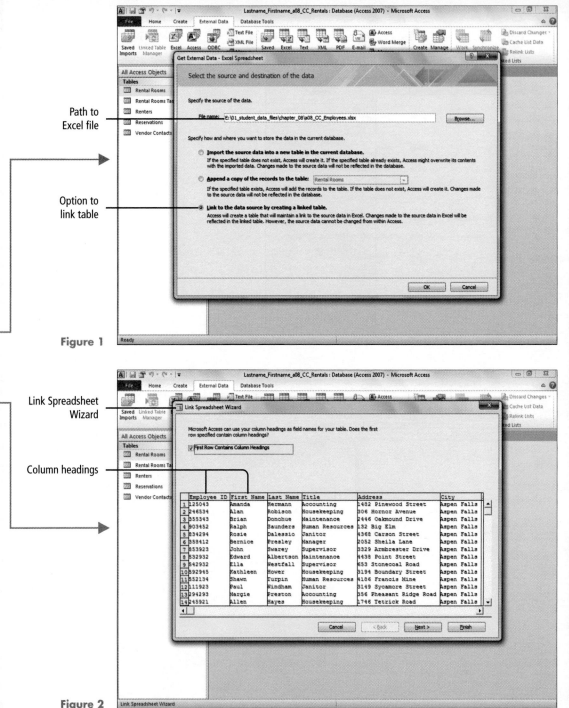

Path to Excel file

Option to link table

Figure 1

Link Spreadsheet Wizard

Column headings

Figure 2

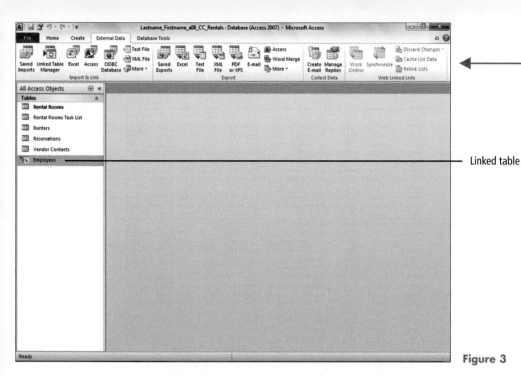

Linked table

Figure 3

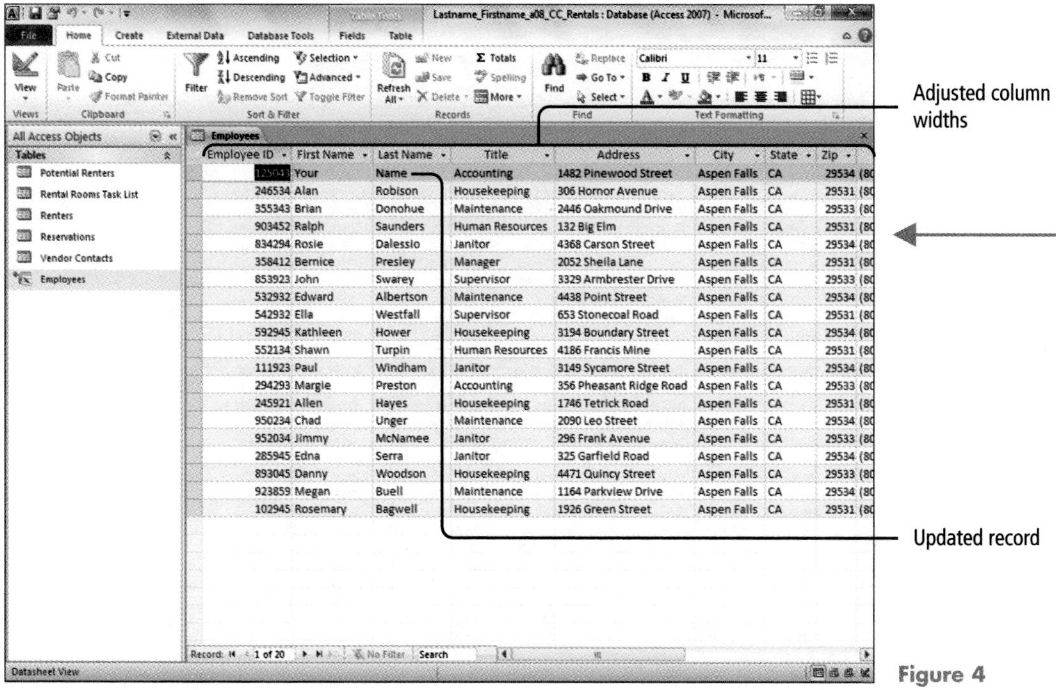

Adjusted column widths

Updated record

Figure 4

6. Click **Finish**, read the displayed message, and then click **OK**. Compare your screen with **Figure 3**.

   In the Navigation Pane, the linked table displays an Excel icon with an arrow to indicate that the table is linked to the Excel file.

7. In the **Navigation Pane**, double-click the **Employees** table.

8. **Close** [«] the **Navigation Pane**. Click the **Select All** button [ ], and then with the [+] pointer positioned between any two column headings, double-click to resize the column widths. **Save** [ ], and then **Close** [×] the table.

9. **Start** [●] Excel, navigate to your student data files, and then open **a08_CC_Employees**.

10. In cells **B2** and **C2**, change the name *Amanda Hermann* to your first and last name. Using your name, **Save** the file as Lastname_Firstname_a08_CC_Employees and then **Close** [×] Excel.

    When data is linked to an Excel table, the data must be updated in Excel.

11. In Access, **Open** [»] the **Navigation Pane**. Double-click the **Employees** table. Verify that the first record displays your name, as shown in **Figure 4**.

12. Click **Save** [ ], and then click **Close** [×] the table.

- **You have completed Skill 3 of 10**

► Data in a spreadsheet often needs to be shaped before it can be imported into Access.

► Before importing data, each record needs to be a row and each field needs to be in the same column. For example, the first names must be in the same column. Duplicate records may need to be deleted so that a primary key can be assigned.

1. **Start** ⊕ Excel. From your student files, open **a08_CC_Renters.xlsx**.

2. Notice that column H has no data. Point to the top of column **H**, and then with the ⬇ pointer, click to select the column.

3. On the **Home tab**, in the **Cells group**, click the **Delete** button, and then compare your screen with **Figure 1**.

The column is removed and Phone becomes the new column H.

4. Scroll down to view row 41, and notice the row has no meaningful data. With the ➡ pointer, click the **row 41** header to select the row. On the **Home tab**, in the **Cells group**, click the **Delete** button.

5. Scroll to the top of the workbook. Click in cell **A1**, and then type PR_ID Press Enter. On the **Data tab**, in the **Sort & Filter group**, click the **Sort A-Z** button ↑. Notice that the *PR_ID* values in rows 10 and 11 are duplicates, as shown in **Figure 2**.

The *PR_ID* column will be the primary key in the Access table.

6. With the **Data tab** displayed, in the **Data Tools group**, click **Remove Duplicates**.

■ **Continue to the next page to complete the skill**

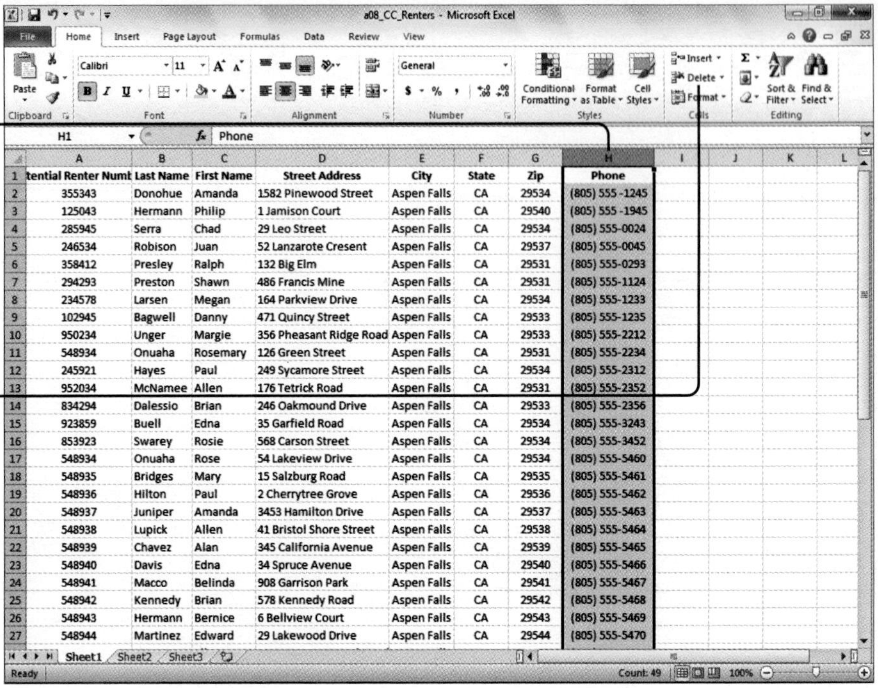

New column H →

Delete button →

Figure 1

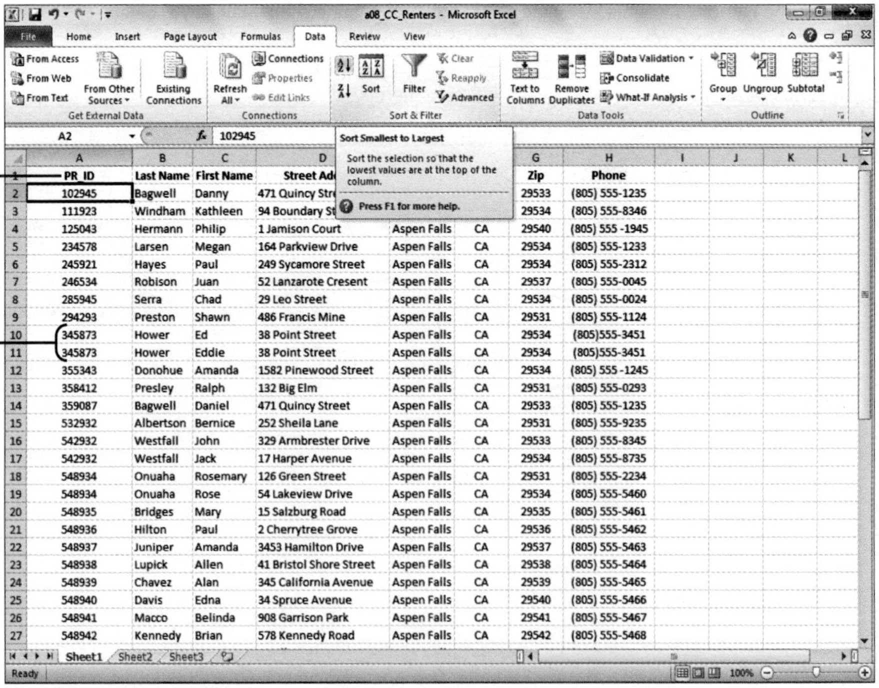

Column label changed →

Duplicate values →

Figure 2

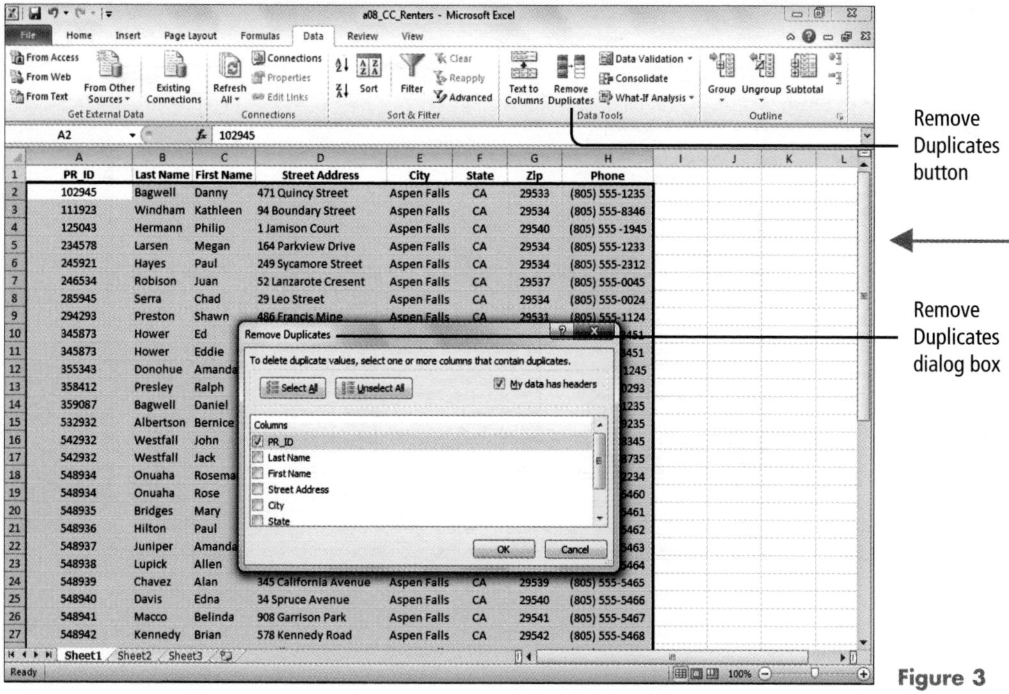

Remove
Duplicates
button

Remove
Duplicates
dialog box

Figure 3

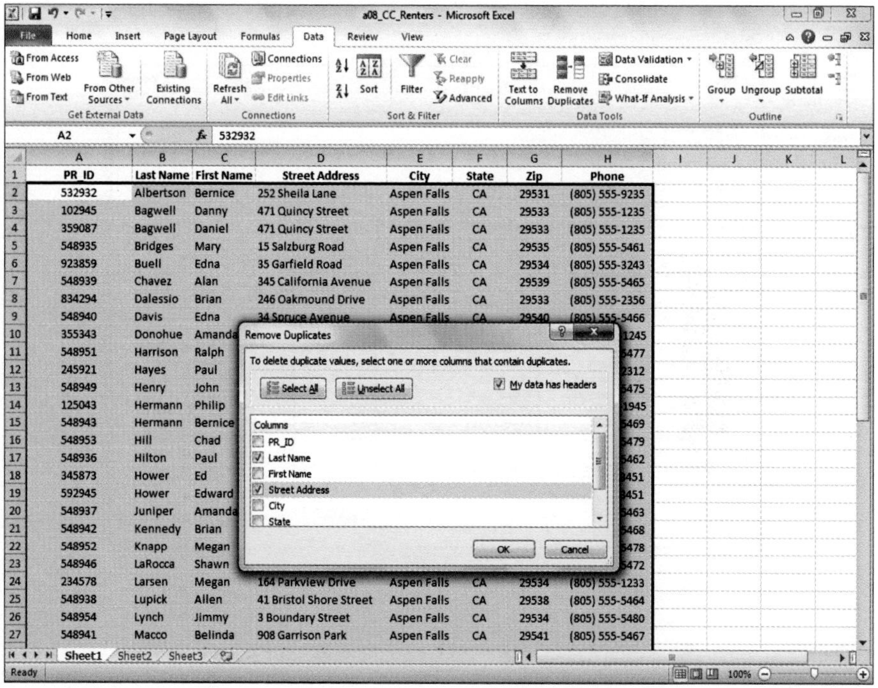

Figure 4

7. In the **Remove Duplicates** dialog box, verify the **My data has headers** check box is selected, and then click the **Unselect All** button. Select the **PR_ID** check box, as shown in **Figure 3**.

8. Click **OK**. Read the message that 4 duplicate values were removed, and then click **OK**.

9. Click anywhere in the **Last Name** column, and then in the **Sort & Filter group**, click the **Sort A-Z** button. In rows 3 and 4, notice that two records exist for *Daniel Bagwell*.

10. In the **Data Tools group**, click **Remove Duplicates**. Click the **Unselect All** button, and then select the **Last Name** and **Street Address** check boxes. Click **OK**, and then compare your screen with **Figure 4**.

11. In the displayed message, click **OK**. Save, and then **Close** Excel.

- **You have completed Skill 4 of 10**

► When an Excel spreadsheet organizes fields and records in columns and rows, the data can be imported to create a new Access table.

► Imported tables store the data in the Access file so the table can be joined to other tables and used to create forms, queries, and reports.

1. In Access, display the **External Data tab**, and then in the **Import & Link group**, click **Excel**.

2. In the **Get External Data – Excel Spreadsheet** dialog box, click **Browse**. Navigate to your **Access Chapter 8** student files and then double-click **a08_CC_Renters.xlsx.** Verify that the option to import the source data into a new table is selected, and then click **OK**.

3. In the displayed **Import Spreadsheet Wizard**, verify that the **Sheet1** data displays, as shown in **Figure 1**.

4. Click **Next**, and then select the **First Row Contains Column Headings** check box.

5. Click **Next** two times, and then select the **Choose my own primary key** option button. Compare your screen with **Figure 2**.

   PR_ID will be the primary key in the new table.

6. Click **Next**, and then in the **Import to Table** box, replace *Sheet1* with Potential Renters

7. Click **Finish**, and then **Close** the **Get External Data – Excel Spreadsheet** dialog box.

■ **Continue to the next page to complete the skill**

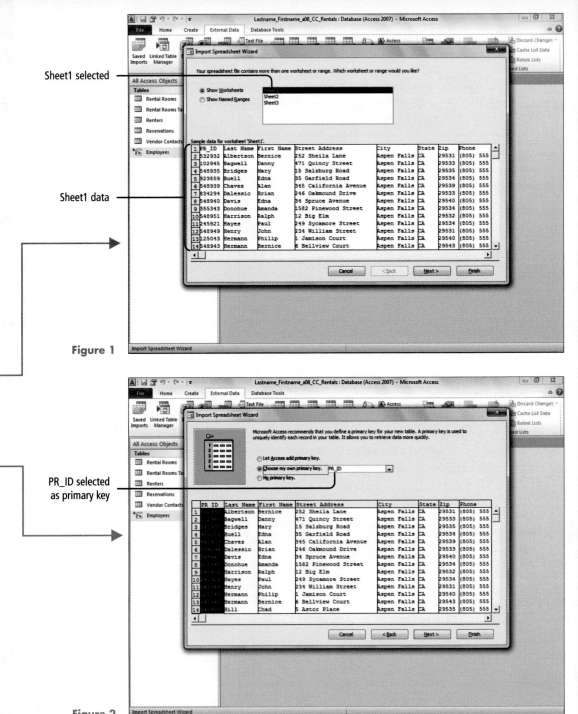

Sheet1 selected

Sheet1 data

Figure 1

PR_ID selected as primary key

Figure 2

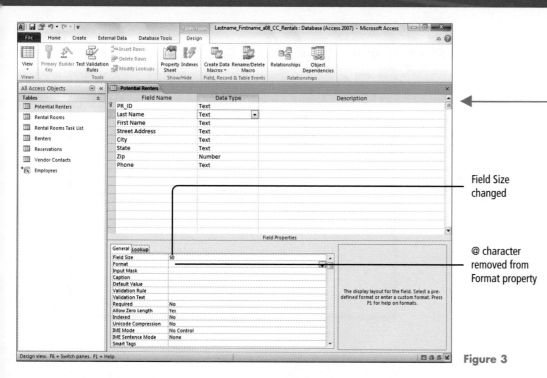

Field Size changed

@ character removed from Format property

Figure 3

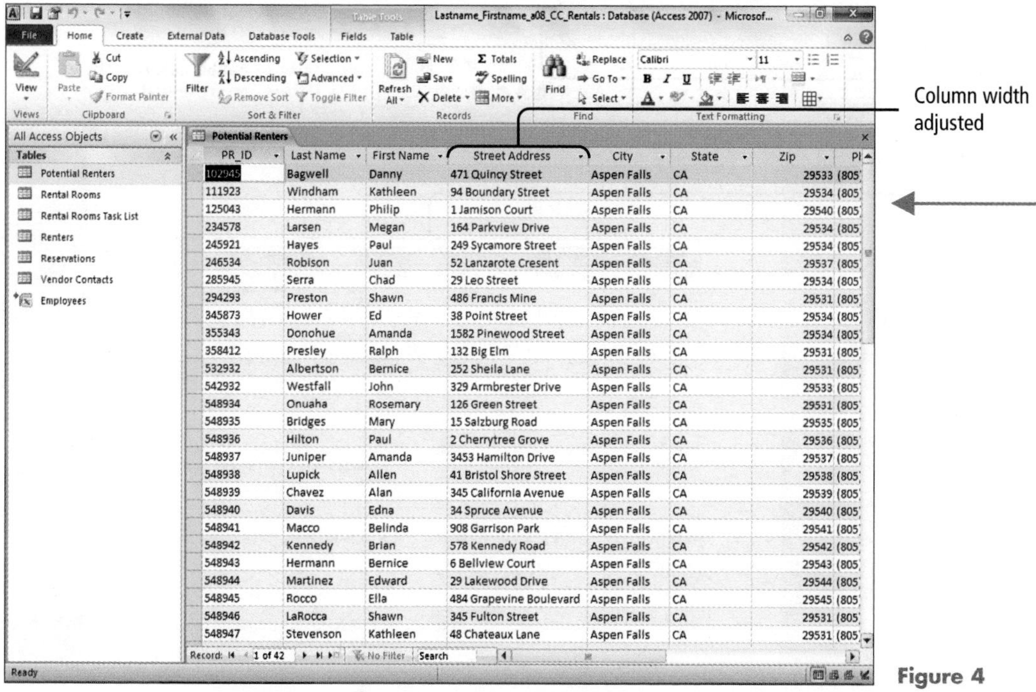

Column width adjusted

Figure 4

8. **Open** the **Potential Renters** table in Design view.

9. Click the **Data Type** box for **PR_ID**, click the displayed box arrow, and then click **Text**.

10. For **PR_ID**, change the **Field Size** property from *255* to *10*

11. Click the **Last Name** field, and then change the **Field Size** to *50* In the **Format** box, delete the @ character. Compare your screen with **Figure 3**.

   By default, text fields imported from Excel have a field size set to 255. The @ character in the Format box indicates that the formatting applied in the Excel worksheet may not have been imported into the Access table.

12. Repeat the technique just practiced to change the **Field Size** to *50* and to delete the @ character in the **Format** box for the following fields: **First Name**, **Street Address**, **City**, **State**, and **Phone**.

13. Click **Save** 🖫. Read the displayed message, and then click **Yes**.

14. Switch to Datasheet view. With the ➕ pointer, double-click to resize the **Street Address** column, and then compare your screen with **Figure 4**.

15. **Save** 🖫, and then **Close** ✖ the table.

■ **You have completed Skill 5 of 10**

▶ Access tables can be exported as Word documents, where they can be formatted as Word tables.

▶ Tables exported from Access to Word are typically saved in the ***Rich Text Format***—a file format designed to move text between different applications while preserving the text's formatting. Rich Text Format files are often referred to as ***RTF*** files.

1. In the **Navigation Pane**, click to select the **Rental Rooms** table. Display the **External Data tab**. In the **Export group**, click **More**, and then click **Word**.

2. In the **Export - RTF File** dialog box, click **Browse**, and then in the **File Save** dialog box, navigate to your **Access Chapter 8** folder. In the **File name** box, replace *Rental Rooms* with Lastname_Firstname_a08_CC_Rooms and then click **Save**.

3. In the **Export - RTF File** dialog box, under **Specify export options**, select the **Open the destination file after the export operation is complete** check box, as shown in **Figure 1**.

   The File name box indicates that the exported file will be saved in the Rich Text Format by displaying an *.rtf* file extension.

4. Click **OK**, and then compare your screen to **Figure 2**.

   On the title bar, *[Compatibility Mode]* indicates that the document is not saved in the Word 2010 file format.

■ **Continue to the next page to complete the skill**

.rtf file extension

Export option selected

Figure 1

Compatibility Mode

Rental Rooms table in Word

Figure 2

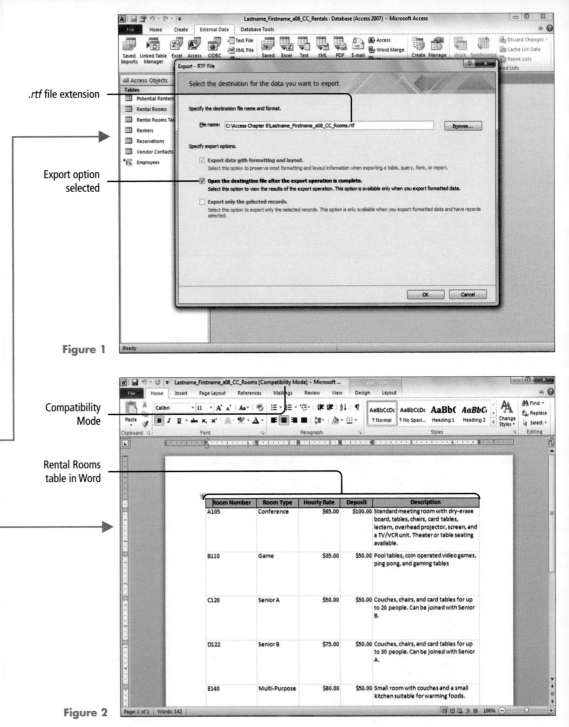

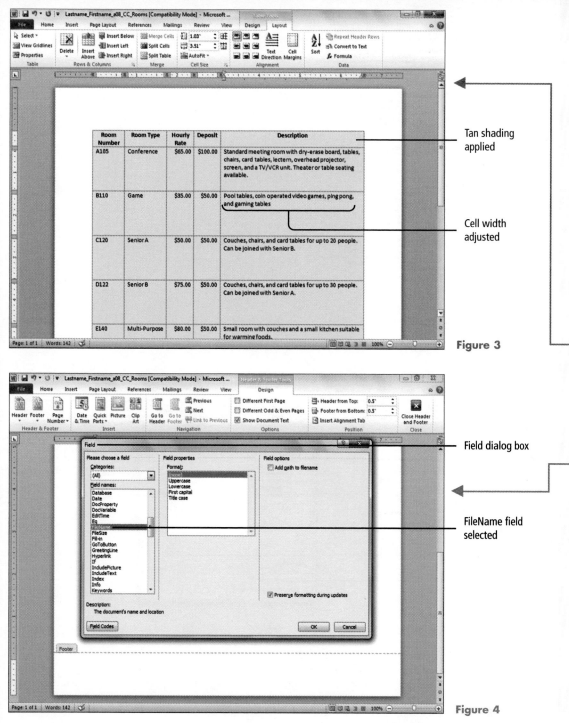

Tan shading applied

Cell width adjusted

Figure 3

Field dialog box

FileName field selected

Figure 4

5. Switch to Access, and then **Close** the **Export - RTF File** dialog box.

6. Switch to Word. Point to the table, and above the table's upper-left corner, click the **Table Selector** button ⊞ to select the entire table.

7. With the entire table selected, on the **Design tab**, in the **Table Styles group**, click the **More** button ▼, and then click the second table style in the second row under **Built-In—Light List - Accent 1**. In the **Table Styles group**, click the **Shading** button, and then click the third color— **Tan, Background 2**.

8. With the entire table still selected, on the **Layout tab**, in the **Cell Size group**, click the **AutoFit** button. In the displayed list, click **AutoFit Contents**. Click anywhere in the table so that it is no longer selected, and then compare with **Figure 3**.

9. On the **Insert tab**, in the **Header & Footer group**, click **Footer**. From the displayed list, click **Edit Footer**. On the **Design tab**, in the **Insert group**, click **Quick Parts**, and then click **Field**. Scroll down the displayed list of fields, and then click **FileName**, as shown in **Figure 4**.

10. In the **Field** dialog box, click **OK**.

11. On the **Design tab**, in the **Close group**, click the **Close Header and Footer** button.

12. Click **Save** 🖫. If you are printing your work for this project, print the Word document. **Close** 🗙 Word.

■ **You have completed Skill 6 of 10**

► *XML* is an acronym for *Extensible Markup Language*—a standard that uses text characters to define the meaning, structure, and appearance of data.

► Because XML stores data in text files, it is a common method for storing data for any database, application, or operating system.

1. From the **Start** menu, click **Computer**. In the displayed folder window, navigate to the student files for this chapter. Right-click **a08_CC_Expenses**. From the displayed shortcut menu, point to **Open with**, and then click **Notepad**. **Maximize** the Notepad window, and then compare with **Figure 1**.

   In an XML file, the text between the < and > characters is called a *tag*. Each data element consists of an opening tag, the data itself, and then a closing tag.

2. **Close** Notepad without saving changes.

3. In Access, with the **External Data tab** displayed, in the **Import & Link group**, click **XML File**.

4. In the **Get External Data - XML File** dialog box, click **Browse**. Navigate to the file **a08_CC_Expenses**. Select the file, and then click **Open**.

5. In the **Get External Data - XML File** dialog box, click **OK**.

6. In the **Import XML** dialog box, expand Expenses. Under **Import Options**, verify that the **Structure and Data** option button is selected, as shown in **Figure 2**.

■ **Continue to the next page to complete the skill**

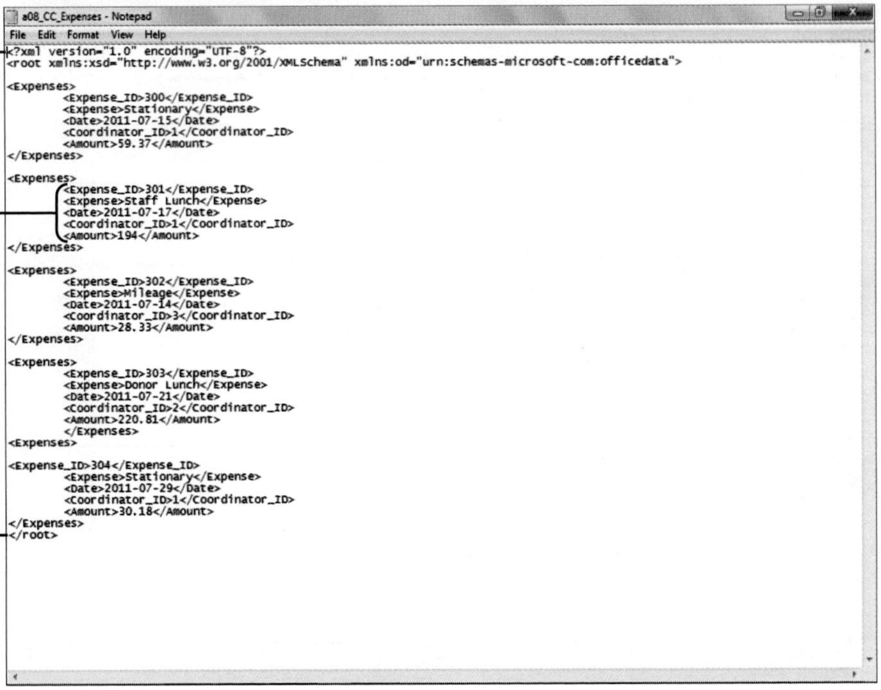

Opening tag

Data

Closing tag

Figure 1

Import XML dialog box

Table name

Field names

Structure and Data option button selected

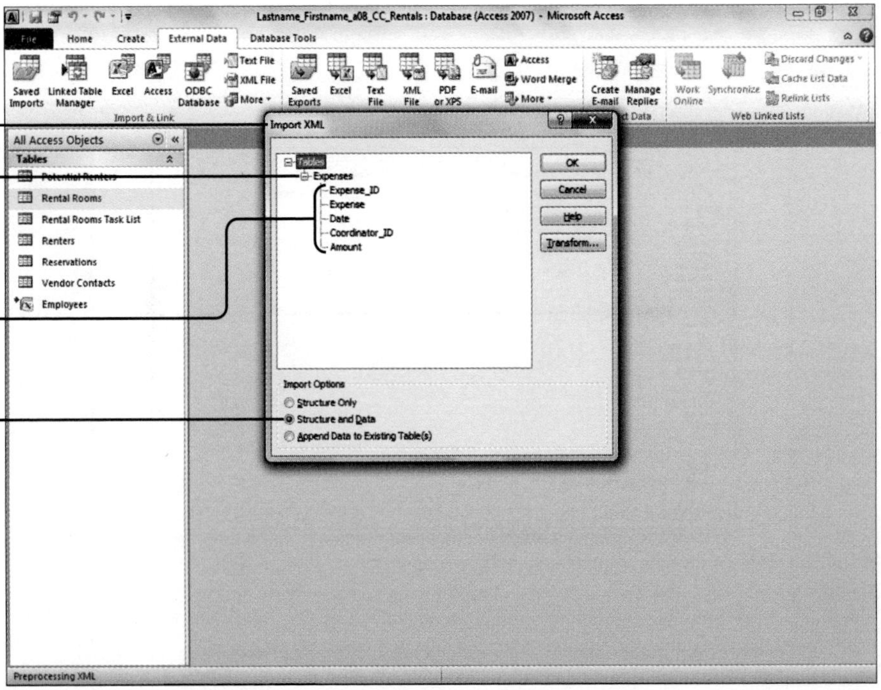

Figure 2

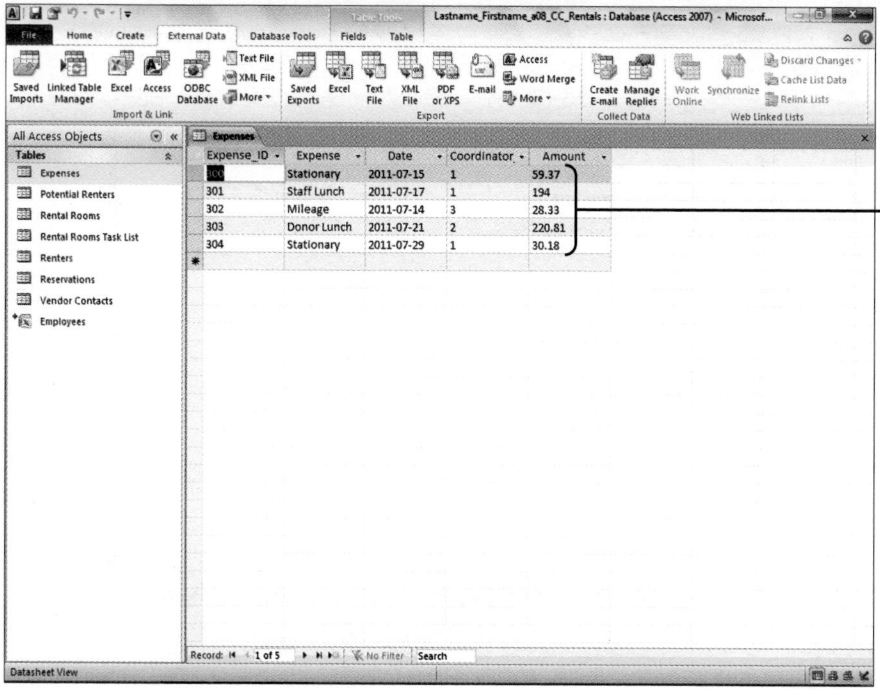

Imported XML data

Figure 3

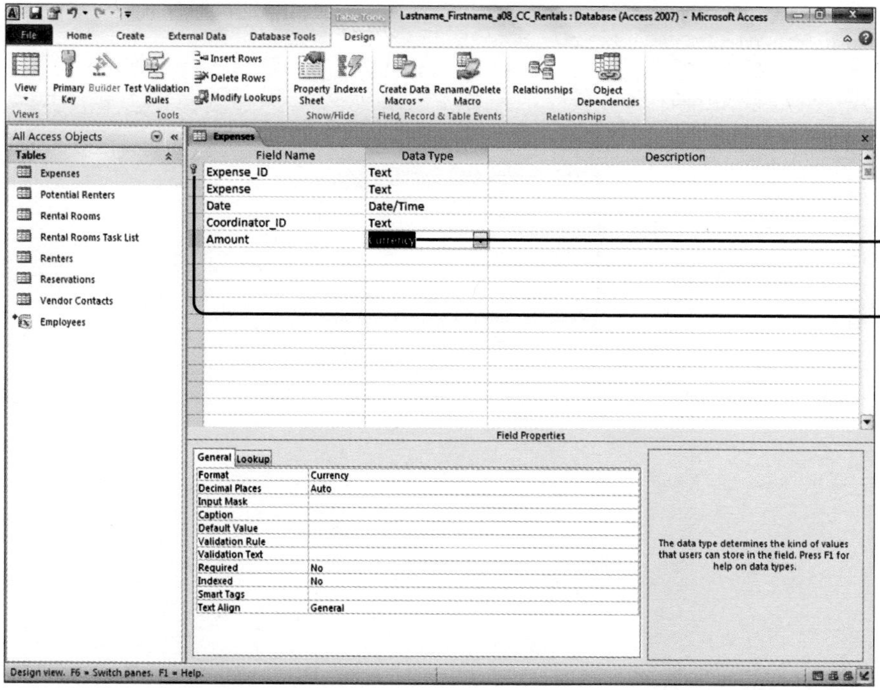

Currency data type

Primary key assigned

Figure 4

7. Click **OK**, and then in the **Get External Data - XML File** dialog box, click **Close**.

The XML tags define the name of the table—*Expenses*—and the name of each field that will be imported.

8. In the **Navigation Pane**, double-click the **Expenses** table, and then compare your screen with **Figure 3**.

9. Switch to Design view. With **Expense_ID** selected, on the **Design tab**, in the **Tools group**, click **Primary Key**.

10. In the **Date** row, click the **Data Type** box, click the displayed arrow, and then click **Date/Time**.

11. For the **Amount** field, change the data type to **Currency**. Compare your screen with **Figure 4**.

12. Click **Save**, read the displayed message, and then click **Yes**. Switch to Datasheet view. In the append row, enter the following data using your own name:

Expense ID	305
Expense	Lunch with Your Name
Date	7/30/2011
Coordinator	1
Amount	$50.00

13. Increase the width of the **Expense** column to display your entire name. If you are to print your work for this chapter, print the table.

14. **Save**, and then **Close** the table.

■ **You have completed Skill 7 of 10**

▶ Access tables can be exported as XML text files.

▶ When exporting an XML file, you can choose to export the data, the structure of the table itself, and/or the table's formatting.

1. In the **Navigation Pane**, click the **Renters** table to select it. On the **External Data tab**, in the **Export group**, click **XML File**.

2. In the **Export - XML File** dialog box, click **Browse**. In the **File Save** dialog box, navigate to your **Access Chapter 8** folder. In the **File name** box, replace *Renters* with Lastname_Firstname_a08_CC_Renters and then click **Save**. Compare your screen with **Figure 1**.

   XML text files are assigned the *.xml* file extension.

3. In the **Export - XML File** dialog box, click **OK**, and then compare your screen with **Figure 2**.

   The Export XML dialog box can export the data—*XML*—the table field properties—*XSD*—and/or the table formatting—*XSL*.

■ **Continue to the next page to complete the skill**

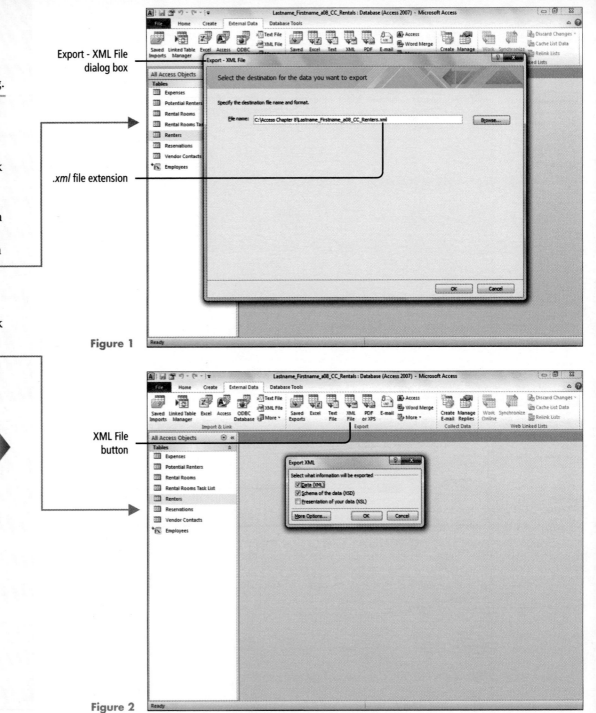

Export - XML File dialog box

.xml file extension

Figure 1

XML File button

Figure 2

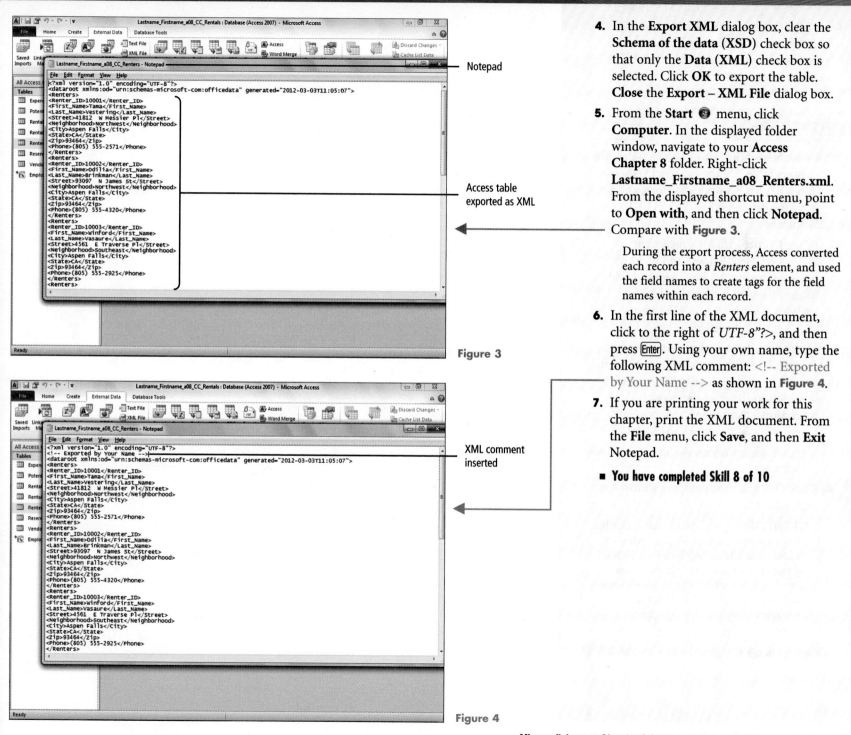

Notepad

Access table
exported as XML

Figure 3

XML comment
inserted

Figure 4

4. In the **Export XML** dialog box, clear the **Schema of the data (XSD)** check box so that only the **Data (XML)** check box is selected. Click **OK** to export the table. **Close** the **Export – XML File** dialog box.

5. From the **Start** 💿 menu, click **Computer**. In the displayed folder window, navigate to your **Access Chapter 8** folder. Right-click **Lastname_Firstname_a08_Renters.xml**. From the displayed shortcut menu, point to **Open with**, and then click **Notepad**. Compare with **Figure 3**.

   During the export process, Access converted each record into a *Renters* element, and used the field names to create tags for the field names within each record.

6. In the first line of the XML document, click to the right of *UTF-8"?>*, and then press [Enter]. Using your own name, type the following XML comment: <!-- Exported by Your Name --> as shown in **Figure 4**.

7. If you are printing your work for this chapter, print the XML document. From the **File** menu, click **Save**, and then **Exit** Notepad.

- **You have completed Skill 8 of 10**

► *HTML (Hypertext Markup Language)* is a language used to create web pages. An *HTML document* is a text file with HTML tags that instruct web browsers how to display the document as a web page.

► Access tables can be exported to a new HTML document.

1. In the **Navigation Pane**, click to select the **Renters** table. On the **External Data tab**, in the **Export group**, click **More**, and then from the displayed list, click **HTML Document**.

2. In the **Export - HTML Document** dialog box, click **Browse** and then navigate to your **Access Chapter 8** folder. In the **File Save** dialog box, type Lastname_Firstname_a08_Renters_HTML and then click **Save**.

3. Under **Specify export options**, select the **Export data with formatting and layout** check box, and then select **Open the destination file after the export operation is complete** check box. Compare your screen with **Figure 1**.

    HTML documents use the *.htm* or *.html* file extension.

4. Click **OK**, and then compare your screen with **Figure 2**.

    The HTML Output Options dialog box has options for formatting the page using an HTML template and options for which set of text characters the HTML document should use. For pages written in languages such as Russian, the special characters available in Unicode may be required.

■ **Continue to the next page to complete the skill**

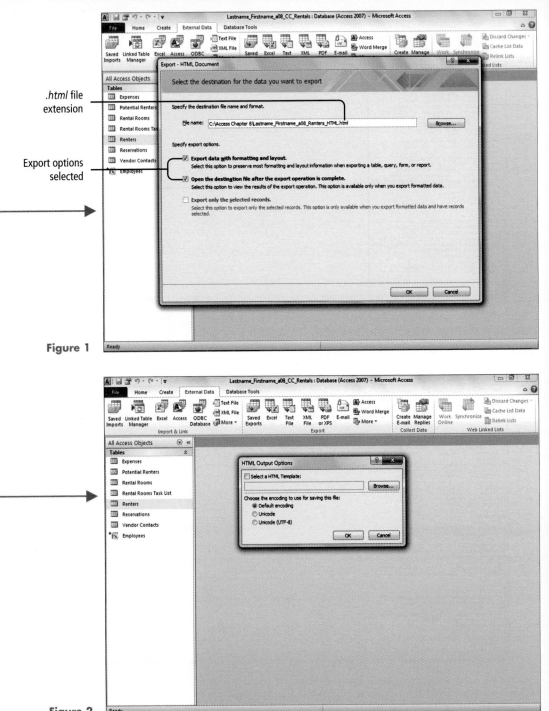

.html file extension

Export options selected

Figure 1

Figure 2

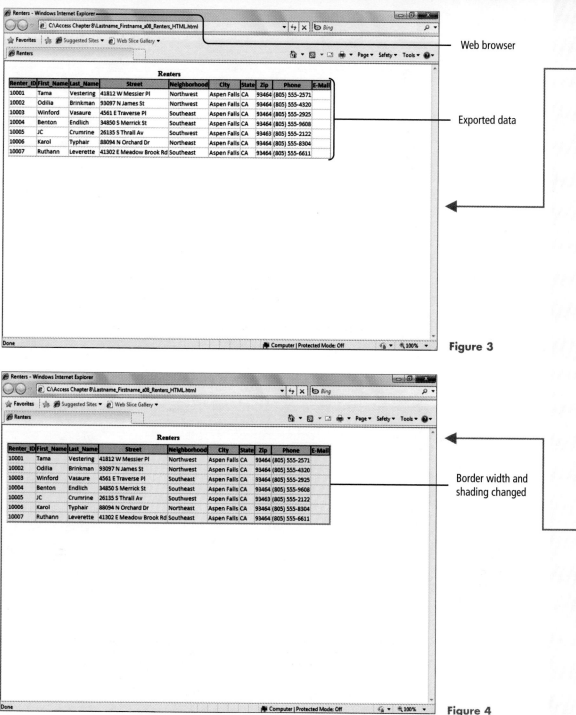

Web browser

Exported data

Figure 3

Border width and shading changed

Figure 4

5. In the **HTML Output Options** dialog box, click **OK**. Wait a few moments for your web browser to display the table, as shown in **Figure 3**.

6. Click **Start** 🔵, and then point to **All Programs**. In the list of programs, scroll as needed, click the **Accessories** folder, and then click **Notepad**. In Notepad, from the **File Menu**, click **Open**. In the **Open** dialog box, click the arrow to the right of **Text Documents (*.txt)**, and then click **All Files**. Navigate to **Lastname_Firstname_a08_Renters_HTML** and then double-click to open the file in Notepad.

7. On the seventh line of text, in the *Table* tag, change *BORDER=1* to BORDER=3 and then change *BGCOLOR=#ffffff* to BGCOLOR=#ffff99

   In HTML, the value assigned to the BORDER attribute determines the width of the border, and the value assigned to BGCOLOR determines the background color. In this manner, HTML sends instruction to the browser.

8. From the **File Menu**, click **Save** 💾, and then **Exit** ❌ Notepad.

9. Switch to your web browser, and then to the right of the address bar, click the **Refresh** button 🔄. Compare your screen with **Figure 4**.

   The table border is wider and the table has a background color of light yellow.

10. **Close** ❌ your web browser.

11. In Access, **Close** the **Export – HTML Document** dialog box.

■ **You have completed Skill 9 of 10**

▶ Data in Access can be linked to a *mail merge document*—a Word document that combines a main document, such as a letter, a sheet of labels, or an envelope, with a data source.

▶ The data source is typically used to insert individual names and addresses into the main document.

1. In the **Navigation Pane**, click to select the **Employees** table. On the **External Data tab**, in the **Export group**, click **Word Merge**.

2. In the displayed **Microsoft Word Mail Merge Wizard**, verify that the **Link your data to an existing Microsoft Word document** option button is selected, and then click **OK**.

3. In the **Select Microsoft Word Document** dialog box, navigate to your student files, and then double-click **a08_CC_Letter**.

4. If necessary, on the taskbar, click the **Word** button to display the letter. **Maximize** the Word window, and then compare your screen with **Figure 1**.

   In Word, the Mail Merge task pane displays at the right. The first two steps of the mail merge have been completed: a mail merge document was created and the Employees table has been selected as the data source.

5. In the **Mail Merge** task pane, under **Step 3 of 6**, click **Next: Write your letter**.

6. Click two lines below the date, and then compare your screen with **Figure 2**.

■ **Continue to the next page to complete the skill**

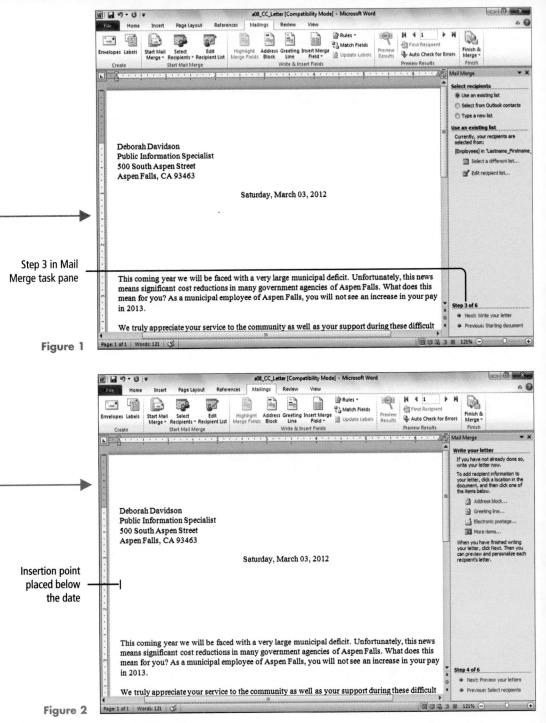

Step 3 in Mail Merge task pane

Figure 1

Insertion point placed below the date

Figure 2

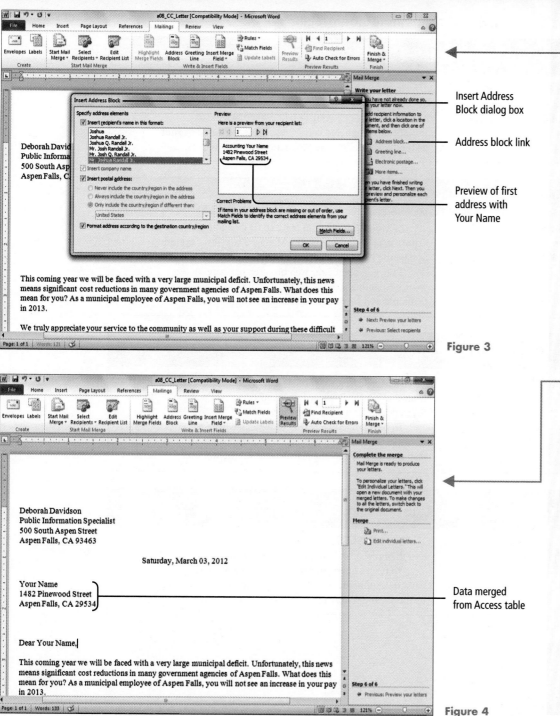

Insert Address
Block dialog box

Address block link

Preview of first
address with
Your Name

Figure 3

Data merged
from Access table

Figure 4

7. In the **Mail Merge** task pane, under **Write your letter**, click **Address block**, and then compare your screen with **Figure 3**.

   The Insert Address Block dialog box inserts data from the data source and displays a preview of the data as it will appear when merged.

8. Under **Specify address elements**, click **Joshua Randall Jr.**—the second format in the list—and then click **OK**.

   Notice that «*Address Block*» displays where the address data will be merged.

9. Click in the empty paragraph below «*Address Block*», and then in the **Mail Merge** task pane, click **Greeting line**. Under **Greeting line format**, click the second box arrow, from the displayed list, click **Joshua Randall Jr.**, and then click **OK**.

10. In the **Mail Merge** task pane, click **Next: Preview your letters**, and then click **Next: Complete the merge**. Compare with **Figure 4**.

11. On the **Mailings tab**, in the **Preview Results group**, click the **Next Record** button ▶. Verify the name *Alan Robison* displays.

12. In the **Preview Results group**, click the **Previous Record** button ◀. Verify that your name displays in the letter, and then, in the **Mail Merge** task pane, under **Merge**, click **Print**. In the **Merge to Printer** dialog box, select the **Current record** option button. If you are printing this project, click **OK** and then click **Print**. Otherwise, click **Cancel**.

13. **Save** the letter as Lastname_Firstname_a08_CC_Letter and then **Exit** Word. **Exit** Access.

Done! You have completed Skill 10 of 10 and your document is complete!

More Skills

The following More Skills are located at **www.pearsonhighered.com/skills**

More Skills ⑪ Save Tables as PDF Documents

Access tables can be saved in the Portable Document Format—*PDF*—so that they can be viewed by any program that can open this type of file—for example, Adobe Reader and web browsers.

In More Skills 11, you will save a report as a PDF document.

To begin, open your web browser, navigate to www.pearsonhighered.com/skills, locate the name of your textbook, and follow the instructions on the website.

More Skills ⑫ Save Export Steps

You can save the steps taken to import or export data as import or export steps. When data needs to be exported or imported frequently, the saved steps can be run from the Manage Data Tasks dialog box.

In More Skills 12, you will export data to Excel, save the export steps, and then use the Manage Data Tasks option to update the Excel file.

To begin, open your web browser, navigate to www.pearsonhighered.com/skills, locate the name of your textbook, and follow the instructions on the website.

More Skills ⑬ Import Objects from External Databases

Objects from an Access database can be imported into another Access database. These importable objects include tables, queries, and reports.

In More Skills 13, you will import a table, query, and report from one Access database into another Access database. You will then add a relationship to the new table.

To begin, open your web browser, navigate to www.pearsonhighered.com/skills, locate the name of your textbook, and follow the instructions on the website.

More Skills ⑭ Update a Database through E-Mail

Data can be collected by sending e-mail messages with a form to collect the desired data. Each recipient fills out the form when he/she replies to the message, and the data is automatically updated in the Access table.

In More Skills 14, you will create and send an e-mail request, and then reply to the request as a recipient.

To begin, open your web browser, navigate to www.pearsonhighered.com/skills, locate the name of your textbook, and follow the instructions on the website.

Key Terms

Online Help Skills

1. **Start** Access. In the upper-right corner of the Access window, click the **Help** button . In the **Help** window, click the **Maximize** button.

2. Click in the search box, type import and then click the **Search** button . In the search results, click **Import or link to data in an Excel workbook**.

3. Click **Troubleshoot missing or incorrect values**. Compare your screen with **Figure 1**.

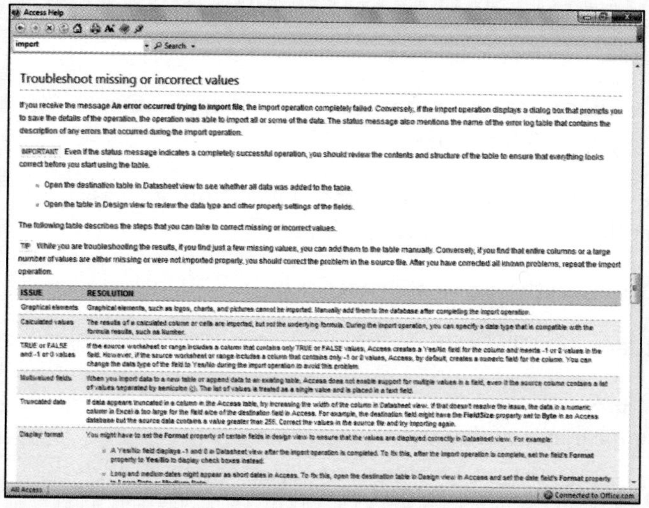

Figure 1

4. Read the section to see if you can answer the following questions: When importing data from Excel, how are calculated fields handled? What is a "key violation error"?

Matching

Match each term in the second column with its correct definition in the first column by writing the letter of the term on the blank line in front of the correct definition.

_____ **1.** A character used to separate fields in a delimited text file.

_____ **2.** A text file in which the data in each column is separated by an identifying character, such as a comma, a space, or a tab.

_____ **3.** A file that stores only the text characters but not the formatting, tab stops, or tables.

_____ **4.** A file format designed to move text between different applications while preserving the text's formatting.

_____ **5.** An Access table type that uses data in another application, such as Excel, but stores that data in the other application.

_____ **6.** This is the text between the < and > characters in an XML file.

_____ **7.** A simple text editor provided with the Windows operating system.

_____ **8.** A standard that uses text characters to define the meaning, structure, and appearance of data.

_____ **9.** A text file with HTML tags that instruct web browsers how to display the document as a web page.

_____ **10.** A process that combines a main document with a data source to create letters, labels, or envelopes.

A Delimited text file

B Delimiter

C HTML document

D Linked

E Mail merge

F Notepad

G Rich Text Format

H Tag

I Text file

J XML

Multiple Choice

Choose the correct answer.

1. A file that stores only the text characters but not the formatting, tab stops, or tables.
   A. Delimited text file
   B. Text file
   C. HTML document

2. A file where data in each column is separated by a character.
   A. Delimited text file
   B. HTML document
   C. XML file

3. This is used to separate fields in a text file and allows the data to be accurately imported to the correct columns in Access.
   A. Image
   B. Number
   C. Delimiter

4. An object that is linked in Access to an object in Excel.
   A. Linked query
   B. Linked table
   C. Linked macro

5. RTF is the acronym for this type of file.
   A. Relative Textural Format
   B. Rich Text File
   C. Rich Text Format

6. This language is a standard that not only details the layout and structure of data but also the meaning of data.
   A. JavaScript
   B. XML
   C. HTML

7. This Windows application enables you to edit both XML and HTML documents.
   A. Notepad
   B. Access
   C. Outlook

8. In XML, the text between "<" and ">" is called this.
   A. Field
   B. Delimiter
   C. Tag

9. Every website is created with this language.
   A. HTML
   B. XML
   C. Java

10. A Word document with links to an external source.
    A. Mail merge
    B. Mail link
    C. Access merge

Topics for Discussion

1. What is the purpose of importing an XML document into Access?

2. How should a text file be formatted before exporting the data to Access?

Skill Check

To complete this database, you will need the following files:

- a08_Car_Attendees
- a08_Car_Awards
- a08_Car_Guests
- a08_Car_Letter
- a08_Car_Show
- a08_Car_Sponsors

You will save your files as:

- Lastname_Firstname_a08_Car_Show
- Lastname_Firstname_a08_Car_Attendees
- Lastname_Firstname_a08_Cars
- Lastname_Firstname_a08_Car_Table
- Lastname_Firstname_a08_Car_Letter

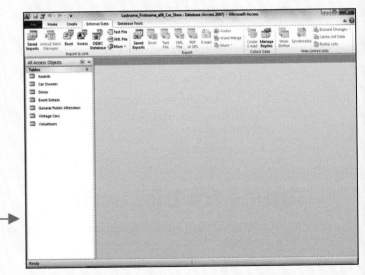

Figure 1

1. **Start** Access. Open **a08_Car_Show**, and save the database in your **Access Chapter 8** folder as Lastname_Firstname_a08_Car_Show Enable the content.

2. On the **External Data tab**, in the **Import & Link group**, click **Text File**. **Browse** to your student data files, and then open **a08_Car_Awards**. In the **Get External Data - Text File** dialog box, click **OK**.

3. In the **Import Text Wizard**, click **Next**, select the **First Row Contains Field Names** check box, and then click **Next** two times. Assign **Award ID** as primary key, and then click **Next**. Name the new table Awards Click **Finish**. Click **Close**.

4. **Start** Excel. Open **a08_Car_Attendees** and save as Lastname_Firstname_a08_Car_Attendees In cell **A1**, change *ID* to GP ID In cells **B2** and **C2**, change the two names to your own first and last names.

5. On the **Data tab**, in the **Data Tools group**, click **Remove Duplicates**. Select only the **GP ID** field, and then click **OK** to delete two duplicate records. Repeat this technique, but select only the **Last Name** and **Street Address** fields to delete two more duplicate records. Compare with **Figure 1**. Click **Save**. **Close** Excel.

6. On the **External Data tab**, in the **Import & Link group**, click **Excel**. **Browse** to your **Access Chapter 8** folder, and then open **Lastname_Firstname_a08_Car_Attendees**. Click **OK**.

7. In the **Import Spreadsheet Wizard**, click **Next**, select the **First Row Contains Column Headings** check box, and then click **Next** two times. Assign **GP ID** as the primary key, and then click **Next**. Name the table General Public Attendees Click **Finish**. Click **Close**. Compare with **Figure 2**.

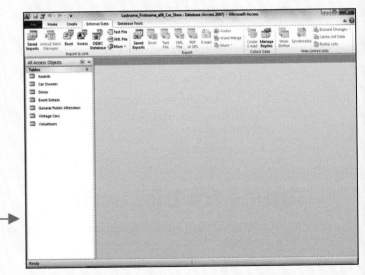

Figure 2

8. Open **General Public Attendees** in Design view, and then for the seven fields with the **Text** data type, change the **Field Size** to 50 and delete the @ character from each **Format** property. Click **Save**, click **Yes**, and then **Close** the table.

 Continue to the next page to complete this Skill Check

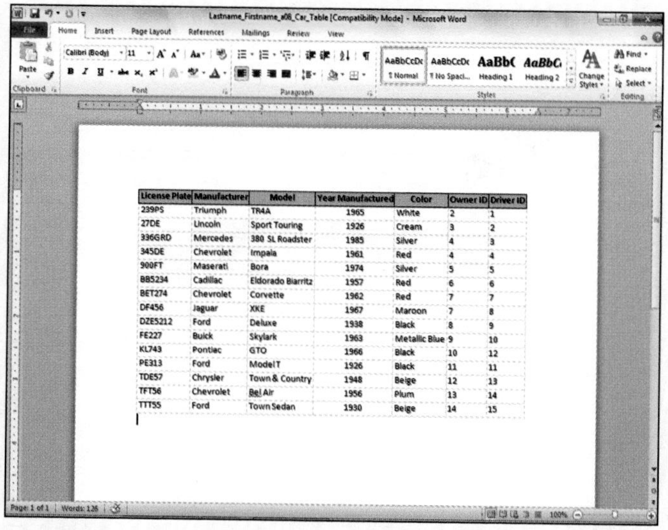

License Plate	Manufacturer	Model	Year Manufactured	Color	Owner ID	Driver ID
239PS	Triumph	TR4A	1965	White	2	1
27DE	Lincoln	Sport Touring	1926	Cream	3	2
336GRD	Mercedes	380 SL Roadster	1985	Silver	4	3
345DE	Chevrolet	Impala	1961	Red	4	4
900FT	Maserati	Bora	1974	Silver	5	5
BB5234	Cadillac	Eldorado Biarritz	1957	Red	6	6
BET274	Chevrolet	Corvette	1962	Red	7	7
DF456	Jaguar	XKE	1967	Maroon	7	8
DZE5212	Ford	Deluxe	1938	Black	8	9
FE227	Buick	Skylark	1963	Metallic Blue	9	10
KL743	Pontiac	GTO	1966	Black	10	12
PE313	Ford	Model T	1926	Black	11	11
TDE57	Chrysler	Town & Country	1948	Beige	12	13
TFT56	Chevrolet	Bel Air	1956	Plum	13	14
TTT55	Ford	Town Sedan	1930	Beige	14	15

Figure 3

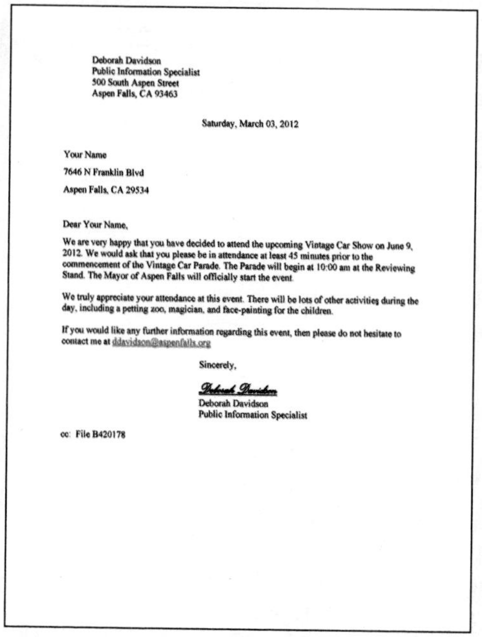

Deborah Davidson
Public Information Specialist
500 South Aspen Street
Aspen Falls, CA 93463

Saturday, March 03, 2012

Your Name

7646 N Franklin Blvd

Aspen Falls, CA 29534

Dear Your Name,

We are very happy that you have decided to attend the upcoming Vintage Car Show on June 9, 2012. We would ask that you please be in attendance at least 45 minutes prior to the commencement of the Vintage Car Parade. The Parade will begin at 10:00 am at the Reviewing Stand. The Mayor of Aspen Falls will officially start the event.

We truly appreciate your attendance at this event. There will be lots of other activities during the day, including a petting zoo, magician, and face-painting for the children.

If you would like any further information regarding this event, then please do not hesitate to contact me at ddavidson@aspenfalls.org

Sincerely,

Deborah Davidson
Public Information Specialist

cc: File B420178

Figure 4

9. In the **Import & Link group**, click **Excel**. In your student data files, open **a08_Car_Guests**. Select the **Link to the data source by creating a linked table** option button. Click **OK**.

10. In the **Link Spreadsheet Wizard**, click **Next**, select the **First Row Contains Column Headings** check box, and then click **Next**. In the **Linked Table Name** box, name the table Invited Guests Click **Finish**, and then click **OK**.

11. On the **External Data tab**, in the **Import & Link group**, click **XML File. Browse** to and then double-click **a08_Car_Sponsors**. Click **OK** two times. Click **Close**.

12. With **Vintage Cars** selected, in the **Export group**, click **Excel. Browse** to your **Access Chapter 8** folder, name the file Lastname_Firstname_a08_Cars Click **OK**. Click **Close**.

13. With **Vintage Cars** selected, in the **Export group**, click **More**, and then click **Word. Browse** to your **Access Chapter 8** folder, name the file Lastname_Firstname_a08_Car_Table and then click **Save**. Select the option to open the destination file, and then click **OK**. Click **Close**.

14. In Word, on the **Layout tab**, apply the **AutoFit Contents** command. Click the **Insert tab**, select the table, click the **Footer** button, and then click **Edit Footer**. In the **Insert group**, click the **Quick Parts** button, and then click **Field**. Under **Field** names, click **FileName**, and then click **OK**. Click the **Close Header and Footer** button, and then compare with **Figure 3**. **Print** the Word document. **Save**, and then **Close** Word.

15. Open the **General Public Attendees** table. On the **External Data tab**, in the **Export group**, click **Word Merge**. In the wizard, click **OK**. In the **Select Microsoft Word Document** dialog box, navigate to and open **a08_Car_Letter**.

16. In Word, in the **Mail Merge** pane, move to **Step 4 of 6**. Click the second blank line below the date, click **Address block**, and then click **OK**. Click in the second blank line below the address block, insert the **Greeting Line**, and then click **OK**.

17. Move to **Step 5 of 6**, and verify that your name displays in the letter, as shown in **Figure 4**. Move to **Step 6 of 6**, and then in the **Mail Merge** task pane, click **Print**. In the **Merge to Printer** dialog box, select the **Current record** option button. If you are printing your work, click **OK**, and then click **Print**. Otherwise, click **Cancel**. Compare your printout to **Figure 4**.

18. **Save As** Lastname_Firstname_a08_Car_Letter, **Exit** Word, Excel, and Access.

Done! You have completed the Skill Check

Assess Your Skills 1

To complete this database, you will need the following files:

- a08_Harvest_Days
- a08_Harvest_Expenses

You will save your files as:

- Lastname_Firstname_a08_Harvest_Days
- Lastname_Firstname_a08_Harvest_Expenses
- Lastname_Firstname_a08_Harvest_Events
- Lastname_Firstname_a08_Harvest_Coordinator
- Lastname_Firstname_a08_Harvest_Table

1. **Start** Access and open the student data file **a08_Harvest_Days**. **Save** the database in your **Access Chapter 8** folder with the name Lastname_Firstname_a08_Harvest_Days

2. Import the comma-delimited text file **a08_Harvest_Expenses**. Use the first row for field names, assign **Expense ID** as the primary key, and name the table Expenses

3. Export the **Expenses** table as an XML file in your **Access Chapter 8** folder with the name Lastname_Firstname_a08_Harvest_Expenses Do not export the data schema—XSD file.

4. **Start** Notepad, and then open **Lastname_Firstname_a08_Harvest_Expenses**. Using your own name, type the following XML comment: <!-- Exported by Your Name --> If your instructor asks you to print your work, print the document. **Save** the file, and then **Exit** Notepad.

5. Export the **Events** table as an HTML document. Save the HTML file in your **Access Chapter 8** folder as Lastname_Firstname_a08_Harvest_Events Export the data with formatting and layout.

6. **Start** Notepad, and then open **Lastname_Firstname_a08_Harvest_Events**.

7. Scroll to the bottom of the document, and then click after *</TABLE>*. Press Enter, and then using your name, type <p>Prepared by Your Name</p> **Save** and **Exit** Notepad. Open **Lastname_Firstname_a08_Harvest_Events** in your web browser. If your instructor asks you to print your work, print the web page.

8. In the **Navigation Pane**, double-click the **Coordinator** table. Add a new record with a **Coordinator ID** of 4 and type the **Coordinator Name** using your name. Export the **Coordinator** table as an Excel file with the name Lastname_Firstname_a08_Harvest_Coordinator Open the spreadsheet in Excel. If your instructor asks you to print your work, print the document. **Exit** Excel.

9. Export the **Coordinator** table into a Word file named Lastname_Firstname_a08_Harvest_Table Format the table with **Blue, Accent 1, Lighter 60%** shading.

10. Compare your project with **Figure 1**. **Exit** Access. **Exit** Word, and then submit as directed.

Done! You have completed Assess Your Skills 1

Coordinator ID	Coordinator Name	Employer	Telephone
1	Marion Davis	Aspen Falls City Hall	(805) 555-6278
2	Tony Besso	Aspen Falls City Hall	(805) 555-3490
3	Philip Cooke	Aspen Falls City Hall	(805) 555-8031
4	Your Name		

Figure 1

Assess Your Skills 2

To complete this database, you will need the following files:

- a08_Police_Dept
- a08_Police_Awards
- a08_Police_Salaries
- a08_Police_Letter
- a08_Police_Apps

You will save your files as:

- Lastname_Firstname_a08_Police_Dept
- Lastname_Firstname_a08_Police_Letter
- Lastname_Firstname_a08_Police_Apps
- Lastname_Firstname_a08_Police_Employees

1. **Start** Access and open the student data file **a08_Police_Dept. Save** the database in your **Access Chapter 8** folder with the name Lastname_Firstname_a08_Police_Dept
2. Link the data in the Excel file **a08_Police_Awards** to create a linked table in Access. Use the first row for column headings and name the table Police Awards
3. Import the Structure and Data of the XML file **a08_Police_Salaries** to create a table named *Employee Salaries.*
4. In the **Employees** table, change the first record—*Felicia Perkins*—to your own first and last name.
5. Merge the **Employees** table with **a08_Police_Letter** as a Word Merge document. In the fourth empty line below the date, insert an **Address block** with the **Joshua Randall Jr.** format.
6. In the second blank paragraph above the letter body, insert a **Greeting line** with the **Joshua Randall Jr.** format. Complete the merge process. If you are printing this project, print the first record in the document. Save the letter in your **Access Chapter 8** folder with the name Lastname_Firstname_a08_Police_Letter and then **Exit** Word.
7. **Start** Excel, and then open the file **a08_Police_Apps. Save** the file in your **Access Chapter 8** folder with the name Lastname_Firstname_a08_Police_Apps
8. Change cell **A1** to App_ID Use the **Remove Duplicates** tool to remove duplicate records for the *App_ID* and *Last Name* columns. There should be *51* unique records remaining after this process. Change the record with the **App_ID** of *5049* to your own name. **Save**, and then **Exit** Excel.
9. In Access, import the data from the Excel file **Lastname_Firstname_a08_Police_Apps**. Use the first row for column headings, assign **App_ID** as the primary key, and then name the table Applicants
10. Export the formatting, and layout of the **Employees** table as an **HTML Document** with the name Lastname_Firstname_a08_Police_Employees If you are printing this project, open the HTML document in a web browser and print. Compare your printout with **Figure 1**.
11. **Exit** all open applications.

Done! You have completed Assess Your Skills 2

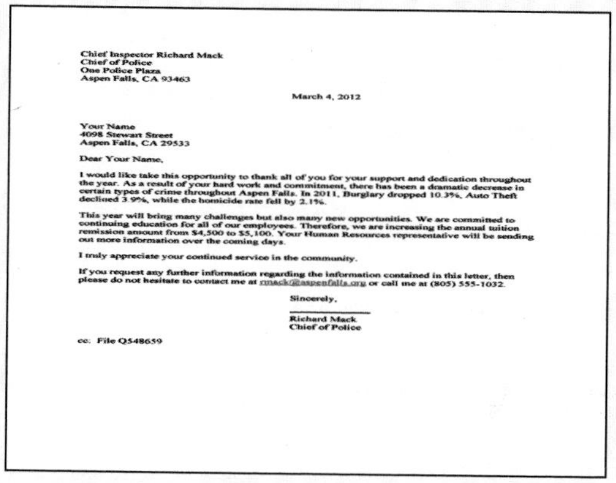

Chief Inspector Richard Mack
Chief of Police
One Police Plaza
Aspen Falls, CA 93463

March 4, 2012

Your Name
4098 Stewart Street
Aspen Falls, CA 29533

Dear Your Name,

I would like take this opportunity to thank all of you for your support and dedication throughout the year. As a result of your hard work and commitment, there has been a dramatic decrease in certain types of crime throughout Aspen Falls. In 2011, Burglary dropped 10.3%, Auto Theft declined 3.9%, while the homicide rate fell by 2.1%.

This year will bring many challenges but also many new opportunities. We are committed to continuing education for all of our employees. Therefore, we are increasing the annual tuition remission amount from $4,500 to $5,100. Your Human Resources representative will be sending out more information over the coming days.

I truly appreciate your continued service in the community.

If you request any further information regarding the information contained in this letter, then please do not hesitate to contact me at rmack@aspenfalls.org or call me at (805) 555-1032.

Sincerely,

Richard Mack
Chief of Police

cc: File Q548659

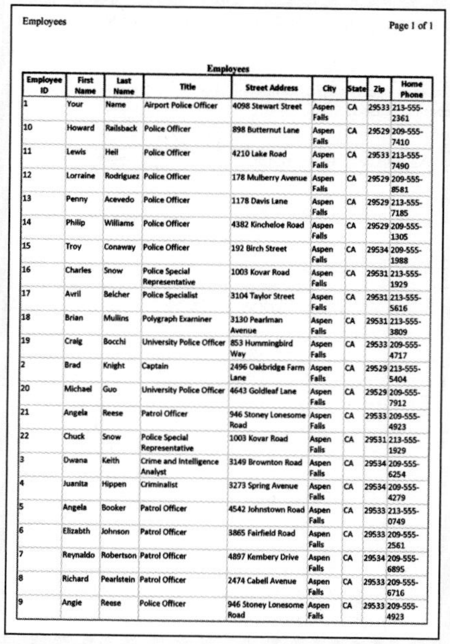

Employees   Page 1 of 1

Employees

Employee ID	First Name	Last Name	Title	Street Address	City	State	Zip	Home Phone
1	Your	Name	Airport Police Officer	4098 Stewart Street	Aspen Falls	CA	29533	213-555-2361
10	Howard	Railsback	Police Officer	898 Butternut Lane	Aspen Falls	CA	29529	209-555-7410
11	Lewis	Heil	Police Officer	4210 Lake Road	Aspen Falls	CA	29533	213-555-7490
12	Lorraine	Rodriguez	Police Officer	178 Mulberry Avenue	Aspen Falls	CA	29529	209-555-8581
13	Penny	Acevedo	Police Officer	1178 Davis Lane	Aspen Falls	CA	29529	213-555-7185
14	Philip	Williams	Police Officer	4382 Kincheloe Road	Aspen Falls	CA	29529	209-555-1305
15	Troy	Conaway	Police Officer	192 Birch Street	Aspen Falls	CA	29534	209-555-1988
16	Charles	Snow	Police Special Representative	1003 Kovar Road	Aspen Falls	CA	29531	213-555-1929
17	Avril	Belcher	Police Specialist	3104 Taylor Street	Aspen Falls	CA	29531	213-555-5616
18	Brian	Mullins	Polygraph Examiner	3130 Pearlman Avenue	Aspen Falls	CA	29531	213-555-3809
19	Craig	Bocchi	University Police Officer	853 Hummingbird Way	Aspen Falls	CA	29533	209-555-4717
2	Brad	Knight	Captain	2496 Oakbridge Farm Lane	Aspen Falls	CA	29529	213-555-5404
20	Michael	Guo	University Police Officer	4643 Goldleaf Lane	Aspen Falls	CA	29529	209-555-7912
21	Angela	Reese	Patrol Officer	946 Stoney Lonesome Road	Aspen Falls	CA	29533	209-555-4923
22	Chuck	Snow	Police Special Representative	1003 Kovar Road	Aspen Falls	CA	29531	213-555-1929
3	Dwana	Keith	Crime and Intelligence Analyst	3149 Brownton Road	Aspen Falls	CA	29534	209-555-6254
4	Juanita	Hippen	Criminalist	3273 Spring Avenue	Aspen Falls	CA	29534	209-555-4279
5	Angela	Booker	Patrol Officer	4542 Johnstown Road	Aspen Falls	CA	29533	213-555-0749
6	Elizabth	Johnson	Patrol Officer	3865 Fairfield Road	Aspen Falls	CA	29533	209-555-2561
7	Reynaldo	Robertson	Patrol Officer	4897 Kembery Drive	Aspen Falls	CA	29534	209-555-6895
8	Richard	Pearlstein	Patrol Officer	2474 Cabell Avenue	Aspen Falls	CA	29533	209-555-6716
9	Angie	Reese	Police Officer	946 Stoney Lonesome Road	Aspen Falls	CA	29533	209-555-4923

Figure 1

Assess Your Skills Visually

To complete this database, you will need the following file:

- a08_Art_Classes

You will save your file as:

- Lastname_Firstname_a08_Art_Classes

Open the database **a08_Art_Classes** located with your student files. Export the data in the **Art Classes** table into a Word document. **Save** the Word document as Lastname_Firstname_a08_Art_Classes and then format the table as shown in **Figure 1**. Apply the **Light List – Accent 1** table style and the **Blue, Accent 1, Lighter 80%** shading. Apply the **Landscape** orientation, and then **AutoFit** the table contents. Submit as directed.

Done! You have completed Assess Your Skills Visually

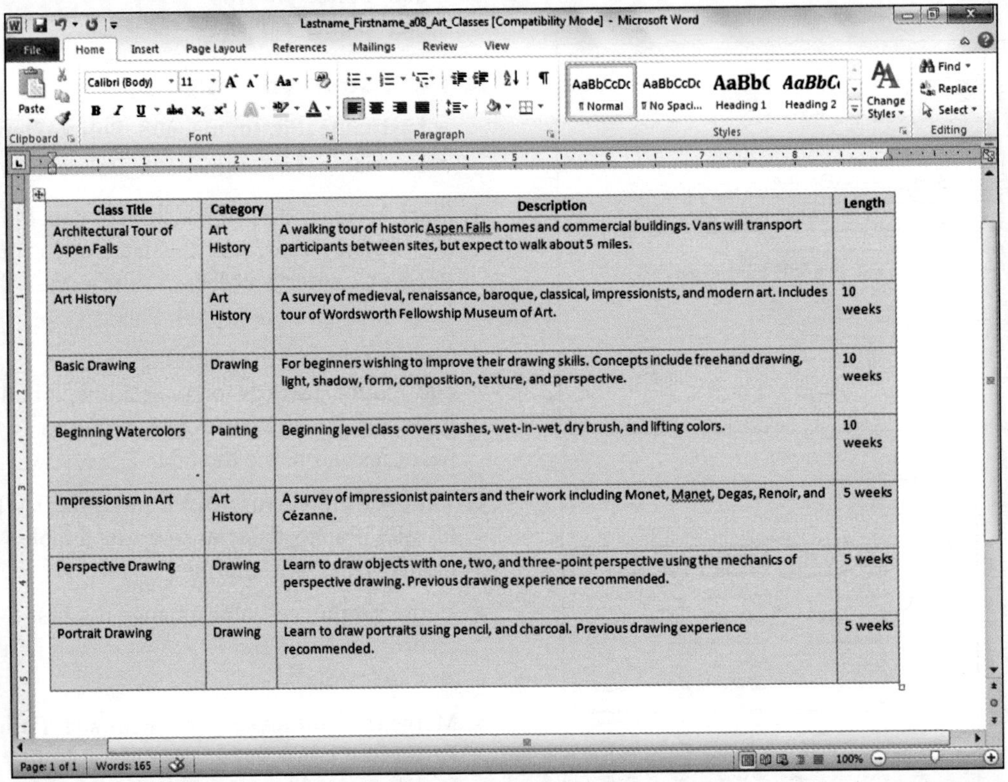

Class Title	Category	Description	Length
Architectural Tour of Aspen Falls	Art History	A walking tour of historic Aspen Falls homes and commercial buildings. Vans will transport participants between sites, but expect to walk about 5 miles.	
Art History	Art History	A survey of medieval, renaissance, baroque, classical, impressionists, and modern art. Includes tour of Wordsworth Fellowship Museum of Art.	10 weeks
Basic Drawing	Drawing	For beginners wishing to improve their drawing skills. Concepts include freehand drawing, light, shadow, form, composition, texture, and perspective.	10 weeks
Beginning Watercolors	Painting	Beginning level class covers washes, wet-in-wet, dry brush, and lifting colors.	10 weeks
Impressionism in Art	Art History	A survey of impressionist painters and their work including Monet, Manet, Degas, Renoir, and Cézanne.	5 weeks
Perspective Drawing	Drawing	Learn to draw objects with one, two, and three-point perspective using the mechanics of perspective drawing. Previous drawing experience recommended.	5 weeks
Portrait Drawing	Drawing	Learn to draw portraits using pencil, and charcoal. Previous drawing experience recommended.	5 weeks

Figure 1

Skills in Context

To complete this database, you will need the following file:

- a08_Cinco

You will save your file as:

- Lastname_Firstname_a08_Cinco

Open the database **a08_Cinco** located with the student files, and then export the **Potential Sponsors** table as an XML file without an XSD file. Name the XML file Lastname_Firstname_a08_Cinco Open the XML file in Notepad. On the first line of the XML document, to the right of *UTF-8*", type <!-- Exported by Your Name --> At the bottom of the document, before the </dataroot> tag, add the XML structure and data to add another record. For the XML structure, follow the pattern of XML tags for the previous record. For the data, use your school's name as the *Sponsor_Name*, your name for the *Contact_Name*, and your

school's main telephone number as the *Contact_Phone*. **Save** the file, and then **Exit** Notepad. Open **Lastname_Firstname_a08_Cinco** with your web browser. If you receive an error, open the XML file in Notepad and carefully check that you entered the record above the closing *dataroot* tag and that each XML tag is exactly the same as the ones in the previous record. Submit as directed.

Done! You have completed Skills in Context

Skills and You

To complete this database, you will need the following file:

- Blank database and Word document

You will save your files as:

- Lastname_Firstname_a08_Skills
- Lastname_Firstname_a08_Skills_Letter

Using the skills you have practiced in this chapter, create a new database with a table listing the names and addresses of at least 10 people that you would like to send a letter to. Save the database as Lastname_Firstname_a08_Skills Write a letter in Word, save it as Lastname_Firstname_a08_Skills_Letter and then close the

letter. In Access, link the table with your saved letter as a mail merge document. Insert an address block and greeting line, and then complete the merge. Submit as directed by your instructor.

Done! You have completed Skills and You

CHAPTER 9

Build Macros and Write VBA Procedures

▶ Macros and Microsoft Visual Basic for Applications (VBA) are used to automate tasks such as opening and navigating forms or entering data.

▶ Macros perform built-in sets of instructions, and VBA programs perform instructions that you write yourself.

Your starting screen will look like this:

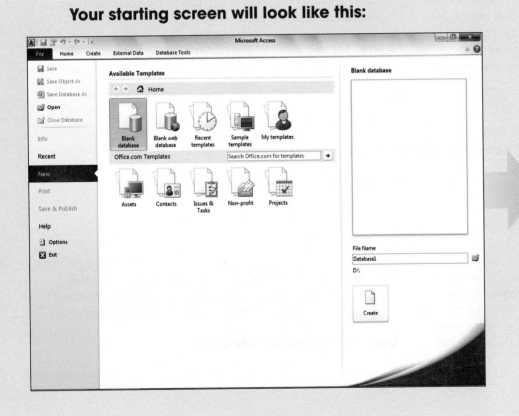

SKILLS

Skills 1-10 Training

At the end of this chapter, you will be able to:

Skill 1 Build and Test Client Macros
Skill 2 Add Comments and Reorder Macro Actions
Skill 3 Add Conditions to Macros
Skill 4 Test Macros with Conditions
Skill 5 Add Command Buttons that Run Macros
Skill 6 Add Quick Access Toolbar Buttons and Convert Macros to VBA
Skill 7 Create VBA Procedures
Skill 8 Write and Debug VBA Code
Skill 9 Write VBA Statements and Work with Variables
Skill 10 Add Conditions to VBA Procedures

MORE SKILLS

More Skills 11 Build Macros that Send Reports via E-Mail
More Skills 12 Build Macros to Navigate Forms
More Skills 13 Run Macros on Startup
More Skills 14 Create Custom Menus

Outcome

Using the skills listed to the left will enable you to create documents like these:

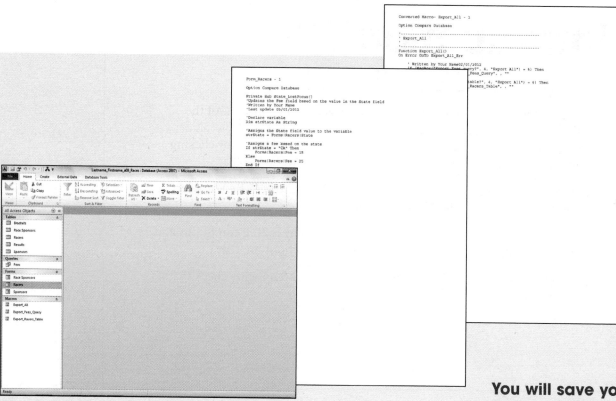

You will save your files as:

Lastname_Firstname_a09_Fees_HTML

Lastname_Firstname_a09_Fees_Workbook

Lastname_Firstname_a09_Races

Lastname_Firstname_a09_Races_Snip

In this chapter, you will create documents for the Aspen Falls City Hall, which provides essential services for the citizens and visitors of Aspen Falls, California.

Introduction

▶ Recall that you can automate tasks by storing actions in a macro. All the actions can then be performed by running the macro. For example, all of the tables in your database can be exported as Excel workbooks by clicking a button on a form or a button added to the Quick Access Toolbar.

▶ You can write instructions in Visual Basic for Applications (VBA) or select prebuilt instructions in the Macro Builder.

▶ Macros and VBA code can help you make decisions by testing conditions and then performing certain actions only when the conditions are true.

▶ While creating macros or VBA programs, you should frequently check that it performs as intended.

Time to complete all
10 skills – 50 to 90 minutes

Find your student data files here:

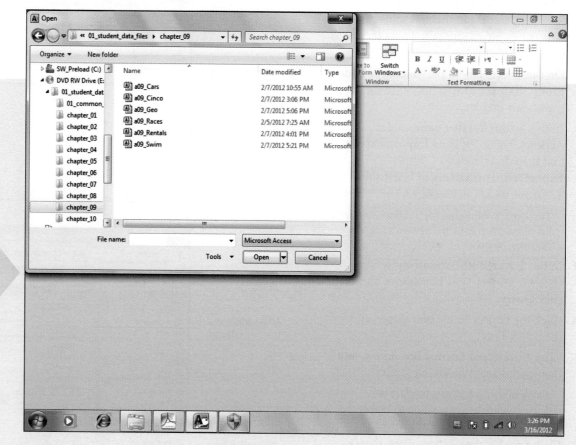

**Student data file needed
for this chapter:**

- a09_Races

► Recall that a macro is an action or group of stored instructions used to automate tasks.

► A macro is created, saved, and named so that it can be used by any other database object for repetitive tasks.

1. **Start** ⊕ Access, and then open **a09_ Races**. Use the **Save As** dialog box to create a **New folder** named Access Chapter 9 Save the database in the new folder as Lastname_ Firstname_a09_Races If necessary, enable the content.

2. On the **Create tab**, in the **Macros & Code group**, click the **Macro** button to display the Macro Builder.

3. In the **Action Catalog pane**, under **Actions**, expand ⊞ **Data Import/Export**, and then double-click **ExportWithFormatting** to insert the action, as shown in **Figure 1**.

   The ExportWithFormatting action displays a list of macro arguments needed to export database objects.

4. In the **ExportWithFormatting** action, click the **Object Type box arrow**, and then click **Query**.

5. Click the **Object Name box arrow**, and then click **Fees**.

6. Click the **Output Format box arrow**, and then click **Excel Workbook (*.xlsx)**.

   These macro arguments instruct the *ExportWithFormatting* action to export the *Fees* query as an Excel workbook.

7. Click **Save** 🖫, type Export_Fees_Query and then click **OK**. Compare your screen to **Figure 2**.

   After they are saved, client macros are listed in the Navigation Pane under Macros so that they can be accessed by other database objects.

■ **Continue to the next page to complete the skill**

Action Catalog pane

ExportWithFormatting action inserted into Macro Builder

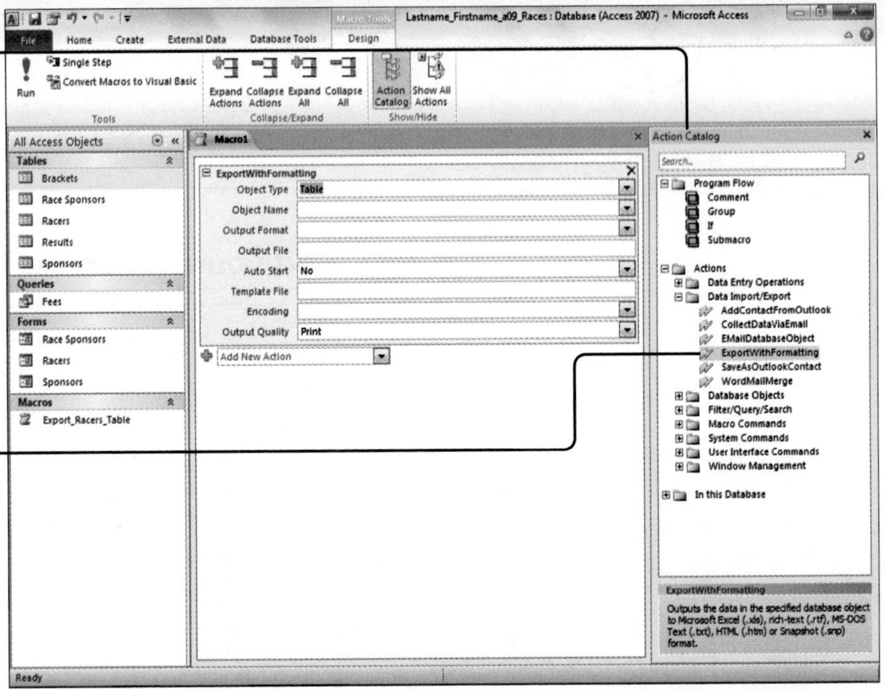

Figure 1

Action arguments selected

Macro name displays in Navigation Pane

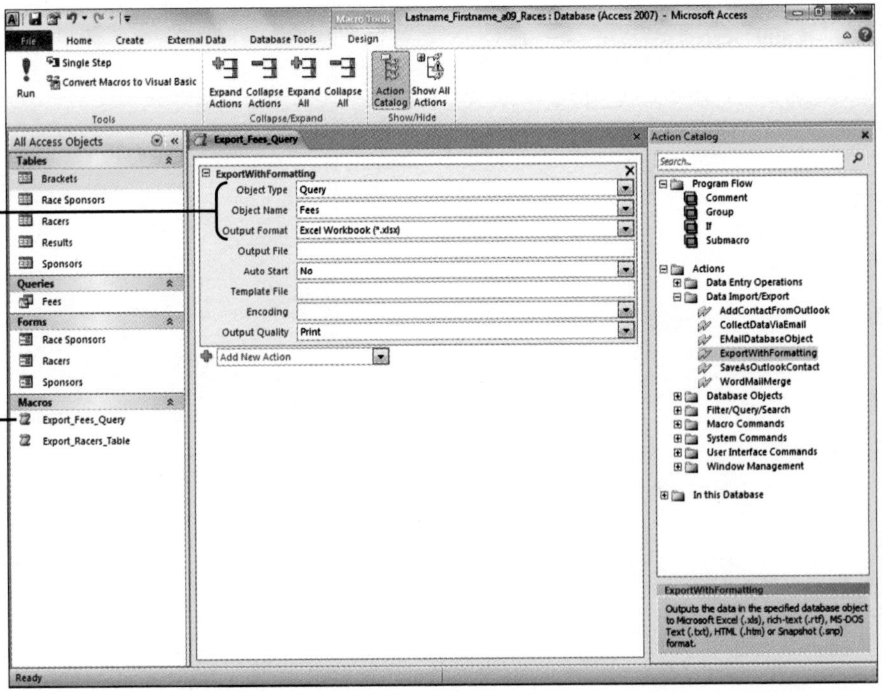

Figure 2

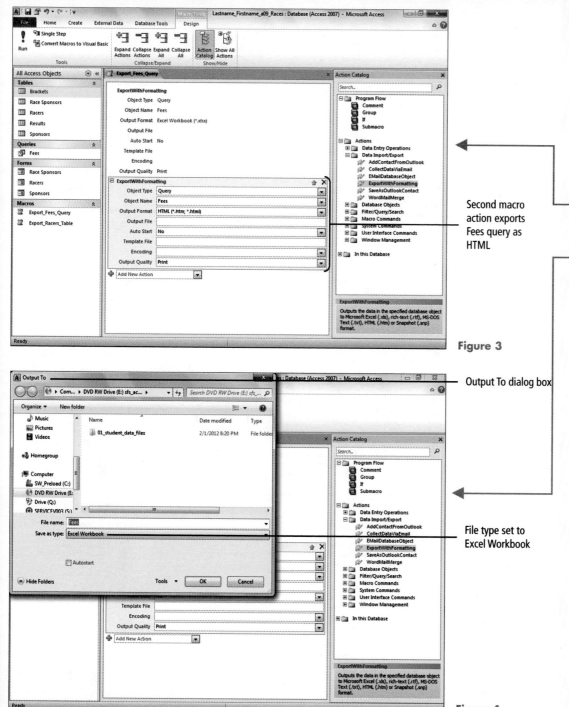

Second macro
action exports
Fees query as
HTML

Figure 3

Output To dialog box

File type set to
Excel Workbook

Figure 4

8. In the macro, click the **Add New Action arrow**, and then from the list, click **ExportWithFormatting** to insert a second query action.

 Macro actions can be selected from the Action Catalog pane or from the Add New Action box in the macro.

9. In the second **ExportWithFormatting** action, repeat the techniques just practiced so that the action exports the **Query** named **Fees** as an **HTML (*.htm, *.html)** file. Compare your screen with **Figure 3**.

10. Click **Save**. On the **Design tab**, in the **Tools group**, click the **Run** button, and then compare your screen with **Figure 4**. If you receive an error message, click **OK**, and then carefully check that your macro actions and arguments match the previous steps.

 The *Output To* dialog box displays with the file type set to Excel Workbook, which indicates that the first macro action ran successfully.

11. In the **Output To** dialog box, click **Cancel** so that the query is not actually exported.

12. In the second **Output To** dialog box, verify that the **File type** is set to **HTML**, and then click **Cancel** so that the query is not actually exported.

 When building macros, it is a good idea to test early and often. This helps isolate and fix potential errors.

- **You have completed Skill 1 of 10**

► **Comments** are remarks added to a macro or VBA code to provide information to those writing or reviewing the macro or VBA code.

► Comments are ignored by Access when the macro or VBA code is run.

1. With the **Export_Fees_Query** open in Design view, click the first macro action to select it.

2. In **Action Catalog pane**, under **Program Flow**, double-click **Comment**. In the comment box just inserted, type Exports Fees query to Excel Select the first action, and then compare your screen with **Figure 1**.

   Comments are colored green to set them apart from the macro actions. Comments begin with /* and end with */ to instruct Access to ignore all of the text between them when the macro is run.

3. Point to the comment so that the **Move up** 🔼, **Move down** 🔽 and **Delete** ☒ icons display. Click **Move up** 🔼 to move the comment above the first macro action.

   Comments should be displayed above each macro action.

4. Below the second action, click the **Add New Action arrow**, and then click **Comment** to insert a second comment. Type Exports Fees query to HTML

5. Repeat the technique just practiced to move the second comment between the first and second macro actions. Select the first action, and then compare your screen with **Figure 2**.

■ **Continue to the next page to complete the skill**

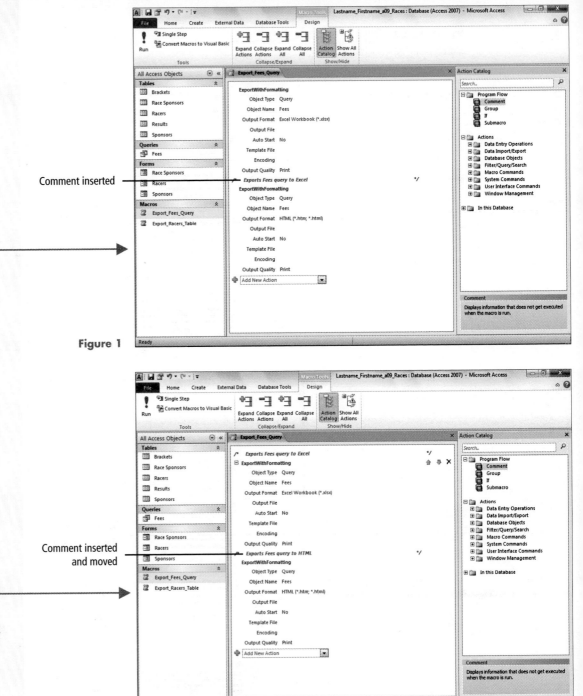

Comment inserted

Figure 1

Comment inserted and moved

Figure 2

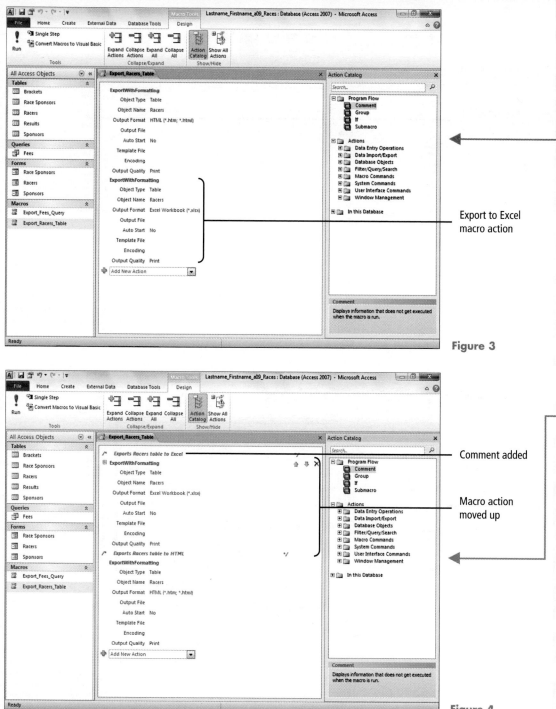

Export to Excel
macro action

Figure 3

Comment added

Macro action
moved up

Figure 4

6. Click **Save** 🔲. Click **Run** to test that the comments have not affected the macro. In both **Output To** dialog boxes, click **Cancel**. **Close** ☒ the macro.

7. In the **Navigation Pane**, right-click **Export_Racers_Table**, and then click **Design View**. Compare your screen with **Figure 3**.

   Unless instructed otherwise, macro actions are performed in the order they are inserted in the macro. Here, the Racers table will be exported as an HTML file, then exported as an Excel file.

8. In the macro, click to select the second macro action. Click **Move up** 🔼.

9. Use either technique practiced earlier to insert a comment with the text Exports Racers table to Excel Move the comment above the first macro action.

10. Insert a second comment with the text Exports Racers table to HTML and then move the comment above the second macro. Select the first action, and then compare your screen with **Figure 4**.

11. Click **Save** 🔲. **Run** the macro to test that it exports the Racers table in the Excel and HTML file formats, but in both **Output To** dialog boxes, click **Cancel**. **Close** ☒ the macro.

    If you accidentally clicked OK instead of Cancel when testing macros, you can delete any files created by the macros.

■ **You have completed Skill 2 of 10**

► Using message boxes and VBA expressions, you can ask for input and then have the macro perform different actions based on the results of that input.

1. On the **Create tab**, in the **Macros & Code group**, click the **Macro** button.

2. In the **Action Catalog pane**, under **Program Flow**, double-click **If**. Compare your screen with **Figure 1**.

> An *If* action is added to the macro. *If actions* provide a conditional expression and then perform an action or series of actions only when the result of the condition is true or false.

3. To the right of the **Conditional Expression** box, click the **Builder** button 🔘 to open the **Expression Builder**.

4. In the **Expression Builder** dialog box, under **Expression Elements**, expand ⊞ **Functions**, and then click **Built-In Functions**. Under **Expression Categories**, scroll down, and then click **Messages**.

5. Under **Expression Values**, double-click **MsgBox**, and then compare your screen with **Figure 2**.

> The Expression Builder inserts the MsgBox action, followed by the arguments used by the MsgBox action.

6. In the expression just inserted, click the <<**prompt**>> argument, and then, including the quotation marks, type "Export Fees query?"

> The *prompt* argument is the message that displays in the message box.

7. Click the <<**buttons**>> argument, and then type 4

> The number *4* instructs the macro to display a message box with two buttons—*Yes* and *No*.

■ **Continue to the next page to complete the skill** ➤

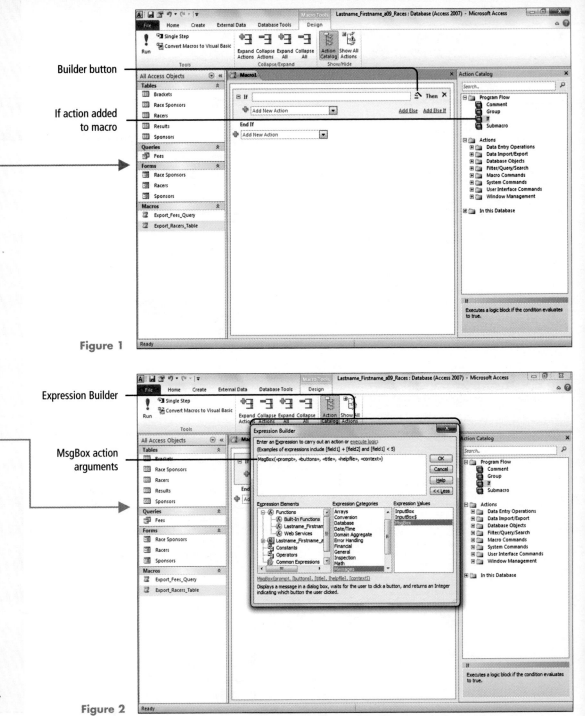

Builder button

If action added to macro

Figure 1

Expression Builder

MsgBox action arguments

Figure 2

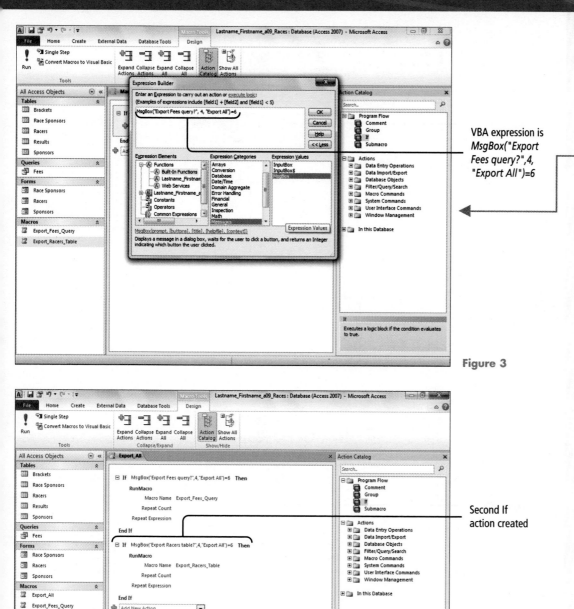

VBA expression is
MsgBox("Export Fees query?",4, "Export All")=6

Figure 3

Second If action created

Figure 4

8. Click the **<<title>>** argument, and then type "Export All" To the right of *"Export All"* delete all the remaining text, commas, and spaces. Do not delete the closing parenthesis.

9. Click to the right of the closing parenthesis, and then type =6 Compare with **Figure 3**.

> When the Yes button is clicked, the numeric value 6 is sent to the expression, and the condition in the expression is true. When the No button is clicked, the numeric value is not 6, and the condition is false.

10. Click **OK**. If an error message displays, close it, open the **Expression Builder**, and carefully check your typing. Be sure to include the quotation marks, commas, and parentheses as described above.

11. Click **Save** 🖫. In the **Save As** dialog box, type Export_All and then press Enter.

12. If necessary, click to select the **If** action. Above the **End If** statement, in the **If action** box, click the **Add New Action box arrow**, scroll down, and then click **RunMacro** to insert the action within the **If** action.

13. Click the **Macro Name arrow**, and then click **Export_Fees_Query**.

14. Below the **End If** statement, click the **Add New Action arrow**, and then click **If** to insert a second If action. In the lower **If** box, type MsgBox("Export Racers table?", 4,"Export All")=6

15. In the second **If** action, add a new action that runs the **Export_Racers_Table** macro. **Save** 🖫. Click a blank area, and then compare your screen with **Figure 4**.

- **You have completed Skill 3 of 10**

► When testing macros with conditions, all possible outcomes should be tested.

► For conditions with Yes/No message boxes, both the Yes and No buttons should be tested.

1. On the **Design tab**, in the **Tools group**, click **Run**, and then compare your screen with **Figure 1**.

   The message box title, prompt, and buttons specified in the expression display.

2. Click **Yes** so that the Export_Fees_Query runs. In the **Output To** dialog box, verify the file type is Excel Workbook, and then click **Cancel**. In the second **Output To** dialog box, verify the file type is HTML, and then click **Cancel**.

   Recall that the file does not actually need to be saved to test if the macro is running correctly.

3. Compare the second message box that displays on your screen with **Figure 2**.

4. Click **Yes** to run the **Racers** table export. In both **Output To** dialog boxes, click **Cancel**.

5. Run the macro again. In the first message box, click **Yes**.

6. In the **Output To** dialog box, navigate to your **Access Chapter 9** folder. In the **File name** box, type Lastname_Firstname_a09 _Fees_Workbook and then click **OK**. In the second **Output To** dialog box, type Lastname_Firstname_a09_Fees_HTML Click **OK**.

■ **Continue to the next page to complete the skill** ➤

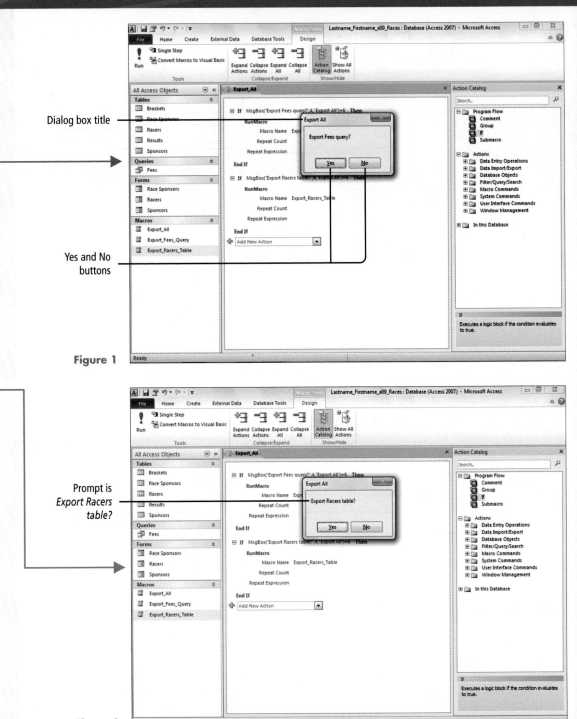

Dialog box title

Yes and No buttons

Figure 1

Prompt is *Export Racers table?*

Figure 2

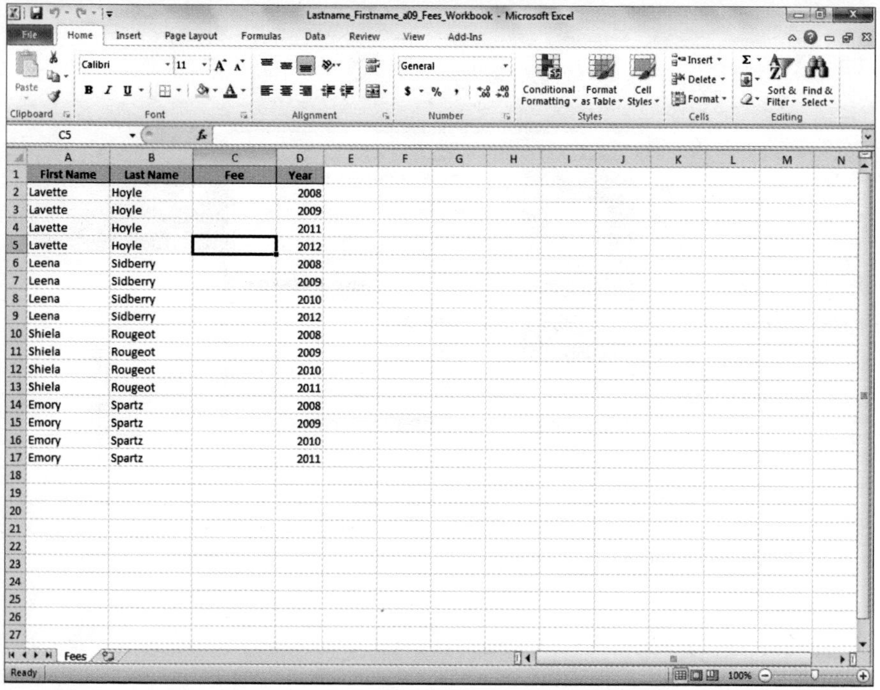

Figure 3

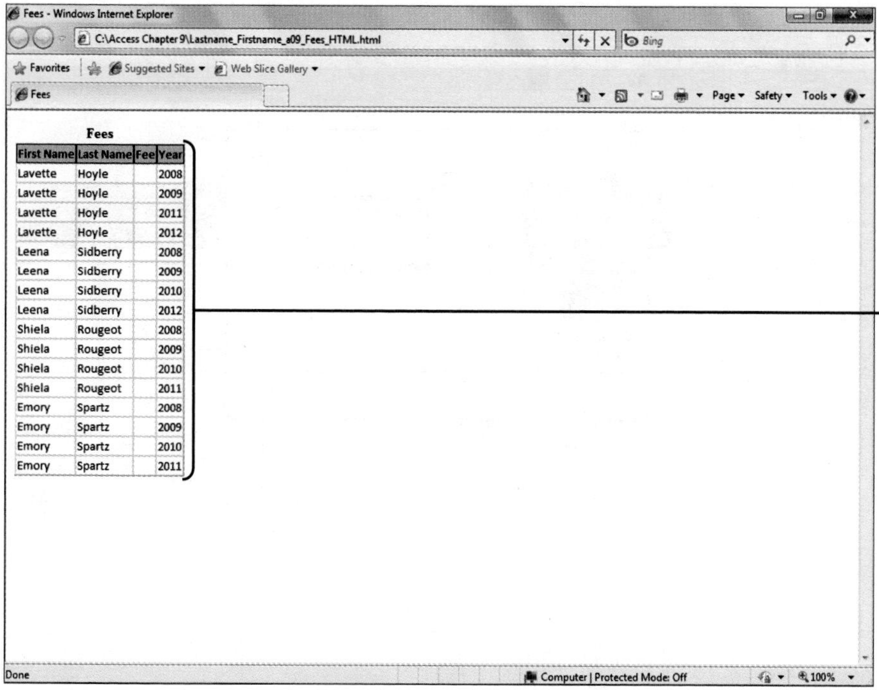

Racers table exported as HTML file

Figure 4

7. In the **Export All** message box asking to export the **Racers** table, click **No**.

8. **Close** ☒ the macro.

9. Click **Start** ⊙, and then click **Computer**. In the folder window, navigate to your **Access Chapter 9** folder. Verify that the Excel file and Web page were saved in the **Access Chapter 9** folder.

10. In the displayed folder window, double-click **Lastname_Firstname_ a09 _Fees_Workbook.** Compare your screen with **Figure 3**.

> The names and contact information for all racers are displayed in an Excel worksheet.

11. **Exit** Excel without saving the changes.

12. From your **Access Chapter 9** folder, double-click **Lastname_Firstname_a09_ Fees_HTML**, and then compare your screen with **Figure 4**.

13. **Close** ☒ your Web browser.

14. **Close** ☒ the **Computer** window.

■ **You have completed Skill 4 of 10**

► Buttons can be added to forms, and actions can then be assigned to the buttons. For example, a button can be set to run a macro when it is clicked.

1. In the **Navigation Pane**, right-click the **Racers** form, and then click **Design View**.

2. On the **Design tab**, in the **Controls group**, click the **Button** button ▦. With the ⊡ pointer, point to the **4 inch** horizontal grid line and about 3 grid dots below the **Detail** bar, and then click one time.

3. In the **Command Button Wizard**, under **Categories**, click **Miscellaneous**, and then under **Actions**, click **Run Macro**. Compare with **Figure 1**.

> Many different actions can be assigned to a button. Buttons are used to open forms, navigate and edit records, or open reports, for example.

4. Click **Next**, and then under **What macro would you like the command button to run?** click **Export_All**.

5. Click **Next**. Select the **Text** option button, and then in the **Text** box, replace the existing text with Export Data as shown in **Figure 2**.

■ **Continue to the next page to complete the skill**

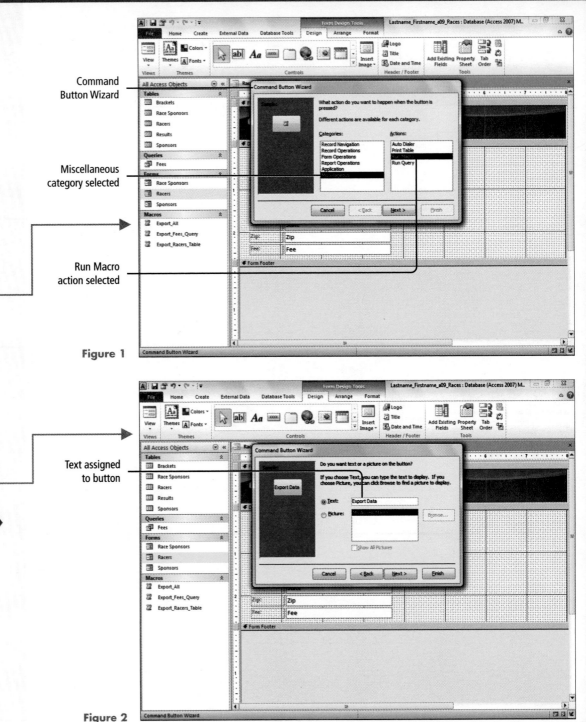

Command Button Wizard

Miscellaneous category selected

Run Macro action selected

Figure 1

Text assigned to button

Figure 2

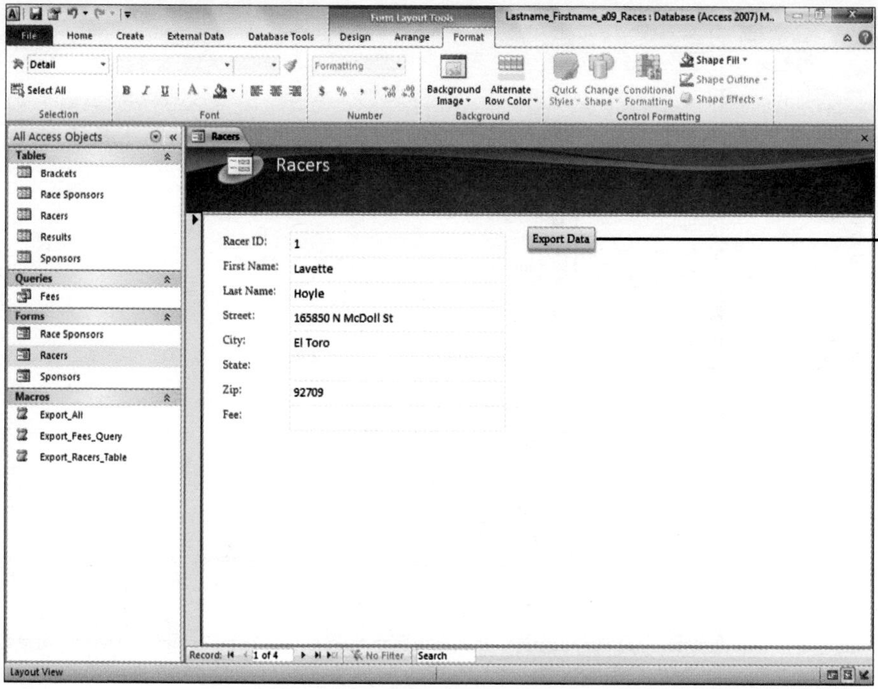

Command button added

Figure 3

Field	Value
Racer ID	Accept AutoNumber
First Name	Craig
Last Name	Johnson
Street	17 Caldone Way
City	Beverly Hills
State	CA
Zip	90210

Figure 4

6. Click **Next**, and then, in the **Name** box, type cmdExport_Racers

   Programmers often assign meaningful names to buttons and other objects so that they can identify them when they write VBA code. The *cmd* prefix helps programmers identify the type of object—here a command button. Object names cannot have spaces.

7. Click **Finish** to complete the wizard and to insert the button.

8. Switch to Layout view, and then click the **Export Data** button. On the **Format tab**, in the **Control Formatting group**, click the **Quick Styles** button. In the gallery, click the sixth choice in the fourth row—**Subtle Effect, Aqua, Accent 5**. Click a blank area of the form, and then compare your screen with **Figure 3**.

9. Switch to Form view. On the Navigation bar, click the **New (blank) record button** ▶. Use the form to enter the record shown in **Figure 4**.

   The *Fee* field has intentionally been left blank.

10. Click the **Export Data** button. In both message boxes displayed by the macro, click **No**.

11. **Save** 🖫, and then **Close** ⊠ the form.

■ **You have completed Skill 5 of 10**

▶ Buttons that perform commonly used Access commands can be placed on the Quick Access Toolbar, also known as the QAT.

▶ Quick Access Toolbar buttons also run macros when they are clicked.

1. Click the **File** button, and then click **Options**.

2. On the left side of the **Access Options** dialog box, click **Quick Access Toolbar**, and then compare your screen with **Figure 1**.

    The Access Options dialog box lists all of the Access commands so that you can add their buttons to the QAT. Here, the popular commands are listed.

3. Click the **Choose commands from arrow**, and then from the list, click **Macros**.

4. Click the **Customize Quick Access Toolbar arrow**, and then from the list, click the choice that displays the path and name of your database file. Compare your screen with **Figure 2**.

    The Quick Access Toolbar can be modified for all databases, or just the currently opened database. Here, the QAT of the current database will be changed.

5. In the list of available macros, click **<Separator>**, and then click the **Add** button.

    A *separator*—a small vertical or horizontal line used to separate choices in a list, toolbar, or menu—will be added to the QAT.

■ **Continue to the next page to complete the skill**

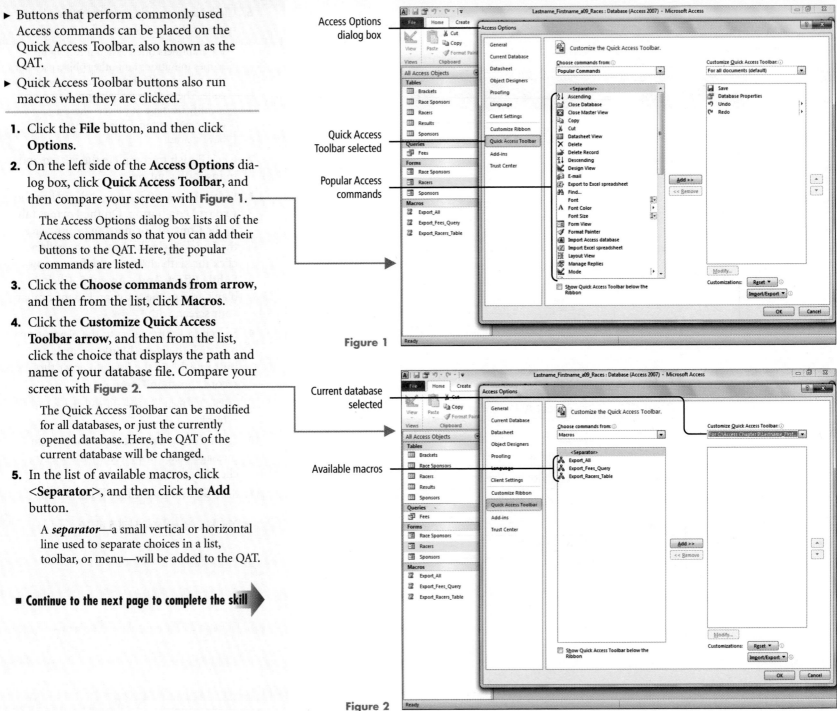

Access Options dialog box

Quick Access Toolbar selected

Popular Access commands

Figure 1

Current database selected

Available macros

Figure 2

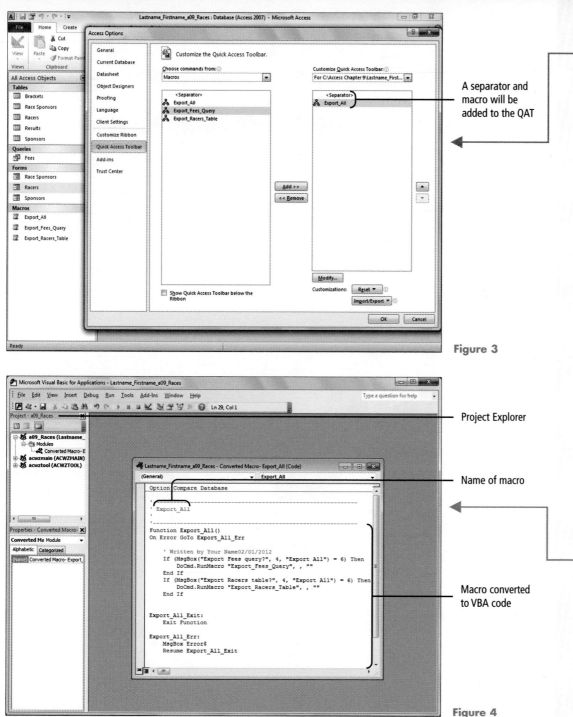

Figure 3

Figure 4

6. In the list of available macros, click **Export_All**, and then click the **Add** button. Compare your screen with **Figure 3**.

7. Click **OK** to close the dialog box. On the **Quick Access Toolbar**, to the right of the last separator, click the macro button to verify that the **Export_All** macro runs. In both of the displayed messages, click **No**.

8. Create a full-screen snip, **Save** it in your **Access Chapter 9** folder as Lastname_Firstname_a09_Race_Snip and then close the **Snipping Tool** window.

9. Open the **Export_All** macro in Design view. Repeat the techniques practiced previously to add a comment. In the **Comment** box, using your own name, type Written by Your Name Press [Enter], and then type the current date in the format: *dd/mm/yyyy*.

10. Click the **Move Up** button as needed to move the comment above the first macro action.

11. Click **Save**. In the **Navigation Pane**, under **Macros**, click **Export_All**. On the **Design tab**, in the **Tools group**, click **Convert Macros to Visual Basic**. In the **Convert macro: Export_All** dialog box, click **Convert**. In the message box, click **OK**.

12. In the **Project Pane**, under **Modules**, double-click **Converted Macro-Export All** and then compare your screen with **Figure 4**.

13. If you are printing this project, from the **File menu**, click **Print**.

14. From the **File menu**, click **Close and Return to Microsoft Access. Close** the **Export_All** macro.

■ **You have completed Skill 6 of 10**

▶ *Visual Basic for Applications (VBA)* is a programming language designed to work within Microsoft Office applications.

▶ VBA is a subset of the Microsoft Visual Basic (VB) programming language and is used to write your own *programs*—stored instructions that tell a computer what to do—that run while you work with Office applications.

1. Open the **Racers** form, and then notice that the Fee field has no data.

2. Switch to Design view, and then on the **Design tab**, in the **Tools group**, click the **Property Sheet** button. On the form, click the **State** text box to display its properties. Click the property sheet **Event tab**, click in the **On Lost Focus box**, and then compare with **Figure 1**.

   The property sheet Event tab displays all the *events*—actions, such as mouse clicks or typing, detected by a running program— that are associated with the *State* control. Here, the On Lost Focus event detects when the insertion point moves out of the *State* text box.

3. On the property sheet **Event tab**, click the **On Lost Focus Build** button ⬚, and then compare your screen with **Figure 2**.

   The Choose Builder dialog box has three options for writing stored instructions: Macro Builder, Expression Builder, and Code Builder.

■ **Continue to the next page to complete the skill**

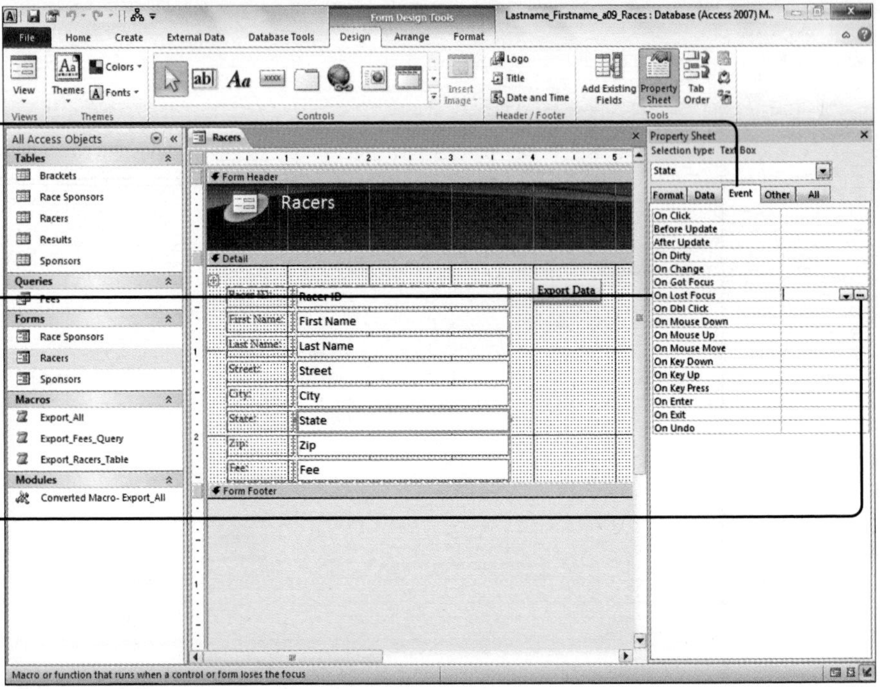

Event tab

On Lost Focus event

Build button displays

Figure 1

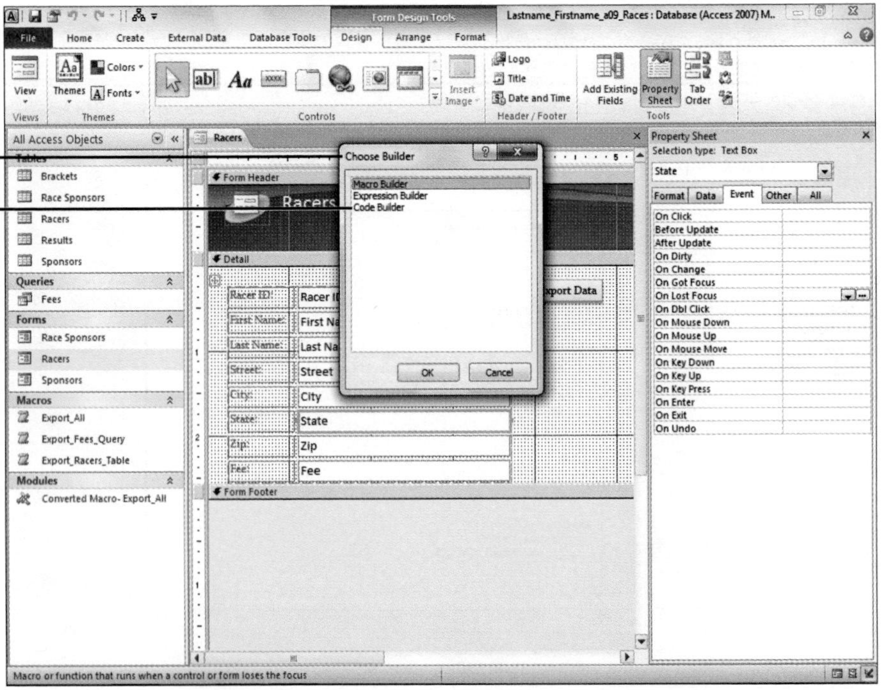

Choose Builder dialog box

Code Builder

Figure 2

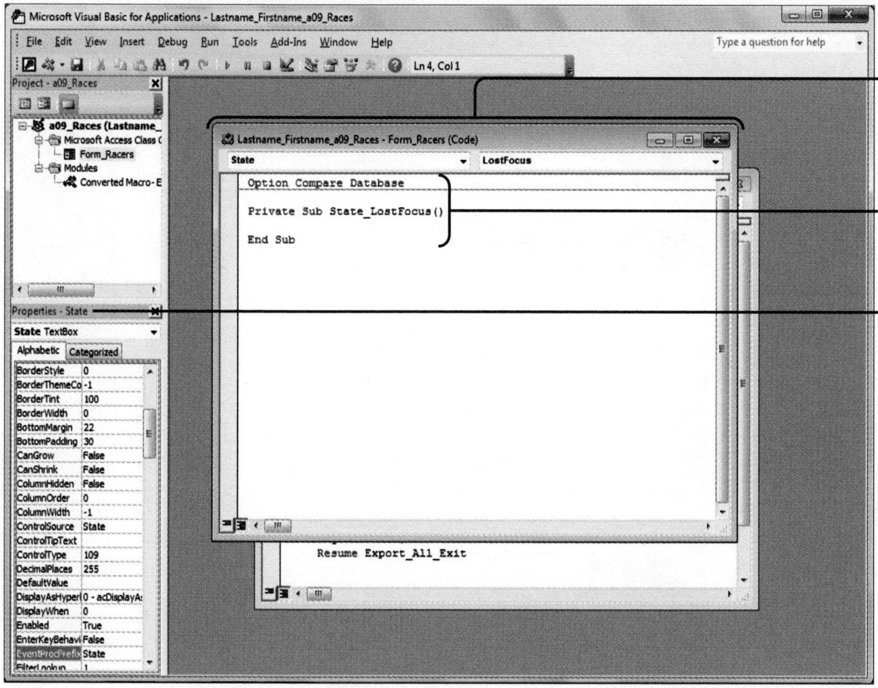

Figure 3

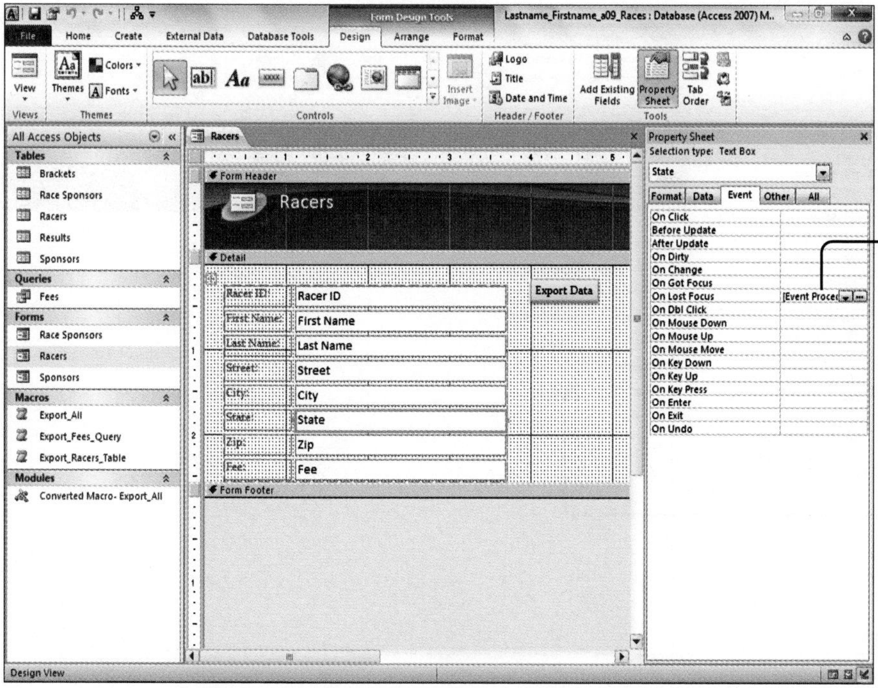

4. In the **Choose Builder** dialog box, click **Code Builder**, and then click **OK**. If the Converted Macro-Export_All window is opened, click the window, and then click Close. Take a moment to familiarize yourself with the Microsoft Visual Basic window, as shown in **Figure 3**.

> The *Visual Basic Editor (VBE)* is a program for writing VBA program code.
>
> The center of the screen is the *Code window* where you write and edit VBA code. Here, the Code window displays the State_ LostFocus *sub procedure*—a group of related statements that is a subset of a program. Sub procedures are often referred to as *subs* or *procedures*.
>
> In the upper-left corner of the VBE window, the Project Explorer is used to manage code windows. In the lower-left corner, the Properties pane lists the current properties for each database object.

5. On the Standard toolbar, click the **Save** button 🖫.

> This action saves the VBA code, but does not save any changes made to the form.

6. On the Standard toolbar, click the **View Microsoft Office Access** button 🔲, and then compare with **Figure 4**.

> The form window is the active window, and the Microsoft Visual Basic window displays as a button on the taskbar.
>
> The On Lost Focus property displays *[Event Procedure]* to indicate that a sub procedure will run whenever the State control loses focus.

7. Save 🖫 the form.

■ **You have completed Skill 7 of 10**

Figure 4

► In VBA, comments begin with a single quotation mark.

► Programmers routinely test their programs in a process called debugging. To *debug* is to find and fix errors in programming code and make sure the program functions as intended.

1. With the **Racers** form open in Design view, in the property sheet, click the **On Lost Focus Build** button ⬚ to return to the Visual Basic Editor. Alternately, you can switch between windows by pressing [Alt]+[F11].

2. In the **Code** window, with the insertion point below *Private Sub State_LostFocus( )*, type the following comments. Be sure each line begins with a single quotation mark:

   'Updates the Fee field based on the value in the State field

   'Written by Your Name

3. Press [Enter], and then verify that the comments display in green, as shown in **Figure 1**.

4. Click **Save** 🖫, and then press [Alt]+[F11] to return to the form. Switch to Form view. Click in the **State** text box, and then press [Tab]. Compare with **Figure 2**.

   Because the code has only comments, screen elements were not changed, the program ran successfully, and the focus moved to the Zip field without generating an error.

■ **Continue to the next page to complete the skill** ▶

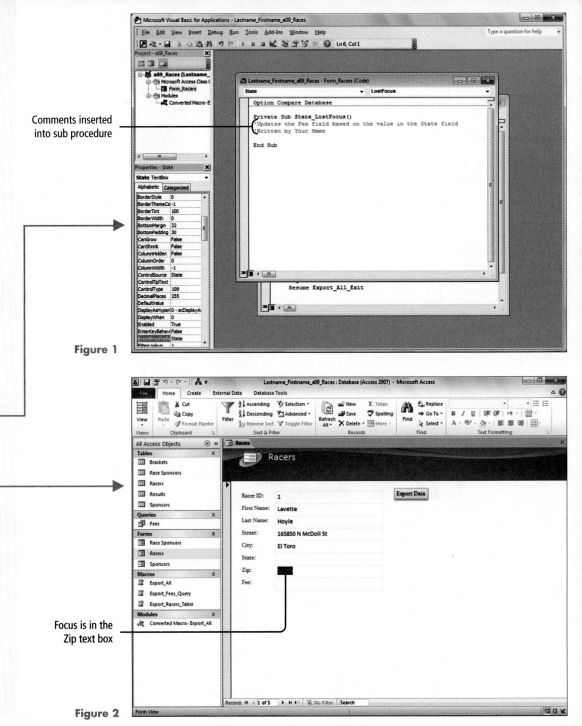

Comments inserted into sub procedure

Figure 1

Focus is in the Zip text box

Figure 2

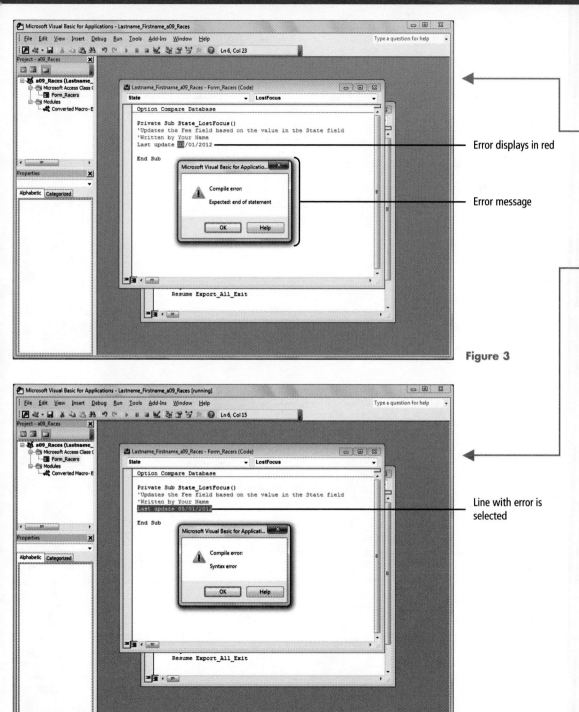

Figure 3

Figure 4

5. Switch to Design view. In the property sheet, click the **On Lost Focus Build** button 🔳 to return to the Visual Basic Editor.

6. In the blank line below your name, type the following without a single quotation mark: Last update 05/01/2012 Press Enter, and then compare your screen with **Figure 3**.

   A message displays that there is an error; in the Code window; the line that generated the error is red.

7. Read the message, and then click **OK**. Press Alt + F11 to return to the form. Switch to Form view. Click in the **State** text box, press Tab, and then compare with **Figure 4**.

   A message displays, and in the Code window, the line with the error is highlighted. The code has a *syntax error*— a code error that violates the rules of a programming language. Here, the error is that a comment does not begin with a single quotation mark.

8. Click **OK**. On the Standard toolbar, click the **Reset** button 🔳 to stop the code from running. In the Visual Basic Editor, to the left of *Last update 05/01/2012*, insert a single quotation mark (') and then click **Save** 🔳.

9. Press Alt + F11 to return to the form. Click in the **State** text box, and then press Tab to verify that the focus moved to the Zip field without creating an error.

   Whenever you see error messages when working with VBA code, you can apply these techniques to reset the procedure. You can then carefully check your typing and test your code again.

■ **You have completed Skill 8 of 10**

► A *statement* is a line in a program that contains instructions for the computer.

► Programs often need to store values in the computer's random access memory (RAM). *Variables* are programming objects that refer to the values stored in RAM.

1. Switch to the **Visual Basic Editor Code window**, click at the end of the last comment and then press Enter two times.

2. Type the comment 'Declare variable and then press Enter.

3. Type the statement Dim strState As String and then press Enter two times. Verify that Dim and As String are blue, as shown in **Figure 1.** ——————————————————➤

   Dim, As, and *String* are **keywords**—words in a programming language that have a particular meaning or purpose.

   strState is the name of the variable, and As String determines the variable's ***data type***—the type of data that can be stored in a variable such as numbers, characters, or dates.

   The *str* prefix indicates to the programmer that the variable will store a ***string***—a sequence of either alpha or alphanumeric characters. Many programmers practice ***Hungarian notation***—a naming convention where the prefixes indicate the type of data or type of object.

4. Type the comment 'Assigns the State field value to the variable and then press Enter.

5. Type the statement strState = Forms! Racers!State Press Enter, and then compare your screen with **Figure 2.** ——————➤

■ **Continue to the next page to complete the skill** ➤

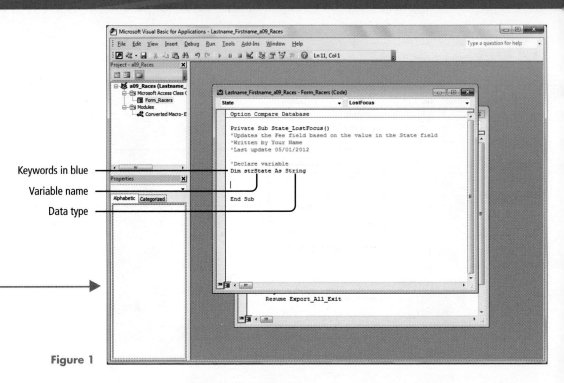

Keywords in blue
Variable name
Data type

Figure 1

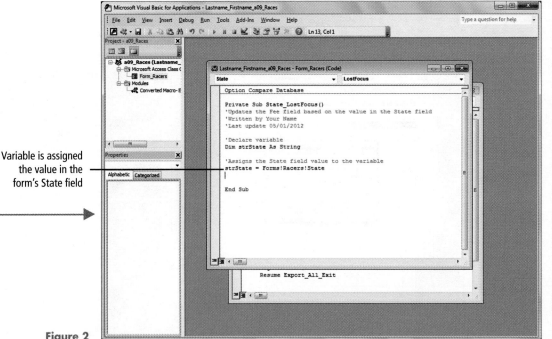

Variable is assigned the value in the form's State field

Figure 2

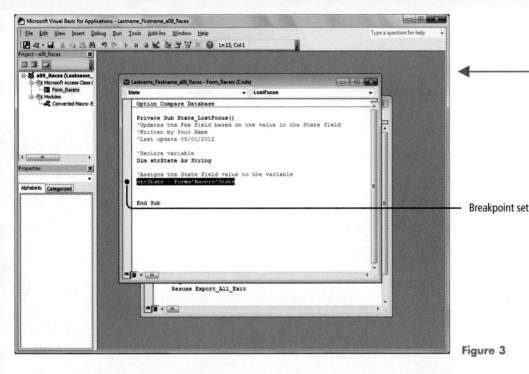

Figure 3

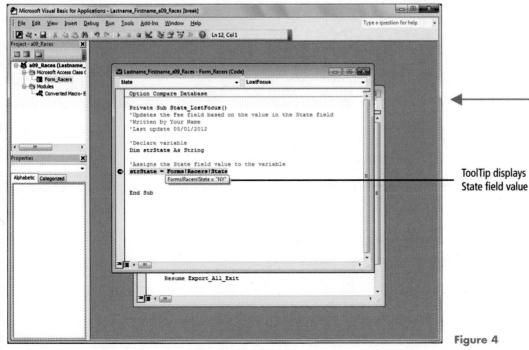

Figure 4

6. In the **Code** window, click in the margin to the left of the statement *strState = Forms!Racers!State*. Compare your screen with **Figure 3**.

> The red dot indicates that a ***breakpoint***—an intentional stop or pause inserted into a program—has been set. When the program runs, it will stop at the breakpoint so that the programmer can more precisely test the code.

7. Click **Save** 🖫, and then press [Alt] + [F11] to return to the form.

8. With the **Racers** form in Form view, in the first record, replace the **State** field value with NY and then press [Tab].

> The Microsoft Visual Basic window opens and the line with the breakpoint is highlighted.

9. Point to the text *Forms!Racers!State*. Read the ToolTip to verify that the **State** field equals *NY*, as shown in **Figure 4**.

10. Point to *strState* and notice the variable has not been assigned a value, as indicated by the ToolTip *strState = ""*.

11. From the **Debug** menu, click **Step Into**. Point to strState and notice the variable has been assigned the correct value, as indicated by the ToolTip *strState = "NY"*.

> In this manner, ***logical errors***—errors where the program runs, but does not produce the intended results—can be found. Here, the program is functioning as intended—the variable is storing the value entered into the State field in RAM.

12. On the Standard toolbar, click the **Reset** button 🔲. From the **Debug** menu, click **Clear All Breakpoints**. Click **Save**.

▪ **You have completed Skill 9 of 10**

Breakpoint set

ToolTip displays
State field value

► To make decisions, programs rely on *control structures*—methods that perform logical tests and perform actions when the conditions are true.

► The *If Then Else control structure* tests if a condition is true. When the condition is true, the program runs one set of statements. Otherwise, a different set of statements are run.

1. In the **Code** window, click in the first blank line below *strState = Forms!Racers! State*, and then press [Enter].

2. Type the comment 'Assigns a fee based on the state and then press [Enter].

3. Type the following control structure indenting the second statement, with the [Tab] key, as indicated, and then compare your screen with **Figure 1**.

    If strState = "CA" Then

        Forms!Racers!Fee = 15

    End If

    Here, the If statement tests if the variable—*strState*—is equal to CA. When it is, the Fee field will be changed to 15. The indented line adds *white space*—optional spacing that visually organizes the code to make it more readable by programmers.

4. Click **Save** 🖫, and then press [Alt] + [F11] to return to the form.

5. In the first record of the **Racers** form, change the **State** to CA and then press [Tab]. Compare your screen with **Figure 2**.

    The VBA code assigned the value *CA* to the variable, and then tested if the variable was equal to *CA*. Since this condition was true, the statement to assign a fee of 15 was executed.

■ **Continue to the next page to complete the skill** ►

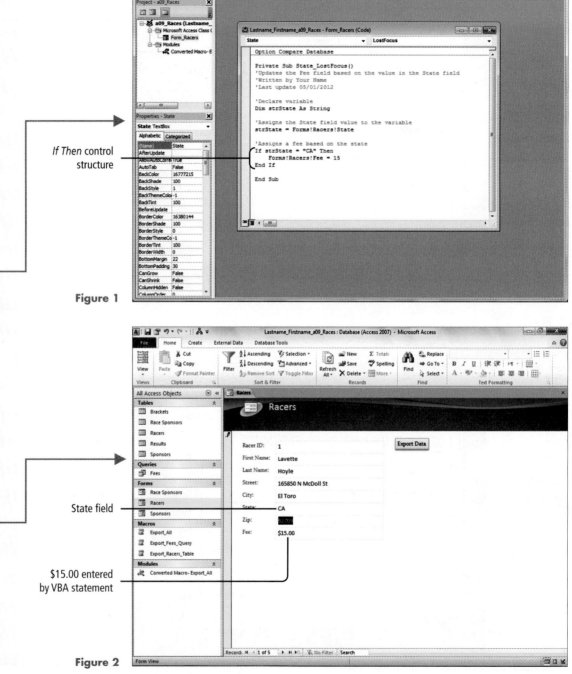

If Then control structure

Figure 1

State field

$15.00 entered by VBA statement

Figure 2

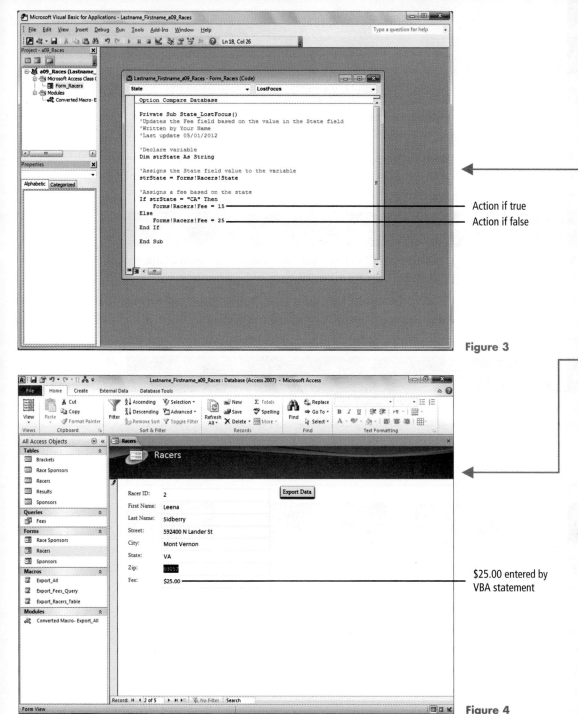

Action if true

Action if false

Figure 3

$25.00 entered by
VBA statement

Figure 4

6. Press `Alt` + `F11` to return to the Visual Basic Editor. In the **Code** window, click to the right of the text *Forms!Racers!Fee = 15*, press `Enter`, and then press `Bksp`.

7. Type the following statements, indenting as indicated:

   Else

      Forms!Racers!Fee = 25

8. Carefully compare your code with **Figure 3**.

   The Else statement specifies what statement should execute when the If condition is *not* true. Here, when the state is not *CA*, the value 25 will be entered into the Fee field.

9. Click **Save** ⊟, and then press `Alt` + `F11` to return to the form.

10. With the **Racers** form in Form view, navigate to the second record, and then change the **State** field to VA Press `Tab`, and verify that a fee of $25.00 is entered into the Fee field, as shown in **Figure 4**.

11. Repeat the technique just practiced to change the state for record **3** to CA and the state for record **4** to MI

12. In the Navigation bar, click the **Next record** button ▶, and then enter your own name and address into the form.

13. Press `Alt` + `F11` to return to the Visual Basic Editor. If instructed to print this project, from the File menu, click Print, and then click **OK**. **Close** the **Microsoft Visual Basic** window.

14. **Close** ✕ the **Racers** form.

Done! You have completed Skill 10 of 10 and your document is complete!

The following More Skills are located at **www.pearsonhighered.com/skills**

More Skills ⑪ Build Macros that Send Reports via E-Mail

A macro can be created that sends reports via e-mail by exporting the report to Microsoft Outlook.

In More Skills 11, you will create a macro to e-mail reports to a client. To complete this project, you will need to work at a computer with Microsoft Outlook 2010 installed and configured to work with your e-mail account.

To begin, open your web browser, navigate to www.pearsonhighered.com/skills, locate the name of your textbook, and follow the instructions on the website.

More Skills ⑫ Build Macros to Navigate Forms

A macro can automate the steps needed to open a form and navigate to a new, blank record. By running the macro, these steps can be performed with a single click.

In More Skills 12, you will create a macro that opens a form and then navigates to a new record.

To begin, open your web browser, navigate to www.pearsonhighered.com/skills, locate the name of your textbook, and follow the instructions on the website.

More Skills ⑬ Run Macros on Startup

When you have several tasks that need to be performed after a database is opened, you can write a macro to perform these tasks automatically.

In More Skills 13, you will create a macro that automatically opens two tables when the database opens.

To begin, open your web browser, navigate to www.pearsonhighered.com/skills, locate the name of your textbook, and follow the instructions on the website.

More Skills ⑭ Write Macros to Create Custom Menus

Macros can be created that display a custom shortcut menu for a report or form. The shortcut menu lists command names that you specify, and each command runs a macro that you associate with that command.

In More Skills 14, you will create a custom menu, with options to save, print, and close.

To begin, open your web browser, navigate to www.pearsonhighered.com/skills, locate the name of your textbook, and follow the instructions on the website.

Key Terms

Online Help Skills

1. **Start** ⊕ Access. In the upper right corner of the Access window, click the **Help** button ⊡. In the **Help** window, click the **Maximize** button.

2. Click in the search box, type vba and then click the **Search** button ⊡. In the search results, click **Introduction to Access Programming**.

3. Scroll down to **Understand Macros**. Compare your screen with **Figure 1**.

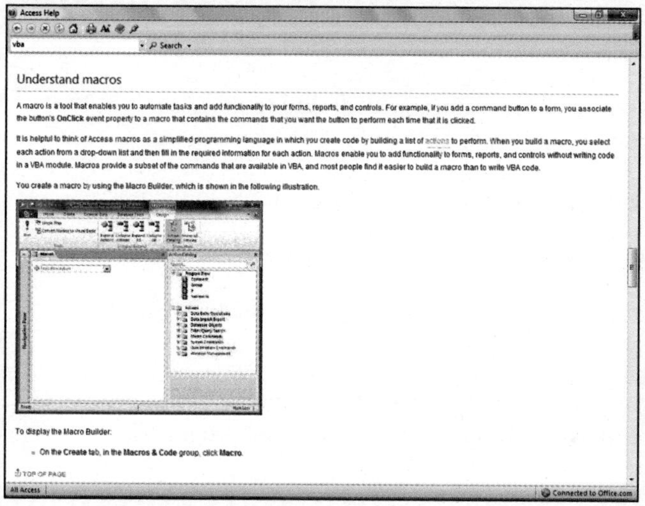

Figure 1

4. Read the section to see if you can answer the following: Macros are related to which programming language? What is the name of the user interface, or window, where macros are created? Name one type of Access object where a macro can be added?

Matching

Match each term in the second column with its correct definition in the first column by writing the letter of the term on the blank line in front of the correct definition.

___ **1.** A remark about the computer program.

___ **2.** A small vertical or horizontal line used to organize choices in a list, toolbar, or menu.

___ **3.** A set of stored instructions that tells a computer what to do.

___ **4.** To find and fix errors in programming code and to make sure the program functions as intended.

___ **5.** A programming object that refers to the values stored in memory.

___ **6.** A sequence of either alpha or alphanumeric characters.

___ **7.** A naming convention where the prefixes indicate the type of data or type of object.

___ **8.** The type of error that does not produce the intended results, even though an error message does not display when the program is run.

___ **9.** A control structure that tests if a condition is true and then performs different actions when the condition is true or false.

___ **10.** This is used to visually organize the code in order to make it more readable by programmers.

A Comment

B Debug

C Hungarian notation

D If Then Else

E Logical Error

F Program

G Separator

H String

I Variable

J White space

Multiple Choice

Choose the correct answer.

1. This provides a conditional expression and then performs an action or series of actions only when the result of the condition is true or false.
   A. Variable
   B. Keyword
   C. If action

2. The event-driven programming language built into Microsoft Office applications.
   A. VBA
   B. Java
   C. C

3. An action such as a mouse click or updating a field detected by a running program.
   A. Breakpoint
   B. Event
   C. Variable

4. The program where you write and edit VBA code.
   A. Code window
   B. Visual Basic Editor
   C. Programming window

5. A group of related statements that is a subset of a program.
   A. Grouping
   B. Task list
   C. Sub procedure

6. Code that violates the rules of a programming language.
   A. Disruptive code
   B. Language infringement
   C. Syntax error

7. A line in a program that contains instructions for the computer.
   A. Statement
   B. Variable
   C. Separator

8. This term is used to describe the value that can be stored in a variable, such as numbers, characters, or dates.
   A. Separator
   B. Data type
   C. Sub

9. An intentional stop or pause inserted into a program.
   A. String
   B. Tab
   C. Breakpoint

10. Methods that perform logical tests and perform actions when the conditions are true.
    A. Procedures
    B. Logical errors
    C. Control structures

Topics for Discussion

1. In this chapter you learned to write stored statements in the Macro Builder and in the Visual Basic Editor. Which method do you think is more efficient and why?

2. If VBA programs can work without adding comments, then why do programmers add them?

Skill Check

To complete this database, you will need the following file:

- a09_Cars

You will save your files as:

- Lastname_Firstname_a09_Cars
- Lastname_Firstname_a09_Cars_Snip

1. **Start** Access. Open **a09_Cars**, and then save the database in your **Access Chapter 9** folder as Lastname_Firstname_a09_Cars If necessary, enable the content.

2. Open the **Cars** form in Design view. In the **Controls group**, click **Button**. In the upper-right corner of the **Form Header**, click the left mouse button.

3. In the **Command Button Wizard**, click **Miscellaneous**, and then click **Run Macro**. Click **Next**, verify that **ExportCarsToHTML** is selected, and then click **Next**. Click in the **Text** box, and then replace the text with Export Cars Click **Finish**. Compare with **Figure 1**. ──────

4. Switch to Form view, and then click the **Export Cars** button. In the **Output To** dialog box, click **Cancel**. **Save**, and then **Close** the form.

5. Click **File**, and then click **Options**. In the left margin, click **Quick Access Toolbar**. Click the **Customize Quick Access Toolbar arrow**, and then click your file name and file path. Under **Choose commands from**, click **Macros**. Click **ExportCarsToHTML**, click **Add**, and then click **OK**. Compare your screen with **Figure 2**. ──────

6. Create a full-screen snip, **Save** it in your **Access Chapter 9** folder as Lastname_Firstname_a09_Cars_Snip and then close the **Snipping Tool** window.

7. On the **Create tab**, in the **Macros & Code group**, click the **Macro** button. Click **Save**. In the **Save As** dialog box, type Export_Cars and press ⏎.

8. Click the **Add New Action arrow**, and then click **RunMacro**. Click the **Macro Name** box arrow, and then click **ExportCarsToHTML**.

9. Click the **Add New Action arrow**, and then click **If**. Click in the **If** box, type MsgBox("Export as Excel Workbook?",4,"Data Export")=6

- **Continue to the next page to complete this Skill Check** ▶

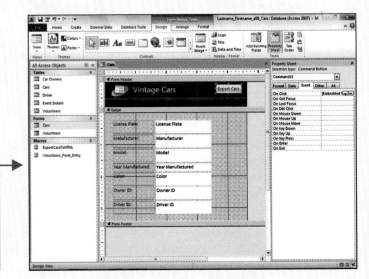

Figure 1

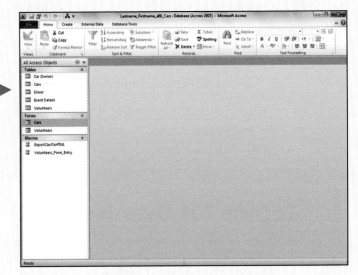

Figure 2

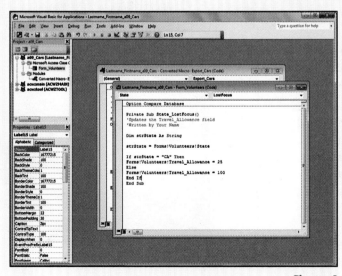

Figure 3

Figure 4

10. Above the **End If** statement, click the **Add New Action arrow**, and then click **ExportWithFormatting**. Click the **Object Name arrow**, and then click **Cars**. Click the **Output Format arrow**, and then click **Excel Workbook (*.xlsx)**.

11. Above the **End If** statement, click the **Add New Action arrow**, and then click **Comment**. Type Prepared by Your Name Move the comment to the beginning of the macro, as shown in **Figure 3**.

12. Click **Save**, and then click **Run**. In the **Output To** dialog box, click **Cancel**. In the message box, click **Yes**. In the **Output To** dialog box, click **Cancel**. Run the macro again, and then in the message box, click **No**.

13. In the **Navigation Pane**, click the **Export_Cars** macro once. On the **Design tab**, in the **Tools group**, click **Convert Macros to Visual Basic**. In the displayed message box, click **Convert**, and then click **OK**. In Project Explorer, double-click the module name to open its code window. From the **File menu**, click **Close and Return to Microsoft Office Access**. **Close** the macro.

14. Open the **Volunteers** form in Design view, display the property sheet, and then click the **State** text box to display its properties. On the property sheet **Event tab**, click the **On Lost Focus** box, and then click the **Build** button. Double-click **Code Builder**.

15. In the **Code** window, below *Private Sub State_LostFocus( )* type the following comment: 'Updates the Travel_Allowance field Press ⏎, and then type the comment 'Written by Your Name

16. Press ⏎ two times. Type Dim strState As String and then press ⏎ two times. Type strState = Forms!Volunteers!State

17. Press ⏎ two times. Type If strState = "CA" Then Press ⏎, and then type Forms!Volunteers!Travel_Allowance = 25 Press ⏎, and then type Else Press ⏎, and then type Forms!Volunteers!Travel_Allowance = 100 Press ⏎, and then type End If Compare your screen with **Figure 4**.

18. If instructed, print the code. Click **Close and Return to Microsoft Office Access**.

19. Click **Save**. Switch to Form view. Press ⟨Tab⟩ five times to update the **Travel_Allowance** field.

20. Click **New (blank) record**, and then add your information to the record.

21. Submit the file as directed by your instructor. **Exit** Access.

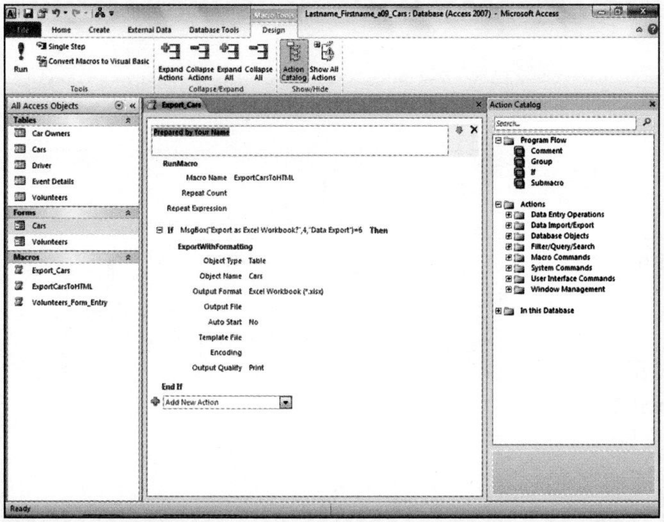

Done! You have completed the Skill Check

Assess Your Skills 1

To complete this database, you will need the following file:

- a09_Cinco

You will save your files as:

- **Lastname_Firstname_a09_Cinco**
- **Lastname_Firstname_a09_Cinco_Snip**

1. **Start** Access and open the student data file **a09_Cinco**. **Save** the database in your **Access Chapter 9** folder with the name Lastname_Firstname_a09_Cinco

2. Create a new macro, and then add the **ExportWithFormatting** action. Set the macro to export the **Events_For_Approval** query as an **Excel Workbook** (*.xlsx). Save the macro as Export_Events_To_Excel and then **Close** the macro.

3. Create a new macro, and then add the **ExportWithFormatting** action. Set the macro to export the **Events_For_Approval** query as an HTML document. **Save** the macro as Export_Events_To_HTML and then **Close** the macro.

4. Create a new macro, and then save the macro as Export_Events Add a **Comment** action, and then in the **Comment box**, type Prepared by Your Name

5. Add an **If** action that displays a message box with the text Export Events to Excel? The message box should display Yes/No buttons and the title Export Request When the **Yes** button is clicked, an action should run the **Export_Query_To_Excel** macro.

6. After the **End If** statement, add an **If** action that displays a message box with the text Export Events as a Webpage? The message box should display Yes/No buttons and the

title Export Request When the **Yes** button is clicked, an action should run the **Export_Query_To_HTML**.

7. **Save**, and then compare your screen with **Figure 1**. **Run** the macro to test all possible outcomes. When the **Output To** dialog box displays, click **Cancel**.

8. Convert the **Export_Events** macro to Visual Basic, and then compare with **Figure 2**. If directed by your instructor, print the code. **Close** the **Code** window, and then **Close** the macro.

9. Add a button to the **Quick Access Toolbar** for the current database that runs the **Export_Events** macro when it is clicked.

10. Open the **Events** form in Design view. In the **Detail** section, on the **1 inch horizontal grid line**, directly below the **Approval** text box, insert a command button. Use the wizard so that the button runs the **Export_Events_To_Excel** macro, displays the text Export to Excel and is named cmdExcelExport

11. Switch to Form view. Create a full-screen snip, Save it in your **Access Chapter 9** folder as Lastname_Firstname_a09_Cinco_Snip and then close the **Snipping Tool** window.

12. **Save**, and then **Close** the form. Submit the files as directed by your instructor. **Exit** Access.

Done! You have completed Assess Your Skills 1

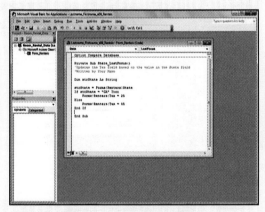

Figure 1

Figure 2

Assess Your Skills 2

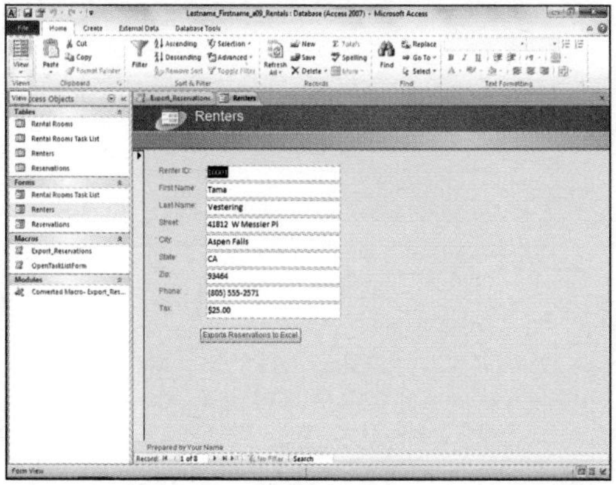

To complete this database, you will need the following file:

- a09_Rentals

You will save your database as:

- Lastname_Firstname_a09_Rentals
- Lastname_Firstname_a09_Rentals_Snip

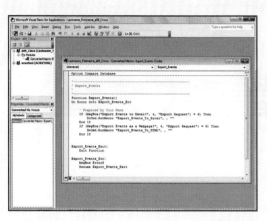

Figure 1

Figure 2

1. **Start** Access and open the file **a09_Rentals**. **Save** the file in your **Access Chapter 9** folder with the name Lastname_Firstname_ a09 _Rentals

2. Open the **Renters** form in Design view, and then click the **State** text box. Display the property sheet, and then create a VBA sub procedure for its **On Lost Focus** event.

3. In the **VBA Code** window, type the comment 'Updates the Tax field based on the value in the State field Press [Enter], and then type 'Written by Your Name

4. Press [Enter] two times, and then type a statement that declares a variable named strState and assigns it the string data type.

5. Press [Enter] two times, and add a statement that assigns the **State** field value in the **Renters** form to the variable.

6. Press [Enter] two times, and then add an **If Then Else** control statement that assigns a **Tax** of 25 for renters from "CA" and a **Tax** of 85 for renters not from "CA" Compare your screen with **Figure 1**.

7. Return to the form, switch to Form view, and then test the macro by using [Tab] key to go through each of the records to update the **Tax** field for each record. If asked by your instructor, print the Code window. **Close** the **Code** window. **Save** and **Close** the **Renters** form.

8. Create a macro that exports the **Reservations** table as an **Excel Workbook** (**.xlsx**). Save the macro as Export_ Reservations Before the first macro action, add the **Comment** Prepared by Your Name **Save**, and then convert the macro to Visual Basic. If asked by your instructor, print the converted VBA code. **Close** the Visual Basic Editor.

9. Open the **Renters** form in Design view. In the **Detail** section, on the **1 inch** horizontal grid line, and below the **Tax** text box, insert a command button. Use the wizard so that the **Export_Reservations** macro runs when the button is clicked. The button's text should be Exports Reservations to Excel and the button should be named the command button cmdExportReservations In the **Form Footer**, insert a Label with text Prepared by Your Name

10. Switch to Form view, and then compare your screen with **Figure 2**. Create a full-screen snip, **Save** it in your **Access Chapter 9** folder as Lastname_Firstname_a09_Rentals_Snip and then close the **Snipping Tool** window.

11. **Save** and **Close** the **Renters** form and **Export_Reservations** macro. Submit the files as directed by your instructor. **Exit** Access.

Done! You have completed Assess Your Skills 2

Assess Your Skills Visually

To complete this database, you will need the following file:

- a09_Geo

You will save your file as:

- Lastname_Firstname_a09_Geo

Open **a09__Geo** and save the database in your **Access Chapter 9** folder as Lastname_Firstname_a09_Geo In the **Events** form, add the four buttons (Table to Excel, Table to HTML, Query To Excel, and Query To HTML), as shown in **Figure 1**. Each button has been formatted with a Quick Style of **Light 1 Outline, Colored Fill – Blue, Accent 1**. Each button should be positioned and formatted as shown and run the corresponding macro provided in the student data file.

Print or submit electronically as directed by your instructor.

Done! You have completed Assess Your Skills Visually

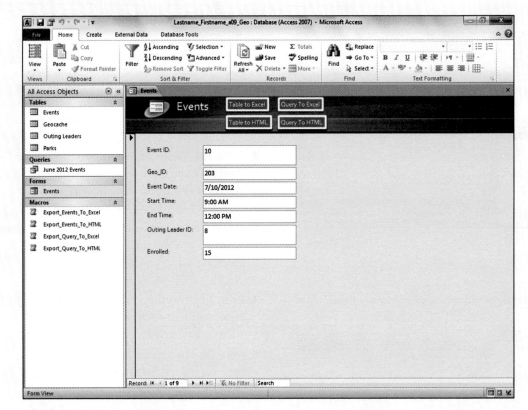

Figure 1

Skills in Context

To complete this database, you will need the following file:

- a09_Swim

You will save your file as:

- Lastname_Firstname_a09_Swim

Open **a09_Swim** and save it in your **Access Chapter 9** folder as Lastname_Firstname_a09_Swim

The **Employees** form has a VBA event procedure with four different errors in the program. Debug the program so that the

correct **Insurance** is entered into the form field. Click through each record to update the entire **Employees** table.

Print or submit electronically as directed by your instructor.

Done! You have completed Skills in Context

Skills and You

To complete this database, you will need the following file:

- New blank Access database

You will save your file as:

- Lastname_Firstname_a09_Skills_and_You

Using the skills you have practiced in this chapter, create a table named Movies with the following field names: **ID, Movie Title,** and **Rating**. For **ID**, use the default **AutoNumber** data type and assign the field as the primary key. Under **Movie Title** enter your 10 favorite movies. Under **Rating**, add your rating of the movie from 1 to 5, with 5 being Excellent. Create an **Export_To_Excel** macro, which exports the **Movies** table to Excel. Create a form

named Movies based on the **Movies** table, and then insert a button that runs the **Export_To_Excel macro**. Save the file to your **Access Chapter 9** folder as Lastname_Firstname_a09_ Skills _and_You

Print or submit electronically as directed by your instructor.

Done! You have completed Skills and You

CHAPTER 10

Administer Databases and Work with SQL

▶ When you will be sharing a database with others, you protect the database so that only authorized individuals can access or change the data.

▶ In SQL view, you work directly with language that Access uses to query tables.

Your starting screen will look like this:

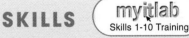

SKILLS

Skills 1-10 Training

At the end of this chapter, you will be able to:

Skill 1 Customize the Navigation Pane

Skill 2 Modify Queries in SQL View

Skill 3 Secure and Encrypt Databases

Skill 4 Change User Account Settings

Skill 5 Create Group and User Accounts

Skill 6 Secure User Accounts

Skill 7 Edit and Test Permissions

Skill 8 Replicate Databases

Skill 9 Synchronize Replicated Databases

Skill 10 Copy and Reset Access Security Settings

MORE SKILLS

More Skills 11 Split Databases

More Skills 12 Add Smart Tags

More Skills 13 Document Databases

More Skills 14 Use the Security Wizard

Outcome

Using the skills listed to the left will enable you to create documents like these:

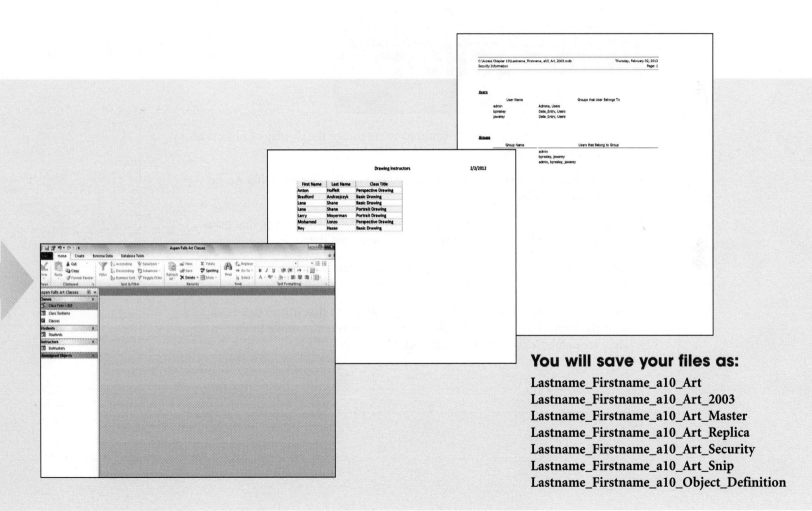

You will save your files as:

Lastname_Firstname_a10_Art
Lastname_Firstname_a10_Art_2003
Lastname_Firstname_a10_Art_Master
Lastname_Firstname_a10_Art_Replica
Lastname_Firstname_a10_Art_Security
Lastname_Firstname_a10_Art_Snip
Lastname_Firstname_a10_Object_Definition

In this chapter, you will create documents for the Aspen Falls City Hall, which provides essential services for the citizens and visitors of Aspen Falls, California.

Introduction

- ▶ The Navigation Pane can be customized to rearrange the display of objects as well as to hide objects.

- ▶ You can enhance queries by working directly with the language that Access uses to query tables.

- ▶ As a database administrator, you can secure the data by requiring that users enter a name and password before they can open the database.

- ▶ After an authorized person has opened a secure database, you can control if he or she can read, write, or delete data from tables.

- ▶ You can make special copies of an online database so that others can work with the copy offline. Later, the changes that everyone has made to the separate database files can be synchronized.

Time to complete all
10 skills – 50 to 90 minutes

Find your student data files here:

> **Open**
>
> « 01_student_data_files ▸ chapter_10   Search chapter_10
>
> Organize ▾   New folder
>
> SW_Preload (C:)
> DVD RW Drive (E:
> 01_student_dat
> 01_common_
> chapter_01
> chapter_02
> chapter_03
> chapter_04
> chapter_05
> chapter_06
> chapter_07
> chapter_08
> chapter_09
> chapter_10
>
> | Name | Date modified | Type |
> |------|---------------|------|
> | a10_Art | 2/2/2012 2:57 PM | Microsoft |
> | a10_Cars | 2/3/2012 11:41 AM | Microsoft |
> | a10_Police | 2/3/2012 10:43 AM | Microsoft |
> | a10_Races | 2/3/2012 7:14 AM | Microsoft |
> | a10_Rentals | 2/3/2012 12:16 PM | Microsoft |
> | a10_Roads | 2/3/2012 1:52 PM | Microsoft |
>
> File name: Microsoft Access
>   Tools ▾   Open   Cancel
>
> Ready

Student data file needed for this chapter:

- a10_Art

► To make it easier to use a subset of database objects, you can create your own categories and groups in the Navigation Pane.

► The Navigation Pane is organized by dragging database objects into the custom groups that you create.

1. **Start** ⊕ Access, and then open **a10_Art**. Use the **Save As** dialog box to create a **New Folder** named Access Chapter 10 Save the database in the new folder as Lastname_Firstname_a10_Art If necessary, enable the content.

2. Click **File**, and then click **Options**. In the **Access Options** dialog box, click **Current Database**.

3. Under **Application Options**, click in the **Application Title** box, type Aspen Falls Art Classes and then compare your screen with **Figure 1**.

4. Under **Navigation**, click the **Navigation Options** button. In the **Navigation Options** dialog box, under **Categories**, click **Custom**.

5. Click the **Rename Item** button, type Aspen Falls Art Classes and then press [Enter].

6. Under **Groups for "Aspen Falls Art Classes"**, click **Custom Group 1**. Click the **Rename Group** button, type Classes and then press [Enter].

7. Click the **Add Group** button, type Students and then press [Enter]. Repeat this technique to add another group named Instructors and then compare your screen with **Figure 2**.

8. Click **OK** to close the **Navigation Options** dialog box, and then click **OK** to close the **Access Options** dialog box. Notice that the application title displays on the Access title bar.

■ **Continue to the next page to complete the skill**

Access Options dialog box

Application Title

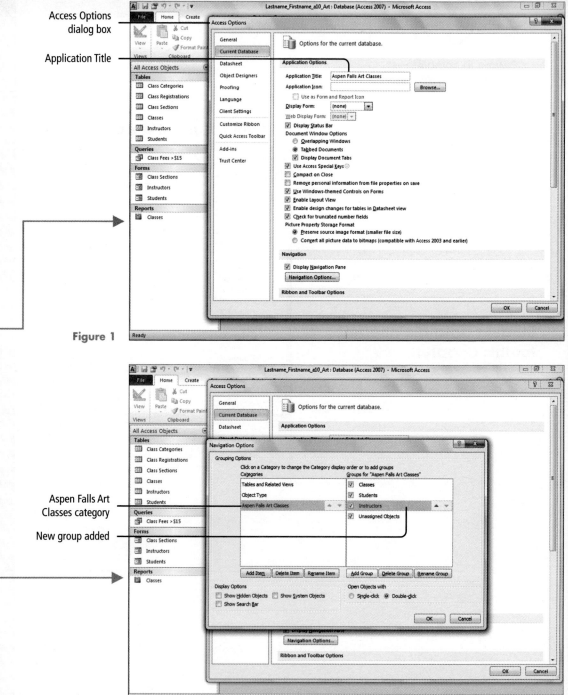

Figure 1

Aspen Falls Art Classes category

New group added

Figure 2

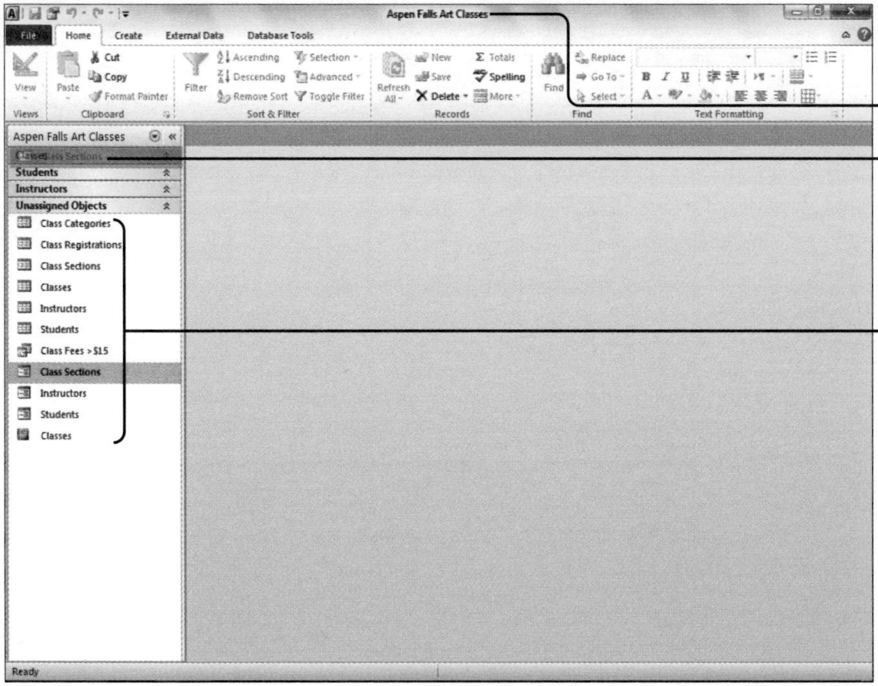

Application title

Form being added
to *Classes* group

Unassigned
objects

Figure 3

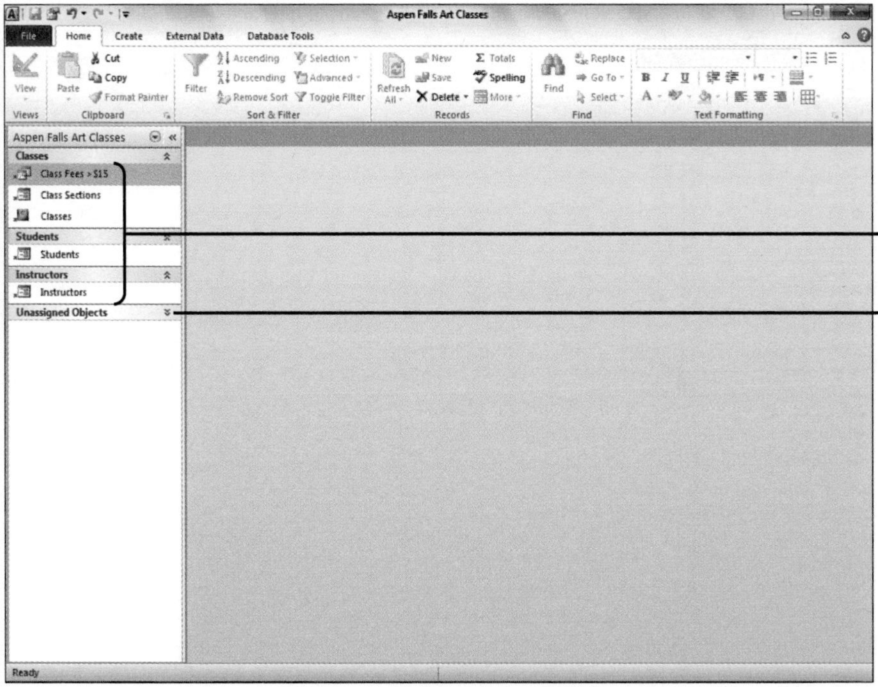

Objects moved to
custom groups

Unassigned Objects
collapsed

Figure 4

9. Click the **Navigation Pane arrow** 🔽 , and then click **Aspen Falls Art Classes**.

10. In the **Navigation Pane**, under **Unassigned Objects**, locate the form named **Class Sections**, as indicated by the **Form** icon 🔳. Drag the form over the **Classes** bar, and when the **Move** 🖐 pointer displays, move the form up, as shown in **Figure 3**, and release the mouse button.

11. Repeat this technique to move the **Instructors** form into the **Instructors** group and the **Students** form into the **Students** group.

12. Move the **Classes** report into the **Classes** group.

13. Move the **Class Fees >$15** query to the **Classes** group.

14. In the **Navigation Pane**, click the **Unassigned Objects arrow** 🔼 to close the group, and then compare your screen with **Figure 4**.

15. Click **Start** 🔵, click **All Programs**, and then open the **Accessories** folder. Click **Snipping Tool**, click the **New button arrow**, and then click **Full-screen Snip**.

16. Click the **Save Snip** button 💾. In the **Save As** dialog box, navigate to your **Access Chapter 10** folder, **Save** the file as Lastname_Firstname_a10_Art_Snip and then **Close** ❎ the **Snipping Tool** window. Print the snips or submit your files as directed by your instructor.

■ **You have completed Skill 1 of 10**

▶ *Structured Query Language (SQL)* is the language used to query database tables.

▶ In Access, all queries are written in SQL, and the SQL statements can be viewed and edited in SQL view.

1. In the **Navigation Pane**, click the **Unassigned Objects arrow** ⊻ to open the group.

2. Display the **Create tab**, and then in the **Queries group**, click **Query Design**.

3. In the **Show Table** dialog box, add the **Instructors** and **Class Sections** tables, and then click **Close**.

4. Click **Save** 🔲, type Drawing Instructors and then press Enter.

5. Add these fields to the design grid in the following order: **First Name, Last Name,** and **Class Title**.

6. In the **Class Title** criteria box, type Like "*Drawing" and then compare with **Figure 1**. ────────

7. In the **Results group**, click **Run**, and then compare with **Figure 2**. ─────────

   The query displays 12 records.

▪ **Continue to the next page to complete the skill** ▶

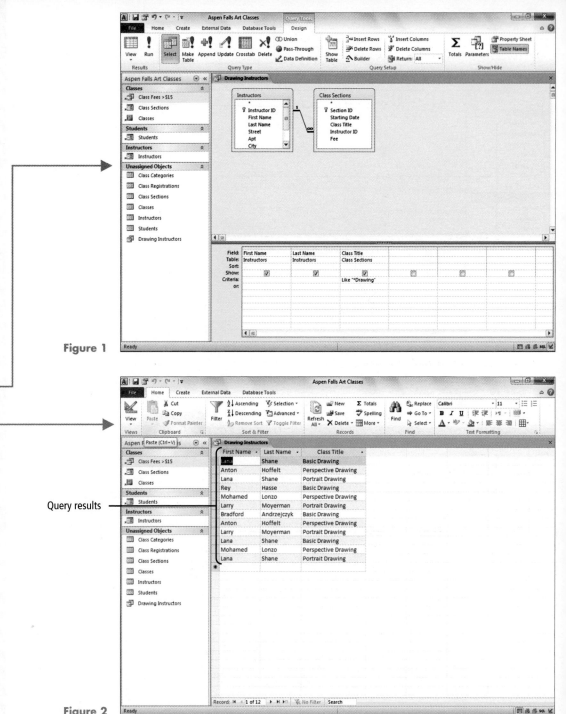

Figure 1

Figure 2

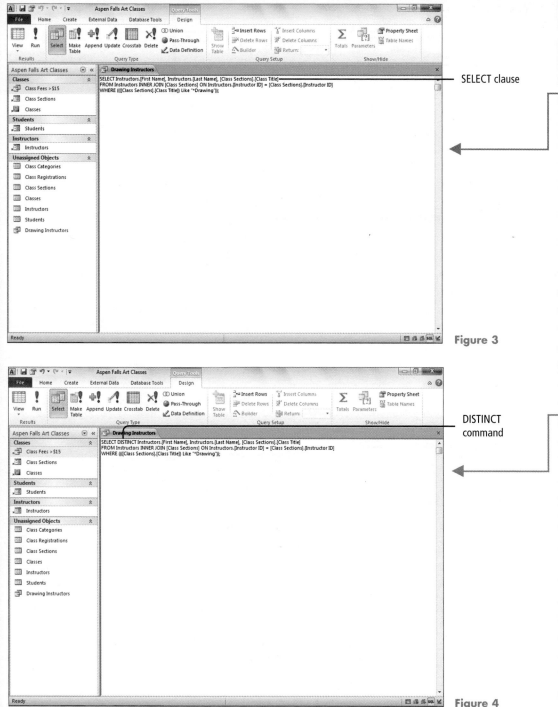

SELECT clause

Figure 3

DISTINCT
command

Figure 4

8. On the **Home tab**, in the **Views group**, click the **View button arrow**, and then, from the displayed list, click **SQL View**. Click a blank area on the **SQL object tab**, and then compare your screen with **Figure 3**.

   In SQL view, the query's underlying SQL statement displays. SQL statements consist of one or more clauses. Here, the **SELECT** clause lists the fields which the query should display. This type of query is called a select query.

   The **FROM** clause lists the table or tables which the query fields are from. In the FROM clause, the **INNER JOIN** clause defines how fields from related tables should be joined.

   The **WHERE** clause identifies the query criteria. In SQL, when two tables have a field with the same name, the field name must be preceded by the table name and a period. When table or field names have spaces, they must be enclosed in brackets ([ ]).

9. In the first clause, click to the right of **SELECT**, add a space, and then type DISTINCT Compare with **Figure 4**.

   DISTINCT is a SQL command that removes duplicate data from the query result. Here, when the same instructor teaches the same class more than once, the class will be listed only one time. In this manner, SQL view can be used to modify Access queries.

10. **Run** the query and verify that seven unique records display. Print the query.

11. Click **Save** 🖫, and then **Close** ⊠ the query. **Close** the database.

   ▪ **You have completed Skill 2 of 10**

▶ To prevent unauthorized access to your database, you can encrypt the database.

▶ *Encryption* is the process of transforming information into a format that cannot be read until the correct password is entered.

1. If necessary, close all open databases. On the **File tab**, click **Open**. In the **Open** dialog box, navigate to your **Access Chapter 10** folder.

2. Click **Lastname_Firstname_a10_Art** one time to select it. In the **Open** dialog box, click the **Open button arrow**, as shown in **Figure 1**.

3. From the displayed list, click **Open Exclusive**. If necessary, enable the content.

   Before a database file can be encrypted, it must be opened in *Exclusive mode*—a mode that prevents others from opening the database while you are working with it.

4. Click **File**, and then click **Encrypt with Password**. Compare your screen with **Figure 2**.

   The Set Database Password dialog box is used to enter and verify the password that will be needed to view the database after it is encrypted.

■ **Continue to the next page to complete the skill**

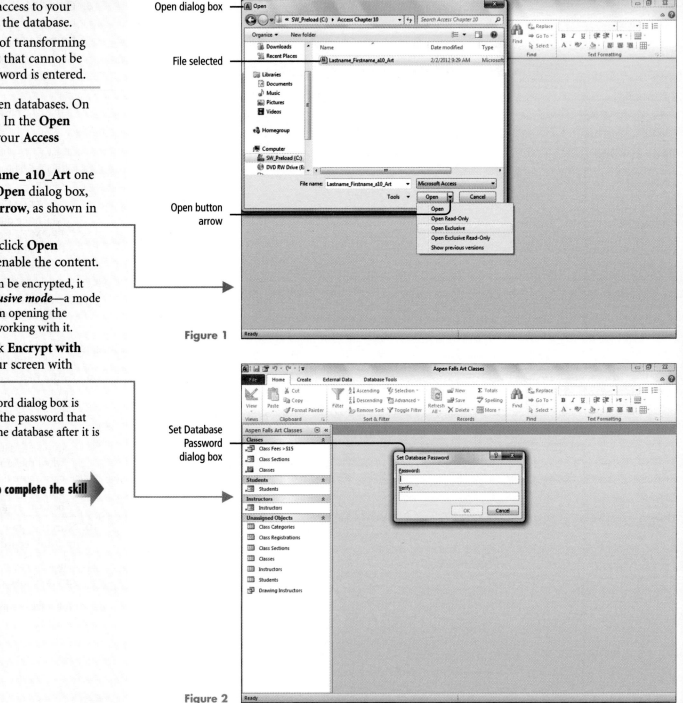

Open dialog box

File selected

Open button arrow

Figure 1

Set Database Password dialog box

Figure 2

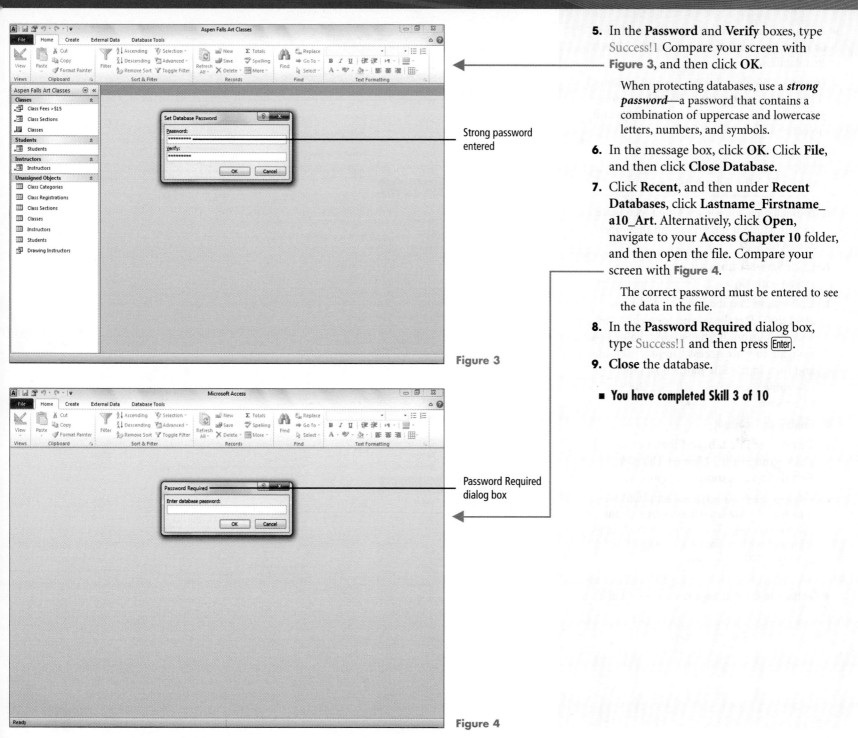

5. In the **Password** and **Verify** boxes, type
Success!1 Compare your screen with
Figure 3, and then click **OK**.

> When protecting databases, use a *strong
> password*—a password that contains a
> combination of uppercase and lowercase
> letters, numbers, and symbols.

6. In the message box, click **OK**. Click **File**,
and then click **Close Database**.

7. Click **Recent**, and then under **Recent
Databases**, click **Lastname_Firstname_
a10_Art**. Alternatively, click **Open**,
navigate to your **Access Chapter 10** folder,
and then open the file. Compare your
screen with **Figure 4**.

> The correct password must be entered to see
> the data in the file.

8. In the **Password Required** dialog box,
type Success!1 and then press [Enter].

9. **Close** the database.

■ **You have completed Skill 3 of 10**

Strong password
entered

Figure 3

Password Required
dialog box

Figure 4

▶ A *user account* provides specific privileges, or rights, to access certain tools and objects in a database.

▶ In Access, the default user account is named Admin. This user account has *administrator privileges*—full access to database tools and objects.

▶ You can prevent others from having administrator privileges by setting a password for the *Admin* user account.

1. In **Backstage** view, click **Open. Navigate** to your student data files, and then open **a10_Art**.

2. Click **Save & Publish**. Compare your screen with **Figure 1**.

3. Under **Save Database As**, click **Access 2002-2003 Database**, and then click the **Save As** button. In the **Save As** dialog box, navigate to your **Access Chapter 10** folder, and then in the **File name** box, type Lastname_Firstname_a10_Art_2003 Click **Save**.

4. Enable the content.

5. Display the **File tab**, and then notice a new group called **Manage Users & Permissions**, as shown in **Figure 2**.

    When a file is saved in the 2002-2003 file format, the Manage Users & Permissions option displays. The features in this group are not available for databases saved in the Access 2010 file format.

■ **Continue to the next page to complete the skill**

Various versions of Access

Save & Publish

Figure 1

Manage Users & Permissions

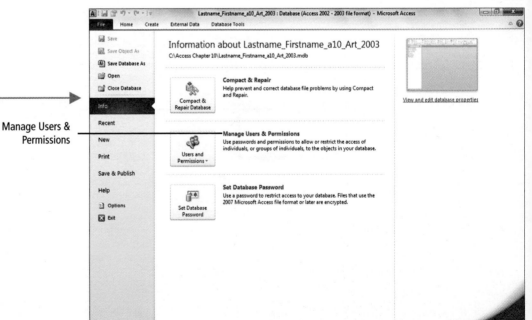

Figure 2

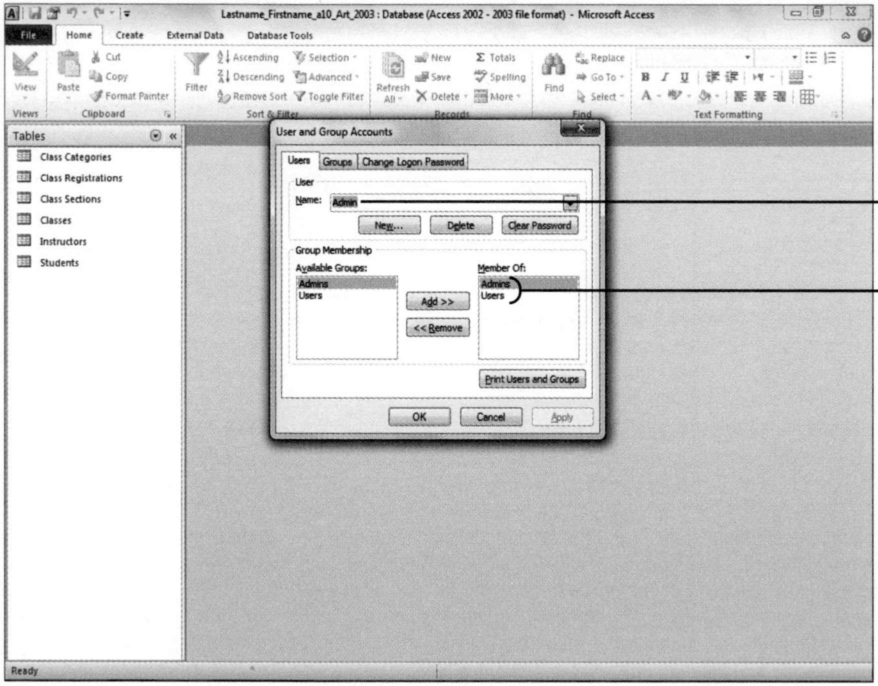

Admin user name

Member of Admins
and Users groups

Figure 3

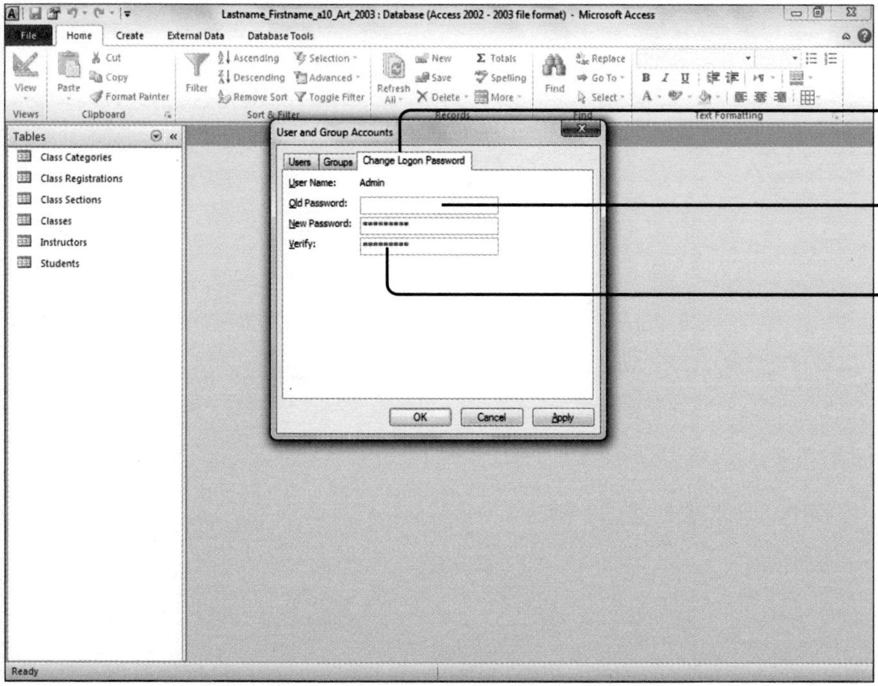

Change Logon
Password tab

Old Password is
blank

New password
entered

Figure 4

6. Click **Users and Permissions**, and then click **User and Group Accounts**. Compare your screen with **Figure 3**.

   The Users and Group Accounts dialog box is used to manage the individuals who will be using the database. Each user account is assigned to at least one *group*—a collection of user accounts that inherit the privileges assigned to the group. Here, the user named Admin is a member of the Admins and Users groups.

7. In the **User and Group Accounts** dialog box, click the **Change Logon Password tab**.

   A *logon* is the combination of user name and password that is needed to access files or features. In Access, the administrator account password is blank until you change it.

8. In the **New Password and Verify** boxes, type Success!2 Compare your screen with **Figure 4**.

   When creating a user for the first time, the Old Password box is left blank.

9. Click **Apply**. Click **OK**, and then **Exit** Access.

10. **Start** Access, and then open **Lastname_Firstname_a10_Art_2003**.

    When a password has been assigned to the Admin user account, the Logon box requests a password.

11. In the **Logon** dialog box, in the **Name** box, delete the existing entry, and then type Admin Press (Tab), and then in the **Password** box, type Success!2 Press (Enter).

■ **You have completed Skill 4 of 10**

- You can create your own user groups and user accounts. You can then add the new users to the desired groups.

- All members of a group inherit the privileges assigned to the group. For example, when you add a user account to the Admins group, that user will have administrator privileges.

1. Click the **File tab**. In **Manage Users and Permissions**, click **Users and Permissions**, and then click **User and Group Accounts**.

2. In the **User and Group Accounts** dialog box, click the **Groups tab**.

3. Click **New**, and then compare your screen with **Figure 1**.

   The New User/Group box is used to name a new user or new group and to assign the *personal ID*—any string between 4 and 20 characters in length that uniquely identifies a group or user.

4. In the **New User/Group** dialog box, in the **Name** box, type Data_Entry

5. Press [Tab], in the **Personal ID** box, type 00001 and then click **OK**.

6. Click the **Users tab**, and then compare with **Figure 2**.

   The new group displays under Available Groups.

■ **Continue to the next page to complete the skill**

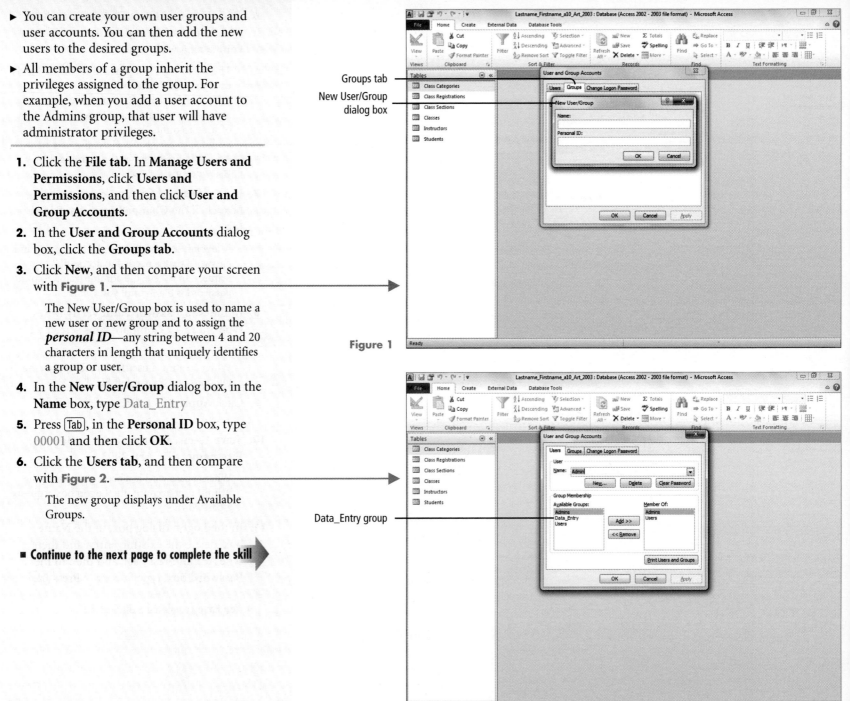

Groups tab

New User/Group dialog box

Figure 1

Data_Entry group

Figure 2

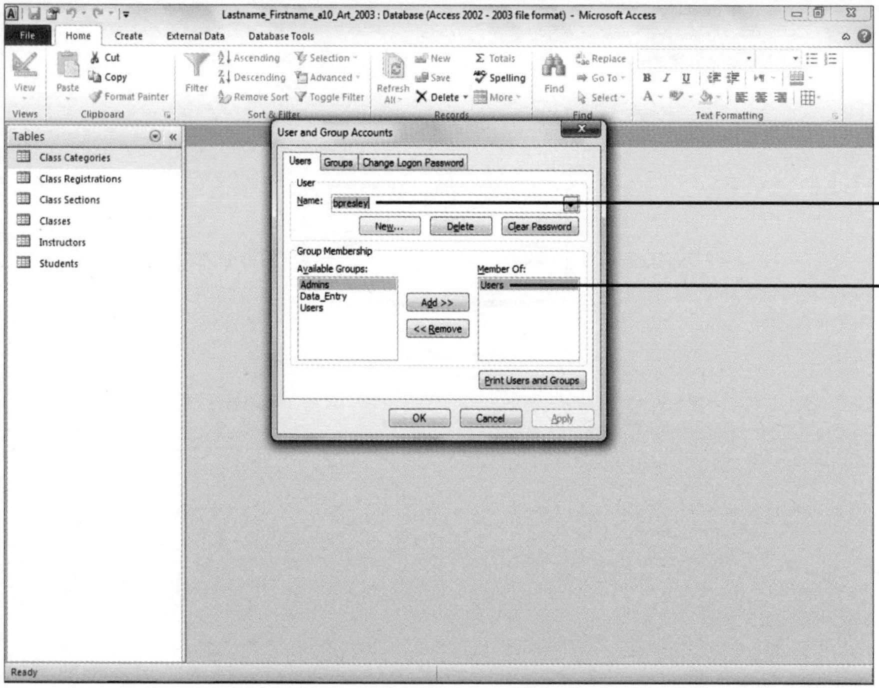

bpresley
user created

Member of
Users group

Figure 3

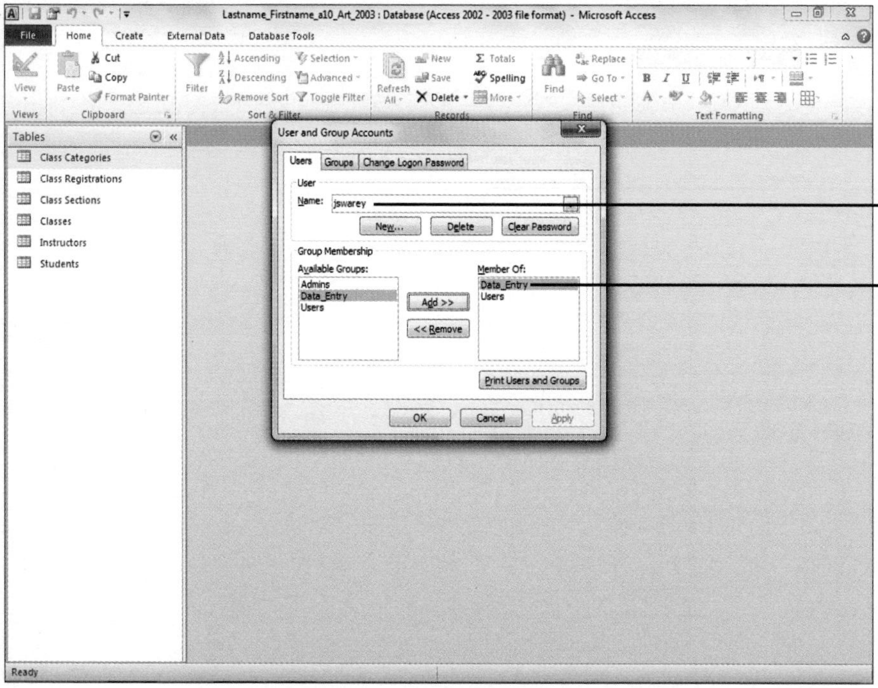

jswarey selected

Member of
Data_Entry group

Figure 4

7. Under **User**, click **New**. In the **New User/Group** dialog box, in the **Name** box, type bpresley Press ⟨Tab⟩, and then in the **Personal ID** box, type 00002 Press ⟨Enter⟩, and then compare with **Figure 3**.

  All users must be members of the Users group.

8. Repeat the technique just practiced to create a new user name jswarey with a personal ID of 00003

9. With *jswarey* selected in the **Name** box, under **Available Groups**, click **Data_Entry**, and then click the **Add** button. Compare your screen with **Figure 4**.

  In this manner, users are assigned to groups.

10. Click the **Name** arrow, and then from the displayed list, click **bpresley**. With **Data_Entry** selected, click the **Add** button to add *bpresley* to that group.

11. Click the **Print Users and Groups** button. With the **Both Users and Groups** option selected, click OK. Save the file as Lastname_Firstname_a10_Object_Definition If requested, print the report.

12. Click **OK** to close the dialog box, and then **Exit** Access.

■ **You have completed Skill 5 of 10**

▶ The password for new users is blank. When the password for a user account is blank, the database is not secure.

▶ After creating new users, either the user or the database administrator must log on as that user to assign a password.

1. **Start ⊕** Access, and open **Lastname_ Firstname_a10_Art_2003**.

2. In the displayed **Logon** box, in the **Name** box, replace the existing entry with jswarey Leave the password blank, and then compare with **Figure 1**. Press Enter.

   Recall that by default, each user's password is blank. Here, the two new users have blank passwords.

3. Click **File**. Click **Users and Permissions**, and then click **User and Group Accounts**.

4. In the **User and Group Accounts** dialog box, click the **Change Logon Password** tab.

5. In the **New Password and Verify** boxes, type Success!3 and then compare your screen with **Figure 2**.

■ **Continue to the next page to complete the skill** ▶

Logon dialog box ——

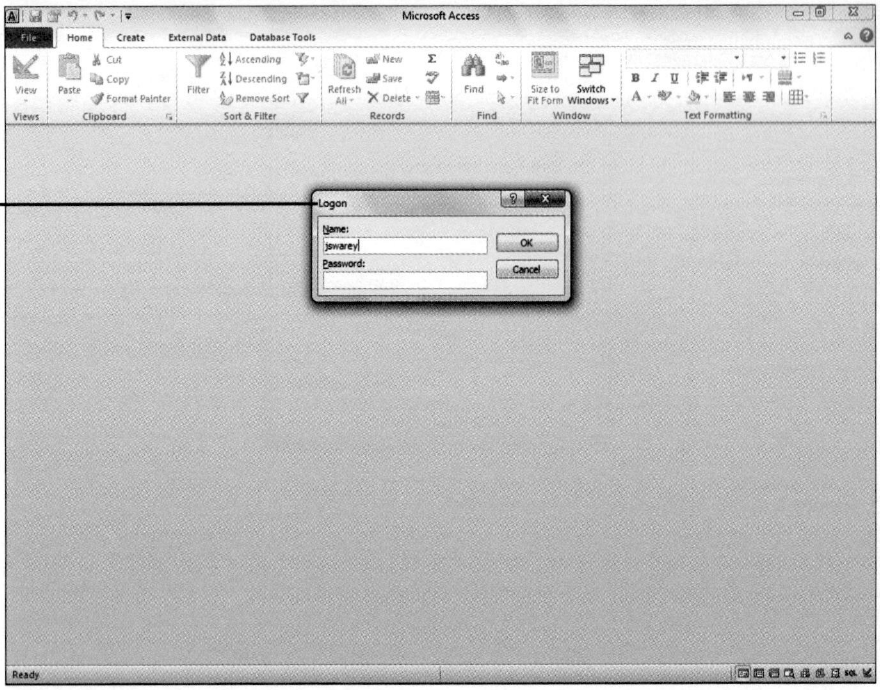

Figure 1

New password entered

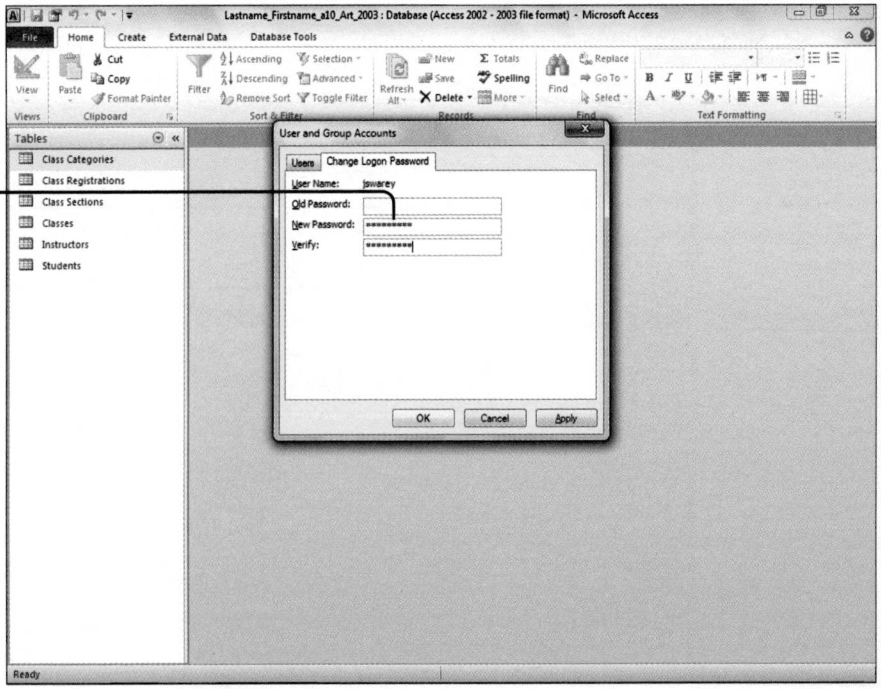

Figure 2

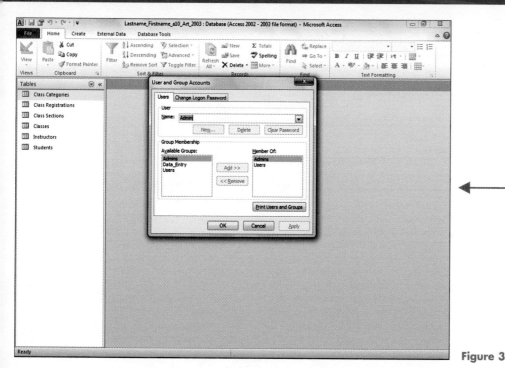

Figure 3

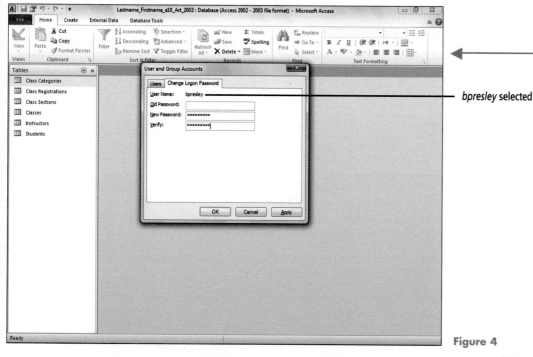

Figure 4

6. Click **Apply**. Click **OK**, and then **Exit** Access.

7. **Start** ⊙ Access, and then open **Lastname_Firstname_a10_Art_2003**.

8. In the displayed **Logon** box, in the **Name** box, type bpresley Leave the password blank, and then press Enter.

9. Click **File**. Click **Users and Permissions**, and then click **User and Group Accounts**. Compare your screen with **Figure 3**.

10. In the **User and Group Accounts** dialog box, click the **Change Logon Password** tab.

11. In the **New Password** and **Verify** boxes, type Success!4 and then compare your screen with **Figure 4**.

12. Click **Apply**. Click **OK**, and then **Exit** Access.

■ **You have completed Skill 6 of 10**

bpresley selected

- User accounts and groups can be granted different *permissions*—sets of rules that control the types of access that a user has to objects in the database.

- Common permissions include reading data, changing data, adding records, deleting records, and modifying the design of tables, forms, or reports.

1. **Start** ⊙ Access, and **open Lastname_ Firstname_a10_Art_2003**. In the displayed **Logon** box, in the **Name** box, replace the existing text with Admin Press (Tab), and then type Success!2 Click **OK**.

2. Click **File**, click **Users and Permissions**, and then click **User and Group Permissions**.

3. In the **User and Group Permissions** dialog box, to the right of **List**, click the **Groups** option button.

4. Under **User/Group Name**, click **Users**. Under **Object Name**, verify that **Class Categories** is selected. Under **Permissions**, clear the **Read Design** check box, and then verify that all the permission check boxes are cleared, as shown in **Figure 1**. ————

    Recall that all user accounts must be a member of the Users group. By default, the Users group has permissions to read, design, and change data in all tables in the database. To set permissions for individual user accounts or groups, the permissions for the Users group need to be removed.

5. Click **Apply**. Under **Object Name**, click **Class Registrations**. Under **Permissions**, clear the **Read Design** check box, and then click **Apply**.

6. Repeat the technique just practiced to clear the **Read Design** check box for the four remaining tables. Compare with **Figure 2**. ————

■ **Continue to the next page to complete the skill**

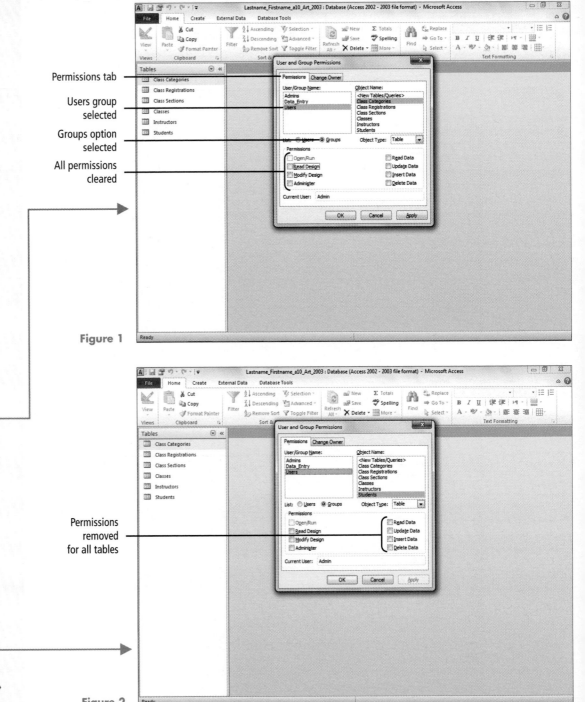

Permissions tab

Users group selected

Groups option selected

All permissions cleared

Figure 1

Permissions removed for all tables

Figure 2

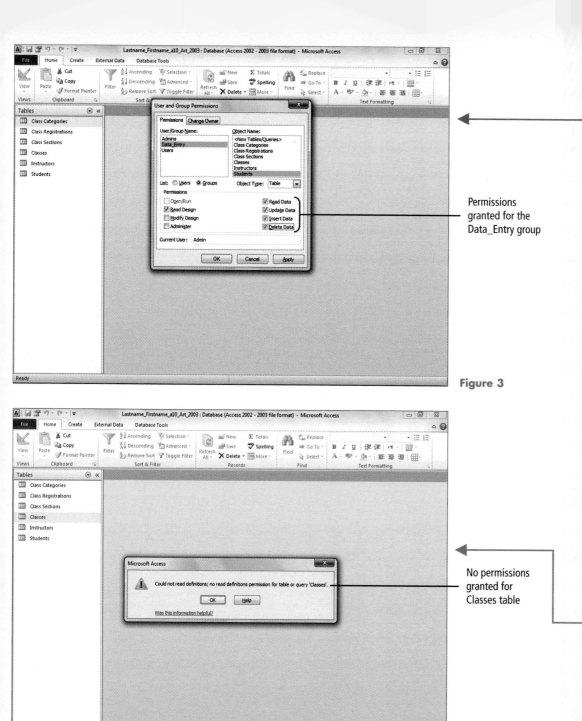

Figure 3

Permissions granted for the Data_Entry group

No permissions granted for Classes table

Figure 4

7. Under **User/Group Name**, click **Data_Entry**. With **Students** still selected, under **Permissions**, select the **Read Data**, **Update Data**, **Insert Data**, and **Delete Data** check boxes. Compare with **Figure 3**, and then click **Apply**.

 By granting permissions to a group, all members of the group inherit those permissions. Here, Bernice Presley—*bpresley*—and John Swarey—*jswarey*—are members of the Data_Entry group. As members of that group, they have permission to read records, change data in records, add new records, and delete records in the Students table. However, they do not have permission to modify the design of the table.

8. In the **User and Group Permissions** dialog box, click **OK**, and then **Exit** Access.

9. **Start** 🌑 Access, and then open **Lastname_Firstname_a10_Art_2003**.

10. In the displayed **Logon** box, in the **Name** box, type *jswarey* and then in the Password box, type Success!3 Press Enter.

11. Open the **Students** table. In the first record, change the **First Name** value to Adrian and then **Close** ⊠ the table.

 You can tell the changes were successful because John Swarey was granted permission to view and update records in the Students table.

12. In the **Navigation Pane**, double-click the **Classes** table, and compare your screen with **Figure 4**. Click **OK**, and then **Exit** Access.

 The message confirms that permissions were not granted to view the Classes table.

■ **You have completed Skill 7 of 10**

▶ When you replicate a database, you create a *replica*—a special copy of a database file where changes made to the copy can be synchronized with changes made to the original.

▶ Replicas can be worked with offline— on a business trip, for example—and then synchronized with the online database later.

1. **Start ⊕** Access, and then click **Open**. Navigate to your student data files, and then click one time to select **a10_Art**. Compare with **Figure 1**.

   When you create a password for the *Admin* account, the password applies to all database files on your computer system or network. Here, the password created in *Lastname_Firstname_a10_Art_2003* is needed to open the current database.

2. Click the **Open button arrow**, and then click **Open Exclusive**. In the displayed **Logon** box, in the **Name** box, type Admin Press [Tab], type Success!2 and then press [Enter].

3. Click **File**, and then click **Save & Publish**. Under **Save Database As**, click **Access 2002-2003 Database**, and then click **Save As**. Navigate to your **Access Chapter 10** folder, and then in the **File name** box, type Lastname_Firstname_a10_Art_Master Click **Save**. Click **Enable Content**.

   Replicated databases must be saved in the Access 2002-2003 file format.

4. Display the **Database Tools tab**. In the **Administer group**, click **Replication Options**, compare your screen with **Figure 2**, and then click **Create Replica**.

■ **Continue to the next page to complete the skill**

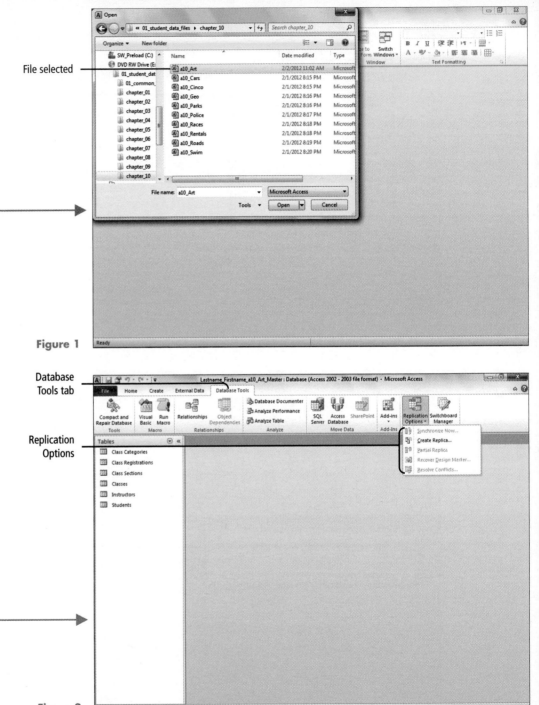

File selected

Figure 1

Database Tools tab

Replication Options

Figure 2

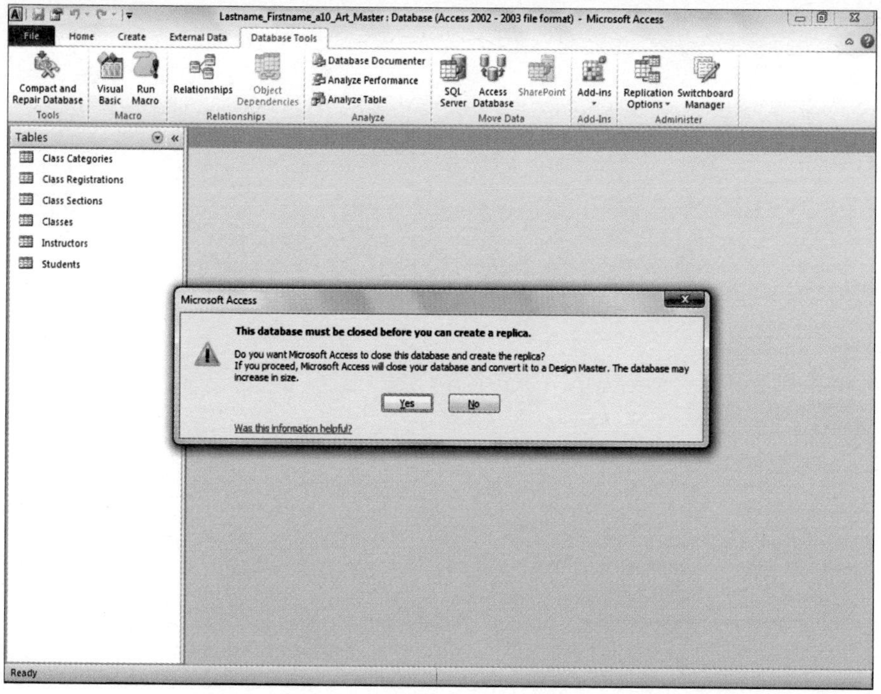

Figure 3

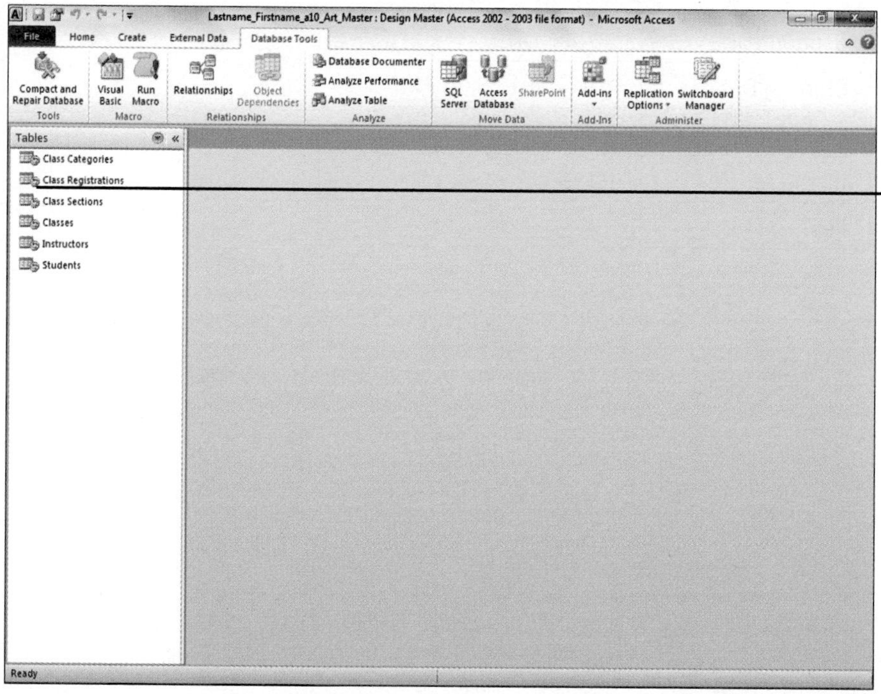

Replication icon

Figure 4

5. Read the displayed message box, and then compare your screen with **Figure 3**.

> The message indicates that the current database will be closed and that a copy of the current database will be created.

6. Click **Yes**.

7. Read the displayed message, and then click **No** so that a backup file is not created.

8. In the displayed **Location of New Replica** dialog box, change the **File name** to Lastname_Firstname_a10_Art_Replica and then click **OK**.

9. Read the displayed message box, and then click **OK**. Compare your screen with **Figure 4**.

> On the title bar, the words "Design Master" indicate that you are working with the original database from which the replica was created. (The *Design Master* is the original database from which a replica was created.) In the Navigation Pane, the replication icon displays next to each table name.

10. Close the database. **Exit** Access.

- **You have completed Skill 8 of 10**

► After changes are made in a replicated copy, the Design Master can be updated to reflect the changes that were made.

1. **Start** ⊕ Access, and then click **Open**. Navigate to your **Access Chapter 10** folder, and then **Open** the file **Lastname_Firstname_a10_Art_Replica**.

2. In the displayed **Logon** box, in the **Name** box, type Admin Press Tab, type Success!2 and then press Enter. If necessary, enable the content. Compare with **Figure 1**.

3. In the **Navigation Pane**, double-click the **Class Sections** table. In the table's **Navigation bar**, click the **New (blank) record** button ⏭.

4. In the new record, enter the data shown in **Figure 2**. When you are done, the Navigation bar should indicate that 26 records are in the table.

5. **Close** ✕ the table, and then close the database.

6. On the **File tab**, click **Open**. Navigate to your **Access Chapter 10** folder, and then open **Lastname_Firstname_a10_ Art_Master**.

■ **Continue to the next page to complete the skill**

Replicated copy opened

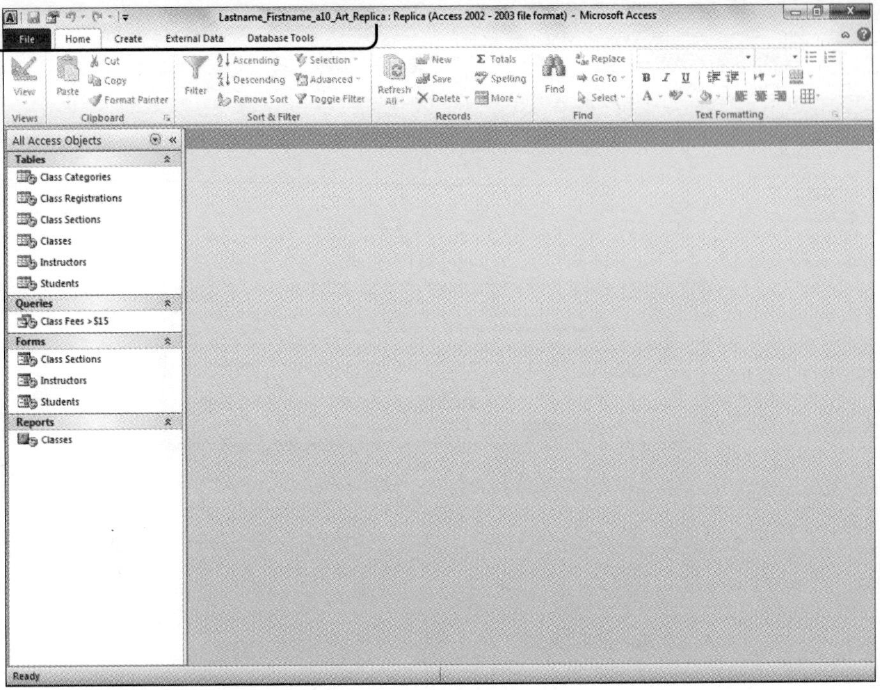

Figure 1

Section ID:	20147
Starting Date:	10/14/2012 7:00 PM
Class Title:	Basic Drawing
Instructor ID:	A121
Fee:	45

Figure 2

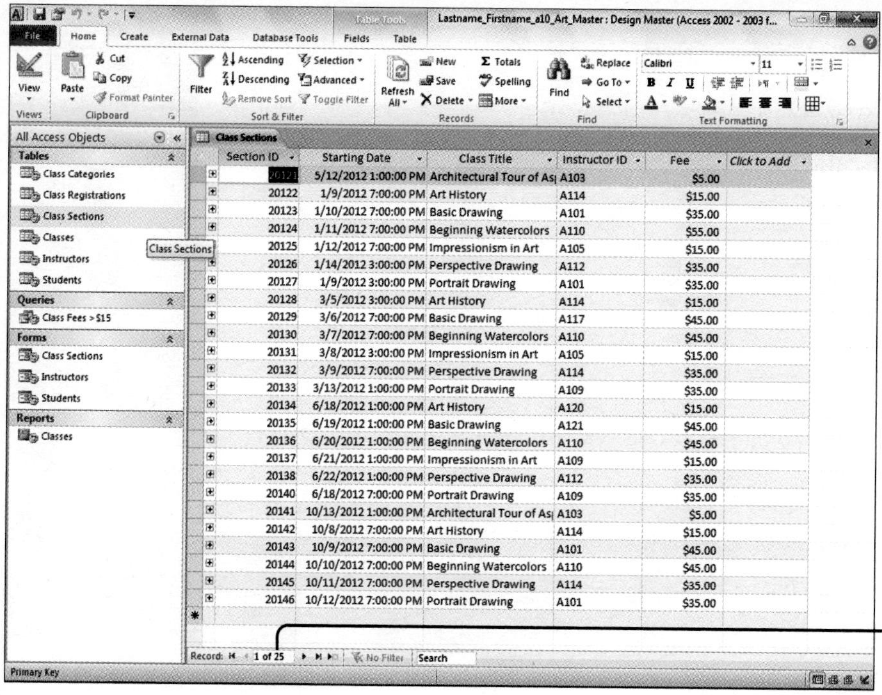

25 records display

Figure 3

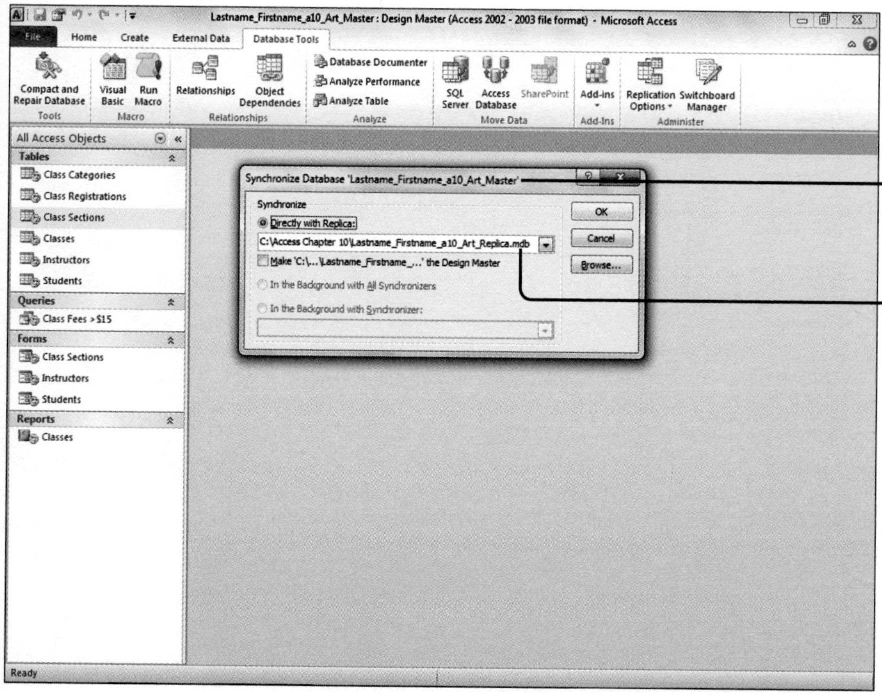

Synchronize Database dialog box

Path of the replica file

Figure 4

7. Click the **Navigation Pane arrow** , and then click **All Access Objects**.

8. Open the **Class Sections** table, and then compare with **Figure 3**.

   The master displays 25 records. The record added in the replicated copy is not in the master database.

9. **Close** the table. On the **Database Tools tab**, in the **Administer group**, click **Replication Options**, and then click **Synchronize Now**. Click **Browse**, navigate to **Lastname_Firstname_a10_Art_Replica**, and then in the **Browse** dialog box, click **OK**. Compare your screen with **Figure 4**.

   The Synchronize Database dialog box synchronizes a master database with the replica that you choose.

10. In the **Synchronize Database 'Lastname_Firstname_a10_Art_Master'** dialog box, verify that the path and name of the replica file are correct, and then click **OK**.

11. Read the displayed message, and then click **Yes**.

12. In the displayed message box, click **OK**.

13. Open the **Class Sections** table and verify that 26 records display.

    Any changes made to the master database will also be made in the replicated copies. In this manner, individuals can work with replicated copies of a database and later update the master database with their changes. Any changes made by co-workers to the master database will be updated in the replicated copy.

14. **Close** the table, and then **Exit** Access.

   ▪ **You have completed Skill 9 of 10**

▶ Because the security settings that you created in this chapter apply to all database files on your computer, you need to return the settings to their default settings.

1. Click the **Start** button 🔵, and then click **Computer**. In the displayed folder window, double-click **Local Disk (C:)**, and then double-click the **Users** folder.

2. In the **Users** folder, locate the folder with your Windows logon name, and then double-click the folder.

3. In the folder window, click the **Organize** button, and then click **Folder and search options**.

4. In the **Folder Options** dialog box, click the **View tab**. Under **Advanced settings**, select the **Show hidden files, folders, and drives** option button, and then click **OK**. Compare with **Figure 1**.

> The *AppData folder* is a hidden folder that stores Access settings.

AppData folder displays

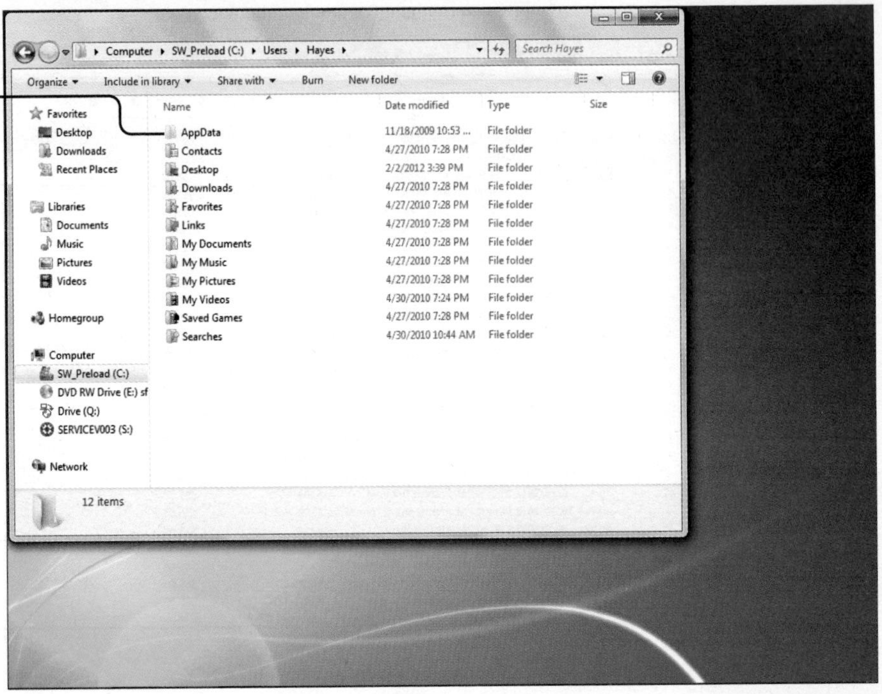

Figure 1

5. Double-click the **AppData** folder, and then double-click to open the displayed **Roaming** folder. Open the **Microsoft** folder, and then open the displayed **Access** folder. Compare your screen with **Figure 2**.

> The System database is typically located at C:\Users\[Logon name]\AppData\Roaming \Microsoft\Access. If not, you may need to search for *System.mdw*.

File path

System file

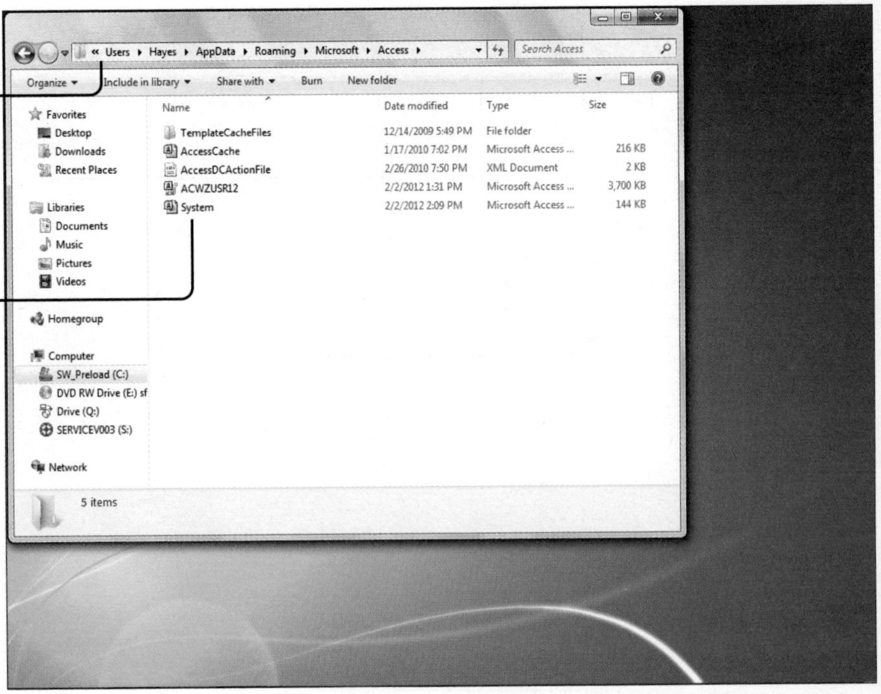

Figure 2

■ **Continue to the next page to complete the skill** ➤

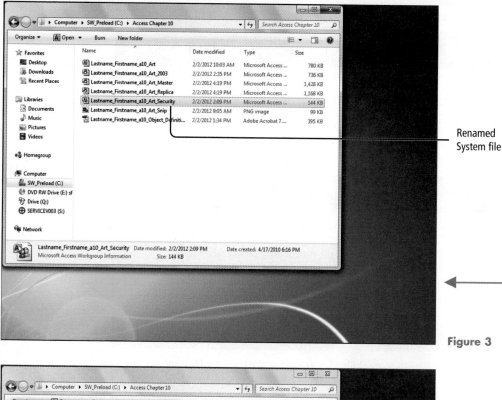

Renamed
System file

Figure 3

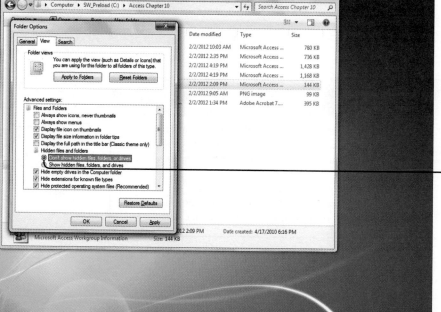

Don't show hidden
files, folders, and
drives selected

Figure 4

6. Right-click the **System** file, and then click **Cut**.

   To reset the security settings, you can delete the database that stores the security settings—*System.mdw*. The next time that Access is opened, this file will be re-created with the default security settings.

7. In the folder window, navigate to your **Access Chapter 10** folder. In the **Access Chapter 10** folder, right-click a blank area, and then from the displayed shortcut menu, click **Paste**.

8. Right-click the pasted file, and from the displayed shortcut menu, click **Rename**. Type Lastname_Firstname_a10_ Art_Security Press [Enter], and then compare your screen with **Figure 3**.

9. Switch back to the previous window. Click **Organize**, and then from the displayed list, click **Folder and search options**.

10. In the **Folder Options** dialog box, click the **View** tab. Under **Advanced settings**, select the **Don't show hidden files, folders, or drives** option button, as shown in **Figure 4**.

11. Click **Apply to Folders**, click **Yes**, and then click **OK**.

12. Submit your files as directed by your instructor.

Done! You have completed Skill 10 of 10 and your document is complete!

More Skills

The following More Skills are located at **www.pearsonhighered.com/skills**

More Skills 11 Split Databases

When you split a database, you move the tables into a separate database. You can then create different databases with different forms, queries, and reports by linking to the separated tables. In this way, you can design multiple views while maintaining a single source of data.

In More Skills 11, you will split a database into two files. You will then create another database that uses the separated tables.

To begin, open your web browser, navigate to www.pearsonhighered.com/skills, locate the name of your textbook, and follow the instructions on the website.

More Skills 12 Add Smart Tags

Using smart tags in datasheets provides the user with a fast way to link to other applications.

In More Skills 12, you will add smart tags to a telephone number column, thereby enabling you to save contacts quickly to Outlook.

To begin, open your web browser, navigate to www.pearsonhighered.com/skills, locate the name of your textbook, and follow the instructions on the website.

More Skills 13 Document Databases

Database administrators often need to document their work. For example, a list of the permissions assigned to each user account or group for each object in the database is often useful. The Database Documenter is used to create detailed reports for the database administrator.

In More Skills 13, you will use the Database Documenter to create a highly detailed report for a database.

To begin, open your web browser, navigate to www.pearsonhighered.com/skills, locate the name of your textbook, and follow the instructions on the website.

More Skills 14 Use the Security Wizard

The Security Wizard can be used to create user accounts, assign passwords, and assign permissions. The Security Wizard provides several prebuilt groups—Backup Operators, for example—with permissions already defined for each group.

In More Skills 14, you will use the Security Wizard to create a new user account and then place the user in the Backup Operators group. You will then test the security settings created by the wizard.

To begin, open your web browser, navigate to www.pearsonhighered.com/skills, locate the name of your textbook, and follow the instructions on the website.

Key Terms

Online Help Skills

1. **Start** 🔵 Access. In the upper-right corner of the Access window, click the **Help** 🔘 button. In the **Help** window, click the **Maximize** 🔲 button.

2. Click in the search box, type sql and then click the **Search** button 🔍. In the search results, click **Introduction to Access SQL**.

3. Scroll down to **SQL CLAUSES**. Compare your screen with **Figure 1**.

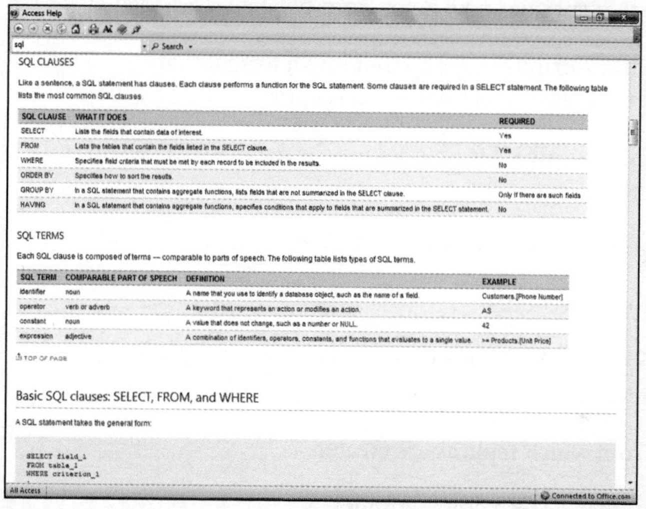

Figure 1

4. Read the section to see if you can answer the following questions: The FROM clause refers to which type of database object? Which clause specifies field criteria that must be met by each record to be included in the results?

Matching

Match each term in the second column with its correct definition in the first column by writing the letter of the term on the blank line in front of the correct definition.

_____ **1.** The language used to query database tables.

_____ **2.** This clause lists the fields that the query should display.

_____ **3.** An SQL clause that specifies how fields from two tables are related.

_____ **4.** The process of transforming information into a format that cannot be read until the correct password is entered.

_____ **5.** A mode that prevents others from opening the database while you are working with it.

_____ **6.** An account type that provides specific privileges to an individual.

_____ **7.** A collection of user accounts.

_____ **8.** The combination of user name and password that is needed to access files or features.

_____ **9.** The database from which replicas are created.

_____ **10.** A hidden folder that stores Access settings.

A AppData folder

B SQL

C Design Master

D Encryption

E Exclusive mode

F Group

G INNER JOIN

H Logon

I SELECT

J User Account

Multiple Choice

Choose the correct answer.

1. The language used to query database tables.
   a. Structured Java
   b. JavaScript
   c. Structured Query Language

2. The clause that lists the fields that the query should display.
   a. FROM
   b. SELECT
   c. WHERE

3. The clause that lists the origin of the table or tables in the query fields.
   a. FROM
   b. SELECT
   c. WHERE

4. An SQL command that removes duplicate data from the query result.
   a. DISTINCT
   b. SELECT
   c. WHERE

5. A password that contains a combination of upper-case and lowercase letters, numbers, and symbols.
   a. Technical password
   b. Hard password
   c. Strong password

6. Provides full access to database tools and objects.
   a. User access
   b. Administrator privileges
   c. Group access

7. Any string between 4 and 20 characters in length that uniquely identifies a group or user.
   a. Strong password
   b. User access code
   c. Personal ID

8. A set of rules that control the types of access a user has to objects in the database.
   a. Permissions
   b. Exclusive mode
   c. Encryption

9. A special copy of a database file where changes made to the copy can be synchronized with changes made to the original.
   a. Shadow copy
   b. Replica
   c. Linked workbook

10. The database that stores the security settings.
    a. System.mdw
    b. Replica
    c. Encrypted file

Topics for Discussion

1. Provide some examples of when you would assign some users access to view certain tables but not allow those users to edit any of the data contained in these tables.

2. In what ways can database information be secured?

Skill Check

To complete this database, you will need the following file:

- a10_Races

You will save your files as:

- Lastname_Firstname_a10_Races
- Lastname_Firstname_a10_Races_2003
- Lastname_Firstname_a10_Races_Replica
- Lastname_Firstname_a10_Races_System

1. **Start** Access. and then open **a10_Races**. Save the database in your **Access Chapter 10** folder as an **Access 2010 Database** named Lastname_Firstname_a10_Races If necessary, enable the content.

2. Click **File**, and then click **Options**. In the **Access Options** dialog box, click **Current Database**. In the **Application Title** box, type AF Triathlon Click the **Navigation Options** button. Under **Categories**, click **Custom**. Click **Rename Item**, and then type AF Triathlon Under **Groups for "AF Triathlon"**, click **Custom Group 1**, click the **Rename Group** button, and then type Racers Click **OK** two times.

3. Click the **Navigation Pane arrow**, and then click **AF Triathlon**. Drag the **Racers** form to the **Racers** group. Compare your screen with **Figure 1.**

4. Open the **Sponsorship** query. On the **Home tab**, in the **Views group**, click the **View button arrow**, and then click **SQL View**. Click to the right of **SELECT**, add a space, and then type DISTINCT

5. Click **Run**, and then verify that 7 records display. Compare your screen with **Figure 2**. Click **Save**, close the query, and then click the **File tab.**

6. Click **Save & Publish**, and then under **Save Database As**, click **Access 2002-2003 Database**. Click **Save As**. Navigate to your **Access Chapter 10** folder, and then in **File name**, type Lastname_Firstname_a10_Races_2003 Click **Save**. Enable the content.

7. On the **Database Tools tab**, in the **Administer group**, click **Replication Options**, and then click **Create Replica**. Click **Yes**, and then click **No**.

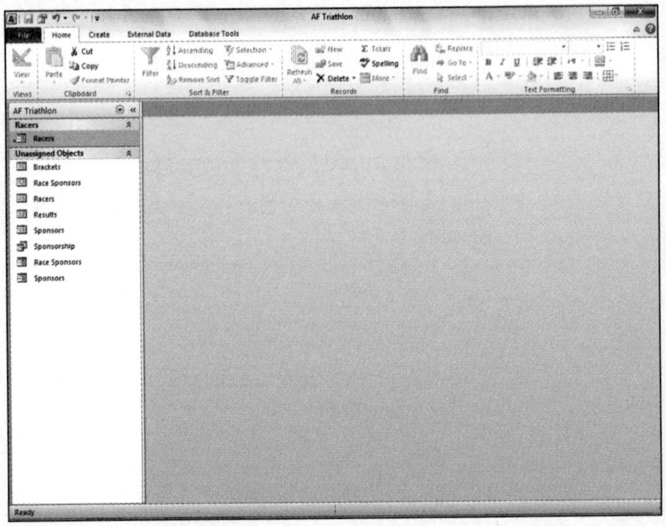

■ Continue to the next page to complete this Skill Check

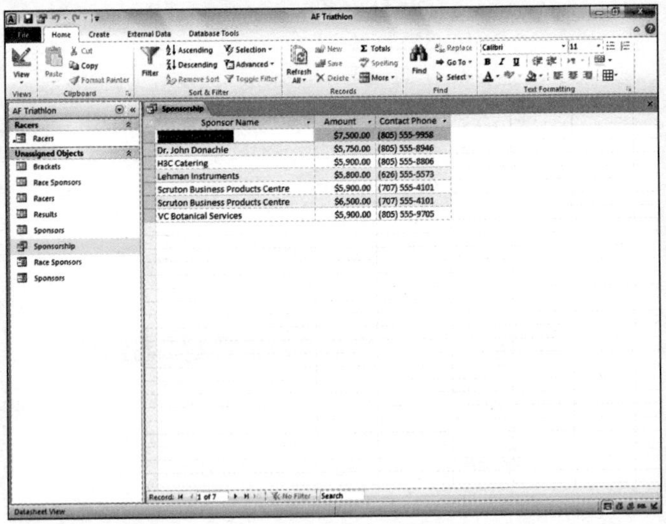

Figure 1

Figure 2

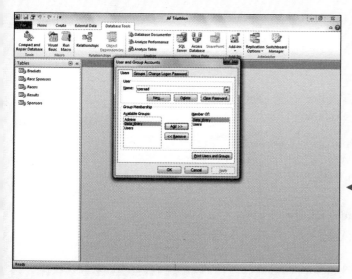

Figure 3

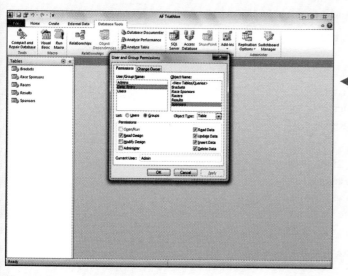

Figure 4

8. In the **Location of New Replica** dialog box, change the **File name** to Lastname_Firstname_a10_Races_Replica and then click **OK**. Click **OK** again.

9. Click the **File tab**, click **Users and Permissions**, and then click **User and Group Accounts**. Click the **Change Logon Password tab**. In the **New Password** box, type Success!2 In the **Verify** box, type Success!2 Click **Apply**.

10. In the dialog box, click the **Groups tab**, and then click **New**. In the **New User/Group** dialog box, type Data_Entry Press ⌨Tab, and then type 00009 Click **OK**.

11. Click the **Users tab**, and then click the **New** button. In the **New User/Group** dialog box, in the **Name** box, type rpersad and then in the **Personal ID** box, type 456456 Click **OK**. Under **Available Groups**, click **Data_Entry**, and then click the **Add** button. Compare with **Figure 3**, and then click **OK**.

12. Click the **File tab**, click **Users and Permissions**, and then click **User and Group Permissions**. In **List**, select the **Groups** option button, and then under **User/Group Name**, click **Users**.

13. Under **Object Name**, click **Brackets**. Under **Permissions**, clear the **Read Design** check box, and then click **Apply**. Repeat this technique to remove the permissions for the **Users** group for the four remaining tables.

14. Under **User/Group Name**, click **Data_Entry**. Under **Object Name**, click **Brackets**. Under **Permissions**, select the **Read Data, Update Data, Insert Data,** and **Delete Data** check boxes, and then click **Apply**. Repeat these techniques to add the same permissions for the four remaining tables. Compare your screen with **Figure 4**, and then click **OK**.

15. **Close** the database, and then click **Open**. In the **Open** dialog box, navigate to the Lastname_Firstname_a10_Races file, and then click once to select the file. Click the **Open button arrow**, and then click **Open Exclusive**. Click the **File tab**, and then click **Encrypt with Password**. In the **Password** box, type Success!1 Press ⌨Tab, and then type Success!1 Click **OK**, and then click **OK** again. **Exit** Access.

16. In a folder window, navigate to **System located at C:\Users\[Your Windows Logon Name]\AppData\Roaming\Microsoft\Access**. If necessary, display hidden files. Cut the file, and then **Paste** it in your **Access Chapter 10** folder. Rename the pasted file Lastname_Firstname_a10_Races_System Submit your files as directed by your instructor.

Done! You have completed the Skill Check

Assess Your Skills 1

To complete this database, you will need the following file:

- a10_Police

You will save your files as:

- Lastname_Firstname_a10_Police
- Lastname_Firstname_a10_Police_2003
- Lastname_Firstname_a10_Police_Replica
- Lastname_Firstname_a10_Police_System

1. **Start** Access and and open **a10_Police**. Save the database in your **Access Chapter 10** folder with the name Lastname_Firstname_a10_Police

2. In the **Application Title**, type Aspen Falls Police In **Navigation Options**, rename the **Custom** category to Aspen Falls Police Rename the **Custom Group 1** to Employees From the **Navigation Pane arrow**, select **Aspen Falls Police**. Drag the **Employee Awards** query to the **Employees group**.

3. In the **Employee Awards** query, add the DISTINCT command so that only 12 records display when the query is run. **Save** and **Close** the query.

4. **Close** the database, and then reopen it in **Exclusive** mode. Encrypt the database using the password Success!1 **Exit** Access.

5. Open **a10_Police**, and then save the database in your **Access Chapter 10** folder as an **Access 2002-2003 Database** file named Lastname_Firstname_a10_Police_2003

6. Change the **Admin** password to Success!2

7. Add a new group named Clerks with a **Personal ID** of 123123 and then add two new users named Data_Entry1 with a **Personal ID** of 1001 and Data_Entry2 with a **Personal ID** of 1002 Add both new users to the **Clerks** group. Logon as Data_Entry1 and then change the password to Success!3

8. Open **Lastname_Firstname_a10_Police_ 2003** in **Exclusive** mode. Log on as *Admin*, and then for the **Users group**, remove all permissions for all the tables.

9. For the **Clerks** group, grant the **Read Data, Update Data, Insert Data**, and **Delete Data** privileges for the **Employees** table.

10. **Close** the database. Navigate to the **System** file. **Cut** and **Paste** the file to your **Access Chapter 10** folder. Rename the pasted file Lastname_Firstname_a10_Police_System

11. Decrypt the file **Lastname_Firstname_a10_ Police**.

12. Open **Lastname_Firstname_a10_ Police_2003**. Create a replica but do not create a backup, and name the replica Lastname_Firstname_ a10_Police_Replica

13. **Close** the database and then open **Lastname_Firstname_a10_Police_2003**. Use the **Employees** table to add a new record with an **Employee ID** of 24 and a **Last Name** using your own last name. Leave the remaining fields blank.

14. Synchronize the **Design Master** database and replica databases.

15. **Close** the database. **Exit** Access.

Done! You have completed Assess Your Skills 1

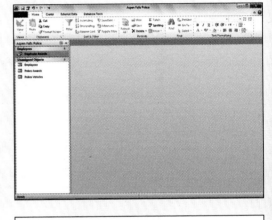

Figure 1

Assess Your Skills 2

To complete this database, you will need the following file:

- a10_Cars

You will save your files as:

- Lastname_Firstname_a10_Cars_2003
- Lastname_Firstname_a10_Cars_Replica
- Lastname_Firstname_a10_Cars_System

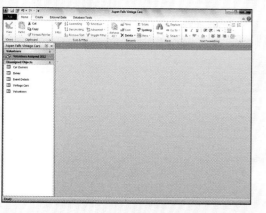

Figure 1

1. **Start** Access and open the student data file **a10_Cars**. **Save** the file as a **2002-2003 Access Database** in your **Access Chapter 10** folder with the name Lastname_Firstname_a10_Cars_2003

2. In the **Application Title**, type Aspen Falls Vintage Cars In **Navigation Options**, rename the Custom category to Aspen Falls Vintage Cars Rename the **Custom Group 1** to Volunteers From the **Navigation Pane arrow**, select **Aspen Falls Vintage Cars**. Drag the **Volunteers Assigned 2012** query to the **Volunteers** group.

3. Change the **Admin** password to Success!2

4. Add a new group named Data_Entry with a **Personal ID** of 7070

5. Add a new user named dbenjes with a **Personal ID** of 7171 Add **dbenjes** to the **Data_Entry** group.

6. For the **Data Entry** group, grant the **Read Data, Update Data, Insert Data**, and **Delete Data** privileges for all five tables.

7. Create a replica of **Lastname_Firstname_a10_Cars_2003**. Do not create a backup, and name the replica Lastname_Firstname_a10_Cars_Replica Close the database.

8. Navigate to the **System** file located at **C:\Users\[Windows Logon Name]\AppData\Roaming\Microsoft\Access**. **Cut** and **Paste** the file to your **Access Chapter 10** folder, and name the file Lastname_Firstname_a10_Cars_System

9. Open **Lastname_Firstname_ a10_Cars_ 2003**. Modify the **Volunteers Assigned 2012** query in SQL view so that the **Volunteer** and **Driver** duplicates are removed and 15 records display. Save, and then Close the query.

10. Synchronize the database, and then **Close** the database.

11. **Exit** Access. If directed, submit the file to your instructor.

Done! You have completed Assess Your Skills 2

Assess Your Skills Visually

To complete this database, you will need the following file:

- a10_Rentals

You will save your database as:

- Lastname_Firstname_a10_Rentals

Open the database **a10_Rentals**, and then save the database in your **Access Chapter 10** folder as Lastname_Firstname_a10_Rentals In **Access Options**, in the **Application Title** box, type AF_Rentals_Your Name In **Navigation Options**, create an Aspen Falls Rentals category and then add a Rooms group to this category. Move the **Room Hosts** query to the **Rooms** group. Edit the **Room Hosts** query in SQL view so that eight records display, as shown in **Figure 1**.

Submit as directed by your instructor.

Done! You have completed Assess Your Skills Visually

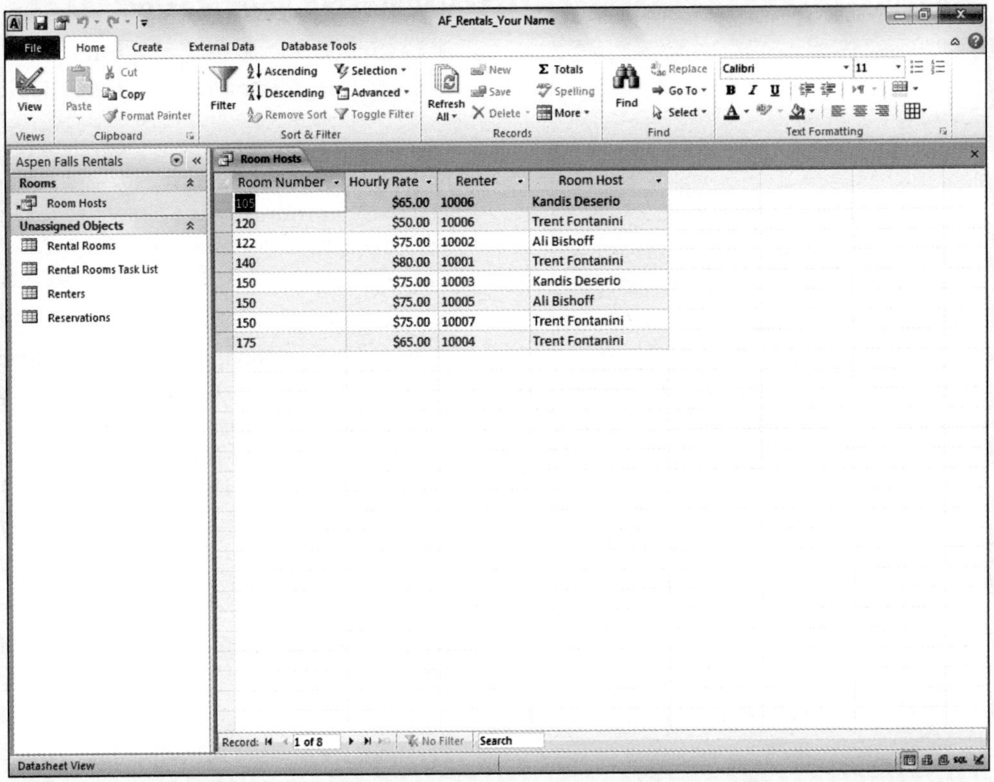

Figure 1

Skills in Context

To complete this database, you will need the following file:

- a10_Roads

You will save your files as:

- Lastname_Firstname_a10_Roads_2003
- Lastname_Firstname_a10_Roads_System

Open **a10_Roads**, and save the database in your **Access Chapter 10** folder as an **Access 2002-2003** file with the named Lastname_Firstname_a10_Roads_2003 Create two user groups named Designers and Data Entry Create user accounts for njones and nbagwan and add them to the **Designers** group. Create the users dberlusconi and gdavis and then add them to the **Data Entry** group. You will decide the **Personal IDs** for the groups and users.

For the **Users** group, revoke all permissions for both tables. For the **Designers** group, grant only the **Read Design** and **Modify**

Design permissions. For the **Data Entry** group, grant the **Read Data, Update Data, Insert Data,** and **Delete Data** permissions.

For the *Admin* account, change the password from blank to Success!1 After you are done, cut and paste the **System** file and rename it Lastname_Firstname_a10_Roads_System Submit as directed by your instructor.

Done! You have completed Skills in Context

Skills and You

To complete this database, you will need the following file:

- New blank Access database

You will save your files as:

- Lastname_Firstname_a10_Contacts_2003
- Lastname_Firstname_a10_Contacts_Replica

Using the skills you have practiced in this chapter, create a new database with a list of 10 of your contacts. Save the database as an **Access 2002-2003** file with the name Lastname_Firstname_a10_Contacts_2003 Create one table called **Contacts** with **Contact_ID, Full_Name, Telephone_Number, Email_Address,** and **Org_ID**. Add another table with a one-to-many relationship called **Organizations**, with the fields **Org_ID** and **Org_Name**. Create a

replica for you to travel with called Lastname_Firstname_a10_Contacts_Replica Add two more contacts to the replicated database, and then synchronize the **Design Master** database with the replica.

Done! You have completed Skills and You

Glossary

Action arguments Additional instructions that determine how a macro action should run.

ActiveX control A control that enables your active application to interact with another application across the Internet.

Administrator privileges Permissions that allow full access to database tools and objects.

Anchored control Stretches, shrinks, or moves whenever the form is resized.

AND logical operator A logical comparison of two criteria that is true only when both criteria outcomes are true.

AppData folder A hidden folder that stores Access settings.

Append row A blank row in a datasheet in which a new record is entered.

Application Parts Prebuilt tables with fields for common information needs.

Asterisk (*) wildcard A wildcard that matches any combination of characters.

Attachment data type An Access data type used to store files such as Word documents or digital photo files.

AutoComplete An IntelliSense menu of commands that match the characters you are typing.

AutoNumber A field that automatically enters a unique, numeric value when a record is created.

Back-end file A file that contains the tables when using the Database Splitter.

Backup operator The person responsible for creating backup copies of the master file.

Between...And operator An operator that finds all numbers or dates between and including two values.

Breakpoint An intentional stop or pause inserted into a program.

Calculated control A text box that displays the result of an expression.

Calculated field A column added to a query that derives its value from other fields.

Caption An Access field property that sets the label that displays in datasheets, forms, and reports.

Cascading delete A referential integrity option where you can delete a record on the one side of the relationship, and all the related records on the many side will also be deleted.

Cascading update A referential integrity option where you can edit the primary key values in one table, and all the related records in the other table will update accordingly.

Category field In a PivotChart, refers to the fields that will appear on the chart's category axis as labels.

Cell The box formed by the intersection of a row and column.

Cell reference A number on the left side and a letter on the top of a spreadsheet that addresses a cell.

Child field A field in a subreport that links the report to its subreport.

Clipboard A temporary storage area that holds text or an object that has been cut or copied.

Code window The window where you write and edit VBA code.

Combo box A control that has a text box and a list that is hidden until you click its arrow.

Command button A control that performs an action or sequence of actions when it is clicked.

Comment A remark added to a macro or VBA code to provide information to those reviewing the macro or VBA code.

Compact and Repair A command that rebuilds database files so that data and database objects are stored more efficiently.

Comparison operator An operator used to compare two values; for example, = (equal to) and < (less than).

Concatenation The process of combining two or more text values to create one text value.

Conditional formatting Changes the appearance of a control based upon a user's display configuration related to the value that appears in a field.

Control An object in a form or report such as a label or text box.

Control grid Cells arranged in rows and columns into which controls are placed.

Control structure Methods that perform logical tests and perform actions when the conditions are true.

Copy A command that places a copy of the selected text or object in the Clipboard.

Criteria The conditions used in a query to select the records you are looking for.

Crosstab query A type of select query that calculates a sum, average, or similar statistic and then groups the results by two sets of values.

Currency data type A number formatted to display the dollar sign and two decimals.

Cut A command that removes the selected text or object and stores it in the Clipboard.

Data field In a PivotChart, refers to the numeric fields that will appear on the chart's value axis.

Data label The text that identifies each data marker on a chart.

Data marker A column, bar, area, dot, pie slice, or other symbol that represents a single point of data.

Data series A collection of related data points used in a chart that is usually represented by a unique color.

Data type Specifies the type of information that a field will hold, for example, text, number, date, and currency.

Database A structured collection of related information about people, events, and things.

Database Documenter An Access tool that provides printable reports about object properties and relationships.

Database management system Software used to manage and interact with the database.

Database object A basic part of a database that allows you to work with the database; for example, tables, queries, forms, and reports.

Database Splitter A wizard that divides a database.

Datasheet An Access view that displays records in rows and fields in columns similar to an Excel spreadsheet.

Date Picker A control that enables you to navigate a calendar and then click the desired date.

Date/Time data type An Access data type that stores numbers in the date or time format.

DBMS See database management system.

Debug To find and fix errors in programming code and make sure the program functions as intended.

Delimited text file A text file where the data in each column is separated by an identifying character such as a comma, a space, or a tab.

Delimiter The character used to separate fields in a delimited text file.

Description An Access field property used to document a field's purpose; it displays in the status bar of the datasheet when field is active.

Design grid The lower half of the Query tab, which lists the fields that will display in the query results.

Design Master The original database from which a replica was created.

Design view A view in which the structure and behavior of database objects are modified.

Dialog box A box where you can select multiple settings.

DISTINCT A SQL command that removes duplicate data from the query result.

Drag To move the mouse while holding down the left mouse button and then to release it at the appropriate time.

Edit To insert text, delete text, or replace text in an Office document, spreadsheet, or presentation.

Encryption The process of transforming information into a format that cannot be read until the correct password is entered.

Entity relationship diagram A visual model used to design the database.

ERD Entity relationship diagram; a visual model used to design the database.

Event An action, such as a mouse click or typing, detected by a running program.

Exclusive mode A mode that prevents others from opening the database while you are working with it.

Expression A combination of fields, mathematical operators, and pre-built functions that calculates values in tables, forms, queries, and reports.

Extensible Markup Language A standard that uses text characters to define the meaning, structure, and appearance of data.

Field A set of common characteristics around which a table is organized.

Field Size An Access field property that limits the number of characters that can be typed into a text or number field.

Find duplicates query A query that searches a field and then displays any records that contain duplicate values. The query can then be used to remove the duplicate values.

Foreign key A field in one table that is also the primary key of a second table; it is used to create a relationship with that table.

Form A database object used to enter new records, delete records, or update existing records.

Format To change the appearance of the text, such as changing the text color to red.

FROM A SQL command that lists the table or tables that query fields are from.

Front-end file A file that contains objects created from tables, such as forms, reports, and queries, when using the Database Splitter.

Gallery A visual display of choices from which you can choose.

Gradient A range of position-dependent colors typically ranging from lighter to darker.

Gradient fill An effect where one color fades into another.

Grid line A line between the cells in a table or spreadsheet.

Group A collection of user accounts that inherit the privileges assigned to the group.

HTML (Hypertext Markup Language) A language used to create web pages.

HTML document A text file with HTML tags that instruct web browsers how to display the document as a web page.

Hungarian notation A naming convention where the prefixes indicate the type of data or type of object.

Hyperlink Text or other object that displays another document, location, or window when it is clicked.

Hyperlink data type An Access data type that stores links to websites or files located on your computer.

If action A macro action that provides a conditional expression and then performs an action or series of actions only when the result of the condition is true or false.

If Then Else control structure Tests if a condition is true.

Indeterminate relationship A relationship that does not enforce referential integrity.

Index Stores the location of records based on the values in a field.

INNER JOIN A SQL command that defines how fields from related tables should be joined.

Input mask A set of special characters that control what can and cannot be entered in a field.

Insertion point A vertical line that indicates where text will be inserted when you start typing.

IntelliSense A technology that displays Quick Info, ToolTips, and AutoComplete as you type expressions.

Is Null This operator returns records when that field has no value.

Junction table The middle table in a many-to-many relationship.

KeyTip An icon that displays in the Ribbon to indicate the key that you can press to access Ribbon commands.

Keyword A word in a programming language that has a particular meaning or purpose.

Label An object on a form or report that describes other objects on the report or form.

Label report A report formatted so that the data can be printed on a sheet of labels.

Layout The arrangement of data and labels in a form or report.

Layout view An Access view used to format a report or form while being able to view a sample of the data.

Left outer join A join type where every record in the one side of the relationship displays even if there is no matching record in the table on the many side of the relationship.

Legend A chart element that identifies the patterns or colors that are assigned to the categories in a chart.

Linked table A table that exists in a different file created by applications such as Microsoft Access, Microsoft Excel, or Microsoft SQL Server.

Live Preview A feature that displays the result of a formatting change if you select it.

Logical error An error where the program runs but does not produce the intended results.

Logon The combination of user name and password that is needed to access files or features.

Lookup field A field whose values are retrieved from another table or from a list.

Macro A sequence of commands that can be performed as one task.

Macro actions Prebuilt sets of instructions that perform tasks when the macro is run.

Macro Builder An object tab with prebuilt commands that you can select and modify to build a macro.

Mail merge document A Word document that combines a main document such as a letter, a sheet of labels, or an envelope, with a data source.

Many-to-many relationship A relationship where one record in either of the outer tables can have many associated records in the other outer table.

Master field A field in a report that is used to link the report to its subreport.

Memo data type An Access data type that stores up to 65,535 characters of text data and the formatting assigned to that text.

Mini toolbar A toolbar with common formatting buttons that displays after you highlight text.

Multiple item form A form that displays records in rows and columns in the same manner that a datasheet does.

Navigation Form Enables you to combine several forms or reports into a single form.

Notepad A program provided with the Windows operating system designed to edit text files.

Null In queries and filters, this means that the field is empty and has no value.

Null Empty A field that has no value is null.

Number data type An Access data type that stores numeric values.

Object In Access, a basic part of a database that allows you to work with the database; for example, tables, queries, forms, and reports.

One-to-many form A main form and a subform that displays all the related records for the record displayed in the main form.

One-to-many relationship A relationship where a record in the first table can have many associated records in the second table.

One-to-one relationship A relationship where each record in one table can have only one corresponding record in the other table.

Option Group A frame with a set of check boxes, toggle buttons, or option buttons.

OR logical operator A logical comparison of two criteria that is true if either of the criteria outcomes is true.

Padding The amount of space between a control's border and other controls on the form or report.

Page footer An area at the bottom of each page that contain labels, text boxes, and other controls.

Page header An area at the top of each page that contains labels, text boxes, and other controls.

Page Layout view A view where you prepare your document or spreadsheet for printing.

Parameter query A query that displays an input box that asks for criteria each time the query is run.

Parent field The field to which a child field is linked.

Paste To insert a copy of the text or an object stored in the Clipboard.

PDF (Portable Document Format) file A file in a format that preserves document layout and formatting, which can be viewed in Adobe Acrobat Reader, a web browser, or another PDF reader.

Permissions Sets of rules that control the types of access a user has to objects in the database.

Personal ID Any string between 4 and 20 characters in length that uniquely identifies a group or user.

PivotChart An interactive graphical representation of summarized data.

PivotTable Provides an interactive way to summarize quickly large amounts of data.

Placeholder character The symbol in an input mask that is replaced as you type data into the field.

Plain Text Characters with no formatting capabilities.

Plot area The area bound by the axes in a chart.

Pop Up form A form that when opened remains on top, even when it is not the active form.

Primary key The field that uniquely identifies each record in a table.

Print Preview An Access view used to work with a report that will be printed.

Program A group of stored instructions that tell a computer what to do.

Protected View A view applied to documents downloaded from the Internet that allows you to decide if the content is safe before working with the document.

Query A database object that displays a subset of the data in response to a specific question.

Query Builder A tool used to create queries within database objects such as forms and reports.

Query design workspace The upper half of the Query tab, which displays the available tables and fields that the query can use.

Question mark (?) wildcard A wildcard character that matches any single character.

Quick Info An IntelliSense box that explains the purpose of the selected AutoComplete.

Quick Start data type A set of fields that can be added with a single click. For example, the Address data type inserts five fields for storing postal addresses.

Quick Start fields Commonly used groups of fields that can be quickly inserted into a table.

Quick Styles Designs with specific background fills, font colors, and shading that can be applied with one click.

RAM The computer's temporary memory.

Read-only mode A mode where you cannot save your changes.

Record The collection of related information that displays in a single row of a database table.

Redundant data Data duplicated in more than one location within a database.

Referential integrity A rule that keeps related values synchronized. For example, the foreign key value must match one of the primary key values in the other table.

Relational database A database that joins two tables by placing common fields in related tables.

Relationship The joining of two tables using common fields.

Replica A special copy of a database file where changes made to the copy can be synchronized with changes made to the original.

Report A database object designed to display table data or query results on the screen or in printed form.

Report footer An area at the end of a report that contains labels, text boxes, and other controls.

Report header An area at the beginning of a report that contains labels, text boxes, and other controls.

Rich Text Text that can be formatted.

Rich Text Format A text format designed to work with many different types of programs.

Right outer join A join type where every record in the many side of the relationship displays even if there is no matching record in the table on the one side of the relationship.

Right-click Click the paragraph with the right mouse button.

RTF The acronym for Rich Text Format.

Screen shot A picture of your computer screen, a window, or a selected region saved as a file that can be printed or shared electronically.

ScreenTip Informational text that displays when you point to commands or thumbnails in the Ribbon.

SELECT A SQL command that lists the fields that the query should display.

Separator A small vertical or horizontal line used to separate choices in a list, toolbar, or menu.

Serial dates The number of days since December 30, 1899, and the fraction of 24 hours that has expired for the day.

SetValue A macro action used to add a value to a field or control.

Shortcut menu A list of commands related to the type of object that you right-click.

Simple Query Wizard A Wizard used to quickly adds fields to a new query.

Single form layout A form that displays one record at a time.

Smart tags A property in which Access recognizes certain types of data and links the data to other applications.

Snip A screen capture created with the Snipping Tool.

Special effect Formatting applied to controls to make them appear raised or sunken in a form or report.

Stacked layout An arrangement where labels display the field names in the left column and text boxes display the corresponding field values in the right column.

Startup macro A macro that runs automatically when an Access database is opened. Can be used to automate common startup tasks, such as opening forms or running queries.

Statement A line in a program that contains instructions for the computer.

String A sequence of either alpha or alphanumeric characters.

Strong password A password that contains a combination of uppercase and lowercase letters, numbers, and symbols.

Structured Query Language (SQL) The language used to query database tables.

Sub procedure A group of related statements that is a subset of a program. Sub procedures are often referred to as subs or procedures.

Subdatasheet A datasheet that displays related records from a related table. The related table must be on the many side of the relationship.

Subform A form contained within another form that displays records related to the other form.

Subreport A report that is inserted into another report.

Summary statistic A calculation for a group of data such as a total, an average, or a count.

Switchboard A form with buttons or links that open other database objects.

Syntax error Code error that violates the rules of a programming language.

System.mdw The database that stores the security settings.

Table The database object that stores the data in rows and columns.

Table Analyzer Searches a table for redundant data and, when it is found, suggests how to split the table into two or more related tables.

Table Design view Used to add fields to a table and to set the properties for those fields.

Table Events Used to register changes to records through the use of macros.

Tag The text between the < and > characters in an XML file.

Text box An object on a form or report that displays the data from a field in a table or query.

Text data type An Access data type that stores up to 255 characters of text.

Text file A file that stores only text characters but not formatting, tab stops, or tables.

Toggle button A button used to turn a feature both on and off.

Triple-click Click three times fairly quickly without moving the mouse.

Typographical error An error created during data entry.

Unique An Access field property that requires that each record contain a unique value.

Unique identifier Another term for primary key.

Unmatched data A condition where the data in one field does not have a corresponding value in a related table.

User account An account that provides specific privileges, or rights, to access certain tools and objects in a database.

Validation message The text that displays in a message box when a validation rule is broken during data entry.

Validation rule A field property that requires specific values be entered into a field.

Variable A programming object that refers to the values stored in RAM.

Visual Basic Editor (VBE) A program for writing VBA program code.

Visual Basic for Applications (VBA) A programming language designed to work within Microsoft Office applications.

WHERE A SQL command that identifies query criteria.

White space Optional spacing that visually organizes the code to make it more readable by programmers.

Wildcard A special character, such as an asterisk, used in query criteria to allow matches for any combination of letters or characters.

Windows Live A free online storage that can be used to save and open your files from any computer connected to the Internet.

Windows Live ID A unique name and password- a Hotmail or Windows Live e-mail user name and password, for example.

Windows Live network A group of people whom you have invited to share files or to chat using Instant Messenger.

Workgroup information file A security-enhanced database in which the user and group permissions created by the Security Wizard are applied.

XML The acronym for Extensible Markup Language.

Yes/No data type An Access data type that stores values that can have one of two possible values for example, yes and no, or true and false.

Index